FIXED INCOME MARKETS AND THEIR DERIVATIVES, 2e

SURESH M. SUNDARESAN

Professor of Finance and Economics
Columbia Business School
Columbia University

SOUTH-WESTERN
THOMSON LEARNING

Australia · Canada · Mexico · Singapore · Spain · United Kingdom · United States

Fixed Income Markets and Their Derivatives, 2e
by Suresh M. Sundaresan

Vice President/Publisher: Jack W. Calhoun
Acquisitions Editor: Mike Mercier
Developmental Editor: Jennifer Baker
Marketing Manager: Julie Lindsay
Marketing Coordinator: Shannon O'Callaghan
Production Manager: Sharon L. Smith
Production Editor: Starratt E. Alexander
Manufacturing Coordinator: Sandee Milewski
Permissions Coordinator: Lorretta Palagi
Verification: Alex Nikolaev
Cover Design: Meighan Depke, Meighan Depke Design
Cover Image: Omega Type, FPG
Cover Design Manager: R. A. M.
Editorial Assistant: Joe Squance
Production House and Compositor: Shepherd, Inc.
Printer: R.R. Donnelley & Sons Company—Crawfordsville Manufacturing Division

Printed in the United States of America
1 2 3 4 5 04 03 02 01

For more information contact South-Western, 5101 Madison Road, Cincinnati, Ohio, 45227 or find us on the Internet at http://www.swcollege.com

For permission to use material from this text or product contact us by
• telephone: **1-800-730-2214**
• fax: **1-800-730-2215**
• web: **http://www.thomsonrights.com**

Library of Congress Cataloging-in-Publication Data
Sundaresan, Suresh M.
  Fixed income markets and their derivatives / Suresh M. Sundaresan.--2nd ed.
     p.   cm.--(Current issues in finance)
  Includes bibliographical references and index.
  ISBN 0-324-00446-X
    1. Fixed-income securities. I. Title. II. Series

HG4650 .S86 2001
332.63'2044--dc21   2001031452

Brief Contents

Contents

Preface

Fixed-income markets have grown tremendously in the last three decades. Nearly two-thirds of the market value of all securities in the capital markets is fixed-income securities. The securities range from a simple zero coupon security, which pays only at its maturity, to securities that have uncertain cash flows with many implicit or explicit optional features. The subject matter of *Fixed Income Markets and Their Derivatives* is extraordinarily rich in market institutions and theories of valuation. In addition, a great deal of empirical evidence on the behavior of interest rates, inflation, default rates, prepayments, and so on, bridges the gap between the richness of market institutions and the relatively sophisticated models of valuation. This book attempts to capture the rich interplay between theory, empirical evidence, and the evolution of market institutions.

ORGANIZATION OF THIS EDITION

The second edition of *Fixed Income Markets and Their Derivatives* presents an integrated, self-contained analysis of the market institutions, theory, and empirical evidence in fixed-income markets and their derivatives. Three new chapters have been added, covering inflation-indexed debt markets, emerging market debt securities, and credit risk models. The sequencing of the chapters has been significantly changed, based on feedback received from users of the text, to promote better continuity and smoother flow. In addition, concepts that are mathematically advanced are presented in appendices to the chapters. The main body of each chapter focuses on applications and examples. Many EXCEL applications are included in this edition to show that the analytical tools developed in the text can be used in real-world applications.

The book has been reorganized into three parts. Part I of the book consists of six chapters that focus exclusively on fixed-income markets and basic analytical tools such as duration, convexity, and yield curve-related mathematics. Chapters 1 and 2 provide an overview of the markets and how they are organized. Chapter 3 describes how the government fixed-income securities market is structured, and describes auction mechanisms in detail. The analytical tools (sometimes known as "bond mathematics") are developed in Chapter 4. In Chapters 5 and 6 we develop concepts of yield curve analysis.

Part II consists of six chapters that cover fixed income markets such as inflation-indexed debt markets, mortgage-backed securities and emerging debt markets, as well as a discussion of portfolio management techniques. Chapters 7 through 11 are devoted to the study of specialized fixed-income securities such as inflation-indexed bonds, agency securities, corporate debt, emerging market debt securities, and so on. Chapter 12 addresses portfolio management issues.

Part III consists of 7 chapters devoted to the study of fixed-income derivatives and the development of options pricing models, including all option-related tools and applications. Chapter 13 provides an overview of the fixed-income derivatives markets. Chapter 14 provides a self-contained development of basic options pricing principles, the Black-Scholes model, and the binomial options pricing model as they apply to fixed-income markets. Chapter 15 analyzes the Treasury futures contracts. Interest rate models and interest rate options pricing are developed in Chapter 16, and Chapter 17 provides a comprehensive treatment of Eurodollar futures markets and interest rate swaps. Credit risk models and credit derivatives are presented in Chapter 18. The last chapter presents risk management principles.

Below are additional details describing the content and objectives of each chapter:

- A comprehensive overview in **Chapter 1** provides a bird's-eye view of the global fixed-income markets and a perspective on key issues. This is done with an eye on institutional features and recent empirical evidence and data.
- A detailed description of how fixed-income markets are organized and who are the key players in the market is presented in **Chapter 2.** Primary dealership system, secondary markets, inter-dealer brokers, and so on, are discussed in detail. Major players (central banks, institutional investors, dealers, etc.) and their roles are discussed.
- **Chapter 3** presents in detail a description and analysis of when-issued markets, auction mechanisms, repo markets, and the financing of securities.
- The tools of bond mathematics, such as yield to maturity, yield to call, accrued interest, modified duration, MaCaulay duration, convexity, and so on, are developed in **Chapter 4.** Over 25 examples using real-life prices and yields are worked out to illustrate these important tools. Many EXCEL applications are provided. For advanced students, more difficult analytical concepts are presented in the appendix. Many applications such as spread trades and butterfly trades are illustrated.
- Yield curve analysis is developed in two parts. The first (in **Chapter 5**) develops how economic news releases take place in capital markets. The role of the central bank in controlling inflation and growth rate of the economy is discussed. The market's anticipation of the central bank's actions and the relationship between business cycle and real interest rates are also developed in this part. The second part (in **Chapter 6**) develops the tools of yield curve analysis, such as spot rates, forward rates, and par bond yield curve. The economics of stripping and reconstitutions are addressed in this part. Throughout we have used real-world prices and yields in developing the concepts of yield curve analysis.
- Inflation-indexed securities have been introduced in the United States and this market is treated in **Chapter 7.** We describe the development of this market and how the inflation-indexed securities are designed. The tax rules associated with this security and their possible effects are also addressed. The duration of inflation-indexed securities are computed and shown to be much higher than

similar nominal bonds. The use of inflation-indexed securities along with nominal securities to extract expected inflation is also discussed.

- The agency and corporate debt securities are described in **Chapter 8.** The special status of agency markets and the possible changes in their status are addressed because of the implications on their pricing as well as for the overall market. The shrinking of the Treasury market and the new benchmark notes programs of the agencies are also discussed. The corporate debt securities such as commercial paper (CP), corporate bonds, and so on, are presented. Both investment grade and high-yield bond markets are described. The process of financial distress, the role of bankruptcy code, credit rating, and so on, are presented in detail.

- The mortgage-backed securities markets are discussed in **Chapter 9.** The focus is on the valuation of securities and the incentives that dictate prepayments.

- Tax-exempt securities markets are analyzed in **Chapter 10.** The steepness of the tax-exempt curve, the practice of yield burning, and the tax clienteles are discussed in this chapter.

- Emerging market debt securities are described in **Chapter 11.** The nature of the market, the absence of a bankruptcy code, the spread behavior, and Brady bonds are discussed in detail.

- **Chapter 12** provides a brief account of portfolio management techniques such as dedicated portfolio construction, indexation, immunization, and so on.

- An overview of the fixed-income derivatives markets is provided in **Chapter 13.** The products that are traded in the listed markets (exchanges) and the products that are traded in the dealer markets are presented. The overall breadth and depth of the markets are assessed.

- **Chapter 14** provides a self-contained treatment of options and their applications in the fixed-income area. The Black-Scholes and the binomial options pricing methods are developed. Their applications are illustrated in an EXCEL setting. Options of cash instruments and futures contracts are priced. Risk management applications are illustrated.

- Treasury futures contracts are analyzed in **Chapter 15.** The contract specifications, recent changes in the contract grade, and the economics behind the determination of cheapest deliverable bonds are presented in the context of real-world examples. Important concepts such as basis, basis after carry, implied repo rate, delivery options, and so on, are discussed in full detail.

- In **Chapter 16** we discuss the Eurodollar futures contracts and the interest rate swap markets. The basic ideas behind their development and valuation principles are shown through realistic examples. The factors that determine the swap rates are analyzed in detail. Caps, floors, collars, and options on swaps are valued.

- **Chapter 17** develops various models of interest rates. The Vasicek model; the Cox, Ingersoll, and Ross model; the Black, Derman, and Toy model, the Ho and Lee model; and the Heath, Jarrow, and Morton model are discussed. Some applications of these models for valuing interest rate derivatives are also shown.

- **Chapter 18** develops credit risk models. The structural model of Merton and its use by KMV in deriving equity-based probabilities of default are analyzed. The development of reduced form models and the pricing of credit derivatives are briefly surveyed.

- The final chapter, **Chapter 19,** develops basic principles of risk management including portfolio value-at-risk (VAR).

ADDITIONAL LEARNING MATERIALS

Each chapter has several questions that test the reader on concepts developed in the chapter, as well as other issues. Some questions are designed based on historical data.

A solutions manual prepared by the author includes an introduction with a suggested course plan, allowing for either a quantitative or non-quantitative approach. The manual also provides solutions to the end-of-chapter questions in the text.

The book support Web site at http://sundaresan.swcollege.com includes additional updated information on bond pricing and hyperlinks to Internet resources mentioned in the text. Instructors and students are encouraged to visit the text's web site, as well as the South-Western Finance web site at http://finance.swcollege.com, where visitors will find resources such as Finance in the News, FinanceLinks Online, Wall Street analysts reports, and the Thomson Investors Network.

ACKNOWLEDGEMENTS

The development of this book covered several years and I owe a debt of gratitude to many people. Several classes of MBA students at Columbia Business School (in my Debt Markets course and Advanced Derivatives course) offered critical comments and suggestions on the class notes that formed the basis for the book. Parts of the manuscript were also used in the training programs at Bankers Trust, Goldman Sachs, Credit Suisse and Morgan Stanley. I am grateful to many participants in these programs for their comments and suggestions.

The book uses results from published research co-authored with a number of my colleagues. In this context my thanks are due to Ron Anderson, Mark Broadie, In Joon Kim, Bruno Montalvo, Kjell Nyborg, Krishna Ramaswamy, Scott Richard, Tong-sheng Sun, Ching Wang, and Fernando Zapatero.

Several of my students have assisted me in the collection and analysis of the data. In particular, I want to thank Quing Du, Rao Aisola, Geoff Zin, G. R. K. Reddy, Tom Gill, Scott McDermott, and Wen-ching Wang for their help. The book has benefited from a critical review by many colleagues who offered valuable insights. I thank the following reviewers:

Stanley M. Atkinson
University of Central Florida

Pierluigi Balduzzi
New York University

Bradford Cornell
University of California, Los Angeles
Director, Bank of America Research Center

Mark R. Eaker
University of Virginia Darden School

Michael Gibbons
Wharton School
University of Pennsylvania

Peter Knez
University of Wisconsin

James T. Lindley
University of Southern Mississippi

Ehud Ronn
University of Texas, Austin

Anthony B. Sanders
The Ohio State University

Chester Spatt
Carnegie Mellon University

Rajiv Sant
Mankato State University

Paul J. Swanson, Jr.
University of Cincinnati

The professional staff at South-Western made the task of writing this book as salubrious as possible. I thank Mike Mercier, Dennis Hanseman, Starratt Alexander, Jennifer Baker, and the staff at South-Western for their help in the completion of the second edition. Finally, I thank my wife, Raji Ayer, for her understanding throughout this project and also for preparing many of the tables, figures, and solutions to problem sets.

Despite careful scrutiny by all involved, a few errors may have gone undetected. I retain responsibility for them. I will be grateful if any remaining errors are brought to my attention so that they can be corrected in the next printing.

Suresh Sundaresan

Part I

Markets, Mechanisms, and Basic Tools

Chapter 1

An Overview of Fixed-Income Securities

Chapter Objectives

The purpose of this chapter is to introduce and describe fixed-income securities and the markets in which they are issued and traded. Chapter 1 will help the reader understand and answer the following questions:

- What are fixed-income securities?
- What are the key categories of players in debt markets, and what are their objectives? In this context, we will examine the following players:
  1. Issuers
  2. Investors
  3. Intermediaries
- What are the sources of risk and return in debt securities? The following sources of risk will be defined and addressed:
  1. Market risk
  2. Credit risk
  3. Liquidity risk
  4. Timing risk
- How are debt securities classified?

In addition, Chapter 1 will provide an overview of each segment of the debt markets in the United States and other leading capital markets in the world. In this overview, the terminology used in each segment will also be defined.

INTRODUCTION

An overview of fixed-income securities markets is useful for many reasons. First, nearly two-thirds of the market value of all the securities that are outstanding in the world are classified as fixed-income securities. This means that a substantial amount of savings are invested in fixed-income securities. Second, most participants in corporate and financial sectors participate in the fixed-income securities market to varying degrees. For example, corporate Treasurers must decide on the types of securities to issue; frequently corporations issue debt securities, such as commercial paper, corporate bonds, and medium-term notes, These securities are part of fixed-income securities markets. While corporations have the choice between the issuance of equity and fixed-income securities, federal government, state governments, and municipalities do not have that choice; they issue only debt securities. Such securities form the core of the fixed-income securities markets. For these reasons, it is important to get a good understanding of the fixed-income markets.

This chapter provides an overview of debt securities, issuers, intermediaries, and buyers and illustrates their diversity. We will provide a simple framework for comparing the risks and rewards of fixed-income securities. In subsequent chapters, we will develop in detail each segment of the fixed-income markets and their derivatives. The pricing of such securities and their risk-return trade-offs will be examined in detail. In addition to providing an overview of these markets, this chapter also introduces the vocabulary and some basic terminology frequently used by professionals in the fixed-income markets.

DEBT SECURITIES

Fixed-income securities are financial claims issued by governments (e.g., the U.S. Treasury, the German Treasury, etc.), government agencies (e.g., the Federal Home Loan Bank [FHLB]), state governments, corporations (e.g., Exxon, GM, etc.), municipalities (e.g., New York City), banks (e.g., Citibank, Barclays, etc.), and other financial intermediaries. The cash flows promised to the buyers of fixed-income securities represent contractual obligations of the respective issuers. Typically, when such contractual obligations are not met, the buyers of fixed-income securities will have the right to take control of the firm that issued such debt securities. Fixed-income securities (or debt securities) are issued, traded, and invested in markets called fixed-income markets (or debt markets).

Figure 1-1 gives a perspective of the debt markets. The sellers of fixed-income securities (governments, agencies, corporations, banks, etc.) share certain common objectives. For example, sellers of securities would like to receive fair value for their securities. In addition, they would like to be able to issue securities that best fit their needs. Some would like to issue simple noncallable debt securities with a fixed maturity date and a fixed coupon; such securities are referred to as **bullet securities.** Others would like to issue securities that are callable, and some would like to issue debt that is convertible. For example, issuers who anticipate that their future credit ratings will improve might put in call features in their debt issue if the market does not share their optimism about the future potential for improved credit reputation. In Figure 1-1, we list some of the objectives of issuers in this market.

The buyers of fixed-income securities are typically large institutions, such as pension funds, insurance companies, commercial banks, corporations, mutual funds, and central banks. In addition, smaller institutions and individual investors also participate in this market. Their objectives might include buying and selling at a fair price and at a narrow bid offer spread, for example. **Bid** is the price at which a dealer is willing to buy and **offer** is the price at which a dealer is willing to sell. Some of the key objectives of the buyers are listed in Figure 1-1. An institution or an individual would sell at the bid to the dealer and buy at the offer from the dealer.

Sundaresan, *Fixed Income Markets and Their Derivatives*, 2e
Errata

Despite careful attention and verification, we detected a few errors in the 2nd edition of *Fixed Income Markets and Their Derivatives* after the initial printing. These errors will be addressed as soon as the text is reprinted. In the meantime, we submit the following corrections and sincerely apologize for any inconvenience to instructors or students using the text.

CHAPTER 1
Page 5: Figure 1-1, the bottom of the figure has been cut off. Below is the complete figure as it was intended to appear.

Issuer of Debt Securities	Financial Intermediaries	Institutional and Retail Investors

Issuers:
1. Governments and their agencies
2. Corporations
3. Commercial Banks
4. States and municipalities
5. Special-purpose vehicles
6. Foreign institutions

Intermediaries:
1. Primary dealers
2. Other dealers
3. Investment banks
4. Credit rating agencies
5. Credit and liquidity enhancers

Investors:
1. Governments
2. Pension funds
3. Insurance companies
4. Mutual funds
5. Commercial banks
6. Foreign institutions
7. Households

Objectives:
1. To sell securities at a fair market price
2. To have orderly and liquid secondary markets in their securities
3. To be able to reverse and modify earlier issuance decisions in response to market conditions efficiently
4. To design and issue debt securities that best suit their needs

Objectives:
1. To provide primary market making services, such as bidding in the auction, underwriting, and distribution
2. To provide orderly market making in the secondary market
3. To provide risk management and asset liability management services
4. To provide proprietary trading activities

Objectives:
1. To buy securities of different risk-return profiles at a fair price
2. To obtain diversification at a low cost
3. To reverse previous decisions at a low cost
4. To have access to risk management services, such as derivatives
5. To get information on credit ratings, etc., at a low cost

Fig. 1-1 *A Schematic Representation of Debt Markets*

Page 24: Refer to paragraph 4. In the last line the term "FNMA" should be replaced by "FHLMC".

Page 28: The second paragraph under *High Yield Debt* incorrectly refers to Table 1-14. It is Table 1-12 that refers to 1997 new issue volume.

Page 63: Refer to Figure 2-6. In the left box the date 10-June-93 should be replaced by 10-Jun-86. In the right box the date 13-June-93 should be replaced by 13-Jun-86.

CHAPTER 3
Page 82: Refer to the first paragraph, lines 16-17. In the sentence that begins, "The bidders on the noncompetitive tender are assured . . ." replace "quantity-weighted average price established" with "stop-out yield established."

CHAPTER 4
Page 141: Refer to figure 4-9. In the Y-axis the number 101.91367 should be replaced by 101.91347.

Page 142: Refer to figure 4-9. In the Y-axis the top number 101.91367 should be replaced by 101.91347.

Page 157: Refer to first equation. It should be replaced by $\text{MD} = \dfrac{\dfrac{\Delta P}{P}}{\Delta y}$

CHAPTER 6
Page 221: Refer to equation (6.16). It should be replaced by $\dfrac{dz_{T-t}}{z_{T-t}} = r(t)dt$

Page 530: Refer to figure 15-7. The Y-axis label should be $\dfrac{\text{Price}}{\text{CF}}$

FIGURE 1-1   *A Schematic Representation of Debt Markets*

Issuer of Debt Securities	Financial Intermediaries	Institutional and Retail Investors

Issuers:

1. Governments and their agencies
2. Corporations
3. Commercial Banks
4. States and municipalities
5. Special-purpose vehicles
6. Foreign institutions

Intermediaries:

1. Primary dealers
2. Other dealers
3. Investment banks
4. Credit rating agencies
5. Credit and liquidity enhancers

Investors:

1. Governments
2. Pension funds
3. Insurance companies
4. Mutual funds
5. Commercial banks
6. Foreign institutions
7. Households

Objectives:

1. To sell securities at a fair market price
2. To have orderly and liquid secondary markets in their securities
3. To be able to reverse and modify earlier issuance decisions in response to market conditions efficiently
4. To design and issue debt securities that best suit

Objectives:

1. To provide primary market making services, such as bidding in the auction, underwriting, and distribution
2. To provide orderly market making in the secondary market
3. To provide risk management and asset liability management services
4. To provide proprietary trading activities

Objectives:

1. To buy securities of different risk-return profiles at a fair price
2. To obtain diversification at a low cost
3. To reverse previous decisions at a low cost
4. To have access to risk management services, such as derivatives
5. To get information on credit ratings, etc., at a

Fixed-income securities are traded in secondary markets, which are typically organized as dealer markets or over-the-counter (OTC) markets known as fixed-income markets that are spread all over the world. The intermediaries in these markets are many. They provide a variety of different functions for a fee. They help issuers in the initial offering of the security, assist in the pricing and distribution of the security, make a secondary market, provide liquidity, and engage in proprietary trading activities. In addition, intermediaries, such as Moody's or Standard and Poor produce information about the credit quality of different issuers. This information, made available for a fee, is an important service provided by intermediaries in the corporate debt market. Other intermediaries exist who provide liquidity and credit enhancements for a fee. Such activities by intermediaries tend to promote a more liquid and efficient debt market. Some of the objectives of financial intermediaries are shown in Figure 1-1.

Debt Securities and Their Risks

Contractual Cash Flows. As noted earlier, debt contracts typically specify explicit rules of compensation to the buyer (investor) during their stated term which is pre-specified at the time of issuance. Usually, payments are contractual. The examples of fixed-income securities provided here illustrate the diversity of the issuers, as well as the diversity of the debt contracts traded in these markets.

FIGURE 1-2   *Interest Rate Risk of a 7.25%, 5-15-2016 T-Bond*

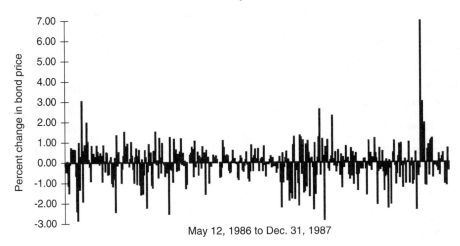

Example 1-1:

7.25%, 5-15-2016 noncallable U.S. T-bond

This debt contract has a compensation of 7.25% (payable semiannually on May 15 and on November 15) of the face amount of the Treasury bond until its maturity date. On the maturity date, in addition to the interest payment, the face amount is also payable. The periodic compensation is referred to as the **coupon** and the remaining life of the claim is referred to as the **time to maturity.**

This is an example of a bullet debt security, which is **default-free** as there is no doubt that the promised payments will be made; thus, investors face no **credit risk.** This is not to say that such an instrument has no risk. Indeed, investors who take a position in this Treasury bond are exposed to a significant **interest rate risk.** For example, the price of this T-bond fluctuated within a period of 18 months (from May 1986 to December 1987) from a minimum of 71.78% of the par amount to a maximum of 101.72% of par. This vividly brings home the interest rate risk of T-bonds. As Figure 1-2 clearly illustrates, the percentage price changes in this T-bond were rather high, reaching a 7% change within a day. An investor who bought a million dollar par value of this T-bond at par was exposed to a great deal of price risk; the value fell as low as $717,800 and went as high as $1,017,200. We will develop and illustrate later the different quantitative measures of interest rate and price risk that are used in practice.

The size of this specific T-bond outstanding in the market is on the order of $10 billion. This rather large size coupled with the fact that there are hundreds of dealers who stand ready to participate in a two-way market indicates that such a security is **liquid.** High liquidity means that investors can buy or sell large amounts easily at a narrow bid-offer spread without an adverse price reaction. The average bid-offer spread for this T-bond during this period was 1.1 basis points. (A **basis point** is one-hundredth of

	Dimension of Risk and Return	Level of Risk Present in the Security 7.25%, 5-15-2016 U.S. T-Bond
TABLE 1-1 *Example 1-1, U.S. Treasury Bond*	Credit risk	Not present
	Interest rate risk	High
	Liquidity risk	Generally very liquid; bid-offer spreads are small
	Timing risk	No uncertainty of timing of cash flows
	Taxation	Taxable only at federal level
	Foreign exchange (FX) risk	None for domestic investor
	Inflation risk	Present
	Future cash flows	Known—no risk
	Event risk	Not present

one percent. Hence, 1.1 basis points is 0.011%, or 0.00011.) The maximum was 4.31 basis points. This illustrates that the T-bond had a very low liquidity risk. The fact that this T-bond was not callable by the Treasury means that the investor has no uncertainty about the timing of the cash flows. Thus, the security has no **timing risk.** For example, if the security can be called by the issuer, the investor will face timing risk. Some securities are subject to **event risk.** This risk arises if the issuer's credit risk suddenly deteriorates or a major recapitalization (such as a leveraged buyout) occurs, adversely affecting the risk of the bond. Note that the T-bond in Example 1-1 has no event risk.

It is useful to classify this security along the dimensions of risk and return as in Table 1-1. The dimensions of risk enumerated in Table 1-1 are generally of great interest to investors in the fixed-income securities markets. (We have not explicitly identified reinvestment risk as a separate risk factor—it may be thought of as part of the interest rate risk dimension.)

Example 1-2:

A $200 million par amount of floating rate notes was issued by Citicorp on June 26, 1978. The coupon of the floater is indexed to the six-month T-bill rates, that is, to the arithmetic average of the weekly market rate for the six-month U.S. Treasury bills as published by the Federal Reserve during the 14 calendar days immediately prior to the last 10 days of February and August. The actual coupon will be this average plus 120 basis points during the period 1979–1983 subject to a minimum of $7\frac{1}{2}$%. For the period 1984–1988, the spread over the average will be 100 basis points subject to a minimum of 7%; and for the period 1989–1998, the spread will be 75 basis points subject to a minimum of $6\frac{1}{2}$%. At the time of issue, Citicorp was rated AAA/AA+. The note matured on September 1, 1998. The floater did not have conversion features but was callable after September 1, 1988, at declining call prices.

The buyer of this floating rate note is subject to very different sources and degrees of risk than the buyer of the U.S. T-bond in Example 1-1. The Citicorp floater has credit risk. In addition, the future cash flows are uncertain as the coupons are indexed to the

TABLE 1-2	Dimension of Risk and Return	Level of Risk Present in the Security: Citicorp Floater
Example 1-2, Citicorp Floater	Credit risk	Present—spreads vary depending on issuer's credit reputation
	Interest rate risk	Relatively low since the coupons are indexed to short rates
	Liquidity risk	Generally not liquid; bid-offer spreads are relatively high
	Timing risk	Callability after 10 years introduces timing risk
	Taxation	Taxable at all (federal, state, and local) levels
	FX risk	None for domestic investor
	Inflation risk	Present
	Future cash flows	Not known
	Event risk	Present

future path of six-month T-bill yields. As Example 1-2 shows, the coupon of debt securities need not always be fixed. The time to maturity is also not necessarily fixed. In Example 1-1, the life was known at the time of issuance. In Example 1-2, the life cannot be predicted; it depends on when the issuer calls or declares financial distress. Table 1-2 summarizes the risks of the Citicorp floater.

When the issuer of a debt claim has a probability of going bankrupt, the debt securities may only be issued with several additional features. We now turn to some of these contractual provisions.

Priority of Cash Flows. This issue is moot for government debt. The power of taxation virtually guarantees promised cash flows. For other issuers of debt securities, debt contracts typically have precedence over residual claims such as equity. When there are multiple issues of debt securities by the same entity (as is typical), priorities and relative seniorities are clearly stated by the issuer in **bond covenants.** This leads to some important variations in debt contracts.

Secured and Unsecured Debt. Secured debt, such as **mortgage bonds,** is backed by tangible assets of the issuing company. In the event of financial distress, such assets may be sold to satisfy the obligations of debt holders. Unsecured debt, known as **debentures** in the United States, is not secured by any assets.

Contingency Provisions. Debt securities sold by issuers that are subject to a positive probability of default typically contain two important contingency provisions.

First, debt contracts specify events that precipitate bankruptcy. In the debt pricing literature, this is known as the **lower reorganization boundary.** An example of such an event is the nonpayment of promised coupon payments. Another example is the failure to make **balloon** payments. (The payment of principal at maturity is often referred to as a balloon payment.) Such events give the debtholders the right to take over the firm. Often, the debt holders may not exercise the right to take over the issuing firm if they feel they could do better by renegotiating with the managers. The lower reorganization boundary is also the point where debtholders may decide whether to enter into a process of workouts and renegotiations or force the firm into formal liquidation. Alternatives such as Chapter 7 or Chapter 11 of the Federal Bankruptcy Act must be considered by the debtholders at this stage. A detailed treatment of these issues is provided in Chapter 8.

Second, debt contracts also specify the rules by which debtholders will be compensated upon bankruptcy and transfer of control. Quite often, the actual payments may differ from the specified payments. Naturally, the value of debt issues is affected in important ways by such provisions and deviations. Often, renegotiations and workouts lead to deviations from the **absolute priority rules,** whereby senior claimholders must be paid before any payments are made to junior claimholders. A fuller discussion of the empirical evidence is provided in Chapter 8.

Most corporate debt issues are **callable** at predetermined prices, which gives the issuer the right to buy back the debt issue at prespecified future times. Most are issued with **sinking fund provisions,** which require that the debt issue be periodically retired in predetermined amounts. Some are **puttable** at the option of the buyer, and some are **convertible** into a prespecified number of shares of common stock of the issuing company. Most convertible debt securities are also callable. Debt securities in different markets also have some idiosyncratic features; many municipal bonds are **serial issues.** In such issues, stated amounts mature at different times and bear different coupons. To understand some of these features, we provide the following additional examples of debt securities.

Example 1-3:

On June 22, 1993, Anheuser Busch issued $200 million par amount of long-term bonds bearing a coupon of 7.375% and maturing in 2023. The bond was rated A1 and was callable after 10 years. Note that this bond is subject to credit risk, interest rate risk, timing risk, etc. Since this is just one of the several debt issues that have been made by the issuer in the past, and since the issuer has a positive probability of defaulting, all the contractual provisions we outlined earlier will have an impact on the pricing of the security.

Example 1-4:

In October 1993, nearly $200 million worth of bonds were issued by the municipality of Detroit. This was a **revenue bond** for the water supply system, which is backed by the revenues generated by the system. The debt had serial issues maturing from 1995 to 2023. The 1995 serial unit was priced to yield 3.40%, and the 2023 unit was priced to yield 5.43%. The issue was tax-exempt and was insured by the Federal Guaranty Insurance Company. The issue was rated AAA by the rating agencies. Unlike the previous examples of debt securities, this municipal issue is tax-exempt in the sense that the interest payments are not taxed at the level of buyers (investors), who are residents of the state of Michigan.

Example 1-5:

> In October 1993, the Federal Home Loan Bank (FHLB) issued $750 million of real-estate mortgage-investment conduit securities. The 30-year, 6.5% mortgage securities were offered by Salomon Brothers and backed by the Government National Mortgage Association (GNMA). The collateral has a weighted average coupon of 7% and a weighted average maturity of 358 months. This debt security is part of a securitized transaction, discussed in detail later in the chapter.

Example 1-6:

> Fujitec Co. (Japan) issued $60 million of Eurobonds with a coupon of 0.875%. The issue was sold with equity warrants that are due to mature on November 10, 1997. Each bond had two warrants attached to it. The warrants should be exercised by October 1997. This is an example of a hybrid debt security, discussed further in Chapter 8. This debt security provides some equity exposure to the investor. Other hybrids, such as convertible bonds, are also popular in the marketplace.

These examples should give the reader a taste of the richness and diversity present in debt securities. We provide a classification of debt securities next.

CLASSIFICATION OF DEBT SECURITIES

Usually, debt securities are classified by issuers and, within each issuer class, they are further classified by maturity sectors.

Treasury (Sovereign) securities comprise U.S. Treasury securities, U.K, gilts, German government bonds (*Bunds*), Japanese government bonds (JGBs), French government bonds (OATs), etc.

Agency securities are debt securities issued by government agencies, such as the Federal Home Loan Bank (FHLB) and the Tennessee Valley Authority (TVA). Debt securities issued by Federal National Mortgage Association (FNMA), and Government National Mortgage Association (GNMA) also fall in this group.

Corporate securities are debt securities issued by corporations. They may be further classified into investment grade corporates and noninvestment grade or high-yield securities.

Mortgage-backed securities are debt securities backed by pools of mortgages.

Asset-backed securities are securities backed by a portfolio of assets, such as credit card receivables.

Municipal issues are debt securities issued by state governments and municipalities.

Emerging market securities are debt securities issued by less-developed and developing countries.

Figure 1-3 presents a perspective of the domestic (U.S.) debt market.

FIGURE 1-3   *Composition of Domestic Taxable Debt Markets*
Total Market Value $4,977 Billion

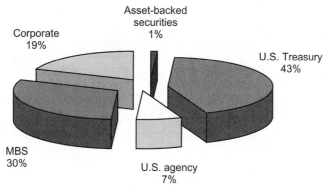

Source: Lehman Brothers (December 1997)

TABLE 1-3   *Outstanding Level of Public and Private Debt 1985–1999* ($ Billions)*

	Municipal	Treasury[1]	Agency Mortgage-Backed[2]	U.S. Corporate*	Fed. Agencies
1985	859.5	1,360.2	372.1	776.5	293.9
1986	920.4	1,564.3	534.4	959.6	307.4
1987	1,010.4	1,724.7	672.1	1,074.9	341.4
1988	1,082.3	1,821.3	749.9	1,195.7	381.5
1989	1,135.2	1,945.4	876.3	1,292.5	411.8
1990	1,184.4	2,195.8	1,024.4	1,350.4	434.7
1991	1,272.2	2,471.6	1,160.5	1,454.7	442.8
1992	1,302.8	2,754.1	1,273.5	1,557.0	484.0
1993	1,377.5	2,989.5	1,349.6	1,674.7	570.7
1994	1,341.7	3,126.0	1,441.9	1,755.6	738.9
1995	1,293.5	3,307.2	1,570.4	1,937.5	844.6
1996	1,296.0	3,459.7	1,711.2	2,122.2	925.8
1997	1,367.5	3,456.8	1,825.8	2,346.3	1,022.6
1998	1,464.3	3,355.5	2,018.4	2,666.1	1,296.5
1999*	1,532.5	3,281.0	2,292.0	3,040.0	1,500.0

Sources: U.S. Department of Treasury; Federal Reserve System; Federal National Mortgage Association; Government National Mortgage Association; Federal Home Loan Mortgage Corporation.

*The Bond Market Association estimates.

[1]Interest bearing marketable public debt.

[2]Includes only GNMA, FNMA, and FHLMC mortgage-backed securities.

The domestic taxable debt markets index is presented in Figure 1-3. U.S. Treasury accounts for 43% of the index and mortgage-backed securities account for 30%. The rest is composed of corporates, U.S. agency, and asset-backed securities. Table 1-3 presents the growth of these markets during the 1985–1999 period.

FIGURE 1-4   *Global Debt Markets (G-7 Markets)*
Total Market Value $4,572 Billion

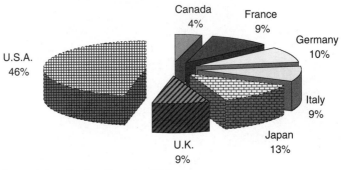

Source: Lehman Brothers (December 1997)

Figure 1-4 presents the global debt markets index. Nearly 70% of the index is accounted for by the United States, Japan, and Germany. The remainder is composed of the United Kingdom, Italy, France, and Canada. A comparison of new issue volume in fixed-income markets with the equity market is provided later in Table 1-12 of this chapter.

Next, we provide an overview of each important segment of the debt market.

U.S. Treasury Market

The United States Treasury regularly issues debt securities with maturities ranging from a few days to 30 years. Such securities are known as Treasury securities. These are regarded by the investment community as risk-free. This is because the U.S. government stands ready to pay the necessary obligations (i.e., coupons and face amounts) to any investor who buys these securities. These securities are backed by the full faith and credit of the U.S. government. The economic power of the United States and the power of the government to levy taxes are obviously two of the important factors in the investor's perception that these securities are default-free. Since a large amount of debt securities are issued by the U.S. government, the Treasury has to schedule regular and frequent auctions to sell these securities. The Treasury securities are auctioned by the U.S. Treasury according to the schedule provided in Table 1-4. Note that the Treasury is auctioning both nominal and inflation-indexed securities. Due to budget surplus the Treasury has started to reduce the issuance of securities and has embarked on a buyback program using some of the surplus. We will discuss this later in the book. We enclose the announcement by Treasury Secretary Lawrence Summers, which outlines the rationale for buying back Treasury securities.

The buyback by the Treasury has threatened the liquidity of the Treasury market and its benchmark status.

TABLE 1-4   *Frequency of Auctions of Treasury Securities, by Maturity, 1985–1999*

Year	Type of Security										
	13-Week	26-Week	52-Week	2-Year	3-Year	4-Year	5-Year	7-Year	10-Year	20-Year	30-Year
1985	Weekly	Weekly	Every 4th week	Monthly	Quarterly	Quarterly	Quarterly	Quarterly	Quarterly	Quarterly	Quarterly
1986										None (1/15/86)	
1987											
1988											
1989											
1990						None (12/31/90)					
1991							Monthly (1/31/91)				
1992											
1993								None (4/15/93)			Semiannually (8/16/93)
1994											
1995											
1996									6×/yr (7/15/96)		3×/yr (8/15/96)
1997									Quarterly (8/15/97)		
1998						None (5/15/98)	Quarterly (8/17/98)				
1999											Semiannually[1]

Source: *Treasury Bulletin.*

Note: Date indicates when a security was first issued under a new schedule or, if discontinued, when a security was last issued.

[1] In August 1999, the Treasury announced that it would discontinue the November auction and issue 30-year bonds in February and August only. All securities are sold by single-price (Dutch) auction procedure.

Statement of Treasury Secretary Lawrence Summers
(January 13, 2000)

This morning I have the pleasure of introducing an important new tool for Treasury's management of the public debt in an era of budget surpluses–debt buybacks. Today we are releasing the final regulations that make this important tool available to us, and announcing our plan to use debt buybacks to benefit American taxpayers as we continue to pay down our nation's debt.

As you all know, FY 1999 produced a budget surplus of $123 billion, the largest ever. Following FY 1998's surplus of $69 billion, we have generated the first back-to-back budget surpluses in over forty years. As a result, we have paid down $140 billion in debt held by the public over the past two years, saving taxpayers the billions of dollars in interest payments that would have been due on that amount. And, while future projections are always uncertain, if the President's fiscal framework is adopted and the current fiscal discipline is maintained, we anticipate paying down the debt held by the public to zero within the next fifteen years.

As I have previously noted, reducing the supply of Treasury debt held by the public brings enormous benefits to our economy.

- It means that less of the savings of Americans will flow into government bonds and more will flow into financing capital investment for American businesses and homes for American families.
- It means that we will be less reliant on borrowings from abroad to finance American investment.
- It means that there will be less pressure on interest rates than there would otherwise have been, and therefore lower borrowing costs for businesses and lower interest payments for American families.

(continued)

At the same time, this success brings a new and welcome debt management challenge for the Federal government. Debt buybacks, which will allow us to repurchase outstanding securities before they mature, are a new tool created to respond to these challenges.

Debt buybacks have several concrete advantages for our Federal debt management:

- First, they allow us to enhance the liquidity of Treasury benchmark securities, which promotes overall market liquidity and should reduce the government's interest costs over time. The issue of liquidity is important, as can be seen in the noticeable difference in yield between recently issued highly liquid benchmark securities and older less liquid debt. This differential is commonly in the range of 20 basis points.
- Second, by paying off debt that has substantial remaining maturity, buybacks enable us to prevent what would otherwise be a potentially costly and unjustified increase in the average maturity of our debt, which has grown from $5\frac{1}{4}$ years in 1997 to $5\frac{3}{4}$ years in 1999 and, absent countervailing action, would be projected to rise to almost 8 years by 2004. Over the long term, this would impose additional cost on the taxpayers to finance our debt.
- Third, by paying off debt, we can make more effective use of excess cash at times of the year when tax revenues exceed immediate spending needs. For instance, last April our cash balances rose from $5 billion to $75 billion due to the receipt of income tax payments.

Each of these benefits contributes to our ability to meet our overall debt management goals, which include achieving the lowest cost financing for American taxpayers, effective cash management, and promotion of efficient capital markets. We plan to use debt buybacks to help us fulfill each of these goals. The rule that is being released today establishes the procedures by which we will conduct debt buybacks. These include:

- An announcement of the range of eligible maturates.
- A multiple-price, reverse auction format.
- Operations will be conducted through the Federal Reserve Bank of New York.
- Only competitive offers will be accepted.
- Settlement will occur two days after the buyback operation.

While the amount of debt that we intend to purchase will be influenced by a number of factors, we expect to buy back as much as $30 billion this year. We will begin conducting buyback operations in the next few months and expect to conduct several in the first half of the year. We plan to gauge the market reaction to our early experiences and adjust our processes and procedures, including the notice period, size, timing, and regularity of the operations. We will prepare the market for our first debt buyback operation by prior public announcement.

Following consultations between OMB and CBO, it has been determined that the most appropriate budget treatment for any purchase premium (or discount) is as a means of financing. This is the section of the budget that includes funds used for debt reduction (or borrowed to finance deficits), seigniorage on coins, changes in Treasury cash balances, and other items that, like debt buybacks, do not represent a true cost to the Federal government.

The Treasury is committed to protecting the interests of the American taxpayer. An era of budget surpluses requires us to adapt by making changes to the way we manage the national debt in a manner consistent with our long-held objectives: achieving the lowest cost of financing for the American taxpayer; maintaining sound cash management practices; and promoting efficient capital markets. Today, we have put in place an important new tool to allow us to manage our nation's debt more efficiently. We look forward to using it to benefit all Americans. Thank you.

TABLE 1-5
On-the-Run Issues, as of
September 5, 1999

Issue	Yield	Coupon	Maturity
3 months	4.91%	—	12/02/1999
6 months	5.13%	—	3/02/2000
1 year	5.20%	—	8/17/2000
2 years	5.62%	5.500%	8/31/2001
5 years	5.77%	6.000%	8/15/2004
10 years	5.89%	6.000%	8/15/2009
30 years	6.02%	6.125%	8/15/2029
Inflation Indexed Treasury			
5 years	3.92%	3.625%	7/15/2002
10 years	4.01%	3.875%	1/15/2009
30 years	4.03%	3.875%	4/15/2029

Source: Bloomberg.

In Chapter 3, we will examine in detail the auction procedures of the U.S. Treasury. For now, it is important to note that the securities are auctioned at **benchmark maturities,** shown in Table 1-4. Recently, the Treasury has discontinued the auction of three-year and seven-year Treasury securities and will auction thirty-year Treasury securities less frequently instead of the quarterly auctions. Newly auctioned securities are known as **on-the-run issues.** The yields of on-the-run Treasury issues are shown in Table 1-5. The yield of a security is its internal rate of return, that is, the discount rate at which its present value of all its future cash flows is exactly equal to its market price. We will describe this concept in detail in Chapter 4.

The investor base for Treasury securities is truly global. Foreign central banks, domestic and foreign banks, pension funds, mutual funds, thrifts, etc., are major buyers of Treasury securities. The extent of participation by foreign investors in the domestic debt securities market is significant.

Securities issued by the Treasury with a maturity of less than or equal to one year at the time of issuance by the Treasury are called **Treasury bills** or **T-bills.** Such securities do not pay any coupons and may be purchased in auctions at a discount to their face value, which is typically $1 million. Treasury bills are thus U.S. Treasury discount obligations that promise the payment of face amount on a predetermined date. T-bills are auctioned by the U.S. Treasury at periodic intervals in the following maturities: 91 days (three months), 182 days (six months) and 364 days (one year). T-bills are perhaps among the most liquid and nominally riskless securities. The bid-offer spreads on newly issued (or the on-the-run issues) are rather small (in the neighborhood of 1 to 2 basis points). Transaction sizes may range from $5 to $100 million. As T-bills become more seasoned and approach their maturity date, their liquidity falls, and investors typically pay a lower price as they require a liquidity premium in yields to buy such seasoned bills.

Treasury securities that pay coupons and that have maturities in the range of 1 to 10 years at the time of issuance are called **Treasury notes (T-notes).** Treasury securities that have maturities in excess of 10 years are called **Treasury bonds (T-bonds).** Maturities of Treasury bonds generally extend to 30 years. The thirty-year T-bond is known as the **long bond.** The Treasury regularly schedules auctions of such securities in the market. U.S. Treasury notes and bonds pay periodic (usually semiannual) coupons in addition to the face amount at maturity. Their prices are quoted in fractions of $\frac{1}{32}$, $\frac{1}{64}$, and sometimes even in $\frac{1}{128}$. (In the bond market, $\frac{1}{32}$ is referred to as a **tick.**) Price quotations do not include the accrued interest (discussed later in Chapter 4). U.S. Treasury coupon obligations may be bought or sold only with accrued interest. This is the amount of the next coupon that the current owner has earned by virtue of owner- ship of the Treasury note or bond. The buyer will have to pay the quoted price (**flat price**) plus the accrued interest. The flat price plus the accrued interest is known as the **full price** or the **invoice price.** The U.S. Treasury no longer issues callable bonds. In the past, it has issued bonds that are callable at par after the **call protection period.** During the call protection period, the Treasury will not call the bonds back. Much of the active trading is usually concentrated in on-the-run issues. For liquid on-the-run is- sues, the bid-offer spreads are typically $\frac{1}{32}$ to $\frac{2}{32}$. Transaction sizes usually range from $5 million face amount to about $50 million or more. Seasoned issues (those is- sued in previous auctions) are known as **off-the-run issues.** For off-the-run issues, the spreads may be much higher. Transaction sizes and bid-offer spreads for off-the-run issues are difficult to predict. In a similar manner, practitioners refer to more seasoned issues as off-off-the-run issues. This is because most recently issued on-the-run issues are the ones about which dealers have the most information. As the issue gets older (and becomes off-the-run), dealers may not have the same level of information about which institutions own the securities and in what amounts.

We illustrate the daily trading volume in on-the-run, off-the-run, and when-issued Treasury markets in Figure 1-5. (The when-issued markets will be presented and dis-

FIGURE 1-5 *Daily Trading Volume of U.S. Treasury Securities*

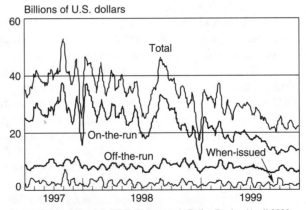

Source: Michael Fleming, FRBNY Economic Policy Review/April 2000.

Notes: The chart plots the 10-day rolling average of the daily trading volume in the interdealer market. The volume figures are reported on a one-way basis (so that a trade between two parties is counted only once) and cover about 65% of the interdealer broker market.

cussed in Chapter 3.) Note that the daily trading volume of on-the-run is by far greater than that of off-the-run.

We also present Table 1-6, which shows why investors regard on-the-run securities to be very valuable generally and especially in a crisis situation. Note that in all benchmark maturities off-the-run securities yield more than on-the-run securities. In a crisis, such as the Russian default in the fall of 1998, investors prefer the more liquid on-the-run securities so that the spread widens even more.

In Figure 1-6, we provide the dollar value of T-bills, T-notes, and T-bonds that were held by private investors and institutions as of September 1999.

The prices of Treasury securities fluctuate a good deal in response to economic and political news. This, in turn, affects the return performance of Treasury securities. In Table 1-7, the yield performance of Treasury thirty-year bonds are shown for the period 1977–1998.

Notice that the yields have ranged from a low of 5.20% in 1998 to a high of 14.88% in 1981. The variability can be severe even within one year; in 1982, the yields dropped from a level of 14.22% in January to a level of 10.54% in December. Such yield volatility coupled with the level of Treasury securities outstanding in the private sector poses very serious risks to portfolio managers and bond dealers. This emphasizes the fact that the absence of default risk does not necessarily imply that such securities are riskless. The plot of the yield (internal rate of return) and the maturity is referred to as the **yield curve.** Typically, as the maturity increases, yield increases. This is referred to as the **"normal"** or **"upward-sloping"** yield curve. Table 1-7 shows that there may

TABLE 1-6 *Off-the-Run/On-the-Run Yield Spreads of U.S. Treasury Coupon Securities*		Basis Points			
	Period	*Two-Year*	*Five-Year*	*Ten-Year*	*Thirty-Year*
	Precrisis: July 1, 1997–Aug. 14, 1998	2.80 (1.80)	4.48 (1.90)	7.87 (1.71)	5.01 (1.71)
	Crisis: Aug. 17, 1998–Nov. 20, 1998	11.62 (5.76)	16.68 (4.89)	6.63 (3.30)	12.99 (4.65)
	Postcrisis: Nov. 23, 1998–Oct. 29, 1999	5.02 (2.37)	17.93 (2.75)	13.55 (6.93)	13.50 (1.83)
	Full sample: July 1, 1997–Oct. 29, 1999	4.72 (3.86)	11.33 (7.14)	10.03 (5.54)	9.36 (4.78)

Source: Michael Fleming, FRBNY Economic Policy Review/April 2000 based on data from Bear Stearns and GovPX.

Note: The table reports the means and standard deviations (in parentheses) of the daily off-the-run/on-the-run yield spreads of the indicated securities. The spreads are calculated as the predicted yields less the market yields, where the predicted yields are those of comparable-duration off-the-run securities as derived from a model of the yield curve estimated with off-the-run prices.

FIGURE 1-6   *Distribution of Marketable Treasury Debt Outstanding, by Type of Security, September 30, 1999*

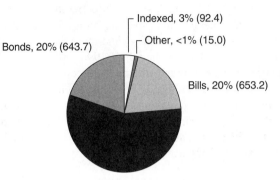

Source: *Monthly Statement of the Public Debt of the United States* (U.S. Department of the Treasury), September 1999.

Note: Numbers in parentheses are amounts outstanding, in billions of dollars.

TABLE 1-7

Thirty-Year T-bond Yields and Yield Spreads

Year	High	Low	Spread of Thirty-Year T-bond Yields over Three-Month T-bill Yields
1977	7.94%	7.64%	NA
1978	8.85%	8.18%	82
1979	10.12%	8.94%	−114
1980	12.40%	9.81%	−51
1981	14.88%	12.14%	−106
1982	14.22%	10.54%	243
1983	11.88%	10.63%	241
1984	13.44%	11.52%	269
1985	11.81%	9.54%	306
1986	9.40%	7.27%	166
1987	10.26%	7.39%	279
1988	9.46%	8.30%	200
1989	9.32%	7.82%	−40
1990	9.17%	8.00%	116
1991	8.55%	7.41%	282
1992	8.10%	7.23%	425
1993	7.47%	5.78%	355
1994	8.16%	6.21%	308
1995	7.93%	5.96%	135
1996	7.06%	6.05%	155
1997	7.09%	5.99%	131
1998	5.95%	5.20%	65
1999	6.48%	5.63%	109

Source: Federal Reserve.

be an overall relationship between the levels of the yields and the shape of the yield curve. This is seen by looking at the average spreads of thirty-year T-bond yields over the three-month T-bill yields. Note that the spread was negative from 1979 to 1981, when the rates rose to very high levels. This implies an **inverted yield curve** during this period. Then the spread became positive again in the period from 1982 to 1988. During 1989, the yield curve was inverted again. In 1999, the yield of 30-year fell below that of 10-year. This is due to the buyback of 30-year bond by Treasury and the belief that 10-year T-note might become the more important benchmark.

Foreign Sovereign Bond Market

There is a large international government securities market. Most of the large bond dealers in the United States also make a market in these securities. These securities have several idiosyncratic features worthy of note. Table 1-8 provides a perspective of the Foreign Sovereign bond market.

Canadian Debt Market. Canadian bonds have a range of maturities from two to thirty years. Typically, the issues are noncallable bullet bonds, although index-linked debt has also been issued recently. As in the U.S. Treasury market, three-month and six-month T-bills are auctioned every week. Two-year to thirty-year maturities are auctioned quarterly.

Gilts. Gilt-edged stock or gilts are British government debt securities. Standard gilts carry fixed, annual coupons and pay the face amount at maturity date. In addition to the standard gilts, the British government issues the following:

- Index-linked gilts, which have coupon and face amounts indexed to the U.K. retail price index
- Convertible gilts, which may be converted into one or more other gilts at specific dates and conversion ratios
- "Irredeemable gilts," which are perpetuals callable at par. **Perpetuals** are securities with no maturity dates.

Coupon payments on gilts are called **dividends.** Typically, withholding taxes are applied to dividends from gilts, although there are gilts which are exempt from this rule. The flat price of a gilt is called the "clean price" and its full price is called the "dirty price." Gilts may be bought or sold cum dividend until 37 days before the next coupon date. The gilt goes exdividend at that point. Some highlights of the gilt markets are shown in Table 1-8. The benchmark issues of the U.K. market are also shown in Table 1-8.

JGBs. The Japanese Government Bond (JGB) market is a large market. JGBs are typically issued with a fixed maturity date, carry a fixed annual coupon (payable semiannually), and are quoted on a simple yield basis. These conventions are analyzed in Chapter 4. Discount bonds are also issued and they are quoted differently, depending

TABLE 1-8 *Foreign Sovereign Bond Market*

Sovereign Market	Highlights
Canadian Bond Market	Maturity range—2 to 30 years. 5 to 10 years most liquid. Market organization—OTC dealer network. Benchmarks—3, 5, and 10 years. Issue procedure—subscription offerings and yield auction. Coupon—semiannual, actual/365 basis.
U.K. government bonds	Market organization—OTC dealer market very active. Issue procedure—multiple price auctions for T-bills. Issue procedure—single price auctions for gilts; "tap issues" also used. Coupon—annual, actual/actual basis.
Japanese Government Bond Market (JGB)	Issued by government of Japan. Classified into Construction bonds, Deficit Financing bonds, and Refinancing bonds. Maturity—10 years is most common. Issues are referred to by their issue number. Coupon bonds are issued with original maturities of 2, 10, and 20 years. Discount bonds are issued with 5 years maturity. Market organization—Trades in Tokyo Stock Exchange. Cash JBG trading occurs on OTC markets. Issue procedure—A part is underwritten by a syndicate of banks, insurance companies, and securities firms. Remaining is issued by auctions. Yield—simple yield to maturity calculations.
German government bonds Federal government (*Bunds*) Federal railways (*Bundesbahn*) Federal post office (*Bundespost*)	Maturity—10 years. Market organization—stock exchanges and OTC dealer markets. Benchmarks—most recent issues. Issue procedure—combination of Dutch auction and fixed allocation to a pool of institutions. Coupon—annual basis.
French government bonds *Obligations Assimilable du Trésor* (OATs)	Accounts for 70% of the market. Maturity range—10 to 30 years. New tranch of 10-year bonds reopened monthly; new tranch of long bonds reopened every two months, and additional issues. Market organization—listed on Paris Stock Exchange, OTC dealer market very active. Benchmarks—10 and 30 years. Issue procedure—Dutch auctions. Coupon—semiannual, actual/actual basis. Special features—some OATs are convertible, some have warrants and some are indexed to short- or long-term rates.
French government notes *Bons à Taux Annuel Normalisé* (BTANs)	Accounts for 30% of the market. Maturity range—1 to 7 years. Typically issued in 2 and 5 years maturities. Market organization—OTC dealer market very active. Benchmarks—2 and 5 years. Issue procedure—Dutch auctions. Coupon—annual, actual/actual basis.

TABLE 1-8   *Continued*

German Benchmarks

Year	Code	Issue/Mat	B/O Price	M Price	M Yld	Page	Source	GMT
2	113683	3.250 15.09.00	99.96–02	99.99	3.253	42166	SOC GEN	16:56
3	113485	8.250 20.09.01	112.69–75	112.72	3.544	42168	SOC GEN	17:01
4	114124	4.500 19.08.02	103.06–12	103.09	3.614	42171	SOC GEN	17:01
5	114127	4.500 19.05.03	103.47–53	103.50	3.649	42172	SOC GEN	17:01
6	113493	6.750 15.07.04	114.69–75	114.72	3.827	42174	SOC GEN	16:49
7	113498	6.500 14.10.05	114.79–85	114.82	4.017	42176	SOC GEN	16:49
8	113501	6.250 26.04.06	113.66–72	113.69	4.087	42177	SOC GEN	17:01
9	113503	6.000 04.07.07	112.43–49	112.46	4.251	42178	SOC GEN	17:01
10	113507	4.750 04.07.08	104.81–87	104.84	4.130	42179	SOC GEN	17:01
30	113508	4.750 04.07.28	92.88–28	93.080	5.211	42182	SOC GEN	17:01

UK Benchmarks

Year	Code	Issue/Mat	M Price	M Yld	Page	Source	GMT
2	8 00	8 07/12/00	105–02	5.42	22491	H S B C	14:34
3	7 01	7 06/11/01	104–22	5.29	22491	H S B C	14:33
4	7 02	7 07/06/02	105–26	5.21	22491	H S B C	14:33
5	6H03	6 1/2 07/12/03	106–13	5.05	22491	H S B C	14:33
6	6T 04	6 3/4 26/11/04	108–14	5.11	22491	H S B C	14:33
7	8H05	8 1/2 07/12/05	119–09	5.21	22491	H S B C	15:17
8	7H06	7 1/2 07/12/06	114–29	5.22	42190	SOC GEN	08:49
9	7Q07	7 1/4 07/12/07	115–00	5.16	22491	H S B C	15:17
10	9 08	9 13/10/08	129–06	5.20	22491	H S B C	15:17
11	8 09	8 25/09/08	126–21	4.837	21122	J P M	16:03
12	6Q10	6 1/4 25/11/10	109–09	5.20	42190	SOC GEN	08:44
15	8 13	8 27/09/13	128–01	5.26	42190	SOC GEN	08:49
20	8T 17	8 3/4 25/08/17	142–11	5.19	42190	SOC GEN	08:49
25	8 21	8 02/06/21	137–26	5.14	22491	H S B C	15:17
30	6 28	6 07/60/28	115–14	5.00	22491	H S B C	15:17

Source: Telerate, 10/25/98.

on whether they have less than or more than a year to maturity. JGBs are callable at any time by the Ministry of Finance. Maturities range from a few years to 20 years. Liquidity tends to be concentrated on a benchmark bond. Often the benchmark bond trades at several basis points below comparable JGBs. High coupon bonds are valued higher in Japan than in other countries, and therefore, they trade at a lower yield. This coupon effect is distinct from the coupon effects that one sees in other international bond markets where high coupon bonds often sell for a higher yield.

German Debt Market. The German debt market has grown recently, due at least in part to the mounting deficits. The long-term government bonds are known as Bunds. They typically have a maturity of 10 years. Five-year notes are also issued by the government. The public debt is held in book-entry form. (This system will be described in Chapter 2.) The benchmark issues are shown in Table 1-8.

French Government Debt. The most important bond issue in the French government market is the *Obligations Assimilable du Trésor* (OAT) (see Table 1-8), which matures in the range of 10 to 30 years. This bond is issued in tranches to increase the supply as needed. Two-year and five-year debt securities are also auctioned.

Agency Securities

Government-sponsored enterprises (GSEs) are private corporations that operate under a charter from the U.S. Congress. The majority of its board of directors are elected by private shareholders. The central function of a GSE is to serve as a financial intermediary. The activities of a GSE will include making loans and loan guarantees to borrowers in certain sectors of the economy identified in the legislation. GSEs are perceived by investors to have an implicit federal government guarantee backing their obligations.

The Federal Home Loan Bank, the Federal National Mortgage Association, and the Federal Home Loan Mortgage Corporation are examples of agencies that routinely issue debt securities. Federal agencies, such as the Tennessee Valley Authority (TVA) and Export-Import Bank, also issue large amounts of debt securities. Federal agencies are, for the most part, privately owned but are sponsored and backed by the federal government. Table 1-9 lists some characteristics of the issuing federal agencies.

The composition of the agency securities market is shown in Figure 1-7. The growth of the agency securities markets during 1985–1999 is shown in Table 1-10. The tremendous growth in FHLB, FNMA, and FHLMC securities is the most obvious fact in Table 1-10.

TABLE 1-9 *Federal Agencies*

Agency	Highlights
Federal Home Loan Bank (FHLB)	FHLB is well capitalized and it issues debt up to 15 years maturity. FHLB has also issued short-term notes and zero coupon bonds.
Federal National Mortgage Association (FNMA) and Federal Home Loan Mortgage Corporation (FHLMC)	Fannie Mae and Freddie Mac were created to promote a liquid secondary market for mortgages. Fannie Mae is a publicly traded corporation. Freddie Mac is smaller than Fannie Mae. These agencies issue debentures, MBS, etc.
Refcorp	This agency was set up to bail out the savings and loans and thrifts. It has issued 40-year bonds.
Tennessee Valley Authority(TVA)	TVA was created to promote the Tennessee River region.
Student Loan Marketing Association (SLMA)	Sallie Mae promotes a liquid secondary market for government-guaranteed student loans. Loans bought by Sallie Mae are insured. Its advances are collateralized; hence, its credit is very good.
Farm Credit System (FCS)	FCS provides low-cost credit to agriculture and fisheries. It has considerable political support.

Agency securities are not direct obligations of the federal government. Even though the probability of default is very small, they trade at a spread to comparable Treasuries. Agency securities are issued in relatively smaller sizes compared with Treasuries and as a result are not as liquid. This factor may also contribute to the spread between Treasuries and agencies. Table 1-10 illustrates the spreads on agency

FIGURE 1-7 *Composition of Agency Debt Market*
Total $327,716 Million (December 1997)

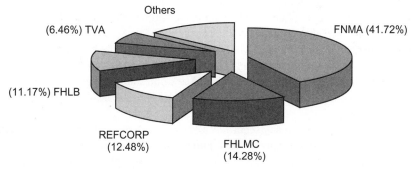

Source: Lehman Brothers.

TABLE 1-10   *Federal and Federally Sponsored Credit Agency Debt Outstanding, 1985–1999:Q3 ($ Billions)*

	Federal Home Loan Banks	*Federal Home Loan Mortgage Corporation*	*Federal National Mortgage Association*	*Farm Credit System[1]*	*Student Loan Marketing Association*	*Tennessee Valley Authority*	*Other[2]*	*Total*
1985	74.4	11.9	93.9	68.9	8.4	16.3	20.0	293.
1986	88.8	13.6	93.6	62.5	12.2	17.2	19.6	307.
1987	115.7	17.6	97.1	55.3	16.5	18.1	21.1	341.
1988	135.8	22.8	105.5	53.8	22.1	18.3	23.2	381.
1989	136.1	26.1	116.1	55.7	28.7	17.9	31.2	411.
1990	117.9	30.9	123.4	54.9	34.2	23.4	49.9	434.
1991	107.5	30.3	133.9	53.5	38.3	22.4	56.9	442.
1992	114.7	29.6	166.3	53.2	39.7	23.6	56.9	484.
1993	139.5	50.0	201.1	54.4	39.8	29.9	56.0	570.
1994	205.8	93.3	257.2	54.4	50.3	27.5	50.3	738.
1995	243.2	120.0	299.2	58.6	47.5	29.4	46.7	844.
1996	263.4	157.0	331.3	61.3	44.8	27.9	40.2	925.
1997	313.9	169.2	369.8	64.8	37.7	27.8	39.4	1,022.
1998	382.1	287.4	460.3	64.7	35.4	26.5	40.0	1,296.
1999:Q3	481.6	341.1	524.9	69.2	41.9	26.4	40.7	1,525.

Source: Federal Reserve System.

[1]Includes Farm Credit Banks and Farm Credit Financial Assistance Corporation.

[2]Includes Defense Department, Export-Import Bank, Federal Housing Administration GNMA certificates of participation, Postal Services, U.S. Railway Association, Financing Corporation, and the Resolution Funding Corporation.

securities issued by FNMA (Fannie Mae). Agency securities operate on a 30-day month and 360-day year convention.

Agency securities, by and large, have a very high credit reputation. The pressure from the U.S. Congress to examine the implicit and explicit guarantees issued by the government to agencies will sooner or later cause the agencies to acquire a high standalone credit reputation. Until then, potential buyers will take into account both the standalone quality and the explicit and implicit guarantees in valuing agency securities. Congress is reexamining the status of GSEs. We discuss this issue in detail in a later chapter dealing with corporate and agency bonds.

Notice that the agency securities range in maturities from a few months to 30 years. Many of them are callable after a short call protection period indicated under the column "Call" in Table 1-11.

In response to treasury buybacks, FNMA has introduced the benchmark program. In Table 1-11, we can see the benchmark notes maturing on 9/15/09 and 9/15/29. Unlike most other bonds in the table, these benchmark notes are noncallable to serve as a genuine alternative to Treasury benchmarks. Similar issues are now being made by the FNMA as well.

The relative supply of agency securities also could influence their valuation. While agency securities generally are noncallable bullet bonds, some issues are quite innovative; Refco has issued 40-year bonds that are eligible for stripping, some agencies have issued zero coupon bonds, and some have optional redemption features. (**Stripping** refers to a practice in which dealers buy a coupon-paying bond and then "strip" all the coupons and principal cash flows and sell them as separate securities.) These provisions require sophisticated techniques for their valuation. About a third of the agency issues tend to have call features. Sallie Mae has issued floaters, and Fannie Mae has issued sinking fund debentures. Many of the Fannie Mae issues have call features.

Corporate Securities

The corporate fixed-income securities market has been the dominant way of raising capital for U.S. corporations in the last few years. Table 1-12 vividly illustrates the importance of this market for corporate funding.

It is clear that the corporate debt market has been used to raise capital several times more than the equity market during the last three years. Falling interest rates may have been the major motivation for this trend. Unlike the Treasury markets, which are characterized by about 200 to 300 issues, each of which has a relatively large size outstanding, the corporate debt market is characterized by thousands of issues, each of which accounts for a small size. A typical corporate issue is of the order of $100 million to $200 million, whereas a typical Treasury auction is of the order of $10 billion to $12 billion.

Much like the Treasury market, newly syndicated corporate issues are actively traded. The seasoned issues, which have been issued a few months earlier, tend to be illiquid and trade at wider bid-offer spreads. Unlike the Treasury issues, most corporate issues tend to have call features or sinking fund features. We alluded earlier in this

TABLE 1-11   *Agency Issues*

Date	Issuer	Amount ($)	Security	Maturity	Call	Coupon	Price	Yield (%)	Spread	Lead(s)
8/30/99	FHLB	25.0	Bonds	9/17/09	2	7.500	100	7.500	162	VINING/ 1ST TENN
8/30/99	FHLB	15.0	Bonds	9/21/06	2	7.000	100	7.000	N.A.	M.KEEGAN
8/30/99	FHLB	15.0	Notes	9/20/01	1	6.200	100	6.200	52.5	1ST TENN
8/27/99	FFCB	250.0	Desig bonds	7/2/01	NC	5.875	99.73	N.A.	40	CSFB/ LEH
8/27/99	FHLB	125.0	Notes	9/20/04	1	7.000	100	7.000	N.A.	BEAR
8/27/99	FHLB	25.0	Notes	9/17/03	2	6.525	100	6.525	N.A.	VINING/ 1ST TENN
8/27/99	FHLB	25.0	Notes	9/22/00	3 Mo	5.900	100	5.900	N.A.	SPEAR
→8/27/99	FNMA	3500.0	Bench notes	9/15/09	NC	6.625	99.87	6.642	84.5	BEAR/ ML/ MSDW ←
8/27/99	FNMA	500.0	Bench notes	5/15/29	NC	6.250	92.4	6.851	93	BEAR/ ML/ MSDW
8/26/99	FHLB	25.0	Bonds	9/16/09	3	7.030	100	7.030	128	1ST TENN/ GS
8/26/99	FHLB	25.0	Bonds	9/14/09	2	7.025	100	7.025	132	1ST TENN/ GS
8/26/99	FHLB	25.0	Notes	3/21/05	6 Mo	7.000	100	7.000	136	1ST TENN/ GS
8/26/99	FHLB	20.0	Notes	9/7/04	1	6.940	100	6.940	129	FUCM
8/26/99	FHLB	15.0	Notes	9/20/04	2	6.625	100	6.625	N.A.	M.KEEGAN
8/26/99	FHLB	15.0	Notes	9/20/04	3	6.530	100	6.530	N.A.	VINING
8/26/99	FHLB	15.0	Notes	3/20/03	1.5	6.375	100	6.375	N.A.	M.KEEGAN
8/26/99	FHLB	150.0	Notes	9/31/01	1	6.150	100	6.150	N.A.	BARCLAYS
8/26/99	FHLB	30.0	Notes	9/21/01	1	6.125	100	6.125	N.A.	NOR/ HUNTN
8/26/99	FHLB	25.0	Notes	3/20/01	3 Mo	6.000	100	6.000	N.A.	WACHOVIA/ NBC
8/26/99	FHLB	3000.0	Jumbo notes	9/17/01	NC	5.875	99.84	5.959	40	SSB/ GS
8/26/99	FHLMC	25.0	Debentures	9/4/03	2	6.500	100	6.500	N.A.	NORWEST
8/26/99	FHLMC	25.0	Debentures	9/7/01	3 Mo	6.250	100	6.250	N.A.	CHASE
8/25/99	FHLB	250.0	Notes	3/1/00	NC	Floats	100	Floats	70	PW/ HSBC/ PIPER
8/25/99	FHLB	25.0	Notes	9/14/06	2	7.040	100	7.040	131	1ST TENN/ GS
8/25/99	FHLB	45.0	Bonds	9/15/06	6 Mo	7.000	100	7.000	N.A.	MK/ CHASE/ LEH
8/25/99	FHLB	15.0	Bonds	9/17/04	3	6.500	100	6.500	N.A.	M.KEEGAN
8/25/99	FHLB	15.0	Bonds	3/15/02	1	6.210	100	6.210	N.A.	M.KEEGAN
8/25/99	FHLB	25.0	Notes	9/17/02	2	6.210	100	6.210	N.A.	DAIN
8/25/99	FNMA	40.0	Notes	9/4/09	2	7.400	100	7.400	N.A.	VINING/ 1ST TENN
8/25/99	FNMA	30.0	MTN	9/1/06	1	7.250	100	7.250	N.A.	1ST TENN/ HSBC
8/24/99	FHLB	25.0	Bonds	9/15/14	1	7.780	100	7.780	N.A.	LASALLE
8/24/99	FHLB	15.0	Bonds	9/17/09	3	7.340	100	7.340	148.5	1ST TENN
8/24/99	FHLB	25.0	Notes	8/28/02	1	6.620	100	6.620	N.A.	PARIBAS
8/24/99	FHLB	15.0	Notes	9/17/03	2	6.525	100	6.525	N.A.	NORWEST
8/24/99	FHLB	25.0	Notes	9/20/01	1	6.220	100	6.220	N.A.	VINING/ NORWEST
8/24/99	FNMA	30.0	MTN	9/1/04	1	7.110	100	7.110	N.A.	M.KEEGAN/ PW

Source: MCM Corporate Watch.

Note: For each agency bond, this table provides useful summary information. To illustrate, let us examine the bond indicated by arrows. This is a FNMA benchmark note, issued in the amount of $3.5 billion on 8/27/99 and maturing on 9/15/09. It is noncallable (NC), bears a coupon of 6.625%, and sold at a price of 99.87% of par value. The yield on this note is 6.642%, and the yield spread over benchmark Treasury was 84.5 basis points. Lead managers of this issue were Bear Stearns, Merril Lynch, and Morgan Stanley Dean Witter.

TABLE 1-12
1997—New Issue Volume

Security	Number Issued	$ Millions
High-grade	1,221	178,152
Public-high-yield	122	30,348
144a-high-yield	534	90,602
Structured	2,196	201,261
Convertible	131	25,163
Common stock	1,282	149,194
IPO	612	65,257

Source: MCM Corporate Watch.

chapter to the question of why such contractual features are present in the corporate debt market. Call features also permit managers to eliminate debt, if necessary. Debtholders might place restrictive covenants that may not allow managers to undertake certain investments or may prohibit certain types of mergers and acquisitions. By having a call feature, managers give themselves the right to take such actions at a predetermined (call) price.

The presence of credit risk, the relative lack of liquidity compared to the Treasuries, and the call features cause the investors to demand a higher yield on corporate issues than on other similar Treasuries. Table 1-13 shows that this is generally the case.

Along the maturity spectrum, the corporate debt issues fall into three groups:

1. Short maturities under a year are in the *money markets sector.* The key corporate debt here is the commercial paper.
2. In the one- to five-year sector are the *medium-term notes.* Floaters also fall in this group.
3. Finally, longer maturities come under the **corporate bonds** classification.

We will discuss these instruments briefly in this chapter and postpone to Chapter 8 a fuller account of the corporate debt.

Commercial Paper. Short-term corporate debt is known as **commercial paper** (CP). The maturity of commercial paper varies anywhere from 30 days to 270 days. CPs, like T-bills, are discount instruments. Maturities less than 270 days may be offered for sale to the public without registration with the Securities and Exchange Commission (SEC).

CPs are quoted on a discount basis. The discount yield of CPs, however, is measured a bit differently from that of a T-bill. Typically, CPs are priced off the London Interbank Offered Rates (LIBOR) of comparable maturities. LIBOR refers to the interest rate at which banks are able to borrow money in interbank market, which is not subject to U.S. regulations. For example, it is usual for a CP trader to say that IBM's 90-day CP trades at 50 basis points below 90-day LIBOR. Many corporations, by virtue of their strong credit reputations, are able to borrow directly from the public at rates that are lower than what they could get at banks. A good CP program provides

TABLE 1-13   *"A"-Rated Individual Issuer Credit Curves: Bid x Ask—Basis Point Spreads to U.S. Treasuries*

"A1" Industrial Issuer Curves												

"A1" Industrial Issuer Curves

Sept. 1, 1999

Treas	5.71	x	5.71	5.77	x	5.77	5.85	x	5.85	5.92	x	5.92
Issuer	*2000*			*2001*			*2002*			*2003*		
BUD	60	x	57	64	x	61	69	x	66	77	x	74
DCX	81	x	78	85	x	82	90	x	87	98	x	95
DOV	69	x	66	73	x	70	78	x	75	86	x	83
F	75	x	72	79	x	76	84	x	81	92	x	89
F	69	x	66	73	x	70	78	x	75	86	x	83
HNZ	45	x	42	49	x	46	54	x	51	62	x	59
→ IBM	46	x	43	50	x	47	55	x	52	63	x	60 ←
MOT	62	x	59	66	x	63	71	x	68	79	x	76
PEP	50	x	47	54	x	51	59	x	56	67	x	64
PPG	73	x	70	77	x	74	82	x	79	90	x	87
Treas	5.95	x	5.95	5.96	x	5.96	5.97	x	5.97	5.99	x	5.99
Issuer	*2005*			*2006*			*2007*			*2008*		
BUD	92	x	89	97	x	94	103	x	100	108	x	105
DCX	113	x	110	118	x	115	124	x	121	129	x	126
DOV	101	x	98	106	x	103	112	x	109	117	x	114
F	107	x	104	112	x	109	118	x	115	123	x	120
F	101	x	98	106	x	103	112	x	109	117	x	114
HNZ	77	x	74	82	x	79	88	x	85	93	x	90
→ IBM	78	x	75	83	x	80	89	x	86	94	x	91 ←
MOT	94	x	91	99	x	96	105	x	102	110	x	107
PEP	82	x	79	87	x	84	93	x	90	98	x	95
PPG	105	x	102	110	x	117	116	x	113	121	x	118

Source: MCM Corporate Watch.

Note: For each corporate issue, this table provides some pricing information. To illustrate, let us examine the IBM issues indicated by arrows. As of September 1, 1999, IBM 2000 bond was trading at a spread of 46 basis points over the Treasury benchmark, which was yielding 5.71%. The IBM 2008 bond was trading at a spread of 94 basis points on the bid side and 91 basis points on the offer side.

the issuing corporation with yet another borrowing strategy. The Federal Reserve produces an index of CP rates by averaging across CP quotes from a randomly selected sample from a roster of CP dealers. This index, known as the Fed AA index, also is a barometer of the CP market. Highly rated CPs trade at rates well below comparable LIBOR, and poorly rated CPs trade well above LIBOR.

Medium-Term Notes (MTNs). This sector starts at maturities exceeding three months and extends to several years. The MTNs can be issued through shelf registration, which provides a great deal of flexibility to the issuer. In a **shelf registration,** the issuer gets blanket approval from the SEC for an amount of debt that may then be issued over a prespecified period of time. This gives the issuer the ability to respond quickly to any rapid changes in interest rates. The structure of the MTNs indexes the issuance cost to the short-term interest rates.

Corporate Coupon Issues. Corporate debt is largely composed of coupon-bearing debt. These coupon obligations are contractual obligations; nonpayment of a coupon payment will provide an option to the debtholders to take control of the firm.

Corporate debt is rated by rating agencies, such as Moodys and Standard and Poor. Depending on the ratings, corporate debt may be either investment grade or non-investment grade ("junk"). Moody's ratings go from Aaa to C. Standard and Poors go from AAA to D. Generally, a bond with a rating of B or less has a high default risk. Investors require a high credit risk premium to hold those securities. Corporate bonds typically have a **mandatory sinking fund** provision. This provision calls for an orderly retirement of debt in scheduled installments. Sometimes issuers also provide an **optional sinking fund** feature whereby they could retire additional amounts. Contractual provisions of corporate bonds typically also have call features. After a call protection period (typically 5 to 10 years from the issue date), the issuer will have the option to call the bonds at face amount plus a predetermined premium schedule. Each corporate issuer may have several layers of debt, and each layer might differ with respect to seniority and security. Debentures in the United States are unsecured debt. On the other hand, mortgage bonds are secured by a lien on specific tangible assets of the issuing firm. Senior debtholders have a prior claim on the assets of the firm in the event of bankruptcy. Subordinated (junior) debtholders will have the residual claim followed by equity holders. All these factors have to be carefully considered in valuing corporate debt securities.

High-Yield Debt. As pointed out earlier, high-yield bonds are those issued by entities that are rated as less than investment grade. Such issues were often made in conjunction with leveraged buyout activities, although more recent issues have been made for raising capital to fund capital projects. This source of capital is important for issuers with poor credit rating as an alternative to bank debt.

High-yield debt can be made through a public offer with investment banks underwriting the issue. Table 1-14 illustrates that in 1997, 122 such issues were made, accounting for $30.368 billion. The so-called Section 144A issues refer to bonds that are only offered to Qualified Institutional Buyers (QIBs) and as Table 1-14 illustrates, over 500 issues were made in Section 144A, accounting for more than $90,000 million. Structured debt issues are customized to fit the needs of issuers. Such issues may have special option features, for example.

High-yield securities come in varied forms. Since the issuers of high-yield bonds tend to have a large amount of debt in their capital structure, their ability to service debt payments is critical to their survival. Hence, most high-yield debt securities are structured so that they carry very low coupons during early years; hence, they tend to sell at a discount. One of the most common structures is referred to as **deferred-interest**

bonds. In these bonds, no coupons are paid for an initial period lasting for several years. This structure gives a chance for the firm to generate sufficient cash flow to service the interest payments later. Similarly **payment-in-kind (PIK) bonds** provide the issuers with the option either to pay cash coupon or offer similar bonds instead of the coupon payments. Step-up bonds pay coupons that increase (stepped up) over life at specified future dates. These structures are discussed in Chapter 8.

Securitized Assets—Mortgage-Backed Securities

In the fixed-income markets, the concept of securitization has led to the development of liquid markets, notably the mortgage-backed securities (MBS) markets. The mortgage market is one of the largest segments in the securities markets. **Securitization** is a process by which illiquid assets are transformed into very liquid financial instruments. Figure 1-8 highlights the key steps involved in the securitization process.

This process requires the following distinct players and steps:

1. **Originator:** Securitization begins with an institution playing the role of the originator. The originator, which can be a private institution, such as an S&L, or a federal agency creates individual mortgages or receivables.

FIGURE 1-8 *Concept of Securitization—Example from Mortgage-Backed Securities*

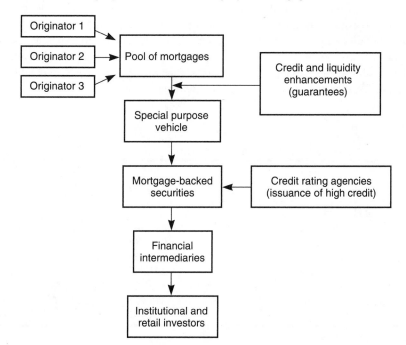

2. **Pooling and standardization:** The assets (loans) are then pooled. Such pools may be created using more than one originator. The pooling activity is performed to create a large enough loan portfolio to interest large institutional investors. The individual loans are standardized along several dimensions: the maturity, the interest rate (fixed or adjustable, levels and indices), the amount of the loan, the geographical location, etc. This standardization makes the cash flows from the pool easier to predict.

3. **Guarantees and credit enhancement:** For a fee, a standardized portfolio is then guaranteed by a federal agency (or a private entity of sufficiently high credit reputation) against default. Such defaults may occur at the level of individual units in the pool (such as a particular homeowner in a pool of mortgages or an account in a pool of credit card receivables) or at the level of issuers. Both classes of default are covered by guarantees. Together, standardization and the guarantee enhance the marketability of the securities that are then issued as claims to the guaranteed cash flows from the pool of assets.

4. **Special purpose vehicle (SPV):** The SPV is created solely to construct the pool of financial assets and then issue the asset-backed securities. The key idea here is to put some distance between the originators and the pool of assets. For instance, the SPV is structured such that the bankruptcy of the originator(s) will not affect the pool of financial assets held by the SPV. This separation is critical in obtaining the necessary credit enhancements, which usually lead to a high credit rating.

This process of pooling, standardizing, and selling claims on guaranteed loans has the effect of improving the liquidity of what might otherwise be illiquid assets. It improves the allocation of risk and resources across different geographical locations. Hopefully, it also reduces the cost of mortgage loans in the mortgage-backed securities markets. Table 1-14 gives a perspective on the size of the mortgage market and the extent to which this market has been pooled and securitized. Note that the size of the

TABLE 1-14 *Mortgage Debt Outstanding in Millions of Dollars*

	1994	1995	1996	1997
Total	4,392,093	4,606,303	4,929,430	5,277,185
Institutional Holders				
Major financial institutions	1,819,806	1,894,420	1,979,114	2,084,728
1. Commercial banks	1,012,711	1,090,189	1,145,389	1,244,210
2. Savings institutions	596,191	596,763	628,335	629,726
3. Life insurance companies	210,904	207,468	205,390	210,792
Pooled mortgages	1,732,347	1,866,763	2,070,436	2,282,566
Federal agencies	315,580	306,774	300,935	292,522
Others	524,360	538,347	578,945	617,369

Source: Federal Reserve, May 1998.

pooled mortgage market is quite large—it is about \$2.3 trillion. The potential for growth in this area is even greater. The process of securitization has transformed this market into a major segment of the fixed-income securities market.

The process of securitization, while resulting in a highly liquid market for mortgage-backed securities, exposes the investors to a unique set of risks. Mortgage-backed securities are created by using a pool of mortgages as the underlying collateral and selling pro rata shares of the cash flows that are generated by the pool of mortgages. In essence, the cash flows generated by the pool are passed through to the investors. The investor holding a mortgage-backed security is holding a proportionate share in the underlying pool, but the homeowners who have taken out mortgages have the right to prepay. For investors in mortgage-backed securities, this leads to the risk of receiving a pro rata share of prepayments that may be made by the homeowners of the pool.

Prepayments occur because homeowners rarely hold mortgages to the stated maturities, which range up to 30 years. They have the option to prepay the loans and do so for many reasons. The following affect prepayments:

- **Drop in interest rates.** When the perceived benefits of low interest rates outweigh the costs of refinancing, refinancing is more attractive.
- **Labor market turnover.** When homeowners move from one job to another, they close out existing mortgage loans and take new ones.
- **Seasonal changes.** Families tend to move in summer and early fall, causing seasonal effects in prepayments.
- **Family circumstances.** Such events as divorces, deaths, and other changes in the family size often lead to refinancing.
- **Housing prices.** When house prices fall, the incentive to prepay is reduced as the homeowners are trapped. When the house prices drop to a very low level, homeowners have a "walk away" option by which they can surrender the house to the bank and walk away from the loan. Clearly, this affects the prepayments during periods when the real estate market is falling.
- **Defaults.** In a pool, when defaults occur, the guarantees go into effect, resulting in additional payments.

MBSs have been structured to handle payments (scheduled and unscheduled) in different ways to suit the preferences of a wide spectrum of investors. One popular class of MBSs is that of **pass-through securities,** which provide the investor with a prorated share of all payments made by the pool, including prepayments. Examples of such securities are GNMAs and FNMAs. GNMAs carry the full faith and credit of the United States, but FNMAs do not have this direct U.S. guarantee. Another type of MBS partitions prepayments according to stated rules. These securities, called collateralized mortgage obligations (CMOs), are typically backed (or collateralized) by pools of mortgages or pass-through securities, such as GNMAs. Each partition will receive prepayments according to set rules. In Chapter 9, we undertake a detailed treatment of this market.

Municipal Issues

Municipalities (state and local governments) issue debt securities regularly. Broadly, such issues may be grouped into the following categories:

- **General obligation bonds,** which are backed by the full faith, credit, and taxing power of the issuer; and
- **Revenue bonds,** which derive their cash flows from specific project revenues.

Municipal issues maturing in one year or less are known as municipal notes and longer term issues are referred to as municipal bonds. The composition of the municipal bond market is provided in Table 1-15.

Municipal issues are smaller in size than those of other securities. In addition, typically they are issued as serial bonds. In serial issues, scheduled parts of the principal (balloon) payments are retired at prespecified maturities. Each specified maturity will carry a distinct coupon. These factors contribute to their low liquidity.

Until very recently, the most distinctive feature of municipal securities was that the interest payments made by municipal securities were exempt from federal taxes (as well as from state and local taxes for local residents), and this caused their yields to be lower, *ceteris paribus.* The Tax Reform Act of 1986 has placed a number of restrictions on the tax exemption status of municipal securities. In effect, the reform has significantly eroded the tax-exempt status of municipal securities. Bonds issued for activities, such as road construction and capital projects, qualify for tax-exempt status. All other issues in which 10% or more of the proceeds are used to finance a project that

TABLE 1-15   *Composition of Municipal Bond (Tax-Exempt Debt) Market in Millions of Dollars*

	1995	1996	1997
By Type of Issue			
General obligation bonds	56,980	60,409	69,934
Revenue bonds	88,677	110,813	134,989
By Type of Issuer			
States	14,665	13,651	18,237
Special district or Statutory authority	93,500	113,228	134,919
Municipality, county, or township	37,492	44,343	70,558
Issues for New Capital	102,390	112,298	127,928
By Use of Proceeds			
Education	23,964	26,851	31,860
Transportation	11,890	12,324	13,951
Utilities and conservation	9,618	9,791	12,219
Social welfare	19,566	24,583	27,794
Industrial aid	6,581	6,287	6,667
Other	30,771	32,462	35,095

Source: Federal Reserve, May 1998.

will be used by a private entity are regarded as private activity bonds. Only qualified private activity bonds are eligible for tax-exempt status. To be considered a qualified private activity bond, the issuer has to meet a number of requirements and fall into certain categories of activities, such as the construction of airports or sewer systems and student development.

In addition, the Tax Reform Law has placed other restrictions on municipals. States are now limited on the amount of partially tax-exempt private activity bonds they can issue every year. Also, prior to the 1986 law, financial institutions (especially commercial banks) were permitted to deduct the interest cost (for tax purposes) incurred in carrying the municipal securities, providing double tax benefits. This was eliminated by the Tax Reform Law of 1986. Municipalities refund bonds when interest rates fall. In a later chapter on municipal bonds, we explore issues connected to municipal refunding.

The tax treatment of municipal securities results in municipals being priced to provide a lower yield compared to very similar Treasury or corporate securities. The market yields of these three fixed-income securities is plotted in Figure 1-9. The possibility that tax benefits may be reduced is a serious risk faced by municipal bond investors. Note that the spreads of municipals have changed a great deal over time. In Chapter 10, we explore the determinants of such spreads. The tax status of municipal bonds tend to attract households, commercial banks, and property and casualty insurance firms to hold most of the municipal debt.

FIGURE 1-9 *Yields of Municipals, Treasuries, and Corporates*

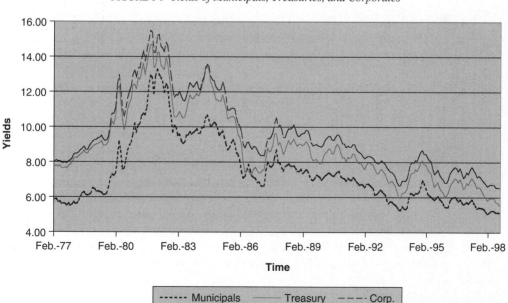

Ecuador: Restructuring the Debt Restructuring

Ecuador, a $14.5 billion economy with debts totaling $13.3 billion, may default on its $6 billion in Brady bonds. On Aug. 25, President Jamil Mahuad said the country would defer a $96 million interest payment due Aug. 28 for 30 days, the Brady grace period. Ecuador, which faces millions more in various external obligations coming due by year-end, says it will attempt an unprecedented restructuring of its Brady debt, but the road will be difficult.

Ecuador's Brady bonds—named after former U.S. Treasury Secretary Nicholas Brady, who drafted the plan to restructure Latin American debt piled up in the 1980s and partly backed by U.S. Treasury securities—are themselves the result of a 1994 debt restructuring. Also, any renegotiation will depend on the government's receiving a loan from the International Monetary Fund. This is needed to restore investor confidence and to support Ecuador's sinking economy, which is expected to contract 7% this year, with inflation of 60%. The sudden Aug. 31 resignation of Finance Minister Ana Lucia Armijos, who was expected to coordinate the whole process, will only complicate matters. Economy Minister Guillermo LAsso will take over.

On Aug. 30, Ecuador signed an IMF loan agreement totaling $1.25 billion, which would go toward bolstering foreign reserves. None of the IMF money can be used to pay debts to prevent selective bailout of private investors. The problem: The loan is contingent upon fiscal measures and banking reforms that are unlikely to pass the opposition-led Congress. Armijos' last official act was to introduce a $4.2 billion IMF-approved budget for 2000, down sharply from $5.2 billion in 1999, that is expected to fuel economic growth of 3% next year and cut inflation to 25%.

So far, the secondary market for other Latin American Bradys has taken the news in stride.

But analysts fear that a default by Ecuador could taint other Brady debt, as well as retard the Latin American recovery by hiking risk premiums on many Latin investments.

BY JAMES C. COOPER & KATHLEEN MADIGAN

Source: *Businessweek Online,* Sept. 13, 1999.

Emerging Markets

A number of developing countries have entered the fixed-income markets recently. Argentina, Brazil, and Mexico have an active market for their debt securities. Here we present an overview of this growing segment of the fixed-income securities market. Since the middle of the 1980s, the emerging markets in debt securities have developed considerable liquidity.

To get a perspective of the importance of emerging markets, we have presented in Table 1-16 the composition of the Lehman Brothers Emerging Markets Index. As of

TABLE 1-16
Lehman Brothers
Emerging Markets Index
Composition

As of December 1997	
Total Dollar Value of Index:	$234,126 Billion
Emerging Americas	72.42%
Emerging Europe	9.98%
Emerging Asia	11.95%
Rest (Middle East and Africa)	5.65%
Total:	100.00%

TABLE 1-17
Brady Bonds in Lehman
Brothers Emerging
Markets Index
(in Millions of Dollars)

Brady bonds	$119,404.26
Local issues	$ 4,907.52
International issues	$114,496.74

December 1997, the value of the index stood at $234 billion. Of these, more than 70% was accounted for by Latin American issuers.

Following the bank loan crisis in emerging markets, bank loans were securitized into debt securities with partial guarantees under the leadership of the Treasury Secretary Nicholas Brady in early 1990s. Such bonds are known as Brady bonds. Table 1-17 presents the importance of Brady bonds in the emerging market index.

We provide a detailed treatment of this market in a later chapter in this book. It is useful to note at this juncture that Brady bonds are obligations of the governments of developing countries. They are perhaps the most liquid of emerging market debt securities. The prices of Brady bonds provide an important signal of market sentiments. Recent default by Ecuador or its emerging market debt vividly illustrates the risks associated with this asset class.

A FRAMEWORK FOR PRICING FIXED-INCOME SECURITIES

Our overview of fixed-income markets highlights the fact that fixed-income securities are exposed to various dimensions of risk. Depending on who the marginal investor is in any specific fixed-income security market and depending on the compensation required by the investor for bearing the risks, the pricing of the security will be affected. To assist the reader in developing some intuition about the relative pricing of fixed-income securities, we provide a simple framework in Table 1-18.

The general approach to pricing fixed-income securities proceeds logically. First, the Treasury securities, which are the most liquid securities and which are free from credit and timing risk, will be priced. Almost every other sector of the fixed-income

TABLE 1-18   *Relative Risk Exposures of Fixed-Income Securities*

Dimension of Risk and Return	Treasury	Agencies	Corporates	MBS	Municipals	Emerging Markets
Credit risk	Absent	Very low	Varies	Very low	Varies	High
Interest risk	Varies	Varies	Varies	Varies	Varies	Varies
Liquidity risk	Very low	Low/moderate	Varies	Low	Varies	High
Timing risk	None	Low	High	Very high	High	Varies
Tax	Only federal taxes	Fully taxable	Fully taxable	Fully taxable	Tax-exempt	Fully taxable
FX risk	None	None	None	None	None	Present
Inflation	Present	Present	Present	Present	Present	Present

securities market is then priced relative to the Treasury benchmark. This requires a theory of risk and return of the Treasury securities. But the valuation of Treasury securities can proceed without a theory of credit risk. To this end, many of the valuation procedures that will be described in detail in this text are for Treasury securities. The pricing of other securities, such as corporate and mortgage-backed securities, requires in addition a theory for pricing default risk and prepayments. In general, the pricing relationship will assume the following form. Let us say that we have been able to determine that the required rate of return on a Treasury security with a certain coupon and maturity is π_t. Then, a similar corporate security with credit risk will have a required return of the form, $\pi_t + \epsilon_t$ where ϵ_t is the compensation for credit risk. In reality, the premium in the required return (as measured by the yields) includes not only a compensation for credit risk but also a compensation for liquidity risk and for any contractual provisions that may be present in the corporate security. Such contractual provisions might include call features, for example. By developing models of credit risk and prepayments, and super-imposing those models on the basic Treasury model, we will be able to value corporate and mortgage-backed securities.

In Table 1-19, we provide a framework for the pricing of debt securities and the logical sequence of steps that are involved in the process.

As shown in Figure 1-9, the relationship between the yields in the Treasury, corporate, and municipal markets over the last two decades shows that the spread's ϵ_t has fluctuated a great deal over time. This suggests that the factors that determine the premium over the Treasury rates can be quite variable over time.

Note that the relative valuation of securities as reflected in the yield spreads has fluctuated a good deal. The pricing of debt securities focuses on the valuation of Treasury securities and on the determination of the spreads at which securities in the other segments of the fixed-income securities markets trade relative to comparable Treasury securities. These issues are taken up in detail in later chapters.

TABLE 1-19   *Pricing of Debt Securities*

	Interest Rate Risk	*Default Risk*	*Contractual Provisions (Options)*	*Other Sources of Risk*	*Required Rate of Return*
Noncallable Treasury	Interest rate risk is critical and must be modeled.	Not relevant	New issues since 1985 are noncallable. There are about 20 callable issues outstanding.	Off-the-run issues may be illiquid.	Compensation for interest rate risk only.
Callable Treasury	Interest rate risk is critical and must be modeled.	Not relevant	The call option held by the Treasury has to be modeled.	Many of them are illiquid.	Compensation for interest rate risk plus a compensation for the timing uncertainty.
Corporate Securities	Interest rate risk is critical and must be modeled.	Issuer's credit reputation is critical. Credit risk must be modeled.	Sinking funds and calls may be present. Investors may have the right to put the bond back to the issuer. Call features may be present.	With the exception of new issues, liquidity is poor in this market.	Compensation for interest rate risk plus a compensation for the timing uncertainty plus a compensation for credit risk minus the value of options held by the investor.
Mortgage-Backed Securities	Interest rate risk is critical and must be modeled.	When housing prices fall, homeowners can "walk away" from the loan, and this affects the cash flows. Credit standing of the pool	The homeowners have the option to prepay and this must be modeled.	Housing prices, seasonal factors, etc.	Compensation for interest rate risk plus a compensation for the timing uncertainty. Additional compensation for lack of liquidity and the credit standing of the structure.

(continued)

TABLE 1-19   *Continued*

	Interest Rate Risk	*Default Risk*	*Contractual Provisions (Options)*	*Other Sources of Risk*	*Required Rate of Return*
Municipal Securities	Interest rate risk is critical and must be modeled.	Issuer's credit reputation is critical. Credit risk must be modeled.	Sinking funds and calls may be present. Investors may have the right to put the bond back to the issuer.	Tax status is critical and must be modeled.	Compensation for interest rate risk plus a compensation for the timing uncertainty plus a compensation for credit risk minus the value of tax benefits held by the investor. Tax risks are present.
Emerging Market Securities	Interest rate risk is critical and must be modeled.	Issuer's credit reputation is critical. Credit risk must be modeled.	Sinking funds and calls may be present. Investors may have the right to put the bond back to the issuer.	Political risk, exchange rate risk, and tax considerations must be modeled.	Compensation for interest rate risk plus a compensation for the timing uncertainty plus a compensation for credit risk plus a compensation for exchange rate and political risks.
Hybrids	Interest rate risk is critical and must be modeled.	Issuer's credit reputation is critical. Credit risk must be modeled.	Sinking funds and calls may be present. Investors may have the right to convert the bond into shares of common stock.	Equity risk is important.	Compensation for interest rate risk plus a compensation for the timing uncertainty plus a compensation for credit risk minus the value of the conversion option held by the investor.

FURTHER READING

Several texts with an emphasis on market institutions in fixed-income markets are available. Notable texts are Fabozzi (1993) and Ray (1993). In addition, there are texts that address topics relating to interest rates, such as Van Horne (1994). Many specialized texts are available, each dealing with one or two segments of fixed-income markets. Ray (1993) provides a detailed account of the Treasury market. Several excellent texts are available on government securities markets. These include Bollenbacher (1988), Garbade (1982), and Scott (1965). Despite the fact that these books are somewhat dated, their treatment of the material is still of considerable value.

Specialized journals are available dealing with each segment of the fixed-income markets. The *Journal of Fixed-Income* publishes papers on topics spanning all segments of the fixed-income markets. Articles in this journal tend to be oriented more toward the practitioners. Other journals, such as the *Journal of Portfolio Management*, also contain articles of general interest to practitioners in the fixed-income area. Other academic journals, such as the *Journal of Finance, Review of Financial Studies, Journal of Financial Economics, Journal of Financial and Quantitative Analysis,* and *Journal of Business,* carry academic papers with an emphasis on theoretical and empirical work in finance. Many influential papers on fixed-income securities have appeared in these journals. Some influential papers on interest rates and term structure theory have also appeared in the *Journal of Political Economy, Econometrica,* and other journals of economics. Real estate and mortgage-backed securities have several academic and practitioner-oriented journals. Two prominent journals are the *Journal of AREUEA* and the *Journal of Real Estate Finance and Economics.* A number of journals, such as *Financial Analysts Journal, Journal of Portfolio Management,* and *Financial Management,* also carry many papers on fixed-income markets.

PROBLEMS

1.1   In the market, highly rated corporate bonds are providing a 2% higher return than comparable Treasury securities. Does this mean that these corporate securities are better investments than Treasury securities? Discuss.

1.2   What types of institutional investors will value liquidity more? Why?

1.3   The fixed-income sector of the U.S. market consists of Treasuries, corporates, mortgage-backed securities, and municipals.

   (a) Provide a brief analysis of each of these segments along each dimension of risk.

   (b) Provide a pecking order among these segments for (i) pension funds, (ii) central banks, and (iii) hedge funds. Explain your conclusions. How would the tax status of these securities affect the pecking order?

1.4   Define the terms T-bills, T-notes, and T-bonds.

1.5   What are the on-the-run, off-the-run, and off-off-the-run issues in the Treasury market? Why is such a distinction important?

1.6   Many corporate bonds have call features or sinking fund features. The issuer has the right to call these bonds at prespecified call prices on prespecified dates. Only a small percentage of Treasury bonds (of late, no Treasuries) have call features. What might be the reasons for this difference? Explain.

1.7   Explain why Treasuries of the same risk tend to sell for a lower yield than corporates of the same risk. Explain why municipals of the same risk tend to sell for a lower yield than either corporates or Treasuries. Using the data in the *Treasury Bulletin,* plot the spreads between long-term corporates, Treasuries, and municipals for the last 20 years. Explain the spread behavior as a function of

    (a) the level of the yields,

    (b) the shape of the Treasury yield curve,

    (c) changes in the tax environment, and

    (d) credit risk.

1.8   Consider an investor with a marginal tax rate of 30%. If municipal securities yield 6% and a comparable corporate yields 7.5%, which is the better investment? Why? Provide a discussion of other factors that will affect the choice between these investments.

1.9   What are special purpose vehicles? Describe their functions in securitization.

1.10   Describe the process of securitization. How does this process help in the overall resource allocation of the economy?

1.11   What are revenue bonds? How do they differ from general obligation bonds?

1.12   Some floating-rate bonds are issued with a put feature, which gives the investor the right to put the floater back to the issuer on preset dates at par. Discuss whether this put is a protection against interest rate risk or credit risk.

1.13   Briefly describe each of the following debt securities and the motivation behind the issuing of such securities. What might be the motivation for investors to invest in these securities?

    (a) Convertible bonds

    (b) Inverse floater

    (c) Payment-in-kind (PIK) bonds

    (d) Zero coupon bonds

    (e) Yankee bonds

1.14   Describe the sectors of fixed-income markets in which institutional investors such as pension funds should not be investing their funds. Why?

1.15   What are the reasons for issuers to raise capital by issuing floating rate securities as opposed to fixed-rate securities?

1.16   Review the publication *Bond Week* by Salomon Brothers for this week. Using the information presented in this publication, write a summary report not exceeding one page highlighting the activities in the fixed-income securities market.

1.17   Bonds in the corporate sector are usually issued with sinking fund provisions. Supply the rationale for this contractual feature. Will it be beneficial to the bondholders? Why?

1.18   You have bought two securities from the same issuer. The first security is a bullet corporate bond with a maturity of 30 years and a coupon (semiannual) of 10%. The second security is a floating-rate bond with a maturity of 30 years. The floater will pay a coupon (semiannual) equal to the prevailing six-month T-bill rate plus 100 basis points. Assume that the floater has no additional contractual provisions and that the ex-coupon dates for the two securities are the same. Explain how you will assess the risks of these two securities.

1.19   Discuss the importance of the emerging market in the fixed-income markets. What is the Brady Plan? How has it affected the emerging market?

REFERENCES

Bollenbacher, G. 1988. *The Professional's Guide to the U.S. Government Securities Markets: Treasuries, Agencies, Mortgage-backed Instruments.* New York: New York Institute of Finance.

Fabozzi, F. (ed.). 1987. Mortgage-Backed Securities: New Strategies Applications and Research. Chicago: Probus.

Fabozzi, F. 1993. *Bond Markets, Analysis and Strategies.* 2nd ed. Englewood Cliffs, NJ: Prentice-Hall.

Fabozzi, F. (ed.). 1994. *Handbook of Fixed Income Securities.* Homewood, IL: Irwin Professional Publishing.

Garbade, K. D. 1982. *Securities Markets.* New York: McGraw Hill.

Ray, C. 1993. *The Bond Market. Trading and Risk Management.* Homewood. IL: Business One Irwin.

Scott, I. 1965. *Government Securities Market.* New York: McGraw Hill.

Stigum, M. 1983. *The Money Market.* Homewood, IL: Dow-Jones Irwin.

Sundaresan, S. 1991–1993. Debt Markets. Columbia University MBA B8308 course binders.

Van Horne. James C. 1994. *Financial Markets Rates and Flows.* 4th ed. Englewood Cliffs, NJ: Prentice-Hall.

SOME USEFUL WEBSITES

1.   http://www.mcmwatch.com/

This site provides useful summary information about money markets, corporate debt financing, Treasury markets, emerging markets, the Federal Reserve and other matters of general interest to fixed-income professionals. The reports are valuable in getting a perspective of the fixed-income markets.

2.   http://www.federalreserve.gov

This is the home page of the Federal Reserve Bank of New York. It has several useful pages, which are well worth looking into. A complete description of the open market operations, as well as the functions of the Fed, is to be found here. Research papers and other publications are also maintained here.

3.   http://www.federalreserve.gov/releases/H15/data.htm

This page contains valuable data for analyzing the spreads in fixed-income markets.

4.   http://www.ustreas.gov/

This is the home page of the department of Treasury, which contains information about Treasury functions, T-bills, T-notes, and bonds. It also contains results on auctions and data for research.

5.   http://www.bankofengland.co.uk/

This is the home page of Bank of England, which contains information about the U.K. market and also about the developments in the Euro-based government bond markets. It also has research papers and other publications of interest.

6.   http:/www.bondmarkets.com/

This is the home page of the Bond Market Association. This is an important website for students of fixed-income markets.

7.   http:/www.bradynet.com/

This site contains a wealth of information about emerging market debt.

Chapter 2

Organization
and Conduct
of Debt Markets

Chapter Objectives

The purpose of this chapter is to describe the organization of debt markets. Chapter 2 will help the reader to understand and answer the following questions:

- What are different forms of market organizations?
- What is adverse selection?
- Who are the key players in debt markets? In this context, we will describe the following players:
  1. Treasury
  2. Federal Reserve
  3. Government agencies
  4. Primary dealers
  5. Interdealer brokers
  6. Investors
- What are the options that the Federal Reserve can use in implementing its monetary policies?
- What are repo markets? How are they used for financing Treasury securities?
- What happened in the May 1991 two-year auctions? What are short squeezes? What was the robe played by Salomon Brothers in that auction?
- What are some of the regulatory issues in debt markets?
- What is transparency in securities markets?

INTRODUCTION

This chapter begins by briefly describing certain market organizations that are relevant to the study of fixed-income markets. We then discuss the salient properties of market organizations that participants take into account in their trading and pricing decisions. Next, we discuss the key players in the Treasury markets and the Treasury market organization. Other segments of the fixed-income markets are then taken up. The regulatory aspects of fixed-income markets in general are addressed in the final section of the chapter. We discuss in particular the scandal in the Treasury markets involving Salomon Brothers and explore its consequences for the future conduct of Treasury auctions and the regulation of the Treasury markets.

MARKET ORGANIZATION

The organization of markets or the market structure refers to the institutional arrangement by which buyers of securities are matched with sellers. Chapter 1 noted that most fixed-income securities markets around the world are organized as over-the-counter (OTC) or dealer markets. We provide below some basic market structures which will serve as a frame of reference for our analysis. The classification that follows is suggested in Garbade (1982), who also provides a more detailed treatment of some of these market organizations.

Direct search is an arrangement in which buyers directly search and identify matching sellers without the benefit of one or more intermediaries. For this structure to come about, the frequency of transactions must be so low that no intermediary finds it economical to provide any service. The costs of search, location, and negotiation are fully borne by the individual transactor (buyer or the seller). As a result, this market structure may frequently lead to trades away from the best possible price. This type of market structure is not of interest in the context of fixed-income security markets and probably is descriptive only of primitive markets with very few buyers and sellers, which are extremely illiquid.

When trading becomes more and more frequent, brokers may find it economical to intermediate (for a fee) and match buyers and sellers at mutually agreed-upon terms. For a **brokered market** to come about, the trading volume in securities must be heavy, and there must be significant economies of scale in the search costs to locate counterparties, so that a direct search is a more costly alternative to buyers and sellers. In addition, transactions away from the best possible price must not be too costly for the buyer and seller. The last condition is necessary because the broker may not be able to execute the order instantaneously. Note that the broker acts as an agent to buyers and sellers. Brokered markets are quite common in the securities industry.

The secondary market for U.S. Treasury is organized as a **dealer market.** More than 1,500 dealers stand ready to buy and sell Treasury securities at bid and offer prices that are widely disseminated to investors either through electronic screens or through telephones. (Bid and offer prices are defined in Chapter 1.) The dealer market structure reduces the time of search compared to brokered markets. Dealers may quote different bid-offer prices for the same security; hence, a limited search for the best price may still be necessary. Dealers, unlike brokers, also take outright positions in securities; thus, they are also exposed to the market risk on their inventories. Depending on the securities, their profits will depend on the market risks, as well as the depth and breadth of their sales force and customer base.

Centralized markets in which all market participants interact simultaneously are known as **auction markets.** These reduce further the cost of search and provide better bid-offer spreads. The centralized open outcry markets, such as the futures and options exchanges, may be thought of as prototypical examples of auction markets. The seller of securities is concerned with designing the mechanism that enables the expected revenues to be maximized. In addition, if the issuer intends to be a repeat seller (such as the U.S. Treasury), then there is an incentive to ensure that the market is free from manipulations. We discuss some of the auction mechanisms used in the Treasury market in Chapter 3.

Properties of Market Organizations

An important trait of a well-functioning market organization is **transparency.** This, loosely interpreted, is the extent to which information about trades, quotes, and other market information, such as volume of trading and open interest, are available to all players in the market. The cost of obtaining such information is also critical. Hence, in a well-functioning market organization, transparency should be present at a sufficiently low cost.

When intermediaries attempt to match potential buyers with potential sellers in a market, they face the risk of trading with either buyers or sellers who have more information than the others about the security or the deal that is about to be transacted. This is referred to as the **adverse selection** problem. A common example is the used-car market. In such markets, the seller of the used car presumably knows a good deal more about the true condition (and the true value) of the car than potential buyers. In order to protect themselves against such trades, the intermediaries will then charge a wider bid-offer spread to all participants in the market. This can be a serious factor in the determination of the bid-offer spread when the availability of relevant information to all participants is not symmetric and the cost of obtaining additional relevant information is significant.

In addition to the adverse selection problem, the intermediaries routinely take large inventory positions in securities and absorb the risk of price fluctuations before such inventories are sold to customers. The risk of the security in a market, the ability to off-load that risk in other markets, and the uncertainty in the cost of financing such inventories will all contribute both to the bid-offer spreads and to the depth of the market.

There is a growing body of literature on what is called the market microstructure that deals with these and other related questions. This literature examines the properties of different market arrangements on such factors as price formation and bid-offer spreads.

Generally, the form of the market organization (OTC or dealer markets, auctions, etc.) has a significant impact on the resulting price processes and bid-offer spreads. In addition, the informational disclosure requirements, the regulatory rules, and the effectiveness of their enforcement also affect the outcome significantly.

Several influential papers, notably Glosten and Milgrom (1985) and Glosten (1987), contain valuable models for the components of bid-offer spreads. One model is that the bid-offer spread consists of two components. The first component is the compensation that the market maker gets due to possible monopoly power, inventory carrying costs, etc. The second component is compensation due to the adverse selection component. When market makers realize that the counterparties with superior information will buy when the price is low relative to the true value and will sell when the price is high relative to the true value, this causes an upward revision of the true price after a buy and a downward revision of the true price after a sell. While most of the available theoretical models are interpreted in the context of equity markets, the basic insights apply to fixed-income markets as well.

The adverse selection component of the bid-offer spread will be less significant if the informational differences between the participants are negligible. Cornell (1993) examines the Treasury market for the presence of private information and adverse selection and concludes that the adverse selection problems are not severe. At the end of this chapter, we briefly review some of the regulatory aspects of fixed-income securities markets that bear on these properties of market organization.

PLAYERS IN GOVERNMENT SECURITIES MARKETS

In this section, the focus will first be on the government securities market. Later, we will describe the organization of other sectors of the fixed-income securities markets.

The government securities market in the U.S has seven major participants:

1. The **U.S. Treasury** is the fulcrum of the government securities market. It is the issuer of short-term and long-term debt securities on a regular basis.
2. The **Federal Reserve System** acts as the agent of U.S. Treasury in issuing U.S. Treasury debt through a computerized book-entry system. Both the initial sale of securities and subsequent transfers are handled by the Federal Reserve System. The conduct of monetary policy, including the open market operations, is also carried out by Federal Reserve (Fed).
3. **Agencies of the U.S. government** also issue securities of varying maturities. These are collectively known as agency debt issues. An overview of this market is in Chapter 1.
4. **Primary dealers** are those banks, bank subsidiaries, diversified investment banks, and specialty firms approved to transact directly with the Fed in its market operations. Currently, there are nearly 30 primary dealers.
5. **Other dealers** routinely trade in U.S. government securities but are not primary dealers. These include depository institutions, securities firms, and specialist firms.
6. **Interdealer brokers** are important players in the government securities market. They conceal the identities of the ultimate sellers and buyers, and act as principals to both sides of the trade.
7. **Investors** throughout the world hold U.S. government securities because they are, perhaps, the most liquid and nominally riskless securities. The investment community in this sector includes central banks, pension funds, insurance companies, commercial banks, corporations, and state and local governments. The Fed itself transacts heavily in government securities, but it does not directly buy securities from the Treasury. It conducts its transactions through primary dealers.

U.S. Treasury

The United States Treasury is responsible for borrowing money in capital markets to meet government expenditures. In addition, it is also vested with the responsibility of tax collection. One of the key tasks connected with these responsibilities is determining the amount and type of debt that must be sold. The U.S. Treasury issues marketable debt securities, such as T-bills, T-notes, and T-bonds. It also issues nonmarketable securities, such as savings bonds, and special issues called cash management bills and foreign-targeted securities. Obviously, the composition of these securities is an important decision. Recently, the U.S. Treasury has started to issue inflation-indexed securities. The U.S. Treasury also decides on the time schedule of issuing debt and, given the large amount of debt that is issued, the Treasury decides on the maturity composition of debt. Lately, the U.S. Treasury has significantly reduced the average maturity by suspending the seven-year benchmark auction and making the 30-year auction twice a year instead of quarterly refunding. The average maturity of U.S. Treasury debt reached a peak of ten years and five months in June 1947 and then followed generally a declining trend until December 1975, when it reached an all-time low of two years and five months. The current average maturity is six years. Decisions about maturity composition affect the supply of Treasury securities in an important way, influencing the pricing of Treasury yield curve across the maturity spectrum. As of 1999, the average maturity stood at five years and six months.

As a third major task, the Treasury must decide on the mechanism for selling Treasury securities to the public. Currently, the Treasury is using the uniform-price or the Dutch auction procedure for selling all its securities. Other countries, such as Canada, use discriminatory as well as Dutch auctions. The next chapter will discuss in detail these auctions, the theory behind them, and the empirical evidence. The schedule of Treasury auctions is provided in Chapter 1.

As of 1999, the U.S. economy was generating considerable surplus. The Treasury was reducing the level of public debt by reducing the quantity auctioned. In fact, as noted in Chapter 1, the Treasury announced that it would buy back outstanding debt to reduce the cost of servicing public debt. Buying back the debt is relatively new in the U.S. Treasury market but has taken place in other Treasury markets, such as the Canadian Government Bond market. Such buybacks may have important consequences for the liquidity of the Treasury market and for its benchmark status.

Federal Reserve

The Fed is vested with the responsibility of conducting monetary policies. These policies control the money in the economy and the level and the course of interest rates of different maturities. In addition, as the equivalent of central bank of the country, the Fed is the "lender of last resort." It also acts as an agent of the Treasury in conducting auctions and in handling payments and collections via electronic transfer systems. Finally, it plays the role of regulator in matters concerning commercial banks, Treasury securities, and derivative assets on interest rates.

The Fed consists of the Board of Governors and the Federal Reserve District Banks. Currently, there are 12 district banks, each with its own branches. The Federal Reserve Board has seven members, one of the members serving as the Chairman. The members are appointed by the President of the United States.

The Federal Reserve System is also responsible for implementing monetary policies. Several policy options are available to the Fed.

1. The Fed can cut or raise the discount rate. The discount window of the Federal Reserve is where the central bank lends funds to depository institutions. Such lending typically takes the form of short-term adjustment credit, seasonal credit, and in some instances longer-term credit. **Discount rate** is the rate that the Federal Reserve charges on short-term adjustment credit. This rate is often viewed by the market as an indicator of monetary policy. The discount rate affects the cost of reserves borrowed from the Federal Reserve. Increases in discount rates generally reflect the central bank's concern over inflationary pressures. Likewise, decreases in discount rates may reflect a concern about economic weakness. The central bank may utilize this tool sparingly or frequently as it sees fit. For example, during the period of December 1990 to mid-1992, the central bank cut the rates seven times from a high of 7% to a low of 3% to activate a sluggish economy. In the period mid-1994 through mid-1995, the Fed increased the discount rate from a low of 3% to a high of 5.25% to combat the threat of inflation. Discount window lending is considered the "lender of last resort" function of the central bank.

2. The Fed can change the reserve requirements. **Reserve requirements** refers to the percentage of deposits that a depository institution must maintain either as cash or on deposit at a Federal Reserve Bank. The central bank is authorized to impose a reserve requirement of 8% to 14% on transaction deposits and up to 9% on non-personal time deposits. Reserve requirements represent a cost to the banks. In recent times, the central bank has imposed a 10% reserve requirement on transaction deposits and none on time deposits.

   The reserve requirements are enforced over a two-week period. The depository institution's **average reserves** over the two-week period ending every alternate Wednesday must equal the required percentage of its **average deposits** in the two-week period ending Monday, two days earlier.

   Increasing the reserve requirements reduces the creation of credit and hence will reduce the economic activity.

3. The Fed can undertake outright transactions in Treasury and federal agency securities in the open market (at market prices) with securities dealers, and official foreign and international accounts maintained at the Federal Reserve Bank of New York.

4. The Fed also can enter into repurchase agreements (repos or RPs) for different terms to maturity.

The Federal Reserve has a committee known as the Federal Open Market Committee (FOMC), which authorizes the tools by which it conducts monetary policies.

Fed Funds Market. The Fed funds market is the market for the reserve balances at the Fed that depository institutions maintain to meet the reserve requirements. The Fed does not pay interest on these reserves and, as a consequence, the depository institutions try to maintain the minimum amount of reserves necessary to conduct their activities. A depository institution that is short of reserves will borrow reserves from a bank that has a surplus in the Fed funds market. Such borrowing and lending can be done either directly by the banks or through brokers. Usually, brokered transactions are of larger average size. Typically, big banks borrow reserves from smaller ones that have surplus reserves. Many of the depository institutions that have a surplus of reserves view the Fed funds market as a means of obtaining liquidity. The daily volume of Fed funds transactions arranged by the brokers exceeds $50 billion.

Fed funds transactions typically take place overnight. Sometimes the Fed funds transactions extend over a term of a few days. It must be recognized that the Fed funds transactions are unsecured lending and borrowing between depository institutions. The term Fed funds market is a lot less liquid than the overnight market.

A typical Fed funds transaction is shown in Figure 2-1. The bank with surplus reserves offers the reserves (typically through a Fed fund broker) to the bank that has a need for such reserves. The selling bank also informs the Federal Reserve Bank in its district, which arranges for the transfer.

The Fed funds rate is a barometer of the activities of the depository institutions and reflects the rate at which banks are able to obtain reserves. The supply and demand in the market for reserves determine the Fed funds rate. The rates go up when the demand for reserves is great and goes down when the demand is sluggish. The behavior of the Fed funds rates from 1954 to 1998 is shown in Figure 2-2. The central bank sets a target Fed funds rate. This target rate is a way for the central bank to signal the cost of credit. A cut in the target rate is viewed as *easing* credit, and an increase in the target rate is viewed as *tightening* credit availability. The actual Fed funds rate will fluctuate in the market, reflecting the market conditions. The central bank will pursue its open market policies to keep the actual Fed funds rate close to the target. When market conditions warrant a change in the target rate, the central bank will change it. Typically, changes in the target Fed funds rate are made in FOMC meetings. We enclose the target Fed funds rate changes that were made in the last few years. The Fed

FIGURE 2-1   *Fed Funds Market Transaction*

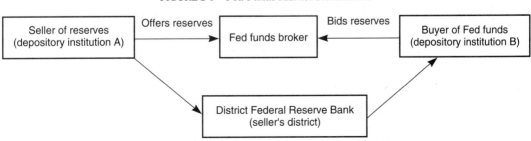

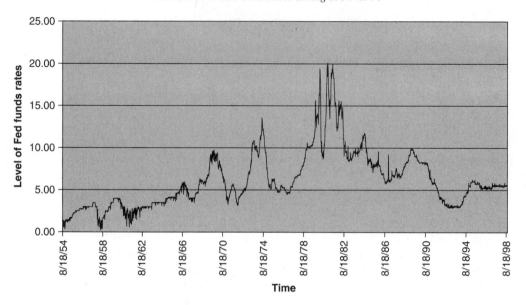

FIGURE 2-2   *Fed Funds Rates during 1954–1998*

Historical Changes of the Federal Funds Rate		
	Change	*New Level*
1995		
February 1	$+\frac{1}{2}$	6
July 6	$-\frac{1}{4}$	$5\frac{3}{4}$
December 19	$-\frac{1}{4}$	$5\frac{1}{2}$
1996		
January 31	$-\frac{1}{4}$	$5\frac{1}{4}$
1997		
March 25	$+\frac{1}{4}$	$5\frac{1}{2}$
1998		
September 29	$-\frac{1}{4}$	$5\frac{1}{4}$
October 15	$-\frac{1}{4}$	5
November 17	$-\frac{1}{4}$	$4\frac{3}{4}$
1999		
June 30	$+\frac{1}{4}$	5
Aug 24	$+\frac{1}{4}$	$5\frac{1}{4}$
Nov 16	$+\frac{1}{4}$	$5\frac{1}{2}$
2000		
Feb 2	$+\frac{1}{4}$	$5\frac{3}{4}$
Mar 21	$+\frac{1}{4}$	6
May 16	$+\frac{1}{2}$	$6\frac{1}{2}$

Source: Federal Reserve.

cut the target rate three times in 1998 largely to provide liquidity to a market that was rocked by the Russian default and hedge fund failures. In 1999 and 2000, the Fed tended to tighten credit to keep inflation under control in a rapidly expanding economy. From time to time, especially around the end of the calendar year, the Fed fund rates go up, resulting in the spikes evident in Figure 2-2. This may be because many big depository institutions drive up the Fed funds rates seasonally.

Open Market Operations. The Fed's discount window is an important monetary policy tool. Under this scheme, the Fed provides credit when there is a shortage; the discount rate is the rate at which the Fed acts as a lender of last resort to the depository institutions. The loans made by the Fed can be directed toward short-term scarcity, seasonal peak loads (as in agriculture) for credit, or distress credit to help depository institutions that are in serious financial trouble.

When the Fed changes its holdings of Treasury securities, it does so in this secondary market. The directives of the Federal Open Market Committee are implemented by the trading desk of the New York Fed. Since its transactions influence the pace of monetary expansion, the Fed is only allowed to participate in outright transactions in the secondary market where Treasury and Federal agency securities are already outstanding. It is not allowed to bid directly in the auctions. The Fed has a wide choice in the type of securities to buy or sell (maturity, coupon, discount, etc.), as well as in the choice of the counterparties. The timing of the Fed's actions is dictated by the forecasts of the reserve demands; the larger the anticipated demand, the greater the purchases of securities. The Fed's portfolio has a diversified maturity composition, as Table 2-1 illustrates. However, the bulk of the Fed's holdings are in U.S. Treasury securities. Nearly 60% of the Treasury holdings are under a maturity of one year.

TABLE 2-1 *Federal Reserve Banks Maturity Distribution and Security Holdings (in Millions of Dollars)*

	March 1999	*April 1999*	*May 1999*
Total Loans	65	68	121
< 15 days	64	40	75
15 < and < 90 days	1	28	47
Total U.S. Treasury Securities	478,416	482,503	488,535
< 15 days	26,785	13,804	9,131
15 < and < 90 days	98,303	103,293	106,365
91 < and < 365 days	134,439	142,071	139,450
1 year < and < 5 years	112,263	115,147	121,571
5 years < and < 10 years	46,598	47,546	49,403
> 10 years	60,029	60,642	62,615
Total Federal Agency Obligations	5,917	3,603	4,808
< 15 days	5,606	3,292	4,545
Others over 15 days	311	311	263

Source: Federal Reserve Bulletin, August 1999.

In addition to outright transactions, the Fed routinely undertakes temporary transactions in which reserves are either injected or drained for a day or two. If, for example, a shortage of reserves is anticipated, the Fed can either buy securities outright, as explained earlier, or temporarily buy the securities with an agreement to sell them back within a day or two. Usually, much larger operations are carried out using the temporary transactions. One strategy used by the Fed in this context is the **matched sale-purchase transactions** (MSP) in which the Fed sells T-bills for immediate delivery through dealers and simultaneously buys them back for delivery in a day or two. These are viewed as two separate transactions.

The Fed also uses repurchase agreements to effect temporary transactions. Reverse repos (explained later) are used by the Fed to either provide or absorb bank reserves. In addition, the Fed transacts on behalf of foreign central banks and official institutions.

Many foreign accounts place a percentage of their U.S. dollar holdings with the Fed in an overnight repo facility. If such holdings are placed in repo using an MSP with the Fed's portfolio, then the reserves will be drained—this is because the funds received by the foreign account stay with the Fed. This is referred to as a **system RP.** When the foreign order can be routed through the market it is referred to as a **customer RP.** Usually, customer RPs signal a modest addition to the reserves, limited by the funds in the foreign accounts. On the other hand, system RPs signal a larger magnitude of reserve adjustments. For a more detailed treatment of the repo transactions by the Federal Reserve, see Meulendyke (1989). As Table 2-2 indicates, the matched transactions account for a large percentage of the Federal Reserve's open market operations. This is closely followed by the repo transactions.

The monetary policies followed by the Fed underwent a major change in October 1979 when Paul Volcker became Chairman. The growth rates in money measures were targeted, and the emphasis of the Fed funds rates was diminished. Figures 2-3 and 2-4 illustrate the wild fluctuations in the levels of interest rates and their volatilities from 1977 to 1998. Note that the period 1980–1983 witnessed very high levels of

TABLE 2-2   *Federal Reserve Open Market Operations (in Millions of Dollars) in U.S. Treasury Securities*

Policy Dimension	Activity	1996	1997	1998
Outright Transaction	Gross Purchases	17,094	44,122	29,926
	Gross Sales	0	0	0
	Redemptions	2,015	1,996	4,676
Matched Transactions	Gross Purchases	3,092,399	3,577,954	4,395,430
	Gross Sales	3,094,769	3,580,274	4,399,330
Repurchase Agreements	Gross Purchases	457,568	810,485	512,671
	Gross Sales	450,359	809,268	514,186

Source: Federal Reserve Bulletin, August 1999.

FIGURE 2-3   *Levels of Interest Rates*

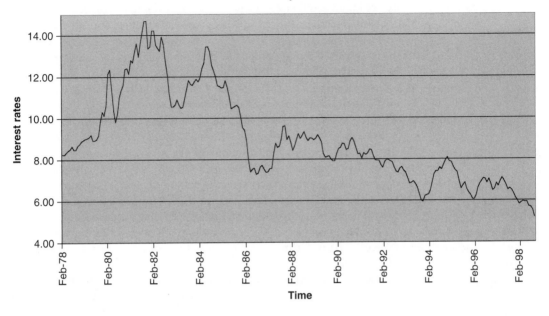

FIGURE 2-4   *Volatility of Interest Rates*

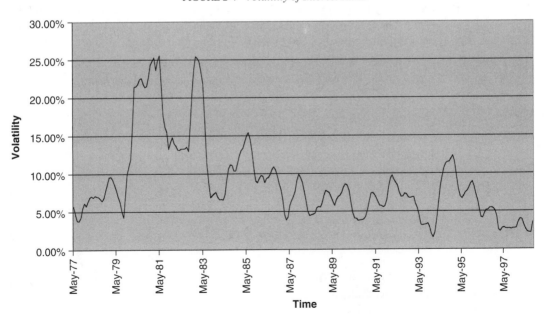

interest rates and very high volatilities as market participants came to grips with the new monetary policy. In addition, the yield curve was inverted for an extended period of time. This is also evident in Table 1-7, where we found that the spreads were negative in 1979–1981.

The Fed, acting as a fiscal agent for the Treasury, conducts the auctions of new Treasury securities. This entails collecting and processing competitive and noncompetitive bids from dealers. These auctions are considered in detail in Chapter 3. T-bills, T-notes, and T-bonds are issued in **book-entry** form. This is a **tiered custodial system.** This system records the ownership of securities in entries on the books of a series of custodians. This system begins with the Treasury and extends through the Federal Reserve Banks, depository institutions, brokers, and dealers to the ultimate owner. The tiered system operates as follows. The Treasury's book-entry will establish the total amount of each issue that is outstanding and the share of each that is held by each Federal Reserve Bank. Each Federal Reserve Bank will record how much of each issue is held by the depository institutions in its district that maintain book-entry accounts with it. The record of each depository institution will establish the amount that is held in its Reserve Bank for other depository institutions that do not maintain accounts at the Fed and for others.

Interest payments, as well as principal payments at maturity, are made by the Treasury, crediting the funds down the custodial tiers just described. Only certain depository institutions may have book-entry accounts at Federal Reserve Banks. Others must have their holdings reflected on the books of a depository institution that, in turn, has holdings through a depository institution. Transfers are made by making appropriate entries. If the transfer of a security takes place within the jurisdiction of a Federal Reserve Bank, no entries will be made at the Fed level or above. All entries will take place below the level of that Federal Reserve Bank.

Here we have only sketched the role of the Federal Reserve. A more comprehensive analysis appears in Hubbard (1991).

Government Securities Dealers

Currently, there are 30 primary dealers in the government securities markets. The following is a list of the primary government securities dealers reporting to the market reports division of the Federal Reserve Bank of New York.

ABN AMRO, Inc.
Aubrey G. Lanston & Co., Inc.
Banc of America Securities, LLC
Banc One Capital Markets, Inc.
Barclays Capital, Inc.
Bear, Stearns & Co., Inc.
Chase Securities, Inc.

CIBC World Markets Corp.
Credit Suisse First Boston Corp.
Daiwa Securities America, Inc.
Deutsche Bank Securities, Inc.
Donaldson, Lufkin & Jenrette Securities Corp.
Dresdner Kleinwort Benson North America, LLC
Fuji Securities, Inc.
Goldman, Sachs & Co.
Greenwich Capital Markets, Inc.
HSBC Securities (USA), Inc.
J. P. Morgan Securities, Inc.
Lehman Brothers, Inc.
Merrill Lynch Government Securities, Inc.
Morgan Stanley & Co., Inc.
Nesbitt Burns Securities, Inc.
Nomura Securities International, Inc.
Paine Webber, Inc.
Paribas Corporation
Prudential Securities, Inc.
SG Cowen Securities Corp.
Salomon Smith Barney, Inc.
Warburg Dillon Read, LLC
Zions First National Bank

In addition to the 30 primary dealers, there are more than 1,500 other dealers who perform a variety of trading and market-making functions in the Treasury market. The primary dealer system was established by the Federal Reserve. The basic advantage of such a system is that the Fed is in a position to conduct its monetary policies efficiently with a small number of well-capitalized dealers. Primary dealers are expected to participate in Treasury auctions, to distribute Treasury securities, and to stand ready to buy or sell securities for customers, that is, act as "market makers." The Fed has an approved list of primary dealers as shown previously. The Fed takes into account such factors as the capital base (financial strength), the customer base, the volume of activity, the commitment to making a market under varied market conditions, and the ability to meet the needs of the Fed when approving a dealer to be one of its primary dealers. Government securities dealers perform several tasks. They make markets for customers, providing relevant information, analysis, and advice to customers; maintain a sales force to accomplish this, do transactions, and win customer loyalty; maintain an inventory of government securities to meet customer needs; absorb and distribute a large chunk of U.S. government securities when securities are sold at auction; and buy and sell securities in the secondary market. The price at which the dealer is willing to buy is called a bid. The price at which a dealer is willing to sell is called an offer.

TABLE 2-3   *Cash Market Transactions of U.S. Government Securities Dealers (Daily Averages in Millions of Dollars)*

Outright Transactions	February 1999	March 1999	April 1999
By type of security			
U.S. Treasury bills	31,811	34,426	28,670
Coupon securities, by maturity			
Five years or less	107,777	96,141	87,799
More than five years	71,489	62,008	53,736
Inflation-indexed	772	402	1,415
Federal agency			
Discount notes	41,355	40,089	37,345
Coupon securities, by maturity			
One year or less	1,796	1,097	1,222
More than one year, but less than			
or equal to five years	7,446	7,640	6,875
More than five years	3,633	3,141	4,625
Mortgage-backed	75,923	69,547	69,382
By type of counterparty			
With interdealer broker			
U.S. Treasury	117,230	106,659	93,341
Federal agency	3,791	4,121	3,904
Mortgage-backed	25,301	23,601	23,682
With other			
U.S. Treasury	94,620	86,316	78,330
Federal agency	50,438	47,846	46,162
Mortgage-backed	50,622	45,946	43,700

Source: Federal Reserve Bulletin, August 1999.

Trading Activities. The volume of daily trading activity by government dealers is large. This is illustrated in Table 2-3, where the transactions in the underlying cash market are reported. These are classified first according to the type of securities and then according to the type of counterparties engaged in the transactions. These statistics reveal some interesting patterns. First, a major percentage of the transactions occurs in the Treasury securities. Mortgage-backed securities form a distant second, followed by the Federal agency securities. This sheds further light on the depth and liquidity of Treasury markets. The classification of trades by counterparties shows a rather interesting pattern— nearly 60% of Treasury transactions occur between dealers and brokers, and only 40% occur between customers and dealers. In sharp contrast, more than 60% of the transactions in mortgage-backed securities occur between customers and dealers. For the Federal agency debt, the customer-driven transactions are even higher at 85%.

These patterns reveal that the dealers take positions in Treasury and other securities not only to make a market in these securities but also to take principal positions. This latter activity is referred to as **proprietary trading** and has been increasingly responsible for a large percentage of dealers' profits and risks. As we shall see later in Chapter 19 on risk management, some significant losses have occurred as a result of these proprietary trading activities.

TABLE 2-4   *Derivatives Transactions of U.S. Government Securities Dealers*
(Daily Averages in Millions of Dollars)

Item	February 1999	March 1999	April 1999
Futures Transactions			
By type of deliverable security			
U.S. Treasury bills	n.a.	0	0
Coupon securities, by maturity			
Five years or less	2,512	2,649	1,947
More than two years	17,132	15,926	11,950
Inflation-indexed	0	0	0
Federal agency			
Discount notes	0	0	0
Coupon securities, by maturity			
One year or less	0	0	0
More than one year, but less than			
or equal to five years	0	0	0
More than five years	0	0	0
Mortgage-backed	0	0	0
Options Transactions			
By type of underlying security			
U.S. Treasury bills	0	0	0
Coupon securities, by maturity			
Five years or less	1,153	1,506	985
More than five years	5,798	5,050	4,657
Inflation-indexed	0	0	0
Federal agency			
Discount notes	0	0	0
Coupon securities, by maturity			
One year or less	0	0	0
More than one year, but less than			
or equal to five years	0	0	0
More than five years	0	0	0
Mortgage-backed	844	825	783

Source: Federal Reserve Bulletin, August 1999.

Table 2-4 provides a summary of the transactions undertaken by dealers in **derivative markets,** such as futures, forwards and options. It is important to note that these markets enable dealers to manage the risk in market making.

In addition, these markets enable dealers to leverage their positions significantly in their proprietary trading activities. Options are mostly on shorter maturity instruments. In Part III, we examine in detail how such derivative products are used in the fixed-income markets.

Position Management. The composition and management of inventory is structured to permit the dealer to sell at a price higher than the cost of acquiring the securities.

(The bid-offer spread is the profit if the price risk of inventory is eliminated.) This calls for the management of the interest rate risk—a primary source of price fluctuations in the government securities market. Dealers manage their own positions, that is, speculate with a view to profit from interest rate fluctuations; thus, dealers position securities to reflect their assessment of future interest rates. A dealer may take "a long position," anticipating a fall in interest rates, or "go short," anticipating a rise in interest rates. Most of the positions are highly leveraged or supported by borrowed funds. Hence, as noted earlier, position management is often the dominant source of variation in profit and capital for securities firms.

The daily average positions of dealers are given in Table 2-5, classified by type of securities. It is of interest to note that the dealers had established significant short posi-

TABLE 2-5   *Positions of U.S. Government Securities Dealers*
(Daily Averages in Millions of Dollars)

Item	February 1999	March 1999	April 1999
Net Outright Positions			
By type of security			
U.S. Treasury bills	4,509	24,510	24,563
Coupon securities, by maturity			
Five years or less	−12,028	−18,124	−14,332
More than five years	1,465	−6,408	−5,060
Inflation-indexed	1,931	1,846	2,618
Federal agency			
Discount notes	18,671	18,189	24,321
Coupon securities, by maturity			
One year or less	3,450	2,683	2,538
More than one year, but less than			
or equal to five years	5,044	5,222	3,991
More than five years	3,146	4,110	6,131
Mortgage-backed	17,432	16,774	12,875
Net Futures Positions			
By type of deliverable security			
U.S. Treasury bills	n.a.	0	n.a.
Coupon securities, by maturity			
Five years or less	459	−910	93
More than five years	−14,876	−12,929	−17,408
Inflation-indexed	0	0	0
Federal agency			
Discount notes	0	0	0
Coupon securities, by maturity			
One year or less	0	0	0
More than one year, but less than			
or equal to five years	0	0	0
More than five years	0	0	0
Mortgage-backed	0	0	0

Source: Federal Reserve Bulletin, August 1999.

tions in certain maturity sectors of the Treasury cash market. In addition, they were holding significant long positions in the mortgage-backed securities market. Their short positions in futures might be to hedge their long positions in the cash market.

The positions shown in Tables 2-3 and 2-4 are huge. How do dealers finance such huge positions? Surely, the capital base of the dealers is not sufficient to support such large positions. The answer is in the market for repurchase agreements or repo markets.

Repo Markets. The single most important source of financing for government dealers is the repo market. Government securities are liquid and default-free; hence, they are excellent collateral. Dealers can borrow money on a collateralized basis to buy such securities. This enables dealers with limited capital to take positions in securities worth billions of dollars. Table 2-6 gives an idea of the financing of a dealer's position.

The repo market is very large—exceeding $600 billion. Repurchase agreements (repos or RPs) are transactions in which one party (say, Party A) buys securities from another (Party B) while agreeing to resell those securities at a later date. Reverse repurchase agreements (or reverse repos) are transactions in which Party A sells securities to Party B while agreeing to repurchase those securities at a later date.

TABLE 2-6   *Financing of Positions of U.S. Government Securities Dealers (Daily Averages in Millions of Dollars)*

Item	February 1999	March 1999	April 1999
Reverse repurchase agreements			
Overnight and continuing	261,190	256,331	251,605
Term	788,073	781,168	818,297
Securities borrowed			
Overnight and continuing	225,926	226,297	212,240
Term	100,463	93,810	102,437
Securities received as pledge			
Overnight and continuing	2,380	2,555	n.a.
Term	n.a.	0	0
Repurchase agreements			
Overnight and continuing	666,536	655,676	677,260
Term	674,687	673,650	711,067
Securities loaned			
Overnight and continuing	11,753	12,875	10,235
Term	5,776	6,122	5,942
Securities pledged			
Overnight and continuing	48,945	48,533	45,650
Term	5,896	7,712	10,700
Collateralized loans			
Total	18,388	18,177	17,891

Source: Federal Reserve Bulletin, August 1999.

Repos and reverse repos may be done on an overnight basis or on a term basis for a specified number of days, ranging from a few days to over 30 days. Many of the repo and reverse repo transactions are done on an overnight basis or for a very short term not exceeding a few weeks at most.

A repo transaction may be viewed conceptually as **secured lending.** There are two parties to any repo transaction. Party A is the owner of the security or the collateral. For example, in a repo transaction Party A may need the money to pay for the securities he is selling to Party B. Party B, who has the cash, will charge interest for agreeing to this transaction. Party A will still retain the rights to any cash flows from the security (i.e., coupons or accrued interest) that he has used to collateralize the loan. Party A, the owner of the collateral, is said to do the repo transaction. Party B, the owner of cash, is said to do the reverse repo transaction. Table 2-7 shows the growth of repo and reverse repo transactions during the 1981–1999 period.

Securities used in repo transactions are referred to as **collaterals,** signifying the secured loan nature of the transaction. The buyer of the collateral does not deliver funds equal to the market value of the collateral; a **hair cut** will be taken from the market value, and only the remainder is delivered to the seller. This is one of the several ways in which credit risk is handled in repo transactions. Important considerations in any repo transaction include the term of the repo transaction (this may be overnight, a week, another specified term, or open), the amount of cash borrowed, and the rate of

TABLE 2-7 *Financing by U.S.* *Government Securities* *Dealers* *Reverse Repurchase and* *Repurchase Agreements*[1] *Average Daily Amount* *Outstanding 1981–1999* *(in Billions of Dollars)*		*Reverse* *Repurchase*	*Repurchase*	*Total*
	1981	46.7	65.4	112.1
	1982	75.1	95.2	170.3
	1983	81.7	102.4	184.1
	1984	112.4	132.6	245.0
	1985	147.9	172.9	320.8
	1986	207.7	244.5	452.2
	1987	275.0	292.0	567.0
	1988	313.6	309.7	623.3
	1989	383.2	398.2	781.4
	1990	377.1	413.5	790.5
	1991	417.0	496.6	913.6
	1992	511.1	628.2	1,139.3
	1993	594.1	765.6	1,359.7
	1994	651.2	825.9	1,477.1
	1995	618.8	821.5	1,440.3
	1996	718.1	973.7	1,691.8
	1997	883.0	1,159.0	2,042.0
	1998	1,111.4	1,414.0	2,525.5
	1999	1,070.1	1,361.0	2,431.1

Source: Federal Reserve Bank of New York.

[1]Figures cover financing involving U.S. government, federal agency, and federal agency MBS securities.

interest upon which the two parties have agreed. Overnight and open repo trades have to be renewed every day, possibly at new rates.

Most Treasury securities may be secured at a rate known as the **general collateral rate.** Thus, from the standpoint of obtaining secured credit, most of the Treasury securities may be close substitutes. Some of the securities may be in demand from time to time owing to a short squeeze or the deliverability in futures market. Such securities may trade at rates that are much lower than the general collateral rate. Such rates are called **special repo rates.** The investor wishing to go "long" in a bond will deliver the bond as collateral to borrow cash at the repo rate. The "long" enjoys the coupon and accrued interest from the bond but is obligated to pay the repo rate. The investor who wishes to go "short" in a bond will borrow the bond and sell it. The cash proceeds of the sale will be posted as collateral. The "short" is entitled to the interest rate (referred to as reverse repo rate) on the cash collateral but is obligated to pay any coupons or accrual of coupon during the period over which he or she is short.

When the bond becomes scarce or valuable due to an unanticipated shortage, it becomes a very attractive collateral. For example, during the fall of 1998 when Russia defaulted and the hedge fund Long-Term Capital Management (LTCM) collapsed, investors rushed to buy Treasury securities in a "flight to quality." In relation to this strong demand, there was a relative shortage. When this happens, the Treasury securities can be pledged as collateral to borrow cash at a low repo rate known as the special repo rate. Long investors will enjoy this specialness. The short investors will be penalized to reflect the fact that buying back the currently scarce treasury security to cover their short position is expensive. Hence, they must accept a low special repo rate on their cash collateral. Generally, repo markets involve large transfers of funds, extend for short terms, and are characterized by small earnings relative to potential changes in the value of the underlying securities or collaterals.

Interest rates in repo markets (repo rates) are generally lower than those on Federal funds due to the collateralized nature of transactions. The Fed funds rates reflect the fact that they are uncollateralized transactions. Repo markets are used by a large number of institutions—corporations, financial institutions, pension funds, commercial banks, etc. In contrast, the Fed funds market is open only to depository institutions. Figure 2-5 provides the historical spreads between the Fed funds rates and the repo rates. Although the Fed funds rates are typically higher than the general collateral repo rates, if the supply of Treasury securities increases and the need to finance the inventory position becomes critical, the repo rates will go up. This sometimes causes the repo rates to become higher than the Fed funds rates. During the first half of 1993, the repo rates often exceeded the general collateral rates.

Repo markets are used extensively by dealers to leverage their business activity; this is a natural outcome as government securities dealers regularly transact in securities that qualify as collaterals. Often, a dealer's capital is an extremely small fraction of the securities holdings: most of the securities are financed in the repo markets. Repo trades are simple to execute and provide the dealers with flexibility. The main alternative to repo financing for dealers is a bank loan, which would be relatively more expensive and less flexible. Dealers with good credit reputations may also use commercial paper to finance some of their activities.

FIGURE 2-5   *Fed Funds Rates Minus Overnight Repo Rates, March 1987 to December 1990*

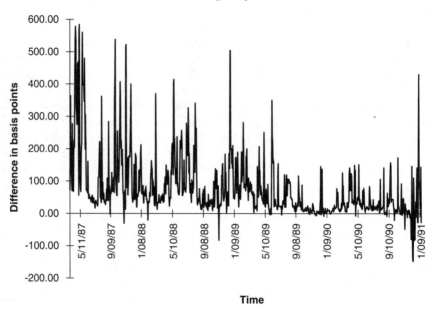

The following example of a simple repo transaction clarifies the mechanics of RPs, as well as the risks involved. Throughout the text, we will treat repo transactions as conceptually equivalent to secured lending and borrowing.

Example 2-1:

On June 10, 1986, Dealer X wished to finance $10 million par amount of a 7.25%, 5-15-2016 T-bond. The dealer wished to carry the position until June 13, 1986. Let us examine this trade. Table 2-8 gives the bid and ask prices in the market during the relevant period. (The prices are given in decimals.)

On June 10, 1986, Dealer X bought the T-bond and delivered it to the repo dealer. (See Figure 2-6.) The repo dealer accepted the T-bond as a collateral and lent cash at the repo rate. Typically, a repo dealer would not lend cash equal to the market price of the T-bond. The dealer would take a hair cut to protect against adverse price movements. Let us say that the dealer charged a hair cut of 0.5% of the market price. Then, the following transactions occurred:

1. The dealer bought the T-bond. Since the dealer bought the bond on June 10, 1986, he paid 94.03 plus accrued interest. The flat price of the T-bond was 94.03, the accrued interest was 0.5122; hence, the full price was 94.5422. On $10 million par, the full price was approximately 9,454,220. (The mechanics of calculating accrued interest are described in Chapter 4.)

	Date	Ask Price	Bid Price
TABLE 2-8	6/10/86	94.16	94.03
Repo Transactions	6/11/86	94.97	94.84
to Finance Positions,	6/12/86	95.03	94.91
7.25%, 5-15-2016, T-Bond	6/13/86	96.91	96.78

FIGURE 2-6   *Repo Transaction*

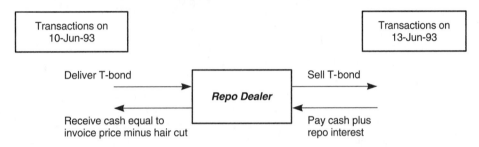

2. The hair cut taken by the repo dealer was 0.5% of market value: $0.5 \times \frac{1}{100} \times$ 9,454,220 = \$47,271.10.
3. Hence, the amount borrowed was 9,484,220 – 47,271.10 = 9,406,948.90.
4. On June 13, 1986, the dealer took possession of the T-bond, and sold it for the full (invoice) price in the market. On that day, the flat price of the T-bond was 96.91 and the accrued interest was 0.5713, so the full price was 97.4813. Hence, on \$10 million par, the full price was approximately \$9,748,130.
5. The repo dealer would be paid the amount borrowed plus the repo rate interest. The interest paid at a repo rate of 6% for three days on the borrowed money was $9,406,948.90 \times 0.06 \times \frac{3}{360} = 4703.47$. Hence, the amount paid for financing at a repo rate of 6% was $9,406,948.90 \times (1 + 0.06 \times \frac{3}{360}) =$ 9,411,652.37.
6. Also, during this period, the bond dealer earned from the T-bond an accrued interest of $(0.5713 - 0.5122) \times 100,000 = \$5,910$. This is reflected in the transaction prices.

The repo transaction itself is shown in Figure 2-6.

Repo trades generally settle on the trade day itself; this is in contrast to Treasury securities in the cash market, which normally settle a day after the trade day.

Note that in Example 2-1, the financing costs are lower than the accrued interest earned over the same period. This is referred to as **positive carry,** reflecting the fact that every day that the bond dealer carries his position in the repo markets, his or her

FIGURE 2-7 *Difference between General Collateral Rates and Special Rates*

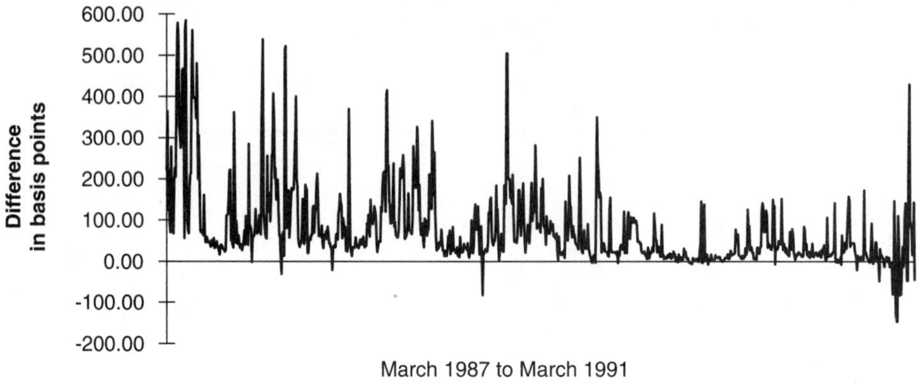

March 1987 to March 1991

interest income provides a cushion exceeding the financing costs. This is typical in a normal or positively sloped yield curve, where the coupons reflect medium-term and long-term yields and the financing costs reflect the short-term yields. On the other hand, when the yield curve is inverted, the yields of the Treasury securities are less than the repo rates, which are short term relative to Treasury securities. This is referred to as **negative carry.** In day-to-day operations, carry can be significant for dealers.

As pointed out earlier, from time to time the repo rates of some securities trade special. In Figure 2-7, we plot the difference between the general collateral rates and the special rates for on-the-run three-month Treasury bills. Note that on-the-run bills have been extremely expensive to borrow in the repo markets. Conversely, the owner of these bills could have borrowed at attractive rates using these bills as collateral—on some days, the repo rates are 500 basis points cheaper than the general collateral rates. We show that there are systematic auction effects in repo rates in Chapter 3. Duffie (1992) and Sundaresan (1994) explore the reasons for these special repos.

Dealers may have a significant repo position (on the order of several billion dollars) which is exactly matched with reverse repo positions. In such situations, the dealer is earning a spread, provided there is no credit risk. The counterparty, who has loaned cash in exchange for the collateral, faces the risk that the other party may not repay the cash plus the repo interest. This risk is mitigated by the fact that the collateral can be sold in the market. If the market value of the collateral drops significantly in relation to the cash loaned plus the interest owed, the credit risk becomes significant. In such situations, the positions may be marked to market, obliging the borrower of the cash to post additional collateral or cash.

Interdealer Brokers

The **inner market** in the government securities market comprises the interdealer brokers. The primary dealers rely on the interdealer brokers for a significant percentage of their trades, as noted in Table 2-3. Interdealer brokers aggregate information about the

TABLE 2-9

Interdealer Brokers,
U.S. Treasury Market

Cantor Fitzgerald
Garban Ltd.
EJV Brokerage, Inc.
Fundamental Brokers, Inc.
Liberty Brokerage, Inc.
RMJ Securities Corp.
Hilliard Farber & Co.

bids and offers posted by various dealers and disseminate that information on computer screens. They do so without revealing the identities of the dealers. This enables the dealers to undertake their proprietary trading activities anonymously. Dealers pay the interdealer brokers commissions for this service. Table 2-9 provides a list of interdealer brokers in the U.S. Treasury market. Of these brokers, Cantor Fitzgerald allow access to their screens not only to all primary dealers and to other dealers but also to other institutions, such as pension funds and banks. In addition, Cantor Fitzgerald make their quotes available through Telerate. Their market share is nearly 25% of the interdealer broker market. Other brokers provide access only to primary dealers. There is a real-time price and quote distribution system known as GOVPX that disseminates information about the Treasury market round the clock. It also shows all the executed trades, best bids, and offers.

Note that the trading volume is huge in the government securities market (about $90 billion per day, on average). In comparison, the equity market's average trading volume is about $6 billion to $6.5 billion a day. The number of transactions per day in the government market, however, is rather small compared to those in the equity market. GOVPX reports that only 2,000 trades occur in the Treasury market per day. In contrast, more than 100,000 trades per day occur in the equity market. The coverage of GOVPX is much poorer compared to the interdealer broker system that is in place. This raises some questions about the transparency of the market. Table 2-10 illustrates the trades executed during a 90-minute window by Garban, one of the interdealer brokers.

Several aspects of Table 2-10 are worthy of note. Note that each transaction is either a "hit" or a "take." If the offer to sell is accepted, it is considered a take. If a dealer's bid to buy is accepted it is considered a hit. Some of the securities are traded on a yield basis. Note, for example, that at 8:34:49 A.M. a six-month when issued (WI) T-bill was traded at a yield at 3.23%. The size of the transaction was $100 million par. Of course, bills always trade in terms of yields. All when-issued transactions trade on a yield basis until the day after the auction. In the last transaction shown in Table 2-10, note that a 6% coupon note maturing on October 15, 1999, was taken at a price of 97.78125. The size of this transaction was $3 million par.

The interdealer broker market has become quite competitive over the last few years. The interdealer brokers provide liquidity for dealers. For this service, they enjoy a commission and a spread. With the entry of Liberty Brokerage, however, the profitability of interdealer brokers has fallen sharply. This is because the dealers (who helped set up Liberty) wanted to lower the costs of trading in the interdealer broker markets.

TABLE 2-10   *Actual Transactions of an Interdealer Broker, November 2, 1992, from 7:12 A.M. to 8:42 A.M.*

Hit or Take	Time	Price or Yield	Coupon	Maturity	Price/Yield	Size
Take	7:12:41 AM	P	4	9/30/94	99.34375	1,000,000
Take	7:35:45 AM	P	6	10/15/99	98.00000	3,000,000
Hit	7:45:13 AM	P	$6\frac{3}{8}$	8/15/02	97.06250	1,000,000
Hit	8:01:16 AM	P	$6\frac{3}{8}$	8/15/02	97.03125	3,000,000
Hit	8:01:26 AM	P	6	10/15/99	97.98438	2,000,000
Hit	8:02:11 AM	P	$5\frac{3}{4}$	10/31/97	99.34375	1,000,000
Hit	8:05:20 AM	P	$5\frac{3}{4}$	10/31/97	99.32813	25,000,000
Take	8:07:02 AM	P	$6\frac{3}{8}$	8/15/02	97.03125	1,000,000
Hit	8:13:36 AM	P	$5\frac{3}{4}$	10/31/97	99.32813	2,000,000
Hit	8:13:59 AM	P	$5\frac{3}{4}$	10/31/97	99.32813	8,000,000
Hit	8:14:50 AM	P	4	9/30/94	99.35156	1,000,000
Hit	8:14:55 AM	P	$5\frac{3}{4}$	10/31/97	99.31250	5,000,000
Hit	8:14:59 AM	P	$4\frac{1}{4}$	10/31/94	99.71875	1,000,000
Hit	8:23:57 AM	P	$5\frac{1}{2}$	11/30/93	101.81250	5,000,000
Hit	8:24:42 AM	P	$6\frac{3}{8}$	8/15/02	96.81250	2,000,000
Hit	8:26:05 AM	P	$7\frac{1}{4}$	8/15/22	95.28125	1,000,000
Hit	8:26:39 AM	P	$7\frac{1}{4}$	8/15/22	95.28125	1,000,000
Hit	8:28:06 AM	P	$6\frac{3}{8}$	8/15/02	96.71875	1,000,000
Hit	8:28:17 AM	P	$5\frac{3}{4}$	10/31/97	99.21875	2,000,000
Hit	8:28:50 AM	P	$7\frac{1}{4}$	8/15/22	95.21875	5,000,000
Hit	8:29:05 AM	P	$5\frac{1}{2}$	11/30/93	101.81250	1,000,000
Hit	8:29:30 AM	P	$7\frac{1}{4}$	8/15/22	95.21875	7,000,000
Hit	8:29:59 AM	P	$7\frac{1}{4}$	8/15/22	95.20313	1,000,000
Hit	8:30:34 AM	P	$5\frac{3}{4}$	10/31/97	99.18750	6,000,000
Take	8:31:36 AM	P	$5\frac{3}{4}$	10/31/97	99.21875	1,000,000
Take	8:31:36 AM	P	$5\frac{3}{4}$	10/31/97	99.21875	8,000,000
Take	8:31:46 AM	P	$7\frac{1}{2}$	5/15/02	104.01560	1,000,000
Take	8:31:53 AM	P	$5\frac{1}{2}$	9/30/97	98.29688	1,000,000
Take	8:31:56 AM	P	$6\frac{3}{8}$	8/15/02	96.75000	1,000,000
Take	8:31:56 AM	P	$6\frac{3}{8}$	8/15/02	96.75000	1,000,000
Take	8:32:16 AM	P	$6\frac{3}{8}$	8/15/02	96.75000	1,000,000
Take	8:32:20 AM	P	$5\frac{3}{4}$	10/31/97	99.21875	1,000,000
Take	8:32:20 AM	P	$5\frac{3}{4}$	10/31/97	99.21875	10,000,000
Hit	8:34:49 AM	P	$4\frac{1}{4}$	10/31/94	99.68750	3,000,000
Hit	8:34:49 AM	P	6 WI	5/06/93	3.23000	100,000,000
Hit	8:35:03 AM	P	6	10/15/99	97.73438	1,000,000
Hit	8:35:08 AM	P	$4\frac{5}{8}$	8/15/95	99.29688	2,000,000
Hit	8:35:12 AM	P	$7\frac{1}{2}$	5/15/02	104.03130	10,000,000
Hit	8:35:20 AM	P	$6\frac{3}{8}$	8/15/02	96.71875	10,000,000
Hit	8:35:45 AM	P	$4\frac{5}{8}$	8/15/95	99.29688	1,000,000
Hit	8:35:47 AM	Y	$5\frac{3}{4}$	10/31/97	99.18750	10,000,000
Hit	8:35:49 AM	P	$7\frac{1}{2}$	5/15/02	104.03130	6,000,000
Hit	8:35:57 AM	P	$6\frac{3}{8}$	8/15/02	96.71875	8,000,000

TABLE 2-10   *Continued*

Hit or Take	Time	Price or Yield	Coupon	Maturity	Price/Yield	Size
Hit	8:36:17 AM	P	1 YR	10/21/93	3.44000	25,000,000
Hit	8:37:30 AM	P	6	10/31/93	102.23440	5,000,000
Hit	8:37:30 AM	P	6	10/31/93	102.23440	6,000,000
Take	8:37:31 AM	P	$7\frac{1}{2}$	5/15/02	104.04690	2,000,000
Take	8:37:33 AM	P	$5\frac{3}{4}$	10/31/971	99.21875	5,000,000
Hit	8:37:47 AM	P	$5\frac{1}{2}$	11/30/93	101.79690	11,000,000
Hit	8:38:15 AM	P	$5\frac{3}{4}$	3/31/94	102.29690	10,000,000
Take	8:38:45 AM	P	$7\frac{1}{2}$	5/15/02	104.09380	1,000,000
Hit	8:38:46 AM	P	$5\frac{1}{2}$	11/30/93	101.79690	2,000,000
Take	8:39:49 AM	P	$7\frac{1}{2}$	5/15/02	104.09380	1,000,000
Take	8:40:09 AM	P	$5\frac{3}{4}$	10/31/97	99.25000	10,000,000
Take	8:40:25 AM	P	$7\frac{1}{4}$	8/15/22	95.25000	1,000,000
Take	8:40:47 AM	P	$7\frac{1}{4}$	8/15/22	95.25000	1,000,000
Take	8:41:14 AM	P	6	10/15/99	97.78125	7,000,000
Take	8:41:14 AM	P	6	10/15/99	97.78125	3,000,000

Source: Garban.

Investors

As was pointed out in Chapter 1, the government securities markets command a rather large pool of institutional customers, including large institutions abroad. Central banks, commercial banks, pension funds, mutual funds, and insurance companies are examples of investors in this market. A more recent addition to this impressive list is the group called hedge funds. A **hedge fund** is a private investment partnership that takes leveraged positions in various segments of the capital markets. A number of such hedge funds are well-capitalized, with assets exceeding more than a billion dollars. Such funds have been known to invest billions of dollars in just a single Treasury issue. The ramifications of such investments for the Treasury auction, secondary market prices, and repo rates are taken up in Chapter 3. Figure 2-8 provides the distribution of ownership of Treasury securities.

Investors tend to be classified according to their investment strategies. For example, some investors are passive, tending to run **indexed portfolios** in which the investor's portfolio is indexed to a broad market index, such as the Lehman Brothers Fixed-Income Index. Other investors follow active portfolio policies. Still others are classified as current yield accounts, and so on.

The broad base of investors with varying investment objectives and strategies necessitates a reasonably large sales force. Most government dealers have a large sales force to cover their customers, providing research reports on interest rates, markets, and instruments; trade ideas and execution; asset-liability management services; etc.

FIGURE 2-8   *Distribution of Treasury Securities, by Ownership, March 31, 1999*

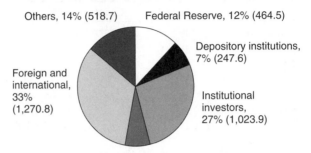

Source: *Treasury Bulletin,* September 1999, tables OFS-1, OFS-2.

Note: Numbers in parentheses are amounts, in billions of dollars. Excludes interest-bearing public debt held in U.S. government accounts (mainly investments in the social security and federal retirement trust funds). For state and local governments, includes about $167.45 billion of nonmarketable Treasury debt. Institutional investors include insurance companies, mutual funds, and pension funds.

ORGANIZATION AND STRUCTURE OF OTHER MARKET SEGMENTS

In this section, we will summarize briefly the organization and structure of other segments of the fixed-income markets. Since the intermediaries are more or less the same players, the focus will be on the issuers and on regulatory matters, which differ significantly from the Treasury markets.

Corporate Debt Market

Two key differences between the Treasury and the corporate markets were noted earlier: there is credit risk in the corporate sector, and there are many more issuers with relatively smaller issues in the corporate market. The existence of credit risk means that there will be efforts to generate information about the credit-worthiness of issuers. This is the task performed by credit rating agencies, such as Moody's, Standard & Poors, and Fitch. There are also organizations that provide credit and liquidity enhancements. For example, a letter of credit is typically issued by a highly rated financial institution to help issuers place commercial paper.

The major Treasury securities dealers, such as Goldman, Sachs and Salomon Brothers, are also the key corporate securities dealers. Typically, such dealers work with corporations to price the new issues of corporate debt and arrange the distribution of the paper to various institutional and retail accounts. Although a small number of bonds are traded on the New York Stock Exchange (NYSE), a substantial percentage of the corporate debt is traded in the dealer market.

In Figure 2-9, we provide an example of the trading activity in corporate bonds in NYSE as reported by the *Wall Street Journal.*

FIGURE 2-9   *Stock Exchange Bond Trading*

WEDNESDAY, OCTOBER 18, 2000

NYSE BONDS

Company	Cur. Yld	Vol	Price	Chg
AES Cp 8s8	8.7	145	91 7/8	-2 1/8
AMR 9s16	9.0	42	100 1/4	- 3/4
ATT 5 1/8s01	5.2	69	99	+11/32
ATT 7 1/8s02	7.1	10	100	...
ATT 6 3/4s04	6.8	39	98 3/4	...
ATT 5 5/8s04	5.9	10	95 1/2	...
ATT 7s05	7.0	15	99 1/2	- 1/4
ATT 7 1/2s06	7.4	19	101	+ 3/8
ATT 7 3/4s07	7.6	52	101 7/8	+1 1/2
ATT 6s09	6.8	50	87 3/4	- 1/2
ATT 8 1/8s22	8.3	172	97 7/8	- 1/2
ATT 8 1/8s24	8.3	86	98 1/8	- 1/4
ATT 8.35s25	8.2	30	101 1/2	...
ATT 6 1/2s29	8.3	133	78 3/8	- 1/2
ATT 8 5/8s31	8.5	11	101	- 7/8
AmGnFn 6 3/4s03	6.6	20	96 3/8	+ 1/4
Amresco 10s03	20.4	101	49	-5
Amresco 10s04	19.6	211	51	-3
ArmWld 9 3/4s08	16.3	20	59 3/4	+1 3/4
BayView 9s07	12.4	100	72 7/8	+4 7/8
BellsoT 8 1/4s04	6.5	20	97 5/8	+ 1/4
BellsoT 7s25	7.6	15	92	-1 1/4
BellsoT 8 1/4s32	8.2	70	100 7/8	...
BellsoT 7 7/8s32	8.0	77	98 5/8	- 3/8
BellsoT 6 3/4s33	8.0	5	84 3/4	...
BellsoT 7 5/8s35	8.0	10	94 7/8	...
BethSt 8.45s05	11.0	29	77	-3 3/8
Bevrly 9s06	9.9	35	90 7/8	+ 3/8
Bordn 8 3/8s16	13.7	84	61	-4 3/4
BoydGm 9 1/4s03	9.4	10	98 1/2	- 1/2
BrnSh 9 1/2s06	10.2	10	93 3/8	- 1/8
CentrTrst 7 1/2s01	cv	316	97 5/8	-3/16
ChaseM 6 1/2s05	6.7	10	97 1/4	...
ChaseM 6 1/2s06	6.5	15	96	- 3/8
ChaseM 6 3/4s08	7.1	2	95 1/8	-1 7/8
ChiqBr 10s09	20.8	15	48	-2 1/2
ClrkOil 9 1/2s04	10.4	76	91 3/8	- 3/8
CoeurDA 7 1/4s05	cv	20	30	-1
Coeur 6 3/8s04	cv	55	35 5/8	+ 3/8
Consec 8 1/8s03	10.3	17	78 7/8	-1 1/2

Company	Cur. Yld	Vol	Price	Chg
Conseco 10 1/2s04	12.8	5	82	-2 1/2
Conseco 10 1/4s02	14.7	225	69 3/4	+2 1/2
DR Hrtn 10s06	10.0	60	100	-1 1/2
DelcoR 8 5/8s07	10.0	20	86	- 1/8
DevonE 4.95s08	cv	25	96	+1
Dole 7s03	7.6	70	92 1/2	- 5/8
Dole 7 7/8s13	9.1	113	86 1/2	- 5/8
DukeEn 5 7/8s01	5.9	10	99	-3/16
DukeEn 6 1/4s04	6.4	27	97	-1 5/8
DukeEn 7 7/8s24	7.8	130	101	...
DukeEn 7s33	7.8	25	89 1/2	- 1/8
FedNM zr19s	...	2	23 3/8	+ 3/8
FedDS 8 1/2s03	8.5	25	100 1/4	- 3/4
Finova 9 1/8s02	10.8	7	84 1/2	+ 1/2
Florsh 12 3/4s02	38.6	11	33	+ 1/2
GEICap 7 7/8s06	7.6	10	104 1/8	...
GMA 6 3/4s02	6.8	50	98 7/8	- 1/8
GMA 7s02	7.0	23	100	- 1/4
GMA 5 7/8s03	6.1	12	96 3/4	- 3/4
GMA dc6s11	6.9	10	87 1/2	+ 1/2
GMA zr15	...	4	316	+5
Hilton 5s06	cv	40	80 1/2	- 1/2
Hollngr 9 1/4s06	9.4	10	98 1/2	...
Honywll zr09	...	185	51 7/8	-1 1/4
IRT Pr 7.3s03	cv	13	95	+1
IBM 6.45s07	6.7	15	96 7/8	- 1/8
IPap dc5 1/8s12	6.9	20	74	+ 1/2
IntShip 9s03	9.0	50	100 1/2	...
KaufB 9 3/8s03	9.8	20	96 1/8	-1 7/8
KaufB 9 5/8s06	9.7	86	99	+1
KerrM 5 1/4s10	cv	4	124	+1
KerrM 7 1/2s14	cv	7	97 1/8	- 1/4
Leucadia 8 1/4s05	8.4	30	98	+1
Lilly 6.57s16	7.1	38	92	+1 1/8
Loews 3 1/8s07	cv	25	86 3/4	+1 1/8
LglsLt 8.2s23	8.3	20	99	...
Lucent 6.9s01	6.9	5	99 1/2	- 5/8
Lucent 7 1/4s06	8.1	31	97 3/4	+ 3/4
MBNA 8.28s26	9.1	42	90 1/2	...
MSC Sf 7 7/8s04	cv	18	91	...
Mascotch 03	cv	20	66	+ 1/2
McDnl 6 5/8s05	6.9	2	96 1/4	-3
Medtrst 9s02	cv	40	90	-2 3/8
NStl 8 3/8s06	20.8	75	40 1/4	-21 5/8

Company	Cur. Yld	Vol	Price	Chg
NETelTel 4 1/2s02	4.7	5	95 1/4	- 1/8
NJBTi 7 1/4s11	7.5	18	97	...
NJBTi 7 3/8s12	7.6	1	97	- 1/2
NYTel 7 3/8s11	7.5	25	98 7/8	+ 3/8
Noram 6s12	cv	5	96	+2
OldRep 7s07	7.6	25	92 1/8	+ 1/8
OreStl 11s03	16.4	150	67	-2
ParkElc 5 1/2s06	cv	45	123	-6 1/2
ParkerD 5 1/2s04	cv	185	85	- 1/4
PhilPt 8.49s23	8.4	10	101 1/2	+ 1/2
PhilPt 7.92s23	8.3	8	95 3/4	- 1/4
Polaroid 11 1/2s06	14.6	403	79	-5
PrmHsp 9 1/4s06	9.4	44	98	...
Quanx 6.88s07	cv	8	86	-2 5/8
RelGrp 9s00f	...	45	10	+1
RelGrp 9 3/4s03f	...	60	6 1/8	+1 1/8
ReynTob 8 5/8s02	8.4	30	95 3/4	- 3/8
ReynTob 8 3/4s04	9.4	10	93	+1
ReynTob 9 1/4s13	10.6	3	87 1/8	- 7/8
RobMyr 63	...	29	95 3/4	...
Safwy 10s01	9.7	50	103	+1 7/8
Safwy 9 7/8s07	9.0	7	110 1/4	+ 1/4
SalSB 03t	...	50	89 1/2	+ 1/2
SilicnGr 5 1/4s04	cv	45	64 1/2	...
Simula 8s04	cv	15	56	+6.
SouBell 6s04	6.2	43	96 1/4	+ 1/4
StdCmcl 07	cv	30	59 1/2	-1 1/2
StdPac 8 1/2s07	9.0	30	95	+2
StoneC 10 3/4s02A	10.9	195	99	+ 3/4
StoneC 10 3/4s02O	10.6	130	101 1/4	- 3/4
StoneC 11 1/2s04	11.7	55	98 5/8	-2 3/8
StoneC 12 1/2s02	12.3	4	99 3/4	- 1/4
TVA 6 1/8s03	6.2	50	98 3/4	+ 3/8
TVA 6s13	6.4	5	94	-2
TVA 6.35s18	7.6	17	83	-3 1/2
TVA 8 1/4s34	8.3	55	99 7/8	...
TVA 8 1/4s42	7.7	13	106 7/8	+ 3/8
TVA 7 1/4s43	7.5	35	96 1/4	+ 3/8
TVA 6 7/8s43	7.5	20	91 5/8	- 7/8
TVA 7.85s44	7.7	18	101 1/2	- 3/4
Tenet 7 7/8s03	8.0	100	98 5/8	- 3/8
Tenet 8s05	8.2	170	97 3/4	+ 3/4
Tenet 8 5/8s07	8.9	219	97 1/2	- 7/8
TrneWar 8.18s07	7.9	15	103 7/8	+ 1/4
TrneWE 7 1/4s08	7.4	36	98 5/8	+ 5/8
TrneWar 9 1/8s13	8.4	60	109 1/4	...
TrneWar 9.15s23	8.4	2	109 1/2	+ 3/8
TolEd 8s03	7.9	7	101	...
TollCp 8 3/4s06	8.8	20	99 3/8	- 1/2
THilfig 6 1/2s03	8.5	5	76 1/8	-4 7/8
US Timb 9 5/8s07	11.0	5	87 1/4	+ 3/8
WsteM 4s02	cv	50	93 1/2	...
Webb 9 3/4s03	10.0	81	97 1/2	-1
Webb 10 1/4s10	11.0	39	93 1/2	...
WebbDel 9 3/8s09	10.9	97	85 3/4	-2 1/4
Weirton 11 3/8s04	16.5	37	69 1/8	-1 7/8
Weirton 10 3/4s05	15.4	78	70	-1
WhlPit 9 3/8s03	9.2	5	102 3/8	...

BOND TABLES EXPLAINED

Bonds are interest-bearing debt certificates. Their value is usually quoted as a percentage, with 100 equaling par, or face value. This table shows the issuing company, then the original coupon rate (interest rate) and the last two digits of the maturity year.

Current yield represents the annual percentage return to the purchaser at the current price. The **Price** column refers to the bond's closing price. A **Chg** is the difference between the day's closing price and the previous daily closing price. A majority of bonds, and all municipal or tax-exempt bonds, are not listed on exchanges; rather they are traded over the counter

Other footnotes:

cv Bond is convertible into stock under specified conditions
cld Called
dc Selling at a discounted price
f Dealt in flat -- traded without accrued interest
k Treasury bond, non resident aliens exempt from witholding tax
m Matured bonds
na No accrual of interest
p Treasury note, non-resident aliens exempt from witholding tax

r Registered
rp Reduced principal
st Stamped
t Floating rate
x Ex interest
vj In bankruptcy or receivership or being reorganized under the Bankruptcy Act, or securities assumed by such companies
wd When distributed
wi When issued
zr Zero coupon issue

AMEX BONDS

Company	Cur. Yld	Vol	Price	Chg
AltLiv 5 1/4s02	cv	73	42	-4
ExcelLeg 9s04	cv	17	83	- 1/2
ExcelLeg 10s04	12.0	6	83 5/8	...
LehB10UnV 03	...	50	98	-4
TrnsLux 7 1/2s06	cv	10	80	+3
TWA 11 3/8s06	29.2	31	39	+1 7/8
Trump 11 1/4s03f	...	25	87	- 1/2

The Securities and Exchange Commission (SEC), which oversees this market, has permitted shelf registration, under which the issuing corporation is not required to disclose the amount of debt it plans to issue or the timing of issuance. By giving a blanket authority to issue debt that is valid for a three-year period, the SEC has significantly enhanced the flexibility of the corporation to issue debt at short notice. This is known as **Rule 415.**

In addition, the market for privately placed corporate debt has expanded significantly in the last few years. The impetus for this growth is the ruling of SEC known as **Rule 144A,** which, among other things, permits the trading of privately placed debt among large institutions known as qualified institutional buyers (QIBs). This has enabled the development of a market for underwriting privately placed debt securities. A detailed treatment of this market is undertaken in Chapter 8.

Price Transparency in the Corporate Bond Market

The corporate bond market differs in a significant way from the Treasury market. Each corporate issue is very small relative to a typical Treasury auction. On the other hand, there are thousands of corporate issuers with varying credit quality. Furthermore, corporate debt contracts vary tremendously in terms of their contractual features, such as calls, puts, conversion features, and linking funds. It is estimated that there are about 400,000 bonds outstanding of which less than 5% is actively traded in any given year. This is in sharp contrast to the trading in the Treasury market, which we saw in Chapter 1. Unlike the GOVPX system, there is no transparent mechanism to discover the prices and values of corporate bonds. One proposal is to ensure that the last transaction price, the spread over Treasury, and the transaction date be made available to potential investors. While this is certainly better than the current situation, given the poor turnover in many bonds, this still may not be sufficiently informative. In addition to this information, it will be valuable to potential investors to know some information on the characteristics of the corporate bond (such as duration, credit rating, contractual features) and the prices and valuations of bonds that are similar to this corporate bond. This way the effects of lacks of active trading can be minimized. Often, for corporate bonds that are not actively traded, a **matrix pricing** scheme is used by dealers whereby such bonds are valued *relative* to more actively traded bonds.

Mortgage-Backed Securities

Agency and mortgage-backed securities are also traded in the dealer market. Typically, the primary dealers and other major dealers in the Treasury market are also the major players in this market. Dealers work closely with Federal agencies, such as FHLB and FHLMC (Freddie Mac), in underwriting new issues, pricing, and market making. Much of the activity in this market is in the primary issuance and structuring. Secondary market trading is not as active as in the Treasury secondary market. Many players are involved in the securitization and creation of mortgage-backed securities besides the dealer and the Federal agency; in Chapter 1, we mentioned some of the other players involved in this process. This market is analyzed in detail in Chapter 9.

Municipal Debt Market

The municipal debt market is similar to the corporate debt market in the sense that there is credit risk; hence, there are rating agencies who produce information about the credit standing of various issuers. In addition, there are credit enhancers and insurers in this market; the American Municipal Bond Assurance Corporation (AMBAC), the Municipal Bond Investors Assurance Corporation (MBIAC), the Financial Guarantee Insurance Company (FGIC), and the Bond Investors Guaranty Insurance Company (BIG) are the insurers in this market.

General obligations bonds must be approved by the taxpayers but revenue bonds do not require the taxpayers' approval. Although municipal issuers are not subject to any issue disclosure requirements (as in the corporate market, where issues must be registered), the sellers of municipal securities are required to produce and disseminate information about the proposed issue. Both negotiated and competitive types of issues are used in the municipal debt market. Typically, the general obligations issues are sold by the competitive system, and the revenue issues are sold by the negotiated system.

As in the Treasury markets, there are brokers' brokers who do not underwrite or carry inventories, or deal with public customers. Two of the biggest brokers' brokers in this market are J. J. Kenny and Chapdelaine. They assist dealers in secondary-market trading activity. In addition, the dealers also use services, such as the blue list, blue list ticker, or munifacts; these are news and wire services in which dealers participate to conduct their secondary-market trading activities.

In the municipal bond market, there is a transactions reporting system that has been developed by the Municipal Securities Rulemaking Board (MSRB). This data includes prices, volume of trading, credit rating, call dates, etc. Electronic dissemination of such information through the World Wide Web should occur in the not-too-distant future.

REGULATION OF FIXED-INCOME MARKETS

Fixed-income markets are largely self-regulated. Although powerful regulators, such as the Federal Reserve and the Securities and Exchange Commission, closely follow this market, by and large this market is left to function on its own.

The Treasury Department has the authority to issue Treasury securities and to set the conditions for their issuance and sale. The responsibility for compliance with and enforcement of the Treasury auction rules also rests with the Treasury. The Federal Reserve, which is the agent of the Treasury in conducting auctions, spot-checks customer bids in the Treasury auctions for their authenticity. In addition, the Federal Reserve has extensive market surveillance responsibility.

There are three major institutions that oversee the regulation of fixed-income securities markets: the U.S. Treasury, the Federal Reserve, and the Securities and Exchange Commission (SEC). These institutions set rules governing the sale of securities, underwriting practices, reporting requirements, audit trails, etc., that have far-reaching implications for the conduct of these markets and the outcomes of trades in these markets.

As part of market surveillance, information on the government securities market is generated and shared by these three regulatory institutions. Effective surveillance requires the timely collection and analysis of relevant information. The Fed currently gets data on market prices, trading volumes, and yields directly from automated computer systems. Telephone surveys of dealers are also used for collecting additional data. Much of the analysis on trading activity and positions of dealers reported in this chapter is based on the data gathered by the Fed for surveillance purposes.

The regulatory tool used to improve market transparency, discussed earlier in this chapter, is improved access to information. Thus, there is a focus on providing increased access to interdealer broker price and volume information. This is not very surprising given that the interdealer broker screen is possibly the best source on current bids and offers and transactions for government securities; timely access to such information allows customers to evaluate the execution quality and depth of current and illiquid issues. As mentioned earlier, GOVPX is the current system used to disseminate information.

In addition, large position reporting and audit trails help prevent manipulations and squeezes in government markets. However, unlike the equity markets, where positions exceeding 5% of a class of equity securities must be disclosed, in debt markets there are no such large positions reporting requirements.

We have already seen some of the rules affecting the issuance of securities. The auction mechanisms for the Treasury have been reviewed and tested by the U.S. Treasury and the Federal Reserve. The sale of corporate bonds comes under the registration requirements and other provisions of the SEC. The underwriting practices in the municipal debt markets are also regulated.

FURTHER READING

The theoretical literature on market organization is vast. Directly relevant to the subject of market microstructure are the academic journals cited in Chapter 1. The profitability of dealers has been analyzed in a relatively old, but still valuable, study by Meltzer and Gert von der Linde (1960). Another useful source is Meulendyke (1989), which focuses more on the Federal Reserve and open market policies. Several economics journals, notably the *Journal of Monetary Economics* and *Journal of Money, Credit and Banking* provide a prominent forum for academic research in this area.

A number of authors have explored the issue of liquidity in fixed-income markets. One paper of special interest in this area is Amihud and Mendelson (1986), examining the bid-ask spread in an asset-pricing framework. Garbade and Silber (1979) investigates the frequency of market clearing in the dealer market as one of the measures of liquidity. Kamara (1987, 1991) explore liquidity of Treasury bills and the effect of market organization on liquidity. Sarig and Warga (1989) and Warga (1992) examine the effect of liquidity on the pricing of bonds.

Squeezes in Treasury auctions and specialness in repo rates have been explored by a number of researchers. Jegadeesh (1993) has investigated this problem using data on secondary market prices. Cornell (1993) has investigated whether an adverse selection component is present in the bid-offer spreads and has concluded that this is a less serious issue in the Treasury markets. Cornell and Shapiro (1989) provide evidence of specialness in repo rates and Duffie (1992) provides a simple model for explaining this specialness. Sundaresan (1994) uses data on general collateral and special repo rates to show that there is a tendency for on-the-run issues to get very special as the next auction date approaches.

PROBLEMS

2.1   Compare the NYSE with the OTC fixed-income markets on the following dimensions:
(a) Average size of trades per day,
(b) Average number of trades per day, and
(c) Total dollar volume traded per day.
How would you go about comparing the liquidity of these two markets?

2.2   Look up the last full year (January to December) of Treasury auctions from the *Treasury Bulletin*. What is the total dollar amount borrowed by the Treasury? How is this amount distributed across different maturities? What is the rate at which the Treasury has borrowed in each maturity sector? What considerations are relevant in determining the maturity composition of Treasury debt?

2.3   (a) Describe briefly: (i) brokered markets and (ii) dealer markets. Explain the key differences between them.
(b) In two separate but simultaneous transactions, security XYZ was transferred at unit prices of $105 and $95. Under what types of market structure would the transactions be possible, and which is the most likely one? Explain your conclusions.
(c) What will be your conclusion if unit prices were $102 and $101.85 in the previous transactions? Why?

2.4   What are the key factors that determine the bid-offer spreads in the U.S. Treasury market? Look up the Bloomberg screen for the Treasury market and document the bid-offer spreads in the Treasury market for all maturity sectors.

2.5   Briefly describe the role played by the Federal Reserve in the Treasury market. What methods are used by the Fed to implement its monetary policies?

2.6   What are Fed fund rates?

2.7   Describe repo markets. What is the relationship between repo rates and Fed fund rates? Under what circumstances can the repo rate be higher than the Fed fund rates?

2.8   Describe the role of primary dealers in the Treasury market.

2.9   What are the risks faced by the dealers in the Treasury market? What are the expected rewards?

2.10   What are the institutions responsible for the regulatory oversight of the Treasury market? In which areas do you think there is a great need for regulatory oversight? Why?

REFERENCES

Amihud, Y., and H. Mendelson. 1986. "Asset Pricing and the Bid-Ask Spread." *Journal of Financial Economics* 17:223–249.

Bollenbacher, G. 1988. *A Professional's Guide to the U.S. Government Securities Markets: Treasuries, Agencies and Mortgage-Backed Instruments.* New York Institute of Finance.

Cornell, B. 1993. "Adverse Selection, Squeezes and the Bid-Ask Spreads on Treasury Securities." *Journal of Fixed Income* 3:39–47.

Cornell, B., and A. C. Shapiro. 1989. "The Mispricing of U.S. Treasury Bonds: A Case Study." *Review of Financial Studies* 2(3):297–310.

Duffie, D. 1992. Special Repo Rates. Stanford University Research Working Paper.

Garbade, K. D. 1982. *Securities Markets.* New York: McGraw Hill.

Garbade, K. D., and W. L. Silber. 1979. "Structural Organization of Secondary Markets: Clearing Frequency, Dealer Activity and Liquidity Risk." *Journal of Finance* 34:577–593.

Glosten, L. R. 1987. "Components of the Bid-Ask Spread and the Statistical Properties of Transaction Prices." *Journal of Business* 42(5):1293–1307.

Glosten, L. R., and P. R. Milgrom 1985. "Bid, Ask and Transaction Prices in a Specialist Market with Heterogeneously Informed Traders." *Journal of Financial Economics* 14:71–100.

Hubbard, G. 1991. *Money the Financial System and the Economy.* Reading, MA: Addison-Wesley.

Jegadeesh, N. 1993. "Treasury Auction Bids and the Salomon Squeeze." *Journal of Finance* 48:1403–1419.

Kamara, A. 1987. "Market Trading Structures and Asset Pricing: Evidence from the Treasury-Bill Market." *Review of Financial Studies* 1:357–375.

Kamara, A. 1991. Liquidity and Short-term Treasury Yields. University of Washington Working Paper.

Meltzer, A., and G. von der Linde. 1960. A Study of the Dealer Market for Federal Securities. Materials prepared for the Joint Economic Committee, 86th Congress.

Meulendyke, A.-M. 1989. *U.S. Monetary Policy and Financial Markets.* Federal Reserve Bank of New York.

Sarig, O., and A. Warga. 1989. "Bond Price Data and Bond Market Liquidity." *Journal of Financial and Quantitative Analysis* 24:367–378.

Scott, I. 1965. *Government Securities Market.* New York: McGraw Hill.

Simon, D. P. 1994. "Underwriting Premium and Informational Advantages at Treasury Coupon Auctions: Evidence from Intraday Quotes." *Journal of Financial Economics* 35:43–62.

Sundaresan, S. 1991–1993. Debt Markets. Columbia University MBA B8308 Course Binders.

Sundaresan, S. 1994. "An Empirical Analysis of U.S. Treasury Auctions: Implications for Auction and Term Structure Theories." *Journal of Fixed-Income* 4:35–50.

U.S. Department of the Treasury, Securities and Exchange Commission, and Board of Governors of the Federal Reserve System. 1992. *Joint Report on the Government Securities Market.* Washington, DC.

Warga, A. 1992. "Bond Returns, Liquidity and Missing Data." *Journal of Financial and Quantitative Analysis* 27:605–617.

SOME USEFUL WEBSITES

1. http://www.bondmarkets.com/

The Bond Market Association website contains very useful data concerning fixed-income markets, research reports, market practices, and regulatory developments.

2. http://www.libnet.com/

The website of Liberty Brokerage gives useful insights into the practices of interdealer brokers.

3. http://www.bloomberg.com/

Excellent website for getting 6–7 yield curve, stock quotes, and interest rates.

4. http://www.ustreas.gov/

Great website for all matters relating to Treasury securities.

5. http://www.msrb.org/

This is a useful website to find data on municipal bond markets.

Chapter 3

Treasury Auctions and Selling Mechanisms

Chapter Objectives

This chapter describes the mechanisms used by the U.S. Treasury to sell its debt securities to investors and evaluates each mechanism. Chapter 3 will help the reader to understand and answer the following questions:

- How do governments sell their debt securities in the world?
- What are discriminatory auctions?
- What are uniform price auctions?
- What is the when-issued market, and what role does it play in the bidding of auctions?
- What are private-value auctions?
- What are common-value auctions?
- What is winner's curse?
- What are short squeezes in auctions?
- How should the U.S. Treasury sell debt to minimize the cost of public debt?

INTRODUCTION

U.S. Treasury securities have been sold to investors for over five decades using auction mechanisms. Unlike auctions of wines or works of art, U.S. Treasury auctions are preceded by forward trading among potential bidders in the auction. This forward market, known as the **when-issued market,** is an integral part of the Treasury bidding and distribution system currently in place. Such when-issued trading is not present in most auctions involving other commodities. In some foreign sovereign bond markets, Treasury auctions are preceded by some form of precommitments by way of when-issued trading. In when-issued trading, the bidders are liable to enter the auction and bid with prior short or long positions. Consequently, this affects their bidding strategies and the outcomes of the auction. In Chapter 2, we discussed an example of a when-issued trade transaction that was executed by an interdealer broker. In addition to the when-issued market, where a significant percentage of the to-be-auctioned securities are sold, there is a secondary market (the resale market) where participants are able to buy and sell the auctioned securities in "spot" trading. When spot trading occurs, the trade usually is settled one day following the trade gate. Therefore, strictly speaking, all transactions are forward transactions. Moreover, as explained in Chapter 2, investors are also able to borrow or lend their securities overnight or for specified terms in repo markets. The when-issued market, the primary auctions market, the repo markets, and the secondary markets compose the integrated mechanism by which Treasury securities are sold to the investing public. In this chapter, we will focus on Treasury auctions and the when-issued markets.

TREASURY AUCTIONS

Throughout the world, auctions are used by governments to sell debt securities. In Appendix A of this chapter, we present a summary of the auction procedures used by the OECD countries to sell their public debt to investors.

Note that countries tend to use two types of auctions to sell their government debt. One procedure is known as multiple-price or multiple-yield auction. In this arrangement, bidders submit multiple bids (prices at which they want to buy and the amount that they want to buy at each price). In the multiple-yield auctions, they submit yields instead of prices. The Treasury will determine the aggregate demand curve consisting of the prices and the amounts demanded by *all* bidders at each price. Then, the Treasury will choose the bids that are highest and allocate the securities at the highest bid. Whatever supply is left will be sold to the next highest bid at that price and so on until the supply is exhausted. This is also known as a **discriminatory** auction, since the Treasury is choosing the bidders on the basis of their bids.

Another type of auction also widely used by the Treasury is the uniform-price or uniform-yield auctions. In this arrangement, bidders also submit multiple bids. The Treasury will determine the aggregate demand curve of the market by aggregating the quantity demanded at each bid. Then the Treasury will choose the price (or yield) at which the supply is equal to aggregate demand. At that bid (stop-out price or stop-out yield) *all* winning bidders get their demand, irrespective of how aggressively they bid. The most aggressive bids get the first priority in the allocation of securities, but there is no price discrimination.

We will now focus more on U.S. Treasury auctions. Since 1999, all U.S. Treasury auctions have been uniform-price auctions. The discriminatory procedure has been discontinued. Nonetheless, we will discuss both types of auctions since both are widely used throughout the global government debt markets as indicated in Appendix A of this chapter.

Over the period 1929 to 1992, the amount of Treasury securities sold steadily increased. To get an idea of the size of this market, consider that in 1981, the Treasury sold $670 billion of marketable Treasury securities. In 1991, the corresponding figure was an astounding $1.70 trillion! Note from Figure 3-1 that after reaching a peak in the late 1990s, the Treasury market has actually began to shrink due to the budget surplus. In fact, the current and projected budget surpluses may actually lead to a substantial reduction in the size of the Treasury market. This depends on whether future surpluses will be spent on other government programs or tax cuts instead of paying down

FIGURE 3-1   *Historical and Projected Agency and U.S. Treasury Debt*

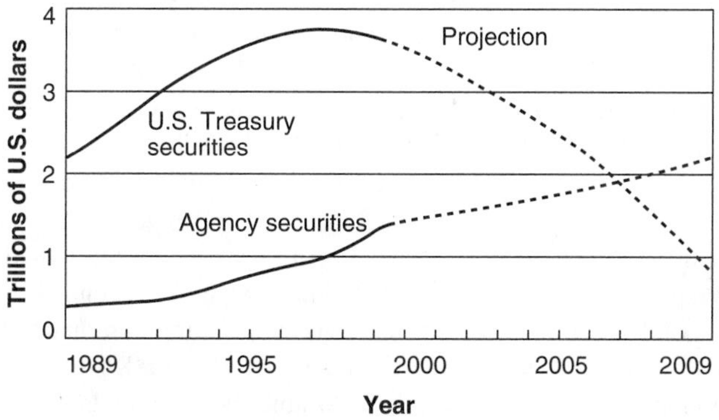

Source: Michael Fleming, FRBNY Economic Policy Review, April 2000.

Note: Figures are reported as of September 30, except for the 1999 agency debt figure, which is reported as of June 30. Treasury debt projections are the CBO's as of July 1999; they assume that current laws and policies remain unchanged, and they exclude debt held in U.S. government accounts. Agency debt projections assume that the market grows at the same rate as the economy (according to CBO projections of GDP).

debt. As noted earlier, the benchmark programs planned by federal agencies may push their market size *above* the Treasury market in the foreseeable future. The Treasury auction procedure has undergone important changes along the way. Prior to the 1970s, the U.S. Treasury used subscription offerings (in which the interest rate was preset and the security was sold at a fixed price), exchange offerings (which permitted investors to exchange maturing issues with new ones at fixed prices), and advanced refunding (which allowed outstanding securities to be exchanged prior to their maturities). These mechanisms are not covered in the text.

In 1970, the Treasury instituted an auction procedure in which the coupons were preset, and investors were asked to bid on the basis of prices. This procedure continued until 1974 when the Treasury stopped setting the coupon prior to receiving bids and switched over to yield auctions. (During the period February 1973 to May 1974, Treasury conducted six uniform-price, sealed-bid auctions.) Until late 1908, the U.S. Treasury sold Treasury bills, notes, and bonds via a sealed-bid discriminating auction. The schedule of auction dates are set as per Treasury auction cycles indicated in Chapter 1. The quantities to be auctioned are posted at the time the auction is announced, typically a week prior to the auction date. The securities are issued one to five days following the auction.

The sequence of events in a typical auction may be best summarized in the context of an actual Treasury auction. Accordingly, we provide in Table 3-1 a typical auction announcement by the U.S. Treasury for five-year, ten-year, and thirty-year quarterly refunding auctions.

Note in Table 3-1 that the announcement of the auction was made on August 2, 2000. The auction date itself varied from August 8 to August 10, 2000, depending on the security being auctioned. On the announcement date, potential bidders know the size of the auction and the maturity, but they do not know the coupon, which is set by the Treasury after all the bids have been submitted on the auction day at 1:00 P.M.

Note that the securities are not issued on the auction date; the issue date itself is August 15, 2000, five to seven days after the auction, depending on the security. The when-issued trading commences on the announcement date (August 2, 2000) and continues until the securities are issued (August 15, 2000). Thus, the when-issued trading commences on the announcement date without the knowledge of the coupon of the issue.

In the case of 10-year T-notes, the when-issued trading commenced on August 2, 2000, and continued until the issue date of August 15, 2000. During the period between the announcement date (August 2, 2000) and the auction date (August 9, 2000), the when-issued trading will be done on the basis of yields as the coupon of the issue is not known until the auction results are posted on the auction date. On the auction date, sealed bids are received at 1:00 P.M. and the Treasury sets the coupon and announces the auction awards approximately one hour after the bids are received (2:00 P.M.). Subsequently, the when-issued trades are done on a price basis. In all when-issued trades, the settlement date is the issue date.

All Treasury securities are eligible for the strips program. Chapter 5 contains a description and an analysis of the Treasury strips market. In brief, this is a market in which zero coupon Treasury securities are created by "stripping" coupon and principal payments. We discuss the need for such securities in Chapter 11 in the context of asset-liability management and the risk properties of strips in Chapters 4 and 5.

Note that until the securities are issued no financing is necessary. Subsequent to the settlement of the issued securities, financing becomes necessary.

The U.S. Treasury is a repeat seller of securities in the market. By designing an optimal mechanism of sale, it can reduce the cost of public debt. Broadly speaking, auctions have been classified into private-value auctions and common-value auctions. In **private-value auctions,** bidders (potential buyers) have their own idiosyncratic valuation of the object that is being auctioned. In **common-value auctions,** bidders have a shared, common value of the object that is being auctioned. Treasury auctions are considered to be common-value auctions, by and large. Excellent survey papers on auctions theory are available. Milgrom (1989) and Engelbrecht-Wiggins (1990) are particularly relevant. In designing an appropriate auction, the Treasury should attempt to get the best possible price and also ensure that the scope for manipulation and squeezes is kept at a minimum to encourage the orderly conduct of auctions. The second objective is particularly relevant given the fact that the Treasury is a repeat seller in the market. As noted at the outset, countries use two types of auctions. We discuss them next.

Uniform-Price Auctions

After experimenting for a few years with uniform-price auctions, since 1992 the U.S. Treasury has decided to sell *all* its securities using the uniform-price auction (or the Dutch) procedure.

TABLE 3-1   *Highlights of Treasury Offerings to the Public, August 2, 2000 Quarterly Financing*

Offering Amount	$10,000 million	$10,000 million	$5,000 million
Description of Offering:			
Term and type of security	$4\frac{3}{4}$-year notes (reopening)	10-year notes	$29\frac{3}{4}$-year bonds (reopening)
Series	E-2005	C-2010	Bonds of May 2030
CUSIP number	912827 6D 9	912827 6J 6	912810 FM 5
Auction date	August 8, 2000	August 9, 2000	August 10, 2000
Issue date	August 15, 2000	August 15, 2000	August 15, 2000
Dated date	May 15, 2000	August 15, 2000	November 15, 1999
Maturity date	May 15, 2005	August 15, 2010	May 15, 2030
Interest rate	$6\frac{3}{4}\%$	Determined based on the highest accepted competitive bid	$6\frac{1}{4}\%$
Amount currently outstanding	$15,426 million	Not applicable	$11,269 million
Yield	Determined at auction	Determined at auction	Determined at auction
Interest payment dates	November 15 and May 15	February 15 and August 15	November 15 and May 15
Minimum bid amount and multiples	$1,000	$1,000	$1,000
Accrued interest payable by investor	$16.87500 per $1,000 (from May 15 to August 15, 2000)	None	$15.62500 per $1,000 (from May 15 to August 15, 2000)
Premium or discount	Determined at auction	Determined at auction	Determined at auction
STRIPS Information:			
Minimum amount required	$800,000	Determined at auction	$32,000
Corpus CUSIP number	912820 ER 4	912820 FT 9	912803 CH 4
Due dates(s) and CUSIP number(s) for additional TINT(s)	Not applicable	Not applicable	Not applicable

The following rules apply to all securities mentioned above:

Submission of Bids:

Noncompetitive bids	Accepted in full up to $5,000,000 at the highest accepted yield.
Competitive bids	(1) Must be expressed as a yield with three decimals, e.g., 7.123%.
	(2) Net long position for each bidder must be reported when the sum of the total bid amount, at all yields, and the net long position is $2 billion or greater for each of the notes and $1 billion or greater for the bond.
	(3) Net long position must be determined as of one half-hour prior to the closing time for receipt of competitive tenders.
Maximum Recognized Bid at a Single Yield	35% of public offering
Maximum Award	35% of public offering

Receipt of Tenders:

Noncompetitive tenders	Prior to 12:00 noon Eastern Daylight Saving time on auction day
Competitive tenders	Prior to 1:00 P.M. Eastern Daylight Saving time on auction day
Payment Terms	By charge to a funds account at a Federal Reserve Bank on issue date, or payment of full par amount with tender. *TreasuryDirect* customers can use the Pay Direct feature which authorizes a charge to their account of record at their financial institution on issue date.

Two types of bids are accepted by the Treasury, competitive and noncompetitive bids. In competitive bids, both prices and quantities are submitted by primary dealers and major institutional investors. Each competitive bidder is allowed to submit multiple bids. The competitive bidders (if successful) are assured of the prices they have bid for the security, although they may not get the entire quantity they bid for. Noncompetitive bids from the public are limited to no more than five million. The total quantity bid by the investors in the noncompetitive tender is subtracted from the aggregate amount of the security that the Treasury has to offer in the auction to determine the amount that will be sold via the competitive bids. The U.S. Treasury will choose the yield at which the aggregate demand exhausts the supply to the competitive tender. This market clearing yield is known as the stop-out yield. (This means that the Treasury starts at the lowest yield and works its way down to the higher yield. At the highest winning yield [stop-out yield] the allocation will be done on a pro rata basis.) It is worth emphasizing that each successful competitive bidder pays the stop-out yield. The bidders in the noncompetitive tender also pay the stop-out yield. The bidders on the noncompetitive tender are assured of the quantities that they bid for at the quantity-weighted average price established in the competitive tender. So, noncompetitive bidders face no quantity uncertainty. Since the Treasury restricts the bids in the noncompetitive sector to $5 million par amount of the auctioned security, only small investors and institutions tend to participate in this sector of the auctions. There is a limit on the maximum amount of securities awarded to a single bidder. Under the 35% rule, the bidder's net long position in the auction at any one yield inclusive of futures, forwards, and when-issued markets may not exceed 35% of the amount of the security in the auction. When the issue is reopened, the net long position will include any position in the outstanding security as well. Once the bidding is completed, the 35% rule is lifted.

The auction awards of the uniform-price sealed-bid auction announced in Table 3-1 is presented in Table 3-2 for the 30-year bonds.

Note that in this auction the Treasury is selling about $5 billion of the 30-year (or more precisely $29\frac{3}{4}$-year) bonds. The coupon of the issue is already known in this case as the Treasury is "reopening" an existing (or an already outstanding) 30-year T-bond. Note from Table 3-2 that the stop-out yield was 5.697%, reflecting the market conditions on the auction date around 1:00 P.M. As noted by arrows in Table 3-2, all noncompetitive and succesful competitive bidders got the bond at 5.697% and paid a price of 107.860. Note that the median yield was 5.688%. About 5% of the bids were 5.65% or lower! All bidders, however, no matter how aggressively they bid, got the bonds at 5.697%. We will discuss the merit of this auction procedure later in the chapter.

Metrics to Assess Auctions. Although only a little over $5 billion of the security was awarded, the Treasury received a total of nearly $18.5 billion worth of bids. The ratio of the bids received to the amount awarded is computed and is used as a metric of how well the auction went; the higher this ratio, the stronger the auction is, *ceteris paribus.* This ratio is called the **bid-cover ratio.** In this auction, the bid-cover ratio was 3·71 as shown in Table 3-2. The uncertainty about the auction outcome is some-

TABLE 3-2   *Treasury Security Auction Results*
Bureau of the Public Debt—Washington, D.C., August 10, 2000

Results of Treasury's Auction of $29\frac{3}{4}$ Year Bonds

This issue is a reopening of a bond originally issued February 15, 2000.

Interest Rate:	$6\frac{1}{4}\%$	Issue Date:	August 15, 2000
Series:		Dated Date:	May 15, 2000
CUSIP No:	912810FM5	Maturity Date:	May 15, 2030
STRIPS Minimum:	$32,000		

High Yield: 5.697%   Price: 107.860

All noncompetitive and successful competitive bidders were awarded securities at the
→ high yield. Tenders at the high yield were allotted 68%. All tenders at lower yields were ←
accepted in full.

Accrued interest of $15.62500 per $1,000 must be paid for the period from May 15, 2000 to
August 15, 2000.

Amounts Tendered and Accepted (in Thousands)

Tender Type	Tendered	Accepted
Competitive	$ 18,550,664	$ 4,985,464
Noncompetitive	15,182	15,182
Public subtotal	18,565,846	5,000,646*
Federal Reserve	723,700	723,700
Foreign Official Inst.	50,000	50,000
Total	$ 19,339,546	$ 5,774,346

Median yield 5.688%: 50% of the amount of accepted competitive tenders was tendered at or below that rate. Low
yield 5.650%: 5% of the amount of accepted competitive tenders was tendered at or below that rate.
Bid-to-Cover Ratio = 18,565,846 / 5,000,646 = 3.71
*Awards to TREASURY DIRECT = $8,035,000

times summarized by the dispersion of the winning bids; in this auction, the difference
between the median yield and the stop-out yield is 5.697 − 5.688 = 0.009 or 0.9 basis
points. Note that the percentage of the awards going to the noncompetitive bids is
rather small; this is also typical. Recall that only retail accounts and small investors
participate in this segment. The $5 million limit also discourages big institutions from
actively bidding in this leg of the auction. The percentage of the awards that went to
the noncompetitive tender is $\frac{15,182}{5,000,646} = 0.30\%$.

Note that the **stop-out yield** was 5.697%; bidders who bid at yields above the
stop-out yield did not win any security in the auction. All the other bidders (who bid
more aggressively in the auction) received the security at a common market clearing
yield of 5.697%. Remember that even the most aggressive bidder paid only 5.697%.
This has important implications for both the level of bidding in these auctions and for
the possible dispersion of the bids.

Discriminatory Auctions

Although the U.S. Treasury no longer uses discriminatory auctions, they are widely used by other governments, as may be seen from Appendix A of this chapter. We, therefore, will briefly illustrate how the discriminatory scheme works.

In discriminatory auctions, typically the governments invite two types of bids: competitive and noncompetitive. In competitive bids, primary dealers submit both prices and quantities. Each competitive bidder is allowed to submit multiple bids. There is typically a ceiling on how much can be submitted in a noncompetitive tender. The government acts as a perfectly discriminating monopolist by awarding the security to the highest bidder and working its way down until the entire amount is sold. (This implies that the government starts at the lowest yield and works its way to the highest yield. At the highest winning yield, all allocation is done on a pro rata basis.) The bidders in noncompetitive tender get the amount that they bid at a yield equal to the weighted average of the winning yields in the competitive tender. We illustrate the allocation in a discriminatory auction that was conducted by Bank of Canada in Table 3-3.

Bank of Canada auctioned off three treasury bills on September 12, 2000. All the bills were issued on September 14, 2000. We will illustrate the auction by focusing on the T-bill maturing on December 21, 2000. Note that $3.2 billion were issued. The lowest (most aggressive) yield submitted was 5.588%, the highest yield (least aggressive) submitted was 5.608%, and the average yield was 5.599%. Since this is a multiple-price auction (indicated by arrows in Table 3-3), the most aggressive winning bidder would have paid a price of 98.51897% of the par. Note from the bottom of Table 3-2 that the noncompetitive tenders are quiet small relative to the competitive tender.

Empirical evidence indicates that the uniform-price auction appears to have a higher bid-cover ratio and a higher dispersion of winning bids. Traders familiar with the bidding process confirm that this is fairly typical in their experience. At first glance, it may appear that the Treasury is losing out: Bidders who bid more aggressively only ended up paying the stop-out yield. The reason for their aggressive bidding is precisely that the bids are not discriminated. Indeed, if lots of bidders bid aggressively, then the stop-out yield will go down, reflecting the overall aggressiveness. This will increase the revenue of the Treasury and lower the cost of public debt.

In both auction mechanisms, bidders face quantity uncertainty. In the uniform-price auction presented, bidders who bid most aggressively were allotted the security first, and as the supply was depleted, the bidders who exactly bid at the stop-out yield ended up receiving less than their total demand. The U.S. Treasury makes a pro rata allocation for bidders at the stop-out yield. Bidders in discriminatory auctions are subject to similar quantity uncertainty. This is a significant quantity risk that should also encourage more aggressive bidding. In addition, bidders may also diversify their bids by submitting multiple price-quantity bids.

The foregoing discussion indicates that the choice of the auction mechanism is of great importance to the seller. In discriminatory auctions, the Treasury is able to act as a perfectly discriminating monopolist. However, this action results in **winner's curse:** The winning bidder knows that he or she will pay a higher price than his or her competitor, with whom he or she has to compete in the secondary market. This creates an incentive to shade down the bids and possibly engage in preauction information shar-

TABLE 3-3   *Treasury Bills—Regular Auction Results*

On behalf of the Minister of Finance, it was announced today that tenders for Government of Canada treasury
bills have been accepted as follows:

Auction Date	**2000.09.12**	
Bidding Deadline	**12:30:00**	
Total Amount	**$6,000,000,000**	

$\rightarrow$ **Multiple Price** $\leftarrow$

Amount	Issue	Maturity	Outstanding After Auction	(%) Yield and Equivalent Price		(%) Allotment Ratio	Bank of Canada Purchase
$3,200,000,000	2000.09.14	2000.12.21	$5,800,000,000	Avg. **5.599**	**98.51897**		**$500,000,000**
				Low **5.588**	**98.52184**		
$\rightarrow$ ISIN: **CA1350Z7BF01**				High **5.608**	**98.51663**	8.42759	$\leftarrow$
$1,400,000,000	2000.09.14	2001.03.15	$1,400,000,000	Avg. **5.745**	**97.21515**		**$100,000,000**
				Low **5.730**	**97.22221**		
ISIN: **CA1350Z7BP82**				High **5.751**	**97.21232**	76.04167	
$1,400,000,000	2000.09.14	2001.09.13	$1,400,000,000	Avg. **5.889**	**94.45291**		**$100,000,000**
				Low **5.875**	**94.46536**		
ISIN: **CA1350Z7BQ65**				High **5.893**	**94.44935**	91.58537	

Value of bids submitted by distributors

Maturity	Total	Noncompetitive
2000.12.21	$7,358,900,000	$12,900,000
2001.03.15	$3,571,500,000	$15,500,000
2001.09.13	$3,129,500,000	$9,500,000

ing. On the other hand, uniform-price auctions significantly reduce winner's curse, but
the Treasury gives up its ability to price discriminate. The trade-offs in this context are
clear. Which auction is more prone to collusion and squeezes? We explore this question later in the chapter.

WHEN-ISSUED TRADING

One of the major features of the U.S. Treasury auction is the "when, as, and if issued"
trading, known simply as when-issued (WI) trading. During the period between the
auction announcement date and the issue date (which as we saw earlier varies from
five to ten days), when-issued trading occurs. This was officially sanctioned in August
1981, and was initiated to encourage trading in Treasury securities after the announcement of the auction but before the securities are actually issued. Prior to the Treasury's
scheduled auction date for a given security, dealers and investors actively participate
in the when-issued market. In this market, dealers and investors may either take long
positions or short positions in the security (to be auctioned by the Treasury) for a future settlement on the issue date. Thus, WI trades are forward contracts with a settlement date equal to the issue date. The trading in this market is done in terms of the

yields at which the security is expected to be issued. The coupon of the issue is announced by the Treasury after all the bids are received. After the coupon is announced, the issue trades on a price basis one day after the auction. Typically, the securities are issued about one to five days following the auction date.

We present a timeline for a 30-year auction in Figure 3-2, and a 10-year auction in Figure 3-3.

FIGURE 3-2   *Timeline for 30-Year Auction as Shown in Table 3-1 (Reopening)*

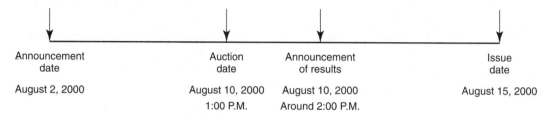

Announcement date	Auction date	Announcement of results	Issue date
August 2, 2000	August 10, 2000 1:00 P.M.	August 10, 2000 Around 2:00 P.M.	August 15, 2000

Status of 30-Year T-Bond

1. From August 2, 2000, to August 15, 2000, the bond trades as a when-issued or WI bond.
2. After August 15, 2000, the bond becomes on-the-run bond.
3. The bond remains on-the-run until the next auction of the 30-year is completed and the new bond is issued. Then this bond becomes off-the-run.
4. The coupon of this 30-year bond is known to the bidders as it is a "reopening" of an existing 30-year T-bond, which has a coupon of 6.25%.

FIGURE 3-3 *Timeline for 10-Year Auction as Shown in Table 3-1*

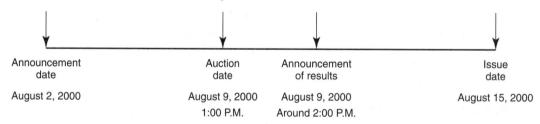

Announcement date	Auction date	Announcement of results	Issue date
August 2, 2000	August 9, 2000 1:00 P.M.	August 9, 2000 Around 2:00 P.M.	August 15, 2000

Status of 10-Year T-Note

1. From August 2, 2000, to August 15, 2000, the note trades as a when-issued or WI note.
2. After August 15, 2000, the note becomes on-the-run note.
3. The note remains on-the-run until the next auction of the 10-year is completed and the new note is issued. Then this note becomes off-the-run.
4. The coupon is set by the Treasury on August 9, 2000, based on the bids submitted by the dealers. During the period August 2, 2000, to August 9, 2000, the note trades on "yield" basis, since the coupon is unknown. After August 9, 2000, the note trades on "price" basis.

TABLE 3-4	Transaction Type	Time of Transaction	Yield	Size of Transaction
When-Issued Trading around Monday, November 2, 1992, Three-Month T-Bill Auction (Maturity Date: February 4, 1993)	Hit	09:03:24 A.M.	3.02000	200,000,000
	Hit	10:05:21 A.M.	3.03000	100,000,000
	Hit	11:38:13 A.M.	3.03000	15,000,000
	Hit	11:52:51 A.M.	3.03000	5,000,000
	Take	12:34:20 P.M.	3.04000	40,000,000
	Take	12:40:11 P.M.	3.04000	25,000,000
	Take	12:48:06 P.M.	3.04000	6,000,000
	Take	12:52:10 P.M.	3.04000	22,000,000
	Hit	01:00:54 P.M.	3.04000	5,000,000
	Take	01:04:23 P.M.	3.04000	14,000,000
	Take	01:06:53 P.M.	3.04000	6,000,000
	Hit	01:08:15 P.M.	3.03500	50,000,000
	Hit	01:58:11 P.M.	3.04500	40,000,000
	Take	02:32:02 P.M.	3.04000	5,000,000
	Take	03:12:08 P.M.	3.04000	25,000,000
	Take	03:35:08 P.M.	3.04000	49,000,000

Source: Compiled from Garban.

As Table 3-4 illustrates, the WI trades can be significant in size; note that the first trade is 200 million. Trades on the order of several hundred million dollars may occur in the WI markets from time to time. The fact that it is a forward transaction allows investors to lock in a price and quantity in the WI market, which would be difficult to do in other markets. Furthermore, as positions in the WI market need not be financed, fairly large positions can be taken and offset in a manner similar to the futures markets. Note in Table 3-4 that eight transactions took place prior to the 1:00 P.M. auction time. During the period after bidding but prior to the announcement of the results at 2:00 P.M. a number of further transactions took place. We will focus on the trading in the windows 1:00 to 2:00 and after 2:00 to determine whether there is strategic postauction buying in the WI market in which some bidders attempt to squeeze others.

The aggregate positions taken in the when-issued market may exceed the total amount of the security that the Treasury has scheduled to auction. As the auction date approaches, such positions are unwound and the positions approach the amount that is to be auctioned. Note that the yields varied from 3.02% in the first trade to 3.04% in the trade at 3:35 P.M. after the auction. A dealer might have sold 100 million par in the WI market in the morning at 3.02% and, after bidding in the auction and finding out the awards, might have covered by buying back 100 million par around 3:00 P.M. at 3.04%, netting a profit of 2 basis points on 100 million without any delivery of securities.

Bidding Strategies

Dealers need to position themselves to bid in auctions. Given the size of the auctions (typically about 10 to 15 billion per auction), it is essential that dealers be in a position to ascertain the demand for the forthcoming auction and be able to hedge any exposure that may result from shortfalls. Such shortfalls may arise in a number of ways. First, dealers may be unable to determine with great precision the demand for the auction—they know only the demands that go through their sales desk and what they see on broker screens. It is possible that many investors will directly bid in the auction without participating in any preauction activities. In this context, a few big customer-driven trades passing through the sales desk of a single bidder could be very valuable private information to the dealer. Second, dealers may face significant uncertainty in the primary auction process as to the amount that they are likely to be awarded; the sealed-bid discriminating auction produces a great deal of uncertainty. It also provides the dealer with a unique opportunity to incorporate private information into bidding.

Dealers get a good idea of the demand for the security (that is going to be auctioned) by participating in the WI market. By filling the demands of customers in the WI market at the prevailing WI yields, dealers get a good estimate of the demand and, importantly, get a market estimate of the level at which they should be bidding. For example, if a dealer has sold in the WI market $700 million at a weighted average WI yield of 6%, the dealer knows that he or she should be bidding in the auction at a slightly higher yield in order to make a profit. Of course, the dealer will condition this information with WI yields just prior to bidding, secondary market yields on similar securities, and so on. The WI market provides the dealer with "demand discovery." This comes at a price: potentially the dealer may win less in the auction than what he or she sold in the WI market. This may lead to a squeeze.

Under which auction mechanism does the dealer have a greater incentive to sell in the WI market? With a discriminating auction, the dealers will be more reluctant to enter the auction with a big WI short position. This is because aggressive bidding in the discriminatory auction will lead them to pay a high price relative to other bidders. On the other hand, in a uniform price auction, they may be more willing to take a big WI short position. This is because they can cover their short position by aggressively bidding in the uniform-price auction, for they know that all dealers pay the same price (namely, the lowest accepted price) in the auction that is uniform.

WINNER'S CURSE AND BID SHADING

Winner's curse refers to the possibility that the aggressive bidder in a discriminatory auction will end up paying too much relative to the market consensus. Anticipating this possibility, bidders will tend to shade down their bids relative to the true value of the security, to minimize the winner's curse and invest considerable resources in preauction information gathering to learn more about the market consensus, so that their bids are not out of line with the market consensus. The Treasury loses money because of the winner's curse but is able to exercise the power of a discriminating monopolist by selling the same security by marching down the demand curve submitted by the bidders.

In the uniform price auction, the Treasury allocates the security at a common price; hence, it gives up the power to discriminate. On the other hand, bidders can be

TABLE 3-5   *Markups in Auctions, a Summary of Evidence*

Source	Data and Sample	Measure of Markup	Size of Markup
Cammack (1991)	T-bills (1973–1984)	Auction average minus average of WI at close on auction date	4 basis points
Spindt and Stolz (1992)	T-bills (1982–1988)	Auction average minus bid of WI at 30 minutes before auction	1.5 basis points
Bikhchandani et. al. (1994)	T-bills (1986–1988)	Auction average minus bid of WI at 1:00 P.M.	1 basis point
Simon (1994a)	Coupon (1990–1991)	Auction average minus bid of WI at 1:00 P.M.	$\frac{3}{8}$ basis point

more aggressive since they pay the same price irrespective of their bids. The incentive to gather preauction information is possibly less in this auction. Therefore, the winner's curse should be less of an issue in uniform price auctions.

In Table 3-5, we summarize the available evidence on the winner's curse. Note that the markup on Treasury bills has varied from 4 basis points to 1 basis point. For coupon issues, Simon (1994a) estimates a markup of about $\frac{3}{8}$ basis point. As shown in Table 3-5, researchers have employed several different methods to assess the success of a particular auction format in achieving a high selling price. The markups have varied from $\frac{3}{8}$ to 4 basis points. To the extent that markups are lower in uniform price auctions, that would be evidence in favor of using it. Nyborg and Sundaresan (1996) suggest that this might be the case.

The U.S. Department of Treasury conducted its own studies in 1995 and 1998. Their results are summarized in Table 3-6. Note that the two-year and five-year notes sold by the uniform-price auction procedure since September 1992 tend to have lower markups when compared to others sold by multiple-price (discriminatory) auction procedure.

Why Did the U.S. Treasury Switch to Uniform-Price Auction?

The arguments presented so far should indicate why the Treasury decided to go with the uniform-price auction. If bidders are more aggressive in the auction, the lowest accepted price (or the highest accepted yield) will go up (down). This is to the advantage of Treasury and hence to the tax payer.

In addition, if discriminatory auctions resulted in higher markups, that will be indicative of less aggressive bidding in Treasury auctions. The choice between discriminatory and uniform-price auction is based on which auction produces (a) more aggressive bidding, (b) less markups, and (c) greater demand discovery prior to bidding. We have already suggested that uniform-price auction is more likely to encourage more

TABLE 3-6 *Average Spreads Between Auction Results and 1:00 P.M. WI Bid Yields (Basis Points, Standard Error in Parentheses)*

		Uniform-Price Period			
Securities	Multiple-Price Period 6/91–8/92	Total 9/92–5/98	Results Released in October Study 9/92–9/95	Results Since October Study 10/95–5/98	Whole Period 6/91–5/98
2-year	0.41** (0.13)	0.20 (0.15)	0.22 (0.25)	0.17 (0.15)	
5-year	0.33** (0.06)	0.22 (0.21)	0.20 (0.32)	0.24 (0.26)	
2- and 5-year	0.37** (0.07)	0.21 (0.13)	0.21 (0.20)	0.21 (0.15)	
3-year	0.50 (0.22)	0.49** (0.09)	0.58** (0.17)	0.39** (0.07)	0.49** (0.09)
10-year	0.56 (0.40)	0.66** (0.14)	0.79** (0.22)	0.53* (0.19)	0.64** (0.13)
30-year	0.36 (0.19)	0.46* (0.17)	0.61* (0.22)	0.29 (0.26)	0.43** (0.13)
3-,10-, and 30-year	0.47** (0.15)	0.55** (0.08)	0.67** (0.11)	0.43** (0.10)	0.53** (0.07)

Source: Department of Treasury, October 1998.

*Significantly different from zero at the 95% level.

**Significantly different from zero at the 99% level.

Note: The 30-year Treasury bond was not included in the October study.

aggressive bidding and less markups. What about demand discovery prior to bidding? The evidence that we summarize next suggests that uniform-price auctions generate more information prior to bidding as compared to discriminatory auctions.

A striking difference between discriminatory and single-price auctions is the pattern of arrival of information. For the 30-year discriminatory auctions, Figure 3-4 shows that the volatility of markups increases *after* the auction. In sharp contrast, for the two-year uniform-price auction (as shown in Figure 3-5) the pattern is the opposite. This suggests that most of the information appears to be released *before* the auction in uniform-price format, whereas there are surprises *after* the auction in the discriminatory format. Clearly, it is better to have more information prior to bidding than receiving it later.

U.S. Treasury went about making this decision cautiously. In September 1992, it inaugurated an experiment with uniform-price auctions for two-year and five-year T-notes. The rest of the benchmarks, including T-bills, were sold by discriminatory or multiple-price auction. In October 1995, the Treasury reviewed the results and

FIGURE 3-4   *Thirty-year Discriminatory Auctions (Auction Average Minus WI Rates and Volatility of WI Rates)*

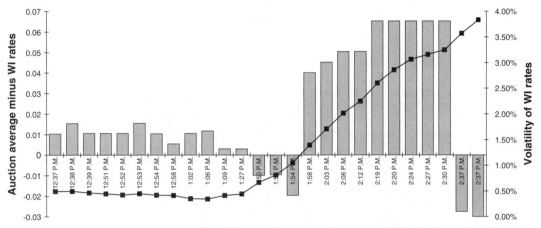

Vertical bars refer to the average markups (the difference between auction average and when-issued rates) across all 30-year auctions at the indicated times on the auction day. Dark squares connected by the solid line plots the volatility of markups.

Source: Nyborg and Sundaresan 1996.

FIGURE 3-5   *Two-Year Uniform-Price Auction (Stop-Out Yield Minus WI Rates and Volatility of WI Rates).*

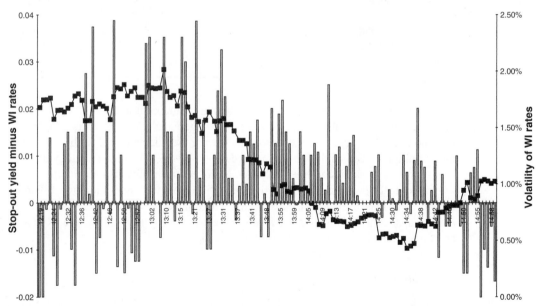

Vertical bars refer to the average markups (the difference between auction average and when-issued rates) across all two-year auctions at the indicated times on the auction day. Dark squares connected by the solid line plots the volatility of markups.

Source: Nyborg and Sundaresan 1996.

decided to continue with the experiment until 1998. In October 1998, the Treasury reviewed the results and decided to switch to uniform-price auctions for *all* securities. We attach a statement by Lawrence Summers, the Deputy Secretary of the Treasury, excerpted from the U.S. Treasury announcing the switch from discriminatory to uniform-price auctions.

While there has been a long-standing interest in the theory of uniform-price auctions, there had been very little empirical analysis when the Treasury inaugurated its experiment with regular uniform-price auctions of 2- and 5-year notes in September 1992. The October 1995 study and this update make valuable contributions to the body of empirical evidence.

The conclusions in this update reinforce those reached in 1995. They provide empirical support for the theoretical proposition that auction participants will bid more aggressively in uniform-price auctions since successful bidders in uniform-price auctions pay only the price of the lowest accepted bid, rather than the actual price they bid, as in the multiple-price approach. Our experience also shows that uniform-price auctions produce a broader distribution of auction awards. These results have important policy implications. The findings indicate that uniform-price auctions can allow the Treasury to make improvements in the efficiency of market operations and reduce the costs of financing the Federal debt. These results are also important in another sense: they provide a clear example of how economic theory can make a significant and direct contribution to public policy. The Treasury is proud to have played a role in bridging the gap between theory and application.

Lawrence H. Summers
Deputy Secretary of the Treasury
October 26, 1998

Treasury Auctions are multiple-unit auctions. Empirical analysis of bids submitted by dealers in Swedish Treasury Auctions suggest the following facts: (1) Bidders respond to uncertainty about the auction by cutting their demand and (2) by submitting more multiple bids than they would have done otherwise. This latter strategy is sometimes referred to as bidder diversification. Many central banks also employ a reservation price. If the bids are not aggressive enough to meet the reservation price, than the central bank may not auction the security. There have been such issue cuts in many countries, such as Portugal and Sweden. Papers by Gordy (1994), Nyborg, Rydquist, and Sundaresan (1999) have addressed these issues.

Short Squeeze

The term "squeeze" is used by market participants to refer to a shortage of supply relative to demand for a particular security, as evidenced by a movement in its price to a level that is out of line with prices of comparable securities—either in outright trading quotations or in financing arrangements (U.S. Department of the Treasury et al. 1992).

A squeeze, which forces some traders to pay very high premiums to borrow the securities they want, is not necessarily illegal. It is illegal, however, if there is collusion in creating a shortage of securities.

It is possible that some investors might enter the auction (and the postauction trading) with a short position. Such investors who are short have obviously borrowed securities (from other investors who are long), which they must buy eventually to cover their short positions. All trades in the when-issued market are settled for delivery and payment on the scheduled issue date. When dealers sell short in the when-issued market, they sell securities that they do not own on the assumption that they can acquire them, either through purchase or loan, in time for delivery.

Dealers typically enter the auction with significant short positions. This situation presents significant risk to the bidders. A bidder who is short and unable to get sufficient quantity of the security in the auction must cover the short position by the issue date by buying in the WI market after the auction. Alternatively, the bidder must borrow the security on the issue date in the repo market to fulfill his or her WI commitments. In such a case, however, the bidder is still short in the security and is exposed to the possibility of a short squeeze. The average short position is 38% of the auction awards according to a study done by the U.S. Treasury in 1992. Even if one or two dealers are relatively more aggressive in the auctions, there could be significant imbalances in dealer long positions relative to their prior short positions. This fact has important implications for both the price behavior and the repo-rate behavior immediately following the auction, as will be shown later. In a short squeeze, one may expect the postauction repo rates (especially during the issue date and the few days immediately following the issue date) to be much lower (later in the chapter, we provide evidence and an explanation as to why this must be the case) and the prices to be correspondingly higher.

The positions of dealers in the auction are substantial, and this compounds the risk of a short squeeze. This is easily seen from the evidence on dealer positions presented in Chapter 2.

Evidence suggests that the primary dealers dominate the competitive awards. According to a study by the U.S. Treasury in the money markets sector, they get 71.5% of the auction awards; in the T-note and T-bond sectors, they get 72% of all the awards. An interesting fact is that the noncompetitive allocation appears to be relatively more important for the T-bills sector.

Primary dealers, depository institutions, and government securities brokers and dealers registered with the SEC may submit competitive and noncompetitive bids for their own accounts, as well as for their customers. Others wishing to bid may do so only for their own accounts. The possibility that one or two dealers could have a commanding position by capturing a major percent of the auction further accentuates the effect of a potential short squeeze.

Implications for Repo Rates

As noted in Chapter 2, Treasury securities may be used as collateral to borrow cash at the repo rate. Also, the cash from the sale of such securities may be used to collateralize short positions. Such cash positions earn reverse repo rates. Bond dealers finance a substantial percentage of their inventory positions in this market. Recall that in a repo contract the security is sold with a simultaneous forward agreement to buy it back at a currently agreed upon price and that, conversely, in a reverse repo transaction the security is purchased and at the termination of the contract (usually overnight) sold back.

It is possible that U.S. Treasury securities that are perfect substitutes in terms of their cash flow pattern will command significantly different repo rates because their collateral values may differ significantly in the repo market. Such differences arise due to the scarcity value of the security in the repo market to cover short positions. This scarcity may arise as a natural outcome of the ex-post-settling-up process by which dealers who are net short cover their positions by either buying or borrowing securities from the dealers who are net long.

When a security is in demand, the owners may be willing to lend that security for cash (as collateral), provided the interest cost on cash is low enough to reflect the demand for the security. The cash will then be used by the owner of the security to earn a spread over the interest cost. Typically, Fed funds or other short-term investments will serve this purpose. This suggests that in a short squeeze the repo rates must fall to induce the owners of securities to lend their securities (sometimes referred to as the special repo rate, see Chapter 2). Note that this process is unique for the on-the-run issues.

When-Issued Trading and Repo Rate Behavior. All trades in the when-issued market are settled after the auction when the securities are actually issued. This fact has empirical implications for the behavior of market prices of the newly auctioned issue in the postauction when-issued trading, and in the cash market prices and the repo rates on the issue date. To see why this is the case, we must remember that, at the end of when-issued trading just prior to the auction, some investors will be net short and some net long. Since each bidder has no private information about other bids, there is residual uncertainty about the bids of other participants in the auction. This fact, coupled with the auction mechanism that introduces quantity uncertainty, implies that it is impossible to guarantee that the short positions will be fully covered by the auction awards. As a consequence, any shortfall must be covered in the postauction when-issued trading and must be settled up on the issue date either in the cash market or in the repo market.

To get an appreciation of these factors, examine Table 3-7, which shows the average of the difference between the general collateral rate and the special rates for all on-the-run issues from the issue date of the current on-the-run security to the issue date of the next on-the-run security.

The summary information in Table 3-7 serves as a useful benchmark. The general collateral rate is the rate applied to most Treasury securities for overnight collateralized lending and borrowing purposes. Dealers generally permit substitution of collaterals in such general collateral agreements. The special rates apply to collateralized transactions where no such substitutions are permitted. As a consequence, it is intuitive why the special rates must be below the general collateral: The owner of a security which is trading special is able to get a much lower rate on collateralized loan transactions. This rent can be substantial. In practice, 90% to 95% of the Treasury securities trade at the general collateral rate. The remaining few exceptions trade special.

As Table 3-7 demonstrates, on-the-run issues trade special as a rule and trade, on average, at 45 to 100 basis points below the general collateral rate. That the spreads are reliably positive is evident from the t-statistics.

Note Table 3-8 how the difference between the general collateral repo rate and the special repo of on-the-run securities *increase* during a crisis. For example, during the period August 17, 1998, to November 20, 1998, Russia defaulted and several hedge funds collapsed. This led to a "flight to quality" wherein investors rush to buy "safe" and "liquid" on-the-run bonds. This extra demand makes on-the-run bonds trade at a special repo rate. The 30-year on-the-run bond (indicated by arrows in Table 3-8) had, on average, a special repo rate that was 211 basis points lower than the general collateral rate! This means that the owner of a 30-year on-the-run bond could have pledged it as collateral (during the crisis) and borrowed cash 211 basis points cheaper, as compared to other similar Treasury securities.

TABLE 3-7   *Repo Rates (Overnight) Summary Statistics, General Collateral—Special Rate (in Basis Points), Sample: 1987–1991*

Statistic	Two-year	Three-year	Five-year	Seven-year	Ten-year	Thirty-year
Number of auctions	57	19	23	18	19	16
Mean	56.57	47.20	67.39	56.22	96.94	69.47
Standard deviation	107.42	82.90	110.31	87.13	130.68	105.82
t-statistic	18.25	19.51	21.03	21.90	25.42	22.22

Source: Sundaresan 1994.

TABLE 3-8   *Repo Specialness of On-the-Run U.S. Treasury Coupon Securities*

Period	Basis Points			
	Two-Year	Five-Year	Ten-Year	Thirty-Year
Precrisis: July 1, 1997–Aug. 14, 1998	21.0 (30.4)	76.9 (80.5)	165.8 (135.8)	120.6 (135.0)
Crisis: → Aug. 17, 1998–Nov. 20, 1998	52.8 (86.6)	126.1 (149.3)	115.6 (143.4)	211.1 ← (164.9)
Postcrisis: Nov. 23, 1998–Oct. 29, 1999	35.3 (48.6)	75.0 (86.2)	200.3 (155.0)	120.1 (123.9)
Full sample: July 1, 1997–Oct. 29, 1999	30.4 (48.5)	81.8 (94.3)	173.9 (146.8)	130.8 (137.4)

Source: Michael Fleming, FRBNY Economic Policy Review/April 2000.

Note: The table reports the means and standard deviations (in parenthesis) of the daily average differences between the overnight general collateral rate and the collateral rates on the indicated on-the-run securities.

TABLE 3-9   *Repo Rates (Overnight) around Auctions, General Collateral—Special Rate (in Basis Points), Sample: 1987–1991*

Benchmark	−4	−3	−2	−1	0	+1	+2	+3	+4
Two-year	90.33	73.17	73.87	60.35	58.07	54.29	38.68	36.89	36.04
	(5.20)	(4.51)	(4.32)	(4.12)	(3.86)	(4.01)	(3.76)	(3.39)	(2.77)
Three-year	121.71	96.18	74.63	37.71	38.18	40.61	37.47	30.36	21.71
	(3.44)	(3.65)	(2.41)	(4.91)	(3.39)	(3.54)	(5.12)	(6.46)	(12.03)
Five-year	153.17	126.19	92.39	72.78	62.80	51.94	79.52	95.00	89.17
	(5.55)	(5.40)	(5.27)	(5.60)	(4.79)	(3.94)	(4.14)	(2.94)	(2.38)
Seven-year	119.11	113.44	93.72	102.64	103.56	50.22	51.05	59.64	24.16
	(4.04)	(4.55)	(4.59)	(4.00)	(3.12)	(5.04)	(3.31)	(2.94)	(3.38)
Ten-year	233.55	189.63	177.90	178.29	147.97	153.92	109.64	99.93	112.55
	(5.63)	(5.02)	(4.43)	(3.74)	(3.71)	(3.50)	(2.81)	(2.70)	(2.90)
Thirty-year	155.19	132.81	131.22	112.75	130.59	83.70	83.08	106.00	111.50
	(4.45)	(3.77)	(4.01)	(3.82)	(2.59)	(3.63)	(3.48)	(2.86)	(3.22)

1. The t-statistics are provided in parentheses.

2. The sample period is from April 1, 1987, to December 1991.

3. Aution date is denoted by 0. The spreads are computed for the nine-day window starting from four days prior to the auction (−4) and ending four days after the auction (+4).

The evidence presented in Table 3-9 clearly demonstrates that during the days prior to auctions, securities become very expensive to borrow, and in some cases, they continue to be expensive for days. This is consistent with the existence of periodic squeezes in Treasury markets over a long period of time. The "auction day effect" is clearly present in the repo rates data. The report from the *New York Times* on short squeezes illustrates this point.

Fed Looks into "Squeeze" in Treasuries

BY JONATHAN FUERBRINGER

The "squeeze" on the Treasury's seven- and 10-year notes has become tight enough to prompt the Federal Reserve Bank of New York to collect information on dealer positions and study the dynamics of the shortage of securities.

A squeeze, which forces some traders to pay very high premiums to borrow the securities they want, is not necessarily illegal. But it can be if there is collusion involved in creating a shortage of securities.

The Federal Reserve Bank, which is collecting the data as part of the broadened market surveillance effort that was started after the Treasury auction scandal involving Salomon Brothers in August 1991, confirmed the special request to dealers for information yesterday.

Hedging Operations

Several dealers said yesterday that they saw nothing happening beyond a normal squeeze on the 10-year note. There is a shortage of the securities because so many dealers have sold them, without actually owning them, as part of hedging operations against large holdings of corporate issues that have been difficult to sell to customers recently.

Two traders, who asked not to be identified, said Yamaichi International, a primary dealer, was at the center of the shortage of seven-year notes.

But Scott E. Pardee, co-chairman of Yamaichi, dismissed the accusations as finger-pointing. "There has been a tendency on the part of people in the center to point fingers at people who are not in the center, so I am not surprised that they are trying to point the finger at us," he said.

Mr. Pardee, a former Federal Reserve official, said traders had done similar finger-pointing at Yamaichi earlier this year in connection with a squeeze of 10-year notes, so his firm was being "scrupulously careful in this." He said the Federal Reserve Bank of New York, in earlier situations, "has done a good job in making sure that no one is sitting on the bonds."

The measure of a squeeze or shortage of notes or bonds is in the repurchase market, where these securities are borrowed. In normal circumstances, a dealer swaps cash for the securities. He lends the cash to the holder of the securities at daily market rates, which are around 3 percent.

But when there is a shortage, the dealer must "pay" by lending that cash at lower than market rates, a move that benefits the dealer who has the securities. Yesterday, the rate on 10-year notes was at zero. while the rate on seven-year notes was around $\frac{1}{8}$ of a percent.

Involvement of the Fed

The Federal Reserve Bank of New York has gathered such data on seven other issues this year, including the five-year note that was auctioned in July, said a spokesman, Peter Bakstansky. "We are trying to better understand the positions in the market and the market dynamics," he said.

In similar instances earlier this year, the information gathered has gone to the interagency working group for Treasury market surveillance, which includes the Treasury, the Fed and the Securities and Exchange Commission.

Under the changes made after the Salomon bidding scandal, the Treasury said it would use its power to make additional securities available to the market to end any acute shortage or squeeze in the market. Although this weapon has not been used, the increased surveillance is part of the first step that would lead to a decision on whether to break up a squeeze.

Squeezes are not unique to the U.S. Treasury market. They occur in other markets as well. In the following box, we reproduce a description of recent squeezes that took place in the Canadian government bond market.

Table 3-9 also provides evidence on the tightness in repo rates surrounding the auction date.

Examples of Recent Squeezes

Case 1: 4% bonds due March 15, 1999

- In August 1997 a very large amount of these bonds was tightly held and some large short positions existed.
- The issue traded as much as 50 basis points below the yield on bonds with a similar maturity, and repo rates occasionally fell well below 1% (general repo rates were about 3.25%).
- The Bank of Canada exchanged $600 million of this issue from its portfolio (through an auction) for bonds with a similar maturity.

Case 2: 1-year treasury bill due August 6, 1998

- The problem developed through the auction process in August 1997.
- The issue was reopened as part of the normal auction cycle in the amount of $1 billion but was still held by only a few parties and there was no available supply to be traded.
- A further reopening of $500 million outside of the regular auction cycle was needed to make some market supply available.

Source: Bank of Canada.

Salomon Brothers Treasury Scandal

As noted earlier, the U.S. Treasury market is generally self-regulated. During the May 1991 two-year auction, however, Salomon Brothers, Inc., one of the major primary dealers, was involved in violations of certain rules of the auction procedure. They submitted bids on behalf of customers without obtaining their authorization. In the process, they ended up controlling a major fraction of the May 1991 two-year note supply, together with some hedge funds. During July and the first half of August 1991, government regulators launched a sweeping investigation of Salomon Brothers Inc., alleging that the firm might have controlled 85% of the two-year Treasury notes that were auctioned on May 22, 1991 (*Wall Street Journal,* August 12, 1991), The SEC broadened its investigation of the Treasury market further by looking at the possibility of widespread collusion and price fixing by more than a dozen investment and commercial banks (*Wall Street Journal,* August 27, 1991), A written report from Salomon Brothers, Inc. opened new areas of investigation for government regulators, and the focus of the investigation widened to include investment firms, such as Paul Tudor Jones' Tudor Investment Corporation and Steinhardt Partners (*Wall Street Journal,* September 5, 1991).

One of the reports of the investigation that appeared in *Wall Street Journal* during this period follows.

Precise Role of Salomon Brothers in May Sale Probed

By Constance Mitchell

NEW YORK—Government investigators—and angry bond dealers—are trying to find out exactly what role Salomon Brothers Inc. and others may have played in an effort to improperly control the market for new two-year Treasury notes in May.

That's one of the issues at the heart of the unfolding scandal that already has besmirched the reputation of Salomon Inc.'s big investment bank unit and the $2.3 trillion Treasury market.

For some time, bond traders had noticed that the price of two-year notes as well as many other shorter-term securities would often rise ahead of their auction date. That's due mainly to demand.

Because the two-year note is the shortest maturing Treasury security with a "coupon" that makes semiannual interest payments, it is highly popular with small and large investors around the world, who tend to buy it at the auction and hold it to maturity. But the price sometimes declines modestly right after the auction, when interest in the note sale fades.

In a strategy designed to profit on the two-year note's trading pattern, many traders and arbitragers would sell the two-year notes "short" ahead of the auction. In a short sale, speculators borrow securities and sell them in hopes of replacing what was borrowed with cheaper securities after the price has fallen. In this case, traders would operate in the "when-issued" market, in which securities are traded before they are actually issued.

But that strategy backfired with a vengeance when something unusual happened at the May 22 auction of $12.26 billion of two-year notes. Instead of declining, the price of the two-year notes jumped sharply and remained at lofty levels for more than a month, causing short sellers and others that needed the notes to be "squeezed" into paying premium prices to cover their positions. Squeezes only occur when securities are heavily concentrated in the hands of a few dealers.

On May 30, one week after the auction, the two-year notes were quoted at a price of $100\frac{5}{32}$ to yield 6.60%, up from an average auction price of $99\frac{29}{32}$ to yield 6.81%. In other words, the $12.26 billion of notes appreciated in value by $30.6 million in just one week.

To make matters worse, the two-year notes became so scarce that the dealers who owned the notes charged exorbitant fees and financing costs when lending them to short-sellers.

From small bond arbitrage operations in Chicago to the New York powerhouses, bond traders across America were badly burned.

"The arbs were hurt the worst; several of the smaller shops went out of business," said Barbara Kenworthy, a portfolio manager at Dreyfus Corp., a mutual fund company that manages about $16 billion of bonds, most of which are Treasurys. A financial firm in Chicago that trades bonds, commodities and foreign exchange said it recently hired two former bond traders who lost their jobs because of the two-year note squeeze.

The pain was so severe and the cries of foul play were so loud that the two-year note squeeze became the talk of the bond market for weeks. More significantly, the Securities and Exchange Commission and the Justice Department's antitrust division began an investigation.

Investigators say Salomon Brothers may have controlled as much as 85% of the notes sold at the auction. The most widespread theory among traders was that Salomon placed huge quantities of bids for itself and on behalf of big clients, rumored to be Michael Steinhardt and George Soros, investment managers that run aggressive "hedge" funds that usually speculate in the stock market.

(continued)

> Last week, Salomon admitted that it had acquired 44% of the notes at the auction. violating Treasury rules that bar anyone from buying more than 35% of a single issue at auction. Traders say Salomon may have controlled far more than that amount through so-called prearranged trades with big investors.
>
> At the time, Mr. Steinhardt acknowledged that his firm owned some two-year notes sold at the May auction. Mr. Soros would not comment. The Securities and Exchange Commission investigators have asked the Steinhardt firm for information about its role in the two-year auction.
>
> When asked by *The Wall Street Journal* in late May to comment on these allegations, Salomon Brothers bond trading manager Paul Mozer became furious and ticked off a list of reasons why he would not comment. When asked for his opinion why the price of two-year notes had risen so sharply, Mr. Mozer said his views about the market were considered by Salomon's sales managers to be "too valuable" to be quoted in the U.S. financial press.

The accusation that somehow the auction was cornered by one dealer, perhaps in collusion with a few major investment firms, has far-reaching implications. The stakes for the U.S. government are obvious: the Treasury auctions in this market frequently, and any questions about the integrity of the marketplace may easily increase the cost of public debt. U.S. Treasury securities have a reputation for safety and liquidity, and are held by major central banks and financial institutions for those reasons. The yields in the U.S. Treasury sector typically form the basis on which agencies, corporations, and banks set their borrowing rates. It is reasonable to say that in each maturity sector Treasury yields represent the floor for the borrowing costs of other major institutions. As a result, it is imperative that the Treasury market be free from corners, squeezes, and manipulations.

The efficiency of the dealer market structure, organized around the primary dealers, has been called into question by many in the wake of the May two-year Treasury note auction. The conventional arguments for the primary dealer system are essentially grounded on the financial strength of the primary dealers and their probity. Some have argued that with a primary dealer system the Treasury does not have to worry about no shows in its auctions. However, this may not be so important given the default-free and liquid nature of the Treasury securities. The fact that Salomon Brothers were able to buy 44% of the May auction casts a shadow on the assumption of probity. Such events clearly point to some of the problems in the current market mechanisms for auctioning Treasury securities.

May Auction of Treasury Notes. To provide a perspective on auctions, we will first examine the results of monthly auctions of two-year Treasury notes during the first half of 1991. Table 3-10 provides a summary of these two-year Treasury note auctions. This not only gives a perspective on the two-year auctions, but it also gives us a broader context in which to evaluate the May 1991 auction.

TABLE 3-10   *Auction of Two-Year Treasury Notes, 1991*

Auction Announcement Date	Jan. 16	Feb. 12	Mar. 20	Apr. 17	May 15	Jun. 19
Tender Date	Jan. 23	Feb. 20	Mar. 26	Apr. 24	May 22	Jun. 25
Maturity of Notes	1/31/1993	2/28/1993	3/31/1993	4/30/1993	5/31/1993	6/30/1993
Tender Time (Noncompetitive)	12 noon EST Jan. 23	12 noon EST Feb. 20	12 noon EST Mar. 26	12 noon EST Apr. 24	12 noon EST May 22	12 noon EST Jun. 25
Tender Time (Competitive)	1 P.M. EST Jan. 23	1 P.M. EST Feb.20	1 P.M. EST Mar. 26	1 P.M. EST Apr. 24	1 P.M. EST May 22	1 P.M. EST Jun. 25
Amount Tender (in Millions) (Noncompetitive)	$1,329	$917	$1,244	$1,317	$1,059	$1,080
Amount Tender (in Millions) (Competitive)	$40,135	$40,068	$29,556	$44,117	$33,801	$37,199
Amount Accepted (Competitive)	$12,619	$12,062	$11,529	$12,006	$13,560	$12,529
Range of Yields (Competitive)	7.08 to 7.09	6.85 to 6.87	7.13 to 7.15	6.99 to 7.00	6.81 to 6.83	7.03 to 7.06
Percent Accepted at Higher Yield (Competitive)	60%	61%	71%	96%	14%	64%

From Table 3-10 we see that the May auction differed in a qualitative way from the rest of the 1991 auctions in that only 14% of the accepted competitive tenders were filled at higher yields. The corresponding percentages for other auctions ranged from a low of 60% to a high of 90%. The unusually large percentage of the competitive bids that were accepted at a lower yield is consistent with aggressive bidding for the Treasury notes during the May auction.

The range of yields from 6.81% to 6.83% in the competitive bids led the Treasury to set a coupon of $6\frac{3}{4}\%$ for the May 1991 issue. This means that the Treasury issued the notes at 99.853% of par. Simon (1994a) reports that the auction bid was 6.81%, as compared to the when-issued rates prior to the auction of around 6.84%. Figure 3-6 (reproduced from Simon 1994a) shows the nature of the yield behavior surrounding the auction.

Postauction Prices. The postauction prices (adjusted for overall movements in relevant interest rates) are an excellent indicator of whether the prices were artificially different from their economic values. To this end, we provide Table 3-11, which documents the postauction yields for a period of six days (including the auction date). The change in the yields between day 0 (the auction date) and day 5 is tabulated in Table 3-12 to give an indication of the postauction price behavior.

A review of Tables 3-11 and 3-12 indicates that in the May 1991 auction, the yields of Treasury notes fell by 20 basis points in the five days following the auction.

FIGURE 3-6   *Two-Year Treasury Note Auctioned May 22, 1991*

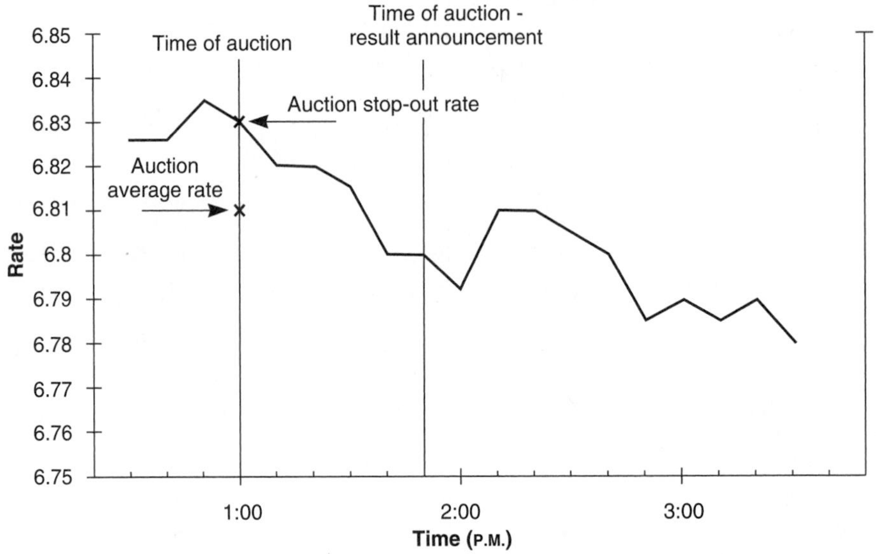

TABLE 3-11   *Yield Behavior after the 1991 Two-Year Treasury Notes Auctions*

Days after Auction Date	June Auction	May Auction	April Auction	March Auction	Feb. Auction	Jan. Auction
0	7.06%	6.81%	7.00%	7.15%	6.87%	7.09%
1	7.03%	6.75%	6.91%	7.07%	6.96%	7.04%
2	6.97%	6.68%	6.89%	7.03%	6.98%	7.08%
3	6.91%	6.69%	6.88%	7.04%	6.97%	7.11%
4	6.96%	6.66%	6.78%	7.01%	7.01%	7.09%
5	6.99%	6.61%	6.80%	6.96%	7.01%	7.07%

TABLE 3-12   *Yield Changes in the 1991 Postauction Period*

	June Auction	May Auction	April Auction	March Auction	Feb. Auction	Jan. Auction
Change in yield after auction date	−7	−20	−20	−19	+4	−2

TABLE 3-13	Days after Auction Date	June Auction	May Auction	April Auction
Spread* Behavior after the Two-Year 1991 Treasury Notes Auctions	0	16	4	5
	1	19	6	–2
	2	21	–1	–3
	3	22	–1	–4
	4	26	–2	–5
	5	24	0	–5

*Spread = on-the-run—off-the run

Taken in isolation, this means little. It is possible that the interest rates simply might have fallen during these five days. To account for this possibility, we need to look at the spread between the May Treasury note and the April Treasury note during this period. As Table 3-13 shows, this spread decreased from 4 to 0 basis points in the same period, suggesting that the May note appreciated in value even after accounting for the overall changes in interest rates.

As Table 3-13 also illustrates, however, the situation was worse in the April auction. The April note appreciated to the tune of 20 basis points in the five days following the auction, and its spread relative to the March note decreased from 5 to –5 basis points in the same period. Thus, the April note prices were driven to a greater extent by idiosyncratic factors.

Since the on-the-run notes and off-the-run notes differ only by a month in their maturity and by little more than 50 basis points in coupons, we do not use duration or more precise measures of risk-adjusted spreads (developed later in Chapter 4) in our calculations. Our suspicion is that adding those corrections would not introduce any qualitative changes in our conclusions.

Postauction Financing Rates. The when-issued (WI) trades are settled on the issue date, which is typically the last business day of the month for two-year auctions. It is, therefore, instructive to look at the financing rates around this period to see if there is any evidence of tightness in the market. Traders noticed significant tightness on the last business day of the auction, as well as during the following weeks. The collateral-specific repo rates for the May two-year were about 75 to 200 basis points lower than the general collateral. When the available supply of a security is limited in relation to its demand, the owners of the security are in a position to squeeze the investors who demand that security. In a well-functioning capital market, close substitutes for that security typically will then become available to meet the excess demand. There are situations, however, where close substitutes will simply not do, and only the specified security can meet the demand of the investors. An example of this situation is the short squeeze, in which short sellers of a security need to buy that security to cover their short positions, despite the fact that many close substitutes (from a cash flow perspective) may be available. In a squeeze, the investors who are long observe that there is an excess demand for a security, and they take advantage of it by extracting economic rents from the investors who are short, either via preposterously low repo rates or via prices that do not reflect the economic value of that security. So a necessary condition for establishing that a squeeze is present in the market is to show that the prices and repo rates are artificially different from their economic values.

In the May 1991 auction, aggressive bidding enabled Salomon Brothers to accumulate a dominant position in the security. The other dealers were obliged to buy back the security from Salomon Brothers at a very high price to cover their short positions that existed beyond their auction awards. This short squeeze is evident in the price of the May 1991 T-note, as well as in the spread relationship between the May 1991 T-note and the previously auctioned April 1991 T-note, as shown in Table 3-13.

Regulatory Implications. Salomon Brothers was fined nearly $300 million. More importantly, in response to these problems, major changes have been introduced in the Treasury markets. (See U.S. Department of the Treasury et al. 1992 for more details.) The Treasury has reserved the right to address the squeeze problem by increasing the supply of newly auctioned securities via reopening. In addition, it may release more collateral into the repo market to minimize the squeeze potential there. The bidding process may also be automated. The possibility of allowing some iterative bidding schemes has also been discussed.

We conclude by noting that the Treasury has been using auction procedures to buy back debt from dealers. In Appendix B of this chapter, we provide a summary of the auction procedure and a recent buyback announcement and results.

FURTHER READING

This chapter has presented an analysis of Treasury auctions, when-issued markets, and repo markets. These topics are typically given short shrift in texts on fixed-income markets. Even in the academic literature, the when-issued markets and repo markets have been treated only recently. Auction theory and mechanism design are active research topics in the economics literature. An excellent survey of auction theory is provided in Milgrom (1989). More directly related to Treasury auctions are Bikchandani and Huang (1993) and Chari and Weber (1992). Academic papers addressing the effect of secondary markets on Treasury auctions, the vulnerability of auction mechanisms to manipulation, and a comparative analysis of uniform-price and discriminatory auctions are provided, respectively, in Bikchandani and Huang (1993), Back and Zender (1993), and Nyborg and Sundaresan (1996). We have already reviewed some papers dealing with winner's curse in auctions. Empirical studies in this area by Cammack (1991); Simon (1994a); and Spindt and Stolz (1992) have examined the presence and the magnitude of winner's curse in discriminatory auctions. Simon (1994b) and Nyborg and Sundaresan (1996) examine uniform-price auctions; the latter study provides explicit comparisons between the two auction formats. Repo markets have been described in detail in an excellent text by Stigum (1990). Academic research in this area includes Duffie (1992) and Sundaresan (1996). The when-issued market and its implications for auctions have been explored by Bickchandani, Edsparr, and Huang (1994) and Nyborg and Sundaresan (1996).

PROBLEMS

3.1   Describe clearly the salient features of the discriminatory auction mechanism used by the U.S. Treasury to sell T-bills, and three-year and ten-year T-notes and thirty-year T-bonds.

3.2   Explain the meaning of the term *winner's curse*. Why should the U.S. Treasury be concerned about the possibility of winner's curse being present in Treasury auctions?

3.3   Explain the role of the when-issued market in the context of Treasury auctions. What are the advantages and disadvantages of when-issued trading?

3.4   Describe clearly the salient features of the uniform-price auction mechanism used by the U.S. Treasury to sell two-year and five-year T-notes.

3.5   Which mechanism, the uniform-price auction or the discriminatory auction, is expected to have a greater degree of winner's curse? Why?

3.6   **(a)** Briefly describe the role of primary dealers in Treasury auctions.
(b) These auctions are preceded by WI trading. Briefly describe the WI market.
(c) Discuss the advantages and disadvantages of WI trading for (i) the ultimate investor, (ii) primary dealers, (iii) the U.S. Treasury, and (iv) the price discovery process.

3.7   Who are likely to be the buyers in the WI market and who are likely to be the sellers? What consequences does the WI market have for the auction prices and the secondary-market prices?

3.8   **(a)** Briefly describe the repo markets.
(b) Describe and explain the differences between general collateral repo rates and special repo rates.
(c) Explain the difference between on-the-run and off-the-run issues.
(d) It appears that on-the-run issues tend to go special more often than off-the-run issues. What are the reasons for this pattern?

3.9   Is there a general association between the level of interest rates and the shape of the yield curve? Review the evidence presented in this chapter and in Chapter 1 in answering this question.

3.10   Is there a relationship between the levels of interest rates and their volatility? Discuss the evidence.

REFERENCES

Back, K., and J. Zender 1993, "Auctions of Divisible Goods: On the Rationale for the Treasury Experiment." *Review of Financial Studies* 6:733–764.

Bikchandani, S. 1988. "Reputation in Repeated Second-Price Auctions." *Journal of Economic Theory* 46:97–119.

Bikchandani, S., and C. Huang 1989. "Auction with Resale Markets: An Exploratory Model of Treasury Bill Markets." *The Review of Financial Studies* 2:311–339.

Bikchandani, S., and C. Huang 1993. "The Economics of Treasury Securities Markets." *Journal of Economic Perspectives* 7:117–134.

Bikchandani, S., P. L. Edsparr, and C. Huang 1994. The Treasury Bill Auction and the When-Issued Market: Some Evidence. M.I.T. Working Paper.

Cammack, E. 1991. "Evidence of Bidding Strategies and the Information in Treasury Bill Auctions." *Journal of Political Economy* 99:100–130.

Chari, V. V., and R. Weber 1992. "How the U.S. Treasury Should Auction Its Debt." Northwestern University Working Paper.

Duffie, D. 1992. Special Repo Rates. Stanford University Research Working Paper.

Engelbrecht-Wiggins, R. 1990. "Auctions and Bidding Models: A Survey." *Management Science* 26:119–142.

Fleming, Michael J. April 2000. The Benchmark U.S. Treasury Market: Recent Performance and Possible Alternatives," *FRBNY Economic Policy Review.*

Friedman, M. 1991. "How to Sell Government Securities." *Wall Street Journal,* August 28.

Fuerbringer, J. 1992. "Fed Looks into 'Squeeze' in Treasuries." *New York Times* September 25: D,1:6,D11.

Gordy, Michael B. 1994. "Structural Analysis of Reservation Price Policy in a Treasury Bill Auction." Board of Governors of the Federal Reserve System.

Nyborg, K., Rydquist, K., and S.M. Sundaresan 1999. "Bidder Behavior in Multi-Unit Auctions: Evidence from Swedish Treasury Auctions." Columbia University Working Paper.

Nyborg, K., and S. Sundaresan 1996. Discriminatory versus Uniform Treasury Auctions—Evidence from When-Issued Transactions, *Journal of Financial Economics* 42:63–104.

Simon, D. P. 1994a. "Markups, Quantity Risk and Bidding Strategies at Treasury Coupon Auctions." *Journal of Financial Economics* 35:43–62.

Simon, D. P. 1994b. "The Treasury's Experiment with Single-Price Auctions in the Mid-1970s: Winner's or Taxpayer's Curse?" *Review of Economics and Statistics* 76:754–760.

Spindt, P., and R. Stolz 1992. "Are U.S. T-bills Underpriced in the Primary Market?" *Journal of Banking and Finance* 16:891–908.

Stigum, M. L. 1989. *The Repo and Reverse Markets.* Homewood, IL: Dow Jones-Irwin.

Stigum, M. 1990. *The Money Market.* Homewood, IL: Dow Jones-Irwin.

Sundaresan, S. 1994. "An Empirical Analysis of U.S. Treasury Auctions: Implications for Auction and Term Structure Theories." *Journal of Fixed Income* 4:35–50.

U.S. Department of the Treasury, Securities and Exchange Commission, and Board of Governors of the Federal Reserve System 1992. *Joint Report on the Government Securities Market.* Washington, D.C.

Vickrey, W. 1961. "Counterspeculation, Auctions, and Competitive Sealed Tenders." *Journal of Finance* 16:8–37.

A Comparison of Procedures Used to Sell Government Debt

Source: Joint Report on Government Securities Market, 1992

OECD Countries: Techniques to Sell Central Government Debt Internally

Australia

General Comments	Auction	Other Sale Methods
The Treasury is responsible for government debt management and the Reserve Bank of Australia is its fiscal agent. There is no permanent lending by the RBA to the government although a short-term overdraft facility at market-related interest rates is available. Australia has surpluses in FYs 1988–91 (ended 6/30/91). This year the economy has been in recession, and a deficit of US$8.4 billion equivalent is estimated in the 1991–92 budget. The types of debt instruments issued are: short-term notes (5-, 13-, and 26-week maturities) sold weekly, and short- (1 to 3 years), medium- (3 to 5 years), and long-term (over 5 years) bonds. Australian government securities are in book-entry form. There are two groups of authorized dealers, with which RBA conducts open market operations. First, 8 "authorized short-term money-market dealers" have a contractual relationship with RBA to provide liquidity to the government securities market. RBA conducts most open market operations through short-term market-makers. Second, there are 18 "reporting bond dealers" through which RBA conducts OMO in bonds. The reporting bond dealers have no privileges or obligations regarding issuance of government debt. The government securities market is informally regulated by the RBA.	All government securities have been sold through *multiple-yield auctions* since 1982. Bids are accepted from parties registered for this purpose with RBA. Any potential bidder that can establish its financial capability can bid without deposit. The minimum competitive bid is US$77,800 equivalent. No limit is set on awards to one entity, nor is there any restriction on the number of bids any entity can submit. Usually reopen outstanding issues rather than issuing new ones. Bids usually amount to 3 to 4 times the amount offered. There is no when-issued trading.	Australian government savings bonds were issued on tap until 1987. The government no longer issues bonds targeted specifically at household savings. The RBA stands ready to fill small orders for marketable government securities (US$780 to US$39,000 equivalent) from its own portfolio at a price prevailing in the market, plus a small service charge. Small amounts can be sold to the RBA under the same terms. From time to time the government, through RBA, has repurchased outstanding bonds for cancellation or has exchanged current issues for older bonds to improve the overall liquidity of the market.

OECD Countries: Techniques to Sell Central Government Debt Internally

Belgium

General Comments	Auction	Other Sale Methods
The Ministry of Finance is responsible for public debt management, and the National Bank of Belgium is its fiscal agent. The government may borrow up to US$485 million equivalent for day-to-day cash management from NBB. In FY 1990 (ended 12/31/90) the budget deficit totaled US$12.69 billion equivalent.	Short-term certificates and "linear" bonds have been sold by *multiple-yield auctions* since January 1991. "Linear" bonds are issued monthly as reopenings of bonds with the same maturity, interest rate, and identifying number. Bids are accepted without deposit from parties registered for this purpose with the NBB.	Long-term public subscription bonds are sold 3 or 4 times per year. The coupon and maturity are set by the MOF and subscriptions are taken for about two weeks. The bonds are targeted to smaller investors. The minimum purchase amount is US$322 equivalent. MOF pays banks a commission for selling them to the public.
The types of debt instruments issued are: short-term bills (3-, 6- and 12-month), long-term public subscription bonds and "linear" bonds maturing in 3 to 15 years. The bills and linear bonds are issued in book-entry form to institutional investors and dealers. Public subscription bonds are in paper form. Most trading is on stock exchanges. The MOF has selected 14 primary dealers to bid in auctions and make secondary markets in short-term bills and linear bonds. Immediately after an auction, they have the sole right to purchase, on a noncompetitive basis at the auction average, additional amounts of the securities. Primary dealers and other intermediaries may be used by NBB to conduct open market operations. The Securities Regulation Fund, established under the authority of the MOF and the NBB regulates participants in the government securities market.	No limit is placed on awards to any one entity, nor is there a limit on the number of bids that can be submitted. The minimum bid is for US$322,000 equivalent for bills and US$1.6 million equivalent for linear bonds. There is no when-issued trading prior to the auction.	

OECD Countries: Techniques to Sell Central Government Debt Internally

Canada

General Comments	Auction	Other Sale Methods
The Department of Finance is responsible for debt management, and works closely with its fiscal agent, the Bank of Canada to develop policy. The budget deficit has been stable at about US$26 billion equivalent for the last 5 years.	About $\frac{3}{4}$ of marketable bonds and all short-term bills are sold in *multiple-yield auctions*. Awards, including awards for customers, are limited to 20 percent of amount offered of bonds and one-third of the amount offered of bills. When-issued trading begins when an issue is announced for auction. No commissions are paid for bonds and bills sold by auction. Canada is moving toward using auctions to sell all marketable securities.	Fixed-price subscription offerings are used for about $\frac{1}{4}$ of marketable bonds; the coupon and price are announced $1\frac{1}{2}$ days before the deadline for subscriptions. The Bank of Canada buys any portion of an issue that the primary distributors do not buy. A commission is paid on bonds sold via the syndicate.
Bonds are bullet maturities with fixed rates and are redeemable at maturity. Bonds mature in 2 to 30 years. Canada auctions each week 3- and 6-month bills and year bills. About 90% of bonds are in book-entry form in the Canadian Depository for Securities. Bills are in bearer paper form.		Canadian savings bonds are sold and the outstanding stock is also repriced each October. They are puttable at any time with accrued interest. Fees are paid for sale and processing of Canada Savings Bonds.
Marketable government bonds are sold only to a group of primary distributors, including commercial banks (5) and investment dealers (55). Primary distributors and all Canadian banks can bid for bills. The Bank of Canada conducts open market operations through 10 jobbers, a subset of the primary distributors. Most trading is over the counter, although some is done through securities exchanges.		
Bank dealers in government securities are regulated by the Canadian federal banking regulator. Other government securities dealers are regulated by provincial securities commissions, the key one of which is the Securities Commission of Ontario.		
Canada began selling index-linked bonds in November 1991.		

OECD Countries: Techniques to Sell Central Government Debt Internally

Denmark

General Comments	Auction	Other Sale Methods
Debt management is the responsibility of the Ministry of Finance, with the central bank as fiscal agent. The budget deficit has widened in recent years, and is estimated at US$6.5 billion equivalent in 1991. The government has a cash account with the central bank, which makes it possible for government borrowing to lead or lag the government's borrowing needs. Main types of securities issued to the public are: fixed and floating rate bonds (5–10 years); notes (1.1 to 2.2 years); and bills (3 and 6 months). Government securities are in book-entry form. In the domestic market there are no primary dealers or private underwriters for government bonds. Trading is over-the-counter and through the Copenhagen Stock Exchange. The government borrows in foreign currencies abroad for exchange stabilization purposes and uses underwriting syndicates to place the securities. Foreign investors participate in the domestic market. The central bank conducts open market operations through the Copenhagen Stock Exchange. Participants in the government securities market are regulated by the Supervisory Authority of Financial Affairs.	Domestically, bills are sold through *uniform-price auction* quarterly. Also, the central bank purchases them and sells them on tap. Banks and non-bank dealers that are connected to the Danish Securities Center, a private non-profit depository clearance and settlement system, can submit bids in auctions. There is no limit on awards to a single bidder. Trading is not permitted prior to the auction.	Treasury notes and bonds are sold on tap. New issues are sold by the central bank through the Stock Exchange. Banks and security brokers accept applications which are passed on to the Stock Exchange like orders for secondary market purchases. The National Bank, acting on behalf of the Treasury, may set new issue yield at its discretion during Stock Exchange sessions. A new note issue is usually sold on tap for nine months after original issue. There are no regulations as to the length of the tap period for bonds. There is a tax-related minimum interest rate rule, which may require closing a tap issue if market yields rise.

OECD Countries: Techniques to Sell Central Government Debt Internally

France

General Comments	Auction	Other Sale Methods
The Ministry of the Economy and Finance is responsible for debt management, and the Bank of France is its fiscal agent. Budget deficits widened in the 1980s, and the deficit amounted to US$18.4 billion equivalent in 1990. The Bank of France does not lend directly to the government. The Treasury has selected 15 primary dealers (SVTs) that are responsible for bidding in auctions, making markets, and providing screen quotations to the public. There are also 2 reporting dealers (CVTs). The primary dealers established an interdealer broker in 1987; only SVTs and CVTs have access to it. The Bank of France executes open market operations through a group of 26 interbank market agents that are selected separately by the Bank. All marketable securities are in book-entry form. Participants in Treasury auctions must have an account at the Bank of France or bid through an institution that has an account at the Bank of France. Secondary market trading is over the counter. The government does not pay commissions to purchasers of marketable securities. Bank participants in the government securities market are regulated by the Banking Commission. The Stock Exchange Operations Commission supervises other participants in the government securities market.	*Multiple-price auctions* are used to sell coupon securities which pay interest annually and principal at maturity. The "fungible" OAT bond, which is the most important security from the standpoints of new issues and trading, matures in 4–30 years and is reopened in new tranches to increase the size of each issue and enhance liquidity. Until midday the day after an auction, each SVT is permitted to submit noncompetitive bids for the most recently auctioned OAT bond at the auction average price in an amount up to 30% of its average awards in the previous 3 OAT bond auctions. The minimum purchase in the auction is US$9.8 million equivalent. The Treasury also auctions 2-year and 5-year fixed rate bonds in a minimum of US$196,000 equivalent. *Multiple-rate auctions* are used to sell short-term bills (maturing in 13, 26, and 52 weeks) issued at a discount. The minimum purchase amount in the auction is US$196,000 equivalent. When-issued trading begins when a security is announced.	There are US$5.9 billion equivalent of 5-year nonmarketable savings bonds outstanding. No effort is made to promote sales of savings bonds.

OECD Countries: Techniques to Sell Central Government Debt Internally

Germany

General Comments	Auction	Other Sale Methods
Ministry of Finance is the issuer and Bundesbank is its fiscal agent. German budget deficits have been widening in recent years, and in FY 1991 is estimated at US$40.0 billion equivalent. Temporary cash advances of up to US$4 billion equivalent are regularly made from the Bundesbank to the government.	Medium-term notes, mostly with 4 years to maturity, have been sold in *multiple-price auctions* since May 1991. A portion of each sale of Bunds has been auctioned since 1990. When-issued trading begins with the announcement of an auction. There is no limit on awards to any one entity. There is no commission paid to entities that are awarded securities in an auction.	Bunds usually have 10 years to maturity. Since July 1990, Bunds have been sold in 3-part sales: (1) negotiated through syndicate, 32%; (2) *multiple-price auctions*, 39%; and (3) Bundesbank market-tending portion, 29%, distributed when the price is favorable to the government. Syndicate allocations have been based on auction awards since October 1991. Commissions are paid to the syndicate for the underwritten portion of securities and those sold on tap.
The most important debt instruments are longer term bonds, called Bunds, and 5-year special notes. Very little financing is done in short-term maturities under one year. All new public debt is in book-entry form.		5-year special notes are issued on tap only to individuals and charitable organizations; when an issue is completed, it is traded in the secondary market.
A 110-member consortium of banks (including 49 affiliated with foreign banks) comprise the syndicate for negotiated placements and the eligible bidders in auctions. Consortium members are selected by the Bundesbank, acting as MOF's agent. The consortium members are also used by the Bundesbank to execute open market operations and to sell government securities on tap. Noncompetitive bidding is through consortium members.		Private placements of short-term paper have been used in the past, but were not done in 1991.
Public debt securities are traded on stock exchanges. The Federal Banking Supervisory Office licenses all entities that trade securities for the accounts of third parties. The eight regional stock exchanges, which are under the supervision of the state (Laender) governments, are SROs and have broad authority to regulate market participants and trading.		

OECD Countries: Techniques to Sell Central Government Debt Internally

Italy

General Comments	Auction	Other Sale Methods
The Treasury Ministry is responsible for debt management and the Bank of Italy is its fiscal agent. Italian budget deficits widened in the 1980s, and the deficit was the equivalent of US$128.4 billion in 1990. The government may borrow directly from the Bank of Italy. Only 4% of the public debt is foreign-owned.	Short-term bills denominated in lire are auctioned in *multiple-price auctions*. The Treasury sets no minimum acceptable price for *multiple-price auctions*. A set amount is reserved for noncompetitive awards. Treasury bills denominated in ECU are sold in *uniform-yield auctions*. Treasury bonds in lire and ECU maturing in 5 to 10 years are sold in *uniform-price auctions*. The government sets the maximum acceptable yield (minimum price) in *uniform yield/price auctions*.	About 9% of the public debt is in the form of small investor savings certificates and deposits in the Post Office System. Once a significant contributor to public financing, this System has declined in importance in recent years.
The government issues: short-term Treasury bills in lire and in ECU; medium and long-term variable and fixed rate bonds in lire and ECU. Short-term bills and longer term bonds indexed to short-term rates account for over 70% of the public debt. The longer maturity is 10 years. More than 90% of marketable government securities are in book-entry form through the Central Depository System run by the Bank of Italy.	Trading begins when new security issues are announced by the Treasury. Minimum competitive bids in all auctions are US$88,550 equivalent of lire or US$73,350 equivalent ECU. While there is no cap on the value of awards, no entity may submit more than 5 bids per auction.	
Most trading is on a wholesale screen-based market, whose participants are regulated by the Bank of Italy. There are 23 primary dealers selected by the Bank of Italy, which uses them together with other market participants to execute open market operations.	Noncompetitive bids are not accepted in uniform price/yield auctions. Participation in the auction is limited to banks, credit institutions, insurance and financial companies and stockbrokers.	
Membership in the screen-based market is voluntary. There are entities acting as dealers that are not subject to any regulatory regime.		

OECD Countries: Techniques to Sell Central Government Debt Internally

Japan

General Comments	Auction	Other Sale Methods
The Ministry of Finance is responsible for debt management and the Bank of Japan is its fiscal agent. Budget deficits have been declining since the mid 1980s. The 1990 deficit was US$22.5 billion equivalent. The Japanese government bond market is the second largest in the world. Most trading is in an OTC market, though some transactions are on the eight stock exchanges. About one-third of OTC trading volume is done through one brokers' broker, which is owned by its members. MOF sells short-term bills and intermediate- and long-term bonds. Monthly sales of 10-year bonds account for 80% of government debt outstanding and are the most actively traded issues in the secondary market. All marketable Japanese bonds are in book-entry form. There are no firms designated as primary dealers, although the market and the underwriting group are dominated by several large participants. The Bank of Japan uses several brokers, which are not part of the underwriting syndicate, as intermediaries to execute open market operations. The government securities market is regulated by the Ministry of Finance.	*Multiple-price auctions* are used for securities maturing in 2, 3, and 6 months and 2, 3, 4, and 20 years. When-issued trading is illegal at any price prior to the auction and is illegal at a discount in the immediate post-auction period. For 10-year bonds, 60% are awarded in *multiple-price auctions* and 40% are distributed through an 833-member syndicate (includes 675 banks and 158 securities firms). Awards are limited to 30% of amount auctioned; thus, 18% of the total of a 10-year. The government pays commissions to purchasers in the auction and to the underwriting syndicate.	The remaining 40% of each 10-year bond is sold through the syndicate, which obtains the bonds at the average of accepted competitive tenders. 5-year bonds are placed fully through the underwriting syndicate, but comprise only a small proportion of total issues. Government compensation bonds to war-surviving families. Such nonmarketable bonds account for only about 1% of government bonds outstanding.

OECD Countries: Techniques to Sell Central Government Debt Internally

Netherlands

General Comments	Auction	Other Sale Methods
The Ministry of Finance is responsible for debt management and the central bank is its fiscal agent. Budget deficits have been declining since the mid 1980s. The deficit amounted to US$12.8 billion equivalent in FY 1991. The central bank may lend temporarily directly to the government in limited amounts. It also purchases government securities through open market operations. The MOF often purchases and sells government bonds to stabilize prices. Bonds maturing in 10 years accounted for 75% of MOF borrowing in 1990/91. Short-term bills were not sold in 1990/91. Subscriptions on original issue are limited exclusively to members of the Amsterdam Stock Exchange (banks and securities broker/dealers). Foreign investors hold 23% of Netherlands government securities. MOF emphasizes debt lengthening and does not borrow in foreign currencies or sell indexed or variable rate securities. Government securities are available in bearer definitive and registered forms. There are no primary dealers. The market for government securities is regulated by the Amsterdam Stock Exchange.	During the late 1980s through early 1991, MOF sold bonds in *multiple-yield auctions*. Since March 1991, however, government bonds have been sold on tap exclusively.	Bonds are all sold on tap. An issue stays open for one or two weeks. There may be when-issued trading before the issue is closed. The government may change the price during the tap period. No fees are paid by MOF to subscribers to tap issues. The minimum purchase amount is US$1.5 million equivalent. Private placements of long-term bonds account for most of the rest of government borrowing. Intermediaries in private placements receive fees from the MOF. Nonmarketable savings bonds are not offered by the government.

OECD Countries: Techniques to Sell Central Government Debt Internally

New Zealand

General Comments	Auction	Other Sale Methods
The Treasury is responsible for debt management and the Reserve Bank of New Zealand is its fiscal agent for internal borrowing. New Zealand had surpluses in FYs 1988–90 and a surplus of US$1.0 billion equivalent in 1991. Nearly half of the debt is owned by foreign investors. The government may borrow from RBNZ.	All marketable securities are sold in *multiple-yield auctions*. There is no limit on the proportion of an auction that can be purchased by any bidder. When-issued trading begins when a security is announced. No commissions are paid by the Treasury to purchasers in auctions. The government does not set a maximum acceptable yield.	Nonmarketable Kiwi bonds are sold to retail investors on tap. They are puttable at a discount, and the minimum purchase is US$600 equivalent. Fees are paid to institutions that handle Kiwi bond transactions. Kiwi bonds account for 3% of internal public debt.
Securities include short-term bills (32% of internal public debt) and government stock maturing in up to 10 years (57% of internal public debt). Outstanding issues are reopened to foster market liquidity.		
All bidders in auctions must be registered with the RBNZ or bid through an entity that is registered. The RBNZ conducts open market operations, including issuing 63-day RBNZ bills, through dealers that are registered with RBNZ as counterparties for open market operations. There are no primary dealers. All marketable debt is in book-entry form. Tenders in auctions are in paper form.		
There is no specific regulation of the government securities market. The RBNZ provides prudential regulation of banks.		

OECD Countries: Techniques to Sell Central Government Debt Internally

Switzerland

General Comments	Auction	Other Sale Methods
The Federal Department of Finance is responsible for debt management and Swiss National Bank is its fiscal agent. The Swiss central government borrows little and the public debt is small. Most governmental activity is carried out by the cantons, or states. Foreign participation in the government securities market is small. The amount is unknown, because all securities are in bearer form.	Swiss Debt Register Claims maturing in 3 and 6 months are issued every two weeks through *uniform-price auctions*. Long-term bonds, which account for the majority of the debt, are sold from time to time through *uniform-price auctions*. No tender price limits are applied. The government gives a rough indication of the desired issue amount.	Bills usually with maturities of 3 to 24 months are sold on a discount basis only to commercial banks. The price is set by the central bank and banks subscribe for a fixed overall amount. Government notes with maturities of 3 to 10 years are sold through private placements on a commission basis.
There are no primary dealers. The Swiss central bank rarely conducts open market operations.	All categories of investors are authorized to participate in auctions. There are no limits on the amount that can be awarded to any bidder in an auction. When-issued trading is permitted prior to the auction. Noncompetitive bids are accepted, and usually are small relative to the size of auctions.	
The government issues a variety of securities including 3- and 6-month bills, medium-term notes and long-term bonds.		
Trading is over-the-counter and through regional stock exchanges. There is no comprehensive government securities regulation. Banks are subject to the supervision of the Federal Banking Commission. The cantons regulate the regional stock exchanges. The cantons of Zurich and Basle, where the most important financial centers are located, license over-the-counter market participants as well as exchange participants.		

OECD Countries: Techniques to Sell Central Government Debt Internally

United Kingdom

General Comments	Auction	Other Sale Methods
The Treasury works closely with the Bank of England (fiscal agent) to develop debt management policy. The budget has been in surplus in recent years, with the surplus in 1991 US$960 million equivalent. The government borrows directly from the Bank of England. Bidding in gilt auctions is open to all investors, either on a competitive basis (minimum of US$960,000 equivalent) or noncompetitive basis (bids from US$1,920 to $960,000 equivalent). The bulk of bids are submitted by primary dealers (18 gilt-edged market makers) either on behalf of customers or for their own account. The GEMMs ensure the liquidity of the secondary market by quoting continuous two-way prices in all gilts in all trading conditions; they have a direct dealing relationship with the Bank of England and exclusive access to interdealer brokers and gilt borrowing facilities. Participants in the gilt-edged market are subject to prudential supervision of the Bank of England. The Securities Investment Board, which is under the Department of Trade and Industry, oversees protection of investors.	*Multiple-price auctions* are used for bills and longer-term debt (gilts). When-issued trading is allowed, beginning with the announcement of auction details. Bank of England has discretion not to allot more than 25% of the amount offered to an individual bidder if to do so would be likely to lead to market price distortion. The Bank of England does not set a minimum price, but securities may not be allotted if the price is unacceptably low. *Minimum price tender* sales are used to sell gilts; bidding is open to all investors. The minimum price is set in advance for fixed-rate gilts. Gilts are allotted at a common price, either minimum price or price at which all gilts offered are sold (if higher). Tenders for index-linked stocks normally have no minimum price, but authorities do not usually allot at a price that they perceive to be below market. Any unsold gilts are bought by the Bank of England for sale on tap to GEMMs.	Bank of England buys gilts that remain unsold from minimum price tender sales; these are subsequently sold on tap to the GEMMs. Guiding principle is that the Bank refrains from selling gilts into a falling market. There usually is a "fallow period" following an auction during which additional amounts are not sold on tap. Gilts can be issued and placed directly with the Bank of England for sale to the GEMMs, in exactly the same way as above. Usually, in the form of *tranchettes* (small additional amounts of existing stocks), but sometimes in larger amounts. Nonmarketable savings instruments are sold to individual investors through Post Offices.

Appendix B

Summary of the Proposed Buy-Back Regulations

The following is a summary of the more important features of the proposed buy-back regulations. These proposed rules are available at the *Federal Register* and at the Bureau of the Public Debt's website at www.publicdebt.treas.gov. The proposed regulations call for a 60-day comment period.

Type of offers: Competitive offers only, no noncompetitives.

Type of operation: A "reverse auction," with a multiple-price process in which successful offerors receive the price at which they offered securities.

Buy-back operation announcement: Treasury would issue a press release, which would include the eligible securities and the total amount of the buyback. Treasury would have the right to buy back less than this amount.

Eligible submitters: Only primary dealers would be allowed to submit offers. This limitation would enable use of FRB New York's open market functionality. Other holders of eligible securities could participate through offers submitted by a primary dealer.

Offer format: On basis of price, to three decimals, in 32nds. For example, 102.172. (third decimal represents 8ths of a 32nd).

Maximum number of offers per security: No limit.

Maximum amount of offers accepted from a submitter: No limit. In other words, no "35 percent" type of limit.

Announcement of results: Treasury would issue a press release. For each security we buy back, the press release would provide the amounts offered and accepted, the highest price accepted, and the remaining privately held amount outstanding. FRB New York would transmit results messages to primary dealers informing them only of the acceptance of the offers they submitted.

Settlement: On the day after the buy-back operation, successful submitters would transfer securities against payment via Fedwire. Definitive securities also eligible for delivery.

Location of rule: 31 CFR Part 375 (a new part).

Source: U.S. Treasury.

Treasury Announces Debt Buyback Operation

On August 17, 2000, the Treasury will buy back up to $1,500 million par of its outstanding issues that mature between November 2021 and November 2026. Treasury reserves the right to accept less than the announced amount.

This debt buyback (redemption) operation will be conducted by Treasury's Fiscal Agent, the Federal Reserve Bank of New York, using its Open Market operations system. Only institutions that the Federal Reserve Bank of New York has approved to conduct Open Market transactions may submit offers on behalf of themselves and their customers. Offers at the highest accepted price for a particular issue may be accepted on a prorated basis, rounded up to the next $100,000. As a result of this rounding, the Treasury may buy back an amount slightly larger than the one announced above.

This debt buyback operation is governed by the terms and conditions set forth in 31 CFR Part 375 and this announcement.

The debt buyback operation regulations are available on the Bureau of the Public Debt's website at www.publicdebt.treas.gov.

Details about the operation and each of the eligible issues are given in the attached highlights.

Highlights of Treasury Debt Buyback Operation (August 16, 2000)

Par amount to be bought back . . . . Up to $1,500 million
Operation date . . . . August 17, 2000
Operation close time . . . . 11:00 A.M. eastern daylight saving time
Settlement date . . . . August 21, 2000
Minimum par offer amount $100,000
Multiples of par $100,000
Format for offers . . . . Expressed in terms of price per $100 of par with three decimals. The first two decimals represent fractional 32nds of a dollar. The third decimal represents eighths of a 32nd of a dollar, and must be a 0, 2, 4, or 6.
Delivery instructions . . . . ABA Number 021001208 FRB NYC/CUST

Treasury Issues Eligible for Debt Buyback Operation (In Millions)

Coupon Rate (%)	Maturity Date	CUSIP Number	Par Amount Outstanding*	Par Amount Privately Held*	Par Amount Held as STRIPS**
8.000	11/15/2021	912810 EL 8	32,267	29,295	18,708
7.250	08/15/2022	912810 EM 6	10,314	9,468	1,032
7.625	11/15/2022	912810 EN 4	9,530	7,929	5,549
7.125	02/15/2023	912810 EP 9	17,850	15,221	7,270
6.250	08/15/2023	912810 EQ 7	22,694	21,207	4,734
7.500	11/15/2024	912810 ES 3	11,100	9,569	7,222
7.625	02/15/2025	912810 ET 1	11,550	10,394	8,077
6.875	08/15/2025	912810 EV 6	12,327	10,555	4,768
6.000	02/15/2026	912810 EW 4	12,905	11,790	1,755
6.750	08/15/2026	912810 EX 2	10,894	9,280	3,023
6.500	11/15/2026	912810 EY 0	11,493	9,803	3,960
		Total	162,924	144,511	66,098

*Par amounts are as of August 15, 2000.

**Par amounts are as of August 14, 2000.

The difference between the par amount outstanding and the par amount privately held is the par amount of those issues held by the Federal Reserve System.

(continued)

Treasury Debt Buyback Operation Results (August 17, 2000)

Today, Treasury completed a debt buyback (redemption) operation for $1,500 million par of its outstanding issues. A total of 11 issues maturing between November 2021 and November 2026 were eligible for this operation. The settlement date for this operation will be August 21, 2000. Summary results of this operation are presented below.

	(amounts in millions)
Offers Received (Par Amount):	$6,879
Offers Accepted (Par Amount):	1,500
Total Price Paid for Issues	
(Less Accrued Interest):	1,760
Number of Issues Eligible:	
For Operation:	11
For Which Offers were Accepted:	8
Weighted Average Yield	
of all Accepted Offers (%):	5.995
Weighted Average Maturity	
for all Accepted Securities (in years):	23.1

Details for each issue accompany this release.

Treasury Debt Buyback Operation Results (August 17, 2000)
(Amounts in Millions, Prices in Decimals)

TABLE I

Coupon Rate (%)	Maturity Date	Par Amount Offered	Par Amount Accepted	Highest Accepted Price	Weighted Average Accepted Price
8.000	11/15/2021	1,234	291	123.593	123.574
7.250	08/15/2022	378	25	114.937	114.937
7.625	11/15/2022	393	235	119.718	119.700
7.125	02/15/2023	503	280	113.781	113.762
6.250	08/15/2023	546	25	103.203	103.200
7.500	11/15/2024	433	330	119.312	119.281
7.625	02/15/2025	503	14	121.031	120.986
6.875	08/15/2025	695	300	111.687	111.671
6.000	02/15/2026	463	0	N/A	N/A
6.750	08/15/2026	1,108	0	N/A	N/A
6.500	11/15/2026	623	0	N/A	N/A

TABLE II

Coupon Rate (%)	Maturity Date	CUSIP Number	Lowest Accepted Yield	Weighted Average Accepted Yield	Par Amount Privately Held*
8.000	11/15/2021	912810EL8	6.016	6.017	29,004
7.250	08/15/2022	912810EM6	6.016	6.016	9,443
7.625	11/15/2022	912810EN4	6.005	6.007	7,694
7.125	02/15/2023	912810EP9	6.000	6.002	14,941
6.250	08/15/2023	912810EQ7	5.991	5.991	21,182
7.500	11/15/2024	912810ES3	5.980	5.982	9,239
7.625	02/15/2025	912810ET1	5.978	5.982	10,380
6.875	08/15/2025	912810EV6	5.969	5.970	10,255
6.000	02/15/2026	912810EW4	N/A	N/A	11,790
6.750	08/15/2026	912810EX2	N/A	N/A	9,280
6.500	11/15/2026	912810EY0	N/A	N/A	9,803

Total Par Amount Offered: 6,879

Total Par Amount Accepted: 1,500

Note: Due to rounding, details may not add to totals.

*Amount outstanding after operation. Calculated using amounts reported on announcement.

Chapter 4

Bond Mathematics

Chapter Objectives

The purpose of this chapter is to lay the mathematical foundations necessary for understanding the instruments and strategies in fixed-income markets. Chapter 4 will help the reader to understand and answer the following questions.

- What are the different methods used to compound cash flows? How do they affect the present and future values?
- What are annuities and perpetuities?
- What is the concept of yield? In particular,
  1. what is yield to maturity?
  2. what is yield to call?
  3. what is current yield?
  4. what is a yield curve?
- What are the different methods used to measure risk? In particular,
  1. what is the price value of a basis point (PVBP) or the dollar value of an 01 (DV01)?
  2. what is Macaulay duration?
  3. what is modified duration?
  4. how should duration be interpreted?
  5. what is convexity?
- How does one hedge interest rate risk?
- How does one apply bond mathematics to trading and risk management to perform
  1. spread trades?
  2. butterfly trades?
- How to use EXCEL to implement bond mathematics functions, such as Price, Yield, Duration, etc.

INTRODUCTION

The analysis of risk and return of fixed-income securities depends extensively on the concept of discounting and, therefore, on the concept of the time value of money. Fixed-income securities are quoted in terms of their yields. The yield of a security is a concept that is closely related to its internal rate of return. There are many measures of yields discussed in this chapter.

TABLE 4-1

Benchmark Treasury
Securities

Maturity	Quoted Price
2	100.02
3	100.20
5	101.23
10	98.25
30	99.01

Many risk measures have been developed for assessing the risk of fixed-income securities and portfolios. Such measures include the price value of a basis point (PVBP) or dollar value of an 01 (DV01), Macaulay duration, modified duration, and convexity. These measures are fully developed and illustrated in this chapter. In addition, the analysis of fixed-income securities requires a thorough understanding of the basics of yield curve. These include the concepts of the spot rates of interest, the forward rates of interest, and the par bond yield curve; these concepts will be discussed in Chapter 5.

It is customary in the fixed-income markets to quote values in terms of yields instead of prices. The relationship between prices and yields and the assumptions implicit in the price-yield relationship are very important. We develop these ideas in stages in this chapter.

The basics of time value of money and discounting are quite important in understanding how fixed-income securities are valued. Much of the ideas are quite basic and are typically covered in an introductory course in finance. Readers interested in a self-contained review of the basic concepts should consult Appendix A at the end of this chapter where we review the time value concepts and illustrate the ideas with many worked-out examples.

Although the process of quoting prices in decimals has begun in the stock market, the prices in fixed-income securities markets are not always quoted in decimals. Treasury prices are quoted in 32nds.

For example, recently the benchmark Treasury securities were quoted as shown in Table 4-1 (in 32nds).

We need to convert prices to decimals to perform financial calculations. The prices that are quoted in 32nds (or any other fraction) can be converted to decimals using the EXCEL function shown next. In a similar manner, we can report a computed price (which will typically be in decimals) into 32nds as shown in Figure 4-1.

COMPUTING YIELDS IN PRACTICE

In practice, we rarely encounter securities with round coupon payments. Before discussing yield calculations in practice, let us review the market conventions and terminology.

FIGURE 4-1   *Price Conventions*

	A	B	C	D	E	F	G	H
1								
2								
3								
4				**EXCEL function to compute prices in decimals**				
5								
6			Maturity	Quoted	Price			
7				Price	(In Decimals)		=DOLLARDE(D9,32)	
8			2	100.02	100.06250			
9			3	100.20	100.62500			
10			5	101.23	101.71875			
11			10	98.15	98.46875			
12			30	99.01	99.03125			
13								
14								
15								
16								
17								
18								
19								

	A	B	C	D	E	F	G	H	I
19									
20									
21									
22									
23				**EXCEL function to quote prices in 32nds**					
24									
25									
26									
27				Maturity	Computed	Quoted			
28					Price	Prices		=DOLLARFR(E30,32)	
29				2	100.25	100.08			
30				3	100.13	100.04			
31				5	98.75	98.24			
32				10	99.02	99.01			
33				30	99.05	99.02			
34									
35									
36									
37									
38									
39									

Debt contracts, such as Treasury bonds, corporate medium-term notes, and municipal bonds, promise to pay periodically a fixed-interest payment, known as the coupon of the security. For example, in Table 4-2 the first Treasury note has a coupon of 4.25%. T-notes have a fixed date, the maturity date, on which they expire; the T-note with the 4.25% coupon matured on August 31, 1994. On the maturity date, T-notes pay the principal amount plus the last coupon payment. The simplest of debt

TABLE 4-2   *Fixed-Income Securities Quotes*

Description	Coupon	Maturity	Price	Yield
Three-month T-bill	NA	12/10/1992	99.267	2.900%
Six-month T-bill	NA	03/11/1993	98.521	2.925%
One-year T-bill	NA	08/26/1993	97.069	3.015%
Two-year T-note	4.25%	08/31/1994	$100\frac{27}{32}$	3.801%
Three-year T-note	4.625%	08/15/1995	$100\frac{31}{32}$	4.269%
Five-year T-note	5.625%	08/31/1997	$101\frac{28}{32}$	5.188%
Seven-year T-note	6.375%	07/15/1999	$103\frac{15}{32}$	5.753%
Ten-year T-note	6.375%	08/15/2002	$100\frac{20}{32}$	6.289%
Thirty-year T-bond	7.25%	08/15/2022	$100\frac{13}{32}$	7.216%
Nineteen-year T-bond	14.00%	11/15/2011	$164\frac{18}{32}$	7.565%

Source: Federal Reserve Bank of New York.

contracts (e.g., noncallable Treasury notes and bonds or noncallable corporate bonds) will only have a periodic fixed coupon plus the principal payment at maturity. Often, however, debt contracts have explicit contractual provisions that render the timing of their cash flows uncertain. For example, some Treasury bonds and many corporate bonds are issued with call features that give the issuer the right to call the securities at prices that are set at issuance. Since the issuer has a greater incentive to call the issue when the interest rates go down, the timing of the cash flows of these securities cannot be predicted with certainty.

Table 4-2 lists the quotes from the Treasury market for selected Treasury securities. The settlement date is September 10, 1992. It is useful to note the distinction between the quoted date, which is the date on which the prices are quoted, and the settlement date, which is the date on which the security and the prices (cash) exchange hands. In all financial calculations, it is the settlement date that is relevant. Typically, the settlement date follows the quoted date by a day or two. The price quotes for the T-bills are in decimals and the yields in basis points. (The quoted yields for T-bills are discount yields, which will be described shortly.) The table gives the prices and yields of three-month, six-month, and one-year T-bills; and the prices and yields of the most recently auctioned T-notes and T-bonds. The prices are quoted in $\frac{1}{32}$. The last entry provides the price and the yield of a callable Treasury bond that matures on November 15, 2011, but can be called at par starting November 15, 2006, on any coupon date.

None of the securities in Table 4-2 has credit risk. They all carry inflation risk, as their payoffs are in nominal currency. With the exception of the 14% T-bond, none of the securities has timing risk. All the T-notes and T-bonds pay intermediate coupons, so the holder may face some risk of reinvestment; this risk arises because the buyer of the bond will not know the rate at which future coupons can be reinvested.

Price and Yields of Treasuries

In practice, the return measure used extensively is yield to maturity. Current yield, yield to call, and yield to worst are also used. To provide a systematic account of these measures, we start with the concept of invoice price of a security.

Invoice price is the price that the buyer of a security has to pay.

Treasury bills are quoted on a discount yield basis. The procedure for obtaining the invoice price from discount quotes is illustrated in Example 4-1.

Example 4-1:

The quotations for settlement on December 14, 1990, for U.S. Treasury bills maturing on May 23, 1991, are shown below.

Quote Date	Bid d	Ask d	Yield
12/14/90	6.78	6.76	7.06

A time line showing the settlement date (SD) and the maturity date (MD) is shown next.

$$\begin{array}{ccc} SD & & MD \\ | \leftarrow & n \text{ days} & \rightarrow | \end{array}$$

The invoice price, P, using the bid discount yield is then calculated as

$$P = 100 \times \left[1 - \frac{n \times d}{360} \right]$$

where the T-bill has n days remaining from the settlement date to maturity and has a discount yield d per \$100 face amount, or

$$P = 100 \times \left[1 - \frac{160 \times 0.0678}{360} \right] = 96.98667$$

$P = 96.98667$.

P is a percentage of the par amount of the Treasury bill. T-bills are traded in \$1 million par, so that the invoice price per million will be \$969,867. (Smaller amounts can also be traded.)

We can use the EXCEL function TBILLPRICE to compute the price of a T-bill given its discount yield as shown in Figure 4-2.

For T-notes and T-bonds, the quoted price or **flat price** is typically not the invoice price. To arrive at the invoice price we add the accrued interest to the flat price. The **accrued interest** is the coupon income that accrues from the last coupon date to the settlement date of the transaction. Example 4-2 illustrates this.

FIGURE 4-2 *EXCEL Function for T-Bill Price*

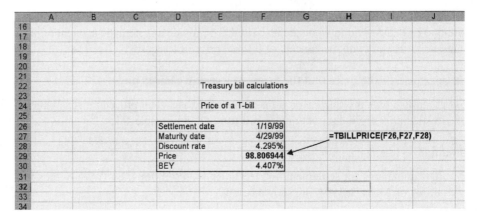

Example 4-2:

The quotations for the December 17, 1991, settlement of a U.S. Treasury bond with an 8% coupon and a maturity date of November 15, 2021, follow. Recall that the price quotations are in $\frac{1}{32}$.

Quote Date	Bid	Ask	Yield
12/17/91	102.29	102.31	7.74

First, we compute the accrued interest. To do this, we determine the last coupon date (LCD), which in this case is November 15, 1991. This is also referred to as previous coupon date (PCD). The next coupon date (NCD) is May 15, 1992. So, the number of days between the NCD and the LCD is 182 days. The number of days between the last coupon date and the settlement date, December 17, 1991, is 32 days. The accrued interest is

$$ai_t = \frac{32}{182} \times \frac{1}{2} \times 8 = 0.7032967.$$

The quoted bid price is $102 + \frac{29}{32} = 102.90625$. Then the invoice price on the bid side is $102.90625 + 0.7032967 = 103.60955$. This is the price at which the owner of the security will be able to sell it. The purchase price will be the quoted ask price plus the accrued interest, $102.96875 + 0.7032967 = 103.6720467$.

Once again, these prices are a percentage of the principal amount, which is usually $1 million. The purchase price per million is, therefore, $1,036,720.47, and the selling price is $1,036,095.47.

We work out another example in which several EXCEL functions are used to compute the accrued interest in Figure 4-3.

FIGURE 4-3   *EXCEL Function for Accrued Interest*

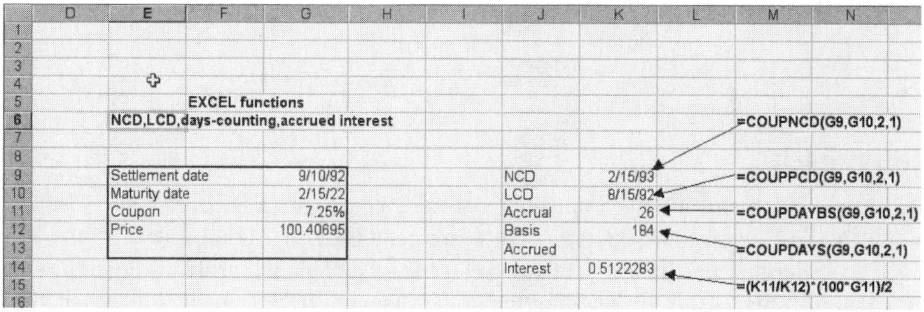

We could also have used the approximation of round number of coupons $N = 60$ to compute the price of the bond using Equation 4.36 as

$$P = \sum_{j=1}^{60} \frac{\frac{8}{2}}{\left(1 + \frac{0.0774}{2}\right)^j} + \frac{100}{\left(1 + \frac{0.0774}{2}\right)^{60}}$$

$$= \frac{8}{0.0774} + \frac{\left(100 - \frac{8}{0.0774}\right)}{\left(1 + \frac{0.0774}{2}\right)^{60}} = 1,030,149.62.$$

The calculations assume a million dollar par value. The yield of a noncallable security is similar to the internal rate of return. The conventions used in the securities industry differ depending on the segment of the fixed-income securities market (Treasury, agencies, MBS, etc.) and on the country (in the United States or the markets abroad). We will illustrate the concept using the domestic Treasury market. First, we consider Treasury bills.

Yield of a T-Bill with $n < 182$ Days:

Consider the same T-bill as in Example 4-1. The **discount yield** is

$$d = \frac{(100 - P)}{100} \times \frac{360}{n}$$

where the T-bill has n days remaining from the settlement date to maturity and sells at a price of P per \$100 face amount. Note that the discount yield has two shortcomings. It uses 360 days per year and it divides the dollar gain (or discount), $100 - P$, by 100. The **bond equivalent yield** or BEY corrects these two shortcomings. For a T-bill with a maturity of less than 182 days, the BEY is calculated as

$$\mathrm{BEY} = \frac{(100 - P)}{P} \times \frac{365}{n}. \tag{4.1}$$

Using this formula, we can identify a simple relation between the discount yield d that traders quote and the BEY,

$$\text{BEY} = \frac{365d}{360 - dn}.$$

Example 4-3:

Thus, using the bid discount quote of 6.78%, we get a BEY of 7.0877%; and using the ask discount quote of 6.76%, we get a BEY of 7.0662%.

Note that the BEY is always greater than d. This is hardly surprising given that we obtain BEY by dividing the dollar discount by P (which is less than 100) and multiplying the result by 365 (which is more than 360). The reported BEY is based on the ask discount quotes. In measuring the return of a T-bill, it is more meaningful to use the BEY than d.

Yield of a T-Bill with $n > 182$ Days:

Equation 4.1 gives the formula for the BEY of a T-bill maturing in fewer than 182 days. When a T-bill has more than six months to maturity, the calculation must reflect the fact that a T-bill does not pay interest, whereas a T-note or T-bond will pay a semiannual interest. The industry convention is to assume that an interest y is paid after six months and that it is possible to reinvest this interest, that is,

$$P\left(1 + \frac{y}{2}\right) + \frac{y}{365}\left(n - \frac{365}{2}\right)\left(1 + \frac{y}{2}\right)P = 100.$$

Solving for y gives the BEY for T-bills with a maturity of more than 182 days as

$$\text{BEY} = \frac{\frac{-2 \times n}{365} + 2\sqrt{\left(\frac{n}{365}\right)^2 - \left(\frac{2 \times n}{365} - 1\right) \times \left(1 - \frac{100}{P}\right)}}{\frac{2 \times n}{365} - 1}. \tag{4.2}$$

Example 4-4:

The quotations for the April 18, 1991, settlement of a U.S. Treasury bill maturing on April 9, 1992, are shown below.

Quote Date	Bid d	Ask d	Yield
4/18/91	5.94	5.92	6.29

Note that $n = 357$ days and the ask discount yield is $d = 0.0592$. First, we calculate the price P as

$$P = 100 \times \left[1 - \frac{357 \times 0.0592}{360} \right] = 94.1293.$$

Substituting this price in Equation (4.2), the formula for the BEY, gives

$$\text{BEY} = \frac{\frac{-2 \times 357}{365} + 2\sqrt{\left(\frac{357}{365}\right)^2 - \left(\frac{2 \times 357}{365} - 1\right) \times \left(1 - \frac{100}{94.1293}\right)}}{\frac{2 \times 357}{365} - 1}.$$

BEY = 6.2802%.

In Figure 4-4, we provide both the discount yields and the bond equivalent yields of a Treasury bill with a May 10, 1993 settlement. Notice that the BEY is always higher than the discount yield and that the difference between these two measures increases with maturity. Table 4-3 provides the T-bill discount yields and BEYs. The on-the-run (benchmark issues) issues are in bold for ready reference. Note that the bid-offer spreads for the bills vary from 2 to 4 basis points.

The EXCEL function TBILLEQ shown in Figure 4-5 calculates the bond equivalent yield of a T-bill. We illustrate this with another example.

We now turn to Treasury coupon issues that are in their final coupon period. Such Treasury issues are known as **short governments** in the industry. As we showed in Example 4-2, the accrued interest is computed using the number of days x between the last coupon date (LCD) and the next coupon date (NCD). Let z be the number of days

FIGURE 4-4   *T-Bill Discount Yield and BEY*

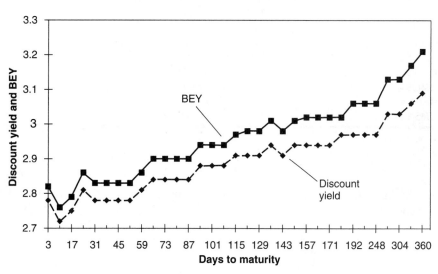

TABLE 4-3   *T-Bill Yield Curve for Settlement on May 10, 1993*

Maturity Date	Days to Maturity	Bid Yield	Ask Yield	BEY	Bid-Ask Spread (Basis Points)
05/13/93	3	2.82	2.78	2.82	4
05/20/93	10	2.74	2.72	2.76	2
05/27/93	17	2.79	2.75	2.79	4
06/03/93	24	2.83	2.81	2.86	2
06/10/93	31	2.8	2.78	2.83	2
06/17/93	38	2.82	2.78	2.83	4
06/24/93	45	2.81	2.78	2.83	3
07/01/93	52	2.82	2.78	2.83	4
07/08/93	59	2.85	2.81	2.86	4
07/15/93	66	2.87	2.84	2.9	3
07/22/93	73	2.88	2.84	2.9	4
07/29/93	80	2.87	2.84	2.9	3
08/05/93	**87**	**2.88**	**2.84**	**2.9**	**4**
08/12/93	94	2.9	2.88	2.94	2
08/19/93	101	2.91	2.88	2.94	3
08/26/93	108	2.92	2.88	2.94	4
09/02/93	115	2.93	2.91	2.97	2
09/09/93	122	2.94	2.91	2.98	3
09/16/93	129	2.95	2.91	2.98	4
09/23/93	136	2.96	2.94	3.01	2
09/30/93	143	2.94	2.91	2.98	3
10/07/93	150	2.97	2.94	3.01	3
10/14/93	157	2.97	2.94	3.02	3
10/21/93	164	2.98	2.94	3.02	4
10/28/93	171	2.97	2.94	3.02	3
11/04/93	**176**	**2.99**	**2.97**	**3.02**	**2**
11/18/93	192	3.01	2.97	3.06	4
12/16/93	220	3.01	2.97	3.06	4
01/13/94	248	3.01	2.97	3.06	4
02/10/94	276	3.05	3.03	3.13	2
03/10/94	304	3.06	3.03	3.13	3
04/07/94	332	3.09	3.06	3.17	3
05/05/94	**360**	**3.11**	**3.09**	**3.21**	**2**

Source: Bloomberg.

between the settlement date (SD) t and the next coupon date, and C be the annual dollar coupon.

$$
\begin{array}{ccc}
LCD & SD & NCD \\
 & |\leftarrow & z\ \text{days} \rightarrow| \\
|\rightarrow & x\ \text{days} & \rightarrow|
\end{array}
$$

FIGURE 4-5   *EXCEL Function for BEY*

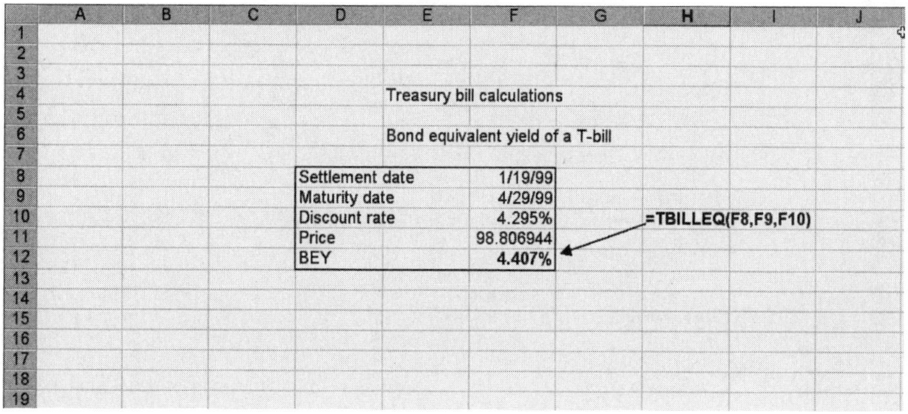

Then the accrued interest at the settlement date ai_t is

$$ai_t = C \times \frac{x - z}{2x}.$$ (4.3)

The invoice price P_t equals the flat price (quoted price) FP_t plus the accrued interest.

The total wealth obtained by selling this security at maturity is $100 + \frac{C}{2}$. The initial investment in the security is the full price paid at the settlement date t, P_t; hence, the rate of return is $\frac{100 + C/2}{P_t} - 1$. Note that this return is earned over a period of z days, so we could annualize the return as

$$\left(\frac{100 + \frac{C}{2}}{P_t} - 1 \right) \times \frac{365}{z}.$$

However, in practice, the yield to maturity of short governments is annualized as

$$y = \left(\frac{100 + \frac{C}{2}}{P_t} - 1 \right) \times \frac{2x}{z}.$$ (4.4)

Similarly, the invoice price is computed using the yield to maturity as

$$P_t = \left(\frac{100 + \frac{C}{2}}{1 + y \frac{z}{2x}} \right).$$ (4.5)

Example 4-5 illustrates how these formulae are applied to debt securities.

The flat price of a short government security can be determined by using the EXCEL function PRICEMAT. This is illustrated by Figure 4-6.

FIGURE 4-6   *EXCEL Function for Short Governments*

	D	E	F	G	H	I	J	K	L	M
5										
6										
7										
8										
9			Short government calculations							
10										
11			Price given yield			⇨				
12										
13			Settlement date		1/19/99					
14			Maturity date		1/31/99	=PRICEMAT(H13,H14,H15,H16,H17)				
15			Issue date		1/31/97					
16			Coupon		5%					
17			Yield		5.120%					
18			Price		99.9809577					
19			Quoted price		99.3139					
20										
21										
22										

Example 4-5:

The quotations for the July 18, 1991, settlement of a U.S. Treasury note with a coupon of 7.75% and a maturity date of November 15, 1991, follow.

Quote Date	Bid	Ask	Yield
07/18/91	100.19	100.21	5.81

In this example, $c = 7.75$, $x = 184$, $z = 120$, $x - z = (SD - LCD) = 64$, and $FP = 100\frac{19}{32}$. The accrued interest $ai_t = 7.75\frac{64}{2 \times 184} = 1.3478$. Thus, the invoice price $P_t = 100\frac{19}{32} + 1.3478 = 101.9415$. Using these in Equation 4.4 gives the yield to maturity

$$y = \left(\frac{100 + \frac{7.75}{2}}{101.9415} - 1 \right) \times \frac{2 \times 184}{120} = 5.816\%. \tag{4.6}$$

The yield of a short government can be determined by the EXCEL function YIELDMAT as shown in Figure 4-7.

The concept of yield to maturity that we have used so far can be extended to Treasury coupon issues with more than one coupon date remaining before the maturity date. Consider a Treasury bond that matures at date T. Let us assume that the settlement date is $t < T$ and that there are N coupon dates remaining. Let z be the number of days between the settlement date and the next coupon date, and x be the number of days between the last coupon date and the next coupon date. Then, given the invoice price P_t, the relation between P_t and y is

$$P_t = \left(\frac{100}{\left(1 + \frac{y}{2}\right)^{N-1+\frac{z}{x}}} \right) + \sum_{j=0}^{j=N-1} \frac{\frac{c}{2}}{\left(1 + \frac{y}{2}\right)^{j+\frac{z}{x}}} \tag{4.7}$$

FIGURE 4-7   *EXCEL Function for Short Governments*

	D	E	F	G	H	I	J	K	L	M
24										
25										
26										
27			Short government calculations							
28										
29			Yield given price							
30										
31			Settlement date		1/19/99		=YIELDMAT(H31,H32,H33,H34,H36)			
32			Maturity date		1/31/99					
33			Issue date		1/31/97					
34			Coupon		5%					
35			Yield		5.121%					
36			Price		99.9809375					
37			Quoted price		99.31					
38										
39										
40										
41										

We can use this formula to find the price P_t given the yield to maturity y or we can solve for y given the price P_t. Equation 4.36 is the price-yield relation for the special case of a round number of coupon payments remaining. Equation 4.7 pertains to the more frequently occurring case. Example 4-6 illustrates its application in determining the yield to maturity of a Treasury bond. As in Example 4-2, this example shows a situation in which the settlement date falls between two coupon dates.

Example 4-6:

The quotations for the January 9, 1992, settlement of a U.S. Treasury bond with a coupon of 8.00% and a maturity date of November 15, 2021, follow.

Quote Date	Bid	Ask	Yield
01/09/92	106.30	107.00	7.41

Typically, bond calculators, such as the HP-12C, are available to handle problems of this sort. Using the bid price, we calculate the invoice price as $P_t = 106 \frac{30}{32} +$ 1.20879 = 108.1463. Then using Equation 4.7, y = 7.418%. Using the ask price, we calculate the invoice price as P_t = 107 + 1.20879 = 108.20879. The yield corresponding to this price is y = 7.413%. Standard spreadsheet packages, such as EXCEL, have functions that calculate yield to maturity once all the other information has been provided.

EXCEL Applications

The prices and yields of government securities with more than one coupon remaining can be determined using the EXCEL functions as shown in Figure 4-8. In computing the yield, we should input the flat price or the clean price. The PRICE function returns the clean price or the flat price.

FIGURE 4-8   *EXCEL Bond Functions*

	D	E	F	G	H	I	J	K	L	M
44										
45										
46				Government bond calculations						
47										
48				Yield given price						
49										
50				Settlement date	1/19/99		=YIELD(H50,H51,H52,H54,100,2,1)			
51				Maturity date	8/15/28					
52				Coupon	5.500%					
53				Yield	**5.182%**					
54				Price	104.78125					
55				Quoted price	104.25					
56										
57										
58										
59										
60										

	D	E	F	G	H	I	J	K	L	M
57										
58										
59										
60										
61										
62										
63				Government bond calculations						
64										
65				Price given yield						
66										
67				Settlement date	1/19/99		=PRICE(H67,H68,H69,H70,100,2,1)			
68				Maturity date	8/15/28					
69				Coupon	5.500%					
70				Yield	5.182%					
71				Price	**104.780595**					
72				Quoted price	104.25					
73										
74										
75										
76										
77										
78										
79										

In Table A-4 using Equation 4.33 (see Appendix A of this chapter), we compute the current yield y_c for different Treasury securities. This can also be expressed as

$$y_c = \frac{c \times 100}{P_t}. \tag{4.8}$$

Loosely speaking, the current yield measures the immediate cash-flow yield and is equivalent to the yield to maturity only if the security is a perpetuity. We can compute the current yield of the bond in Example 4-6 as

$$y_c = \frac{8}{108.1463} = 7.397\%. \tag{4.9}$$

	Yield	Price
TABLE 4-4 *Price versus Yield to Maturity of a T-Bond*	10.00%	81.0625
	9.50%	85.1875
	9.00%	89.6875
	8.50%	94.5938
	8.00%	100.0000
	7.50%	105.9063
	7.41%	**107.0000**
	7.00%	112.4375
	6.50%	119.6563
	6.00%	127.6250

Settlement date: January 9, 1992
Maturity date: November 15, 2021
Coupon: 8.00%

The price column reports the flat prices. The bold row represents the price and the yield to maturity on January 9, 1992. Yields have been rounded down to two decimals.

Some bonds are callable. For such bonds, it is customary to also calculate **yield to call.** Consider the callable bond in Table 4-2 which has a coupon of 14%, matures on November 15, 2011, but is callable on November 15, 2006, for the first time. After the first call date, the bond is callable on every coupon date. The call price is 100. The yield to call is calculated assuming that the bond is callable on the first call date. We report in Table 4-2 the yield to maturity of the bond to be 7.565%. For this bond, using the flat price = $164\frac{18}{32}$, coupon = 14%, settlement date of September 10, 1992, and the first call date November 15, 2006, as the maturity date, we get yield to call to be 6.821%.

In practice, when market yields are below the coupon rate, it is customary to report the yield to call. The reasoning is that the bond is likely to be called as the yields are relatively low. On the other hand, when the market yields are above the coupon rate, typically, yield to maturity is reported since the likelihood of a call is low.

We now introduce **yield curve,** a concept used extensively in the industry. Yield curve is the plot of yield to maturity (along the y-axis) against the time to maturity (along the x-axis).

Price-Yield Relationship. Price and yield have an inverse relationship, as was shown earlier in the chapter; as the price increases, the yield falls, and vice versa. We can see this relationship clearly by varying the yield in Equation 4.7 and computing the prices associated with each yield. For the Treasury bond in Example 4-6, this process results in Table 4-4.

The actual price of the T-bond and its actual yield to maturity for the settlement date are indicated in boldface. Note that as the yield increases from 7.41% to 10%, the price falls from 107.00 to 81.0625. Note that the rate of change in price for a given change in yield depends on the level of the yield; the price change is greater at low levels of yield and lower at high levels of yield. For a 50-basis-point drop from 6.50% to 6.00% in yield, the price increases by almost 8 full points. However, for the 50-basis-point drop from 10.00% to 9.50% in yield, the price increases by only about 4.2 points. This property is referred to as the **convexity** of the price-yield relation. We will investigate this more formally later.

Observations on Yields

The yield to maturity is based on the internal rate of return, but the industry conventions about its calculation change depending on the market segment and the security. For example, the day-count methods differ from market to market. The Treasury market convention is based on actual day counts, while the corporate market convention is based on 30/360 day counts. In the Treasury market, the industry convention ignores holidays. If the maturity date of a security happens to be a holiday, the yield to maturity is still calculated as if the cash flow at maturity date would be paid on that date. In addition, the yield to maturity uses the number of days between the last coupon date and the next coupon date as the basis for its computation (see equation 4.7). As this varies from 181 to 184 days, another inaccuracy is introduced into the yield to maturity calculation.

A more fundamental problem arises from the fact that the internal rate of return implicitly assumes a reinvestment rate equal to the currently prevailing (on the settlement date) internal rate of return throughout the life of the security. To see that this is the case, let us consider the price-yield relationship in a simplified setting in which t is the settlement date, T is the maturity date, and the coupons are paid at intervals of six months. Assuming that there are N round semicoupon payments remaining, $N = 2T$. The price is then

$$P_t = \frac{C}{\left(1 + \frac{y}{2}\right)} + \frac{C}{\left(1 + \frac{y}{2}\right)^2} + \frac{C}{\left(1 + \frac{y}{2}\right)^3} + \cdots + \frac{C + 100}{\left(1 + \frac{y}{2}\right)^{2T}}. \tag{4.10}$$

Cross multiplication results in

$$P_t \times \left(1 + \frac{y}{2}\right)^{2T} = C \times \left(1 + \frac{y}{2}\right)^{2T-1} + C \times \left(1 + \frac{y}{2}\right)^{2T-2} + \cdots + C + 100. \tag{4.11}$$

The left-hand side of the equation (4.11) represents the cash flow that may be obtained by investing the price for a period of T years at a yield to maturity of y. On the right-hand side, we find that all coupons are assumed to be reinvested at y. This is a serious shortcoming in the use of the yield to maturity as a measure of return. Nevertheless, as explained at the outset, associated with every price is a yield. In this sense, the yield to maturity is best thought of as a way to convey the price or the value of the security.

RISK AND DEBT SECURITIES

In this section, we define several measures of price risk. First, we derive analytical expressions that assume a round number of coupons. Then, we consider applications to Treasuries that do not have a round number of coupons.

Price Risk

The risk of a bond is the change in its price due to changes in the interest rates in the market. If P is the price of the bond and y is the yield of the bond, then a measure of the risk of the bond is the change in price of the bond for a change in its yield. This is denoted by $\frac{\partial P}{\partial y}$. Let us try to get some intuition by looking at an example. Consider a bond with one year to maturity. If it pays 4% coupon semiannually on a par value of $100, it is currently yielding 6%. The price of the bond is

$$P = \frac{4}{1 + \frac{0.06}{2}} + \frac{104}{\left(1 + \frac{0.06}{2}\right)^2} = 101.91347.$$

This is shown in Figure 4-9.

We want to know what will happen to its price if the yields change by a small amount, say, one basis point to 6.01%. The new price will be

$$P^1 = \frac{4}{1 + \frac{0.0601}{2}} + \frac{104}{\left(1 + \frac{0.0601}{2}\right)^2} = 101.903764.$$

Figure 4-10 shows the old and the new prices.

We can approximate the risk $\partial P/\partial y$ by

$$\frac{P - P^1}{6.01\% - 6.00\%} = (101.91347 - 101.903764) \times 10,000$$

$$= \$97.053.$$

FIGURE 4-9   *Price Risk*

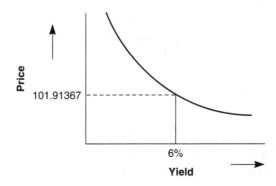

FIGURE 4-10   *Price Risk*

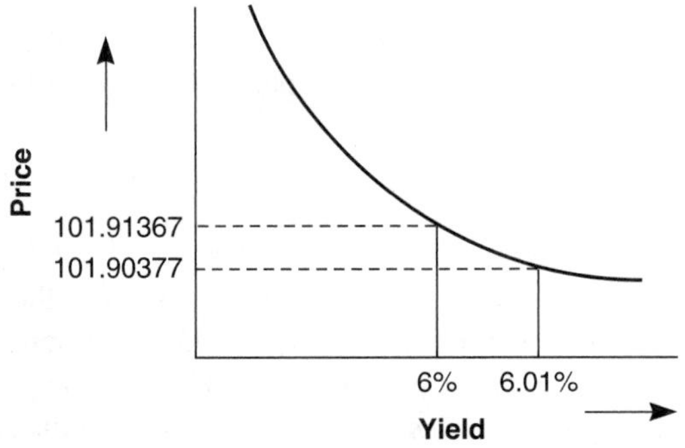

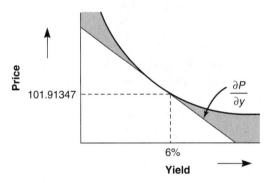

FIGURE 4-11   *Price Risk*

Roughly, we are estimating the slope of the tangent to the price-yield relationship at 6% yield. This is shown in figure 4-11.

The shaded area between the tangent and the price-yield curve is the pricing error incurred when we ignore the convexity.

Given a bond with a round number of coupon payments remaining, the price risk (or equivalently the interest rate risk) can be calculated exactly. We define the price risk as $-\frac{\partial P}{\partial y}$, where the negative sign denotes that the price decreases as the yield increases. Differentiating the Equation 4.36 with respect to y and simplifying, we get the price-risk formula,

$$-\frac{\partial P}{\partial y} = \frac{C}{y^2}\left[1 - \frac{1}{\left(1 + \frac{y}{2}\right)^N}\right] + \frac{N\left(100 - \frac{C}{y}\right)}{2\left(1 + \frac{y}{2}\right)^{N+1}}. \tag{4.12}$$

Typically, the price risk is scaled by a factor of 100 to reflect a change in price for a percentage change in yield. We denote this measure of price risk as Δ_p and write it as

FIGURE 4-12   *Price Risk versus Yield*

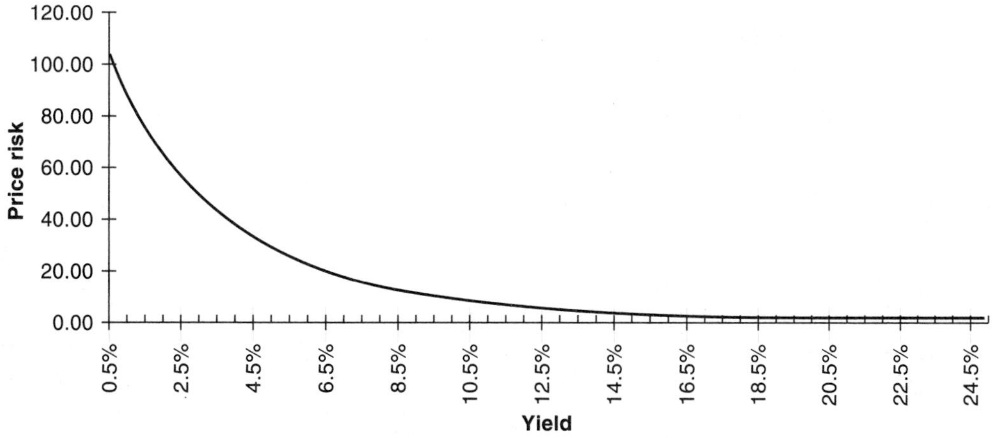

$$\Delta_p = \frac{-\frac{\partial P}{\partial y}}{100} = \frac{1}{100}\left(\frac{C}{y^2}\left[1 - \frac{1}{\left(1+\frac{y}{2}\right)^N}\right] + \frac{N\left(100 - \frac{C}{y}\right)}{2\left(1+\frac{y}{2}\right)^{N+1}}\right). \qquad (4.13)$$

This price-risk measure is the slope of the tangent to the price-yield curve at yield y.

Example 4-7:

Consider a bond with a dollar coupon of $C = 10$ per annum paid semiannually and with 80 round coupons remaining ($N = 80$). For this 40-year bond, the price risk at a yield of 9% ($y = 0.09$) is computed as

$$\Delta_p = \frac{-\frac{\partial P}{\partial y}}{100} = \frac{1}{100}\left(\frac{10}{0.09^2}\left[1 - \frac{1}{\left(1+\frac{0.09}{2}\right)^{80}}\right] + \frac{80\left(100 - \frac{10}{0.09}\right)}{2\left(1+\frac{0.09}{2}\right)^{81}}\right) \qquad (4.14)$$

$\Delta_p = 11.86.$

In the same way, we can compute the price risk for each yield level and plot the result, as shown in Figure 4-12. Notice that the price risk is higher at lower yield levels and progressively falls as the yield increases.

This is most easily seen when N approaches ∞ and

$$\Delta_p = \frac{1}{100} \times \frac{C}{y^2}.$$

When $C = 10$ and $y = 0.09$, the price risk of the perpetuity is $\Delta_p = \frac{1}{100} \times \frac{10}{0.09^2} = 12.346$. Note that this price risk is not significantly different from that of the bond with 40 years maturity. Figure 4-13 compares the price risks of a 10%, 40-year bond and of a

FIGURE 4-13   *Price Risks of a 40-Year Bond and of a Perpetuity*

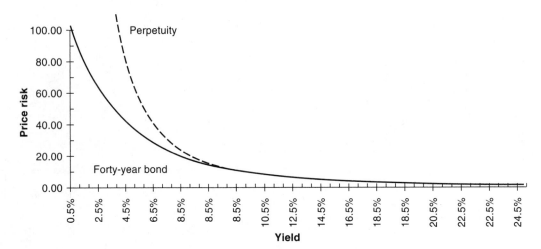

perpetuity. Note that at yields near the coupon, the price risks are indistinguishable. Only at very low-level yields do we find that the perpetuity becomes much more convex than the 40-year bond.

PVBP or Dollar Value of 0.01

The measure of price risk Δ_P is useful. In the industry, several related measures are used; one of these is the **price value of a basis point** (PVBP), defined as the change in the price of a bond per *basis point change* in its yield. Typically, PVBP is expressed in dollars per million. In such cases,

$$\text{PVBP (per \$1 million par)} = \Delta_P \times 100. \qquad (4.15)$$

Example 4-8:

Consider the bond in Example 4-8, with a dollar coupon of $C = 10$ per annum paid semiannually and with 80 round coupons remaining ($N = 80$). For this bond, the price risk at a yield of 9% ($y = 0.09$) was found in Example 4-7 to be 11.86. By using the relationship between PVBP and Δ_P in Equation 4.15, we can compute

$$\text{PVBP (per \$1 million par)} = 11.86 \times 100 = \$1,186 \text{ per million.}$$

PVBP is also referred to as the dollar value of 0.01 or DV01.

Example 4-9:

Consider the T-bond in Example 4-6. Its price P_1 at yield $y_1 = 7.4138\%$ is 106.9914. Then the price P_2 is 106.8651 when the yield is $y_2 = 7.4238\%$ (1 basis point over y_1). Let $\Delta P = P_1 - P_2$ and $\Delta y = y_1 - y_2$. Then the PVBP is defined as

$$PVBP = -\frac{\Delta P}{\Delta y} \times 10,000.$$

We multiply by 10,000 to express this in dollars per million dollar par. The negative sign simply reflects the fact that prices and yields move in opposite directions.

For this example, 0.1262865 is the change in price for a 1 basis-point change in yield, which is $\frac{1}{100}$th of 1% and the PVBP = 1262.865.

By Taylor series approximation, we can write the change in price as

$$\Delta P = \frac{\partial P}{\partial y} \times \Delta y + \frac{1}{2}\frac{\partial^2 P}{\partial y^2} \times \Delta y^2 + o(3). \tag{4.16}$$

where $o(3)$ refers to terms in Δy raised to an exponent of 3 or more. If we were to ignore quadratic terms and beyond, then we get the useful approximation that

$$\Delta P \approx \frac{\partial P}{\partial y} \times \Delta y. \tag{4.17}$$

In terms of Example 4-9,

$$P_2 \approx P_1 - \left(PVBP \times \frac{1}{10,000}\right) \text{ or } P_2 = 106.9914 - 0.1262865 = 106.8651.$$

Example 4-10:

The PVBP of Treasury bills is computed in practice as (remembering that a basis point is $\frac{1}{100}$th of 1%)

$$PVBP = \frac{z}{360} \times 1,000,000 \times \frac{1}{100 \times 100}.$$

Recall that z is the number of days between the settlement date and the next coupon date (or the maturity date, in the case of T-bills), or PVBP = $\frac{z}{360} \times 100$. Hence, a 90-day T-bill will have a PVBP of $25 per million par of the security.

Duration

Another concept widely used to measure risk is duration. Two related measures are used in the industry: **Macaulay duration** and **modified duration.** Macaulay duration has several interpretations:

- Duration is the **discounted time-weighted cash flow of the security divided by the price** of the security. In this sense, the duration measures the average time taken by the security, on a discounted basis, to pay back the original investment; the longer the duration, the greater the risk.
- Duration is the **price elasticity,** which is the percentage change in price for a percentage change in yield; in this sense, the greater the duration of a security, the greater the risk of the security.
- Duration is the **fulcrum in the timeline of security's life,** where the reinvested cash flows exactly balance out the present value of the remaining future cash flows.

We will consider all these interpretations in detail in the context of the example below.

Duration as Discounted Time-weighted Cash Flows. Consider a zero-coupon bond with a maturity of three years yielding 5% (yield to maturity). Consider also a three-year bond paying a coupon of 5% per annum also yielding 5% yield to maturity. For simplicity we assume annual coupons.

The price of the three-year zero is $\frac{100}{1.05^3}$ = 86.3838. The discount factors for the first three years

$$1.05^{-1} = 0.952381,$$

$$1.05^{-2} = 0.907029,$$

and

$$1.05^{-3} = 0.863838.$$

The discounted time-weighted cash flow definition of duration works as follows for the zero coupon bond. Each cash flow is multiplied by the number of years elapsed before it is paid. Then the time-weighted cash flow is discounted back. For year 1, this approach produces

$$0 \times 1 \times 0.952381.$$

This is due to the fact that at year 1, no cash flow is paid.

For year 2, this approach produces

$$0 \times 2 \times 0.907029.$$

Again, this is due to the fact that at year 2, no cash flow is paid. For year 3, this approach produces

$$100 \times 3 \times 0.863838.$$

This is because at year 3, the zero coupon bond pays 100. The total of all these discounted time-weighted cash flows divided by the price of the bond is the duration of the bond:

$$D = \frac{0 \times 1 \times 0.952381 + 0 \times 2 \times 0.907029 + 100 \times 3 \times 0.863838}{86.3838}$$

$$= 3 \text{ years for the three-year zero-coupon bond.}$$

We can produce similar calculations for the coupon bond. Its duration can be computed as

$$D = \frac{5 \times 1 \times 0.952381 + 5 \times 2 \times 0.907029 + 105 \times 3 \times 0.863838}{100}.$$

This can be simplified as

$$D = \frac{4.761905 + 9.07029478 + 272.1088}{100} = \frac{285.941}{100} = 2.859.$$

Note that the coupon bond has a duration which is less than the zero-coupon bond even though both bonds have the same maturity of three years and the same yield. This is because a coupon bond pays its interest payments well before maturity, leading to a lower duration. (See Figures 4-14 and 4-15.)

FIGURE 4-14   *Understanding Duration and Its Interpretations (Duration as a Measure of Time to Cash Flows): Zero-Coupon Bond Example*

	A	B	C	D	E	F	G	H	I
12									
13			**INPUTS**						
14			Coupon=	0%	Yield=	5%			
15									
16			Year	1	2	3			
17			Cash flows	0	0	100			
18									
19			Price=	86.38376	◄———	=F17/(1+F14)^3			
20									
21			Year	1	2	3			
22									
23			Time-weighted						
24			cash flows	0	0	300			
25									
26			Discount factors	0.952381	0.907029	0.863838	◄———	=1/(1+F14)^3	
27									
28			Discounted						
29			time-weighted						
30			cash flows	0	0	259.1513	◄———	=F26*F24	
31									
32			Sum of discounted						
33			time-weighted			259.1513	◄———	=SUM(D30:F30)	
34			cash flows						
35									
36			Duration			3	◄———	=F33/D19	
37									

FIGURE 4-15   *Understanding Duration and Its Interpretations (Duration as a Measure of Time to Cash Flows): Coupon Bond Example*

	A	B	C	D	E	F	G	H	I	J
11										
12										
13			**INPUTS**							
14			Coupon=	5%	Yield=	5%				
15										
16			Year	1	2	3				
17			Cash flows	5	5	105				
18										
19			Price=	100	◄———	=D17/(1+F14)+E17/(1+F14)^2+F17/(1+F14)^3				
20										
21			Year	1	2	3				
22										
23			Time-weighted							
24			cash flows	5	10	315				
25										
26			Discount Factors	0.952381	0.907029	0.863838	◄———	=1/(1+F14)^3		
27										
28			Discounted							
29			time-weighted							
30			cash flows	4.761905	9.070295	272.1088	◄———	=F26*F24		
31										
32			Sum of discounted							
33			time-weighted			285.941	◄———	=SUM(D30:F30)		
34			cash flows							
35										
36			Duration			2.85941	◄———	=F33/D19		
37										
38										

Duration as Elasticity of Interest Rates. **Duration is also the price elasticity, which is the percentage change in price for a percentage change in yield.** Formally, the elasticity measure of duration is referred to as the Macaulay duration and is represented by

$$D = -\frac{\partial P}{\partial y}\frac{1+y}{P}. \tag{4.18}$$

Another related measure is **modified duration** (MD). **Modified duration is the percentage change in price for a change in yield.** Modified duration is denoted as

$$MD = -\frac{\partial P}{\partial y}\frac{1}{P}. \tag{4.19}$$

For this example, we can also use these equations to compute the Macaulay and modified durations. Note that the duration in Equation 4.18 can be represented as

$$\frac{PVBP \times (1 + y)}{P}.$$

As shown in Figure 4-16 for the zero-coupon bond, PVBP is 246.86 per million dollars par amount. Dividing this by its price and multiplying the result by $(1 + y)$, we get the duration as

$$D = \frac{246.86 \times 1.05}{86.3838} = 3.$$

In the same manner, we can compute the duration of the coupon bond, as shown in Fig. 4-17. The PVBP of the coupon bond is 272.38. Its duration is

$$D = \frac{272.38 \times 1.05}{100} = 2.85.$$

The modified duration for the zero-coupon bond is

$$MD = \frac{246.86}{86.3838} = 2.857.$$

and the modified duration of the coupon bond is

$$MD = \frac{272.38}{100} = 2.72.$$

Duration as a Fulcrum of Cash Flows. Consider in Table 4-5 the investment of $86.3838 in the zero-coupon bond. It provides a cash flow of 100 after three years and nothing in between. After how many years from the date of investment will the investment in the zero (net of any reinvested cash inflows) be exactly equal to the present value of the *remaining* future cash inflows? In the case of zero-coupon bond, this question is easy to answer. The only future cash inflow is $100 after three years. The current investment of $86.38376 will exactly grow to $100 after three years. The cash

FIGURE 4-16   *Understanding Duration and Its Interpretations (Duration as Price Elasticity):*
Zero-Coupon Bond Example

	A	B	C	D	E	F	G	H	I	J	K	L
11												
12												
13			**INPUTS**									
14			Coupon=	0%	Yield=	5%						
15												
16			Year	1	2	3						
17			Cash flows	0	0	100						
18												
19			Price=	86.38376 ◄		=D17/(1+F14)+E17/(1+F14)^2+F17/(1+F14)^3						
20			at 5%									
21												
22			Price									
23			at 4.99%	86.40845 ◄		=D17/(1+F14-0.0001)+E17/(1+F14-0.0001)^2+F17/(1+F14-0.0001)^3						
24												
25												
26			PVBP	246.8578 ◄		=(D23-D19)*10000						
27												
28			Duration	3.000572 ◄		=D26/D19*(1+F14)						
29												

FIGURE 4-17   *Understanding Duration and Its Interpretations (Duration as Price Elasticity):*
Coupon Bond Example

	A	B	C	D	E	F	G	H	I	J	K
11											
12											
13			**INPUTS**								
14			Coupon=	5%	Yield=	5%					
15											
16			Year	1	2	3					
17			Cash flows	5	5	105					
18											
19			Price=	100 ◄		=D17/(1+F14)+E17/(1+F14)^2+F17/(1+F14)^3					
20			at 5%								
21											
22			Price								
23			at 4.99%	100.0272 ◄		=D17/(1+F14-0.0001)+E17/(1+F14-0.0001)^2+F17/(1+F14-0.0001)^3					
24											
25											
26			PVBP	272.3758 ◄		=(D23-D19)*10000					
27											
28			Duration	2.859946 ◄		=D26/D19*(1+F14)					
29											
30											
31											
32											

price of the zero and the present value of the future cash flows exert exactly the same
force at three years, which is the duration of the zero. To see this note that

$$86.3838 \times 3 = PV(100) \times 3.$$

Hence, the fulcrum is after three years. This is pictured in Table 4-5.

For the coupon bond, this is a bit trickier. As we consider any future date as a possible fulcrum, there may be some cash inflows from the security before that future
date. These cash inflows have to be reinvested. Note that in Table 4-5, we have the
fulcrum at 2.859 years. This is arrived at by balancing two sets of cash flows as shown
in the following equation. Investment carried forward at 5% *net* of all the coupon cash
flows carried forward:

$$100 \times (1.05)^{2.859} - 5 \times (1.05)^{1.859} - 5 \times (1.05)^{0.859} = 104.285.$$

TABLE 4-5   *Duration as a Fulcrum Balancing the Present Value of Cash Flows*

Duration as a Measure of Time to Cash Flows				*Duration as a Measure of Time to Cash Flows*			
Coupon = 0%	**Yield =**	5%		**Coupon =** 5%	**Yield =**	5%	
Price = 86.3838				**Price =** 100.00			
Year	0	1	2	3	Year	0	1	2	3
Cash flows	−86.38	0		0	100	Cash flows	−100.00	5		5	105

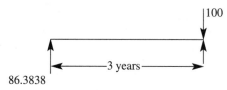

(1) The price $P = 86.3838$ exerts a force equal to $86.3838 \times 3 = 259.1514$
(2) The present value of 100 exerts a force equal to $86.3838 \times 3 = 259.1514$

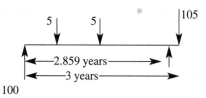

(1) The price $P = 100$ exerts a force equal to 100×2.859 285.9
(2) The present value of all cash inflows
      exert a force equal to $PV(5) \cdot 1 + PV(5) \cdot 2 + PV(105) \cdot 3 = 285.9$

Present value of the terminal cash flows:

$$\frac{105}{1.05^{3-2.859}} = 104.285.$$

Of course, this equality will hold at any other point as well. A comparison, however, of the forces exerted indicated that duration is the fulcrum, as is evident from the next equation.

$$100 \times 2.859 = PV(5) \times 1 + PV(5) \times 2 + PV(105) \times 3$$

EXCEL Applications

We can compute the duration and the modified duration of bonds using EXCEL functions as shown in Figure 4-18.

FIGURE 4-18   *EXCEL Functions*
Modified and McCaulay Duration

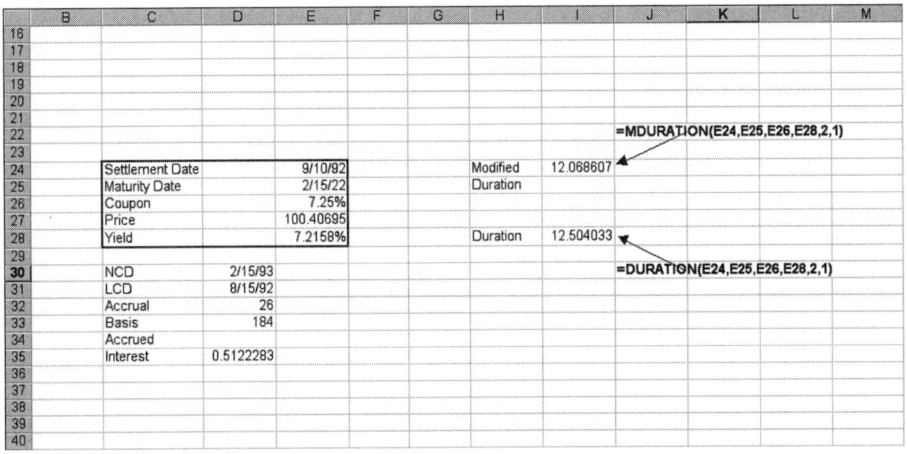

	B	C	D	E	F	G	H	I	J	K	L	M
16												
17												
18												
19												
20												
21												
22									=MDURATION(E24,E25,E26,E28,2,1)			
23												
24		Settlement Date		9/10/92			Modified	12.068607				
25		Maturity Date		2/15/22			Duration					
26		Coupon		7.25%								
27		Price		100.40695								
28		Yield		7.2158%			Duration	12.504033				
29												
30		NCD	2/15/93						=DURATION(E24,E25,E26,E28,2,1)			
31		LCD	8/15/92									
32		Accrual	26									
33		Basis	184									
34		Accrued										
35		Interest	0.5122283									
36												
37												
38												
39												
40												

TABLE 4-6   *PVBP and Modified Duration*

Security	Coupon	Maturity	Yield to Maturity	Prices	MD	PVBP
T-note	4.25%	8/31/1994	3.801%	$100\frac{27}{32}$	1.88	189
T-note	4.625%	8/15/1995	4.269%	$100\frac{31}{32}$	2.71	274
T-note	5.625%	8/31/1997	5.188%	$101\frac{28}{32}$	4.29	438
T-note	6.375%	7/15/1999	5.753%	$103\frac{15}{32}$	5.47	571
T-note	6.375%	8/15/2002	6.289%	$100\frac{20}{32}$	7.25	733
T-bond	7.25%	8/15/2022	7.216%	$100\frac{13}{32}$	12.12	1223

Example 4-11:

The quotations for the September 10, 1992, settlement of on-the-run U.S. Treasury notes and bonds are provided in Table 4-6. For each security, we also indicate the MD and the PVBP.

PVBPs are calculated by using the yields. First, the price is calculated. Then the yield is increased by 1 basis point, and the price is recalculated at the new yield. The price difference is multiplied by 10,000 to get the PVBP.

Note that,

$$MD = \frac{PVBP}{P}.$$

This can be easily verified from Table 4-6. Consider the T-bond. The accrued interest is 0.5122, so the invoice price is $100\frac{13}{32}$ + 0.5122 = 100.91845. The PVBP per million dollars face is 1,223; hence, the modified duration is $\frac{1,223}{100.91845}$ = 12.12.

Consider Equation 4.43, which is the definition of Macaulay duration. Set $C = 0$ in Equation 4.43. Recall that for a zero-coupon bond, the price is given by

$$P = \frac{100}{\left(1 + \frac{y}{2}\right)^{2T}}.$$

Substituting this in Equation 4.43, we note that for a zero-coupon bond $D = T$.

The fact that the duration of zero-coupon bonds is equal to their maturity is very important. Thirty-year zeroes are available in the market; they will have a duration of 30 years. If a company (such as an insurance company) has liabilities with a long duration, then by buying 30-year zero-coupon bonds, it can match the duration of the liabilities to the duration of assets. Stated differently, the interest rate sensitivity of the assets will be matched to the interest rate sensitivity of the liabilities. This is known as asset-liability management, and we will explore this concept in detail in Part II.

Coupon Effect on Duration

The duration measure that we have developed is extensively used in the industry. A feature of this measure is that the duration undergoes discrete changes when coupons are paid. This is shown in Figure 4-19.

Using the third interpretation of duration from Table 4-5, it is easy to see that when a coupon is paid, the fulcrum has to move more to the right to balance the pres-

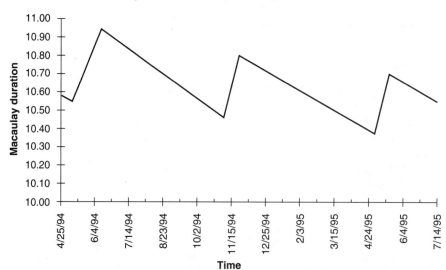

FIGURE 4-19   *Effect of Coupon Payments on Duration*
Coupon Dates: 5/15/94, 11/15/94, and 5/15/95

ent value of cash flows. This increases the duration. As time passes, the maturity of the bond declines, leading to a decrease in duration. These observations explain why we observe a sawtooth pattern in the duration of bonds over time.

Properties of Duration and PVBP

The finding that the duration of a zero-coupon bond is equal to its maturity means that the zero-coupon bond is the most interest-rate-elastic security for a given maturity class. It is easy to verify that **duration is generally increasing in maturity, decreasing in coupons and yield to maturity as shown earlier.** The duration of coupon bonds will be less than their maturity. **Clearly, as time passes, duration will change.** This requires some attention in portfolios of assets and liabilities whose durations are held the same. Note in Table 4-6 that the security with the highest duration (or PVBP) also had the highest yield to maturity.

PVBP and Duration of Portfolios

In appendices B and C at the end of this chapter we have shown how to derive the PVBP and duration of portfolios of fixed-income securities. We illustrate the ideas with Examples 4-12 and 4-13. The PVBP of a portfolio is simply the par value weighted PVBP of individual securities in the portfolio. The duration of the portfolio is the weighted sum of durations of each security in the portfolio. Each weight represents the market-value based proportion of that security as a fraction of the total market value of the portfolio.

Example 4-12:

The quotations for the September 10, 1992, settlement of on-the-run U.S. Treasury notes and bonds are provided in Table 4-6. Consider a portfolio which has a $200 million par amount of the 7.25% T-bond and a $100 million par amount of the 4.25% T-note. What is the PVBP of this portfolio?

Let us define the units of securities in par values of $1 million each. Then, we have 200 units of $7\frac{1}{4}\%$ T-bond and 100 units of $4\frac{1}{4}\%$ of T-note. Let n_1 be the units of $7\frac{1}{4}\%$ T-bond and n_2 be the units of $4\frac{1}{4}\%$ T-note. Then

$$n_1 = 200 \text{ and } n_2 = 100. \text{ Then PVBP}_1 = 1,223 \text{ and PVBP}_2 = 189.$$

$$\text{Then, PVBP}_p = 200 \times 1,223 + 100 \times 189 = 263,500.$$

The portfolio will lose $263,500 per basis point increase in the yield.

Example 4-13:

Let us reconsider the portfolio that has a $200 million par amount of the 7.25% T-bond and a $100 million par amount of the 4.25% T-note. What is the duration of this portfolio?

The invoice prices are $P_1 = 100\frac{13}{32} + 0.5122 = 100.91845$ and $P_2 = 100\frac{27}{32} + 0.1174 = 100.96115$. The market value of the portfolio (in millions) is $200 \times 1.0091845 + 100 \times 1.0096115 = 302.79805$. Hence, $x_1 = \frac{200 \times 1.0091845}{302.79805} = 0.6666$ and $x_2 = \frac{100 \times 1.0096115}{302.79805} = 0.3334$. As given in Table 4-6, $MD_1 = 12.12$ and $MD_2 = 1.88$; then the portfolio duration is $0.6666 \times 12.12 + 0.3334 \times 1.88 = 8.71$.

Spread Trades

This section illustrates how the theoretical concepts that have been developed are applied to set up trading strategies. Consider the data in Tables 4-7 and 4-8.

A trader is evaluating the shape of the yield curve for settlement on December 2, 1991. The yield spread between the 30-year T-bond and the two-year T-note stands at 266 basis points. The trader is expecting this spread to significantly increase in a few days; in other words, the trader is expecting the yield curve to get steeper. The trader wants to set up a trade that will break even if the spread stays at 266 basis points and make money if the spread widens. Of course, he or she is willing to accept the risk that there will be a loss if the yield curve were to flatten; that is, if the spread actually decreases.

How can the trader implement the trade reflecting his or her view about the yield curve? The overall yields may either go down or go up, but it is the spread that the trader is betting on. Let us consider two scenarios, presented in Table 4-9, in which the trader's expectations come true. In scenario 1, two-year yields fall by 20 basis points but the 30-year yields fall only by 10 basis points. This leads to a steepening of the

TABLE 4-7 Thirty-Year T-Bond, Coupon 8.75%, Maturity 5/15/2020	Bid	Ask	Yield	Settlement Date	Accrued Interest	PVBP
	108.8405	108.903	7.96%	12/2/1991	0.408654	1200.643
	109.0806	109.1431	7.94%	12/3/1991	0.432692	1204.999
	109.8076	109.8701	7.88%	12/4/1991	0.456731	1218.246

TABLE 4-8 Two-Year T-Note, Coupon 5.50%, Maturity 11/30/1993	Bid	Ask	Yield	Settlement Date	Accrued Interest	PVBP
	100.3735	100.4360	5.30%	12/2/1991	0.03022	187.3602
	100.4664	100.5289	5.25%	12/3/1991	0.04533	187.34
	100.5967	100.6592	5.18%	12/4/1991	0.06044	187.4086

TABLE 4-9 Possible Scenarios	Yield Two-Year T-Note	Yield Thirty-Year T-Bond	Spread
Scenario 1	5.1	7.86	276
Scenario 2	5.5	8.36	286

yield curve. In scenario 2, precisely the opposite happens. The two-year yields increase by 20 basis points and the 30-year by 30 basis points, resulting in a steeper curve.

First, the trader recognizes that for the spreads to increase in a bullish market, the two-year yields must drop by much more than the thirty-year yields. Similarly, in a bearish market, the two-year yields must increase by much less than the thirty-year yields. This calls for a long position in the two-year T-note and a short position in the 30-year T-bond.

Second, the trader must determine the amount of the two-year T-note to buy and the amount of the 30-year T-bond to short. This is where the concepts that we have developed come in handy. The trader will want to set up the trade such that

$$n_2 \times \text{PVBP}_2 = n_{30} \times \text{PVBP}_{30}$$

where n_2 is the number of two-year T-notes and n_{30} is the number of 30-year T-bonds. This ensures that the price risk of two-year notes is offset by the price risk of 30-year bonds for small interest rate changes.

If $n_{30} = 100$ million par amount, then we can compute n_2

$$n_2 = n_{30} \frac{\text{PVBP}_{30}}{\text{PVBP}_2}.$$

$$n_2 = 100 \times \frac{1200.6435}{187.3642} = 641.$$

So, the trader will go long in 641 million par amount of the two-year T-note and go short in 100 million par amount of the 30-year T-bond.

Precisely how are these transactions arranged? Let us review the repo diagram in Figure 4-20. The trader posts 641 million par amount of the two-year T-note as collateral and borrows the cash. Ignoring the hair cut (margin), the trader will borrow the entire market value at a repo rate of 5%. This way he or she is long in the two-year T-note and is entitled to its coupon. In addition, the trader will borrow and sell 100 million par amount of the 30-year T-bond and post the cash proceeds as collateral. Ignoring the hair cut (margin), the trader will earn, on the entire cash proceeds, an interest income at a repo rate of 4.90%. This way he or she is short in the 30-year T-bond and is obliged to make restitution for any coupon payments. We summarize the key transactions related to this trade in Table 4-10.

The profitability of the spread trade depends on a number of factors, including the following:

- The bid-offer spreads. The trader buys at the offer price and sells at the bid price. The wider the bid-offer spread, the less profitable the trade.
- The repo rates. If the repo rates are low, the trader pays less to borrow but also receives less on the cash collateral.
- Special rates. If the security that is long goes special (see Chapter 3), then the trader makes more money, as it is possible to borrow cheap by using that collateral. Conversely, if the security that is short goes special, the trader will lose money.
- Hair cut (margin). The trader will have to post some margin, and this will reduce the profitability as well.

FIGURE 4-20   *Repo Diagram*

Transactions on December 2, 1991

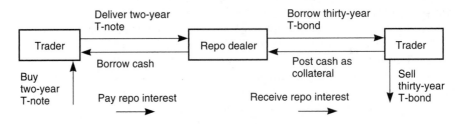

Transactions on December 4, 1991

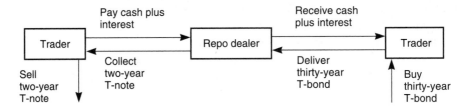

TABLE 4-10   *Summary of Transactions in Spread Trade*

Date	Transactions	Cash Flows
12/2/87	Borrow cash and pay for the two-year T-note. Post two-year T-note as collateral. $(100.4360 + 0.03022) \times 10,000 \times 641 =$	(643,988,470)
	Borrow 30-year T-bond and sell. Post cash as collateral. $(108.8405 + 0.408654) \times 10,000 \times 100 =$	109,249,154
12/4/87	Sell two-year T-note. Per 641 million par, this becomes	
[1]	$(100.5967 + 0.0604) \times 10,000 \times 641 =$	645,212,011
	Repay the amount borrowed plus repo interest. Per 641 million par, this becomes	
[2]	$643,988,470 \times \left(1 + 2 \times \frac{0.05}{360}\right) =$	(644,167,356)
[3]	Collect the cash plus interest. $109,249,154 \times \left(1 + 0.049 \times \frac{2}{360}\right) =$	109,278,894
	Buy the 30-year T-bond to cover the short position.	
[4]	$(109.8701 + 0.4567) \times 10,000 \times 100 =$	(110,326,800)
	Profits (Losses): [1] + [2] + [3] + [4]	(3,251)

The exposure is high: the trader is long 641 million of the two-year T-note and short in 100 million of the long bond. Being wrong about the spread expectations could lose the trader money. The credit risk also has to be factored in. Margins (hair cuts), mark-to-market provisions, and other policies should be considered in this context.

The concepts that we have developed thus far ignored the fact that duration changes with yield. We take up this issue next.

CONVEXITY

As we saw earlier, the slope of price-yield relationship changes with yield levels. Furthermore, the slope of the tangent becomes steeper as the interest rates (yields) fall. This leads to what is known as convexity of the price-yield curve. We will illustrate this with an example.

Consider a bond with a coupon of 7.25% maturing on 2/15/2022. Assume that the settlement date is 9/10/1992. The bond is quoted at a (flat) price of 100.40695. What is its convexity?

The yield of the bond at the current price can be computed to be 7.216%. Let us increase the yield by 1 basis point to 7.226% and recalculate the price, which is 100.28478.

The PVBP is $(100.40695 - 100.28678) \times 10,000 = 1223$. It is easy to verify that the modified duration of the bond is 12.12. By the definition of modified duration, we have

$$MD = \frac{\Delta \frac{P}{P}}{\Delta y}$$

or

$$\frac{\Delta P}{P} = MD \times \Delta y.$$

In this example, $\frac{\Delta P}{P} = 12 - 12 \times \frac{0.01}{100} = 0.1212\%$. We interpret this as follows: for a *small* change in market yields, the percentage change in the price of the bond is 0.1212%. What if the yield changes by 200 basis points? Using the same arguments

$$\frac{\Delta P}{P} = 12.12 \times \frac{200}{100} = 24.24\%.$$

A change of 24.24% in price is

$$\$100.40695 \times 10,000 \times 0.2424 = \$243,386.45$$

per million par. The new price (predicted by modified duration) is $100.40695 \times (1 - 0.2424) = 76.06831$ (rounded to five decimals).

Of course, we can compute the bond price at a new yield of 7.216% + 200 basis points using the price-yield curve. The new price is 80.16387. Hence, the actual change is $100.40695 - 80.16387 = 20.24308$. The change predicted by modified duration is

FIGURE 4-21   *Convexity Effect*

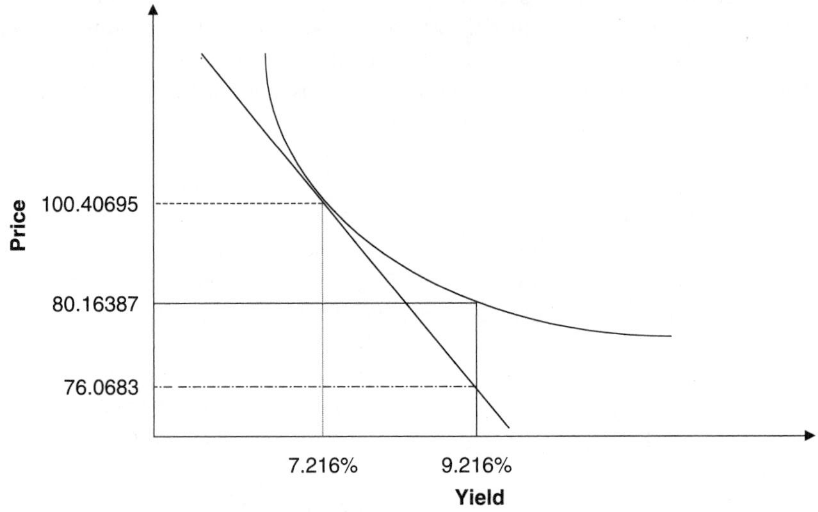

$100.40695 \times 0.2424 = 24.33865$. The difference is due to the *convexity* of the price-yield curve and it equals $24.33865 - 20.24308 = 4.09557$.

This is shown in Figure 4-21.

Recall that we have ignored second-order effects of yield changes on price changes by focusing on measures, such as PVBP and D or MD, which are essentially related to the first derivative of the price with respect to the yield.

Example 4-14:

- We illustrate the idea with a specific example. We consider a two-year zero yielding 10%. We work with annual compounding.
- The convexity of a bond is the change in the slope of the price-yield curve, for a small change in the yield. The second derivative of the price-yield curve provides the basis for the convexity calculations. The price of a two-year zero and its interest rate risk can be presented as follows:

$$P = \frac{100}{(1 + y)^2}$$

$$\frac{\partial P}{\partial y} = -\frac{100 \times 2}{(1 + y)^3}$$

- For a two-year zero, the second derivative is

$$\frac{\partial^2 P}{\partial y^2} = \frac{100 \times 2 \times 3}{(1 + y)^4}.$$

We define convexity as

$$Cx = \frac{1}{2} \frac{\partial^2 P}{\partial y^2} \frac{1}{P}.$$

- Then, using the definition of modified duration, we can express the percentage price change as (See Equation 4.16.):

$$\frac{\Delta P}{P} = -MD \times \Delta y + Cx(\Delta y)^2.$$

Note that the convexity effect on percentage price is positive as seen from the sign of the second term. This is referred to as the **gain from convexity.** We can explicitly compute convexity either using the formula or by using the PVBP estimates.

- Note that PVBP is an estimate of the slope of the price-yield curve. Using this, we can get an estimate of convexity as follows:

$$PVBP = \frac{\Delta P}{\Delta y}.$$

An estimate of convexity is then

$$Cx = \frac{1}{2} \frac{\Delta PVBP}{\Delta y} \frac{1}{P}.$$

For the two-year, the price at 10% is 82.6446. Its PVBP at 10% is 150.2425. Its PVBP at 10.01% is 150.2015.

$$\Delta PVBP = (150.2425 - 150.2015) \times 10,000 = 410$$

$$Cx = 410 \times \frac{1}{2} \times \frac{1}{82.6446} = 2.481$$

- We can also use the cash flow-based formula to get the second derivatives as

$$\frac{\partial^2 P}{\partial y^2} = \frac{100 \times 2 \times 3}{(1 + y)^4} = \frac{600}{1.10^4} = 409.81.$$

Note that this is very close to our estimate based on estimated second derivative. In general, it is much easier to work with the estimate of convexity based on PVBP. When bonds pay coupons and they have many periods to maturity, the estimates based on PVBP are quite easy to implement.

From Equation 4.16 we get

$$\frac{\Delta P}{P} = -MD \times \Delta y + Cx + \Delta y^2 + o(3). \tag{4.20}$$

We find that the convexity contributes to the price change favorably. The gain from convexity is $Cx \times P \times \Delta y^2$. In the example the gain from convexity is $2.28 \times 100.84375 \times (0.01)^2 = 0.023$.

Holding maturity and yield to maturity fixed, the convexity decreases as the coupon increases. Convexity increases with duration. (Appendix D at the end of this chapter shows a derivation of convexity.)

Bullet versus Barbell Securities

Let us consider Table 4-11, which provides the statistics for three zero-coupon bonds or Treasury strips. Using the concepts we have developed, we can easily verify the table entries corresponding to modified duration, gain from convexity, and PVBP. Let us consider a portfolio which has $100 million par amount of the strip maturing on August 15, 2002. Is it possible to replace this strip with a portfolio of the other two strips, which mature on August 15, 1997 and August 15, 2012, respectively, such that there is no cash outlay and the PVBP remains the same?

Let n_i be the number of strip i; we require that the cash proceeds from the sale of strip 2 be sufficient to buy the requisite amounts of strip 1 and strip 3.

$$n_2 P_2 = n_1 P_1 + n_3 P_3 = V_p \qquad (4.21)$$

We further require that the modified duration of the strip that is sold is equal to the modified duration of the portfolio that is purchased.

$$MD_2 = \frac{n_1 P_1}{V_p} MD_1 + \frac{n_3 P_3}{V_p} MD_3 \qquad (4.22)$$

From the table, we substitute $n_2 = 100$, $MD_1 = 4.7995$, $MD_2 = 9.5982$, $MD_3 = 19.1776$, $P_1 = 76.86$, $P_2 = 50.99$, and $P_3 = 21.60$, So the two conditions are

$$100 \times 50.99 = n_1 \times 76.86 + n_3 \times 21.60$$

and

$$9.5982 = \frac{n_1 \times 76.86 \times 4.7995 + n_3 \times 21.60 \times 19.1776}{100 \times 50.99}.$$

Solving, we get $n_1 = 44.20$ and $n_3 = 78.79$. The portfolio we have created by selling strip 2 is very similar but not identical to the strip 2 that we sold. To see why this is the case, we need to analyze the effects of changes in yields on strip 2 and on the portfolio we have created.

Note that by construction, at the prevailing market yields (underlined in Table 4-12) the market value of the strip 2 and its PVBP are exactly matched by those of the barbell

TABLE 4-11   *Treasury Strips, Settlement Date: September 9, 1992*

Security (Strips)	Maturity Date	Price	Yield	Modified Duration	Gain from Convexity	PVBP
1	8/15/1997	76.86	5.41	4.8	0.1270	369
2	8/15/2002	50.99	6.90	9.6	0.4838	489
3	8/15/2012	21.60	7.84	19.2	1.8838	414

portfolio. When there is a parallel shift in the yields, the value of the barbell portfolio dominates the value of the bullet (strip 2) security. Consider what happens to the portfolio when the yields drop. The PVBP of the barbell portfolio, given in the last column, exceeds the PVBP of strip 2. This indicates that the barbell portfolio will benefit more from the reduction in yields. On the other hand, as the yields go up, the PVBP of the barbell portfolio is always lower than that of strip 2. As a consequence, the barbell portfolio will lose less value as compared to strip 2.

Trades of this sort, in which an intermediate maturity security is sold (bought) and two securities whose maturities straddle the intermediate maturity are bought (sold) are known as **butterfly trades.** To get a better perspective, we have plotted in Figure 4-22 the amount by which the barbell portfolio exceeds the strip 2 at different levels of yields.

Note that the convexity effect really kicks in only at very high or very low yield levels. In fact, for ±100 basis points change in yields, the effect of convexity is hardly evident. A critical assumption we have maintained throughout this discussion is that the shift in yields is parallel. This assumption is especially suspect when there is a

	y_2	P_2	$PVBP_2$	y_1	y_3	V_p Barbell	$PVBP$ Barbell
TABLE 4-12 *Convexity Effect, Bullet versus Barbell*	5.00%	61.23	5.936	3.51%	5.94%	61.76	6.559
	5.10%	60.64	5.876	3.61%	6.04%	61.11	6.456
	5.20%	60.06	5.817	3.71%	6.14%	60.47	6.355
	5.30%	59.48	5.758	3.81%	6.24%	59.84	6.255
	5.40%	58.91	5.700	3.91%	6.34%	59.22	6.158
	5.50%	58.34	5.642	4.01%	6.44%	58.61	6.063
	5.60%	57.78	5.585	4.11%	6.54%	58.01	5.969
	5.70%	57.22	5.529	4.21%	6.64%	57.42	5.877
	5.80%	56.67	5.473	4.31%	6.74%	56.84	5.787
	5.90%	56.13	5.418	4.41%	6.84%	56.26	5.698
	6.00%	55.59	5.363	4.51%	6.94%	55.70	5.611
	6.10%	55.06	5.309	4.61%	7.04%	55.14	5.526
	6.20%	54.53	5.256	4.71%	7.14%	54.59	5.442
	6.30%	54.01	5.203	4.81%	7.24%	54.05	5.360
	6.40%	53.49	5.150	4.91%	7.34%	53.52	5.279
	6.50%	52.98	5.099	5.01%	7.44%	53.00	5.200
	6.60%	52.47	5.047	5.11%	7.54%	52.48	5.123
	6.70%	51.97	4.997	5.21%	7.64%	51.97	5.046
	6.80%	51.47	4.947	5.31%	7.74%	51.47	4.971
	6.90%	50.98	4.897	5.41%	7.84%	50.98	4.898
	7.00%	50.49	4.848	5.51%	7.94%	50.50	4.826
	7.10%	50.01	4.799	5.61%	8.04%	50.02	4.755
	7.20%	49.53	4.751	5.71%	8.14%	49.54	4.685
	7.30%	49.06	4.703	5.81%	8.24%	49.08	4.617
	7.40%	48.59	4.656	5.91%	8.34%	48.62	4.550
	7.50%	48.13	4.610	6.01%	8.44%	48.17	4.484

FIGURE 4-22   *Effect of Convexity: Bullet versus Barbell*

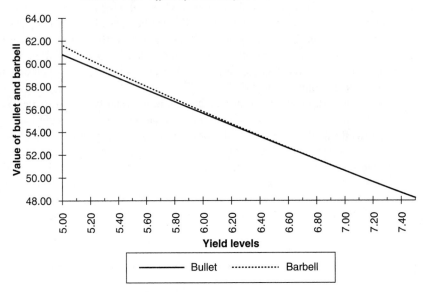

large change in the levels of the yields. Hence, the analysis presented previously should not be construed to mean that convexity is necessarily a desirable attribute.

FURTHER READING

A number of papers have explored the concepts of duration and convexity. A lucid analysis of duration appears in Ingersoll, Skelton, and Weil (1978). The problem of computing duration when interest rates are uncertain is addressed in Cox, Ingersoll, and Ross (1979) in the context of a specific model of term structure. Using duration to "immunize" portfolios is considered by Bierwag (1977). In immunization strategy, the duration of assets is set equal to that of liabilities, through careful choice of asset-liability mix. Since duration measures interest rate sensitivity, in such portfolios assets and liabilities will have the same interest rate sensitivity and hence will be well-hedged with respect to interest rate movements. The issue of convexity is addressed in Klotz (1985) and Yawitz (1986).

PROBLEMS

4.1   An investor buys a face amount $1 million of a six-month (182 days) Treasury bill at a discount yield of 9.25%. What is the cost of purchasing these bills? Calculate the bond equivalent yield. Indicate clearly the formula you used, and show all the steps in your calculations. Recalculate the bond equivalent yield if the T-bill has a maturity of 275 days.

4.2   On November 18, 1987, a $7\frac{7}{8}\%$ T-bond maturing on May 15, 1990, was quoted at $99\frac{29}{32}$ for settlement on November 20, 1987. The last coupon was paid on November 15, 1987.
   (a) What is the invoice price of the T-bond?
   (b) What is the yield on the T-bond?

4.3   What is the price of a 10-year zero-coupon bond priced to yield 10% under each of the following assumptions?
   (a) Annual yield.
   (b) Semiannnual yield.
   (c) Monthly yield.
   (d) Daily yield.

Explain the differences you found. What is the continuous limit?

4.4   In the following table, fill in the indicated blanks. Show all the steps in your calculations on separate sheets. Duration is denoted by D, coupon by C, and yield by Y. The settlement date is February 15, 1986.

Bond Mathematics	C	Y	Maturity Date	Price	D	Value of 0.01
	9%	9.00%	5/15/xx	100.00	5.0	xxxx
	0%	9.00%	2/15/92	xxx.xx	x.x	xxxx
	10%	9.00%	2/15/96	106.50	6.66	xxxx

4.5   Using the information in the following table, construct a $100 million portfolio with a Macaulay duration of 5.0. Supply the missing information in the table. The settlement date is February 15, 1986.

Duration of Portfolios	C	Y	Maturity Date	Price	D
	0%	9.12%	5/15/90	70.00	xx.xx
	9%	x.xx%	2/15/xx	110.00	6.00

4.6   On November 15, 1986, you bought $10 million (face amount) of a 7.50% T-bond maturing on November 11, 2016, at a yield of 7.60%. All coupons were reinvested at 5% yield. The bond was sold on June 20, 1987, at a yield of 7.50%. Calculate the annualized rate of return from this transaction. Show all the key steps.

4.7 (a) Assuming that the settlement date is August 15, 1986, determine the duration of the T-bond from the following table. From the duration formula, estimate the price of the T-bond for a yield change of +10 basis points.
   (b) Repeat the analysis at yield levels of 5%, 6%, 7%, 8%, 10%, 11%, and 12%.
   (c) For these yield levels, determine the actual price from price-yield formula.
   (d) Compare the estimated price with the actual price. Explain the deviations. (Use a spreadsheet program, such as EXCEL or Lotus 123, to handle this problem.)

Duration of a T-Bond	C	Y	Maturity Date	Price	D
	10%	9.00%	11/15/98	107.3043	xx.xx

4.8   Reconsider Problem 4.7. You may now estimate the prices at different yield levels by using both duration and convexity. Compare the estimated prices with the actual price and explain the deviations.

4.9   An investor expects a strong market rally. Assume that the yield-curve shifts will be parallel (i.e., all yields change by the same amount irrespective of maturities). In order to get the highest return over the rally, which of the following securities should be chosen by the investor: (i) the security with the highest duration, (ii) the security with the lowest yield value of $\frac{1}{32}$, or (iii) the security with the highest dollar value of 0.01? Explain your answer.

4.10   **Spreadsheet Problem.** Use *Wall Street Journal* quotes to solve this problem. Compute the spread between the current five-year T-note and the current thirty-year T-bond. Anticipate that this spread will narrow significantly in a month's time. Structure a spread trade using these two securities. The trade must be positioned in the market for a repurchase agreement using weekly term repo rates. Assume that the one-week term repo rates are 3.00% to 3.05%. One leg of the trade will have 100 million par amount of the long bond. Set up the trade as of today and carry the position for five days. Unwind the trade at the end of five days, and report the details of your trade and your position market-to-market using the *Wall Street Journal* prices.

4.11   **Spreadsheet Problem.** Use *Wall Street Journal* quotes to solve this problem. Determine the invoice prices, PVBP, yield value of $\frac{1}{32}$, and the modified duration of all on-the-run securities. Explain your findings.

4.12   **Spreadsheet Problem.** Use *Wall Street Journal* quotes to solve this problem. You are a pension-fund manager with 100 million par amount of the current seven-year T-note. You would like to swap out of this seven-year T-note and replace it with a portfolio of the current five-year T-note and the current ten-year T-note. The trade, however, should be self-financing: The proceeds from the sale of the seven-year T-note should exactly cover the cost of the portfolio of the five-year and ten-year T-notes. In addition, the PVBP of the seven-year T-note must be equal to the PVBP of the portfolio you plan to purchase.

   (a) Determine the amount of five-year and ten-year T-notes you must buy.

   (b) Is the new portfolio identical to the security you sold? Explain.

REFERENCES

Bierwag, G. 1977. "Immunization, Duration and the Term Structure of Interest Rates." *Journal of Financial and Quantitative Analysis* 12:725–743.

Chance, D. M. 1990. "Default, Risk and the Duration of the Zero Coupon Bonds." *Journal of Finance* 55:265–274.

Cox, J., J. Ingersoll, and S. Ross 1979. "Duration and the Measurement of Basis Risk." *Journal of Business* 52:51–61.

Ingersoll, J. E., J. Skelton, and R. L. Weil 1978. "Duration Forty Years Later." *Journal of Financial and Quantitative Analysis* 13:627–650.

Kidder, Peabody, and Co. 1987. Applications of Duration and Convexity for the Analysis of Callable Bonds. Fixed-Income Group.

Klotz, R. 1985. Convexity of Fixed-Income Securities. Salomon Brothers.

Yawitz, J. 1986. Convexity: An Introduction. Financial Strategies Group, Goldman Sachs.

Appendix A

Basic Time Value Concepts

DISCOUNTING

The rate at which money placed in interest-bearing accounts grows depends on the method used for computing the interest payments and reinvestment assumptions. There are two methods of interest calculation, simple interest and compound interest. Compound-interest calculations vary with respect to the number of compounding intervals used in any given period.

To illustrate, let y be the interest rate (annualized) in decimals, that is, 8% or 0.08, let N be the number of years from today, and let FV be the future value of an investment made today after N years. First, consider the case of **simple interest** calculations. Consider investing P (in dollars) today for x days at a simple interest rate of y. The amount that will be available from the account at the end of x days will be

$$P \times \left(1 + y \times \frac{x}{365}\right).$$

When $x = 365$, or when the money is placed in the account for one year, the future value will be $P \times (1 + y)$. Consider a simple interest calculation in which a bank agrees to pay 6% annual (simple) interest on a deposit of $1,000 placed in the bank for 90 days. At the end of 90 days, the total amount will be

$$1,000 \times \left(1 + 0.06 \times \frac{90}{365}\right) = \$1,014.795.$$

Simple interest is used in repo markets and in some money market instruments. Often, in simple interest calculations, one year is assumed to have 360 days. If this market convention is used, then for the example illustrated previously, the total amount will be

$$1,000 \times \left(1 + 0.06 \times \frac{90}{360}\right) = 1,015$$

It is also used in some government bond markets. However, most securities compound their interest payments.

The **future value** of investing P today for N years at an annual interest rate y (with annual interest payments) is

$$FV = P \times (1 + y)^N \tag{4.23}$$

165

If the interest is **compounded semiannually,** that is, we are paid interest at the end of a half year and we earn interest on that interest, then what will be the future value of our capital? At the end of a half year, we will have

$$P \times \left(1 + \frac{y}{2}\right).$$

We reinvest this for another half year, and at the end of the year earn an amount equal to

$$P \times \left(1 + \frac{y}{2}\right) \times \left(1 + \frac{y}{2}\right) = P \times \left(1 + \frac{y}{2}\right)^2.$$

So, with semiannual compounding, the terminal value is

$$FV = P \times \left(1 + \frac{y}{2}\right)^2.$$

The future value of setting aside P today for N years (with m compounding intervals per year) is

$$FV = P \times \left(1 + \frac{y}{m}\right)^{N \times m}. \tag{4.24}$$

As we increase m to ∞, we get a future value with continuous compounding of

$$FV = P \times e^{yN}. \tag{4.25}$$

Generally, we can convert from one method of compounding to another. If we are given the annually compounded interest rate $\hat{y}$, we can convert it to the semiannually compounded interest rate y using

$$\left(1 + \frac{y}{2}\right)^2 = (1 + \hat{y}).$$

Table A-1 records the future values of $100 at a 5% interest rate under annual, semiannual, quarterly, and continuous compounding. Note that the value differences resulting from the number of compounding intervals per year are rather small for maturities of 1 to 10 years. At the end of one year, the simple interest earned is $5, whereas with continuous compounding the interest earned is $5.13. Clearly, the more frequent the compounding, the more interest is earned on interest.

A security that pays C (in dollars) per period for n periods is known as an **annuity.** We can determine the future value of an annuity that pays C for two years as follows. The first year's payment can be reinvested for one more year at a rate y to get, at the end of year two, an amount

$$C \times (1 + y).$$

This, added to the payment of C at the end of year two, gives a future value of

$$FV = C + C(1 + y).$$

TABLE A-1   *Future Value Table*

Years to Maturity	Annual Compounding	Semiannual Compounding	Quarterly Compounding	Continuous Compounding
1	105.00	105.06	105.09	105.13
2	110.25	110.38	110.45	110.52
3	115.76	115.97	116.08	116.18
4	121.55	121.84	121.99	122.14
5	127.63	128.01	128.20	128.40
6	134.01	134.49	134.74	134.99
7	140.71	141.30	141.60	141.91
8	147.75	148.45	148.81	149.18
9	155.13	155.97	156.39	156.83
10	162.89	163.86	164.36	164.87
11	171.03	172.16	172.74	173.33
12	179.59	180.87	181.54	182.21
13	188.56	190.03	190.78	191.55
14	197.99	199.65	200.50	201.38
15	207.89	209.76	210.72	211.70
16	218.29	220.38	221.45	222.55
17	229.20	231.53	232.74	233.96
18	240.66	243.25	244.59	245.96
19	252.70	255.57	257.05	258.57
20	265.33	268.51	270.15	271.83

We use an annual interest rate of 5%. Equation 4.23 has been used to calculate annual compounding, and Equation 4.24 has been used to calculate semiannual compounding (with $m = 2$) and quarterly compounding (with $m = 4$). Equation 4.25 has been used to calculate continuous compounding.

Multiplying the previous equation by $(1 + y)$ gives

$$FV(1 + y) = C(1 + y) + C(1 + y)^2.$$

Subtracting the first equation from the second and simplifying gives

$$FV = \frac{C}{y}\{(1 + y)^2 - 1\}.$$

The future value of an annuity C for N years with an annual interest payment is

$$FV = C \times \left[\frac{(1 + y)^N - 1}{y}\right]. \tag{4.26}$$

We may rewrite Equation 4.26 as

$$FV = \frac{C}{y} \times [(1 + y)^N - 1].$$

Example A-1 illustrates the use of this formula.

Example A-1:

Consider a loan in which a payment of $C = 100$ per annum has to be made for the next 10 years. Let the interest rate y be equal to 9%. Then, the future value of this loan is

$$FV = \frac{100}{0.09} \times [(1 + 0.09)^{10} - 1] = 1,519.29. \tag{4.27}$$

For holders of securities which promise cash flows at future dates, the concept of **present value** (PV) is important. What is the present value (PV) of one dollar to be received N years from today? The present value (with annual compounding) is

$$PV = 1 \times (1 + y)^{-N}. \tag{4.28}$$

Therefore, the PV of one dollar received after N years with m interest compounding intervals per year is

$$PV = 1 \times \left(1 + \frac{y}{m}\right)^{-N \times m}. \tag{4.29}$$

And as m approaches ∞, we get the present value corresponding to continuous compounding

$$PV = 1 \times e^{-yN}. \tag{4.30}$$

Example A-2:

Consider a case in which $100 will be paid 10 years from now and the interest rate is 5% compounded continuously. In this case, the present value is

$$PV = 100 \times e^{-0.05 \times 10} = 60.65.$$

In Table A-2, we tabulate the present value of $100 to be paid at maturities ranging from one to 20 years at a discount rate of 5% under four different compounding methods.

The present value of an annuity C for N years with annual compounding is

$$PV = C \times \left[\frac{1 - \frac{1}{(1 + y)^N}}{y}\right]. \tag{4.31}$$

This equation can be rewritten as

$$PV = \frac{C}{y} \times [1 - (1 + y)^{-N}].$$

Example A-3:

Consider an annuity of $100 per year for the next 10 years at an interest rate of 9%. What is the present value of this annuity?

TABLE A-2   *Present Value Table*

Years to Maturity	Annual Compounding	Semiannual Compounding	Quarterly Compounding	Continuous Compounding
1	95.24	95.18	95.15	95.12
2	90.70	90.60	90.54	90.48
3	86.38	86.23	86.15	86.07
4	82.27	82.07	81.97	81.87
5	78.35	78.12	78.00	77.88
6	74.62	74.36	74.22	74.08
7	71.07	70.77	70.62	70.47
8	67.68	67.36	67.20	67.03
9	64.46	64.12	63.94	63.76
10	61.39	61.03	60.84	60.65
11	58.47	58.09	57.89	57.69
12	55.68	55.29	55.09	54.88
13	53.03	52.62	52.42	52.20
14	50.51	50.09	49.87	49.66
15	48.10	47.67	47.46	47.24
16	45.81	45.38	45.16	44.93
17	43.63	43.19	42.97	42.74
18	41.55	41.11	40.88	40.66
19	39.57	39.13	38.90	38.67
20	37.69	37.24	37.02	36.79

We use an annual interest rate of 5%. Equation 4.27 has been used to calculate annual compounding, and Equation 4.28 has been used to calculate semiannual compounding (with $m = 2$) and quarterly compounding (with $m = 4$). Equation 4.29 has been used to calculate continuous compounding.

$$PV = \frac{100}{0.09} \times [1 - (1 + 0.09)^{-10}] = 641.77.$$

As N approaches ∞, we get the present value of a perpetuity,

$$PV = \frac{C}{y}.$$

Note that as y increases, P falls and that as y decreases, P increases. **This illustrates that the present value and the interest rate used for discounting are inversely related.**

YIELDS

The **internal rate of return** of a bond, denoted by y and sometimes referred to as the **yield to maturity,** is the rate of discount at which the present value of the promised future cash flows equals the price of the security.

In this section, we explore this concept assuming annual compounding, then semi-annual compounding, and finally continuous compounding.

Annual Compounding

The price P of a bond that pays annual dollar coupons of C for N years, per \$100 of face value, is

$$P = \frac{C}{1+y} + \frac{C}{(1+y)^2} + \frac{C}{(1+y)^3} + \cdots + \frac{C+100}{(1+y)^N}. \tag{4.32}$$

Assuming that there is no default, the price of a bond (in equilibrium) will equal the present value of promised future cash flows.

Let us define the percentage coupon c such that $C = c \times 100$. Then, an important result derived from Equation 4.32 is that when $c = y$, $P = 100$. In a similar way, we can verify that

$$c > y \quad \Rightarrow \quad P > 100$$

and

$$c < y \quad \Rightarrow \quad P < 100$$

where the symbol $\Rightarrow$ denotes "implies."

We, therefore, conclude that when the coupon of a security is set equal to its yield to maturity, the security will sell at par.

Thus, we know that when the coupon of a security is greater than (less than) its yield to maturity, the security will sell at a premium (discount) to its par.

Note that Equation 4.32 can be written by recognizing that it is an N-year annuity paying C per period plus the terminal payment of 100. This enables us to write the price P as

$$P = \frac{c \times 100}{y} \times [1 - (1+y)^{-N}] + \frac{100}{(1+y)^N}.$$

The first term on the right-hand side is the present value of an annuity that pays c per period for N years. The second term on the right-hand side is the present value of the terminal balloon payment of 100.

In Table A-3, we provide the prices and yields of three U.S. Treasury notes. The yields in this market vary from 8.47% to 8.49%. The T-note with a coupon of 7.0% is selling at a considerable discount. The T-note with a coupon of 9.5% is selling at a premium, and the T-note with a coupon of 8.5% is selling close to par. The prices are in 32nds, as noted in Chapter 2.

TABLE A-3	Coupon	Maturity	Bid	Ask	Yield
T-Note Prices and Yields					
on June 21, 1990,	8.5%	08/15/1995	100.01	100.03	8.47%
Par, Premium,	9.5%	05/15/1994	103.05	103.09	8.49%
and Discount	7.0%	01/15/1994	95.13	95.17	8.48%

Another measure known as the **current yield** is defined as the dollar coupon of the security divided by its price, or

$$y_c = \frac{C}{P}. \tag{4.33}$$

Note from Example A-3 that the present value of a perpetuity is $PV = \frac{C}{y}$. If we choose y to be the yield of perpetuity, then the PV of perpetuity is also its price. If we denote the price by P, then $P = \frac{C}{y}$. Rearranging, we get $y = \frac{C}{P}$, which is precisely (4.33).

Note, therefore, that the current yield assumes that the bond is a perpetuity, an assumption that is more reasonable for long-term bonds.

Semiannual Compounding

The U.S. Treasury market uses semiannual compounding. The price of a default-free bond which has a round number N of coupons remaining trading at a semiannual yield y is given by

$$P = \frac{\frac{C}{2}}{1 + \frac{y}{2}} + \frac{\frac{C}{2}}{\left(1 + \frac{y}{2}\right)^2} + \frac{\frac{C}{2}}{\left(1 + \frac{y}{2}\right)^3} + \cdots + \frac{\frac{C}{2} + 100}{\left(1 + \frac{y}{2}\right)^N}. \tag{4.34}$$

Using summation notation, we can simplify Equation 4.34 as

$$P = \sum_{j=1}^{N} \frac{\frac{C}{2}}{\left(1 + \frac{y}{2}\right)^j} + \frac{100}{\left(1 + \frac{y}{2}\right)^N}. \tag{4.35}$$

The first term, with the summation sign, is the present value of all future semiannual coupons, and the second term is the present value of the balloon payment. For a bond with exactly N round coupon payments that matures in $\frac{N}{2}$ years, we can specify a simple analytical relationship between the price of the bond and its semiannually compounded yield. This price-yield formula is represented as

$$P = \frac{C}{y} + \frac{100 - \frac{C}{y}}{\left(1 + \frac{y}{2}\right)^N}. \tag{4.36}$$

C is the dollar coupon. As before, $C = c \times 100$, where the coupon rate c is in percent (i.e., if $c = 0.05$, the coupon rate is 5%), then Equation 4.36 becomes

$$P = \frac{c \times 100}{y} + \frac{100 - \frac{c \times 100}{y}}{\left(1 + \frac{y}{2}\right)^N}.$$

Example A-4:

Consider a bond with a dollar coupon of $C = 10$ per annum and with 10 round coupons remaining so that $N = 10$. For this bond, the price at a yield of 9% ($y = 0.09$) may be computed as

$$P = \frac{10}{0.09} + \frac{100 - \frac{10}{0.09}}{\left(1 + \frac{0.09}{2}\right)^{10}} = 103.9564. \tag{4.37}$$

As before, from Equation 4.36 when the coupon rate c is equal to the yield to maturity y, $P = 100$. Also, when N approaches ∞

$$y = \frac{c \times 100}{P}.$$

We can see that the current yield $\frac{c \times 100}{P}$ is probably a better approximation for the yield to maturity when N is large.

To verify this intuition, we provide in Table A-4 the semiannual yields and the current yields of two U.S. Treasury securities with different maturities. The current yield of the long bond is its dollar coupon divided by its ask price at which it can be purchased. So, current yield is $\frac{8.75}{99 + 29/32} = 8.758\%$, which is close to its semiannual yield. For the T-note maturing on August 15, 1998, the current yield is $\frac{9.125}{103 + 21/32} = 8.803\%$, which is 19.30 basis points higher than its yield to maturity.

TABLE A-4   *Comparison of Yields of Two U.S. Treasury Securities, Settlement on August 15, 1990*

Coupon	Maturity	Bid Price	Ask Price	Yield Semiannual	Current Yield
8.75%	08/15/2020	99.27	99.29	8.76%	8.758%
9.125%	08/15/1998	103.17	103.21	8.61%	8.803%

FIGURE A-1   *Price-Yield Relationship, Coupon = 10% and N = 80.*

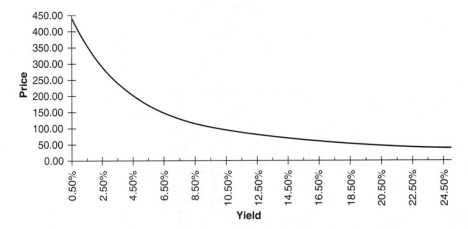

Figure A-1 shows the price-yield relationship for a 10% (annualized) coupon bond having 80 semiannual coupon periods with round number of coupons. Notice that the price-yield relation is convex to the origin. Figure A-1 indicates that the bond is much more elastic at low interest rates than it is at higher interest rates.

Continuous Compounding

If we assume continuous compounding, then the price of a bond with continuously compounded yield to maturity y is

$$P = 100e^{-y \times N} + \int_0^N e^{-y \times t} C \ dt. \tag{4.38}$$

Example A-5:

Consider a bond with a continuously compounded yield of 9%. Let the dollar coupon $C = 10$. Let $N = 10$ years. For this bond, the price at a yield of 9% ($y = 0.09$) is

$$P = 100e^{-0.09 \times 10} + \int_0^{10} 10e^{-0.09t} \ dt = 106.59. \tag{4.39}$$

All these variations in yields are important. Eurobonds pay annual coupons, the U.S. Treasury pays semiannual coupons, and GNMAs make monthly payments. As the coupons become more frequent, it becomes more accurate to assume continuous compounding. This is a very useful concept.

Appendix B

Derivation of Duration Formula

Generalizations—Price-Yield and Duration

It is useful to represent the price-yield relationship in Equation (4.10) in a compact form using the summation sign as in Equation 4.40, where C is the dollar coupon in each coupon period and $2T$ is the number of coupon periods.

$$P_t = \sum_{j=1}^{2T-1} \frac{C}{\left(1 + \frac{y}{2}\right)^j} + \frac{C + 100}{\left(1 + \frac{y}{2}\right)^{2T}}. \tag{4.40}$$

Differentiating Equation 4.40 with respect to y produces

$$\frac{\partial P_t}{\partial y} = \sum_{j=1}^{2T-1} \frac{-C \times \frac{j}{2}}{\left(1 + \frac{y}{2}\right)^{j+1}} - \frac{(C + 100) \times \frac{2T}{2}}{\left(1 + \frac{y}{2}\right)^{2T+1}}.$$

Dropping the time subscript, we can write the price sensitivity as

$$\frac{\partial P}{\partial y} = -\frac{1}{2\left(1 + \frac{y}{2}\right)} \left[\sum_{j=1}^{2T-1} \frac{C_j}{\left(1 + \frac{y}{2}\right)^j} + \frac{(C + 100)2T}{\left(1 + \frac{y}{2}\right)^{2T}} \right]. \tag{4.41}$$

Macaulay duration with semiannual compounding is given by

$$D = -\frac{\partial P}{\partial y} \frac{\left(1 + \frac{y}{2}\right)}{P}.$$

Recall that duration (D) can be considered to be the discounted average time to the security's future cash flows. Equation 4.41 can be rewritten as

$$\frac{\partial P}{\partial y} \frac{1}{P} = -\frac{1}{2\left(1 + \frac{y}{2}\right)P} \left[\sum_{j=1}^{2T-1} \frac{C_j}{\left(1 + \frac{y}{2}\right)^j} + \frac{(C + 100)2T}{\left(1 + \frac{y}{2}\right)^{2T}} \right].$$

174

Rearranging, we get

$$
-\frac{\partial P}{\partial y}\frac{\left(1+\frac{y}{2}\right)}{P} = \frac{1}{2P}\left[\sum_{j=1}^{2T-1}\frac{C_j}{\left(1+\frac{y}{2}\right)^j} + \frac{(C+100)2T}{\left(1+\frac{y}{2}\right)^{2T}}\right]
\tag{4.42}
$$

or,

$$
D = \frac{1}{2P}\left[\sum_{j=1}^{2T-1}\frac{C_j}{\left(1+\frac{y}{2}\right)^j} + \frac{(C+100)2T}{\left(1+\frac{y}{2}\right)^{2T}}\right].
\tag{4.43}
$$

Note that the right-hand side is the time-weighted discounted cash flows expressed as a fraction of the price of the security. We can express duration in units of years by rewriting Equation 4.43 slightly as

$$
D = \frac{1}{2P}\left[\sum_{j=1}^{2T}\frac{C_j j}{\left(1+\frac{y}{2}\right)^j}\right]
\tag{4.44}
$$

where $C_j = C$ for $j = 1, 2, \ldots, 2T - 1$ and $C_{2T} = C + 100$. Let us set $x_j = \frac{1}{P}\left[\frac{C_j}{(1 + y/2)^j}\right]$ so that

$$
D = \frac{1}{2}\sum_{j=1}^{2T}(x_j \times j)
\tag{4.45}
$$

It is easy to verify that $\Sigma_{j=1}^{2T}x_j = 1$ and that, therefore, we can interpret duration as the weighted average time to future cash flows. The units will be years. Example B-1 illustrates how to use Equation 4.45 to calculate duration.

Example B-1:

Examine Table B-1. Column 3 lists the timing of the cash flows in days from the settlement date. Column 4 expresses this in semiannual periods by dividing the days by 181 to find the current basis. The time-weighted cash flows are shown in column 5. The discount factors are shown in column 6. The weights x_j are presented in column 7. Given this data, the present value of the time-weighted cash flows is computed as

$20,076 \times 0.9824 + 41,678 \times 0.9637 + 62,928 \times 0.9458 + 4,062,431 \times 0.9278$

$= 3,888,528.$

The invoice price (per million dollars par) of the bond is $1,009,612.

The Macaulay duration then can be obtained by dividing the present value of the time-weighted cash flows by the invoice price

$$
D = -0.5 \times \frac{3888528}{1009612} = 1.93 \text{ years.}
$$

TABLE B-1   *Macaulay Duration of a T-Note*

(1)	(2)	(3)	(4)	(5)	(6)	(7)
					Discount Factor,	
		Number of	Semiannual	Time-		
Coupon	Cash	Days from	Periods from	weighted		
Dates	Flows,	Settlement	Settlement,	Cash Flows,	$\dfrac{1}{\left(1+\frac{y}{2}\right)^{j}}$	
	C		j	$C \times j$		x_j
2/28/93	21,250	171	0.9448	20076	0.9824	0.02068
8/31/93	21,250	355	1.9613	41678	0.9637	0.02028
2/28/94	21,250	536	2.9613	62928	0.9458	0.01991
8/31/94	1,021,250	720	3.9779	4062431	0.9278	0.93849

Settlement date: September 10, 1992
Maturity date: August 31, 1994
Coupon: 4.25%
Yield to maturity: 3.801%
Flat price: 100.84375
Accrued interest: 0.1174

Note that we can get the same results by applying Equation 4.45:

$$D = \frac{1}{2}[0.9448 \times 0.02068 + 1.9613 \times 0.02028 + 2.9613 \times 0.01991 + 3.9779 \times 0.93849]$$

$$= 1.926.$$

Turning to modified duration, it is easy to verify that

$$MD = \frac{D}{\left(1+\frac{y}{2}\right)}.$$

Referring back to the Taylor series approximation in Equation 4.17, ignoring the quadratic terms and beyond, we can see that

$$\frac{\Delta P}{P} \approx \frac{\partial P}{\partial y} \times \frac{1}{P} \Delta y.$$

Using Equation 4.19, this is the same as

$$\frac{\Delta P}{P} \approx -MD \Delta y. \tag{4.46}$$

For Example B-1, we can compute the modified duration as $MD = \frac{1.926}{1+0.03801/2}$ $= 1.89$.

Appendix C

Portfolio Risk Measures

So far, we have looked at the risk measures of a single security. It is important to see whether these concepts can be generalized to many securities. Consider a portfolio consisting of n_1 units of security 1, n_2 of security 2, . . . , and n_m of security m. Let P_i be the invoice price of security $i = 1, 2, . . . , m$. The value of the portfolio V_p can be written as

$$V_p = n_1 P_1 + n_2 P_2 + n_3 P_3 + \cdots + n_m P_m. \tag{4.47}$$

In our notation $n_1 = 100$ indicates a par value of \$100 million of bond 1. The yield to maturity of a single security was defined earlier. It is natural to extend this concept to a portfolio of securities. Let us define C_{l_j} as the lth cash flow from security j. Assume also that security j expires at T_j, paying its last cash flow. Then,

$$P_j = \sum_{l=1}^{T_j} \frac{C_{l_j}}{\left(1 + \frac{y_j}{2}\right)^{l_j}}.$$

The portfolio value is

$$V_p = \sum_{j=1}^{m} n_j P_j = \sum_{j=1}^{m} \sum_{l=1}^{T_j} \frac{C_{l_j} n_j}{\left(1 + \frac{y_p}{2}\right)^{l_j}}.$$

where the yield to maturity of the portfolio is y_p and is the internal rate of return of the cash flows of the entire portfolio.

From Equation 4.47 we get

$$\frac{\Delta V_p}{\Delta y} = n_1 \frac{\Delta P_1}{\Delta y} + n_2 \frac{\Delta P_2}{\Delta y} + n_3 \frac{\Delta P_3}{\Delta y} + \cdots + n_m \frac{\Delta P_m}{\Delta y} \tag{4.48}$$

Here we have assumed that the yield curve is flat, or $y_j = y$ for all j. In addition, we assume that the changes $\Delta y_j = \Delta y$ for all j. This is called a parallel shift in the yield curve.

From this we get

$$\text{PVBV}_p = n_1 \text{PVBP}_1 + n_2 \text{PVBP}_2 + n_3 \text{PVBP}_3 + \cdots + n_m \text{PVBP}_m. \tag{4.49}$$

In deriving this result, we have assumed that the shifts in the yields are parallel; in other words, that the yields of all securities increase by one basis point.

We can use the same logic to derive the duration of a portfolio of fixed-income securities as shown next.

Reconsider Equation 4.47 that describes the portfolio value V_p. Let $D(p)$ be the Macaulay duration of the portfolio. Then,

$$D(p) = \frac{dV_p}{dy} \times \frac{\left(1 + \frac{y}{2}\right)}{V_p}.$$

Using Equation 4.48 for the value of the portfolio, we may write this as

$$D(p) = -\frac{\left(1 + \frac{y}{2}\right)}{V_p}\left[n_1 \times \frac{\partial P_1}{\partial y} + n_2 \times \frac{\partial P_2}{\partial y} + \cdots + n_m \times \frac{\partial P_m}{\partial y}\right].$$

This can be rewritten as

$$D(p) = -\frac{\left(1 + \frac{y}{2}\right)}{V_p}\left[n_1 V_1 \times \frac{\partial P_1}{\partial y}\frac{1}{V_1} + n_2 V_2 \times \frac{\partial P_2}{\partial y}\frac{1}{V_2} + \cdots + n_m V_m \times \frac{\partial P_m}{\partial y}\frac{1}{V_m}\right].$$

Simplifying, we get

$$D(p) = \left[-\frac{\left(1 + \frac{y}{2}\right)}{P_1}\frac{n_1 P_1}{V_p}\frac{\partial P_1}{\partial y} - \frac{\left(1 + \frac{y}{2}\right)}{P_2}\frac{n_2 P_2}{V_p}\frac{\partial P_2}{\partial y} - \cdots - \frac{\left(1 + \frac{y}{2}\right)}{P_m}\frac{n_m P_m}{V_m}\frac{\partial P_m}{\partial y}\right].$$

Let $x_i = \frac{n_i P_i}{V_p}$ be the fraction of the portfolio held in security i. Define $D(i)$ to be the Macauley duration of security i. Obviously, $x_1 + x_2 + \cdots + x_m = 1$. It then follows that

$$D(p) = [x_1 D(1) + x_2 D(2) + \cdots + x_m D(m)]. \qquad (4.50)$$

In a similar way, we can derive the corresponding result for modified duration of a portfolio as

$$MD(p) = [x_1 MD(1) + x_2 MD(2) + \cdots + x_m MD(m)] \qquad (4.51)$$

Once again, it is important to note that we have assumed a parallel shift in the yields of all the securities in the portfolio. In addition, we are assuming that the securities have no default risk and that they are bullet securities with no call or sinking-fund features.

A comparison of the expressions for portfolio durations in Equations 4.50 and 4.51 with the portfolio PVBP in Equation 4.49 highlights one important difference. **To calculate the portfolio PVBP, we use par values. On the other hand, to compute portfolio durations, we use proportions of market values.**

Appendix D

Derivation of Convexity

We now want to recognize the presence of the quadratic term $\frac{1}{2}\frac{d^2P}{dy^2} \times \Delta y^2$ in (4.33). Differentiate Equation 4.42 with respect to y and simplify to get

$$\frac{\partial^2 P}{\partial y^2} = \frac{1}{4\left(1+\frac{y}{2}\right)^2}\left[\sum_{j=1}^{2T-1}\frac{C_j(j+1)}{\left(1+\frac{y}{2}\right)^j} + \frac{(C+100)2T(2T+1)}{\left(1+\frac{y}{2}\right)^{2T}}\right]. \qquad (4.52)$$

The convexity Cx as defined earlier is

$$Cx = \frac{1}{2}\frac{\partial^2 P}{\partial y^2}\frac{1}{P} \qquad (4.53)$$

Note that convexity of a security is always positive. Another measure, known as **dollar convexity,** DCx is obtained by multiplying Cx by the price P.

For bonds with exactly N round coupons remaining, the second derivative can be written as

$$\frac{\partial^2 P}{\partial y^2} = \left[\frac{N(N+1)\left(100-\frac{C}{y}\right)}{4\left(1+\frac{y}{2}\right)^{N+2}} - \frac{CN}{y^2\left(1+\frac{y}{2}\right)^{N+1}} - \frac{2C}{y^3}\left[\frac{1}{\left(1+\frac{y}{2}\right)^N}-1\right]\right].$$

Example D-1:

Reconsider the T-note in Table B-1. The calculations pertaining to convexity are shown in Table D-1.

To obtain the second derivative, we first evaluate the sum $3.835 + 11.895 + 23.576 + 1,876.323 = 1,915.630$. We then divide the sum by $\left(1+\frac{y}{2}\right)^2$. The result is $1,844.841$. We divide this quantity by 4 to get the second derivative. This is 461.21. The convexity is then obtained by dividing this by the invoice price and then by 2. The result is $Cx = 2.28$.

TABLE D-1   *Convexity of a T-Note*

Coupon Dates	Cash Flows, C	Number of Days from Settlement	Semiannual Periods from Settlement, j	Time-weighted Cash Flows, $Cxj(j+1)$	Discount Factor $\dfrac{C \times j(j+1)}{\left(1+\frac{y}{2}\right)^j}$
2/28/93	2.1250	171	0.9448	3.9043	3.835
8/31/93	2.1250	355	1.9613	12.3423	11.895
2/28/94	2.1250	536	2.9613	24.9479	23.576
8/31/94	102.1250	720	3.9779	2,022.2377	1,876.323

Settlement date: September 10, 1992, Maturity date: August 31, 1994
Coupon: 4.25%, Yield to maturity: 3.801%
Flat price: 100.84375, Accrued interest: 0.1174

Chapter 5

Yield Curve Analysis—1
Determinants of Interest Rates

Chapter Objectives

This chapter explains the connection between the state of the economy and the interest rates. The following issues are addressed in the chapter.

- What are business cycles? How do they influence the level of interest rates and the shape of the yield curve?
- What is the evidence on business cycles in the United States?
- What are the key macroeconomic factors that influence interest rates? What is the effect of macroeconomic news releases on the term structure?
- How does the central bank act in different stages of the business cycle? How does its action affect interest rates.
- What are real rates of interest and how are they related to nominal rates of interest?

INTRODUCTION

In this chapter, we will explore the relationship between the aggregate economic activity of the economy and the behavior of interest rates. We will show that the state of the economy relative to the business cycle (i.e., whether the economy is expanding or contracting) influences the level of the interest rates and the shape of the yield curve. This sets the stage for how the central bank of the country attempts to maintain stability and promote employment without fueling inflation. This will turn out to depend crucially on the target Fed funds rate. The central bank chooses the level to achieve its objectives. We will present evidence on the Federal Reserve's policies in this regard. The macroeconomic factors that determine the levels of interest rates and how news releases concerning macroeconomic factors influence the term structure of interest rates are also presented in this chapter.

We present the Fisherian separation result and the manner in which real rates, expected inflation rates, and nominal rates are related. Evidence on inflation rates is also presented.

BUSINESS CYCLE AND THE YIELD CURVE

Many economic factors influence the level and volatility of interest rates in an economy. Typically, economies display periods of economic growth and expansion followed by periods of decline and contraction. This pattern is referred to as the **business cycle.** The cyclical behavior of the economy can have major consequences for the welfare of individuals, firms, and financial institutions. A rapidly growing economy reduces unemployment and drives up the demand for labor. This, in turn, can increase the rate of growth of wages and result in inflationary growth. An increase in inflation can drive the interest rate high. The growth rate of an economy depends on a number of factors, including the supply of capital and the productivity of capital and labor. The capital may come from domestic savings if the rate of savings is high, or it can flow from abroad if foreign capital finds the growth of U.S. economy and the potential return attractive.

To understand these issues in a systematic way, let us review the behavior of the U.S. economy over the last four decades. National Bureau of Economic Research (NBER) attempts to track the cyclical behavior of the U.S. economy. Table 5-1 illustrates how frequently the U.S. economy goes through these cycles.

The U.S. economy is enjoying a period of growth and expansion since early 1991 as shown in Table 5-1. Prior to this, the economy has undergone many recessionary periods. For example, the period of July 1990 to March 1991 was a period of contraction. The lengths of the periods of expansion and contraction can vary from one business cycle to another (see Figure 5-1). The expansion that began in November 1982 lasted over seven years. The expansion that began in 1991 is in its ninth year. The behavior of macroeconomic variables is related to the overall aggregate economic activity. Variables such as industrial production, consumption, business investment, residential investment, government purchases, and so forth, tend to move in the same direction of the overall economic activity. They are often referred to as **procyclical** economic variables. In fact, some of these variables may even help policy makers and investors to forecast whether the economy is headed for a recession or expansion. Likewise, there are other economic variables, such as unemployment, which goes up in contractions and goes down in expansions. These are known as **countercyclical** economic variables. Among the financial variables, equity prices, nominal interest rates, and real interest rates are important economic variables that are related to the overall economic activity.

To understand how business cycles may affect the yield curve, let us take a look at a hypothetical economy that has reached the **trough** of the cycle. The key economic variables, such as GNP, industrial production, and so forth, would have fallen. The central bank will attempt to revive the economy by lowering the target Fed funds rate. It will follow policies to *ease* credit, thereby stimulating the economy. When short-term interest rates are reduced, typically the yield curve will steepen and become positively sloped.

As the stimulated economy starts to grow out of recession, the demand for credit will increase. This may start to increase the interest rates in the economy. As the economy expands, the demand for labor increases and wages will increase. This will cause inflation to go up and can further drive up the level and volatility of interest rates. In fact, as the economy approaches the peak, the yield curve may become *inverted,* due in part to the central bank's attempts to *tighten* credit by increasing short-term interest rates to reduce inflationary pressures.

TABLE 5-1 *U.S. Business Cycle Expansions and Contractions*

Contractions (recessions) start at the peak of a business cycle and end at the trough.

Business Cycle Reference Dates		Duration in Months			
Trough	*Peak*	*Contraction*	*Expansion*	*Cycle*	
		Trough from Previous Peak	*Trough to Peak*	*Trough from Previous Trough*	*Peak from Previous Peak*
December 1854	June 1857	—	30	—	—
December 1858	October 1860	18	22	48	40
June 1861	April 1865	8	*46*	30	*54*
December 1867	June 1869	*32*	18	*78*	50
December 1870	October 1873	18	34	36	52
March 1879	March 1882	65	36	99	101
May 1885	March 1887	38	22	74	60
April 1888	July 1890	13	27	35	40
May 1891	January 1893	10	20	37	30
June 1894	December 1895	17	18	37	35
June 1897	June 1899	18	24	36	42
December 1900	September 1902	18	21	42	39
August 1904	May 1907	23	33	44	56
June 1908	January 1910	13	19	46	32
January 1912	January 1913	24	12	43	36
December 1914	August 1918	23	*44*	35	*67*
March 1919	January 1920	*7*	10	*51*	17
July 1921	May 1923	18	22	28	40
July 1924	October 1926	14	27	36	41
November 1927	August 1929	13	21	40	34
March 1933	May 1937	43	50	64	93
June 1938	February 1945	13	*80*	63	*93*
October 1945	November 1948	*8*	37	*88*	45
October 1949	July 1953	11	*45*	48	*56*
May 1954	August 1957	*10*	39	*55*	49
April 1958	April 1960	8	24	47	32
February 1961	December 1969	10	*106*	34	*116*
November 1970	November 1973	*11*	36	*117*	47
March 1975	January 1980	16	58	52	74
July 1980	July 1981	6	12	64	18
November 1982	July 1990	16	92	28	108
March 1991		8	—	100	—
Average, all cycles:					
1854–1991 (31 cycles)		18	35	53	53*
1854–1919 (16 cycles)		22	27	48	49**
1919–1945 (6 cycles) 18		35	53	53	
1945–1991 (9 cycles) 11		50	61	61	
Average peacetime cycles:					
1854–1991 (26 cycles)		19	29	48	48***
1854–1919 (14 cycles)		22	24	46	47****
1919–1945 (5 cycles)		20	26	46	45
1945–1991 (7 cycles)		11	43	53	53

From the U.S. Department of Commerce, *Survey of Current Business, October 1994,* Table C-51.

Figures printed in **bold italic** are the wartime expansions (Civil War, World Wars I and II, Korean War, and Vietnam War); the postwar contractions, and the full cycles that include the wartime expansions.

* 30 cycles   *** 25 cycles

** 15 cycles   **** 13 cycles

FIGURE 5-1   *Lengths of Last Five Expansions and Contractions*

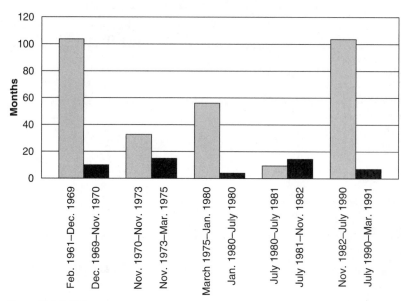

Source: Kettell 1999.

It should be clear that the overall economic activity and the monetary policies followed have a big impact on the level of interest rates, the shape of the yield curve, and the volatility of the interest rates.

Economic Variables and News Releases

In the fixed-income markets, investors follow the economic variables very closely. The investors form expectations about the levels of these variables. As and when the actual values of these variables are released by the relevant government agencies, the market will attempt to digest the information to see if there are some "surprises" relative to the consensus and if so what they may say about future interest rates. Table 5-2 describes a list of economic variables that are widely followed by investors.

For example, the consumer price index (CPI) is an important indicator of inflation risk. If it goes up beyond a consensus estimate, then it will make a big impact on market prices. An unexpected increase may signal a tightening move from the Central Bank, which may increase the interest rates. This will have an adverse impact on the prices of fixed-income securities in general. Investors watch out for such announcements each month. The schedule of economic announcements for the month of September 2000 is indicated in Table 5-3.

TABLE 5-2 *Major Economic Reports and Their Degree of Impact on Financial Markets*

Report	Description	Degree of Impact	Typical Release Date	Released by	Period Covered
Consumer Price Index	The Consumer Price Index measures the average change in prices for a fixed basket of goods and services	High	10th business day	Labor Dept. Bureau of Statistics	Prior month
Durable goods	One of a series of manufacturing and trade reports. Focuses on new orders	Moderate	18th business day	Commerce Dept. Census Bureau	Prior month
Employment	A survey of households providing very timely information on the rate of unemployment	Very high	First Friday of the month	Labor Dept. Bureau of Statistics	Prior month
Gross Domestic Product	Gross Domestic Product measures the value of items produced within the United States	Very high (for initial estimate)	20th business day	Commerce Dept. Bureau of Economic Analysis	Prior quarter
Housing starts	Measures new residential units started. Most significant for the financial markets during turning points in the business cycle	Moderate	15th business day	Commerce Dept. Census Bureau	Prior month
Industrial production	Industrial production measures output in manufacturing mining and utility industries	Moderate	15th business day	Federal Reserve Bank	Prior month
Merchandise trade	Details the monthly exports and imports of US goods	Moderate to high	Third week of the month	Commerce Dept. Census Bureau	Two months prior
NAPM	The (National Association of) Purchasing Managers Index is a composite index of new orders, production, supplier deliveries inventories, and employment	High	First business day of the month	National Association of Purchasing Management	Prior month
Producer Price Index	The Producer Price Index measures the average domestic change in prices, less discounts received, by wholesale producers of commodities	High	10th business day	Labor Dept. Bureau of Statistics	Prior month
Retail sales	A measure of consumer spending, reporting sales of both nondurable and durable consumer goods	High	Mid-month	Commerce Dept. Census Bureau	Prior month
Unemployment insurance claims	Reflects actual initial claims for unemployment insurance filed with state unemployment agencies	Moderate	Every Thursday	Labor Dept. Employment and Training Administration	Prior week ending Saturday

Source: Kettell 1999.

TABLE 5-3   *Scheduled Economic Announcements in September 2000*

<table>
<tr><td colspan="5" align="center">September 2000</td></tr>
<tr><td align="center">Monday</td><td align="center">Tuesday</td><td align="center">Wednesday</td><td align="center">Thursday</td><td align="center">Friday</td></tr>
<tr>
<td></td>
<td></td>
<td></td>
<td></td>
<td valign="top">

1

ECRI Future Inflation Gauge
for August
L: −1.1%
A: −0.5%

Construction Spending (C3)
for July
C: 0.3%
L: −1.7%
A: −1.6%

Employment Situation
for August
C: 255,000
L: −108,000
A: −105,000

NAPM Index
for August
C: 52.3
L: 51.8
A: 49.5
</td>
</tr>
<tr>
<td valign="top">**4**</td>
<td valign="top">

5

Vehicle Sales
for August
C: 14.3
L: 17.1
A: 17,396.9
</td>
<td valign="top">

6

Employment Situation (Germany)
for August
L: 9.3% Unemployment
A: 9.3% Unemployment

NAPM Non-Mfg.
for August
L: 55.5%
A: 60.0%

Productivity and Costs
for 2000Q2
L: 5.7%
A: 5.7%

Semiconductor Billings
for July
L: 5.2%
A: 4.0%
</td>
<td valign="top">

7

Employment Situation (Australia)
for August
L: 6.3% Unemployment
A: 6.4% Unemployment

GDP (France)
for 2000Q2
L: no data
A: 0.7%

Jobless Claims
for 09/02/2000
L: 318,000
A: 316,000

Oil and Gas Inventories
for 09/01/2000
L: 286.7 MB
A 289.5 MB

Wholesale Trade (MWTR)
for July
L: 1.4%
A: −0.3%
</td>
<td valign="top">

8

Labor Force Survey (Canada)
for August
L: 6.8% Unemployment
A: 7.1% Unemployment

Consumer Credit (G19)
for July
C: $10.0 billion
L: $12.0 billion
A: $9.4 billion
</td>
</tr>
</table>

TABLE 5-3 *Continued*

September 2000

Monday	Tuesday	Wednesday	Thursday	Friday
11	**12**	**13**	**14**	**15**
● GDP (Japan) *for 2000Q2* **L:** 2.4% **A:** 1.0	Richmond Fed Manufacturing Survey *for August* **L:** 3.0 **A:** 19.0 Index of Online Shopping *for August* **L:** no data **A:** 70.7	GDP (Australia) *for 2000Q2* **L:** 5.0% **A:** 5.3% Employment Situation (United Kingdom) *for August* **L:** 3.7 % Unemployment **A:** 3.6 % Unemployment Current Account *for 2000Q2* **C:** −$108.0 billion **L:** −$102.3 billion **A:** −$106.1 billion Oil and Gas Inventories *for 09/08/2000* **L:** 289.5 MB **A:** 288.5 MB Import and Export Prices *for August* **L:** 0.0% **A:** 0.2%	Jobless Claims *for 09/09/2000* **L:** 316,000 **A:** 324,000 PPI *for August* **C:** 0.2% **L:** 0.0% **A:** −0.2% Retail Sales (MARTS) *for August* **C:** 0.2% **L:** 0.7% **A:** 0.2%	CPI *for August* **C:** 0.2% **L:** 0.2% **A:** −0.1% Industrial Production *for August* **L:** 0.4% **A:** 0.3% Business Inventories (IV) *for July* **C:** 0.6% **L:** 0.9% **A:** 0.2% ECRI Weekly Leading Index *for 09/01/2000* **L:** no data **A:** −1.0%
18	**19**	**20**	**21**	**22**
NAHB Housing Market Index *for September* **L:** 61 **A:** 61	GDP (Argentina) *for 2000Q2* **L:** 0.9% **A:** 0.8% Housing Starts (C20) *for August* **C:** 1.54 million **L:** 1.51 million **A:** 1.53 million	Beige Book 2:00 PM Oil and Gas Inventories *for 09/15/2000* **L:** 288.5 MB **A:** 286.1 MB International Trade (FT900) *for July* **C:** −$30.7 billion **L:** −$30.6 billion **A:** −$31.9 billion	Jobless Claims *for 09/16/2000* **L:** 324,000 **A:** 308,000 Philadelphia Fed Survey *for September* **C:** 7.5 **L:** 14.1 **A:** 8.2 Treasury Budget *for August* **C:** −$9.0 billion **L:** $4.8 billion **A:** −$10.4 billion Employment Situation (Mexico) *for August* **L:** 2.0% Unemployment **A:** 2.6% Unemployment	SEMI Book-to Ratio *for August* **L:** 1.23 **A:** 1.24 ECRI Weekly Leading Index *for 09/15/2000* **L:** −1.0% **A:** −0.4%

TABLE 5-3   *Continued*

September 2000

Monday	Tuesday	Wednesday	Thursday	Friday
25	**26**	**27**	**28**	**29**
Existing Home Sales *for August* **C:** 4.85 million **L:** 4.79 million **A:** 5.27 million	Employment Situation (Brazil) *for August* **L:** 7.2 % Unemployment **A:** 7.1 % Unemployment Consumer Confidence *for September* **C:** 141.0 **L:** 141.1 **A:** 141.9	GDP (United Kingdom) *for 2000Q2* **L:** 3.0% **A:** 3.2% Durable Goods (Advance) *for August* **C:** 2.5% **L:** −12.4% **A:** 2.9% Oil and Gas Inventories *for 09/22/2000* **L:** 286.1 MB **A:** 285.6 MB	Agricultural Prices *for September* **L:** −1.0% **A:** 1.0% Jobless Claims *for 09/23/2000* **L:** 308,000 **A:** 287,000 GDP *for 2000Q2* **C:** 5.3% **L:** 5.6% **A:** 5.6% Help Wanted Index *for August* **L:** 82 **A:** 78 Online Help Wanted Index *for September* **L:** no data **A:** 132.0	GDP (Canada) *for July* **L:** 4.7% **A:** 4.6% Employment Situation (France) *for August* **L:** 9.7% Unemployment **A:** 9.6% Unemployment Employment Situation (Hong Kong) *for August* **L:** 5.0% Unemployment **A:** 4.9% Unemployment Employment Situation (Japan) *for August* **L:** 4.7% Unemployment **A:** 4.6% Unemployment Chicago PMI *for September* **L:** 46.5 **A:** 51.4 Personal Income *for August* **C:** 0.3% **L:** 0.3% **A:** 0.4% GDP (India) *for 2000Q1* **L:** 7.2% **A:** 5.8% ECRI Weekly Leading Index *for 09/22/2000* **L:** −0.4% **A:** 0.0%

Source: Economic Calendar, *The Dismal Scientist,* www.dismal.com/economy/releases/calendar.asp, September 30, 2000.

A = Actual

C = Consensus estimate

L = Last period

Consensus Estimate Source: Thomson Global Markets

Empirical research indicates that much of the trading activity tends to occur following news releases. Such activities tend to be more intense where the news release represents a "surprise" relative to the market consensus.

Central Bank and the Interest Rates

We have seen in earlier chapters how a change in the monetary policy can alter interest rates in a substantial manner. The central bank plays a very important role in maintaining financial stability and balancing economic growth and unemployment with controlling inflation risk. A fast-growing economy may result in a low unemployment rate but may fuel inflation. The anticipated actions of the central bank and any surprises perceived by the market in the actions of central bank can influence the course of interest rates as well. The role of the Federal Reserve in this context has been discussed in Chapter 2 of this book in some detail. We show how the Fed has changed its target Fed funds rate since 1999 in Figure 5-2. Note that the target rate has increased from 4.75% in January 1999 to 6.50% in May 2000 as it attempts to contain inflation risk in an expanding economy. Note from the NBER business cycle dates, this is a period of expansion and low unemployment. In this period, the Fed is increasing the interest rates to keep the inflation risk low.

FIGURE 5-2   *Moving Target*

► Since June of last year, the Federal Reserve has raised its target on the Fed funds rate from 4.75% to 6.50%. The chart shows when each new target was initiated. Notice that day-to-day fluctuations around the target can be quite volatile.

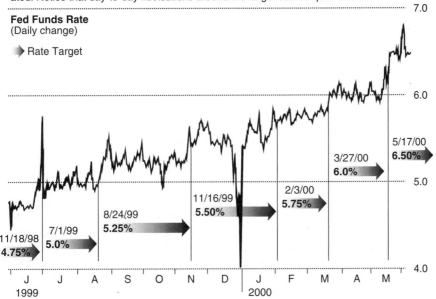

The central bank's actions and the stage of the business cycle that the economy is in should also become clearer by examining the Fed funds target history shown in Table 5-4.

TABLE 5-4

*Fed Funds Rate
Target History*

Date	Fed Funds Rate Target	Fed Action
05/16/00	6.50%	Raised 50 basis points
03/21/00	6.00%	Raised 25 basis points
02/02/00	5.75%	Raised 25 basis points
11/16/99	5.50%	Raised 25 basis points
08/24/99	5.25%	Raised 25 basis points
06/30/99	5.00%	Raised 25 basis points
11/17/98	4.75%	Cut 25 basis points
10/15/98	5.00%	Cut 25 basis points
09/29/98	5.25%	Cut 25 basis points
03/25/97	5.50%	Raised 25 basis points
01/31/96	5.25%	Cut 25 basis points
12/19/95	5.50%	Cut 25 basis points
07/06/95	5.75%	Cut 25 basis points
02/01/95	6.00%	Raised 50 basis points
11/15/94	5.50%	Raised 75 basis points
08/16/94	4.75%	Raised 50 basis points
05/17/94	4.25%	Raised 50 basis points
04/18/94	3.75%	Raised 25 basis points
03/22/94	3.50%	Raised 25 basis points
02/24/94	3.25%	Raised 25 basis points
09/04/92	3.00%	Cut 25 basis points
07/02/92	3.25%	Cut 50 basis points
04/09/92	3.75%	Cut 25 basis points
12/20/91	4.00%	Cut 50 basis points
12/06/91	4.50%	Cut 25 basis points
11/06/91	4.75%	Cut 25 basis points
10/31/91	5.00%	Cut 25 basis points
09/13/91	5.25%	Cut 25 basis points
08/06/91	5.50%	Cut 25 basis points
04/30/91	5.75%	Cut 25 basis points
03/08/91	6.00%	Cut 25 basis points
02/01/91	6.25%	Cut 50 basis points
01/09/91	6.75%	Cut 25 basis points
12/19/90	7.00%	Cut 25 basis points
11/14/90	7.50%	Cut 25 basis points
10/29/90	7.75%	Cut 25 basis points
07/13/90	8.00%	Cut 25 basis points
12/20/89	8.25%	Cut 25 basis points
11/06/89	8.50%	Cut 25 basis points
10/18/89	8.75%	Cut 25 basis points

Note, for example, that the Fed cut the target rate from July 1990 through March 1991 from 8.00% to 6.00%. Note from Figure 5-1 that this was a period of recession/contraction. The Fed continued to cut the rate until September 1992 to a level of 3% to bring the economy to an expansionary mode.

Taylor's Rule

In order to gain some insight into how the target Fed funds rate is set, Taylor (1993) has proposed a simple rule. The target Fed funds rate is set to meet the Fed's objective to maintain a stable economy and meet employment goals. The key to this is the notion of a natural rate of unemployment, defined as a level below which the economy is growing at a too rapid rate fueling inflation. For example, if the natural rate of unemployment is 4.5% and the actual rate of unemployment is 4%, then the demand for labor in the economy is very high. This will drive up wages, and inflation will increase. Clearly, what constitutes a natural rate of unemployment will depend on whether there has been a structural change in the core productivity of the economy. In a highly productive economy, the natural rate may actually decline and a higher growth rate of economy is possible without triggering inflation risk.

Taylor also postulated that the target rate will depend on what the target inflation rate for the economy is. According to Taylor's rule, the target rate should be set as follows:

$$\begin{matrix} \text{Target} \\ \text{rate} \\ \text{(Fed} \\ \text{funds)} \end{matrix} = \begin{matrix} \text{Equilibrium} \\ \text{real} \\ \text{rate} \end{matrix} + \begin{matrix} \text{Current} \\ \text{inflation} \\ \text{rate} \end{matrix} + 0.5 \begin{bmatrix} \text{Difference between} \\ \text{actual and targeted} \\ \text{inflation rate} \end{bmatrix} + 0.5 \begin{bmatrix} \text{Output} \\ \text{gap} \end{bmatrix}$$

In this context, the output gap is the percentage difference between the actual GDP and the potential GDP. The output gap is also related to the unemployment variable. Taylor's rule will suggest that when the output gap is positive (i.e., when the actual GDP growth is higher than potential GDP growth), then the target rate should increase. Likewise, if the actual inflation rate is higher than the target, the Fed funds rate should increase. Taylor's rule has proved to be a valuable tool in understanding how the central bank sets target rates.

A Simple Model of Real Rate of Interest

First, let us focus on the determinants of the real rate of interest. In an economy with no opportunity for lending or borrowing, the real rate of interest is determined by the investment opportunities and the preferences of investors for savings or consumption.

To see this point, review Figure 5-3, which represents a stylized two-date setting (date 0 and date 1). The investor is assumed to have at date 0 a wealth of W_0. The preferences of the investor are represented by the indifference curves shown in Figure 5-3. By investing a part of the wealth, the investor is able to transform the current wealth into future wealth, and hence into future consumption. Thus, by allocating an investment of I, the investor consumes $W_0 - I$ at date 0 and is able to consume an amount

FIGURE 5-3   *Investment Opportunities and Investor Preference*

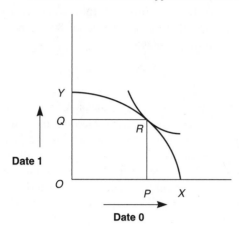

Notes:

1. Initial endowment is represented by *OX*. In the absence of riskless lending and borrowing opportunities, an amount *PX* will be invested in the production-opportunity set. This produces an amount *PR*.

2. The present value of the wealth is *OX*.

3. The consumption pattern is *(OP, OQ)*.

equal to $f(I)$ at date 1, where $f(I)$ is the production associated with an investment of I units at date 0. The optimal level of investment is determined by the propensity of the investor to save; the higher the patience level of the investor, the more will be saved toward investment for future consumption. The indifference curves in Figure 5-3 illustrate that the point of tangency is the optimal level of investment. If $U(c_0, c_1)$ is the utility function for current and future consumption denoted by c_0 and c_1, respectively, then the optimal investment decision arises out:

$$\max_{c_0, c_1} U(c_0, c_1)$$

subject to

$$c_0 = W_0 - I$$

and

$$c_1 = f(I).$$

The optimal investment strategy I^* is given by

$$f'(I) = \frac{\frac{\partial U}{\partial c_0}}{\frac{\partial U}{\partial c_1}} = \frac{dc_1}{dc_2}. \tag{5.1}$$

FIGURE 5-4   *Investment Opportunities, Riskless Lending/Borrowing, and Investor Preference*

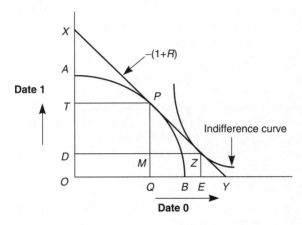

Notes:

1. Initial endowment is represented by *OB*. In the presence of riskless lending and borrowing opportunities, an amount *QB* will be invested in the production-opportunity set. This produces an amount *PQ*. Note that the optimal investment occurs at the tangency point, where the marginal return from production opportunity equals the riskless rate.

2. The present value of the wealth is *OQ* + *PQ*/(1 + *R*) = *OQ* + *QY* = *OY*.

3. The present value of consumption is *OE* + *ZE*/(1 + *R*) = *OE* + *EY* = *OY*.

4. Amount borrowed at date 0 is *EQ*.

5. Amount repaid at date 1 is *EQ*(1 + *R*) = *PM*.

Note that the marginal rate of return from investment $f'(I)$ is set equal to the marginal rate of substitution between current and future consumption. Thus, the investment opportunities and the propensity to save interact to determine the optimal level of investment. Under certainty, the marginal rate of return must also be the real rate of return $1 + R$. Two intuitive relationships emerge in this admittedly stylized setting:

- The higher the productivity of the investment-opportunity set, the higher will be the real rate of interest.
- The greater the propensity to save, the lower will be the real rate of interest.

One of the important features of this stylized analysis is that the investment decisions and consumption decisions are tightly aligned, because investment in the production-opportunity set is the only way to save for the future.

What would happen if riskless lending and borrowing opportunities were provided in addition to the production-opportunity set? This situation is presented in Figure 5-4. Note that the welfare of the investor is improved in this new situation as consumption can be transferred from one date to another in two ways. In addition to using the production technology, the investor is able to borrow or lend at a rate R. Borrowing against future wealth gives the investor important additional flexibility in this new situation. In a stylized way, the investor can be thought of as investing an amount I in the production technology such that

$$f'(I) = 1 + R. \tag{5.2}$$

With diminishing marginal returns to scale, the investment will be carried up to a level where the marginal return is exactly equal to the riskless rate. Then, the present value of the investor's endowments $\{W_0 - I, f(I)\}$ is given by

$$PV = W_0 - I + \frac{f(I)}{1 + R}. \tag{5.3}$$

Now, the investor is free to choose any consumption bundle (c_0, c_1) that satisfies the following condition:

$$PV = c_0 + \frac{c_1}{1 + R}.$$

In other words, any consumption bundle that has the same present value as the present value of the resources can be consumed by the investor. The precise consumption bundle will naturally depend on the preferences of the investor as shown in Figure 5-4. These arguments suggest the relationship between the marginal productivity of capital, investments, and real interest rates.

One important implication of the foregoing analysis is that the optimal investment decision I^* is independent of the consumption decision. This result is known as the **Fisherian separation result.** Another important implication is that the wealth of the consumer in the current situation has improved to the point given by the present value of the investor's resources in Equation 5.3.

Note that the real rate of return depends on a number of factors, such as the savings rate and the productivity (marginal rate of return) of the economy. In general, we may denote the real rate of interest as $R(x)$ where x is the vector of factors that may influence the real rate of interest. As an empirical matter, while the real rates of interest change over time depending on the evolution of the relevant factors, volatility of the real rates is generally low.

In a historical context, real rates of interest are quite high. In part, this is due to low inflation rates. The estimated real rates on a one-year T-bill is about 3%, which is in excess of 1% over the historical estimates. We will show later in this chapter that in order to estimate real rates we need to estimate the expected inflation and the inflation risk premium. This implies that real rates are forward-looking. If they are high, then they can be interpreted as a constraint on economic growth. This view is based on the premise that high real rates point to aggressive Fed tightening. On the other hand, if the productivity of the economy is very high, then the real rates simply reflect a robust economy with very productive opportunities.

Nominal Interest Rates

While the real rate of interest is an important economic concept, in most markets the focus is on the nominal rate of interest. Because most economic transactions occur in terms of the local currency, the nominal interest rate denominated in the local currency is of utmost importance to many players in the capital markets. The nominal rate of interest differs from the real rate due to inflation.

Inflation risk is primarily due to the fact that the future price of a typical consumption bundle denominated in the local currency could differ from the current price level of the same consumption bundle. Many factors, such as the demand for money and supply of money, influence inflation. Let us denote $p(y)$ as the price level where y is the vector of factors that may influence the price level. Then, the nominal rate of interest will typically depend on both factors $\{x, y\}$. In general, these factors may be correlated with each other, and their correlation properties may be important in the determination of the nominal interest rate.

It is also possible that some of the factors in x may also be factors in y; factors that influence the real rate may have an effect on the nominal rate of interest, and vice versa. One such interaction was suggested by Mundell (1963), who argued that an increased inflation risk will make nominally denominated financial assets much less valuable, thereby forcing investors to save more to compensate for the loss in the value of their savings due to increased inflation. The real effect of increased savings, as discussed earlier, is to reduce the real interest rate. It has also been argued that the volatility (risk) of inflation will affect the real rate of interest. Intuitively, we expect the factors determining the price level to induce a lot more volatility in the nominal rate of interest than the factors determining the real rate of interest.

The relationship between nominal and real rates of interest is known as the **Fisher effect,** and it has been at the core of much of the empirical work on interest rates. The basic premise behind this relation is the notion that investors will require a compensation for inflation risk in order to hold securities whose returns are in nominal terms. Thus, an investor holding a 90-day Treasury bill will require a compensation for the possible loss in the purchasing power of dollars in 90 days. This compensation is the expected inflation rate.

Suppose that the price level at date t is p_t and at date $T > t$ is $\tilde{p}_T$. Then, the inflation rate $\tilde{\pi}_t$ between dates t and T is defined as

$$\tilde{\pi}_t = \frac{\tilde{p}_T}{p_t} - 1.$$

Note that the price level at date T is uncertain. As a consequence, the inflation rate $\tilde{\pi}_t$ is also uncertain. In Figure 5-5, we plot the realized inflation rates in the U.S. economy as given by the percentage change in the consumer price index over the last two decades.

Inflation is often measured by looking at the rate of change of the Consumer Price Index (CPI). The core CPI measure and the overall CPI rates from 1984 through 1999 are shown in Figure 5-5. The core CPI rate excludes food and energy, which are

FIGURE 5-5   *Inflation Since 1984*

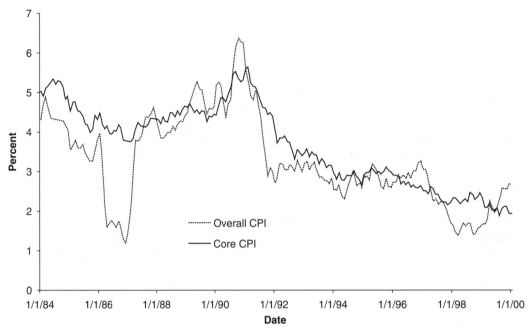

Source: B. Sack 2000.

part of the overall CPI. The inflation rate appears to have been dropping since 1991 by both measures. The overall CPI measure fluctuates more than the core CPI measure but appears to revert toward the core CPI. The oil price shocks in 1986, 1990, and in 1999–2000 contributes to the transitory fluctuations in the overall CPI measure of inflation. The fluctuations in the realized inflation rates vividly demonstrates the risk associated with financial assets. The holder of a T-bill at date t will get a nominal return

$$r_t = \frac{100}{b_t} - 1$$

where b_t is the nominal price of the Treasury bill at date t. The real price of the T-bill at date t is $\frac{b_t}{p_t}$, and the real value of par amount to be received at date T is $\frac{100}{p_T}$. Hence, the real rate of return is $\tilde{R}_t$ is

$$\tilde{R}_t = \frac{\frac{100}{p_T}}{\frac{b_t}{p_t}} - 1.$$

Remembering that $1 + \tilde{\pi}_t = \frac{p_T}{p_t}$ and $1 + r_t = \frac{100}{b_t}$ we get the real rate of return as

$$1 + r_t = (1 + \tilde{R}_t) \times (1 - \tilde{\pi}_t). \tag{5.4}$$

Note that the nominal rate of return of the T-bill is known with certainty. The inflation rate, dependent on the uncertain price level at date T, introduces an element of uncertainty in the real rate of return. Let us rewrite Equation 5.4 and simplify it as

$$1 + \acute{r}_t = 1 + \tilde{R}_t + \tilde{\pi}_t + \tilde{R}_t\tilde{\pi}_t.$$

Taking the expected value, we get the relationship between the nominal rate of interest and the expected real rate of interest:

$$r_t = E[\tilde{R}_t] + E[\tilde{\pi}_t] + E[\tilde{R}_t\tilde{\pi}_t].$$

Remember that the expectation of a product of two random variables is the sum of the product of the expectations and the covariance between the two random variables. Hence,

$$E[\tilde{R}_t\tilde{\pi}_t] = E[\tilde{R}_t]E[\tilde{\pi}_t] + \text{Cov}[\tilde{R}_t, \tilde{\pi}_t].$$

Using this and simplifying we get

$$E_t[R_t] = \frac{r_t - E_t[\pi_t] - \text{Cov}[R_t, \pi_t]}{1 + E_t[\pi_t]}. \tag{5.5}$$

Note that the expected real rate of return associated with holding a nominal security, such as a T-bill, depends on the covariance between the real rate of return and the inflation rate.

Ignoring second-order effects, we can write

$$E_t[R_t] = r_t - E_t[\pi_1]. \tag{5.6}$$

This is the Fisher effect, linking nominal interest rates, expected real interest rates, and the expected rate of inflation. Note that if the real rates do not vary a lot, then changes in expected inflation rates are fully captured by the changes in the nominal rates of interest. If the changes in expected inflation rates affect real activity, such as investments, however, they may well affect the real rates as well. In such a case, nominal rates may not fully respond to the changes in inflation rates. In the development of the Fisher effect, we considered T-bills, which have a known nominal return. A similar relation holds for securities whose nominal return is uncertain due to the reinvestment risk of coupon income.

We have not considered the effect of taxes on Fisher relation. Darby (1975) has suggested that the effect of taxes (ignoring second-order effects) will be to modify the relation as follows:

$$E_t[R_t] = r_t \times (1 - \tau) - E_t[\pi_t]$$

where τ is the tax rate. The key implication of taxes, under the Darby formulation, is that the nominal rate will be more elastic for a given change in the real rate. The real rate behavior in the U.S. economy is shown in Figure 5-6.

A number of authors have attempted to test the extent to which the Fisher effect holds in real life. Two papers that have been influential in this area are Fama (1975) and Fama and Gibbons (1982).

FIGURE 5-6   *Real Rate Fluctuations during 1975–1985*

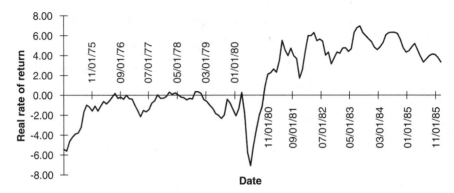

TABLE 5-5

Inflation Rates

Period	Mean Rate of Inflation	Volatility of Inflation
1940–1989	4.58%	3.97%
1940–1949	5.56%	5.91%
1950–1959	2.22%	2.19%
1960–1969	2.53%	1.76%
1970–1979	7.42%	3.43%
1980–1989	5.13%	3.18%
1953–1971 (Fama)	2.31%	1.76%

Source: Table from Smith and Spudeck, *Interest Rates: Principles and Applications,* copyright © 1993 by The Dryden Press, reprinted by permission of the publisher..

Fama (1975) tests for the presence of the Fisher effect by regressing the nominal rates of interest with the realized inflation rate. He uses the regression specification:

$$\pi_t = a_0 + a_1 r_t + \epsilon_t$$

where π_t is the realized inflation rate, r_t is the nominal rate of interest, and ϵ_t is the error term in the regression. Fama starts with the Fisher equation $E_t[R_t] = r_t - E_t[\pi_t]$ but makes the assumption that the real rates are constant. Then, the realized inflation rate π_t should be the expected inflation rate, $E_t[\pi_t]$ plus a level of random noise, ϵ_t. This leads to the regression specification used by Fama. His approach avoids the estimation of the expected inflation rate. Fama uses one-month Treasury bills in his tests, and his sample period covers 1953 through 1971. Note that under the Fisher effect, the coefficient of the nominal rate r_t, which is a_1, should be equal to 1. In addition, a_0 should be negative. Fama tests these hypotheses and finds that the Fisher effect cannot be rejected. He finds that in most of the sample period, a_1 was close to unity.

It has been argued that Fama's result is primarily due to the fact that the sample period he chose is one in which the volatility of interest rates was very low. As Table 5-5 indicates, there are other sample periods in which inflation rates showed a much greater variability. In these other sample periods with higher volatility, the nominal rates do not fully adjust to changes in inflation rate. This is not entirely surprising given that Fama was testing the joint hypothesis that the real rate is constant and that the Fisher effect is present in the data. During periods of higher volatility, one would expect the real rates also to display some variation. In fact, in a later paper, Fama and Gibbons (1982) find evidence that the real rates fluctuate with the levels of real activity in the economy. They also find evidence that a_1 is close to unity.

Inflation Risk on Interest Rates

Macroeconomic news releases that contain information about the future outlook for inflation can influence the prices of fixed-income securities. Several news releases, such as the overall CPI, core CPI, overall PPI (Purchasing Power Index), nonfarm payrolls, retail sales, and the National Purchasing Managers (NAPM) survey of industrial conditions, contain information about future inflation. The impact of a news release depends on the "surprise," which is the difference between the released value and the market expectations. Sack (2000) measured the "surprise" component by using a measure of the expected value from a survey conducted by money market services about a week prior to the macroeconomic news release. He found that both nominal yields and inflation compensation reacted strongly to surprises in news releases.

CONCLUSION

In this chapter we have identified the connections between interest rates and the state of the economy. The importance of macroeconomic news announcements on the levels of interest rates, and the shape of the yield curve was also addressed. With this background, we proceed to analyze the yield curve more precisely in Chapter 6.

PROBLEMS

5.1.   Distinguish real rates of interest and nominal rates of interest. Identify three factors that determine the real rate of interest.

5.2.   Summarize the evidence provided by Fama (1975) and Fama and Gibbons (1982) on the effect of inflation on the real rate of return and investment.

5.3.   What is the Fisher effect? How have the levels of interest rates in the economy and their volatility affected the presence of the Fisher effect?

5.4.   What is the relationship between the shape of the yield curve and the stage of the business cycle? Explain.

5.5.   If the risk of inflation is high, how will the central bank attempt to reduce that risk? Why?

5.6.   What is the Taylor rule? Explain the logic behind this rule.

REFERENCES

Darby, M. R. 1975. "The Financial and Tax Effects of Monetary Policy on Interest Rates." *Economic Inquiry* 13:266–276.

Fama, E. 1975. "Short-Term Interest Rates as Predictors of Inflation." *American Economic Review* 65(3):269–282.

Fama, E., and M. Gibbons 1982. "Inflation, Real Returns and Capital Investment." *Journal of Monetary Economics* 9(3):297–323.

Mundell, R. 1963. "Inflation and Real Interest." *Journal of Political Economy* 71:280–283.

Sack, Brian 2000. "Deriving Inflation Expectation from Nominal and Inflation-Indexed Treasury Yields," Board of Governors of the Federal Reserve System.

Smith, S. D., and R. E. Spudeck 1993. *Interest Rates: Principles and Applications.* Dryden Press, 1993 (The College Outline Series).

Kettell, Brian 1999. "Fed-Watching." Harlow, *Financial Times,* Prentice Hall.

Taylor, J.B. 1993. "Discretion versus Policy Rules in Practice," Carnegie-Rochester Conference Series on Public Policy, 39(0), pages 195–214.

SOME USEFUL WEBSITES

1.   http://www.nber.org

This is the website of NBER. It contains a wealth of resources on business cycles, research papers, and data.

2.   http://www.dismal.com

This is a very useful website to get an overall understanding of the institutions, economic releases, etc.

Chapter 6

Yield-Curve Analysis—2
Term Structure of Interest Rates

Chapter Objectives

This chapter provides the building blocks for the analysis of the yield curve and the concept of the term structure of interest rates. Chapter 6 will help the reader to understand and answer the following questions:

- What is meant by the volatility of interest rates? How does it differ across yields of different maturities?
- What is the term structure of interest rates?
- How can coupon bonds be built as a portfolio of zero-coupon bonds?
- What are the concepts of the term structure of interest rates?
    1. What are spot rates of interest?
    2. What are forward rates of interest?
    3. What does it mean to extract spot rates from the coupon-bond prices?
    4. What is par bond yield curve?
- What are strips? What is meant by reconstitutions?
- What economic considerations are involved in stripping and reconstituting bonds?

INTRODUCTION

Chapter 5 developed the connections between the state of the economy and the course of interest rates. We showed that many factors, such as the stage of the business cycle, central bank actions, and surprises in economic news releases, influence interest rates. In this chapter, we develop the analytical tools needed to manage risks associated with changes in interest rates. We also extend many of the concepts developed in Chapter 4. We show that nonparallel movements occur frequently in the market. We develop the concept of zero-coupon curve. One of the underpinnings to the pricing of fixed-income securities is the fact that most coupon-bearing bonds can be properly viewed as a portfolio of zero-coupon securities. This interpretation is valid so long as there is no credit risk, and no options are held by issuers to call or by investors to put or convert. We also develop concepts, such as the spot rate of interest, forward rate of interest, and par bond yield curve.

We then introduce the strips markets and discuss the relationship between strip and spot rates. Finally, some practical issues that are relevant in the estimation of zero-coupon bond prices from the yield curve are presented.

YIELD-CURVE ANALYSIS

Yield curve is a term used to describe the plot of yield to maturity against time to maturity or against a risk measure, such as the modified duration of debt securities in a certain market segment (such as Treasury). By incorporating the expectations of diverse participants in the marketplace, the shape of the yield curve succinctly captures and summarizes the cost of credit for loans of various maturities. The shape of the default-free yield curve is, therefore, of considerable interest to practitioners in the financial markets.

Recall that the concepts of duration and convexity are strictly valid only when the movements in the yield curve are parallel. To remind yourself what we mean by parallel shifts in yield curve, examine Table 6-1 and Figure 6-1, which illustrate parallel shifts: all the yields go up or go down by precisely the same amount. Note that when

TABLE 6-1

Parallel Shifts in Yields of Securities

Maturity in Years	Current Level of Yields	Parallel Shift by +100 Basis Points	Parallel Shift by −100 Basis Points
0.25	4.5%	5.5%	3.5%
0.5	5.0%	6.0%	4.0%
1	6.0%	7.0%	5.0%
2	7.2%	8.2%	6.2%
3	8.0%	9.0%	7.0%
5	9.5%	10.5%	8.5%
7	11.0%	12.0%	10.0%
10	12.0%	13.0%	11.0%
30	13.0%	14.0%	12.0%

FIGURE 6-1   *Parallel Shifts in Yield Curve*

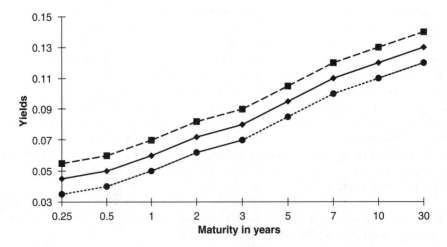

the yield to maturity of the three-month T-bill goes up from 4.5% to 5.5%, the yield to maturity on the thirty-year T-bond also increases from 13% to 14%. Both securities experience an increase of 100 basis points in their yields.

How realistic is the parallel shift assumption? To examine this question, we begin by presenting first the shape of the yield curve at selected points in time and noting the shifts in the shape of the yield curve over time.

Over the last several decades, the Treasury yield curve has assumed different shapes. We review briefly some sample periods to illustrate this richness over time. In Figure 6-2, we provide the shape of the default-free yield curve during June 1981. Figure 6-3 provides the shape as of April 1982, and Figure 6-4 as of December 1982.

FIGURE 6-2   *Inverted Yield Curve (June 1981)*

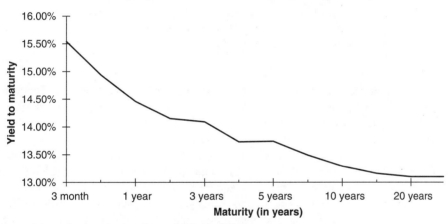

Source: Salomon Brothers, *Analytical Record of Yields, 1982.*

FIGURE 6-3   *Humped Yield Curve (April 1982)*

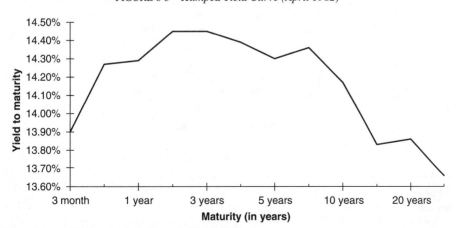

Source: Salomon Brothers, *Analytical Record of Yields, 1982.*

FIGURE 6-4   *Normal Yield Curve (December 1982)*

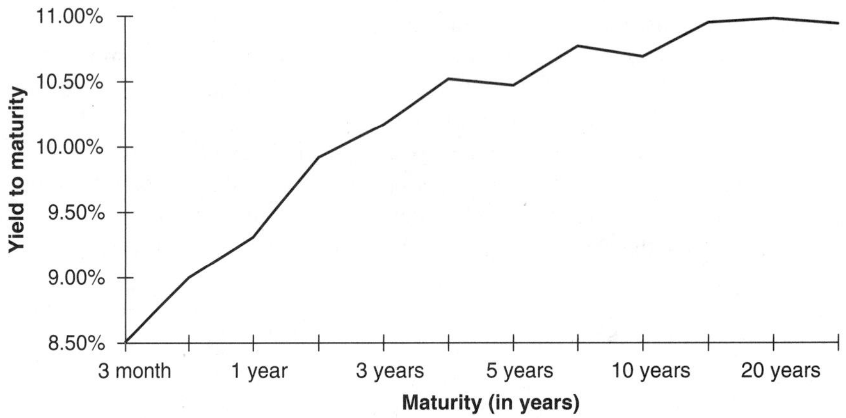

Source: Salomon Brothers, *Analytical Record of Yields,* 1982.

Figure 6-2 shows that the yield curve was steeply inverted during June 1981. That is to say that the short-term yields were at around 15.50%, which is a level much higher than the long-term yields, which were around 13.00%. Note that the overall levels of interest rates were quite high all across the maturity spectrum.

In Figure 6-3, we note that within a year's time the yield curve had become humped. Compared to June 1981, short-term interest rates had fallen, but the long-term interest rates have increased. The yields start at around 13.90% and increase to about 14.50% at a maturity of two years (hump at two years) and then drop to about 13.70% at 30 years. At the end of 1982 (just eight months after April 1982), the yield curve becomes normal or upward sloping, as shown in Figure 6-4. The levels of interest rates, however, have fallen significantly. Short-term rates begin at 8.50% and long-term rates end at around 11.00%. While Figures 6-2 to 6-4 represent a particularly volatile period, such nonparallel shift in the yield curve are encountered from time to time.

To get an idea of the risk associated with nonparallel shifts in the yield curve, examine Figure 6-5, where the spread between the ten-year yields and two-year yields are plotted for the period November 1988 to February 1991. Note that the spread started at about 50 basis points in late 1988 and reached a low of −42 basis points in early 1989, leading to an inverted yield curve during the first half of 1989. Later, the spread became positive and reached a high of 110 basis points toward the beginning of 1991. Note that periodically the yield curve becomes inverted and that nonparallel shifts appear to be pervasive.

In this discussion, we have chosen to work with data for specific maturities: 3 months, 6 months, 1 year, 2 years, 3 years, 4 years, 5 years, 7 years, 10 years, 15 years, 20 years, and 30 years. In reality, there are over 100 Treasury securities that are outstanding in the marketplace, ranging in maturity from a few days to 30 years. In order to get additional insights into the shape of the yield curve and the pattern of its changes, we need to examine the volatility of short-term and long-term interest rates.

FIGURE 6-5   *Spread between Ten-Year Yields and Two-Year Yields, in Basis Points*

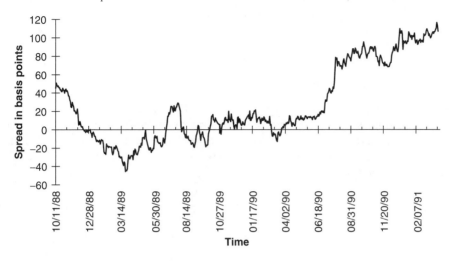

Volatility of Short and Long Rates

Volatility measures the variability of interest rates relative to their expected average levels. Loosely speaking, volatility measures the degree of variation of any variable around its mean. Given historical observations, we can estimate the volatility. It stands to reason that the degree of variation, as well as the mean of the interest rates, change with time as the economic determinants of interest rates change. For example, the short rates of interest changed significantly between 1978 and 1983. As we saw in Chapter 2, this was, in part, due to a change in the monetary policy that was effected by the Fed. (This is an extreme example in the sense that the entire structure underlying interest rates was affected.) The levels of interest rates and their volatility might systematically incorporate the changes in the factors that affect them. As a consequence, the time series of interest rates might exhibit a systematic clustering effect. The estimation procedures used for volatility vary significantly in their levels of sophistication. Some do not explicitly account for the fact that the volatilities exhibit clustering effects; others do.

The traditional approach to estimating volatility looks at a predetermined amount of historical information of a certain frequency (daily, weekly, monthly, etc.) and then computes the standard deviation of that series. This is then annualized and reported as the volatility estimate. The next level of sophistication assigns different weights to different historical observations. For example, more recent observation can be given greater importance. In markets where the liquidity is high and where many transactions occur in any given day, intraday prices or the high-low prices may be used for the purpose of estimating volatility. Later in the book, we will introduce the concept of implied volatilities, whereby volatility estimates are obtained by using the prices of a derivative asset and a pricing framework for the derivative asset. Finally, the GARCH (generalized autoregressive and conditional heteroskedastic) models postulate specific relationships between the level of current volatility and their historical levels in their estimation procedures. The interested reader is referred to Bollerslev and Engle (1993). We present the traditional approach to estimating later in this chapter.

Price-Based versus Yield-Based Volatility

It is useful to distinguish between price-based and yield-based volatilities in the context of fixed-income securities markets. The prices of fixed-income securities tend to par as their maturity dates approach. The price-yield relation that we developed earlier can be used to derive one volatility given the other. For example, we showed that the modified duration is given by

$$\text{MD} = -\frac{dP}{dy}\frac{1}{P}, \tag{6.1}$$

where P is the price and y is the yield of the fixed-income security. Price-based volatility is the standard deviation of the rate of change in prices. Let us denote the price-based volatility as $\sigma_p = \sigma\left(\frac{dP}{P}\right)$. The yield-based volatility is the standard deviation of the percentage change in yields. Denote the yield-based volatility as $\sigma_y = \sigma\left(\frac{dy}{y}\right)$. Then from the expression for the modified duration, we can derive the relationship between price-based volatility and yield-based volatility as follows.

From Equation 6.1, we get

$$\frac{dP}{P} = -\text{MD} \times dy.$$

From the previous expression, we can derive

$$\sigma_P = \sigma_y \times y \times \text{MD}. \tag{6.2}$$

We can use Equation 6.2 to transform price-based volatility into yield-based volatility and vice versa. Thus, the procedures for estimating the price-based volatility can easily be used to compute the yield-based volatility. We illustrate the traditional approach to estimating volatility in Example 6.1.

Example 6-1:

To provide a concrete illustration, consider the 7.25%, 05152016 Treasury bond. We used the prices and yields of the 7.25%, 05152016 Treasury bond over the period May 9, 1986 to June 20, 1986.

Let P_t denote the price at date t and y, denote the yield at date t. Then, the traditional volatility measure is computed as follows:

1. Compute the natural log of the price ratio $R_t = \ln\left(\frac{P_{t+1}}{P_t}\right)$ for each date t in the sample, where $t = 0, 1, \ldots N$. Note that this is the same as the difference in the log of the prices, $[\ln P_{t+1} - \ln P_t]$, at dates $t + 1$ and t.
2. Compute the mean $\mu = \left(\frac{\sum_{t=0}^{N} R_t}{N}\right)$ of the natural log of the price ratio.

FIGURE 6-6   *Price-Based Volatility and Yield-Based Volatility*

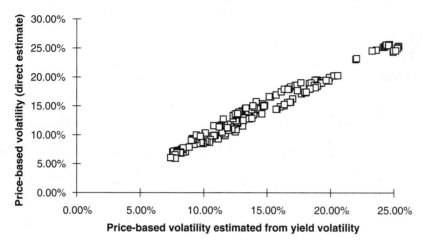

3. Calculate the squared deviations for each t as $x_t = (R_t - \mu)^2$.

4. Then, the traditional daily volatility estimate is

$$\sqrt{\frac{\sum_{i=1}^{N-1} (x_i)}{N-1}}.$$

5. And the traditional *annual* volatility estimate σ_P is

$$\sigma_P = \sqrt{\frac{\sum_{i=1}^{N-1} (x_i) \times 252}{N-1}}.$$

This recognizes that there are 252 trading days per year, on average. Using the data from May 9, 1986, ($t = 0$) to June 23, 1986, ($t = N$), we estimated the price-based volatility on June 24, 1986. This turns out to be 19.36%.

Using the relationship between price-based volatility and yield-based volatility, we can compute the yield volatility as well. In the financial markets, both price and yield volatilities are used. The volatility of the yield for the period is 21.44%.

Using Equation 6.2, we can also estimate the price-based volatility from the yield-based volatility that we estimated. As can be seen from Figure 6-6, these two estimates appear to differ just by a scaling factor.

Evidence on Volatility

When we examine the volatility of interest rates of different maturities, we note that the short-term rates are much more volatile than long-term rates. A clue to this pattern

FIGURE 6-7   *Volatility and the Level of Interest Rates*

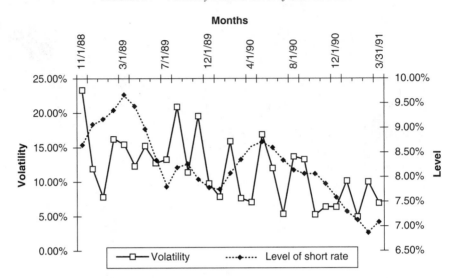

is present in Figures 6-2 through 6-4. Note how the short-term rates changed much more dramatically than long-term rates between June 1981 and April 1982. In addition, as the yield curve moved from a humped shape in April 1982 to an upward-sloping shape in December 1982, the short rates fell by over 500 basis points, whereas the long rates fell by under 250 basis points. Using the data on the Treasury markets, we estimated the short-rate volatilities and long-rate volatilities for various monthly subperiods from November 1988 to March 1991.

The volatilities display two discernible patterns. First, short-term volatilities are generally higher than long-term volatilities, although there are some exceptions in the sample period. Second, the volatility appears to be related to the level of the interest rates and the shape as captured by the average spread between ten-year and two-year T-notes. During this sample period, short-term rates (two-year) have varied from a minimum of 6.87% to a high of 9.67%, a range of 280 basis points. In contrast, long-term rates (ten-year) have varied from a minimum of 7.83% to a maximum of 9.35%, a range of 152 basis points. Thus, the range of the short-term rate is nearly twice that of the long-term rate. This pattern is consistent with what we saw in Figures 6-2 through 6-4. Out of the 29 months from November 1988 to March 1991, during 20 months the volatility of the short rate exceeded the volatility of the long rate.

In Figure 6-7, we provide the association between the level of interest rates and the volatility. Note that there is a general positive association between the level of the short rate and its volatility. In other words, the volatility of rates appears to be level dependent and tends to increase with the levels. As Figure 6-8 shows, during periods of inverted yield curves, the volatility levels are very high and short-rate volatility more often exceeds long-rate volatility.

These considerations are important for several reasons. First, in the specification of a satisfactory model of the term structure it is necessary to incorporate this feature

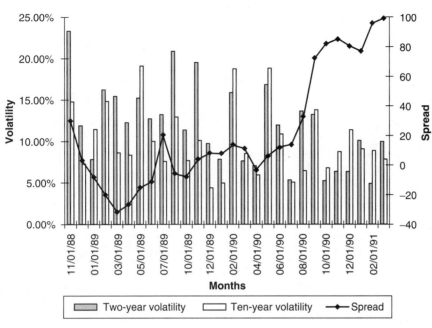

FIGURE 6-8   *Volatility and the Shape of Yield Curve*

of interest-rate volatility. Second, the pricing and hedging of many interest-rate deriv-ative products are significantly influenced by the volatility, and it is important to in-corporate the differential volatility of short-term and long-term interest rates in their valuation.

Yield versus Maturity and Duration

The yield curve, as mentioned earlier, is the plot of yield to maturity as a function of time to maturity or of modified duration. In Figure 6-9, we depict the yield curve on January 15, 1991. All Treasury notes and bonds that were outstanding on that day (for settlement on January 17, 1991) are represented in the figure. In Figure 6-10, we have represented the yield curve as a plot between yield to maturity and modified duration.

To illustrate the problems of drawing sensible inferences from this yield curve, we should note first that on that day over 200 Treasury notes and bonds were outstand-ing in the market. Over 20 outstanding bonds are callable by the Treasury at par on any coupon day during the last five years of the bond's stated life.

Coupon Effect

In each maturity sector, there are clusters of Treasury securities of varying vintages, coupons, and contractual provisions. For example, as noted in Table 6-2, there are five Treasury securities maturing on February 15, 1993, ranging in coupons from 6.75% to

FIGURE 6-9   *Yield Curve on January 15, 1991, First Plot*

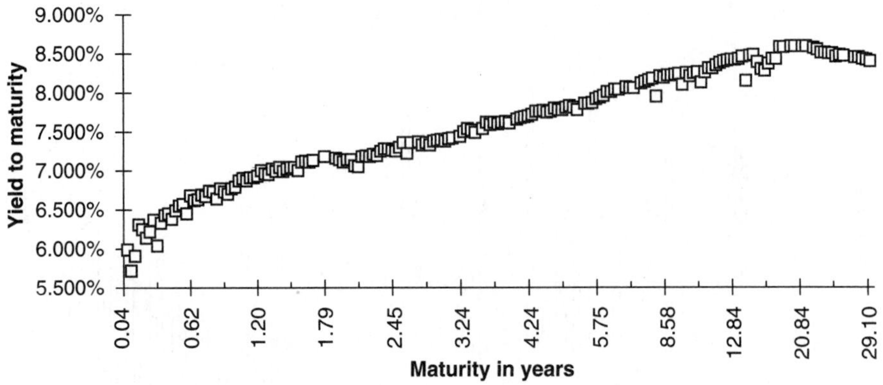

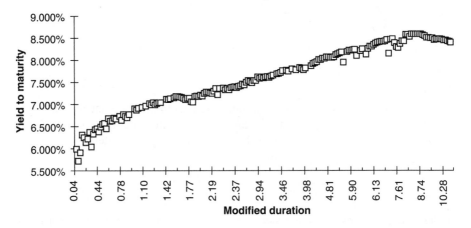

Maturity in years

FIGURE 6-10   *Yield Curve on January 15, 1991, Second Plot*

Modified duration

10.875%. The modified durations of these five securities were practically identical, yet their yield to maturity varied from a low of 7.05% to a high of 7.19%. Note that high-coupon securities generally yield higher. This pattern is by no means an accident: Three securities were maturing on May 15, 1993, and the security with a coupon of 10.125% was yielding 7.28%, whereas the security with a coupon of 7.625% was yielding 7.25%. This difference of 3 basis points is well outside the bid-offer spread and, hence, is of economic significance. Similar situations can be noted in the long end of the yield curve. The 8.5% coupon T-bond maturing on February 15, 2020, has a modified duration of 10.42 years and has a yield to maturity of 8.42%. In comparison, the 9% coupon T-bond maturing on November 15, 2018, with a modified duration of 10.41 years, has a yield to maturity of 8.45%, which is higher by 3 basis points.

TABLE 6-2   *Selected Treasury Notes and Bonds Prices and Yields Quoted: January 15, 1991.*
Settlement: January 17, 1991

Coupon (rounded)	Maturity or First Call Date	Price $(in \frac{1}{32})$	Modified Duration	Maturity (in years)	Yield
6.75000%	2/15/93	99.05	1.85	2.08	7.06%
7.87500%	2/15/93	101.10	1.83	2.08	7.05%
8.25000%	2/15/93	101.31	1.83	2.08	7.18%
8.37500%	2/15/93	102.06	1.82	2.08	7.19%
10.87500%	2/15/93	106.29	1.78	2.08	7.18%
7.62500%	5/15/93	100.21	2.07	2.33	7.25%
8.62500%	5/15/93	102.25	2.06	2.33	7.28%
10.12500%	5/15/93	105.28	2.03	2.33	7.28%
9.00000%	11/15/18	105.23	10.40	27.85	8.45%
8.87500%	2/15/19	104.13	10.24	28.10	8.45%
8.12500%	8/15/19	96.19	10.43	28.59	8.43%
8.50000%	2/15/20	100.24	10.42	29.10	8.42%
8.75000%	5/15/20	103.21	10.63	29.35	8.40%
8.75000%	8/15/20	103.22	10.43	29.60	8.40%

Source: Federal Reserve Bank, New York.

What are the reasons for high-coupon securities to trade at a slightly higher yield even though the duration is the same? Many institutional investors with long-dated liabilities might prefer low-coupon securities, which tend to have a longer duration. As noted in Chapter 4, higher duration means a higher sensitivity to interest rates. Such assets may be ideal to match the interest-rate sensitivity of long-dated liabilities. Pension funds and insurance companies are examples of such institutional investors. They may drive up the price of low-coupon securities, thereby bringing down their yields.

The process of auctions may also contribute to this pattern. The Treasury attempts to sell the security close to par; this means that as the rates decrease, the newly issued security will tend to have a lower coupon, and a number of issues that were issued in the recent past will become high coupons. Thus, the relative supply of high coupons will be larger. This tends to lower their price and increase their yield. Of course, exactly the reverse will occur when the rates increase. There may be tax considerations as well. High-coupon bonds that pay higher interest may subject certain investors to a greater tax exposure. If such investors are the marginal holders of these bonds, they may demand a higher yield. Conversely, low-coupon bonds may be accepted at a lower yield.

The regulatory restrictions faced by institutions may also play a part. In Japan, certain institutions are not permitted to pay dividends from capital gains; they are permitted to pay dividends only from interest income. They prefer high-coupon bonds. As a result, high-coupon bonds in Japan have tended to exhibit lower yield in many periods. We explore further the effect of taxes on the pricing of fixed-income securities later in the text.

Liquidity Effect

The newly issued securities (the on-the-run issues) tend to be more liquid; we showed evidence of this in Chapter 1. As such, they will sell at a higher price. In other words, they command a liquidity premium while off-the-run issues will be cheaper, *ceteris paribus,* because of their illiquidity. This pattern is obvious for the 30-year T-bonds in the last section. Recall that the on-the-run T-bond (8.75% coupon, maturing on August 15, 2020) was trading at a yield of 8.40%, whereas the old 30-year T-bond (8.50% coupon, maturing on February 15, 2020) was trading at a higher yield of 8.42%.

The liquidity effect is probably best seen by comparing Treasury bills with Treasury notes and bonds that have the same maturity. In Table 6-3 we present all the T-bills that were traded on January 15, 1991, for settlement on January 17, 1991. Consider the bill maturing on May 16, 1991, trading at a yield of 6.31%. In the market, a T-note with a coupon 8.125% maturing on May 15, 1991, was yielding 6.37%. Although both are riskless and are virtually identical, the T-note is cheaper than the T-bill by 6 basis points.

Generally, T-bills are more expensive than off-the-run T-notes and T-bonds, as is borne out in Figure 6-11. In Figure 6-12, we illustrate this fact based on more recent data.

Warga (1992) shows that recently issued bonds (on-the-run) are priced to reflect a premium of about 55 basis points per annum compared to otherwise identical bonds. Table 6-4, taken from Warga's paper, vividly illustrates that off-the-run issues are priced at a discount relative to on-the-run issues across a duration range of 20 to 84 months.

TABLE 6-3   *U.S. Treasury Bills Quoted: January 15, 1991. Settlement: January 17, 1991.*

Maturity	Bid	Ask	Yield	Maturity	Bid	Ask	Yield
01/24/1991	5.09	5.05	5.13	05/23/1991	6.13	6.11	6.33
01/31/1991	5.36	5.32	5.41	05/30/1991	6.13	6.11	6.34
02/07/1991	5.46	5.38	5.47	06/06/1991	6.11	6.09	6.32
02/14/1991	5.60	5.58	5.68	06/13/1991	6.13	6.11	6.35
02/21/1991	5.82	5.80	5.91	06/20/1991	6.15	6.13	6.38
02/28/1991	5.83	5.79	5.91	06/27/1991	6.09	6.07	6.33
03/07/1991	5.99	5.97	6.10	07/05/1991	6.19	6.17	6.44
03/14/1991	6.00	5.98	6.12	07/11/1991	6.17	6.15	6.43
03/21/1991	6.00	5.98	6.13	07/18/1991	6.16	6.14	6.42
03/28/1991	5.99	5.97	6.12	08/01/1991	6.21	6.19	6.48
04/04/1991	6.03	6.01	6.17	08/29/1991	6.21	6.19	6.49
04/11/1991	6.02	6.00	6.17	09/26/1991	6.18	6.16	6.47
04/18/1991	6.05	6.03	6.21	10/24/1991	6.27	6.25	6.59
04/25/1991	6.12	6.10	6.29	11/21/1991	6.27	6.25	6.61
05/02/1991	6.11	6.09	6.29	12/19/1991	6.20	6.18	6.55
05/09/1991	6.11	6.09	6.29	01/16/1992	6.20	6.18	6.58
05/16/1991	6.12	6.10	6.31				

FIGURE 6-11   *Liquidity Effects in Yield Curve*

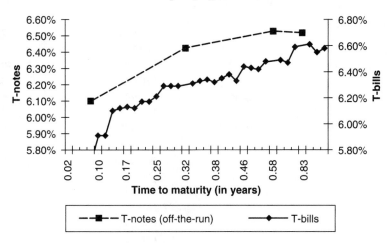

FIGURE 6-12   *Yield Curve for Treasury Securities, September 23, 1999*

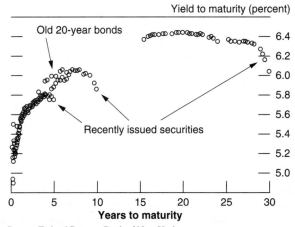

Source. Federal Reserve Bank of New York.

Note that most recently issued securities have generally a lower yield
when compared to previously issued (old) securities. This is due to the
higher liquidity of new issues.

With so many issues outstanding, it is very difficult to estimate the correct yield at
any given maturity date. We need a good benchmark at each maturity date clearly indicating the yield at that maturity date. In addition, there are some maturity dates for
which no issues are present in the market. In order to develop estimates of yields at
those maturities, we need a benchmark as well. This leads us to the concept of term
structure.

TABLE 6-4

EM-Based Mean Differences—All Bonds Minus "On-the-Run" (Figures are in basis points per annum.)

Duration Range (Months)		Mean Difference*
20–24	Portfolio 1	47.6
	t-stat	3.5
28–32	Portfolio 3	40.6
	t-stat	2.4
36–40	Portfolio 5	55.9
	t-stat	4.1
40–44	Portfolio 6	38.5
	t-stat	1.6
44–48	Portfolio 7	65.2
	t-stat	3.5
48–52	Portfolio 8	131
	t-stat	5.3
56–60	Portfolio 10	7.16
	t-stat	0.25
60–64	Portfolio 11	101
	t-stat	3.1
64–72	Portfolio 12	56.5
	t-stat	1.9
72–84	Portfolio 13	8.67
	t-stat	0.2

Source: Warga, 1992.

*Measured in basis points per annum.

TERM-STRUCTURE ANALYSIS

In order to develop a sharp intuition about the shape of the yield curve and the factors that underlie the levels and the shape, we need a more parsimonious representation of the yield curve than Figure 6-9. It is in this context that we define the term structure of interest rates.

Term structure of interest rates refers to the relationship between the yield to maturity of default-free zero coupon securities and their maturities.

Often, the yield to maturity on a default-free zero-coupon (pure discount) bond is termed the **spot rate of interest.** The relationship between the spot rate of a pure discount bond and its maturity is referred to as the **spot curve.** In order to get a better handle on the pricing of zero-coupon bonds, we first develop the pricing principles for a default-free pure discount bond.

Pure Discount Bonds

The concept of term structure is best developed in terms of pure discount bonds or zero-coupon bonds. We define the notation for the price of a zero, suggested earlier, more formally as z_t, the price of a pure discount bond that pays \$1 in t periods from now. We assume that the discount bonds are free from default risk. (The treatment of credit risk requires the modeling of economic factors that lead to financial distress and of the negotiations between creditors and borrowers in times of financial distress. In addition, such factors as liquidation costs, cash flow generating capacity of the borrower, etc. become relevant. We consider such factors in Chapter 8 in the context of corporate debt.) Examples of default-free zero-coupon securities are T-bills (considered in Chapter 4) and zero-coupon securities obtained by stripping U.S. Treasury securities. The analysis of strips is taken up later in this chapter.

Bootstrapping Procedure. Spot rates are associated with specific maturities. Thus, the spot rate y_j for a pure discount bond maturing j years from now may be defined as the discount rate at which the present value of the promised terminal cash flow of the pure discount bond is equal to its price. If z_{j-t} is the price at date t of a pure discount bond paying \$100 in $j - t$ periods, then

$$z_{j-t} = \frac{100}{(1 + y_j)^{j-t}}, \tag{6.3}$$

where y_j is the spot rate of interest on a zero-coupon bond with a time to maturity of $j - t$.

Often, we are confronted with situations where the prices of coupon bonds are readily available, but zero-coupon prices are difficult to get. So, it is necessary to try to estimate zero-coupon bond prices based on the prices of coupon bond prices. A procedure known as bootstrapping is used for this purpose. This procedure is illustrated in Example 6-2.

Example 6-2:

Consider the problem of finding the pure discount bond prices from the coupon bond prices that are available. Table 6-5 gives data for three bonds for a period of three years. Note that Bond 1, which matures in a year's time, has a coupon of 5% (annual) and is selling at a price of 99.50. Bond 2, which matures two years from now, pays a coupon of 6% (annual) and is selling at a price of 101.25. Finally, Bond 3, which pays a coupon of 7%, matures three years from now and is selling at a price of 100.25.

Let P_i be the price of bond i. Let c_i denote the dollar coupon associated with bond i. Then, we can denote the price of the first bond as

$$P_1 = \frac{100 + C_1}{(1 + y_1)}. \tag{6.4}$$

TABLE 6-5	Bond	Price	Year 1	Year 2	Year 3
Prices, Coupons, and Maturities	1	99.50	105	0	0
	2	101.25	6	106	0
	3	100.25	7	7	107

$P_1 = 99.50$ and $C_1 = 5$. Thus, Equation 6.4 becomes

$$99.50 = \frac{100 + 5}{(1 + y_1)}. \tag{6.5}$$

Solving for y_1, we get a one-year spot rate of interest of 5.53%. The one-year implied zero, z_1, is defined as

$$z_1 = \frac{1}{1 + y_1}. \tag{6.6}$$

Substituting $y_1 = 5.53\%$ in the equation and solving, we get $z_1 = 0.9476$. More generally, we can use Equation 6.4 to solve for the one year zero price as follows:

$$z_1 = \frac{1}{1 + y_1} = \frac{P_1}{100 + C_1}$$

Once the price P_1 and the coupon C_1 of the one-year coupon bond are known, we can solve for z_1, the zero-coupon bond price.

Armed with the knowledge of y_1, we can determine y_2. To do this, recognize that the price of Bond 2 can be written in terms of the two spot rates of interest as

$$P_2 = \frac{C_2}{1 + y_1} + \frac{100 + C_2}{(1 + y_2)^2}. \tag{6.7}$$

Note that the first coupon C_2, which will be paid at year 1, is discounted at the one-year spot rate of interest. The final payment $100 + C_2$, paid in year 2, is discounted at the second-year spot rate of interest. Substituting $P_2 = 101.25$, $C_2 = 6$, and $y_1 = 5.53\%$, we get

$$101.25 = \frac{6}{1 + 0.0553} + \frac{100 + 6}{(1 + y_2)^2}. \tag{6.8}$$

Solving for y_2, we get $y_2 = 5.32\%$. The implied zero for two-year maturity may be found by

$$z_2 = \frac{1}{(1 + y_2)^2} \tag{6.9}$$

$$z_2 = 0.9015.$$

	Maturity (Years)	Implied Zero	Spot Rate
TABLE 6-6 *Implied Zeroes and Spot Rates*	1	0.9476	5.53%
	2	0.9015	5.32%
	3	0.8159	7.02%

As before, using Equation 6.7, we can solve in a general way for z_2 as follows:

$$z_2 = \frac{1}{(1 + y_2)^2} = \frac{P_2 - C_2 z_1}{100 + C_2}.$$

The computed values for z_1, P_2 and C_2 are used to solve for z_2.

Proceeding in this way, we can determine y_3 and z_3 as well. The price of Bond 3 may be written as

$$P_3 = \frac{C_3}{1 + y_1} + \frac{C_3}{(1 + y_2)^2} + \frac{100 + C_3}{(1 + y_3)^3}. \tag{6.10}$$

Note that in the previous equation, the only unknown quantity is y_3, the three-year spot rate of interest. Substituting for the values of P_3, C_3, y_1, and y_2, we get

$$100.25 = \frac{7}{1 + 0.0553} + \frac{7}{(1 + 0.0532)^2} + \frac{100 + 7}{(1 + y_3)^3}. \tag{6.11}$$

Solving for y_3, we obtain $y_3 = 7.02\%$. Then

$$z_3 = \frac{1}{(1 + y_3)^3} \tag{6.12}$$

$$z_3 = 0.8159.$$

The results are presented in Table 6-6.

Note that this example is hypothetical and is intended just to illustrate the concept of building the spot curve from coupon bonds. In this and earlier examples, we have used premium and discount coupon bonds, which in a real transaction have coupon effects discussed earlier. In addition, bonds may not be available at every maturity sector. Some maturity ranges are spanned by bonds that are callable. In Table 6-2, we note that callable bonds dominate the maturity range 2002 to 2009. So, the problem of building implied zeroes is far from being as simple as suggested by the examples so far.

Before proceeding to address this important estimation problem, we briefly state the general relationship between coupon bond prices and spot rates of interest.

In Example 6-2, we used the information on coupon bond prices as input to derive the zero-coupon bond prices. Let us denote the information about coupon bonds as Matrix **A**:

$$\mathbf{A} = \begin{bmatrix} 105 & 0 & 0 \\ 6 & 106 & 0 \\ 7 & 7 & 107 \end{bmatrix}.$$

Let us denote by

$$\mathbf{p} = [99.50, 101.25, 100.25]'$$

the vector of bond prices, and let

$$b = [z_1, z_2, z_3]$$

be the vector of zeroes. Then, the zero bond prices and the coupon bond prices satisfy the relation

$$\mathbf{p} = \mathbf{Ab}.$$

We then solve for the zero prices by inverting matrix $\mathbf{A}$:

$$\mathbf{b} = \mathbf{A}^{-1}\mathbf{p}.$$

While in Example 6-2 this process worked well, in practice this will be problematic. The reason is that matrix $\mathbf{A}$ is sparse in many maturity sectors; there may not be any liquid coupon bonds available in certain maturity sectors. However, the approach, with suitable modifications, can be used in situations where there is a large number of bonds (here $\mathbf{A}$ is only a 3×3 matrix). Generally, the price (at date 0) P_n, of a bond maturing in n years and paying an annual coupon of C dollars per year may be represented as

$$P_n = \frac{C}{1 + y_1} + \frac{C}{(1 + y_2)^2} + \cdots + \frac{100 + C}{(1 + y_n)^n}.$$

Using the relationship in Equation 6.3 that the zero prices $z_j = \frac{1}{(1 + y_j)^j}$, we can write

$$P_n = Cz_1 + Cz_2 + \cdots + Cz_n + 100z_n.$$

The bootstrapping procedure then uses the previous relationship recursively:

1. First, we compute z_1 as

    $$z_1 = \frac{P_1}{100 + C_1},$$

    where C_1 is the coupon of the one-year bond and P_1 its price.
2. With the knowledge of z_1, we next proceed to estimate z_2 as

    $$z_2 = \frac{P_2 - C_2 z_1}{(100 + C_2)},$$

    where C_2 is the coupon of the two-year bond and P_2 its price.
3. Proceeding this way, we can estimate the last zero-bond price P_n as

    $$z_n = \frac{P_n - [C_n z_1 + C_2 z_2 + \cdots + C_{n-1} z_{n-1}]}{(100 + C_n)}.$$

The bond is assumed to pay a coupon of C_n per year. When bonds pay semiannual coupons, the same idea is used with minor modifications. For example, the price of a one-year bond with exactly two semiannual coupons outstanding can be written as:

$$P = \frac{\frac{C}{2}}{\left(1 + \frac{y_1}{2}\right)} + \frac{100 + \frac{C}{2}}{\left(1 + \frac{y_2}{2}\right)^2}.$$

In general, we can write bond prices with semiannual compoundings as

$$P = \frac{\frac{C}{2}}{\left(1 + \frac{y_1}{2}\right)} + \frac{\frac{C}{2}}{\left(1 + \frac{y_2}{2}\right)^2} + \cdots + \frac{\left(100 + \frac{C}{2}\right)}{\left(1 + \frac{y_N}{2}\right)^N},$$

where there are N coupon payments. Note that with exactly N coupon payments remaining, the time to maturity in years T will be $\frac{N}{2}$.

Par Bond Yield Curve. A concept that is used in the industry is the par bond yield curve. It is the relationship between the yield to maturity and time to maturity of bonds that sell at their par value. We illustrate this concept by looking again at Example 6-2. To obtain the par bond yield curve, we begin with a one-year bond. If a one-year bond is issued to sell at par, what will be its coupon? The present value of the coupon and the bullet payment must equal 100. Or,

$$100 = \frac{100 + x_1}{1 + y_1},$$

where x_1 is the dollar coupon of the par bond. We conclude from this equation that $x_1 = 5.53$. We now turn attention to the two-year par bond. The present value of its coupons and balloon payments must equal the par amount. Or,

$$100 = \frac{x_2}{1 + y_1} + \frac{100 + x_2}{(1 + y_2)^2},$$

where x_2 is the two-year par bond coupon. Using $y_1 = 5.53\%$ and $y_2 = 5.32\%$, we get

$$100 = \frac{x_2}{1 + 0.0553} + \frac{100 + x_2}{(1 + 0.0532)^2}$$

or, $100 = 0.9476x_2 + (100 + x_2)0.9015.$

Solving, we get the two-year par bond coupon to be $x_2 = 5.327$.

Finally, the three-year par bond must satisfy the requirement that the price (100) should be equal to the present value of its cash flows. Or,

$$100 = \frac{x_3}{1 + y_1} + \frac{x_3}{(1 + y_2)^2} + \frac{100 + x_3}{(1 + y_3)^3}$$

or, $100 = 0.9476x_3 + 0.9015x_3 + 0.8159(100 + x_3).$

Solving, we get the three-year par bond coupon to be $x_3 = 6.908$.

Since for a par bond, yield to maturity must be equal to its coupon rate, we conclude that the par bond yield curve for the next three years must be:

Par Bond Yield Curve

Years to Maturity	Par Bond Yield
1	5.530%
2	5.327%
3	6.908%

The concept of par bond yield curve is extremely useful in real life. For example, a corporate treasurer wishing to issue a three-year AAA corporate note will wish to know the three-year par bond yield in the Treasury market since the yield of the corporate note will be at a spread over a similar Treasury.

So far, we considered annual and semiannual compounding. Now we turn to continuous compounding.

Continuous Compounding. The yield to maturity y_T at date t of the pure discount bond maturing at date T is the continuously compounded rate at which the bond appreciates to the par amount at maturity date. It is defined as

$$z_{T-t} \times e^{y_T \times (T-t)} \equiv 1 \tag{6.13}$$

Solving for the yield to maturity, we get

$$y_T = \frac{-\ln z_{T-t}}{(T-t)}. \tag{6.14}$$

A snapshot at date t of the yield to maturity y_T for various values of T is known as the term structure of interest rates in continuous-time framework. These rates are also known as the zero yields or the spot yields.

The par bond yield in continuous compounding can be defined in the following manner. The price of a bond with a maturity of N and paying a flow dollar coupon at a rate of C_N continuously may be expressed as the discounted value of all the coupons plus the discounted value of the balloon payment. This is stated as

$$P = 100 z_{N-t} + C_N \int_t^N z_{s-t} \, ds.$$

As we show in Chapter 4, for par bonds, the coupon should be equal to the yield to maturity. If we can identify a par bond, then $C_N = 100 y_N$. Using this and the fact that $P = 100$ for par bonds, we get

$$100 = 100 z_{N-t} + 100 y_N \int_t^N z_{s-t} \, ds. \tag{6.15}$$

Equation 6-15 is very important in the sense that once we have the par bond information, the pure discount bond prices can be extracted from the par bond curve.

If there is no uncertainty in interest rates, then to preclude riskless profits the instantaneous holding-period return on bonds of all maturities must be the same and equal to the instantaneous riskless spot rate $r(t)$. Formally, we can say that

$$\frac{d_{z_{T-t}}}{z_{T-t}} = r(t)\ dt. \tag{6.16}$$

The condition in equation (6.16) is simply a requirement that riskless profits do not exist in well-functioning capital markets. If this condition fails to hold, there will be profitable arbitrage opportunities. For example, let us say that at a particular instant, a thirty-year bond provides a higher return than a two-year note. Then by buying the thirty-year bond and selling the two-year note, it should be possible to make riskless profits. To prevent such opportunities, in an efficient capital market securities must satisfy the condition in Equation 6.16.

In addition, since the pure discount bond must converge to par at maturity, we must require that

$$z_o = 1. \tag{6.17}$$

We can solve Equation 6.16 subject to the convergence condition in Equation 6.17. The yield curve is then given by the solution shown in Equation 6.18.

$$z_{T-t} = e^{-\int_t^T r(s)ds} \tag{6.18}$$

The important implication of Equation 6.18 is that the knowledge of the instantaneously riskless spot rate completely specifies the term structure of interest rates. This becomes evident when we note that the right-hand side of Equation 6.18 depends only on the path of instantaneous spot rates of interest.

FORWARD RATES OF INTEREST

Given a set of pure discount bond prices $b(t, T)$, we can calculate a set of forward rates defined on date t as $f_t(T_1, T_2)$. This forward rate can be locked in on date t for a loan starting on date $T_1 \geq t$ and maturing at $T_2 \geq T_1$.

How do we determine the forward rate on date t, so that we can lock the rate in for a loan that begins on date T_1 and matures on date T_2 (naturally, $T_2 \geq T_1 \geq t$)? In Table 6-7, we consider the strategy of investing one dollar on date t at a rate of y_1 to get $(1 + y_1)^{T_1-t}$ on date T_1. We then sell forward these proceeds on date T_1 at a forward rate of $f_t(T_1, T_2)$ to get $(1 + y_1)^{T_1-t} \times [1 + f_t(T_1, T_2)]^{T_2-T_1}$ on date T_2. Note that there is no risk in this transaction, since the forward rates are established on date t. (We ignore the credit risk that may arise from the nonperformance by any of the counterparties.) These are indicated in Transactions 1 and 2 in Table 6-7. Of course, we can instead invest on date t at a rate y_2 to get $(1 + y_2)^{T_2-t}$ on date T_2 (Transaction 3).

Note that transactions 1 and 2 together require an investment of one dollar on date t, as does Transaction 3. To prevent riskless profits, both strategies must produce the same cash flow at date T_2; hence, we must have

$$(1 + y_1)^{T_1-t} \times (1 + f_t(T_1, T_2))^{T_2-T_1} = (1 + y_2)^{T_2-t}.$$

TABLE 6-7   *Forward Rate*

Transaction	Cash Flow on Date t	Cash Flow on Date T_1	Cash Flow on Date T_2
1. Invest \$1 on t at rate y_1, maturing on T_1.	−1	$(1 + y_1)^{T_1 - t}$	
2. Sell forward the proceeds from Transaction 1 on date T_1 at a forward rate $f_t(T_1, T_2)$, maturing on date T_2.	0		$(1 + y_1)^{T_1 - t}[1 + f_t(T_1, T_2)]^{T_2 - T_1}$
Total	−1	0	$(1 + y_1)^{T_1 - t}[1 + f_t(T_1, T_2)]^{T_2 - T_1}$
3. Invest \$1 at rate y_2, maturing on T_2.	−1		$(1 + y_2)^{T_2 - t}$

Solving this equation, we get the forward rate

$$f_t(T_1, T_2) = \left[\frac{(1 + y_2)^{T_2 - t}}{(1 + y_1)^{T_1 - t}} \right]^{\frac{1}{T_2 - T_1}} - 1. \qquad (6.19)$$

This is illustrated in Example 6-3.

Example 6-3:

Let $y_1 = 8\%$, $y_2 = 9\%$, $t = 0$, $T_1 = 1$, and $T_2 = 2$. Using Equation 6.19, the forward rate at date 0 for the period starting date 1 and ending date 2 is

$$f_0(1, 2) = \frac{1.09^2}{1.08} - 1 = 10.009\%.$$

The same concept also applies to pure discount bonds as trading instruments. This is shown in Table 6-8, where

$$f_t(T_1, T_2) = \frac{z_{T_1 - t}}{z_{T_2 - t}} - 1. \qquad (6.20)$$

Table 6-8 shows how to lock in forward rates by trading in spot securities. Equations 6.19 and 6.20 illustrate that the current term structure contains the relevant information for the forward rates of interest. We may synthesize forward contracts from the spot term structure as follows. We have seen that the current term structure thus defines a series of forward rates. A forward rate between two future dates k and l, where $l \geq k$, is a currently agreed-upon rate at which one may borrow or lend on date k for maturity on date l. Let the spot rates on date t be y_k and y_l for dates k and l, respectively.

TABLE 6-8   *Forward Rate, Pure Discount Bonds*

Transaction	Cash Flow on Date t	Cash Flow on Date T_1	Cash Flow on Date T_2
1. Long the discount bonds maturing on T_2	$-z_{T_2-t}$		$+1$
2. Short $\dfrac{z_{T_2-t}}{z_{T_1-t}}$ discount bonds maturing on T_1	$+z_{T_1-t} \times \dfrac{z_{T_2-t}}{z_{T_1-t}}$	$-\dfrac{z_{T_2-t}}{z_{T_1-t}}$	
Net	0	$-\dfrac{z_{T_2-t}}{z_{T_1-t}}$	$+1$

Then the forward rate, $f_t(k, l)$, must satisfy the condition:

$$(1 + y_l)^{l-t} = (1 + y_k)^{k-t} \times [1 + f_t(k, l)]^{l-k}. \tag{6.21}$$

Setting $k = t + 1$ and $l = t + 2$, we get the one-period forward (one-period) rate

$$(1 + y_2)^2 = (1 + y_1)^1 \times [1 + f_t(t + 1, t + 2)]. \tag{6.22}$$

Solving, we find the forward rate

$$f_t(t + 1, t + 2) = \frac{(1 + y_2)^2}{(1 + y_1)^1} - 1.$$

Equation 6.22 is a special case of Equation 6.20 and was used in Example 6-3.

The difference between the forward rates and the spot rates is referred to as the **term premium.** Often, this term premium is thought to contain some information about the changes in the expected spot rate of interest. Some hypotheses about term structure have postulated relationships between forward rates (which can be computed today) and the expected future spot rates, allowing us to write the coupon bond prices in terms of the forward rates.

Our analysis makes it clear that the coupon bond prices incorporate information about the discount factors. We now provide a detailed example of computing forward rates.

Example 6-4:

The prices of pure discount bonds are provided in Table 6-9 for four maturities. Using this as the basic data, we can compute all the applicable forward rates, as well as the par bond yields.

Note that the forward rates at year 0 may be computed for the future periods 1 to 2, 1 to 3, 1 to 4, 2 to 3, 2 to 4, and 3 to 4. In effect, there are six forward rates that we can compute at year 0.

The forward rate at date 0 for the period 1 to 2 may be calculated as follows. We recognize that taking one dollar at date 0 and investing it in a one-period zero

TABLE 6-9
Pure Discount Bonds

Maturity Date	Price	Yield
1	0.9500	5.263%
2	0.9000	5.409%
3	0.8500	5.567%
4	0.7900	6.070%

at 5.263% and then rolling that forward at date 1 until date 2 at the currently fixed forward rate of $f_0(1, 2)$ must yield the same dollar amount as investing at date 0 in a two-period loan at a rate of 5.409%. This leads to the equation:

$$1 \times (1 + 0.05263) \times [1 + f_0(1, 2)] = (1 + 0.05409)^2.$$

Solving, we get

$$[1 + f_0(1, 2)] = \frac{(1 + 0.05409)^2}{(1 + 0.05263)} = 1.0556$$

$$f_0(1, 2) = 5.56\%.$$

In a similar way, the forward rate at date 0 for the period 2 to 3 may be calculated as follows. We recognize that taking one dollar at date 0 and investing it in a two-period zero at 5.409% and then rolling that forward at date 2 until date 3 at the currently fixed forward rate of $f_0(2, 3)$ must yield the same dollar amount as investing at date 0 in a three-period loan at a rate of 5.567%. This leads to the equation:

$$1 \times (1 + 0.05409)^2 \times [1 \times f_0(2, 3)] = (1 + 0.05567)^3.$$

Solving, we get

$$[1 \times f_0(2, 3)] = \frac{(1 + 0.05567)^3}{(1 + 0.05409)^2} = 1.0588$$

$$f_0(2, 3) = 5.88\%.$$

The forward rate at date 0 for the period 3 to 4 may be calculated as follows. We recognize that taking one dollar at date 0 and investing it in a three-period zero at 5.567% and then rolling that forward at date 3 until date 4 at the currently fixed forward rate of $f_0(3, 4)$ must yield the same dollar amount as investing at date 0 in a four-period loan at a rate of 6.070%. This leads to the equation:

$$1 \times (1 + 0.05567)^3 \times [1 + f_0(3, 4)] = (1 + 0.06070)^4.$$

Solving, we get

$$[1 + f_0(3, 4)] = \frac{(1 + 0.06070)^4}{(1 + 0.05567)^3} = 1.0759$$

$$f_0(3, 4) = 7.59\%.$$

Now we compute the forward rates $f_0(1, 3)$, $f_0(1, 4)$, and $f_0(2, 4)$.

The forward rate at date 0 for the period 1 to 3 may be calculated as follows. We recognize that taking one dollar at date 0 and investing it in a one-period zero at 5.263% and then rolling that forward at date 1 until date 3 at the currently fixed forward rate of $f_0(1, 3)$ must yield the same dollar amount as investing at date 0 in a three-period loan at a rate of 5.567%. This leads to the equation:

$$1 \times (1 + 0.05263) \times [1 + f_0(1, 3)]^2 = (1 + 0.005567)^3.$$

Solving, we get

$$[1 + f_0(1, 3)]^2 = \frac{(1 + 0.05567)^3}{(1 + 0.05263)} = 1.1177$$

$$f_0(1, 3) = 5.72\%.$$

The forward rate at date 0 for the period 1 to 4 may be calculated as follows. We recognize that taking one dollar at date 0 and investing it in a one-period zero at 5.263% and then rolling that forward at date 1 until date 4 at the currently fixed forward rate of $f_0(1, 4)$ must yield the same dollar amount as investing at date 0 in a four-period loan at a rate of 6.070%. This leads to the equation:

$$1 \times (1 + 0.05263) \times [1 + f_0(1, 4)]^3 = (1 + 0.0607)^4.$$

Solving, we get

$$[1 + f_0(1, 4)]^3 = \frac{(1 + 0.0607)^4}{(1 + 0.05263)} = 1.2025$$

$$f_0(1, 4) = 6.34\%.$$

The forward rate at date 0 for the period 2 to 4 may be calculated as follows. We recognize that taking one dollar at date 0 and investing it in a two-period zero at 5.409% and then rolling that forward at date 2 until date 4 at the currently fixed forward rate of $f_0(2, 4)$ must yield the same dollar amount as investing at date 0 in a four-period loan at a rate of 6.070%. This leads to the equation:

$$1 \times (1 + 0.05409)^2 \times (1 + f_0(2, 4))^2 = (1 + 0.0607)^4.$$

Solving, we get

$$[1 + f_0(2, 4)]^2 = \frac{(1 + 0.0607)^4}{(1 + 0.05409)^2} = 1.1392$$

$$f_0(1, 4) = 6.74\%.$$

Generally, we can compute forward rates in this manner for various forward dates in the future. What are the problems with these concepts in practice? The first difficulty arises from the fact that there are few benchmark maturities. As noted in Chapter 3, there are only eight benchmark maturities: 3 months, 6 months, 1 year, 2 years, 3 years, 5 years, 10 years, and 30 years. This means that there are significant gaps in the 5-year to 10-year maturity sectors and in the 10-year to 30-year maturity sectors. Second, the frequency of auctions is low in the 30-year sector and in the quarterly refunding maturity sectors. This means that even the on-the-run issues may not trade at or near par on dates further away from the auction date. These complications not withstanding, we will show that it is possible to develop good spot-rate curves based on limited information about the par bond yield curve. We apply the bootstrapping principle to real-life data next.

PRACTICAL CONSIDERATIONS

We will now apply the bootstrapping concepts. Consider the $11\frac{5}{8}\%$ Treasury security maturing January 15, 1992. We can write its price as

$$P = \frac{\frac{11.625}{2}}{1 + \frac{y}{2}} + \frac{105.8125}{\left(1 + \frac{y}{2}\right)^2}. \tag{6.23}$$

Since the settlement date is just two days after the coupon date, let us ignore the accrued interest and treat the full price as $P = 104.5313$. Solving Equation 6.23 we get $y = 6.859\%$. Recall that this procedure assumes a reinvestment rate equal to yield to maturity and that this assumption is unsatisfactory, especially for long-term bonds. A timeline for this security appears in Figure 6-13. When Equation 6.23 is applied to the full price of the bond (with two days accrued interest), we get a yield of 6.79%, which is closer to the actual yield of the bond in the market.

What is the appropriate discount rate for discounting the first coupon that will be paid on July 15, 1991? An off-the-run Treasury security in the market was maturing on July 15, 1991. It has a coupon of 13.75% and sells at $103\frac{15}{32}$. Its yield is found using the equation:

$$103.46875 = \frac{106.875}{1 + \frac{y_1}{2}}. \tag{6.24}$$

Thus, the yield y_1 by solving Equation 6.24 is 6.584%. (We are again ignoring the accrued interest for simplicity.) Therefore, it seems reasonable to discount the first coupon of the Treasury security maturing on January 15, 1992, at 6.584%. Since we estimated y_1 by looking at a security that had no intermediate coupon but had only a bullet payment of 106.875, it is called an implied zero yield or the spot yield. How do

FIGURE 6-13   *Timeline*

1/15/91	7/15/91	1/15/92
Transaction	Coupon	Maturity
date	date	date

we estimate the implied zero yield y_2 for the date January 15, 1992? Let us again use the price of the 11.625% bond maturing on January 15, 1992, as in Equation 6.23. Then,

$$104.53125 = \frac{\frac{11.625}{2}}{1 + \frac{y_1}{2}} + \frac{105.8125}{\left(1 + \frac{y_2}{2}\right)^2}. \tag{6.25}$$

Note that we are now using y_1 to discount the first coupon and y_2 to discount the second payment, which includes the bullet. Since everything in the equation except y_2 is known, we can solve for y_2, the implied zero yield for January 15, 1992. Using $y_1 = 6.584\%$ and solving, we get $y_2 = 6.867\%$. Generally, the procedure that we have described uses a distinct discount rate for each maturity. Such a formulation has very different implications for the reinvestment rates of intermediate coupons. Consider the two-period security:

$$P = \frac{\frac{c}{2}}{1 + \frac{y_1}{2}} + \frac{100 + \frac{c}{2}}{\left(1 + \frac{y_2}{2}\right)^2}. \tag{6.26}$$

Multiplying through by $\left(1 + \frac{y_2}{2}\right)^2$ and simplifying, we get

$$P \times \left(1 + \frac{y_2}{2}\right)^2 = \frac{c}{2} \times \frac{\left(1 + \frac{y_2}{2}\right)^2}{1 + \frac{y_1}{2}} + \left(100 + \frac{c}{2}\right). \tag{6.27}$$

Note that the reinvestment rate for the first coupon is

$$\frac{\left(1 + \frac{y_2}{2}\right)^2}{1 + \frac{y_1}{2}}.$$

As seen earlier in this chapter, this is nothing more than the forward rate at date 0 for the forward period from date 1 to date 2. Recall from Table 6-8 that these rates can be locked in by trading in spot instruments that are available at the current time.

Notice how in our analysis of the yield curve, which is about coupon-paying securities, we have moved on to a discussion of zero-coupon securities. To see this connection in a more transparent manner, consider the strategy of replicating the cash flows of the 11.625% security using T-bills that are zero-coupon securities. This strategy is illustrated in Table 6-10. On January 15, 1991, we buy 100 million par of an 11.625% bond maturing on January 15, 1992. This is shown as Transaction 1. To replicate this, we can buy 5.8125 million par amount of the T-bill maturing on July 11, 1991. (Note from Table 6-3 that there are no T-bills maturing exactly on July 15, 1991.) The T-bill matures on July 11, 1991, paying $5.8125 million, which replicates the coupon cash flow from the bond. The ask price of the bill is easily calculated from the discount rate of 6.15% (given for this T-bill in Table 6-3) as 97.01, which is used in Transaction 2

TABLE 6-10	Transaction on 1/15/91	Cash on 1/15/91	Cash on 7/15/91	Cash on 1/15/92
Coupon Bond as a Portfolio of Zeroes *Quoted: January 15, 1991.* *Settlement: January 17, 1991*	1. Buy 100 million par of 11.625% T-bond.	−104.53125	5.8125	105.8125
	2. Buy 5.8125 million par of T-bill maturing on 7/11/91.	-5.8125×0.9701 $= (-5.6387)$	5.8125 (July 11)	
	3. Buy 105.8125 million par of T-bill maturing on 1/16/92.	-105.8125×0.9375 $= (-99.1992)$		105.8125 (Jan. 16)

of Table 6-10. To replicate the last coupon and the balloon payment, we buy 105.8125 million par of the T-bills maturing on January 16, 1992 (as there are no bills maturing exactly on January 15, 1992). The ask discount rate is 6.18% (see Table 6-3, last entry) leading to a price of 93.7513. On maturity, these bills will match the cash flows from the bond. If the bills and the bond were equally liquid and the relevant maturity dates and coupon dates coincided, this strategy would have been perfect. If P is the price of the bond on January 15, 1991 (denoted by date 0), $b(0, 1)$ is the price of the T-bill on January 15, 1991, for maturity on July 11, 1991 (denoted by date 1), and $b(0, 2)$ is the price of the T-bill on January 15, 1991, for maturity on January 16, 1992 (denoted by date 2), then we may write a no-arbitrage condition as

$$P = c \times z_1 + (100 + c) \times z_2. \tag{6.28}$$

The foregoing equation says that the coupon bond is a portfolio of zero coupon securities. Of course, in reality T-bills, as we have seen, are more expensive than bonds, so the replicating strategy is likely to be more expensive. Consider the cost of the replicating strategy. The total cost is

$$5.8125 \times 0.9701 + 105.8125 \times 0.9375 = 104.8379,$$

which is well in excess of the cost of the bond, 104.5313, that we tried to replicate.

The accrued interest of the bond between January 15, 1991, and the settlement date January 17, 1991, is approximately:

$$\frac{2}{365} \times 0.11625 \times 100 = 0.0637.$$

Adding this to the bond price, we get $104.5313 + 0.0637 = 104.595$. Note that the T-bill portfolio is still more expensive.

This analysis, however, does illustrate that the coupon bond prices contain information about the prices of pure discount bonds. If the prices of coupon bonds are out of alignment with those of pure discount bonds, after accounting for liquidity and coupon effects, there will be profitable trading opportunities without any risk. Ideally, to abstract from the liquidity effects present in bills, we would like to use coupon securities. Since there are coupon effects in these securities, we should use those coupon securities that sell close to or at par in constructing the implied zero-coupon bond prices. We will illustrate this later in the chapter. More generally, this analysis indicates that the schedule of coupon bond prices and pure discount bond prices must stay in alignment to preclude profitable trading opportunities.

HYPOTHESES OF TERM STRUCTURE

A number of hypotheses have been advanced concerning the term structure of interest rates. They attempt to relate interest rates on pure discount bonds of differing maturities with forward rates, expected spot rates, and so on. We provide a very brief overview of some of these hypotheses.

Expectations Hypothesis

One of the most popular hypotheses is the expectations hypothesis. There are many versions of this hypothesis, which was formally developed by Hicks (1946) and Lutz (1940). One version of the expectations hypothesis says that current forward rates are unbiased predictors of future spot rates. Let $f_t(k, k+1)$ be the forward rate at date t for a one-period loan between two future dates k and $k+1$. Let R_k^* be the unknown one-period spot rate at date k. Then the expectations hypothesis says,

$$f_t(k, k+1) = E_t[R_k^*]. \tag{6.29}$$

Thus, the forward rate $f_t(k, k+1)$ is the expected value of the future one-period spot rate denoted by R_k^* at date k. This version is referred to as the **unbiased expectations hypothesis.**

Another version says that the guaranteed return that one gets during the interval $[t, T]$ by holding a $(T - t)$-period bond should be equal to the expected return from rolling over a series of single-period bonds. This may be formally stated as

$$\frac{1}{z_{T-t}} = E_t[(1 + r_t)(1 + r_{t+1}) \cdots (1 + r_{T-1})]. \tag{6.30}$$

The left-hand side of Equation 6.3 represents the return associated with holding a discount bond to its maturity. The right-hand side is the expected return associated with rolling over one dollar from date t to date T in a sequence of one-period maturity bonds at varying future one-period rates of return $\{r_s\}$.

Yet another version of this hypothesis states this in terms of yields. In this version, the yield to maturity of the discount bond at date t is specified in the left-hand side.

$$\left[\frac{1}{z_{T-t}}\right]^{\frac{1}{T-t}} = E_t\left[\{(1 + r_t)(1 + r_{t+1}) \cdots (1 + r_{T-1})\}^{\frac{1}{T-t}}\right] \tag{6.31}$$

Liquidity-Premium Hypothesis

The liquidity-premium hypothesis says that current forward rates differ from future spot rates by an amount known as the liquidity premium.

$$f_t(k, k + 1) = E_t[R_k^*] + \pi_t(k, k + 1) \qquad (6.32)$$

Thus, the forward rate $f_t(k, k + 1)$ is the expected value of the future one-period spot rate denoted by R_k^* at date k plus the liquidity premium, which depends on the term of the loan. Hicks (1946) argues that there will be a "normal backwardation," whereby the forward spot rate will exceed the expected future spot rate by the amount of the liquidity premium. The idea here is that borrowers may prefer to borrow long term to avoid future uncertainties in the supply of capital. On the other hand, lenders will prefer to lend short. Speculators will then bridge this gap by borrowing short and lending long, provided they are compensated by the liquidity premium.

Segmented-Markets Hypothesis

The segmented-markets hypothesis says that different maturity sectors represent distinct markets with their own demand and supply forces. Culberston (1957) argues that different investors may have strong maturity preferences. Sometimes such preferences are also driven by regulatory constraints. Modigliani and Sutch (1967) propose a preferred habitat theory in which investors have a preferred maturity and will only deviate from their preferred maturity if they are offered a premium. As Cox, Ingersoll, and Ross (1981) have suggested, preferred habitat theory may be viewed as a special case of the liquidity-preference hypothesis in which the preferred habitat is short-term bonds, and long-term bonds are held only if they offer liquidity premiums.

Local-Expectations Hypothesis

The local-expectations hypothesis (LEH) says that all bonds provide the same expected rate of return over very small holding periods. It turns out that the LEH is the only hypothesis that is free from arbitrage. Formally, this hypothesis is stated as

$$\frac{E_t[z_{T-(t+1)}]}{z_{T-t}} = 1 + r_t. \qquad (6.33)$$

The expected one-period return during the interval $[t, t + 1]$ on a bond maturing at date T is equal to the one-period return r_t on a bond at date t maturing at date $t + 1$.

These hypotheses are widely used to gain insight into the pricing of term structure. In a later chapter, we will apply the LEH to value bonds and interest rate derivatives.

STRIPS MARKETS

Through the Federal Reserve book-entry system, the Treasury permits certain securities to be stripped. These are called STRIPS or strips—Separate Trading of Registered

*I*nterest and *P*rincipal *S*ecurities. Under this program, Treasury securities may be maintained in the book-entry system operated by the Federal Reserve Banks in such a way that it is possible to trade, in book-entry form, interest and principal components as direct obligations of the U.S. Treasury. The Treasury first made eligible for strips the 10-year and 30-year issues that were made as part of the quarterly refunding on February 15, 1985. Currently, about $115 billion worth of U.S. Treasury issues have been stripped into coupon and principal components. Effective May 1, 1987, securities held in stripped form became eligible for **reconstituting,** as well. Only 30-year (long) bonds and 10-year notes are eligible for stripping.

The effect of the shape of the yield curve on the percentage of reconstituting is shown in Figure 6-14. The spread between the thirty-year and two-year yields is used as a proxy for the shape of the yield curve. Note that this proxy appears to have a strong correlation to the amount of reconstituting.

It should be stressed that strips are not implied zeroes. Strips are traded securities directly subject to demand and supply. Implied zeroes are estimated pure discount functions derived from the prices of coupon-paying Treasury securities. Yet, as expected, implied zeroes provide a benchmark for assessing the relative richness or cheapness of Treasury securities.

Treasury strips are popular securities, and they are traded in OTC markets by dealers. In addition, exchanges have also shown an interest in making a market in these securities. As shown in the *Wall Street Journal* article, AMEX has shown an interest in making a market in strips.

FIGURE 6-14   *Reconstitutions and the Shape of Yield Curve*

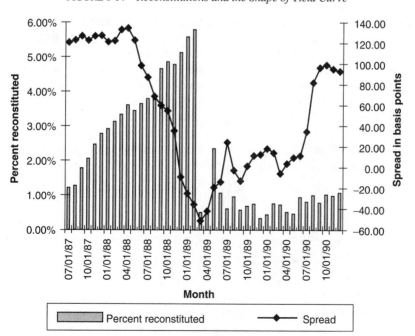

Amex Sells Zero-Coupon Strips

NEW YORK—The American Stock Exchange said it began trading zero-coupon bonds based on U.S. Treasury notes or bonds.

The securities, commonly referred to as strips, allow for separate trading of the interest and principal portions of U.S. Treasury notes and bonds. A zero-coupon security makes no periodic interest payments, but instead is sold at a deep discount to its face value, which the buyer receives at maturity.

Source: Reprinted by permission of *The Wall Street Journal,* December 19, 1990, p. C10. Reprinted with permission of *The Wall Street Journal,* © 1990 Dow Jones & Company, Inc. Permission conveyed through Copyright Clearance Center, Inc.

Why would investors want to hold zero-coupon securities? Several motivating factors are at work here. We saw in Chapter 4 that the duration of Treasury coupon securities change with interest rates and the passage of time. As a result, investors who buy Treasury coupon securities to hedge against their liabilities (by matching the duration of assets with liabilities) may have to frequently rebalance their positions. When a 30-year zero-coupon bond is purchased, its duration is always its time to maturity irrespective of interest rates. This may significantly reduce the need to rebalance positions. Furthermore, note from Table 6-2 that the maximum duration that may be achieved in the Treasury market using the current 30-year T-bond maturing on August 15, 2020, is 10.44 years. There may be many institutional investors holding liabilities with a duration of 15 or more years, and for these investors, strips may be the only realistic alternative. A 30-year strip has a duration of 30 years and may thus be preferred by investors with long-dated liabilities for hedging purposes. If there are many such investors, the strong demand for such securities may drive up the prices of long-dated strips and bring down their yields. Later, we will present evidence supporting this.

Moreover, when a Treasury coupon bond is purchased, the investor is obliged to buy a bundle of cash flows; the 30-year T-bond in Table 6-2, maturing on August 15, 2020, is a bundle of 60 coupon payments (8.75% payable on February 15 and August 15 of every year) and a balloon payment on August 15, 2020. This exposes the investor to reinvestment risks if cash flows are needed to fund liabilities only at selected points in time in the future. Then the investor may be better off buying a few strips and customizing the cash flows to suit the profile of liabilities.

Strip Yields

The prices of Treasury coupon strips and principal-only strips as of January 15, 1991, are plotted in Figures 6-15 and 6-16, respectively. The prices themselves are shown in Tables 6-11 and 6-12, respectively, along with their yields.

Example 6-5:

Let us illustrate the pricing of strips to get a better appreciation of zero-coupon securities. Consider the strip maturing on November 15, 2000, in Table 6-11. Its

FIGURE 6-15   *Price of Treasury Coupon-Only Strips*

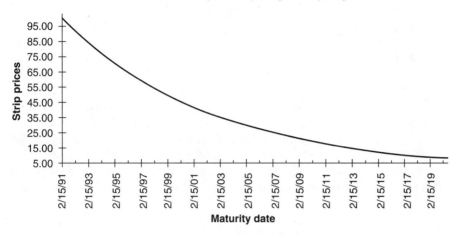

FIGURE 6-16   *Prices of Treasury Principal-Only Strips*

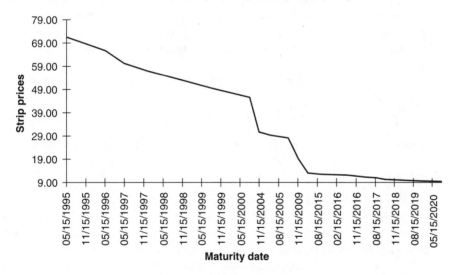

price was 44.34 and its yield 8.45%. The convention in the strips market is semi-annual compounding. The price of the strip for settlement on January 17, 1991 (denoted by t), and maturing on November 15, 2000 (denoted by j) is $Z_{j-t} = 44.34$. By semiannual compounding,

$$Z_{j-t} = \frac{100}{\left(1 + \frac{y_j}{2}\right)^{j-t}},$$
(6.34)

where y_j is the yield to maturity. Note that for this strip, $y_j = 0.0845$, $j = 11/15/2000$, and $t = 1/15/1991$. The time to maturity, $j - t$, in years is 9.8411. In semiannual terms, the time to maturity, $j - t$, is 19.6822. If we substitute $y_j = 0.0845$, and $j - t = 19.6822$, we will get $b(t, j) = 44.29$, which is different from the market price of the strip. This difference is due to the market convention used for pricing strips. Similar to the pricing of Treasury coupon securities, discussed in Chapter 4, semiannual periods are used in computing the maturity of the strip. For this strip, the next coupon date is May 15, 1991, and the last coupon date is November 15, 1990. So, the current coupon period is 181 days. Since the settlement date is January 17, 1991, the number of semiannual periods to the next coupon date is $\frac{[5/15/1991] - [1/17/1991]}{181} = 0.6519$. In addition, there are 19 whole semiannual periods remaining until maturity, so there are 19.6519 semiannual periods in all until maturity. Using this information, the price of the strip may be calculated as

$$\frac{100}{\left(1 + \frac{0.0845}{2}\right)^{19.6519}} = 44.34. \tag{6.35}$$

When the strip has a maturity which is less than the current coupon period, then the simple interest convention is used for pricing. Note that the yield of zeroes in Table 6-11 generally increases with maturity; but after the August 15, 2006, maturity, yields begin to decline, suggesting that long-dated strips are relatively more valued in the market by investors. The strip prices plotted in Figures 6-11 and 6-12 are downward-sloping functions.

To preclude riskless profits, the following restrictions must hold on the pure discount functions:

$$Z_1 \geq Z_2 \geq \ldots \geq Z_n. \tag{6.36}$$

To see why this must be the case, let us consider the prices of strips in Table 6-11.

Example 6-6

Suppose the February 15, 1992, strip is priced at 92.96 as shown in Table 6-11, but the May 15, 1992, strip was priced at 93.00 (instead of 91.37 as shown in Table 6-11). Then the following arbitrage strategy can be put in place: Sell the more expensive strip (if necessary, short it) maturing on May 15, 1992, at a price of 93.00, and buy the cheaper strip maturing on February 15, 1992, at 92.96. This nets a cash flow of 0.24. On February 15, 1992, collect the par amount of 100.00, and earn interest on it by placing it in overnight funds until May 15, 1992, when you will have more than enough money to cover the short position (by paying 100.00).

Therefore, the restriction in Equation 6.36 must hold.

TABLE 6-11   *Treasury Coupon-Only Strip Yields and Prices*

Maturity Date	Yield	Price	Maturity Date	Yield	Price	Maturity Date	Yield	Price
2/15/91	6.10	99.52	5/15/01	8.55	42.13	8/15/11	8.70	17.33
5/15/91	6.48	97.93	8/15/01	8.55	41.24	11/15/11	8.70	16.97
8/15/91	6.60	96.31	11/15/01	8.57	40.31	2/15/12	8.70	16.61
11/15/91	6.60	94.78	2/15/02	8.62	39.26	5/15/12	8.70	16.27
2/15/92	6.88	92.96	5/15/02	8.64	38.37	8/15/12	8.70	15.92
5/15/92	6.92	91.37	8/15/02	8.64	37.55	11/15/12	8.70	15.59
8/15/92	7.06	89.62	11/15/02	8.64	36.78	2/15/13	8.69	15.29
11/15/92	7.09	88.05	2/15/03	8.65	35.96	5/15/13	8.69	14.97
2/15/93	7.29	86.17	5/15/03	8.68	35.09	8/15/13	8.69	14.65
5/15/93	7.37	84.51	8/15/03	8.67	34.38	11/15/13	8.68	14.38
8/15/93	7.43	82.85	11/15/03	8.67	33.67	2/15/14	8.67	14.10
11/15/93	7.35	81.55	2/15/04	8.69	32.87	5/15/14	8.67	13.81
2/15/94	7.59	79.50	5/15/04	8.70	32.15	8/15/14	8.66	13.55
5/15/94	7.64	77.93	8/15/04	8.70	31.46	11/15/14	8.65	13.30
8/15/94	7.70	76.31	11/15/04	8.70	30.81	2/15/15	8.65	13.02
11/15/94	7.68	74.95	2/15/05	8.71	30.11	5/15/15	8.65	12.75
2/15/95	7.85	73.05	5/15/05	8.71	29.48	8/15/15	8.65	12.48
5/15/95	7.88	71.58	8/15/05	8.71	28.85	11/15/15	8.63	12.28
8/15/95	7.91	70.10	11/15/05	8.65	28.49	2/15/16	8.62	12.05
11/15/95	7.83	69.03	2/15/06	8.72	27.61	5/15/16	8.61	11.83
2/15/96	8.01	67.11	5/15/06	8.72	27.03	8/15/16	8.60	11.60
5/15/96	8.06	65.65	8/15/06	8.72	26.46	11/15/16	8.59	11.39
8/15/96	8.10	64.21	11/15/06	8.71	25.94	2/15/17	8.57	11.21
11/15/96	8.11	62.93	2/15/07	8.72	25.35	5/15/17	8.56	11.01
2/15/97	8.21	61.32	5/15/07	8.72	24.82	8/15/17	8.55	10.80
5/15/97	8.26	59.93	8/15/07	8.72	24.29	11/15/17	8.54	10.61
8/15/97	8.29	58.60	11/15/07	8.72	23.78	2/15/18	8.52	10.44
11/15/97	8.31	57.36	2/15/08	8.72	23.28	5/15/18	8.51	10.26
2/15/98	8.35	56.04	5/15/08	8.72	22.79	8/15/18	8.49	10.10
5/15/98	8.37	54.84	8/15/08	8.72	22.30	11/15/18	8.48	9.92
8/15/98	8.39	53.64	11/15/08	8.72	21.84	2/15/19	8.43	9.84
11/15/98	8.39	52.56	2/15/09	8.71	21.41	5/15/19	8.42	9.67
2/15/99	8.45	51.24	5/15/09	8.71	20.96	8/15/19	8.38	9.57
5/15/99	8.46	50.16	8/15/09	8.71	20.52	11/15/19	8.34	9.49
8/15/99	8.47	49.08	11/15/09	8.71	20.09	2/15/20	8.29	9.42
11/15/99	8.47	48.09	2/15/10	8.70	19.70	5/15/20	8.24	9.37
2/15/00	8.49	47.01	5/15/10	8.70	19.29	8/15/20	8.23	9.20
5/15/00	8.49	46.05	8/15/10	8.70	18.87			
8/15/00	8.49	45.09	11/15/10	8.70	18.48			
11/15/00	8.45	44.34	2/15/11	8.70	18.09			
2/15/01	8.54	43.05	5/15/11	8.70	17.71			

Source: Bear Stearns.

TABLE 6-12

Treasury Principal-Only
Strip Yields and Prices

Maturity	Yield	Price
5/15/1995	7.89	71.55
8/15/1995	7.90	70.13
11/15/1995	7.91	68.77
2/15/1996	7.97	67.24
5/15/1996	8.03	65.75
11/15/1996	8.09	63.00
5/15/1997	8.22	60.07
8/15/1997	8.24	58.79
11/15/1997	8.27	57.51
2/15/1998	8.27	56.35
5/15/1998	8.31	55.07
8/15/1998	8.32	53.91
11/15/1998	8.32	52.84
2/15/1999	8.34	51.68
5/15/1999	8.34	50.65
8/15/1999	8.34	49.61
11/15/1999	8.35	48.58
2/15/2000	8.35	47.58
5/15/2000	8.36	46.59
8/15/2000	8.37	45.59
11/15/2004	8.72	30.73
5/15/2005	8.72	29.44
8/15/2005	8.72	28.81
2/15/2006	8.59	28.13
11/15/2009	8.87	19.52
2/15/2015	8.61	13.14
8/15/2015	8.61	12.59
11/15/2015	8.59	12.39
2/15/2016	8.54	12.28
5/15/2016	8.49	12.17
11/15/2016	8.49	11.68
5/15/2017	8.48	11.23
8/15/2017	8.46	11.05
5/15/2018	8.44	10.45
11/15/2018	8.38	10.18
2/15/2019	8.35	10.06
8/15/2019	8.28	9.84
2/15/2020	8.20	9.66
5/15/2020	8.18	9.53
8/15/2020	8.14	9.44

Source: Bear Stearns.

EXTRACTING ZEROES IN PRACTICE

Recall from our bootstrapping procedure, that given a set of par bond coupons and maturities, it is possible for us to extract the spot rates of interest. Once we know the spot rates of interest, we can compute the relevant implied forward rates of interest. Let us consider the problem of building the spot curve. The par bond data have to be gleaned first. We present in Table 6-13 the securities that traded close to par. Note that not all bonds are selling at precisely the par amount. The bonds also clearly vary with respect to their liquidity. Notwithstanding these facts, we will use this information to extract the implied zeroes and the spot curve.

Since the data are sparse, we need to develop a smooth curve-fitting procedure. A number of approaches have been used in the academic literature and in practice. We will briefly review some of these approaches and use a nonlinear curve-fitting scheme that has been suggested to illustrate the idea in the context of the market conditions on January 15, 1991.

Generally, the task of extracting zero prices from the yield curve is complicated by the following factors, as pointed out earlier:

1. There are few issues that sell at par at any point. In Table 6-2, we can only identify a handful of issues (listed in Table 6-13) that sell close to par out of more than 200 issues that are outstanding in the market.
2. To obtain zero prices for all future maturities, we just do not have enough information in the yield curve. We do not have coupon bonds selling close to par maturing at every point in the future.

The approach to this problem is to start by specifying a simple function that describes the zero function. For example, we may specify that

$$Z_{T-t} = F(T - t, \underline{x}), \tag{6.37}$$

TABLE 6-13
Par Bond Data

Coupon	Maturity Date	Price	Yield to Maturity	Years to Maturity
$6\frac{5}{8}\%$	2/15/92	$99\frac{22}{32}$	6.87%	1.0795
$7\frac{1}{4}\%$	8/15/92	$100\frac{8}{32}$	7.00%	1.5781
$7\frac{1}{4}\%$	12/31/92	$100\frac{6}{32}$	7.11%	1.9836
$7\frac{5}{8}\%$	12/31/94	100	7.61%	3.9562
8%	1/15/97	$100\frac{2}{32}$	7.96%	6.0000
$8\frac{1}{8}\%$	2/15/98	$100\frac{7}{32}$	8.06%	7.0849
$8\frac{1}{2}\%$	2/15/20	$100\frac{24}{32}$	8.42%	29.0986

where $\underline{x}$ is a vector of parameters that are to be estimated. We can then postulate that, under ideal conditions, the coupon bond prices are portfolios of zero-coupon bond prices. For bond i that pays a dollar coupon of C_i at date j, we can write

$$P_{\text{model}, i} = \sum_{j=t}^{T_i} C_i Z_{j-t} + 100 Z_{T_i - t}, \qquad (6.38)$$

where bond i matures at date T_i. According to the model, we expect the price of the coupon bond i to be given by $P_{\text{model}, i}$. Let P_i be the market price of bond i. Then, the zero extraction problem may be stated as

$$\min_{\underline{x}} (P_i - P_{\text{model}, i})^2$$

subject to Equations 6.32 and 6.33. Once this is done, we can use the estimated $\underline{x}$ in Equation 6.32 to determine all the zeroes as estimates from the model. Given the estimated zero prices, we can estimate the forward rates as shown earlier.

In a recent paper, Diament (1993) has suggested an approach which falls broadly into the framework just described. Diament assumes that the yield to maturity of *par bonds* be described by the functional form:

$$y(t, T) = \frac{a_1(T - t)^{a_2} + a_3}{a_4(T - t)^{a_2} + 1}. \qquad (6.39)$$

In this functional form, there are four parameters (a_1, a_2, a_3, a_4) that need to be estimated using the data provided in Table 6-13. We will assume that all the bonds in Table 6-13 are selling at par for the purposes of estimation. Once this functional form is estimated, we get the values of (a_1, a_2, a_3, a_4). The results of the estimation lead to the following fitted equation for the par bond curve.

$$y(t, T) = \frac{0.06486(T - t)^{1.92727} + 0.06751}{0.7671(T - t)^{1.92727} + 1}. \qquad (6.40)$$

The implied zeroes and the spot curve are then extracted in a manner similar to the procedures illustrated earlier. The resulting implied zeroes and the spot rates are provided in Table 6-14. To get an idea of how well they describe reality, we also present in Figure 6-17 the spot and the strip rates. We are using implied zeroes as a benchmark for the strips market. If the implied zero prices and the strips prices are out of line, then there may be a lack of alignment between the coupon bond prices and the strips prices that can be exploited for profits. Note that in deciding whether to strip certain strippable Treasury securities, dealers must compare the price of the strippable security to the sum of the prices of each strip that will be obtained from that coupon security. Thus, if a 30-year bond is strippable, dealers will compare the price of the 30-year bond with the sum of the prices of the 61 strips that they will get by stripping. Note that there are 60 (semiannual) coupon payments and one principal payment, equaling 61 strips. It is possible that the dealer will sell some of the strips at a price below the implied zeroes of identical maturities. The dealer will sell other strips at a price higher than the implied zeroes of identical maturities.

TABLE 6-14 *Extracted Implied Spot Rates*

Maturity in Years	Strip Rates	Implied Spot Rates	Maturity in years	Strip Rates	Implied Spot Rates	Maturity in Years	Strip Rates	Implied Spot Rates
0.08	6.10%		10.09	8.54%		20.09	8.70%	
0.32	6.48%		10.33	8.55%		20.34	8.70%	
0.58	6.60%		10.58	8.55%		20.59	8.70%	
0.83	6.60%		10.84	8.57%		20.84	8.70%	
1.00		6.99%	11.00		8.59%	21.00		8.76%
1.08	6.88%		11.09	8.62%		21.09	8.70%	
1.33	6.92%		11.33	8.64%		21.34	8.70%	
1.58	7.06%		11.58	8.64%		21.59	8.70%	
1.83	7.09%		11.84	8.64%		21.84	8.70%	
2.00		7.28%	12.00		8.63%	22.00		8.77%
2.08	7.29%		12.09	8.65%		22.10	8.69%	
2.33	7.37%		12.33	8.68%		22.34	8.69%	
2.58	7.43%		12.58	8.67%		22.59	8.69%	
2.83	7.35%		12.84	8.67%		22.84	8.68%	
3.00		7.59%	13.00		8.66%	23.00		8.78%
3.08	7.59%		13.09	8.69%		23.10	8.67%	
3.33	7.64%		13.33	8.70%		23.34	8.67%	
3.58	7.70%		13.59	8.70%		23.59	8.66%	
3.83	7.68%		13.84	8.70%		23.84	8.65%	
4.00		7.85%	14.00		8.68%	24.00		8.78%
4.08	7.85%		14.09	8.71%		24.10	8.65%	
4.33	7.88%		14.33	8.71%		24.34	8.65%	
4.58	7.91%		14.59	8.71%		24.59	8.65%	
4.83	7.83%		14.84	8.65%		24.84	8.63%	
5.00		8.06%	15.00		8.70%	25.00		8.79%
5.08	8.01%		15.09	8.72%		25.10	8.62%	
5.33	8.06%		15.33	8.72%		25.34	8.61%	
5.58	8.10%		15.59	8.72%		25.59	8.60%	
5.83	8.11%		15.84	8.71%		25.85	8.59%	
6.00		8.22%	16.00		8.71%	26.00		8.79%
6.08	8.21%		16.09	8.72%		26.10	8.57%	
6.33	8.26%		16.33	8.72%		26.34	8.56%	
6.58	8.29%		16.59	8.72%		26.59	8.55%	
6.83	8.31%		16.84	8.72%		26.85	8.54%	
7.00		8.34%	17.00		8.73%	27.00		8.80%
7.08	8.35%		17.09	8.72%		27.10	8.52%	
7.33	8.37%		17.34	8.72%		27.34	8.51%	
7.58	8.39%		17.59	8.72%		27.59	8.49%	
7.83	8.39%		17.84	8.72%		27.85	8.48%	
8.00		8.43%	18.00		8.74%	28.00		8.80%
8.08	8.45%		18.09	8.71%		28.10	8.43%	
8.33	8.46%		18.34	8.71%		28.34	8.42%	
8.58	8.47%		18.59	8.71%		28.59	8.38%	
8.83	8.47%		18.84	8.71%		28.85	8.34%	
9.00		8.50%	19.00		8.75%	29.00		8.80%
9.08	8.49%		19.09	8.70%		29.10	8.29%	
9.33	8.49%		19.34	8.70%		29.35	8.24%	
9.58	8.49%		19.59	8.70%		29.60	8.23%	
9.84	8.45%		19.84	8.70%		30.00		8.81%
10.00		8.55%	20.00		8.76%			

FIGURE 6-17   *Spot Rates versus Strip Rates on January 15, 1991*

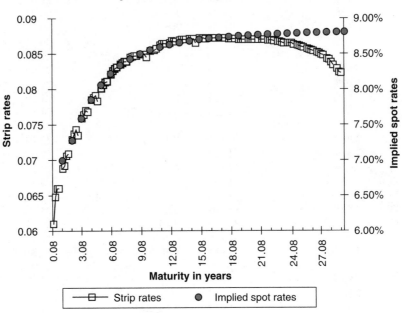

The overall profitability of stripping is evaluated by the expression (where P_i is the price of a strip maturing at date i and P_{bond} is the price of the bond which has been stripped):

$$\pi = \sum_{i=1}^{61} P_i - P_{\text{bond}}.$$

If π is positive, then there is a potential for profits from stripping. Note that the dealer should use those strip prices at which he or she can actually sell all the strips in computing the profits π. If $\pi < 0$, then there is a potential for profits by reconstituting the bond; the dealer will buy all the strips and put the 30-year bond back together.

It is clear that the Treasury coupon security prices contain a great deal of information about the prices of strips. The spot rates and the strip rates are very closely aligned at lower maturities. At intermediate maturities, the spot rates are a bit below strip rates. At the long end, however, strip rates are well below the spot rates of interest.

We have illustrated the extraction of spot rates of interest from the par bond yield curve using a specific statistical (curve-fitting) approach. There have been many approaches presented in the academic literature for fitting a yield curve. In Nelson and Siegel (1987), it is suggested that the discount bond prices are a nonlinear function of time to maturity $T - t$ as shown by

$$Z_{T-t} = \left(\frac{1}{1 + r_s} \right)^{T-t}$$

and

$$r_s = \theta_0 + (\theta_1 + \theta_2)\frac{1 - e^{\frac{-T-t}{\lambda}}}{\frac{T-t}{\lambda}} + \theta_2 e^{\frac{T-t}{\lambda}}.$$

The parameters θ_1, θ_2, and λ will have to be estimated to get the pure discount factors. A simple curve-fitting approach of the sort presented here has been used by McCulloch (1975) and Litzenberger and Rolfo (1984). It should be emphasized that all these methods are curve-fitting procedures; as such, they are statistical in their approach and generally do not have a sound economic foundation.

FURTHER READING

There is a large literature in the area of the term structure of interest rates. The behavior of short and long rates is explored in Campbell and Shiller (1984). A number of papers have examined the estimation of the term structure. Notable contributions in this area include Langtieg (1980), Roley (1981), and McCulloch (1971). The tax effect on term structure is examined by Jordon (1984), Litzenberger and Rolfo (1984), and Schaefer (1981). A number of books have addressed the problem of the term structure of interest rates; notable ones include Malkiel (1966), Meiselman (1962), and Roll (1972).

PROBLEMS

6.1   A 90-day T-bill is trading at 8.25% and may be financed at a 30-day term repo of 8%. What is the break-even rate on the future 60-day T-bill created by this transaction? Show all steps in your analysis.

6.2   Assume the following spot rate (zero-coupon) curve for this problem.

Zero Curve	Years	0.5	1.0	1.5	2.0	2.5
	Rate	7.50	7.75	8.00	8.00	8.00

(a) If all bonds were priced consistently with this curve, what would be the price of a two-year semiannual, 14% coupon security? Why?

(b) Under what circumstances will you expect the value of the total package (coupon bond) to differ from the sum of its component parts (strips)? Why?

6.3   Suppose that the one-year spot rate of interest at time 0 is 8%, and the two-year spot rate is 8.50%. What is the one-year forward rate for year 2? Why?

6.4   Summarize different versions of the expectations hypothesis. What does the expectations theory of term structure say about the relationship between forward rates for one-year loans one year from now and the one-year spot rates one year from now?

6.5   The data in the next table reflects the conditions on October 8, 1985.

Settlement on October 8, 1985	Coupon	Maturity	Price
	9%	9-30-1987	$100\frac{3}{32}$
	$10\frac{5}{8}\%$	8-15-2015	100

(a) Calculate the yield to maturity, PVBP, and yield value of $\frac{1}{32}$ of each security. What is the yield spread?

(b) You expect that the yield curve will flatten, but you have no clue as to whether the overall interest rates will rise or fall. Using the two securities, suggest a spread trade that is consistent with your expectations.

6.6   Assume the following spot rate (zero-coupon) curve for this problem.

Spot Curve					
Years	0.5	1.0	1.5	2.0	2.5
Rate	11.00	10.50	10.00	9.50	9.00

Two-year bonds that are strippable and paying a coupon of 10.375% are selling at a yield of 10%. Is it worthwhile to strip them and sell the stripped pieces? Or is it better to sell them as a unit? (Assume that you own them and that the strips may be sold at spot yields.)

REFERENCES

Bollerslev, T., and R. Engle 1993. "Common Persistence in Conditional Variances." *Econometrica* 61:167–186.

Brown, S. J., and P. H. Dybvig 1986. "The Empirical Implications of the Cox, Ingersoll, Ross Theory of the Term Structure of Interest Rates." *Journal of Finance* 41:617–630.

Campbell, J. Y., and R. J. Shiller 1984. "A Simple Account of the Behavior of Long Term Interest Rates." *American Economic Review* 74:44–48.

Cox, J. C., J. Ingersoll, and S. Ross 1981. "A Re-examination of Traditional Hypotheses about the Term Structure of Interest Rates." *Journal of Finance* 36:769–799.

Culbertson, J. M. 1957. "The Term Structure of Interest Rates." *Quarterly Journal of Economics* 71:489–504.

Diament, P. 1993. "Semi-empirical Smooth Fit to the Treasury Yield Curve." *Journal of Fixed Income* 3(1):55–70.

Dobson, S. W., R. Sutch, and D. Vanderford 1976. "An Evaluation of the Alternative Empirical Models of the Term Structure of Interest Rates." *Journal of Finance* 31:1035–1065.

Echols, M. E., and J. W. Elliott 1976. "A Quantitative Yield Curve Model for Estimating the Term Structure of Interest Rates." *Journal of Financial and Quantitative Analysis* 11:87–94.

Hicks, J. R. 1946. *Value and Capital.* 2nd ed. London: Oxford University Press.

Jordan, J. V. 1984. "Tax Effect in Term Structure Estimation." *Journal of Finance* 39:393–406.

Langetieg, T. C. 1980. "A Multivariate Model of the Term Structure." *Journal of Finance* 35:71–97.

Litzenberger, R. H., and J. Rolfo 1984. "An International Study of Tax Effects on Government Bonds." *Journal of Finance* 39:1–22.

Lutz, F. A. 1940. "The Structure of Interest Rates." *Quarterly Journal of Economics* LV:36–63.

Malkiel, B. 1966. *The Term Structure of Interest Rates.* Princeton, NJ: Princeton University Press.

McCallum, J. 1978. "The Expected Holding Period Return, Uncertainty and the Term Structure of Interest Rates." *Journal of Finance* 30:307–323.

McCulloch, J. 1971. "Measuring the Term Structure of Interest Rates." *Journal of Business* 44:19–31.

McCulloch, J. 1987. "The Monotonocity of the Term Premium: A Closer Look." *Journal of Financial Economics* 18:185–192.

McCulloch, J. H. 1975. "The Tax-Adjusted Yield Curve." *Journal of Finance* 30:811–830.

Meiselman, D. 1962. *The Term Structure of Interest Rates.* Englewood Cliffs, NJ: Prentice Hall.

Modigliani, F., and R. Sutch 1967. "Debt Management and the Term Structure of Interest Rates: An Empirical Analysis of Recent Experience." *Journal of Political Economy* 75(Supplement): 569–589.

Nelson, C. R., and A. F. Siegel 1987. "Parsimonious Modelling of Yield Curves." *Journal of Business* 60(4):473–489.

Roberts, G. S. 1980. "Term Premiums in the Term Structure of Interest Rates." *Journal of Money, Credit and Banking* 12:184–197.

Roley, V. V. 1981. "The Determinants of the Treasury Yield Curve." *Journal of Finance* 36:1103–1126.

Roll, R. 1972. *The Behavior of Interest Rates.* New York: Basic Books, Inc.

Salomon Brothers. *Analytical Record of Yields* (1982).

Sargent, T. J. 1972. "Rational Expectations and the Term Structure of Interest Rates." *Journal of Money, Credit and Banking* 4:74–97.

Sarig, O., and A. Warga 1989. "Bond Price Data and Bond Market Liquidity." *Journal of Financial and Quantitative Analysis* 24(3):367–378.

Schaefer, S. 1981. "Measuring a Tax Specific Term Structure of Interest Rates in the Market for British Government Securities." *Economic Journal* 91:415–438.

Shiller, R., and J. McCulloch 1987. The Term Structure of Interest Rates. National Bureau of Economic Research Working Paper 2341.

Stambaugh, R. 1988. "The Information in Forward Rates: Implications for Models of the Term Structure." *Journal of Financial Economics* 21:41–70.

Van Horne, J. C. 1965. "Interest Rate Risk and Term Structure of Interest Rates." *Journal of Political Economy* 73:344–351.

Van Horne, J. C. 1966a. "Interest Rate Expectations and the Shape of the Yield Curve and Monetary Policy." *Review of Economics and Statistics* XLVIII:211–215.

Van Horne, J. C. 1966b. "Reply." *Journal of Political Economy* 74:633–635.

Warga, A. 1992. "Bond Returns, Liquidity and Missing Data." *Journal of Financial and Quantitative Analysis* 27(4)605–617.

Wood, J. H. 1963. "Expectations, Error and the Term Structure of Interest Rates." *Journal of Political Economy* 71:160–171.

Appendix A

Zero Extraction

We illustrate the zero extraction problem in a more realistic setting. Table A-1 provides data on 13 Treasury issues for settlement on 10/9/98. In Table A-1 we have also computed the accrued interest and the invoice prices for both bid and ask.

In Table A-2, we have provided the cash flow matrix **A** for this problem. In constructing this matrix, note that we have used semiannual coupons for six-month intervals. We can construct the implied zeroes based on both bid and ask prices. First, we need to invert cash flow matrix **A.**

A has 13 rows and 13 columns spanned by the cells C27 through 039. To obtain the inverse we must first mark off a 13 × 13 space in the worksheet where we want the inverse to be placed. Then we insert the command

$$= \text{MINVERSE (C27:039)}$$

followed by pressing simultaneously CONTROL, SHIFT, and ENTER keys. In this example we wanted the inverse to be placed in the cells B45 through N57. Table A-3 shows the inverse of cash flow matrix. Each row corresponding to the maturity date

TABLE A-1   *Basic Information about the Coupon Curve*

Settlement Date: 10/9/98

| | | In 32nds | | | | | In Decimals | |
Maturity	Coupon	Bid Clean	Ask Clean	No. Days Accrued	Basis	Accrued Interest	Bid Dirty	Ask Dirty
2/15/99	5.000%	100.05	100.07	55	184	0.7473	100.90353	100.96603
8/15/99	8.000%	103.00	103.02	55	184	1.1957	104.19565	104.25815
2/15/00	8.250%	105.10	105.12	55	184	1.2330	106.54552	106.60802
8/15/00	8.750%	107.29	107.31	55	184	1.3077	109.21399	109.27649
2/15/01	11.750%	116.16	116.18	55	184	1.7561	118.25611	118.31861
8/15/01	7.875%	109.10	109.12	55	184	1.1770	110.48947	110.55197
2/15/02	14.250%	130.10	130.12	55	184	2.1298	132.44226	132.50476
8/15/02	6.250%	106.09	106.11	55	184	0.9341	107.21535	107.27785
2/15/03	6.250%	107.02	107.04	55	184	0.9341	107.99660	108.05910
8/15/03	5.750%	105.21	105.23	55	184	0.8594	106.51563	106.57813
2/15/04	5.875%	106.22	106.24	55	184	0.8781	107.56556	107.62806
8/15/04	7.250%	113.24	113.26	55	184	1.0836	114.83356	114.89606
2/15/05	7.500%	115.29	115.31	55	184	1.1209	117.02717	117.08967

TABLE A-2   Cash Flow Matrix

	B	C	D	E	F	G	H	I	J	K	L	M	N	O
26		2/15/99	8/15/99	2/15/00	8/15/00	2/15/01	8/15/01	2/15/02	8/15/02	2/15/03	8/15/03	2/15/04	8/15/04	2/15/05
27	2/15/99	102.5	0	0	0	0	0	0	0	0	0	0	0	0
28	8/15/99	4	104	0	0	0	0	0	0	0	0	0	0	0
29	2/15/00	4.125	4.125	104.125	0	0	0	0	0	0	0	0	0	0
30	8/15/00	4.375	4.375	4.375	104.375	0	0	0	0	0	0	0	0	0
31	2/15/01	5.875	5.875	5.875	5.875	105.875	0	0	0	0	0	0	0	0
32	8/15/01	3.9375	3.9375	3.9375	3.9375	3.9375	103.9375	0	0	0	0	0	0	0
33	2/15/02	7.125	7.125	7.125	7.125	7.125	7.125	107.125	0	0	0	0	0	0
34	8/15/02	3.125	3.125	3.125	3.125	3.125	3.125	3.125	103.125	0	0	0	0	0
35	2/15/03	3.125	3.125	3.125	3.125	3.125	3.125	3.125	3.125	103.125	0	0	0	0
36	8/15/03	2.875	2.875	2.875	2.875	2.875	2.875	2.875	2.875	2.875	102.875	0	0	0
37	2/15/04	2.9375	2.9375	2.9375	2.9375	2.9375	2.9375	2.9375	2.9375	2.9375	2.9375	102.9375	0	0
38	8/15/04	3.625	3.625	3.625	3.625	3.625	3.625	3.625	3.625	3.625	3.625	3.625	103.625	0
39	2/15/05	3.75	3.75	3.75	3.75	3.75	3.75	3.75	3.75	3.75	3.75	3.75	3.75	103.75

TABLE A-3   Inverse of Cash Flow Matrix

	A	B	C	D	E	F	G	H	I	J	K	L	M	N
42														
43														
44														
45	2/15/99	0.009756	0.000000	0.000000	0.000000	0.000000	0.000000	0.000000	0.000000	0.000000	0.000000	0.000000	0.000000	0.000000
46	8/15/99	-0.000375	0.009615	0.000000	0.000000	0.000000	0.000000	0.000000	0.000000	0.000000	0.000000	0.000000	0.000000	0.000000
47	2/15/00	-0.000372	-0.000381	0.009604	0.000000	0.000000	0.000000	0.000000	0.000000	0.000000	0.000000	0.000000	0.000000	0.000000
48	8/15/00	-0.000378	-0.000387	-0.000403	0.009581	0.000000	0.000000	0.000000	0.000000	0.000000	0.000000	0.000000	0.000000	0.000000
49	2/15/01	-0.000479	-0.000491	-0.000511	-0.000532	0.009445	0.000000	0.000000	0.000000	0.000000	0.000000	0.000000	0.000000	0.000000
50	8/15/01	-0.000309	-0.000317	-0.000329	-0.000343	-0.000358	0.009621	0.000000	0.000000	0.000000	0.000000	0.000000	0.000000	0.000000
51	2/15/02	-0.000522	-0.000535	-0.000556	-0.000579	-0.000604	-0.000640	0.009335	0.000000	0.000000	0.000000	0.000000	0.000000	0.000000
52	8/15/02	-0.000222	-0.000227	-0.000237	-0.000246	-0.000257	-0.000272	-0.000283	0.009697	0.000000	0.000000	0.000000	0.000000	0.000000
53	2/15/03	-0.000215	-0.000222	-0.000229	-0.000239	-0.000249	-0.000264	-0.000274	-0.000283	0.009697	0.000000	0.000000	0.000000	0.000000
54	8/15/03	-0.000192	-0.000197	-0.000205	-0.000214	-0.000223	-0.000236	-0.000245	-0.000274	-0.000294	0.009721	0.000000	0.000000	0.000000
55	2/15/04	-0.000191	-0.000196	-0.000204	-0.000212	-0.000221	-0.000234	-0.000243	-0.000261	-0.000269	-0.000277	0.009715	0.000000	0.000000
56	8/15/04	-0.000227	-0.000233	-0.000242	-0.000252	-0.000263	-0.000279	-0.000290	-0.000311	-0.000320	-0.000330	-0.000340	0.009650	0.000000
57	2/15/05	-0.000227	-0.000232	-0.000242	-0.000252	-0.000263	-0.000278	-0.000289	-0.000310	-0.000319	-0.000329	-0.000339	-0.000349	0.009639

contains entries that tell us the amount of coupon securities to be bought or sold to synthetically create a zero. For example, in row 45 corresponding to the maturity date of 2/15/99 the entry in cell B45 is 0.009756. This means the following: if we buy 0.009756 of coupon bonds maturing on 2/15/99, we get $1 at 2/15/99. (This is verified by noting that $0.009756 \times 102.50 = 1$.) Similarly, corresponding to date 8/15/99, we must sell −0.000375 of the coupon bond maturing on 2/15/99 and buy 0.009615 of the coupon bond maturing on 8/15/99 to synthetically create a zero-coupon bond maturing on 8/15/99. We can check this as follows:

Cash flows on 2/15/99

$$-0.000375 \times 102.5 + 0.009615 \times 4 = 0$$

Cash flows on 8/15/99

$$0.009615 \times 104 = 1$$

In this sense, the entries in the inverse matrix carry important information about how to create a zero-coupon bond from a portfolio of coupon bonds.

Part II

Fixed-Income Markets and Portfolio Management

Chapter 7

Inflation-Indexed
Debt Markets

Chapter Objectives

This chapter describes indexed bond markets in different parts of the world. The following issues are explored in this chapter:

*   What are Treasury Inflation Protected Securities (TIPS)?
*   How do the yields of TIPS differ from those of nominal government securities?
*   What are the important contractual and tax provisions of TIPS?
*   Are TIPS useful in generating forecasts of future inflation?
*   How does one measure the duration of TIPS?

INTRODUCTION

We have noted in earlier chapters that the Treasury securities epitomize risk-free securities. While it is certainly true that nominal securities issued by the U.S. Treasury are liquid, default-free, and carry certain tax advantages (exemption from local and state taxes), they are still subject to the risk of inflation. The United States began to sell indexed Treasury securities in January 1997. These securities have little inflation risk, and they enjoy the same advantages of the nominal securities issued by the Treasury in the sense that they are default-free, reasonably liquid, and exempt from local and state taxes. These securities are known as **Treasury Inflation Protected Securities,** or simply **TIPS.** The principal value of TIPS is indexed to the nonseasonally adjusted (NSA) U.S. City average all items Consumer Price Index for all Urban Consumers (CPI-U). In Table 7-1, we provide the recent prices and yields of TIPS that have been auctioned in three benchmark maturities. For comparison, we have also provided the prices and yields of nominal Treasury securities in the same benchmark maturities in Table 7-2.

As is customary, the prices are quoted in 32nds. Note that the yields of TIPS are much lower than the yields of nominal Treasury nominal securities. This is due to the fact that the TIPS compensate the investors for inflation risk, as we will explain later in this chapter, whereas the nominal Treasury securities do not offer any such compensation for realized inflation that did not conform to the expected inflation rate at the time they were issued.

The government is in a unique position to sell inflation-indexed securities. It is reasonable to suggest that no other institution can offer such securities with any

TABLE 7-1
Prices and Yields of TIPS as of October 10, 1999

Benchmark	Coupon	Maturity Date	Price	Yield
5 year	3.625%	7/15/2002	99-10	3.89%
10 year	3.875%	1/15/2009	98-02	4.13%
30 year	3.875%	4/15/2029	95-22	4.13%

Source: Bloomberg 1999.

TABLE 7-2
Prices and Yields of Nominal Treasury Benchmarks as of October 10, 1999

Benchmark	Coupon	Maturity Date	Price	Yield
5 year	6.000%	8/15/2004	100-07	5.95%
10 year	6.000%	8/15/2009	99-23+	6.03%
30 year	6.125%	8/15/2029	99-01	6.20%

Source: Bloomberg 1999.

credibility. The Treasury is currently auctioning TIPS in the five-year, ten-year, and thirty-year benchmark maturities. It is using the Dutch auction scheme (uniform-price auction) to sell these securities as explained in Chapter 3. To attract a broad spectrum of investors, Treasury is selling inflation bonds or the so called I-bonds, which are now available in denominations of $50, $75, $100, $500, $1,000, and $5,000. Their earnings are indexed to inflation just like TIPS, and they are exempt from local and state taxes. Under some circumstances when the I-bonds are used for paying tuition and fees at eligible postsecondary educational institutions, all the earnings can qualify for exemption from federal taxes as well.

The design and the issuance of TIPS is a hallmark event in the history of U.S. Treasury markets. If this market is developed by the Treasury as a significant borrowing mechanism, then TIPS can serve as the ultimate benchmark for measuring the cost of borrowing in real terms. The total amount is around $15 billion, which is a very small fraction of overall Treasury debt. In this chapter, we will present an overview of global indexed government bond markets and take up in detail the U.S. indexed bond market. Indexation is by no means a new idea. Indexing means that the cash flows of the bonds (such as coupons and principal payments) are tied to some underlying index. In the 1700s, debt contracts were tied to the price of silver. In the 1930s, many debt securities were indexed to gold prices in the United States. As the debt markets and the bank loan markets developed, however, much of the contacting has continued to be in nominal terms as opposed to being in indexed form. This is despite the fact that many economists have persuasively argued for the use of indexed debt contracts by the government. The interest in issuing and investing in indexed debt securities is obviously tied to the perception of the risk of inflation. Certainly, as the inflation risks became significant in some economies, indexation began to take hold. Tables 7-3 and 7-4 summarize the development of indexed debt markets in the world.

Table 7-3 summarizes the countries that issue inflation-indexed bonds now. As Table 7-3 vividly demonstrates, many countries have experimented with the issuance of

	Country	First Issue Date	Index Used
	Australia	1985	Consumer prices
	Brazil	1991	General prices
	Canada	1991	Consumer prices
	Chile	1967	Consumer prices
	Colombia	1995	Consumer prices
	Czech Republic	1997	Consumer prices
	Greece	1997	Consumer prices
	Hungary	1995	Consumer prices
	Iceland	1995	Consumer prices
	Israel	1955	Consumer prices
	Mexico	1996	Consumer prices
	New Zealand	1995	Consumer prices
	Poland	1992	Consumer prices
	Sweden	1994	Consumer prices
	Turkey	1997	Consumer prices
	United Kingdom	1981	Consumer prices
	United States	1997	Consumer prices

TABLE 7-3

Current Issuers of Inflation-Indexed Government Bonds

Source: "Gilts and the Gilt Market Review 1996/97," Bank of England, List of Current Issuers of Inflation-Indexed Government Bonds, 1997.

TABLE 7-4 *Summary of Major International Indexed Government Bond Markets March 31, 1997*

	Australia	Canada	Israel	Sweden	United Kingdom	United States
Total amount outstanding uplifted (US$ bn)	3.9	5.8	27.3	14.8	84.4	7.4
Total outstanding as a percentage of total marketable government debt	4.4%	1.7%	72.0%	8.1%	17.8%	0.2%
Average daily turnover 1996 ($ mn)	53.5	24.0[a]	26.7	Infrequent trading	358.9	n.a.
Number of bonds	7	2	200+	5	13	1
Longest maturity	2020	2026	2011	2020	2030	2007
Coupon frequency	Quarterly	Semiannual	Annual[b]	Annual	Semiannual	Semiannual
Frequency of inflation index publication	Quarterly	Monthly	Monthly	Monthly	Monthly	Monthly
Length of lag	[c]	3 months	1 month	$2\frac{1}{2}$ months	8 months	3 months
Current method of issue	Multiple-yield auction	Single-yield auction	Multiple-price auction	Yield tap	Price tap	Single-yield auction
Basis of trade	Real yield	Real price	Nominal price	Real yield	Nominal price	Real price
Strippability	No	Yes; not fungible	No	No	No	Yes; not fungible

Source: "Gilts and the Gilt Market Review 1996/97," Bank of England, Summary of Major International Indexed Government Bonds, March 31, 1997.

a. This is the figure for 1995.

b. While Israel's fixed rate indexed bonds pay coupons annually, floating rate indexed bonds pay semiannual coupons.

c. The formula is based on the average percentage change in the CPI over the two quarters ending in the quarter which is two quarters prior to that in which the next interest payment falls.

	Country	Time of Introduction	Rate of Inflation
	Mexico	1989	114.80%
	Argentina	1972	34.80%
	Brazil	1964	69.20%
	Chile	1966	22.20%
	Israel	1955	12.30%
	Australia	1985	4.50%
	New Zealand	1977	2.8%

TABLE 7-5

Timing of Introduction of Indexed Bonds

Source: Campbell and Shiller, 1996.

indexed bonds. Note that the underlying indices have not varied much: most countries have used the consumer prices as the index, but some have used wholesale prices, gold prices, wage index, etc. The inflation-indexed bonds market has taken hold in many countries, including Australia, Canada, Israel, and the United Kingdom. As should be clear, the United States is a relatively late entry into this market. Table 7-4 reports the volume of trading and the contractual charateristics of inflation-indexed bonds. Many Latin American countries (and a few others) tended to issue indexed bonds when the rate of inflation ran very high. Campbell and Shiller (1996) report the time of introduction of indexed bonds and the rate of inflation at that time in Table 7-5.

Note that with the exception of Australia and New Zealand, most of the other countries have issued indexed bonds when the inflation rates are high. Indexed bonds represent a large chunk of the Israel debt market and a small but significant part of the U.K. gilt market. In the United States, Treasury has indicated that the indexed debt issues will be made in sufficient amounts to make this market a liquid one. What might be the motivation for government to issue debt that is indexed to inflation? What types of investors might prefer inflation-indexed bonds as opposed to nominal bonds? We turn to these questions now.

PROS AND CONS

1. The benefits associated with indexed bonds have been articulated by many economists. Friedman has argued that the government is solely responsible for inflation, which expropriates the capital of investors in the Treasury securities. By offering inflation-indexed securities, government will protect the welfare of investors who lent money to the government in the first place. Moreover, by offering inflation-indexed bonds, government gives itself a strong incentive to pursue anti-inflationary policies. This incentive can be also encouraged by forcing the issuance of nominal securities in the shorter end of the yield curve. This obliges the Treasury to refinance every time the short-term debt matures. Unless the inflation rate is kept low, such refinancing costs can be potentially high. The basic idea behind these arguments is the following: either short-term nominal debt (requiring frequent refinancing) or inflation-indexed bonds will reduce the gov-

ernment's incentive to inflate. One might argue that of these two approaches, inflation-indexed bond issuance provides a more cost-effective approach in the sense that we substitute by the one-time issuance cost of indexed bonds the multiple issuances associated with short-term debt and frequent refinancing. Any inflationary adjustment simply increases the principal of the indexed security and is thus a forced savings rather than an outright cash payout. Thus, the issuance of inflation-indexed bonds simultaneously eliminates the moral hazard problem associated with the issuance of a long-term nominal debt and also reduces the need to roll over and refund short-term nominal debt.

2. Others have argued that indexed securities may provide a useful function in providing information about future expected inflation rates. This can be extremely helpful to monetary authorities. While this is true in principle, it is a good deal more complicated to extract the market's expectations of inflation rates by using the prices of TIPS and other nominal Treasury securities. There are several reasons for this. First, most indexed bonds have lags in indexing. This lag is necessary as the CPI numbers have to be compiled and distributed before the coupons and accrued interest of TIPS can be computed. (We show through several examples how this is done later in this chapter.) The presence of this lag limits the usefulness of TIPS as a forecaster of expected inflation rates. Second, the tax treatment of TIPS will definitely influence the pricing and yields of TIPS. How the taxes affect yields and how they interact with real and nominal yields is still an unresolved question. Third, investors will typically require a risk premium associated with the inflation risk. This risk premium has to be estimated and the manner in which it affects the expected inflation rate has to be determined. This is a difficult task as well. Finally, there is an issue as to the differences in the liquidity of the nominal and TIPS market in any given maturity sector. For example, let us say that we are interested in examining the yields of 30-year TIPS with the yield of 30-year nominal Treasury security (long bond). The liquidity of the long bond is a lot higher than the 30-year TIP, and this can make the task of inferring inflationary expectations that much more difficult. These problems notwithstanding, however, TIPS can potentially improve our understanding of expected inflation rates in the economy once it becomes a significant part of the government's borrowing strategy.

3. Treasury has also argued that the issuance of indexed bonds might reduce the cost of public debt. The reasoning is as follows: by offering securities that are indexed to inflation, the Treasury is able to attract investors who are very averse to inflation risk. Such investors will be willing to pay a higher price to buy securities that are default-free and that are indexed to inflation. From the perspective of investors, inflation-indexed bonds may prove to be attractive as well. For example, families that are saving for retirement or college may wish to buy inflation-indexed bonds as their expenses are expected to increase with inflation. Likewise, institutions, such as pension funds and insurance companies, which may have liabilities that are highly correlated with inflation rate, may wish to include a significant amount of inflation-indexed bonds in their assets. Pension funds, which manage assets on behalf of defined-benefits plans, may be particularly an important

class of investors who might benefit from investing in indexed bonds. With the introduction of TIPS, first-time investors have a reliable financial security to hedge in the long-term against the risks of inflation.

4. The revenues and expenditures of the federal government are affected by the rate of inflation. Tax revenues tend to be positively correlated with the rate of inflation. This is not surprising given that the taxes are based on the nominal income of citizens and corporations. On the other hand, the expenditures of the federal government may not be so clearly correlated with the rate of inflation. In fact, by borrowing in indexed securities, both the revenues and the expenditures will be sensitive to the rate of inflation.

5. In the short run, the market for TIPS is likely to be not very liquid due to the relatively small amounts that are currently outstanding in the market. This may imply wider bid-offer spreads until the market develops some depth. Some investors may also be averse to the idea of investing in bonds, which provide lower yields. It is also possible that the investors in TIPS do not trade actively: they may hold TIPS to dedicate the cash flows of TIPS to meet indexed liabilities. This may mean that the volume of trading in TIPS will be lower than that in nominal Treasury securities. This certainly appears to be the case in the United Kingdom where both indexed gilts and nominal gilts are available.

6. One risk associated with investing in the inflation-indexed bond is the risk that the index may undergo some future changes, which may adversely affect the investors who currently hold the security. Congress on occasion has instituted studies to overhaul the way CPI is calculated. There have been opinions that the CPI is overstated, and Cost Of Living Adjustments (COLA) are too generous. This represents a risk in much the same way that the tax treatment of municipal bonds have from time to time been questioned by the Congress, leading to some uncertainty in the municipal bond spreads.

DESIGN OF TIPS

The design of TIPS is central to its potential success or failure. Roll (1996) in his insightful analysis of TIPS identifies the following key features in the design of TIPS:

*   Choice of index
*   Indexation lag
*   Maturity composition of TIPS
*   Strippability of TIPS
*   Tax Treatment
*   Cash flow Structure

Choice of Index

The Treasury's design of TIPS was based on extensive consultations with the participants in the industry and is continuing to evolve based on the feedback that it has received. The key question in the design of TIPS is the choice of the index. As we noted

in Table 7-1, different countries have used different indices. Various market participants within the same country may have preferences for different indices. Several can-
didates exist in the market: the Consumer Price Index (CPI), wage indexes, indexes related to the costs of industrial production, and indexes that are related to other
important items in the household's expenses. There are many important considerations
in the choice of the index. The integrity of the index must be beyond any doubt: the
index should be maintained and updated in a scrupulous manner so that it reflects the
true cost of a representative consumption basket. It must be maintained by an agency
that is independent of the government to avoid any conflicts or "moral hazard" problems whereby the index may be manipulated. In the United States, the CPI is reported
by the Bureau of Labor Statistics which is within the Department of Labor. This Bureau operates independently of the Department of Treasury providing it with indepen-
dence over the calculation of the CPI. It might have been better if a nongovernment
agency were vested with the responsibility for the maintenance and upkeep of the
index. The danger that investors might face in the choice of the index is the possibility
that the composition of the index and the method of its calculation might change in future in a way that adversely affects them. The CPI is the nonseasonally adjusted U.S.
city average all items consumer price index for all urban consumers. This is published
monthly by the Bureau of Labor Statistics. The CPI measures the average change in
prices over time in a fixed market basket of goods and services, including food, cloth-
ing, shelter, fuels, transportation, medical services, and drugs. The weights used in the
CPI reflect their importance in the spending of urban households in the United States.
The weights are updated periodically to reflect any changes in the consumer expendi-
ture patterns. The Treasury's choice of the CPI-U is a good one as it is an index that is
widely tracked by investors and dealers in the fixed-income markets. Roll (1996) suggests that other indices tied to college tuition expenses or medical care expenses might
be attractive to investors and may be politically attractive as well. The retail price
index is used in the gilts market in the United Kingdom, and an index of general price
level is used in Brazil. French government agencies have used indexes that are tied to
the price of electricity, gas prices, coal prices, and the cost of rail travel.

Indexation Lag

If the indexed bond is perfectly indexed so that its payoffs reflect at every instant the
prevailing inflation rate, then such a bond will carry no risk at all with respect to the
inflation factor. Practical considerations, however, dictate that the indexed bonds will
never be perfectly indexed. It is nearly impossible with the existing technology to adjust the coupon payment to reflect the inflation rate up to the last minute. This is due
to the fact that the inflation numbers have to be computed by the Bureau of Labor and
the process takes time. Thus, there is an unavoidable delay between the time the inflation is measured and the time the cash flows are indexed to the measured inflation
rate. Figure 7-1 illustrates the nature of this delay.

   This makes the indexed bond have some residual exposure to the inflation risk.
For example, an investor in month t knows that the indexing for the principal at month
$t + 1$ will not reflect the current inflation rate. This lag in indexing is probably a more

FIGURE 7-1 *Lags in Indexing for TIPS*

Time in months
The indexing at month *t* is based on the
index value in month *t* - 2. During the period
from month *t* to month *t* + 1, the inflation
rate is obtained by linear interpolation
of the CPI between *t* - 2 and *t* - 1.

serious issue for short-term indexed securities when the volatility associated with the inflation risk is very high.

Maturity Composition of TIPS

The U.S. Treasury has auctioned TIPS in five-year, ten-year, and thirty-year maturity sectors. The decision to issue TIPS in the long-term maturity sectors is a very strong credible signal by the Treasury that it intends to keep the inflation rate low. In addition to issuing TIPS in long maturity sectors, the Treasury also has allowed stripping of securities, which implies that long-dated strips that are indexed to inflation will be available to investors. In the Canadian Treasury bond market, already inflation-indexed bonds have been stripped. Now indexed strips have maturities ranging from a few months to more than 25 years. Such index-linked zeroes offering "real returns" may be quite valuable to institutions that have indexed liabilities with long maturities. The decision to offer TIPS in a broad maturity spectrum will clearly improve the TIPS products that will be offered by the dealers. In TIPS, under normal inflationary conditions, the nature of inflation-indexing "back loads" the cash flows. With longer maturities, this effect will be even stronger.

Strippability of TIPS

The Department of the Treasury has allowed the TIPS to be stripped. Because of the nature of indexing, which we discussed earlier, the strips were not fungible. As of March 1999, however, the Treasury has announced certain changes that will allow for all the interest-only strips from Treasury inflation-indexed securities with the same maturity date to be interchangeable (i.e., fungible). This is likely to promote liquid markets for stripped interest-only inflation-indexed securities and could potentially increase the overall demand for the underlying TIPS.

The maturity dates of the real interest strips and their CUSIP numbers are shown in Figure 7-2.

Note that investors can now buy long-dated real strips to hedge against inflation. This should prove to be very attractive to tax-sheltered retirement accounts, such as IRAs and Keogh plans, as well as to pension funds and insurance companies. These strips can be particularly useful in the annuities market to fund retirement benefits that are indexed to inflation.

FIGURE 7-2 *Interest Strips from TIPS*

(TIIN) Due	912833	(TIIN) Due	912833
July 15, 1999	D2 3	April 15, 2009	J2 7
January 15, 2000	D3 1	October 15, 2009	J3 5
July 15, 2000	D4 9	April 15, 2010	J4 3
January 15, 2001	D5 6	October 15, 2010	J5 0
July 15, 2001	D6 4	April 15, 2011	J6 8
January 15, 2002	D7 2	October 15, 2011	J7 6
July 15, 2002	D8 0	April 15, 2012	J8 4
January 15, 2003	D9 8	October 15, 2012	J9 2
July 15, 2003	E2 2	April 15, 2013	K2 5
January 15, 2004	E3 0	October 15, 2013	K3 3
July 15, 2004	E4 8	April 15, 2014	K4 1
January 15, 2005	E5 5	October 15, 2014	K5 8
July 15, 2005	E6 3	April 15, 2015	K6 6
January 15, 2006	E7 1	October 15, 2015	K7 4
July 15, 2006	E8 9	April 15, 2016	K8 2
January 15, 2007	E9 7	October 15, 2016	K9 0
July 15, 2007	F2 1	April 15, 2017	L2 4
January 15, 2008	F3 9	October 15, 2017	L3 2
July 15, 2008	F4 7	April 15, 2018	L4 0
January 15, 2009	F5 4	October 15, 2018	L5 7
April 15, 1999	F6 2	April 15, 2019	L6 5
October 15, 1999	F7 0	October 15, 2019	L7 3
April 15, 2000	F8 8	April 15, 2020	L8 1
October 15, 2000	F9 6	October 15, 2020	L9 9
April 15, 2001	G2 0	April 15, 2021	M2 3
October 15, 2001	G3 8	October 15, 2021	M3 1
April 15, 2002	G4 6	April 15, 2022	M4 9
October 15, 2002	G5 3	October 15, 2022	M5 6
April 15, 2003	G6 1	April 15, 2023	M6 4
October 15, 2003	G7 9	October 15, 2023	M7 2
April 15, 2004	G8 7	April 15, 2024	M8 0
October 15, 2004	G9 5	October 15, 2024	M9 8
April 15, 2005	H2 9	April 15, 2025	N2 2
October 15, 2005	H3 7	October 15, 2025	N3 0
April 15, 2006	H4 5	April 15, 2026	N4 8
October 15, 2006	H5 2	October 15, 2026	N5 5
April 15, 2007	H6 0	April 15, 2027	N6 3
October 15, 2007	H7 8	October 15, 2027	N7 1
April 15, 2008	H8 6	April 15, 2028	N8 9
October 15, 2008	H9 4	October 15, 2028	N9 7
		April 15, 2029	P2 0

Tax Treatment

Taxation of inflation-indexed bonds pose a special issue: should the appreciation in the principal amount due to inflation and the resulting increase in coupon be taxed? The United States Treasury says they must be taxed. In fact, the periodic adjustments to the principal is to be treated as current income for tax purposes. This produces a "phantom income" that is subject to taxation. At high enough inflation rates, taxable investors may experience negative cash flows from TIPS. This is a serious disadvantage associated with investing in TIPS. In sharp contrast to the tax treatment in the United States, the capital gains accruing due to inflation in index-linked gilts in the United Kingdom are exempt from taxation. For a taxable investor, this can be an advantage. The tax treatment accorded to TIPS in the United States is much like the tax treatment accorded to Treasury strips from nominal Treasury securities. In the case of strips as well, the investor must recognize a periodic taxable income, and this produces a negative cash flow as well. There is a large clientele for strips (tax-deferred vehicles, such as the IRA and pension funds), and by the same reasoning, there will be a clientele for TIPS as well. Roll (1996) argues that taxing inflation accruals may, in fact, be necessary to improve the liquidity of the TIPS market. Absent taxes on inflation accruals, TIPS will trade at very low yields, and tax-exempt institutions will prefer nominal securities, which are likely to have higher pre-tax yields. Since tax-exempt institutions represent a significant pool of investment capital, this will lead to an illiquid market for TIPS. While this observation is correct, the bulk of the index-linked gilts in the United Kingdom are held by pension funds! Bank of England reported in one study that the pension funds and insurance companies in the United Kingdom account for nearly 80% of the investment in the indexed-gilt market. In part, this incentive may be tied to the extent to which these pension funds are required to fully fund their indexed liabilities.

Cash Flow Structure

There are varying cash flow structures, beginning with a simple zero-coupon structure to the United States TIPS structure, which is based on the Canadian inflation-protected bonds. We will briefly outline the different structures and review their relative merits. To simplify presentation, we will think of CPI as the index used in the cash flow structure, although any index may be used in the following described structures. Let CPI_t be the level of the index at date t, and let CPI_T be the level of the index on the maturity date.

1. **Indexed zero-coupon structure:** This will pay at maturity date the amount equal to

$$\text{Maturity Payments} = 100\,\frac{CPI_T}{CPI_t}.$$

This structure is the simplest and perhaps the most elementary unit of a real bond. As we have seen earlier, stripping produces a security of this type except that the indexation lags will make the strip from TIP different from the pure zero-coupon structure that we have described previously. Note that the zero-coupon structure presents no reinvestment risk and presents the best protection from the risk of inflation. Such countries as Canada, the United States, and Sweden have indexed zeroes either through stripping or by outright issuance. From the perspective of forecasting, expected inflation rates, as well the zero-coupon structure, is probably the best. Pension funds and insurance companies should find this ideal in putting together indexed annuities without the risk of reinvestment. Unfortunately, the tax treatment in many countries would generate negative cash flows to taxable investors who must recognize the accrual of interest as well as inflation in this structure. This may be one reason why we do not see this structure widely used in indexed bond markets.

2. **Principal Indexed Structure:** This is the structure used by Canada and the United States. On coupon date s, the TIPS in the United States pay the amount

$$\text{Coupon Payments} = 100 \times \frac{CPI_s}{CPI_t} \times \text{At-Issue Coupon Rate.}$$

At maturity the payments from TIP will be

$$\text{Maturity Balloon Payments} = Max\left[100, 100\frac{CPI_T}{CPI_t}\right].$$

Note that the United States TIPs provide the investor with a put option at maturity that allows them to put the bond back to the Treasury at par even if at maturity $CPI_T < CPI_t$. The presence of an embedded put option is obvious once we write the payoff at maturity as

$$\text{Maturity Balloon Payments} = 100\frac{CPI_T}{CPI_t} + Max\left[0, 100 - 100\frac{CPI_T}{CPI_t}\right].$$

3. **Interest Indexed Structure:** On coupon date s, the interest indexed real bond will pay the amount.

$$\text{Coupon Payments} = 100 \times \text{At-Issue Coupon Rate} + 100 \times \left[\frac{CPI_s}{CPI_t} - 1\right].$$

Basically, the coupon payment has the standard at-issue coupon rate determined in the auction, plus the realized rate of inflation.

REAL YIELDS, NOMINAL YIELDS, AND INFLATION RISK PREMIUM

In order to understand the differences between TIPS and nominal Treasury securities, we need to examine the relationship between nominal and real yields. To simplify matters, let us examine the relationship between the yields of a nominal zero-coupon bond (say, a strip from nominal Treasury security) and a real zero-coupon bond (such as a strip from a TIP).

Let the price of a nominal zero at time t paying a dollar at time $t + 1$ be $\$p_N$. Then, the nominal return i on this zero can be defined as

$$p_N(1 + i) = 1.$$

Let us assume that the consumer price index can be bought and sold. If CPI_t is the consumer price index at time t and CPI_{t+1} is the consumer price index at time $t + 1$, then the (uncertain) rate of inflation between these two dates denoted by π_t can be found as follows:

$$CPI_t(1 + \pi_t) = CPI_{t+1}. \tag{7.1}$$

The expected rate of inflation is then,

$$E[\pi_t] = \frac{E(CPI_{t+1})}{CPI_t} - 1. \tag{7.2}$$

The real return on the nominal zero-coupon bond is uncertain. The nominal zero pays at date $t + 1$ a real amount (in units of the consumer price index) of $\frac{1}{CPI_{t+1}}$. The real return on the nominal bond depends on the future consumer price index and is, therefore, uncertain. Hence, the real return on the nominal zero denoted by R_N is found by comparing the real investment at date t with the real cash flow at date $t + 1$ as shown:

Transaction at Date t	Real Investment at Date t	Real Cash Flow at Date t + 1
Buy a Nominal Zero	$\dfrac{p_N}{CPI_t}$	$\dfrac{1}{CPI_{t+1}}$

The real rate of return on the nominal bond is then defined as

$$\frac{p_N}{CPI_t} \times [1 + R_N] = \frac{1}{CPI_{t+1}}.$$

Or, we can write the real return on the nominal zero as

$$1 + R_N = \frac{\dfrac{CPI_t}{CPI_{t+1}}}{p_N} = (1 + i)\frac{CPI_t}{CPI_{t+1}}. \tag{7.3}$$

Writing this in terms of expected returns, we get

$$1 + E[R_N] = (1 + i)\, E\left[\frac{CPI_t}{CPI_{t+1}}\right]. \tag{7.4}$$

We will now consider a real zero-coupon bond. Let its nominal price (in dollars) at time t be $\$p_R$. At time $t + 1$, this bond will pay the index ratio of $\frac{CPI_{t+1}}{CPI_t}$ to the holder. Then, the real return R_R on this real zero is certain because we know at time t that this zero will pay $\#\frac{1}{CPI_t}$ units of the consumer price index at date $t + 1$. This certain real rate of return can be found as before by comparing the real investment at date t with the real cash flow at date $t + 1$ as shown:

Transaction at Date t	Real Investment at Date t	Real Cash Flow at Date $t + 1$
Buy a Real Zero	$\dfrac{p_R}{CPI_t}$	$\dfrac{\dfrac{CPI_{t+1}}{CPI_t}}{CPI_{t+1}}$

The real rate of return on the nominal bond is then defined as

$$\frac{p_R}{CPI_t} \times [1 + R_R] = \frac{1}{CPI_t} \Rightarrow p_R = \frac{1}{1 + R_R}. \tag{7.5}$$

Since the real rate of return on the nominal bond is uncertain, we will demand a risk premium for holding that bond. This is because the actual inflation rate could differ from the expected rate of inflation. This is referred to as the inflation risk premium. Using Equations 7.4 and 7.5 and requiring that the nominal zero carries an inflation risk premium of y, we get

$$(1 + E(R_N)) = (1 + R_R)(1 + y). \tag{7.6}$$

Note that the term $E\left[\frac{CPI_{t+1}}{CPI_t}\right] = 1 + E[\pi_t]$ is one plus the expected inflation rate.

In order for us to express the nominal yield in terms of expected inflation rate, we use (7.4) in (7.6) to get

$$(1 + i)E\left[\frac{1}{1 + \pi_t}\right] = (1 + R_R)(1 + y). \tag{7.7}$$

Unfortunately, we can show (by virtue of Jensen's inequality) that

$$E\left[\frac{CPI_t}{CPI_{t+1}}\right] = E\left[\frac{1}{1 + \pi_t}\right] > \frac{1}{1 + E[\pi_t]}.$$

Let us write $E\left[\frac{1}{1+\pi_t}\right] = \frac{1}{(1+E[\pi_t])(1+x)}$, where x is the convexity effect. The previous equation suggests that the relationship between nominal yields and real yields is affected by the inflation risk premium and the expected inflation rate. Under some simplifying assumptions, we can write the nominal yield as

$$1 + i = [1 + R_R][1 + y][1 + E(\pi_t)](1 + x),$$

where x is the convexity effect. Ignoring this effect for a moment and omitting the second order effects, we can write down the relationship between the nominal rates and the expected real rates as follows:

$$i = R_R + y + E(\pi_t).$$

This relationship explains why in Table 7-1 the yields on TIPS are so much lower than the yields on nominal securities of similar maturities. This difference will persist even on a duration-adjusted basis. This equation also explains why it is difficult to extract the information about the expected inflation rates as the inflation risk premium also enters the right-hand side. As the expected inflation rates change, so does the inflation risk premium. This is readily seen by noting that the changes in the nominal rates of interest arise from changes in the expected inflation rates and the changes in the inflation risk premium.

Note that in our analysis we did not incorporate the effects of lags in indexing to inflation. This is likely to cause the inflation risk premium to go up. Although the delay in the United States market is two months in the gilts markets, the delay can be as high as eight months.

To get a better perspective on how the yields on TIPS have performed over time, we provide Figure 7-3, which plots over the period 1997–1999 the yields on both 10-year nominal securities and 10-year inflation protected securities. Not surprisingly, the yields on nominal securities are much more volatile than the yields on TIPS. This is because much of the inflation risk is already reflected in the principal value of TIPS, whereas the nominal securities have a fixed principal and coupon. The yields of TIPS also reflect the poor liquidity of the market. Dupont and Sack (1999) report that 50% of the largest price changes in TIPS took place around auctions of TIPS. The liquidity of TIPS is lower than nominal treasury securities. As a consequence, investors prefer the more liquid securities in periods of financial distress. Note that during the second half of 1998 (Russian default, hedge funds crisis), nominal yield fell dramatically, even though the yields of TIPS did not change by much. Finally, inflationary expectations and risk premium play an important part in the behavior of yields.

CASH FLOWS, PRICES, AND YIELDS OF TIPS

Computing the cash flows from TIPS is much more complicated than computing the cash flows from nominal Treasury securities. A detailed treatment of this can be found in the Federal Register, published by the Department of Treasury, dated February 6, 1997. This section is drawn heavily from the rules and regulations laid out in that Federal Register. Interest on TIPS is paid on a semiannual basis. The Treasury issues TIPS with a fixed coupon rate. This rate remains a constant throughout the life of the security. This coupon rate is applied to the principal value, which is indexed to the CPI as described earlier. On any coupon payment date, the dollar value of interest is obtained by multiplying the coupon rate by the inflation-adjusted principal on the coupon payment date. The inflation adjustment is done by multiplying the par amount of the bond by the relevant index ratio. The key variables in the calculation of index ratios as of any date t (which can be a coupon payment date) are the CPI_t, which is the reference index number on date t and the reference index number on the issue date 0, which we denote as CPI_0. When the dated date is different from the issue date, then we use the index number as of the dated date instead of the index number as of the issue date. Then, the index ratio IR_t is defined as follows:

$$IR_t = \frac{CPI_t}{CPI_0}.$$

FIGURE 7-3 *Yields on Nominal and Indexed Treasury Securities and Indicators of Inflation, 1997–1999*

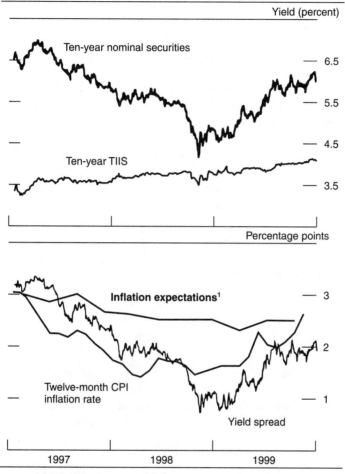

Source: Federal Reserve Bulletin—"The Treasury Securities Market: Overview and Recent Developments" by Dominique DuPont and Brian Sack (Dec 1999).
Note: Yield data are based on most recently issued securities and extend through October 1999; yield spread is yield on ten-year nominal securities less yield on ten-year TIIS. Expectations data and CPI data extend into the third quarter.
[1]Median expectation of CPI inflation over the next ten years among professional forecasters surveyed by the Federal Reserve Bank of Philadelphia.

It is to be noted that the reference index number for the first day of any calendar month is the *CPI* for the third preceding calendar month. For example, the reference *CPI* applicable to April 1, 1996, will be the *CPI* of January 1, 1996, of that year, which only gets reported in February 1996. This lag affects the effectiveness of TIPS against inflation risk as we will see later. The reference *CPI* for any other day of the month is then obtained by simple linear interpolation. For example, let us say that we are interested in figuring out the index ratio for April 15 (which is the issue date of a TIP) of a year. Then,

$$CPI_{\text{April 15}} = CPI_{\text{April 1}} + \frac{14}{30}[CPI_{\text{May 1}} - CPI_{\text{April 1}}].$$

Now the $CPI_{\text{April 1}}$ = The Nonseasonally Adjusted CPI-U for January 1996 = 154.40 (from the Bureau of Labor).

Likewise, $CPI_{\text{May 1}}$ = The Nonseasonally Adjusted CPI-U for February 1996 = 154.90 (from the Bureau of Labor).

Combining these, we get

$$CPI_{\text{April 15}} = 154.10 + \frac{14}{30}[154.90 - 154.40] = 154.63333.$$

Now we have the reference index number for the issue date as 154.63333. The index ratio for April 16 will then be computed simply as

$$IR_{\text{April 16}} = \frac{CPI_{\text{April 16}}}{CPI_{\text{April 15}}}.$$

Note that we can now compute the $CPI_{\text{April 16}}$ as

$$CPI_{\text{April 16}} = 154.10 + \frac{15}{30}[154.90 - 154.40] = 154.65000.$$

Therefore, the index ratio for April 16, 1996 is

$$IR_{\text{April 16}} = \frac{CPI_{\text{April 16}}}{CPI_{\text{April 15}}} = \frac{154.65000}{154.63333} = 1.00011.$$

This way, the index ratios can be computed for each day. Let us examine how these calculations will affect the coupon payments through Example 7-1.

Example 7-1:

A TIP was issued on April 15, 1996, with a coupon rate of 3.5%. The first interest payment date for this TIP is October 15, 1996. The reference CPI number for the issue date of April 15, 1996, was 120.00. The reference CPI number for October 15, 1996, was 135.00. Then, for a par value of $1,000,000, what is the coupon income on October 15, 1996?

The indexed principal is

$$1,000,000 \times \frac{135}{120} = 1,125,000.$$

The coupon income is then

$$1,125,000 \times \frac{0.035}{2} = 19,687.50.$$

The accrued interest and the settlement price of TIPs can be computed in a manner similar to nominal Treasury securities. We illustrate the accrued interest calculations in Example 7-2.

Example 7-2:

The Treasury issued an inflation-indexed bond with a CUSIP number 9128272M3, with the following particulars: The issue date was February 6, 1997, and the dated date was January 15, 1997. The issue was reopened on April 15, 1997. The bond is to mature on January 15, 2007. The reference CPI number for the dated date stood at 158.43548. The coupon rate of the bond is 3.375%.

The Treasury published the following CPI numbers for the months preceding July 1997, as shown in Figure 7-4.

What is the accrued interest on this TIP as of July 2, 1997?

To answer this question, we must first compute the index ratios as in Example 7-1. Based on the information in the problem, we can compute the index ratios for the month of July 1997.

The previous coupon date is January 15, 1997, and the next coupon date is July 15, 1997. The accrued interest is simply

$$\frac{\text{\# days between 7/2/1997 and 1/15/1997}}{\text{\# days between 7/15/1997 and 1/15/1997}} \times \left[\frac{3.375\%}{2}\right] \times 100 \times 1.01112.$$

The formula is identical to the way we compute the accrued interest for nominal Treasury securities except that we multiply the result by the index ratio as of the settlement date, which is 1.01112 for July 2, 1997. The resulting accrued interest is 1.58371. (We obtain the index ratio for July 2, 1997 from Figure 7-5 as 1.01112.)

The prices and yields can also be computed in exactly the same manner as we did for nominal Treasury securities, except that the invoice price will have to reflect the index ratio level as of the settlement date. We illustrate these calculations next in Example 7-3.

Example 7-3:

The U.S. Treasury issued a TIP with the following particulars shown in Figure 7-6.

For the settlement date of October 18, 1999, the clean (flat) price of this bond was 97.953125. What is the yield of this indexed bond? What is its invoice price?

As in the previous example, it is necessary to compute the index ratios first.

FIGURE 7-4 *CPI Numbers for the Months Preceding July 1997*

CPI-U(NSA) March 1997	160.00
CPI-U(NSA) April 1997	160.20
CPI-U(NSA) May 1997	160.10

FIGURE 7-5 *Index Ratios*

Day	Calendar Day	Ref. CPI	Index Ratio
July 1, 1997	1	160.20000	1.01114
July 2, 1997	2	160.19677	1.01112
July 3, 1997	3	160.19355	1.01110
July 4, 1997	4	160.19032	1.01108
July 5, 1997	5	160.18710	1.01106
July 6, 1997	6	160.18387	1.01104
July 7, 1997	7	160.18065	1.01101
July 8, 1997	8	160.17742	1.01099
July 9, 1997	9	160.17419	1.01097
July 10, 1997	10	160.17097	1.01095
July 11, 1997	11	160.16774	1.01093
July 12, 1997	12	160.16452	1.01091
July 13, 1997	13	160.16129	1.01089
July 14, 1997	14	160.15806	1.01087
July 15, 1997	15	160.15484	1.01085
July 16, 1997	16	160.15161	1.01083
July 17, 1997	17	160.14839	1.01081
July 18, 1997	18	160.14516	1.01079
July 19, 1997	19	160.14194	1.01077
July 20, 1997	20	160.13871	1.01075
July 21, 1997	21	160.13548	1.01073
July 22, 1997	22	160.13226	1.01071
July 23, 1997	23	160.12903	1.01069
July 24, 1997	24	160.12581	1.01067
July 25, 1997	25	160.12258	1.01065
July 26, 1997	26	160.11935	1.01063
July 27, 1997	27	160.11613	1.01061
July 28, 1997	28	160.11290	1.01059
July 29, 1997	29	160.10968	1.01057
July 30, 1997	30	160.10645	1.01055
July 31, 1997	31	160.10323	1.01053

FIGURE 7-6 *Profile of a TIP*

CUSIP NUMBER:	9128274Y5
DATED DATE:	15-Jan-99
ORIGINAL ISSUE DATE:	15-Jan-99
ADDITIONAL ISSUE DATE:	15-Jul-99
MATURITY DATE:	15-Jan-09
Ref CPI on DATED DATE:	164

First we need to compile the CPI-U information for the months preceding October 1999. This is shown in Figure 7-7.

Then we compute the index ratios for the month of October 1999, as shown in Figure 7.8.

FIGURE 7-7 *Monthly CPIs*

CPI-U (NSA) June 1999	166.2
CPI-U (NSA) July 1999	166.7
CPI-U (NSA) August 1999	167.1

FIGURE 7-8 *Index Ratios*

Month	Calendar Day	Year	Ref. CPI	Index Ratio
October	1	1999	166.70000	1.01646
October	2	1999	166.71290	1.01654
October	3	1999	166.72581	1.01662
October	4	1999	166.73871	1.01670
October	5	1999	166.75161	1.01678
October	6	1999	166.76452	1.01686
October	7	1999	166.77742	1.01694
October	8	1999	166.79032	1.01701
October	9	1999	166.80323	1.01709
October	10	1999	166.81613	1.01717
October	11	1999	166.82903	1.01725
October	12	1999	166.84194	1.01733
October	13	1999	166.85484	1.01741
October	14	1999	166.86774	1.01749
October	15	1999	166.88065	1.01756
October	16	1999	166.89355	1.01764
October	17	1999	166.90645	1.01772
October	18	1999	166.91935	1.01780
October	19	1999	166.93226	1.01788
October	20	1999	166.94516	1.01796
October	21	1999	166.95806	1.01804
October	22	1999	166.97097	1.01812
October	23	1999	166.98387	1.01819
October	24	1999	166.99677	1.01827
October	25	1999	167.00968	1.01835
October	26	1999	167.02258	1.01843
October	27	1999	167.03548	1.01851
October	28	1999	167.04839	1.01859
October	29	1999	167.06129	1.01867
October	30	1999	167.07419	1.01875
October	31	1999	167.08710	1.01882

FIGURE 7-9 *Yield of a TIP*

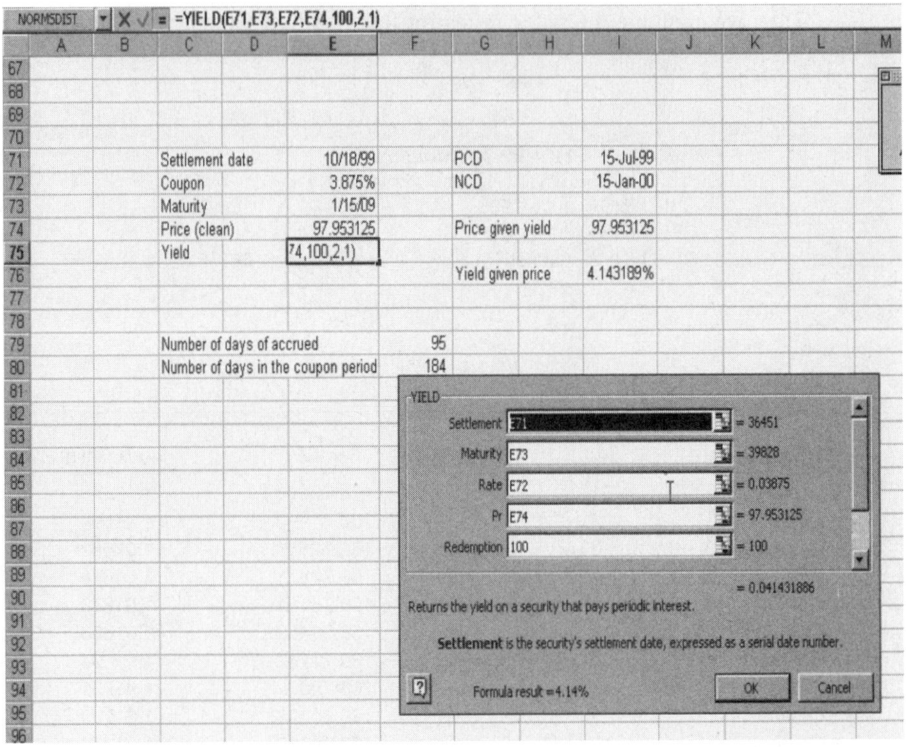

Based on the information, we must first compute the accrued interest. Note that the previous coupon date is July 15, 1999, and the next coupon date is January 15, 2000. The accrued interest is based on the index ratio on the settlement date which is 1.01780.

$$\text{Accrued Interest} = \frac{95}{184} \times \frac{3.875\%}{2} \times 100 \times 1.01780 = 1.018146$$

The settlement price can be computed by adding the accrued interest to the clean price and then multiplying the result by the index ratio. The flat price must first be multiplied by the index ratio, and to this we add the accrued interest to get the invoice price as shown.

$$\text{Invoice Price} = [97.953125 \times 1.01780] + 1.018146 = 100.714836$$

The yield of the TIP can be computed by using the EXCEL yield function in exactly the same way as we did for nominal Treasury securities. We illustrate the yield calculation in Figure 7-9.

DURATION OF TIPS

The measurement of duration of TIPS is always with respect to the real rate of interest. If the TIPS are perfectly indexed then they will carry no inflation risk and, therefore, will have a zero duration with respect to the inflation rate. However, the duration of TIPS with respect to the real rate will be a lot higher than the duration of a comparable nominal Treasury security with respect to its nominal yields. This is because the real rates are far lower than the nominal yields [see Table 7-1 and Table 7-2]. As the yields drop, the duration will increase. In addition, we may also expect the duration of TIPS with respect to nominal yields to be higher in a period of inflation. This is because much of the inflation accruals are back loaded, including the indexed balloon payments at maturity. To illustrate the intuition, we present the duration of TIPS and nominal Treasury securities in Figures 7-10 and 7-11, respectively.

FIGURE 7-10 *TIPS*

Settlement date 10/10/99

Coupon	Maturity	Price	Yield	Duration
3.625%	7/15/02	99.3125	3.89%	2.63
3.875%	1/15/09	98.0625	4.13%	7.78
3.875%	4/15/29	95.6875	4.13%	17.21

FIGURE 7-11 *Nominal Treasury Securities*

Settlement date 10/10/99

Coupon	Maturity	Price	Yield	Duration
6.000%	8/15/04	100.21875	5.95%	4.24
6.125%	8/15/09	99.734375	6.03%	7.48
6.125%	8/15/29	99.03125	6.20%	13.85

A New Leader in the Bond Derby?

Business Week; New York; April 5, 1999; Anne Tergesen; Amy Dunkin

Full Text: *Copyright 1999 The McGraw-Hill Companies, Inc.*

With Wall Street pundits fixated on deflation, the idea of buying Treasury bonds that protect you against inflation seems as crazy as preparing for a communist takeover. But guess what? Treasury Inflation-Indexed Securities are actually a great deal right now. Even if the consumer price index rises only 1.7% annually over the next three decades—a mere tenth of a percentage point above the current rate—buy-and-hold investors will be better off with 30-year inflation-protection securities, commonly known as TIPS, than with conventional Treasuries.

(continued)

If inflation rises more, not an unrealistic assumption given that the CPI has gained an average of 3.1% a year since 1926, TIPS would be an even better buy. Indeed, long-term bond prices have fallen while yields have risen almost a half percentage point since Jan. 1 amid worries over a hot economy, tight labor markets, and resurgent oil prices. But TIPS, which work by indexing the principal for inflation, have rallied. That may spur interest at the government's next auction of 30-year TIPS, tentatively slated for Apr. 15.

TIPS have yet to catch on with individual investors, who have bought only a fraction of the $75 billion issued so far, says Dan Bernstein, research director at Bridgewater Associates, a Westport (Conn.) money manager. Individuals have shied away from TIPS because they're hard to understand and less liquid than ordinary Treasuries.

Slowing inflation has also given people a reason to stay away. If you buy a conventional $1,000, 30-year bond at today's 5.5% rate, you are guaranteed $55 in interest payments each year, no matter what the inflation rate is, until you get your principal back in 2029. Let's say you buy TIPS, now yielding 3.9% plus an adjustment for the consumer price index, and inflation falls to 0.5% from the current 1.6%. Because of the lower inflation rate, you'll get only $44 annually. Nevertheless, even if the economy falls into deflation, you'll get the face value of the bonds back at maturity.

LESS VOLATILE. But if inflation spikes up, TIPS would outshine conventional bonds. For example, a $1,000, 30-year TIPS with a 4% coupon would yield $40 in its first year. If inflation rises by three points, your principal would be worth $1,030. The $30 gain plus the interest would translate into a 7% total return.

TIPS are attractive for another reason: They're one-quarter to one-third as volatile as conventional Treasuries because of their built-in inflation protection. So investors who use them are less exposed to risk, says Christopher Kinney, a manager at Brown Brothers Harriman. As a result, a portfolio containing TIPS can have a higher percentage of its assets invested in stocks, potentially boosting returns without taking on more risk.

Even so, the price of TIPS can change. If the Federal Reserve hikes interest rates, they'll fall. If it lowers rates, they'll rise. That won't be a concern if you hold the TIPS until maturity, of course.

If you're sold on TIPS, you can buy them without commission, with a minimum order of $1,000, at auction via the Treasury Direct program (www.publicdebt.treas.gov, or 800 943-6864). You can also buy them, for a fee, through a broker or bank. If you don't want to hold individual securities, three mutual funds buy inflation-protected debt. They are Pimco Real Return Bond fund, 59 Wall Street Inflation-Indexed Securities fund, and American Century Inflation-Adjusted Treasury fund. The first two invest at least 65% of their assets in U.S. and foreign inflation-protected securities, while American Century is wholly in U.S. issues.

As with zero-coupon debt, it's best to hold inflation-protected assets in a tax-deferred account, such as a 401(k) or individual retirement account. That's because holders of TIPS have to pay federal taxes on the annual interest and the amount by which the principal is increased for inflation—even though they won't see a dime of the latter until the bond matures or is sold. Mutual funds have to pay out the interest and any inflation adjustment in the principal but are still best suited for tax-deferred accounts to take advantage of the compounding of interest and principal over time. If you're more concerned about inflation than deflation, take advantage of Treasury Secretary Robert Rubin's pet project. But take care to keep your gains away from Uncle Sam for as long as possible.

The Case for TIPS:

- They'll outperform conventional Treasuries if inflation rises only slightly—a likely scenario given that it's at a 30-year low
- They're much less volatile than conventional Treasuries
- "Real," or inflation-adjusted, yields are now 3.9%. That's nearly double the historic average real yield on long-term government bonds

Data: Ibbotson Associates, *BUSINESS WEEK.*

CONCLUSION

We have provided an overview and an analysis of the inflation-indexed bond markets. This is a relatively new development in the U.S. Treasury market, although the idea has been around for a very long time and some states in the United States issued indexed bonds centuries ago. We expect these securities to be an important part of the asset allocation decisions of major institutional investors, such as pension funds, 401-K plans, and other retirement vehicles. Households with tuition liabilities may also find this a useful investment vehicle. We expect the market for indexed bonds to develop and grow in the next decade to a level and depth that it will become an integral part of the global fixed-income markets.

PROBLEMS

7.1   What are TIPS? Why do they yield less than similar nominal Treasury securities?

7.2   Go to the United States Treasury website.

http://www.publicdebt.treas.gov/of/ofinflin.htm

Using the information in that Web site, explain the opportunities that investors have in the TIPS market. Using the data on CPI and index ratios provided in the Web site, compute the invoice prices of TIPS in the market.

7.3   Alan Greenspan, the chairman of the Federal Reserve, made the following remark concerning the advantages of introducing TIPS:

> . . . By routinely monitoring the markets for the indexed and unindexed debt instruments, the Federal Reserve could extract the market's evaluation of the consequences of policy operations.

Do you agree with his view? What are the potential problems of inferring inflationary expectations from market prices of TIPS?

7.4   Visit the following website.

http://www.bloomberg.com/markets/

Within this website, go to the Treasury securities page and look up the quotes for TIPS. Verify for each TIP, the yield given the price in the website.

7.5   Should the taxation on inflation accrual be eliminated? What do you think will be the consequences for the liquidity of the TIPS market if the taxes on inflation accrual is eliminated?

7.6   What are the potential risks associated with investing in TIPS?

7.7   Explain the factors that determine the spread between the yield of a strip from a TIP and a strip from a nominal Treasury security with the same maturity.

7.8   Explain the differences between CPI and Producer Price Index (PPI). What constituencies will prefer to have a Treasury bond indexed to PI rather than CPI?

7.9   Compute the duration of the current 30-year nominal Treasury bond and the duration of the current 30-year TIP. Explain the differences that you found.

7.10   Why do you think that there is no market for private label issues of inflation-indexed bonds?

REFERENCES

Campbell, J., and R. Shiller 1996. "A Score Card for Indexed Government Debt." NBER Working Paper 5587.

Deacon, M., and A. Derry 1998. *Inflation-Indexed Securities.* London: Prentice-Hall Europe, 233 pages.

Dupont, D., and B. Sack 1999. The Treasury Securities Market: Overview and Recent Developments, Federal Reserve Bulletin, December, 785–806.

Federal Debt: Answers to Frequently Asked Questions-An Update, May 1999, United States General Accounting Office.

Federal Register 1997. Rules and Regulations, Department of Treasury, Vol. 62, No. 3, January 6, 1997.

Roll, R. 1996. "U.S. Treasury Inflation-Indexed Bonds: The Design of a New Security." *Journal of Fixed-Income Research* 12: 9–28.

Vankudre P., and P. Lindner 1997. "Risk Characteristics of TIPS compared to Nominal Treasury Securities." Lehman Brothers, Fixed-Income Research.

Vankudre P., P. Lindner, and A. Aurora 1997. "Treasury Inflation-Protected Securities: Opportunities and Risks." Lehman Brothers, Fixed-Income Research.

Chapter 8

Agency and Corporate Debt Markets

Chapter Objectives

This chapter describes agency, corporate, and hybrid securities. The theory of corporate debt pricing is also presented. Empirical evidence on financial distress and workouts is offered. The following questions are addressed in this chapter:

- What are Government Sponsored Agencies (GSEs)?
- Should GSEs be accorded special benefits?
- What is commercial paper (CP) and how is it rated?
- How is the corporate bond market classified?
- What are the contractual provisions in the corporate bond market? In particular, what are the following:
  1. Sinking funds
  2. Calls
  3. Puts
- What is bankruptcy code, and what is its importance?
- How big are the high-yield market and the Section 144A market?

INTRODUCTION

U.S. government agencies, corporations, and financial institutions raise capital by issuing a variety of debt securities in the capital market. In this chapter, we will classify the agency and corporate debt securities, describe the market institutions, and discuss the relevant attributes of each security from the standpoint of their risk and return. We will present some empirical evidence on the maturity composition, risk premiums, and contractual provisions that are used in agency and corporate debt. We will also summarize the available theories on the valuation of corporate debt securities. Empirical evidence on financial distress and restructuring will also be evaluated.

We begin by providing an overview of the agency securities markets. We examine in detail the contractual provisions of agency debt, the yield curve in the agency market, and the term structure of risk premiums in the agency market. We describe some of the key federal agencies and some recent developments in this market.

The corporate debt market is then analyzed. We present an overview of the corporate market and compare the evidence with the evidence reported for the period

1980–1991 by Crabbe (1991). After documenting the credit risk distribution, default premiums, and contractual provisions in the corporate debt market, we review the evidence on financial distress, rate of defaults, and recoveries in the corporate debt market. Finally, we examine the hybrids market, where securities, such as convertible bonds, contain both equity and fixed-income exposures.

CLASSIFICATION OF AGENCY DEBT

In Chapter 1, we provided an overview of the U.S. Government agencies that actively participate in the debt markets. In this chapter, we provide a more detailed treatment of this important segment of the fixed-income markets. The agency market consists of a federally sponsored agency that issues securities and federal agencies that do not directly issue securities—they tend to borrow from the Federal Financing Bank.

Federal Agencies

There are at present eight major federally sponsored agencies. Until 1987, there were only five such agency issuers: the Federal Farm Credit Board (FFCB), the Federal Home Loan Bank (FHLB), the Federal Home Loan Mortgage Corporation (FHLMC, also referred to as Freddie Mac), the Federal National Mortgage Association (FNMA, also referred to as Fannie Mae), and the Student Loan Marketing Association (SLMA, also referred to as Sallie Mae). The purpose of these agencies is to help promote credit availability in key sectors of the economy, such as the farm sector, housing sector, and educational sector. In 1987, the Farm Credit Financial Assistance Corporation (FCFAC) was created. The problems in the savings and loan association led to the creation of the Financing Corporation (FICO) in 1987 and the Resolution Trust Corporation (RTC) in 1989. Although only the securities issued by FCFAC are backed by the full faith and credit of the U.S. government, generally, agency securities are regarded as safe securities. The credit risk in agency securities is considered to be small.

Government sponsored enterprises (GSEs) were created to promote the availability of credit to housing. The GSEs devoted to housing are (a) Fannie Mae, (b) Freddie Mac, and (c) the Federal Home Loan Bank System. Over the last decade, GSEs have grown substantially both in terms of their issuances and the volume of debt securities that are outstanding. To gain a perspective, Figure 8-1 shows GSE security issuances during the period 1990 through 1999. From less than $20 billion dollars issue in 1990, the issuances have exceeded $30 billion in 1999.

In Table 8-1, we show the volume of agency securities that is outstanding in the market. In 1999, the outstanding volume exceeded $1.2 trillion, making the agency market a very significant part of the fixed-income securities market.

Note in particular the dramatic growth in FNMA, FHLB, and Freddie Mac agency debt. One reason for this growth has been the budget surplus, which has led to a reduction in the U.S. Treasury market. FNMA introduced a benchmark Notes program in 1998, which calls for the regular issuances of noncallable debt securities.

FIGURE 8-1   *GSE Security Issuance*

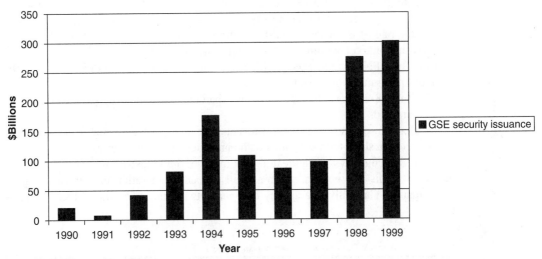

Source: Federal Reserve *Flow of Funds.*

TABLE 8-1   *Federal and Federally Sponsored Credit Agency Debt Outstanding 1985–1999:Q3 ($ Billions)*

	Federal Home Loan Banks	Federal Home Loan Mortgage Corporation	Federal National Mortgage Association	Farm Credit System[1]	Student Loan Marketing Association	Tennessee Valley Authority
1985	74.4	11.9	93.9	68.9	8.4	16.3
1986	88.8	13.6	93.6	62.5	12.2	17.2
1987	115.7	17.6	97.1	55.3	16.5	18.1
1988	135.8	22.8	105.5	53.8	22.1	18.3
1989	136.1	26.1	116.1	55.7	28.7	17.9
1990	117.9	30.9	123.4	54.9	34.2	23.4
1991	107.5	30.3	133.9	53.5	38.3	22.4
1992	114.7	29.6	166.3	53.2	39.7	23.6
1993	139.5	50.0	201.1	54.4	39.8	29.9
1994	205.8	93.3	257.2	54.4	50.3	27.5
1995	243.2	120.0	299.2	58.6	47.5	29.4
1996	263.4	157.0	331.3	61.3	44.8	27.9
1997	313.9	169.2	369.8	64.8	37.7	27.8
1998	382.1	287.4	460.3	64.7	35.4	26.5
1999:Q3	481.6	341.1	524.9	69.2	41.9	26.4

Sources: *Federal Reserve System;* Bond Market Association.

[1]Includes Farm Credit Banks and Farm Credit Financial Assistance Co.

This was followed by the Reference Notes program by Freddie Mac and the tap issuances program by FHLB. In effect, the GSEs are trying hard to provide an alternative to the U.S. Treasury to serve as benchmarks to the rest of the fixed-income markets. If the rate of issuances by GSEs continues at this pace, this market will surpass the Treasury market within a decade, especially if the budget surplus continues to prevail. Both FNMA and Freddie Mac have announced the introduction of benchmark bill programs with weekly auctions.

As Table 8-2 shows, the agency issues span the entire maturity range from two to thirty years as of 1999.

A closer inspection of Table 8-3 reveals that much of the agency debt issuance is concentrated in short-term securities with maturities of one year or less.

This fact coupled with the feature that many of the longer-term issues are callable implies that this is a good sector for small to medium duration investments of high credit quality. Currently, the agency debt markets are not as liquid as Treasury mar-

TABLE 8-2   *Agency Debt Issues (Agency Issue Sizes in $ Billions)*

Issue	*FNMA Benchmark*	*Freddie Mac Benchmark*	*FHLB Global*	*FHLB Tap*
2-year	—	5.0	3.0	3.5
3-year	3.0	5.0	3.0	3.4
5-year	6.5	3.0	—	2.0
7-year	3.5	6.0	—	1.1
10-year	3.5	6.0	—	0.6
30-year	4.25	—	—	—

Source: Fleming 2000.

TABLE 8-3
Short- and Long-Term Federal Agency Debt Issuance 1990–1999 ($ Billions)

Year	Short Term[1]	Long Term	Total
1990	581.7	55.2	636.9
1991	717.5	80.8	798.3
1992	817.1	109.7	926.9
1993	1,255.4	146.5	1,401.9
1994	2,098.1	157.7	2,255.9
1995	3,302.6	228.1	3,530.7
1996	4,246.7	277.9	4,524.6
1997	5,428.0	323.1	5,751.2
1998	5,757.3	590.3	6,347.6
1999	6,538.2	536.3	7,074.4

Sources: Federal Home Loan Bank; Federal Home Loan Mortgage Corporation; Federal National Mortgage Association; Student Loan Marketing Association; Tennessee Valley Authority; Federal Farm Credit Bank; Bond Market Association.

[1]Includes discount notes and maturities of one year or less.

kets. As noted earlier, however, with their ambitious benchmark programs, this situation might change soon. The average trading volume of federal agency securities is shown in Table 8-4.

Note that more than 90% of the transactions are with customers.

There are other agencies that do not directly issue securities but do so via the Federal Financing Bank, such as the Tennessee Valley Authority (TVA) and the Government National Mortgage Association (GNMA).

Agency issues that are not a part of noncallable benchmark programs tend to be callable. These issues are priced relative to a Treasury security of similar maturity. Often, their yields are quoted as a spread over the benchmark Treasury security. The issues traded at spreads varying from 1 to 150 basis points, depending on the terms of the issue. All agency securities are regarded as virtually free from credit risk. They are rated AAA. When they are not rated, they are assumed to be of the highest quality. While this is generally the case, the financial strength of the agency is also a very important factor in determining the spread at which that agency's debt will trade relative to the Treasury.

Many players in the market including the U.S. Treasury have some concerns about the growth of the agency debt market. One concern is that the spurt in the growth of agency debt market is threatening to "crowd out" comparable corporate securities. This may in turn require that corporate debt securities offer higher spreads. As the article from Investment Dealers Digest argues, the agency benchmark issues have started to attract a much wider investment base.

The U.S. Treasury is concerned with the growth of the agency market from a public policy perspective.

In the early 1980s, Fannie Mae became insolvent on a mark-to-market basis. A combination of government initiatives, such as legislative tax relief and regulatory forebearance, coupled with a decline in interest rates allowed FNMA to solve its financial problems. If a similar situation were to happen today, it might lead to a significant

TABLE 8-4 *Average Daily Trading Volume of Federal Agency Securities*[1] *1991–1999 ($ Millions)*	Year	Transactions with Interdealer Brokers	Transactions with Others	Total
	1991	1,541.0	4,170.0	5,711.0
	1992	1,239.0	4,874.0	6,113.0
	1993	1,442.0	7,497.0	8,939.0
	1994	1,285.0	14,735.0	16,020.0
	1995	738.0	22,958.0	23,696.0
	1996	773.0	30,296.0	31,069.0
	1997	1,240.0	38,978.0	40,218.0
	1998	2,362.0	45,234.0	47,596.0
	1999*	4,119.0	50,447.0	54,567.0

Sources: Federal Reserve Bank of New York; Bond Market Association.

*As of December 31, 1999.

[1]Average daily trading volume in federal agency securities by primary dealers with interdealer brokers and primary dealers with others.

Growth in Agency Debt Is Being Felt in Corporate Market

THE INVESTMENT DEALERS' DIGEST: IDD, NEW YORK, JAN. 3, 2000, JEFFREY KEEGAN.

While most fixed-income professionals are upbeat about the corporate bond market heading into 2000, there's a growing consensus that competition from the burgeoning federal agency debt programs has pushed spreads permanently wider.

Jumbo debt issues from the likes of Fannie Mae and Freddie Mac are making up a larger proportion of the investment-grade bond market than ever, and are securing the time and money of portfolio managers previously devoted to corporates and mortgage securities. In short, the rapid growth of agency debt is making the high-grade market a crowded place.

"There's no doubt that corporate spreads have been pushed out because the agencies have increased the overall supply of spread product," said one bond analyst.

The investor base for agencies is beginning to include many new institutions that are attracted to the bullet structures, predictability and liquidity that make the agency securities appealing corporate substitutes. Agencies raised a total of $139 billion through their jumbo debt programs last year, with Freddie Mac raising $50 billion and Fannie Mae issuing a total of $55 billion in jumbo deals, according to Salomon Smith Barney. Other agency issuers have also contributed, with the Federal Home Loan Bank System issuing some $34 billion in bellwether deals.

Based on the detailed funding calendars that Freddie and Fannie have created for 2000, that level of issuance should increase even further next year. Freddie should issue more than $65 billion and Fannie could be on deck to top $60 billion. As the market grows, bond pros predict that it will continue to attract the attention of corporate and mortgage investors, making it difficult for corporate spreads to return to the tighter levels that were the norm just two years ago.

Freddie, Fannie and others have been aggressively moving into new products and increasing their share of new mortgage origination. There are no indications that the agencies are looking to slow down, and with projections for further cuts in U.S. Treasury supply ahead, it's likely that the agencies will continue to increase their issuance as their investor base expands and grows. Agencies issued about 80% more term debt in 1999 than did the U.S. Treasury, coming in at about $250 billion.

A Shift in Indices

With Treasury issuance on the decline and the agencies on the upswing, agency debt is coming to represent a larger percentage of the widely followed fixed-income indices, a shift that encourages portfolio managers to mirror the move. In addition, mortgage portfolio managers have stepped up their activity in the market, keying on the fact that the difference between mortgage spreads and agency spreads helps drive the activity of the agencies, according to Michael Schumacher, agency strategist at Salomon Smith Barney.

The jumbo programs were designed to accomplish exactly what corporate bond pros say they are currently seeing in the market. Corporate and mortgage investors are being attracted to the agency market by the consistent issuance schedule and the sheer size and liquidity that the deals offer. In addition, the agencies have now begun extending the maturity of their deals in a further effort to tap into the long-term investor base. Both Fannie Mae and Freddie Mac came to the market with 30-year issues this year, seizing the interest of a sizable group of corporate buyers.

"Corporate bond portfolio managers are drawn to the more long-end issuance," said one FIG banker, "and the calendars make it easier for non-specialists to participate in the market."

bailout by tax payers. In order to avoid systemic risk, it is necessary that GSEs are subjected to the market discipline as any other financial institution. GSEs now enjoy the following benefits:

1. GSE debt and mortgage-backed securities are exempt from registration with the Securities and Exchange Commission.
2. The GSEs are exempt from state and local corporate income taxes.
3. The GSEs have a line of credit from the Treasury that authorizes the Treasury to purchase up to $2.25 billion of FNMA and Freddie Mac obligations and up to $4 billion of the FHLB obligations.
4. Banks are permitted to make unlimited investments in GSEs' debt securities, whereas there are limits placed on their investments in any other company's debt securities.
5. GSE securities are eligible as collateral for public deposits and for loans from Federal Reserve Banks and Federal Home Loan Banks.
6. GSE securities are lawful investments for federal fiduciary and public funds.
7. GSEs are authorized to use Federal Reserve Banks as their fiscal agents, including issuing and transferring their securities through the book-entry system maintained by the Federal Reserve.

These advantages are significant, and they make the agency securities much more attractive to institutional investors. When one recognizes that FNMA and Freddie Mac are publicly traded companies owned by their stockholders, it is unclear as to why the benefits enjoyed by these agencies should continue. At the time the agencies were created, the infrastructure for credit to the housing sector was ill-developed. These agencies have done a tremendous job of improving the flow of housing credit. Given the current sophisticated market structure for housing credit, it is not clear that government subsidized agencies are necessary, especially given the potential for costly bailouts and the incentive to take on excessive leverage.

Market Conventions

A number of agency issues tend to have a maturity of six months or nine months. These agency securities tend to make interest payments at maturity (IAM). Agency yields are calculated on the assumption that all months have 30 days (even February, which actually has 28 or 29 days, and August, which actually has 31 days). We can write the yield of an IAM agency security as

$$P + ai = \frac{I + 100}{\left(1 + y\frac{n}{360}\right)},$$ (8.1)

where P is the quoted price of the agency security in $\frac{1}{32}$, I is the interest payable at maturity, ai is the accrued interest, and n is the number of days between the settlement date and the maturity date using the 30-day convention. The yield of the IAM agency is denoted by y.

Let $n = 200$ days, using the 30-day counting convention and 6% be the stated interest for the agency. Let us also assume that the number of days between the issue date and the settlement date is 45, using the 30-day counting convention. Then we can compute $I = 6 \times \frac{245}{360} = 4.0833$. The accrued interest $ai = 6 \times \frac{45}{360} = 0.75$. If the quoted price of this agency security is 100, then we can write

$$100 + 0.75 = \frac{4.0833 + 100}{\left(1 + y\frac{200}{360}\right)}. \tag{8.2}$$

Solving, we get the yield of the agency equal to 5.955%.

The convention for agency securities with multiple interest payments is similar. If c is the rate of coupon, then the yield y is calculated as in Equation 8.3. Let us assume that the settlement date is $t < T$ and that there are N coupon dates remaining. Denote by z the number of days between the settlement date and the next coupon date, and by x the number of days between the last coupon date and the next coupon date. Then,

$$P_t + ai_t = \left(\frac{100}{\left(1 + \frac{y}{2}\right)^{N-1+\frac{z}{x}}}\right) + \sum_{j=1}^{j=N} \frac{\frac{c}{2}}{\left(1 + \frac{y}{2}\right)^{j-1+\frac{z}{x}}}. \tag{8.3}$$

The critical point to remember is that all days are counted using the 30-day conventions.

CORPORATE DEBT MARKET

There are six categories of corporate credit. By far the biggest of these is the corporate bond market, which accounts for nearly 40% of the market. This is followed by bank loans (25.8%) and the commercial paper market (22.8%). These three sources of credit account for more than 85% of the corporate credit market. The remainder is accounted for by medium-term notes, international bonds, and asset-backed securities.

While credit risk is perhaps the most important factor in the corporate debt market, it is useful to note that the issuance and refunding and call activities tend to occur in periods of relatively low interest rates. To underscore this point, we present Figure 8-2. Note how as AAA rates fell during the period 1990 to 1993, the corporate bond issuance activity picked up significantly. All corporations have a valuable timing option; they can issue debt now or wait and issue it later. The advantage of issuing now is to take advantage of the interest tax shield or capture the net present value of projects that can be financed using debt issuance. On the other hand, by waiting and issuing debt later, they may be able to take advantage of any drop in interest rates. At low enough interest rates, this waiting option is worth exercising, and the corporation will issue debt or refund to take advantage of low rates.

Credit Risk of Issuers

The most important dimension that distinguishes corporate debt from Treasury debt is the fact that the issuer in the corporate market is an institution that has some credit

FIGURE 8-2   *Total Corporate Bond Issuance and AAA Corporate Rates*

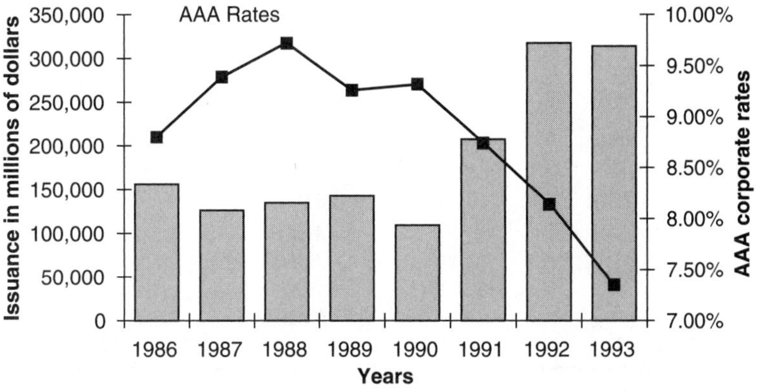

TABLE 8-5

*Long-Term Credit Rating
Categories for Corporate
Debt*

Description	Moody's	S&P
Investment grade bonds		
Gilt-edge, prime maximum safety	Aaa	AAA
Very high grade, high quality	Aa1	AA+
	Aa2	AA
	Aa3	AA−
Upper medium grade	A1	A+
	A2	A
	A3	A−
Lower medium grade	Baa1	BBB+
	Baa2	BBB
	Baa3	BBB−
Junk bonds (high yield)		
Low grade speculative	Ba1	BB+
	Ba2	BB
	Ba3	BB−
Highly speculative	B1	B+
	B2	B
	B3	B−

risk. Corporate debt securities are rated by various rating agencies, such as Moody's and Standard and Poor. Table 8-5 provides the rating categories currently in use for long-term corporate debt. Corporate securities that are rated below Baa3 (Moody's) or BBB (S&P) are considered "speculative" or "junk" or "noninvestment grade."

We begin our study of the corporate debt market by examining the commercial paper market.

TABLE 8-6   *Financing Methods—A Comparison*

	1997		1998 (Until Nov. 23)	
	No.	*$ million*	*No.*	*$ million*
1. High-grade corporate	1221	178,152	1142	160,605
2. Public high yield	122	30,368	100	18,031
3. 144 A—high yield	534	90,602	496	85,336
4. Agency	3508	217,506	3136	198,288
5. Structured	2196	201,261	1948	177,479
6. Straight preferred	186	27,816	171	26,302
7. Convertible	131	25,163	127	22,885
8. Common stock	1282	149,194	1202	140,524
9. IPO	612	65,257	579	63,035
10. Total		985,299		892,485

Source: McCarthy, Crisanti, and Maffei 1998.

Financing in Agency/Corporate Markets

To gain a perspective of financing in the agency and corporate market, let us review Table 8-6, which summarizes the financing activities in 1997 and 1998 in the United States.

The corporate issues (investment grade and high yield) accounted for a total of $263 billion in 1998, which was about 30% of all the financing in the markets represented in Table 8-6. When we take into account structured debt issues and convertible debt issues, the corporate issues account for 52% of all financing.

Commercial Paper

The commercial paper market is among the oldest of all the corporate credit markets in the United States. The market can be traced back to 1869, and its growth was fueled by the demand for corporate credit, which exceeded the supply of bank credit. Many companies directly accessed the lenders via the commercial paper market. Several new issuers also entered the market, as did new investors, such as the money market mutual funds that primarily invest in commercial paper. Today, commercial paper is an important source of short-term credit for large, high-quality borrowers.

Commercial paper is a short-term corporate discount security. It is typically unsecured, and the issuer is obligated to repay the principal amount to the holder of the commercial paper at maturity. Typically, maturities are limited to 270 days or less. Commercial paper maturities can be customized to meet the needs of issuers and investors. Much of the liquidity in the market is concentrated in the maturity range of 30 to 45 days. Generally, commercial paper is traded in denominations of $100,000 or more. The market is typically dominated by large borrowers with very high credit reputations. The largest commercial paper issuers tend to sell their commercial paper directly to investors. Such issuers are known as direct issuers. In 1991, there were about

TABLE 8-7
Short-Term Credit
Rating Categories
for Commercial Paper

Description	Moody's	S&P
Prime	P-1+	A-1+
Prime-1	P-1+	A-1
Prime-2	P-2+	A-2
Prime-3	P-3+	A-3
Not Prime	N.P.	C

75 such direct issuers. Other issuers, whose number is in excess of 1,500, sell their commercial paper through one or more dealers. Major commercial paper dealers are Goldman Sachs, Merrill Lynch, Lehman Brothers, and First Boston. In 1991, these four dealers accounted for more than 90% of the dealer-placed commercial paper. It should be stressed that while the dealers make a secondary market in commercial paper, most commercial paper is held to maturity.

Under the Securities Act of 1933, corporations do not have to register with the Securities and Exchange Commission (SEC) in order to issue CPs. This represents savings in time commitment and resources. This exemption is subject to the issuer meeting certain conditions, which vary with the type of the commercial paper program. These are described later. Further, by issuing CPs, corporations are able to directly access the capital market for short-term capital without having to rely on intermediaries, such as commercial banks, for their financing needs. For highly rated corporations, this is a real advantage as they are able to borrow at rates below the London interbank offered rates (LIBOR), or at "sub-LIBOR" rates. Most issuers in this market enjoy a rating of P-2/A-2 or better. (Table 8-7 lists the rating categories.)

Commercial paper may be purchased by investors subject to the Investment Company Act of 1940. The investors tend to segment this market based on the issuer's credit reputation and origin (domestic or foreign). Investors of commercial paper are money market mutual funds, insurance companies, pension funds, corporations, and banks, among others.

A significant proportion of the commercial paper market is issued under section 3(a)(3) of the Securities Act of 1933. The exemption from registration under this section is derived provided the proceeds from the issuance of commercial paper are used to fund current transactions and the maturity is limited to under 270 days. Commercial paper under this program may be purchased by all investors. In contrast, commercial paper issued under section 4(2) of the act specifies a different set of restrictions in order for the issuer to qualify for exemption from registration. Such issues may be sold only to certain investors, they may not be publicly offered, and they may not be purchased by investors with intent to resell.

Under section 3(a)(2) of the act, letter of credit (LOC)-backed commercial paper may be issued with exemption from registration. Such issues are guaranteed by the U.S. commercial bank. The LOC is issued to protect investors by substituting the credit reputation of the issuer of the LOC for the credit reputation of the issuer of the CP. For the LOC, the issuer pays a fee.

How important are these ratings? There is evidence that suggests that the initial ratings of commercial paper affects common stock returns. Nayar and Rozeff (1994) show that highly rated CP issues made by industrial users (without letter of credit) are often accompanied by significant positive returns. Rating downgrades, notably those that result in an exit from the CP market, are accompanied by significant negative returns. There is some evidence that the initial rating and subsequent rating changes convey important information to investors.

Corporate Bonds

In the corporate bond market, corporations issue securities to raise long-term capital. The investor in the corporate bond market is a creditor to the corporation and has a prior claim to the assets of the corporation, over the equity holders. For example, interest payments to corporate debt must be paid before dividends are paid to equity holders. As we will see later, in the event of financial distress, bondholders have certain rights over how the assets of the firm are distributed. For these reasons, corporate bonds are referred to as senior securities.

Similar to commercial paper issues, the corporate bond issues are regulated by the Securities Act of 1933. The issuer of corporate bonds must comply with the registration requirements of the SEC prior to the public offering of bonds. In addition, corporate debt securities also come under the Trust Indenture Act of 1939. Under the provisions of this act, a trustee must be appointed to represent the bondholders. Typically, a bank or a trust company will act as the trustee. Moreover, all contractual provisions between the issuer of corporate bonds and the trustee must be presented in a written form. This is known as the indenture provisions and is filed along with the registration documents.

Corporate debt securities may be grouped along several dimensions. One category that is used is to classify them according to different sectors of the economy. These sectors follow:

- Finance companies
- Industry
- Telephones
- Utilities
- Yankee issues
- Noninvestment-grade or junk issues

Corporate bonds trade at a spread over Treasuries to compensate the investors for (a) credit risk, (b) liquidity risk, (c) contractual features, and (d) tax disadvantages. To get a sense of the corporate yields, we present Table 8-8.

Aaa yields have varied from a low of 6.5% in 1998 to a high of 14.2% in 1981. The Baa yields peaked to 16.1% in 1982 but reached a low of 7.2% in 1998.

In Figure 8-3, we plot the spreads for two credit qualities: AAA and BAA. Two points are worthy of note. First, the spreads are significant for both rating categories. Second, the spreads are highly variable. Clearly, BAA spreads are much higher than

TABLE 8.8

Moody's Corporate Bond Yield Averages (Percentage Long-Term Annual Averages[1] 1980–1999)

Year	Aaa	Aa	A	Baa	Avg. Corp
1980	11.9	12.5	12.9	13.7	12.7
1981	14.2	14.7	15.3	16.0	15.1
1982	13.8	14.4	15.4	16.1	14.9
1983	12.0	12.4	13.1	13.6	12.8
1984	12.7	13.3	13.7	14.2	13.5
1985	11.4	11.8	12.3	12.7	12.0
1986	9.0	9.5	9.9	10.4	9.7
1987	9.4	9.7	10.0	10.6	9.9
1988	9.7	9.9	10.2	10.8	10.2
1989	9.3	9.5	9.7	10.2	9.7
1990	9.3	9.6	9.8	10.4	9.8
1991	8.8	9.1	9.3	9.8	9.2
1992	8.1	8.5	8.6	9.0	8.5
1993	7.2	7.4	7.6	7.9	7.5
1994	8.0	8.1	8.3	8.6	8.3
1995	7.6	7.7	7.8	8.2	7.8
1996	7.4	7.5	7.7	8.1	7.7
1997	7.3	7.5	7.5	7.9	7.5
1998	6.5	6.8	6.9	7.2	6.9
1999	7.0	7.3	7.5	7.9	7.4

Sources: *Moody's Investors Service;* Bond Market Association.

[1]Maturities 20 years and above.

FIGURE 8-3   *Corporate Spreads*

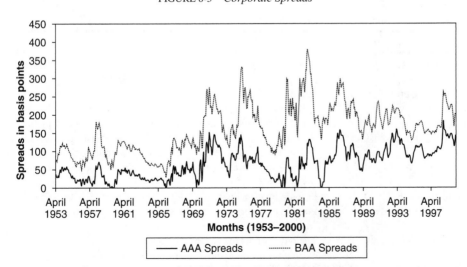

AAA spreads and are much more variable. While the tax and liquidity factors do contribute to the levels of the spread, the variability of spreads is most likely due to perceptions of changes in default risk. Note that the spreads widen around crisis in the market. The stock market crash in 1987, the high-yield market collapse in 1981, and the Russian default in 1998 all contributed to spikes in the corporate spreads.

Contractual Provisions in Corporate Debt

Corporate borrowers and lenders negotiate to arrive at the contractual provisions for corporate debt. In Table 8-9, we summarize some of the key contractual provisions.

Typically, lenders would demand periodic coupon payments. Fulfilling this contractual obligation is a signal that the borrower sends to the lender that the operating cash flows are sufficient to meet contractual obligations. In addition, bondholders frequently require sinking fund provisions, which mandate that borrowers amortize the principal payments over the life of the bond. Failure to comply with sinking fund provisions can lead to default and eventually to bankruptcy.

Let us review the corporate bonds that were issued during the period 1977 to 1990, listed in Table 8-10 (derived from Crabbe [1991]). Note that the number and the percentage of corporate bonds issued with call features has fallen steadily since 1977. As of 1990, only about 20% of the bonds are callable. In addition, the average maturity of debt has also fallen over time. In a perfect capital market, call features should be of no consequence; the gains to the firm are exactly offset by the discount in the sale price imposed by bondholders to compensate them for potential losses. In reality, however, in most corporations there are what are known as "agency problems." These problems arise because corporations are run by managers who should act as agents of

TABLE 8-9   *Contractual Provisions of Corporate Debt Contracts*

Provision	Description
Call features	Enable issuers to call after a call protection period. The call price is typically at a premium to par, and it declines with time.
Refunding provisions	Enable issuers to refund using cheaper sources of debt finance. Refunding restrictions mean that cheaper sources of debt may not be used to refund debt, although the debt may be callable.
Sinking fund provisions	Require investors to retire an outstanding debt issue periodically. The bonds may be retired at par (on a pro rata basis). Some bonds may be either retired at par or through open market purchases.
Putable bonds	Provide investors with the right to put the debt back to the issuer.
Convertible bonds	Provide investors with the right to convert bonds into a specified number of shares of common stock.
Bonds with warrants	The buyer of debt is also provided with warrants that give the right to buy the issuer's shares of common stock.

stockholders. Managers, however, will act in their own interests, and unless suitable compensation contracts are put in place, the actions of managers may not necessarily be in the best interest of the stockholders. Some of these agency problems follow:

Asymmetric Information. If the firm has favorable information about future cash flows that it is unable to communicate credibly at the time of debt issuance, then it has an incentive to issue debt with call features. Once the favorable information gets released, the firm can call the debt back. Often insiders (managers) know more about the firm and its future prospects than do creditors. This means that the creditors will want to design the debt contract in such a way as to minimize any potential costs that the managers might impose. Another consequence of asymmetric information is that the issuance of new equity typically results in a fall in the company's stock price. Thus, the equity issues tend to have "informational costs."

Underinvestment. If, after financing with noncallable debt, favorable projects arrive, then part of the gains will accrue to the bondholders. Then the managers of the firm might forego attractive projects. This underinvestment problem can also be mitigated through the issuance of callable debt.

Risk Shifting. The firm has incentives to take on projects with greater risk when the debt is noncallable. If the risks pay off, the firm gets all the benefits, and the bondholders only get the contracted amount. On the other hand, if the risks do not pay off, the firm can appeal to its limited liability and walk away from its obligations. Including a conversion feature helps to mitigate this problem.

TABLE 8-10   *Investment-Grade New Issues 1977–1990*

Year	Total Value	Percentage Noncallable	Number of Issues	Percentage Noncallable	Mean Maturity
1977	16.22	1	182	1	25.71
1978	13.64	1	138	1	25.28
1979	17.53	2	144	2	23.64
1980	27.29	6	248	5	19.28
1981	24.30	2	190	3	16.89
1982	23.80	18	252	21	14.28
1983	18.62	17	195	21	17.70
1984	24.77	31	212	34	11.66
1985	46.74	24	346	25	14.94
1986	94.11	34	641	32	16.98
1987	65.97	51	447	49	13.35
1988	51.51	47	343	45	12.09
1989	57.95	69	342	63	13.06
1990	55.99	85	319	78	12.78

Source: Crabbe 1991.

Power to the Creditors

By Eric S. Hardy

The traditional corporate bond is rigged against investors. When interest rates rise, it falls in value, just like a Treasury bond. But, unlike Treasury bonds, many corporate bonds don't rise much when interest rates fall. That's because corporate issuers of these bonds reserve the right to call them in early, at only a slight premium over the issue price. Heads you lose, tails you break even.

You can grab back some of this power by buying a bond with a built-in put option. This put gives you the right, but not the obligation, to sell the bond back to the issuer prior to maturity. The put exercise price is usually at par value. Puttable bonds are also generally noncallable—that is, the issuer does not have the right to force you to redeem early.

Nothing is free on Wall Street. You pay for this put feature in the form of reduced yield. Dennis Adler, a corporate bond stategist at Salomon Brothers, says the yield sacrifice on a noncallable 30-year A-rated corporate bond that can be put to the issuer at five par five years out is perhaps 20 basis points (a fifth of a percentage point).

Redeeming Virtue

Issuer	Coupon	Maturity	Moody's Rating	Amount Issued ($mil)	Recent Price	Yield to Put	Yield to Maturity	Date of First Put	Yield Sacrifice*
Columbia/ HCA Healthcare	8.360	4/15/24	A3	$150	$101.21	7.46%	8.25%	4/15/04	0.41%
Corning	7.625	8/1/24	A2	100	99.36	7.72	7.68	8/1/04	0.62
Eastman Chemical	7.625	6/15/24	Baa1	200	96.90	8.05	7.90	6/15/06	0.42
Eaton	8.000	8/15/06	A2	100	102.56	6.10	7.66	8/15/96	0.33
NBD Bank	8.250	11/1/24	Aa3	250	102.20	7.92	8.07	11/1/04	0.50
New England Telephone	7.875	11/15/29	Aa2	350	102.77	6.11	7.65	11/15/96	0.91
New Jersey Bell	7.850	11/15/29	Aaa	150	103.66	6.92	7.55	11/15/99	0.61
Pennsylvania Power & Light	7.700	10/1/09	A2	200	101.86	7.21	7.49	10/1/99	0.48
RJR Nabisco	6.800	9/1/01	Baa3	100	97.83	7.79	7.23	9/2/97	1.19
Torchmark	8.250	8/15/09	A3	100	101.27	7.28	8.10	8/15/96	0.34

These corporate bonds feature a built-in put option: You get at least one chance to cash in the bond early at par value. You exercise this right if interest rates rise or if the issuer's credit quality deteriorates.

*Yield forfeited by favoring puttable bond over nonputtable bond of comparable maturity and credit quality.

Sources: Bloomberg Financial Markets; Salomon Brothers Fixed Income Research.

Giving up some yield makes sense for someone who is nervous about his principal. If worry about a coming spike in interest rates has kept you from buying long bonds at all, then puttables are definitely worth a look.

One important caveat here: Almost all bond puts are "European-style," meaning they can be exercised only for a very short time—perhaps on one specific day. Still, having only one day to redeem a bond is better than having none at all.

A few municipal bonds and about 900 corporate issues have some kind of put feature. But note that for many of the corporate issues, the put becomes exercisable only after a change in corporate control. These are called poison puts and are seldom of value to the investor. They are installed to protect the management.

The table lists ten noncallable corporate bonds that can be put back to the issuer no matter who controls the company. In evaluating bonds like these, don't look at the maturity with your usual frame of reference. Often it's better to think of the put exercise date as the maturity.

To illustrate, look at the NBD Bank 8.25s of 2024. The Aa3-rated bond currently sells for 102 to yield 8.1% to maturity. But because the bond can be sold back to NBD at par on Nov. 1, 2004, it is easier to think of this as a ten-year bond yielding 7.9% to maturity. You'll redeem the bond in 2004 if interest rates have climbed or NBD's credit quality has deteriorated.

Alternatively, if rates have fallen and NBD still looks like a good bank, then you will hang on to the paper. At that point you will have, in effect, a new 20-year bond yielding 8.25% to maturity. In this light, your 30-year bond with a 10-year put becomes a 10-year bond with an attached call option on a 20-year bond. With bonds like this one the creditor is in the driver's seat.

EVIDENCE ON DEFAULTS AND FINANCIAL DISTRESS

Moody's defines default as a situation where an issuer misses or delays a contracted interest or principal payment. This definition includes the following circumstances:

- The issuer offers a package of new securities that has a diminished financial obligation. This may occur in distressed exchange offers.
- The exchange has the purpose of helping the issuer to avoid default.
- Delays in payments within the grace period provided in the indenture are also considered default.

A comprehensive study of defaults during the period 1970–1993 is provided in Moody's Investors Service (1994). Highlights of this study serve as a useful frame of reference for the modeling of corporate bonds. During a 24-year period of the study, the following was found:

- 614 issuers defaulted on corporate debt securities valued at over $93 billion.
- Highly rated firms had much less of a chance of defaulting than poorly rated firms, given the data on defaults across rating categories.
- Senior debt securities had a much higher recovery rate than did junior debt securities.

TABLE 8-11   *Default Data, One-Year Default Rates by Year and Rating*

Year	Aaa	Aa	A	Baa	Ba	B	Investment Grade	Speculative Grade
1970	0.00	0.00	0.00	0.30	8.40	21.60	0.10	10.90
1971	0.00	0.00	0.00	0.00	1.50	0.00	0.00	1.60
1972	0.00	0.00	0.00	0.00	0.50	11.80	0.00	3.70
1973	0.00	0.00	0.00	0.50	0.50	3.40	0.20	1.40
1974	0.00	0.00	0.00	0.00	0.00	6.90	0.00	1.40
1975	0.00	0.00	0.00	0.00	1.60	3.00	0.00	2.30
1976	0.00	0.00	0.00	0.00	1.10	0.00	0.10	1.40
1977	0.00	0.00	0.00	0.30	0.60	8.80	0.00	1.90
1978	0.00	0.00	0.00	0.00	1.10	5.30	0.00	1.80
1979	0.00	0.00	0.00	0.00	0.50	0.00	0.00	0.40
1980	0.00	0.00	0.00	0.00	0.00	4.40	0.00	1.50
1981	0.00	0.00	0.00	0.00	0.00	4.10	0.00	0.70
1982	0.00	0.00	0.20	0.30	2.60	2.20	0.20	3.40
1983	0.00	0.00	0.00	0.00	1.00	6.00	0.00	3.40
1984	0.00	0.00	0.00	0.60	0.50	7.30	0.20	3.50
1985	0.00	0.00	0.00	0.00	2.00	8.70	0.00	4.40
1986	0.00	0.00	0.00	1.10	1.90	11.60	0.30	5.70
1987	0.00	0.00	0.00	0.00	2.60	5.30	0.00	4.00
1988	0.00	0.00	0.00	0.00	1.50	5.70	0.00	3.40
1989	0.00	0.30	0.00	0.50	2.70	8.60	0.20	5.80
1990	0.00	0.00	0.00	0.00	3.30	12.90	0.00	8.80
1991	0.00	0.00	0.00	0.20	5.10	13.10	0.00	9.50
1992	0.00	0.00	0.00	0.00	0.20	6.40	0.00	3.80
1993	0.00	0.00	0.00	0.00	0.50	5.20	0.00	3.10

Source: Moody's Investors Services 1994.

Table 8-11 lists the yearly default rates across different rating categories. In Figure 8-4, we provide the information for investment-grade and speculative-grade debt securities.

The probability of default and the likely recovery rates in the event of default play an important role in the valuation of corporate debt securities. In the models of pricing corporate bonds, these factors are given much prominence. We shall review the corporate debt pricing models after a treatment of the junk bond market and the private placement market next.

Bankruptcy Code

Corporate debt securities come under the rubric of a bankruptcy code, which defines the rights and responsibilities of creditors and borrowers in the event of default. Bankruptcy code is the mechanism that anchors the process of coordination, renegotiation, and restructuring a financially troubled borrower and formalizes the access to the borrower's collateral. In the United States, bankruptcy code has three important provisions:

FIGURE 8-4   *Default Rates of Investment-Grade and Speculative-Grade Corporate Debt*

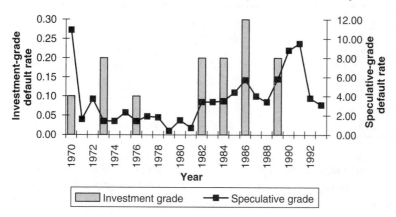

1. **Automatic stay:** After an event that leads to default, the borrower may seek protection under the bankruptcy code. During this time, an "automatic stay" on all payments to creditors is enforced. This is also referred to as a "standstill" agreement. This provision is to ensure that there is no "rush to the gate" by some creditors, who may have an incentive to "cut a deal" with the borrower at the expense of others. The period of automatic stay varies from country to country. The knowledge that automatic stay will be enforced upon default sets the stage for a more orderly process of financial reorganization.

2. **Active role for the bankruptcy court:** The judiciary authority plays an active role in supervising the process of reorganization. The court's rulings are binding on all parties. Moreover, major decisions cannot be taken without the approval of the court.

3. **Debtor in control:** Upon bankruptcy filing, the borrower remains in control under the U.S. bankruptcy code. At the request of the creditors, bankruptcy court can change the management.

In addition, the code provides for what is known as supra-priority financing. This provision allows for new financing (under financial distress), which can be senior to existing creditors. This provision, which is subject to the approval of the court, is used to deal with any liquidity problems during restructuring. In addition, the code admits a non-unanimity provision, whereby a reorganization plan requires only a majority approval by lenders (in numbers) and two-thirds by value in all classes of debt. This provision helps in mitigating any "holdout" problems by small creditors. Table 8-12 sets out the key provisions and their implications.

Chapter 7 of the code allows for the liquidation of the assets of the firm and distribution to the creditors. Chapter 11 provides for continued control by the borrowers with the mandate to reorganize the firm. The bankruptcy code also provides for an Absolute Priority Rule (APR), whereby the senior creditor's claims are first met before the claims of junior creditors are satisfied. Even though the code provides for APR

TABLE 8-12   *Highlights of Bankruptcy Code*

Bankruptcy Code Provision	Effect on Corporate Debt Valuation
1. Ability to liquidate (chapter 7 provision of the code)	Sets a benchmark for negotiations. It is the "outside option" that the creditors have and represents a lower bound for what they can get by negotiations.
2. Chapter 11 of the code (seeking bankruptcy protection)	Sets an orderly process for restructuring under the supervision of bankruptcy court. This is the benchmark that parties use for workouts.
3. Automatic stay	Mitigates coordination problems with multiple creditors.

often in renegotiations, the APR is violated by mutual consent. The bankruptcy code has a strong influence on the growth of corporate bond markets and spreads. An inefficient code with costly litigation will hinder the development of bond markets as lenders will be unwilling to extend credit, ex-ante. A bankruptcy code that is widely perceived to be "borrower friendly" will lead to higher spreads in the bond markets as lenders require a higher compensation for participating in such a market. Likewise, a "lender-friendly" bankruptcy code may lead to lower spreads.

High-Yield Bonds

An important segment of the corporate debt market is the high-yield or junk bond market. Table 8-13 summarizes the new issuance activity in the junk bond market during the period 1977 to 1993. After a tentative initial period (1977–1982), this market became quite active in the period 1983 to 1989. Much of the new issuance during this period can be attributed to leveraged buyout (LBO) activities. The market collapsed subsequently, with the new issues accounting for less than 2% of the market in 1990. The market appears to have stabilized with the new issues of around 20% of the market in 1993.

Financial Distress

Central to the understanding of corporate debt is the process by which financial distress is managed. This is especially important for poorly rated debt, which are subjected to a higher probability of incurring financial distress. John (1993) surveys and synthesizes the factors pertaining to financial distress. He proposes that financial distress happens when the liquid assets of the firm are not sufficient to meet the obligations of the firm's debt contracts. Thus, financial distress can be thought of as a mismatch between the firm's current assets and its current obligations.

It can be handled in a number of ways:

1. The existing assets can be partially liquidated. This will improve the liquidity of the firm and stave off financial distress. The disadvantage of this approach is that there are also liquidation costs (both direct and indirect).

TABLE 8-13   *New Issues of High-Yield Bonds*

Year	Total Number of Issues	Par Amount in Millions	Total Corporates in Millions	High-Yields as a Percentage of Corporates
1977	61	1,040.2	26,314.2	3.95
1978	82	1,578.5	21,557.2	7.32
1979	56	1,399.8	25,831.0	5.42
1980	45	1,429.3	36,907.2	3.87
1981	34	1,536.3	40,783.8	3.77
1982	52	2,691.5	47,208.9	5.70
1983	95	7,765.2	38,372.9	20.24
1984	131	15,238.9	82,491.5	18.47
1985	175	15,684.8	80,476.9	19.49
1986	226	33,261.8	156,061.3	21.31
1987	190	30,522.2	126,134.3	24.20
1988	160	31,095.2	134,791.9	23.07
1989	130	28,753.2	142,790.7	20.14
1990	10	1,397.0	109,284.4	1.28
1991	48	9,967.0	207,300.9	4.81
1992	245	39,785.2	317,605.7	12.52
1993	341	57,163.7	313,897.8	18.21

Source: *This Year in High Yield—The Journal of Global High Yield Bond Research* (1994), Merrill Lynch and Co., New York.

2. The firm can enter into a process of negotiation with the debtholders and reconfigure the debt obligations. This may entail a reduction in the liabilities of the firm or a deferment of the payments. Such debt restructuring will involve the following:
- Reducing the coupons and/or the principal obligations
- Increasing the maturity of the debt
- Accepting the equity of the company in lieu of some of the outstanding obligations

3. The firm can issue additional claims to achieve the liquidity necessary to avoid financial distress.

Note that the process of managing financial distress involves financial reorganization either on the asset side or on the liability side or both. It can be accomplished either out of court or within the formal bankruptcy codes that are applicable. The traditional approach to managing financial distress is for either the debtor or the creditor of the distressed firm to file for bankruptcy protection under Chapter 11. The debtor will then have the right to propose a reorganization within 120 days from the filing date. The process of financial reorganization may involve the creditors, and the 120-day period may be extended by the court, if it is deemed necessary. The plan is then evaluated by the debtholders who may either accept or reject it. Chapter 7 of the bankruptcy code is used to liquidate the firm if the reorganization plan is not accepted. The liquidation costs associated with court-supervised procedures can be quite high both in terms of the resources and in terms of the time it takes to complete the process.

The following key empirical regularities associated with financial reorganizations in the 1980s are well-documented:

- Bankruptcies are costly both because of direct costs and because of disruptions in the firm's activities.
- Bankruptcy procedures give considerable scope for opportunistic behavior by the various parties involved.
- Deviations from the absolute priority of claims are common.

During the period 1983 to 1999, the new issue volume of high-yield bonds grew from $95 billion in 1983 to $150 billion in 1988. (See Figure 8-5.) The new issue volume fell to about $100 billion in 1999. One of the factors contributing to this fall was the flight to quality induced by the Russian default in 1998 and hedge fund failures. Another factor was the increased number of defaults. In Figure 8-6, we have displayed the default rates during 1996 to 1999. Notice the steady increase in default rates during the period August 1998 to December 1999. Compared to $7.9 billion of high-yield defaults in 1998, in 1999 the defaults increased to $22.3 billion.

Altman (1992) classifies junk bonds into three categories:

1. Bonds that were originally issued as investment-grade debt and that subsequently were downgraded to below the investment-grade status. Such issues are referred to as "fallen angels." Altman (1992) estimates that such issues account for 25% of the market.
2. Bonds that were rated as noninvestment-grade at the time of issuance. The proceeds of such debt issues were allocated primarily for normal business activity. Such issues account for another 25% of the market.

FIGURE 8-5   *High Yield Issuance Activity*

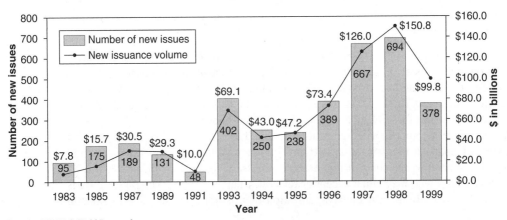

3. The remaining 50% of the junk bond issues that are outstanding were primarily issued for large corporate restructuring. They were issued during the active LBO
period from 1986 to 1989.

High-yield debt provides an alternative for issuers who would otherwise rely on
commercial bank debt. Borrowers in the commercial bank debt market may be subject
to restrictive covenants. In the junk bond market, issuers typically are subject to one or
more of the following covenants:

- **Aggregate debt limitations** specify a bound below which the issuer must main-
  tain the total level of debt.
- **Restrictions on dividend payments** ensure that profits are not diverted to stock-
  holders to the detriment of debtholders.
- **Restrictions on mergers, consolidations, and the sale of assets** by the issuing
  firm.
- **Credible third party guarantees and credit enhancements.**
- **Minimum standards on working capital levels.**

Altman and Nammacher (1987) point out that the high-yield debt market subjects issuers to less restrictive covenants than does private placement. Junk bonds are typically issued in on deferred-payment basis. The idea here is to initially offer a lower
coupon and progressively increase the coupons as the firm is able to shed its excessive
debt and regain its vitality. Such issues are known as **step up issues.** Another structure
that helps in mitigating the temporary liquidity problems is the payment-in-kind (PIK)
bonds that do not pay cash coupons but instead pay additional bonds in lieu of
coupons.

FIGURE 8-6   *Default Rates during 1996–1999*

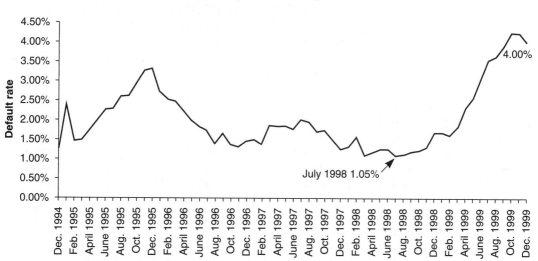

Sources: Bond Investors Association; Moody's Investors Service; CSI High Yield Research.

In striking contrast to investment-grade debt issues, a significant amount of junk bonds are issued with call features. The junk bonds are currently held by large financial institutions. A number of factors, however, have limited the attractiveness of junk bonds to major institutions. Risk-based capital standards have encouraged insurance companies and banks to invest in better quality assets than junk bonds. Credit-rating agencies have become concerned with the lack of liquidity in the junk bond market. Mutual Benefit Life Insurance Company in 1991 was unable to meet the redemptions, at least in part, of the junk-bond investments. In addition, life insurance companies have suffered losses in this market. The insurance subsidiary of the First Executive Corporation suffered significant losses in this market. These observations notwithstanding, the junk bond market appears to have stabilized into a relatively tenacious segment of the debt market.

Private Placements

Historically, private placements of debt issues tend to complement the public issues. This market, in which the issuers are not required to disclose any information to the public, tends to place debt with a few large reputable institutions. Such issues are exempt from registration with the SEC. There have been significant changes in the privately placed debt market since 1990, when the Securities and Exchange Commission (SEC) adopted the Rule 144A. This rule allows large institutions that are relatively sophisticated to trade privately placed debt freely among themselves. Such institutions are referred to as qualified institutional buyers (QIBs). QIBs have a discretionary investment of $100 million or more in such debt securities. This definition automatically includes life insurance companies, pension funds, commercial banks, and finance companies. Many of the debt offerings in this market are underwritten and offer several features of the public debt market without the disclosure requirements.

The section 144A market has become particularly important for high-yield markets as well. Figure 8-7 shows that section 144A issues account for more than 75% of new issues in recent years.

Term Structure of Credit Risk Premia

In Figure 8-8, we show the results of Sarig and Warga (1989a). They plot the spreads against the maturity for different credit ratings. Note that for high-quality firms as the maturity increases, the spreads increase. For poorly rated firms, exactly the opposite is the case. We present in Table 8-14 the credit spreads for different rating categories.

In a recent paper, Carey, Prowse, Rea, and Udell (1993) analyze this market in considerable detail. To get an idea of the increasing importance of this debt market, review the information in Table 8-15. The private placement of debt is about 75% of the public issues of debt. By and large, however, privately placed debt tends to have a much shorter average maturity than public issues. The borrowers in the private debt market are small- and medium-sized issuers with over 65% of the issues falling in the 10–100 million-issue size category with a median issue size of 34 million. In contrast, the median issue size in the public debt market is 150 million. In the privately placed

FIGURE 8-7   *High Yield New Issues by Quarter (by Par Amount)*

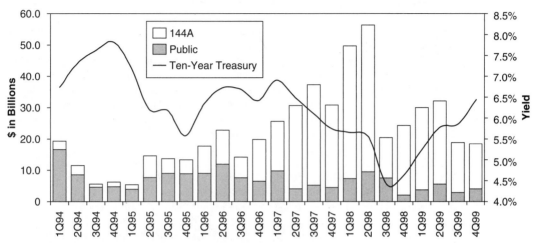

Source: *CSI High Yield Research.* Includes only U.S. dollar-denominated issues.

FIGURE 8-8   *The Term Structure of Risk Premia*

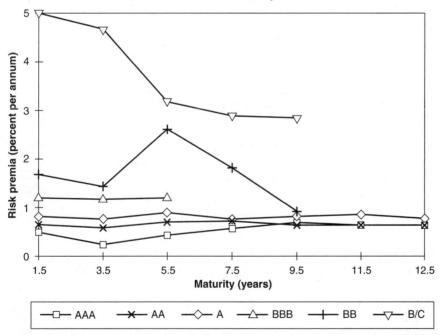

Yield spreads for corporate zero-coupon bonds, February 1985 through September 1987. Maturity numbers (horizontal axis) correspond to the average maturity of each cell in Table 8-15. Average yield spreads are calculated as follows: in each month the yield to an individual corporate bond has subtracted from it the yield to a zero-coupon government strip with identical maturity. If no government strip with identical maturity existed, the yields on the two strips with maturities most closely bounding the corporate bond were interpolated to obtain the appropriate risk-free zero-coupon yield. These yield differences were then averaged across bonds in a given month and then across time to produce the results.

TABLE 8-14   *Yield Spreads for Corporate Zero-Coupon Bonds*

Average yield spreads are calculated over the period February 1985 through September 1987 as follows: In each month, the yield to an individual corporate bond has subtracted from it the yield to a zero-coupon government strip with identical maturity. If no government strip with identical maturity existed, the yield on the two strips with maturities most closely bounding the corporate bond were interpolated to obtain the appropriate risk-free zero-coupon yield. These yield differences were then averaged across bonds in a given month and then across time to produce the results reported for each cell. The unrated column contains bonds from a mixture of ratings and should not be taken to be the lowest rating group. The figures are in percent per annum, and the number of observations is reported below the yield.

Maturity	AAA	AA	A	BBB	BB	B/C	Unrated
0.5–2.5 years	0.410	0.621	0.775	1.326	1.670	4.996	3.081
	21	74	123	48	64	41	38
2.5–4.5 years	0.232	0.562	0.736	1.275	1.495	4.650	3.232
	11	99	251	152	79	117	96
4.5–6.5 years	NA	0.620	0.778	1.405	2.730	3.365	3.197
		114	221	59	58	125	119
6.5–8.5 years	NA	0.620	0.660	NA	1.878	2.959	3.443
		96	138		51	80	119
8.5–10.5 years	0.626	0.575	0.816	NA	0.989	2.912	3.099
	24	69	97		10	10	88
10.5–12.5 years	NA	0.566	0.854	NA	NA	NA	2.478
		64	110				64
12.5 plus years	0.544	0.544	0.740	NA	NA	NA	2.516
	64	501	510				278

Source: Sarig, O., and Warga, A., *Journal of Finance* 1989.

TABLE 8-15	Type of Issue	1975–1980	1981–1985	1986–1991
Gross Issuance by Nonfinancial Companies, in Billions of Dollars	Public	21.00	35.60	87.60
	Private	14.70	19.80	64.80

Source: Carey, Prowse, Rea, and Udell 1993.

debt issues there are no registration costs, and for smaller issues there are no underwriting expenses—an important lack of expense for small- and medium-sized issuers.

    The lenders in this market are typically life insurance companies. They find private-debt issues more attractive from a risk-return standpoint, and they impose restrictive covenants to better manage the risk. It is also possible for lenders to, for example, customize sinking-fund schedules to manage their risk better. Other covenants may include call protection, minimum net worth requirements, and debt ceilings. In addition to life insurance companies, pension funds and finance companies also are big lenders in this market.

The privately placed debt market, since the advent of Rule 144A, has tended to become more liquid. It has also attracted foreign issuers.

CONCLUSION

This chapter described the agency and corporate debt markets. The institutional features of these debt markets were described, and empirical evidence on the maturity composition, the risk premiums, and the sizes of different sectors of these markets were presented. We also reviewed the available theory and empirical evidence on financial distress and corporate-debt valuation. A brief study of hybrid instruments, such as convertible debt, was also provided.

PROBLEMS

8.1   What are agency debt securities? Identify the eight major federally sponsored agencies.

8.2   Explain the role of the Resolution Trust Corporation (RTC).

8.3   Briefly describe the roles of the agencies FHLB, SLMA, and FFCB.

8.4   Most agency securities are callable. What are the reasons for this?

8.5   Who are the major rating agencies? Describe the rating conventions. Identify the rating ranges for investment- and noninvestment-grade corporate debt.

8.6   Explain why many investment-grade corporate bonds issued during late 1980s and early 1990s do not have call features, whereas bonds issued prior to these periods do have call features.

8.7   Explain why junk bonds have call features.

8.8   **(a)** What is the motivation for providing sinking-fund provisions in bonds?
(b) Consider the Eurobond in the following table that will repay a total of 75 million in three equal payments beginning in Year 4.

Sinking Period	Principal Amount Repaid	Years to Repayment
1	25 million	4 years
2	25 million	5 years
3	25 million	6 years

Assume that the holder of this bond will receive an annual coupon of 10%. (i) Write out the cash flow pattern of this bond. (ii) Assume that the sinking-fund requirements are met by buying the bond back at par. How will you go about computing the yield to maturity of the bond?

8.9   What are the key reasons for an issuer to use the commercial paper market for short-term funds?

8.10   What are the different sectors of the corporate bond market? Briefly describe each sector.

8.11 (a) What procedures are available for managing financial distress?

(b) Explain the following terms: (i) Chapter 7, (ii) Chapter 11, (iii) prepacks, (iv) exchange offers, (v) workouts.

8.12 Identify the key differences between junk bonds and investment-grade bonds.

8.13 What is Rule 144A? How has it affected the corporate debt market?

8.14 Describe briefly the privately placed corporate debt market. Who are the typical lenders? What are the pros and cons of borrowing in this market?

8.15 Describe the model used by Merton (1974) to value corporate debt. What are his major conclusions? Critique the model.

8.16 Briefly explain how you will incorporate (i) costly liquidations, (ii) opportunistic debt service, and (iii) deviations from absolute priority in a model of valuing corporate debt.

REFERENCES

Altman, E. 1992. "Revisiting the High-Yield Bond Market." *Financial Management* 21(2):78–92.

Altman, E., and S. Nammachar 1987. *Investing in Junk Bonds: Inside the High Yield Debt Market.* New York: John Wiley & Sons.

Carey, M. S., S. D. Prowse, S. D. Rea, and G. F. Udell 1993. "Recent Developments in the Market for Privately Placed Debt." *Federal Reserve Bulletin* 79(2):77–92.

Crabbe, L. 1991. *Callable Corporate Bonds: A Vanishing Breed.* Washington, D.C.: Board of Governors of the Federal Reserve System.

John, K. 1993. "Managing Financial Distress and Valuing Distressed Securities: A Survey and a Research Agenda." *Financial Management* (Special issue on financial distress) 22(3):60–78.

Merton, R. C. 1974. "On the Pricing of Corporate Debt: The Risk Structure of Interest Rates." *Journal of Finance* 29:449–470.

Moody's Investor Service 1994. *Corporate Bond Defaults and Default Rates, 1970–1993.* Moody's Investor Service, Global Credit Research.

Nayar, N., and M. S. Rozeff 1994. "Ratings, Commercial Paper and Equity Returns." *Journal of Finance* 49:1431–1449.

Sarig, O., and A. Warga 1989a. "Some Empirical Estimates of the Risk Structure of Interest Rates." *Journal of Finance* 44(5):1351–1360.

Chapter 9

Securitization and Mortgage-Backed Securities

Chapter Objectives

This chapter introduces the concepts of securitization, mortgages, and mortgage-backed securities. A concise description of the primary mortgage market is provided. The mortgage contract and the right to prepay are analyzed in detail. The following questions are addressed:

- What are fixed-rate and adjustable-rate mortgages?
- What factors influence prepayments?
- How are prepayments measured?
- What are mortgage-backed securities, and how they are priced?
- What are collateralized mortgage obligations (CMOs), and how are they structured?
- What is an option-adjusted spread (OAS)?

INTRODUCTION

In this chapter, we will first investigate in detail the process of securitization. Its application to mortgage-backed securities markets will be discussed. We will then address the primary focus of this chapter, mortgage-backed securities. We describe the underlying mortgage market and the types of mortgage loans. Next, we evaluate prepayments, which are critical to the understanding of mortgages and mortgage-backed securities. The factors that determine prepayments and various measures of prepayments are described. We then describe the process by which mortgage-backed securities are created and illustrate the valuation principles that are used for pricing mortgage-backed securities.

SECURITIZATION

One of the most exciting developments in securities markets in recent times has been securitization. Stated simply, it is a framework in which some illiquid assets of a corporation or a financial institution are transformed into a package of securities backed by these assets, through careful packaging, credit enhancements, liquidity enhancements, and structuring. For example, the accounts receivables constitute an important asset of most corporations, yet this asset has credit risk stemming from the varying credit reputations of the counterparties. The terms of the accounts receivables could also differ from one counterparty to another counterparty, depending on the transactions. In effect, the combination of credit risk and the idiosyncratic nature of each component in the account receivables makes them illiquid. The basic steps that are involved in securitization are outlined in Chapter 1.

Motivations for Securitization

Securitization was briefly explored in Chapter 1. Some of the major factors that motivate securitization follow.

Many financial institutions find it desirable to reduce the size of their balance sheet. By carving out certain items in their balance sheet via securitization and selling them to investors, the size of the balance sheet can be reduced. For example, the accounts receivables of a corporation may be used to back the issue of commercial paper known as asset-backed commercial paper. The motivation for downsizing the balance sheet is simple. If the revenues remain the same and the size of the balance sheet goes down, then the return on equity will increase; moreover, less capital is needed to meet the capital-requirements standards that have been mandated by regulatory authorities.

The process of securitization permits poorly rated corporations to participate in certain segments of the capital markets that are otherwise unavailable to them. For example, the commercial paper market, where typically only highly rated corporations participate, is now increasingly attracting poorly rated issuers who are able to use the process of securitization to leverage segments of their balance sheet.

Securitization also enables the firm to transfer some risk to investors and reduce the size of the firm. In the process, firms are able to prepare the ground for major capital structure changes.

The Players in Securitization

There are several players involved in the process of securitization. The assets originate with some firm. Often, the firm whose assets back the security is referred to as the **originator.** These assets are then acquired from the originator by the issuer. The issuer typically achieves a bankruptcy remote status by creating a **special purpose vehicle (SPV).** The SPV assures that the pool of assets is held distinct from the originator, so the bankruptcy or insolvency of the originator will have no consequences on the status of the pool of assets held by the SPV.

Often, a **trustee** will be appointed to ensure this. The trustee's job is to ensure that the issuer complies with all the stated obligations. The collection and disbursement of cash flows is yet another responsibility. Often, this requires prudent reinvestment decisions.

FIGURE 9-1   *The Process of Securitization*

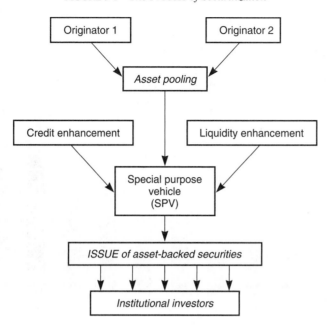

The steps involved in the securitization process and the players are shown in Figure 9-1 (see also Chapter 1). The originators pool their assets according to certain standards. The asset pool is then held in a SPV within an appropriate legal framework so that the originator's financial status is of no consequence to the investors. The process also typically involves **credit and liquidity enhancements.** This is a process in which third parties guarantee to investors the credit-worthiness and timely payments of contractual obligations. The concept of securitization has been applied extensively in the mortgage market to which we turn now.

MORTGAGES

Homeownership in most countries is achieved through a mortgage that is, in essence, a secured loan. The family that wishes to own a home will typically pledge the home as collateral and borrow money from the lender, who is typically a bank or a financial institution. Every month, the homeowner will pay an amount, which is credited toward the payment of interest and the outstanding principal amount that has been borrowed. In the event of a default, the lender has the right to take over the home and dispose of it in the market to recover the outstanding balance. The mortgage market has grown dramatically as shown in Figure 9-2.

FIGURE 9-2   *Total U.S. Mortgage Debt Growth*

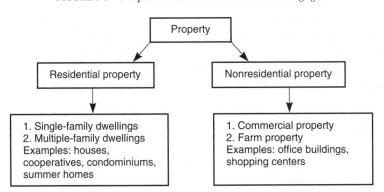

Source: Federal Reserve *Flow of Funds Accounts of the United States.*

FIGURE 9-3   *Properties Used as Collateral in Mortgages*

```
                          ┌──────────────┐
                          │   Property   │
                          └──────────────┘
                   ┌─────────────┴─────────────┐
                   ▼                           ▼
        ┌──────────────────────┐   ┌──────────────────────┐
        │ Residential property │   │ Nonresidential property │
        └──────────────────────┘   └──────────────────────┘
                   │                           │
                   ▼                           ▼
    ┌───────────────────────────┐  ┌───────────────────────────┐
    │ 1. Single-family dwellings│  │ 1. Commercial property    │
    │ 2. Multiple-family        │  │ 2. Farm property          │
    │    dwellings              │  │ Examples: office buildings,│
    │ Examples: houses,         │  │ shopping centers          │
    │ cooperatives, condominiums,│ │                           │
    │ summer homes              │  │                           │
    └───────────────────────────┘  └───────────────────────────┘
```

Although this example deals with homeownership, it applies to commercial properties as well. The terms residential property and nonresidential property are used in the real estate market to distinguish the type of property that is used as a collateral. A schematic classification is shown in Figure 9-3.

Primary Mortgage Market

To understand the risks and incentives present in the mortgage market, it is useful to begin with the primary mortgage market, where lenders and borrowers interact to consummate their transactions. The lender (typically a mortgage banker, commercial bank, or other financial institution) reviews applications for mortgage loans from different potential and present homeowners. The original lender is referred to as the originator. The mortgage originator underwrites the loan, processes the necessary documents, and provides the funds to the homeowner (borrower). While homeowners are the principal mortgage borrowers, farmers and commercial institutions also use mortgage financing. Homeowners are classified into single-family and multifamily units by the lenders. More than 95% of the loans in the residential market are originated by thrifts, commercial banks, and mortgage bankers. The lending institution collects a fee for its services. This fee, known as the **origination fee,** is a small percentage of the loan. On a $200,000 loan, such a fee may be 1 point, or 1% of $200,000 = $2000. Lenders also charge processing fees for carrying out certain activities that are discussed later.

The borrowers are typically homeowners. The lender collects a fair amount of information from the potential borrowers to minimize the risk of default. Typically, before a loan is approved, the following data are gathered:

- Information about the borrower's credit history and about other loans and liabilities that the borrower has. The basic motivation here is to compare the loan amount and the resulting mortgage payments with the net income of the borrower less payments toward prior obligations. A rule of thumb used by many lenders requires that the mortgage payments are less than 28% of the borrower's pretax monthly income. This puts an upper bound on the loan that can be taken by the borrower.
- Information about the borrower's net worth and liquidity.
- An assessment of the value of the property. A policy limit is then set on the **loan-to-value (LTV) ratio** and the down payments that are expected from borrowers. LTV ratios depend on a number of factors, such as the nature of the property, the levels of interest rates, and the credit conditions. For instance, lenders may require that the borrowers make a down payment of 5% to 25% of the appraised property value. Loans extended in this manner are known as conventional mortgages. Such loans are not insured by government agencies.

Several forms of insurance programs exist in the primary mortgage market to ensure orderly payments on the loans. If the LTV is greater than 80%, then lenders will typically require the borrowers to purchase private mortgage insurance. Usually, the uninsured portion of the loan will be less than 70% to 75% of the value of the home. Government agencies, such as the Federal Housing Administration (FHA) and the Veterans Administration (VA), provide mortgage insurance, which is intended to cover low-income and middle-income families. FHA and VA mortgages tend to require smaller down payments than do conventional mortgages. FHA and VA also impose

TABLE 9-1

Government Mortgage Limits 1980–1994

Year	Conventional	FHA	VA
1980	$93,751	$90,000	$100,000
1981	$98,500	$90,000	$110,000
1982	$107,000	$90,000	$110,000
1983	$108,300	$90,000	$110,000
1984	$114,000	$90,000	$110,000
1985	$115,300	$90,000	$110,000
1986	$133,250	$90,000	$110,000
1987	$153,100	$90,000	$110,000
1988	$168,700	$101,250	$144,000
1989	$187,600	$101,250	$144,000
1990	$187,450	$124,875	$184,000
1991	$191,250	$124,875	$184,000
1992	$202,300	$124,875	$184,000
1993	$203,150	$151,725	$184,000
1994	$203,150	$151,725	$184,000

Source: Mortgage Product Analysis, Merrill Lynch, December 1994, New York.

limits on the amount of mortgages they provide; Table 9-1 illustrates how these limits have changed over the 1980 to 1994 period.

When private insurance is taken by the lender, the cost is passed on to the borrower through a higher borrowing rate. Borrowers can also obtain insurance in the market from insurance companies.

After a scrutiny of these factors, the lender accepts a pool of applications and extends loans to acceptable borrowers. Note that such a loan portfolio, an asset in the bank's balance sheet, has a market value that is highly sensitive to the levels of interest rates. This arises from the fact that the borrowers (homeowners) have the option to refinance their loans by prepaying their loans and taking on new loans when mortgage interest rates fall. In addition, most of the bank's liabilities are CDs, FRNs, and other short-term instruments. This means that the cost of funds to most financial institutions is tied to the levels of short-term interest rates. On the other hand, the revenues from such assets such as mortgage-loan portfolios are tied to longer-term interest rates, as the mortgage rates on 15-year and 30-year FRMs tend to be at a spread over respective Treasury counterparts. Thus, the banks have a duration mismatch and, therefore, have a natural yield-curve risk. If the yield curve were to invert, then the cost of funding the loan exceeds the revenues, unless other asset-liability management techniques are used. These techniques include securitization, issuing adjustable-rate mortgages, and matching the duration of assets and liabilities using the derivative markets. Lenders are subject to the risk of default; this is less of a problem to the extent that the value of the property is greater than the loan at the time of default.

After extending several loans, the originator ends up with a loan portfolio. If he decides to sell this portfolio (to book a profit), then there are well-established institutions in the market to help accomplish this task in an efficient manner. There are organizations, such as the Federal Home Loan Mortgage Corporation and the Federal National Mortgage Association, which buy loan portfolios and pool them to make them sufficiently attractive for institutional investors. For a loan portfolio to be purchased by these agencies (see Chapter 8), they must be **conforming loans** meeting certain standards. Loans not satisfying these standards are called **nonconforming loans.** The government agencies play a critical role in enhancing mortgage credit. In addition, there are private entities that also buy nonconforming loans. Together, the government agencies and these private entities play the role of conduits. Most commercial and investment banks have subsidiaries that act as private conduits.

Loans (whether they are pooled or not) must be serviced. A number of activities must be performed in servicing loans. These activities include the following:

- Maintaining the status of individual loans in terms of outstanding principal, prepayments, and delinquency records
- Collecting scheduled interest payments, principal payments, and prepayments
- Handling delinquencies, defaults, and foreclosures
- Making payments to owners of the loan portfolio

There is a servicing fee charged by the financial institutions that provide these services.

One of the choices that the household makes in the mortgage market is the type of loan it takes. In the following sections, we will focus on residential mortgage loans. The conventional residential mortgage loan falls under two categories: (1) fixed-rate mortgages (FRM) and (2) adjustable-rate mortgages (ARM).

Fixed-Rate Mortgages (FRMs)

FRMs differ from other fixed-income securities with promised common coupon payments. Typically, Treasuries, corporates, agencies, and Eurobonds pay semiannual or annual coupon payments. Mortgages typically pay **monthly cash flows.** In addition, mortgages are **amortizing,** with payments assigned toward both interest and principal.

FRMs have level pay structures, but there are other structures, such as graduated-payment mortgages (GPMs), that are also issued from time to time. In GPMs, the initial monthly payments are set somewhat low; then the monthly payments are steadily increased to a prespecified level within five years or so. After this period, the monthly payments are set at that level for the remaining period of the mortgage. In GPMs, because the initial payments are low, the outstanding balance might actually increase, leading to **negative amortization** during the first few years of the mortgage.

The traditional mortgage is the 30-year fixed-rate mortgage with level monthly scheduled payments. This is an amortizing loan, wherein level monthly payments are scheduled over 360 months so that the loan is retired at the end of 360 months. Although 30-year FRMs are common, there have also been active originations of 15-year FRMs in the market.

We illustrate the calculation of monthly payments, interest components, and principal components for a standard 30-year FRM next. Let F_0 be the face value of the loan that was taken, let n be the original term of the loan in months, and let R be the

TABLE 9-2   *Effect of Interest Rates on Scheduled Monthly Payments for Two Terms of Fixed-Rate Mortgages (Original Loan: $100,000)*

Interest Rate	5.00%	5.50%	6.00%	6.50%	7.00%	7.50%	8.00%	8.50%	9.00%	9.50%	10.00%
30-Year FRM	536.82	567.79	599.55	632.07	665.30	699.21	733.76	768.91	804.62	840.85	877.57
15-Year FRM	790.79	817.08	843.86	871.11	898.83	927.01	955.65	984.74	1014.27	1044.22	1074.61

annualized interest that is specified in the FRM. Then, the monthly payments x are computed as shown in Equation 9.1, where $r = \frac{R}{12}$.

$$x = F_0 \times \frac{r(1+r)^n}{[(1+r)^n - 1]} \tag{9.1}$$

These monthly scheduled payments are applied toward both interest and principal. In Table 9-2, we illustrate the effect of R, the annualized interest rate on the monthly payments. As R increases from 5% to 10%, note that the monthly payments increase significantly, from $536.82 to $877.57 for 30-year FRMs.

If we denote F_t as the outstanding balance at the end of month t after that month's payments have been made, then,

$$F_t = F_{t-1} + \left(\frac{R}{12} \times F_{t-1}\right) - x. \tag{9.2}$$

Then the principal payments will be simply

$$F_{t-1} - F_t. \tag{9.3}$$

The interest payments for the month t are given by

$$\frac{R}{12} \times F_{t-1}. \tag{9.4}$$

Figure 9-4 shows the pattern of scheduled interest and principal payments over the life of the mortgage. Note that in the early part of the life of the mortgage, most of the monthly payments x are applied toward repaying the interest component of the loan. It is toward the end of the life of the mortgage that the payments toward principal constitute a major part of the monthly payments. As the mortgage gets older, the outstanding principal balance declines and, as a consequence, the interest payments decline. Since the monthly scheduled payments are fixed, this means that the scheduled principal payments will increase.

The 15-year FRM has higher monthly scheduled payments than a 30-year FRM. To compare these payments, we provide the monthly payments with the interest and principal components for both FRMs in Table 9-2.

FIGURE 9-4   *Scheduled Interest and Principal Payments on a $100,000 30-Year Fixed-Rate Mortgage at 8%*

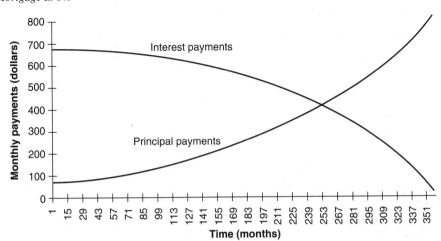

Adjustable-Rate Mortgages (ARMs)

ARMs permit the interest payments to be reset at periodic intervals to prespecified short-term interest rates. The most commonly used short-term indexes are the constant maturity one-year Treasury rate and the Cost-of-Funds Index (COFI), which is the weighted-average cost of funds for the thrift institution members of the Federal Home Loan Bank of San Francisco.

Since ARMs shift fluctuations in interest rates to the borrowers, the asset-liability management problems of lenders that we alluded to in our general discussion are mitigated. The only exposure that the lender has with a plain-vanilla ARM without caps is the exposure to interest rates during the period between the resets. To the extent the interest-rate risk to the lender is reduced, any resulting benefits will, at least in part, be passed on to the homeowners as a lower cost of borrowing. As we saw in Chapter 5, short-term interest rates are more volatile and, as such, ARMs can subject borrowers to a significant amount of risk if the rates increase unexpectedly. If the homeowners are unable to meet the increased monthly payments resulting from such increases in short-term interest rates, defaults can occur.

It is rarely the case that ARMs are issued without additional contractual features. Typically, ARMs include prespecified interest-rate caps. These caps limit the maximum interest rate that the borrower will pay in case the index rates increase dramatically. Often, ARMs carry caps on reset dates, as well as a cap rate applicable throughout the life of the ARM. ARMs also have payment caps.

When the payment cap becomes binding (due to an increase in the short-term rates), the borrower pays the specified capped amount. During this period, the principal amount of the loan may actually increase. This is referred to as negative amortization.

Initially, when the ARM is offered to the borrowers, a below-market initial rate is specified in the contract. This is known as the teaser rate. To summarize, ARM has the following contractual features:

- A reference rate or an index. This can be the one-year constant maturity T-bill or the eleventh district COFI, etc.
- Reset frequency: monthly, semiannual or annual
- Spread over the reference rate
- Lifetime cap on rates
- Periodic cap on rates
- Payment caps
- Teaser rate

Currently, ARMs account for over 50% of the market share.

ARMs allowed more families to qualify for mortgages. In mid-1984, ARMs accounted for approximately two-thirds of the conventional mortgage loans. ARM market share has fluctuated over time, from about 40% in 1981 to a high of 66% in 1984. It has become an established part of the mortgage market. ARM portfolios are more often held by the originators as investments. In 1984, such government agencies as GNMA and FNMA began the securitization of ARMs. Despite these programs, ARMs are not securitized to the same extent as FRMs.

PREPAYMENTS

Mortgages permit the homeowners to prepay their loans. This prepayment provision introduces timing uncertainty into the originating bank's cash flows from its loan portfolio. For example, if the bank originates a pool of mortgages with a weighted-average rate of 8% and six months later the mortgage rates drop significantly below 8%, say to 7%, then the loan portfolio is certain to experience significant prepayments as borrowers rush to refinance their mortgages with less-costly loans. The lender has a long position in the mortgage loan that entitles him or her to monthly scheduled payments, but has also sold an option to the homeowners that gives them the right to prepay the loan when the circumstances demand it. This means that the bank cannot predict the future cash flows from its loan portfolio with certainty. Clearly, the option to prepay will be priced into the loan by the bank, and the borrower will pay a higher interest rate on the loan as a consequence.

Factors Affecting Prepayments

Prepayments of mortgages are driven by a number of factors, each of which merits further elaboration (see also Chapter 1).

Refinancing Incentive. Perhaps the most important reason for prepayments is the refinancing incentive. If the market rates for mortgage loans drop significantly below the rate that a borrower is paying, then the borrower has a very strong reason to prepay as long as the borrower is able to qualify for a new loan. This incentive means that the prepayments accelerate in periods of falling interest rates, especially when there is a belief in the market that the rates have bottomed out.

Seasonality Factor. Families typically do not move during the school year. Things remaining equal, families will move during the period from the middle of June through the first week of September; this results in increased prepayments during this part of the year. This can be thought of as the seasonality factor or the school-year factor.

Age of the Mortgage. During the early part of the mortgage loan, interest payments far exceed the principal component. This, in part, means that the interest savings associated with refinancing are greater during the earlier part of the mortgage loan. We expect the prepayments to be greater during the earlier part of the life of the loan and then stabilize afterward; indeed, prepayments are higher when the life of the loan is in the range of 2 to 8 years. In addition, when a mortgage is more than 25 years old, there may be an incentive to pay it off in order to secure the property's title. The speed of prepayments slows for loans in the age range 10 to 25 years.

Family Circumstances. A number of factors pertaining to family circumstances lead to the prepayment. These factors include marital status (often divorce decisions lead to prepayment) and job switching.

Sometimes, the inability of a household to make the monthly payment (due to job loss or disability) leads to default; under some circumstances, this can precipitate a prepayment. As noted earlier, there are two forms of mortgage insurance. In one form, the lender initiates the insurance and the policy guarantees that the insurance company will pay some or all of the loan in the event the homeowner defaults. In the other form, initiated by the homeowner, the insurance company will pay off the loan obligations in the event of a death of the insured person.

Further, if a family moves (due to such factors as increasing family size, job switches, etc.) and if the loan is assumable, then when the family moves, the next family that moves into the home can assume the mortgage. If the loan is not assumable, it has to be paid in full, which results in prepayments.

Housing Prices. The price of the home is yet another factor in prepayment. The housing price affects the LTV ratio, which in turn affects the ability of the household to qualify for refinancing. When the housing prices increase, the LTV decreases. This enhances the ability of the homeowner to refinance if the going interest rates and family circumstances warrant refinancing. On the other hand, when the housing prices drop, the LTV ratio increases; this diminishes the ability of the homeowner to qualify for refinancing, even if other factors favor refinancing.

The relationship between the asset value of the mortgage and the value of the house thus affects the prepayment incentives.

Asset Value of Mortgage =
Current Face Value of Mortgage − Current Market Value of Mortgage

Mortgage Status (Premium Burnout). The relationship between the contractual inter-est rate in a mortgage loan and the going mortgage interest rates is a major determi-nant of the value of the loan. If the contractual interest rate r is greater than the going interest rate R, then the loan is a prime candidate for prepayment. Such mortgages are referred to as **premium mortgages.** If $r < R$, then the mortgage is said to be a **dis-count mortgage.** We would expect premium mortgages to prepay faster. There is some empirical evidence indicating that the premium mortgages, after some prepay-ments, tend to stabilize. An initial drop in rates leads to significant prepayments. A subsequent drop does not produce a similar level of prepayments. Hence, a number of premium mortgages remain outstanding. This is referred to as **premium burnout.** We have already hinted at some reasons why this might happen.

Mortgage Term. Evidence suggests that the rate of prepayments depends on other fac-tors as well. For example, the rate of prepayment of FRMs with a maturity of 15 years differs from the rate of prepayment of FRMs with a maturity of 30 years. Waldman, Schwalb, and Feigenberg (1993) present the following evidence:

- For current coupon and discount coupon securities, prepayments from 15-year mortgages have been 11% faster than 30-year mortgages during the period 1983 to 1992.
- For high-coupon securities, prepayments from 15-year mortgages have been 5% slower than 30-year mortgages during the period 1986 to 1992. The seasoning of the mortgage appears to have a significant impact on the speed of prepayment.

Measures of Payments

There are different measures of prepayments used in the industry to determine the rate of prepayment. These measures are grounded in certain assumptions that must be un-derstood by investors in the mortgage markets. We will discuss each of these measures in turn. All these measures have been developed in the context of mortgage-backed se-curities. However, they are useful even at the level of individual loans.

Twelve-Year Retirement. This is perhaps the simplest and the least important measure of prepayment. It assumes that the mortgage is prepaid exactly after 12 years. If this assumption is made, we can add the prepayments at the end of 12 years to the sched-uled payments. The cash flows of the mortgage loan in the absence of default can then be determined for all future months. This measure is clearly inconsistent with what we know about the factors that determine prepayments.

Constant Monthly Mortality. This measure assumes that there is a constant probabil-ity that the mortgage will be prepaid following the next month's scheduled payments. For instance, consider the assumption that there is a 0.50% probability that the mort-gage will be prepaid following the first month.

This 0.50% probability is referred to as the single monthly mortality rate, or SMM. Using the SMM, we can compute the probability that the mortgage will be retired in the next month. It depends on two factors: (a) the probability that the mortgage will survive the first month, $1 - 0.50\% = 99.50\%$, and (b) the mortality rate for month 2 (given that it survived the first month), which is 0.50%. So, the probability that the mortgage will be retired in month 2 is $0.50\% \times 99.50\% = 0.4975\%$. Using this, we can say that the probability that the mortgage will be retired in month 3 is $(1 - 0.4975\%) \times 0.50\% = 0.4975\%$ and so on.

Usually, an annual prepayment rate known as the conditional prepayments rate (CPR) is used to measure the speed of prepayments. Given an annual CPR, we can estimate the SMM. Remember that the probability the mortgage will survive a month is $(1 - \text{SMM})$. For a period of one year, the probability of survival is $(1 - \text{SMM})^{12}$. This is set equal to $(1 - \text{CPR})$. So, we get:

$$(1 - \text{SMM})^{12} = 1 - \text{CPR},$$

or

$$\text{CPR} = 1 - (1 - \text{SMM})^{12}.$$

If SMM = 1% (per month), then CPR is 11.36%. In our example, SMM = 1% implies that 1% of the outstanding principal is paid down each month. This measure (CPR) is used widely in the industry to measure prepayments.

As the constant of monthly mortality increases, the probability that the mortgage will be retired early increases; this is useful for computing the prepayments associated with a loan portfolio.

Note that this approach is inconsistent with the fact that the prepayment increases during the first few years, then stays at a relatively low level, and increases again toward the end of the loan period.

FHA Experience. The Federal Home Administration (FHA) has a large database on actual prepayments of mortgages of different vintages. This data forms the basis for computing the probability that a loan will be retired during any given year.

The probability is computed as follows. The FHA data is organized as a series, giving the probability that the new mortgage will survive to the end of any given year, where years are indexed from 1 to 30. Let x_t be this probability. Then, the probability that the mortgage will be retired during any given year t is

$$p_t \equiv x_{t-1} - x_t.$$

The conditional probability that the mortgage will survive through the year t, given that it has survived until the year $t - 1$ is denoted by y_t, and is computed as

$$y_t = 1 - \frac{p_t}{x_{t-1}} = \frac{x_t}{x_{t-1}}.$$

Once we have the conditional probability y_t of a mortgage surviving through the year t, given that it has already survived through year $t - 1$, we can use that information to derive the conditional monthly survival probabilities by invoking additional assumptions about the monthly probabilities. For instance, if we assume that the conditional monthly probabilities within each year are constant (say, z_i for year i) then we must have

$$z_i^{12} = y_i \Rightarrow z_i = y_i^{\frac{1}{12}}.$$

These derived monthly probabilities are referred to as the 100% FHA experience. Unlike the CPRs, 100% FHA experience does not decline with the age of the mortgage.

Example 9-1:

58% of the mortgage pool is expected to survive 10 years and 54% of the pool is expected to survive 11 years. Using this estimate, we may conclude that the prepayment in the 11th year will be 4%, assuming the 100% FHA experience.

Investors use this information and adjust it for different speeds (i.e., 50% FHA experience, 200% FHA experience).

Prepayments measured on the basis of FHA experience, while useful, nonetheless present some problems. Since FHA mortgages are assumable, the speed of prepayments tends to be underestimated.

PSA Experience. The Public Securities Association (PSA) convention assumes that 0.2% of the principal is paid in the first month and will increase by 0.2% in each of the following months, finally leveling out at 6% until the maturity. This convention is referred to as the 100% PSA. By scaling up or down, one can construct different PSA measures. Figure 9-5 shows the prepayment rates for 100% PSA, 150% PSA, and 200% PSA.

FIGURE 9-5   *PSA Prepayment Conventions*

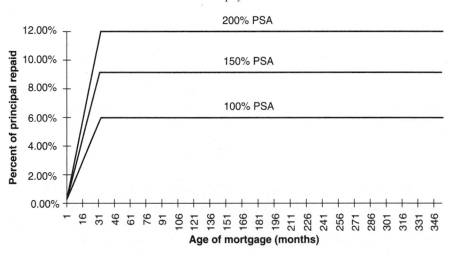

The PSA standard benchmark was introduced in July 1985. *It is not a model of prepayments but used as a benchmark in the industry.* Mathematically, 100% PSA benchmark can be expressed as follows:

$$\text{Months 1 to 30: CPR} = 6\% \times \frac{t}{30},$$

where t is the number of months since the origination of the loan, or

$$\text{Months} > 30: \text{CPR} = 6\%.$$

Basically, the seasoning effect of mortgages is incorporated through a linear increase in prepayments and is based on FHA 30-year FRMs.

Mortgage Cash Flows with Prepayments

With the basics of the mortgage contract in place, we can now see how the monthly cash flows of the mortgage loan contract can be projected into the future. We can construct future cash flows from a single loan with a face value of $100,000 and a rate of 9%. The mortgage loan has a life of 30 years. Prepayments are assumed to occur at a rate of 100% PSA. We detail the calculations next:

- First, using the prepayment rate assumption, we can compute the SMM for month $t = 1$ as follows:

$$\text{CPR} = 6\% \times \frac{1}{30} = \frac{0.06}{30} = 0.002$$

$$\text{SMM} = 1 - (1 - CPR)^{\frac{1}{12}} = 1 - (1 - 0.002)^{\frac{1}{12}} = 0.00167$$

As noted earlier, the method of calculating SMM is the same until $t = 30$. After $t = 30$, CPR = 6% until the loan is retired. Note that SMM = 0.005143 after $t = 30$ until the end.

- Second, total mortgage payments at $t = 1$ are obtained by applying Equation 9.1 with $F_0 = 100,000$, $n = 360$ and $r = \frac{0.09}{12}$. We get the payment x at $t = 1$ to be 804.62. We calculate the interest payment by multiplying the outstanding balance with the monthly interest rate. For $t = 1$, we get $100,000 \times \frac{0.09}{12} = 750$.
- The scheduled principal payment at $t = 1$ is obtained by subtracting the interest payments from the total mortgage payments: $804.62 - 750 = 54.62$.
- Finally, prepayments at $t = 1$ are computed by applying SMM to the remaining principal:

$$= 0.000167 \times [100,000 - 54.62]$$

$$= 16.67$$

- Total principal outstanding at $t = 2$ is obtained by subtracting the total principal payments at $t = 1$ from 100,000 to get:

$$100,000 - [54.62 + 16.67] = 99,928.70.$$

FIGURE 9-6   *Prepayments of a Single Loan at 100% PSA*

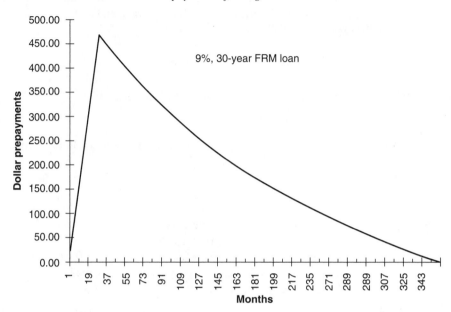

• We then apply the procedure each time to get the projected future cash flows of the mortgage loan.

Figure 9-6 plots the prepayments of this loan with the 100% PSA assumption.

It is important to understand the effect of prepayments on the loan value. The value of the loan with prepayments is compressed to the outstanding balance as interest rates fall. In comparison, the value of a noncallable loan increases as the rates fall.

MORTGAGE-BACKED SECURITIES (MBS)

Historical Overview

We begin our discussion of the mortgage-backed securities markets by first providing a summary of how they developed.

In traditional mortgages, prior to securitization, home buyers obtain loans (via borrowing) from mortgage originators. Typically, originators (mortgage banks, thrifts, etc.) lend to many home buyers; thus, they end up with a loan portfolio. Such loan portfolios may either be held by the originator or sold to other investors. The demand for credit, therefore, comes from home buyers, and the mortgage originators supply the necessary credit. When the demand exceeds the supply in a region, thrifts will sell their loan portfolio (which they originated) in order to supply additional credit. When the supply exceeds the demand in a region, thrifts will buy loan portfolios from other regions. Often, redistribution of mortgage credit from capital-surplus to capital-deficit regions is necessary, and to accomplish this, usually the loans are sold and bought by thrifts and mortgage banks around the country. When the overall demand for credit grows at a rate that cannot be sustained by suppliers of credit, the deposit base of lenders may simply be unable to support the demand for credit. For a liquid secondary market in mortgage loans to develop, it is necessary that some of the following conditions are met:

- The originators must continue to service the loans.
- The loans must be standardized with respect to maturity, coupons, and so on.
- There must be a credible guarantee regarding the performance of home buyers in paying the loan back.

The strong demand for mortgage credit precipitated the following sequence of events. In 1934, the FHA was set up to insure home loans. In 1938, the Fannie Mae was created; its mission was to provide a secondary market for FHA and Veterans Administration (VA) mortgage loans, provide additional liquidity to the mortgage market, and improve the distribution of investment capital. Fannie Mae was set up as a wholly owned government corporation. In 1944, the VA loan guarantee program was set up.

By 1954, Fannie Mae was partly owned by private shareholders and partly by the government. In 1968, it was split into the Government National Mortgage Association (GNMA or Ginnie Mae) and Fannie Mae. At present, Fannie Mae is a private corporation whose shares are listed on the New York Stock Exchange (NYSE). The U.S. Treasury, at its discretion, may buy up to $2.25 billion worth of Fannie Mae's debt. GNMA is wholly government owned. All of its operations are financed by Treasury borrowings, interest on holdings, guarantee fees, and other fees. The mission of GNMA is to supply and stimulate credit for mortgages through its secondary market activities. GNMA guarantees FHA- and VA-based mortgage-backed securities (MBS).

In 1970, the Federal Home Loan Mortgage Corporation (Freddie Mac) was created by Congress. Freddie Mac provides a link between mortgage lenders and capital markets. It buys from savings and loan institutions, mortgage bankers, and commercial banks, and sells mortgage pass-through securities. It began with an initial capital of $100 million funded by 12 Federal Home Loan Banks through nonvoting common stock.

A comparison of the agencies and their pass-throughs is presented next.

Agency and Private Pass-Through Securities: A Comparison

1. **GNMA:** GNMA finances FHA and VA loans. Typically, the loans are from single-family, low-income households. GNMA pass-through securities are guaranteed by GNMA and are issued by GNMA-approved originators and servicers. The loans are packaged in sizes of one million or more and placed with a trustee. Upon acceptance of loan documentation, GNMA assigns a pool number, which identifies the security to be issued. The originator or the servicer then issues pass-through securities, which are sold to investment bankers for distribution.

GNMA tends to require a greater degree of homogeneity of the mortgages within a given pool. Pools tend to have a single type (single-family, 30-year fixed, for example), and the mortgages carry the same interest rate. For single-family pools, the mortgage interest is 50 basis points higher than the pass-through rate: the 50 basis points covers the servicing fee and the guarantee fees. In the GNMA II program, there is more diversity in the underlying loans. Also under the GNMA II program, a central paying and transfer agent consolidates all the payments to the security holders in one monthly check, but there is a delay associated with this process.

The GNMA guarantee of full and timely payment of interest and principal is backed by the full faith and credit of the U.S. Government. GNMA covers low-income (house price less than $152,000) homes. Historically, prepayments are less volatile relative to other agency pass-throughs.

2. **FNMA:** This agency's stocks trade in the NYSE. FNMA buys conventional mortgages and operates a swap program, whereby loans of any age can be swapped into FNMA-issued participation securities. Such a swap can be beneficial to the lenders in the sense that the lenders can use the FNMA-issued securities as collaterals in reverse repurchase agreements.

    FNMA also provides the guarantee of full and timely payment of interest and principal, but this guarantee is not backed by the full faith and credit of the U.S. Government. However, FNMA does have a $2.25 billion credit with the U.S. Treasury. FNMA pools are much more heterogeneous when compared to the pools in the GNMA. FNMA pools may have mortgages with rates that vary by more than 200 basis points, and the loans may be new or seasoned. FNMA covers both FHA and VA loans, as well as conventional loans, which have a much higher value. Due to this and due to the greater diversity of loans, prepayments are much more volatile.

3. **FHLMC:** This agency also buys FHA, VA, and conventional mortgages, and operates a swap program whereby loans of any age can be swapped into Freddie Mac-issued participation securities. As noted earlier, such a swap can be beneficial to the lenders in the sense that the lenders can use the Freddie Mac-issued securities as collaterals in reverse repurchase agreements.

    FHLMC also provides the guarantee of full and timely payment of interest and principal. This guarantee, however, is not backed by the full faith and credit of the U.S. Government, but Freddie Mac has a $2.25 billion credit with the U.S. Treasury. Freddie Mac pools are much more heterogeneous when compared to the pools in the GNMA. Freddie Mac pools may have mortgages with rates that vary by more than 200 basis points, and the loans may be new or seasoned. FHLMC buys FHA and VA, as well as conventional loans, which have a much higher value. Due to this and due to the greater diversity of loans, prepayments are much more volatile.

4. **Private labels:** These are nonagency pass-through securities that create a secondary market for nonconforming loans, which are conventional loans that fail to

meet the size limits and other requirements placed by the agencies. Private pass-throughs trade at a spread over the agency pass-throughs.

Creation of MBS

Only FHA and VA loans qualify for conversion to GNMA pass-through MBS. The loan pool must have some standard features in terms of coupon, single-family or multifamily, maturity, and so on. The minimum size of the pool is $1 million for single-family loans. GNMA II permits mortgages with different interest rates to be included in the same pool.

The following steps are taken in issuing mortgage-backed securities:

1. The originators forward the loan portfolio to GNMA with the appropriate documentation, requesting GNMA's commitment to guarantee the securities to be backed by the pooled mortgage portfolio.
2. GNMA reviews the application. If the review is favorable, then a pool number is assigned, and the commitment is issued.
3. The originators transfer the mortgage documents to custodial agents and send the required pool documents to GNMA.
4. Anticipating the issuance of the GNMA guarantee, the originators solicit advance commitments from dealers, investment banks, and so on, to sell a specified amount of the securities at a set price and yield.
5. GNMA reviews the documentation and issues the guarantee.

The originators continue to service the loans: collecting the monthly interest and principal payments, remitting the net amount of the servicing fee to the security holders, and issuing monthly account statements.

GNMAs are not debt obligations of the issuers. They represent real estate assets. The servicers collect 50 basis points per annum of the outstanding principal balance of each mortgage for servicing and the GNMA guarantee. GNMA gets 6 basis points per annum of 50 for its guarantee. Figure 9-7 illustrates the basics of creating an MBS.

FIGURE 9-7   *Creating Mortgage-Backed Securities (an Example)*

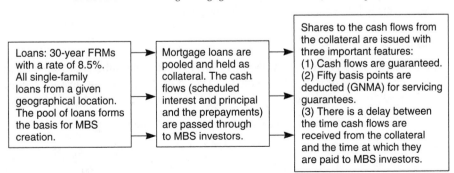

Cash Flows and Market Conventions

Amount of Cash Flow. In principle the cash flows (scheduled interest, principal and prepayments) from the underlying pool of mortgages are passed through to the investors in the mortgage-backed security with the exception of fees. Servicing fees and guarantee fees will be subtracted from the cash flows generated by the loan portfolio that is backing the mortgage-backed security. These fees vary from one agency security to another. For GNMAs, the fees are as follows:

- Forty-four basis points are retained by the servicer for servicing the loans and guarantees.
- GNMA will get 6 basis points for its guarantee. The issuer essentially guarantees GNMA against any defaults by homeowners. GNMA guarantees against defaults by the issuer.
- These fees mean that the investors in the mortgage-backed security will get 50 basis points less than the coupon of the loan portfolio.

Timing of Cash Flow. Homeowners tend to make their scheduled payments during the first half of each month. The payments to the investors in mortgage-backed securities occur on the 15th of the next month. Market participants refer to this as a 45-day delay. This delay varies from one agency security to another. In reality, the actual delay is a good deal less than that.

Market Conventions. Investors buying an agency security, such as a GNMA, must understand the market conventions. GNMAs are quoted in $\frac{1}{32}$, similar to Treasury securities. The prices quoted refer to percentages of the outstanding principal balance in the underlying pool. This requires the calculation of the outstanding balance, which in turn requires compilation of the scheduled interest and principal payments, as well as any prepayments. For these computations, the servicing institutions calculate a pool factor. The definition of **pool factor** $p_f(t)$ is

$$p_f(t) = \frac{B_t}{P}, \qquad (9.5)$$

where B_t is the balance at date t, and P is the original balance.

Example 9-2:

Consider a $100 million par value of GNMA issued some time ago. Currently, it has a pool factor of 0.9 and is quoted at a price of $93\frac{16}{32}$. To an investor who is holding 20 million original par of this GNMA, its market value can be computed as

Par value remaining $= 20 \times 0.9 = 18$ million

Market value $= 18 \times 0.9350 = 16.83$ million.

As in the Treasury markets, this price is the flat price to which the accrued interest is added to determine the invoice price.

The usual settlement practice is to settle two days following the trade date. The first settlement date for any month occurs around the middle of the month. The reason for this is simple: It takes that long to compute and distribute the pool factors. The procedure for computing accrued interest is as follows. The accrued interest ai_t is

$$ai_t = \frac{SD - M}{30} \times c \times \frac{1}{12} \times B,$$

where SD is the settlement date, M is the first day of the month within which t falls, B is the principal balance, and c is the coupon rate.

Example 9-3:

In Example 9-2, let us assume that the coupon rate $c = 9\%$ and that $SD - M$ is 20 days. Then, the accrued interest is

$$ai_t = \frac{20}{30} \times 9 \times \frac{1}{12} \times 18 \times 10,000 = 90,000.$$

Note that the accrued interest calculations differ from Treasuries in important ways. First, interest accrues from the first day of the month; in Treasury markets, the last coupon date is the relevant date from which interest accrues. In the case of GNMA, the convention is actually over 360, as the example illustrates. Note that this means that an investor buying a GNMA in April for settlement in the middle of April (say, April 15) is buying a pro rata share in the outstanding principal balance of a mortgage pool as of the end of March. This investor will expect to receive on May 15 the interest on the balance, computed as of the end of March, plus any prepayments during the month of April.

When agency pass-through securities are traded, they are identified with some key characteristics of the underlying pool. A pool number is assigned that enables investors to learn about the features of the underlying pool, such as whether the pool is fixed or adjustable, the issuer, and the weighted-average coupon. Sometimes trades in securities occur before key features of the underlying pool become available. Such trades are referred to as TBA (to be announced) trades. In TBA trades, investors do not know the pool numbers on the trade date, but they will know them before the settlement date.

Prepayment Evidence. GNMA prepayment history is reported in Table 9-3 for two subsample periods: 1979–1984 and 1989–1991. Note the decline in prepayments after the peak in 1979. The increase in the levels of interest rates accounted for this decline until 1982. During the 1987 to 1991 period, prepayments were stable, although at a

TABLE 9-3
GNMA Prepayment
History

	1979–1984					
	Coupon $7\frac{1}{2}\%$ (1977)		Coupon 8% (1977)		Coupon $9\frac{1}{2}\%$ (1979)	
Year	CPR	PSA	CPR	PSA	CPR	PSA
1979	7.5	141	6.7	149	—	—
1980	3.1	51	3.0	51	1.0	46
1981	1.1	18	1.3	21	1.4	30
1982	0.8	13	0.9	15	1.3	21
1983	2.7	46	2.8	46	2.5	41
1984	2.5	42	2.4	41	2.4	39

	1987–1991					
	Coupon 9% (1986)		Coupon $9\frac{1}{2}\%$ (1986)		Coupon 8% (1987)	
Year	CPR	PSA	CPR	PSA	CPR	PSA
1987	1.6	74	2.6	117	—	—
1988	3.5	78	5.0	107	1.6	52
1989	4.7	79	6.2	105	2.7	52
1990	5.3	89	6.8	114	3.6	59
1991	6.4	107	8.7	145	4.2	70

Source: Mortgage Product Analysis, Merrill Lynch (December 9, 1994).

much higher level relative to the 1980 to 1984 period. The steep increase in 1991 is due to the decline in refinancing rates. This trend continued on into the 1992 to 1993 period (not reported here) as well. For the same reason, higher-coupon GNMAs have faster prepayments, as seen during the 1987 to 1991 period: the $9\frac{1}{2}\%$ GNMA has faster prepayments relative to the 9% GNMA.

Institutional Investors and MBS. MBS comprise a sector in which a number of institutional investors participate. Since MBS are backed by mortgage loans and are guaranteed, credit risk is not a major factor. Investors pay more attention to the nature of the collateral, structure of the issue, and the extent to which there is overcollateralization. For the agency-backed pass-throughs, the main risk is the prepayment risk. The investor buys a pro rata share of the cash flows. If there is a drop in interest rates, prepayments will occur and will be passed through. Figure 9-8 shows the prepayment history for 1988 to 1995. Note the extraordinary increase in prepayments from 1993 to 1994. Despite the prepayment risks, MBS have become an important part of portfolios of institutional investors as the article from *Pension World* (1993) illustrates.

FIGURE 9-8   *Prepayment History (1988–1995)*

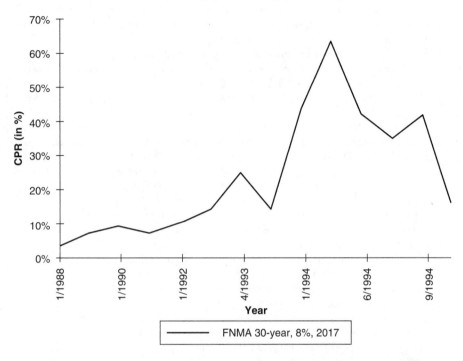

Managers Breathing Easier after Attacks

By Ray Wise

Emerging from their bunkers after three massive prepayment attacks, managers of mortgage portfolios are breathing easier. They see interest rates nudging higher in the months ahead, and a flat-to-slightly-rising rate environment would give Ginnie Mae's an edge over comparable Treasury bonds.

The Treasury Department is curtailing auctions of 30-year bonds in favor of short-to-intermediate maturities. This augurs pressure on the shorter-term Treasuries, causing better relative performance by Ginnie Mae's later this year, says portfolio manager Garitt Kono of the New York-based Dreyfus Corporation.

True, interest rates recently extended their protracted decline, chasing yields on 30-year Treasuries to record lows. "Eventually, though, the rate decline is going to end. Once you get a reversal, you will see more investors coming into the mortgage-backed market," predicts portfolio manager Mike Kennedy of Chicago-based Stein Roe & Farnham.

(continued)

Technically, the market in mortgage-backed securities looks pretty solid, notes managing director Kay Willcox of Prudential Investment Corp., Newark, N.J. There is a dearth of attractive alternatives; high-grade corporates, for example, are burdened by tight yield spreads. Moreover, reflecting prepayment, underweighting of MBS is widespread. Having recently turned positive on this asset class, fixed-income manager Francis H. Trainer of New York-based Sanford C. Bernstein & Co. has a 23% weighting in MBS; that's up sharply from the 13% he carried last September, but well below a market weighting of 29%.

Yet roaring bulls abound. "Ginnie Mae's yield 20% more than Treasuries, with the same credit quality. I think this is a terrific time for the mortgage-backed market," says managing director David H. Glen of Scudder, Stevens & Clark, Boston. "We are trying to load up mortgages. You've got an opportunity here." "The mortgage market is an attractive long-term place to put money, despite the interest-rate declines," adds portfolio manager Amy Swanson of Boston-based State Street Research & Management, Inc.

Falling rates encourage home owners to refinance their mortgages, minimally causing return of principal and reinvestment risk to MBS holders; in the case of a premium coupon, capital loss also results.

The likelihood that prepayment may remain at a high level for months doesn't deter Swanson from being bullish on mortgage securities. "They have good value relative to corporates and Treasuries. It's okay to incur prepayment. You are still earning a handsome return over Treasuries," the money manager notes.

Prepayment risk is managed by Swanson in three ways: applying a worst-case scenario to a mortgage certificate and deciding whether it is worth owning at its current price; trying to anticipate interest-rate changes, and focusing on current coupons. The portfolio of Chris Ray of Putnam Management Co., Boston, who worries less about rate declines than about the possibility that rates may rise sharply, is barbell-shaped; it is focused on 7%–7.5% and 9.5%–10% coupons.

Until fairly recently, conventional wisdom held that widespread mortgage refinancings required fueling by an interest-rate drop of 150 to 200 basis points. That rule-of-thumb has been rendered totally obsolete by the proliferation of refinancing options. Seeking to capitalize on the new environment, mortgage bankers beating the bushes for business have sweetened the deals considerably.

The disparities between interest-rate-sensitive mortgage refinancings on one hand, and all the rest, on the other, have widened. The latter category is secular, fairly predictable and reflects the housing industry cycle.

Example: A young couple living in an apartment with a one-year-old child buys a house from a family needing a bigger spread.

Refinancings driven mainly by steeply falling home loan costs can come so swiftly and unpredictably as to seem like a capital-market manifestation of chaos theory. Prepayment risk can be managed but not eliminated. On the other hand, without that risk, there would be no reason for Ginnie Mae's to out-yield Treasuries.

High-yielding alternatives to mortgage securities are "few and far between," says vice president Leslie Finnemore of Colonial Management Associates, Boston.

In order to better serve investors, the cash flows from mortgage loans are packaged differently in collateralized mortgage obligations (CMOs). This is taken up next.

COLLATERALIZED MORTGAGE OBLIGATIONS (CMOs)

CMOs represent an innovative way to redistribute the cash flows from a pool of mortgages or mortgage-backed securities to various investor classes. Recall that investors in mortgage-backed securities get a pro rata share of the cash flows of the security, including prepayments. CMOs, through careful structuring, can offer varying levels of protection against prepayment.

CMOs were first issued in June 1983 when the FHLMC issued a $1 billion security. The CMO issuance is backed by pools of residential mortgages or mortgage-backed securities, such as GNMAs, which serve as the collateral. The collateral is guaranteed by the GNMA, the FNMA, or the FHLMC.

CMO Structure

CMOs tend to be rated AAA or Aaa by the rating agencies. The key to this high credit reputation is the basic requirement that the cash flows generated by the underlying mortgages or the agency securities are more than sufficient to meet the obligations of all tranches, even under the most extreme prepayment assumptions. Let us review some of the characteristics of general CMO structures.

- The credit risk is minimized by having a credible third party (such as a Federal agency or a AAA insurance company) guarantee the cash flows.
- The amount of collateral is set such that even under the most pessimistic prepayment assumptions, the total value of the bonds issued will be less than the value of the collateral. The typical worst-case assumption requires that all premium mortgages be immediately prepaid and all discount mortgages have zero prepayments.
- CMOs pay semiannual or quarterly payments, but the underlying collateral or mortgages make monthly payments. This means that there is some reinvestment of the cash flows from the underlying collateral. Typically, conservative assumptions about the reinvestment rates are made by the rating agencies. Sometimes, the rates that the issuer can get on guaranteed investment contracts (GICs) are used as indicators of possible reinvestment rates.
- The CMO must be heavily overcollateralized. The purpose of this overcollateralizing is to create an insurance cushion that helps to offset any cash flow shortages that may result due to a fall in reinvestment income from the underlying monthly cash flows.

The cash flows from the collateral are divided and allocated to several classes or tranches of bonds. Currently, there are two basic CMO structures: (1) sequential structure and (2) planned amortization class (PAC) structure.

TABLE 9-4

Generic Sequential CMO Structure

Tranche	Principal (in $ millions)	Coupon	Average Life (in years)	Yield
A	150	9.00%	2.50	2 yr T + 100
B	70	9.00%	6.00	5 yr T + 120
C	100	9.00%	10.00	10 yr T + 125
Z	30	9.00%	18.90	30 yr T + 175

Agency collateral: FNMA

Weighted-average coupon (net): 9.00%

Weighted-average coupon (gross): 9.70%

Pricing speed: 200% PSA

CMO Sequential Structure. A typical generic CMO sequential structure (see Table 9-4) has four tranches. Specific rules dictate how the cash flows (including prepayments) from the collateral are allocated to each tranche. The total cash payment to each tranche is also set ahead of time. The first tranche is allotted a stated coupon. In addition to this coupon, the first tranche will also be allotted any prepayments that are made. Until the first tranche is fully retired, no payments are made to the other tranches, except that the second and third tranches will receive the predetermined coupon amounts. The prepayments are passed through to the second tranche only after the first is fully retired. In this sense, each tranche successively receives prepayments as soon as its immediate predecessor is retired. The last (here the fourth) tranche is called the **Z bond** and receives no cash flows until all earlier tranches are fully retired. The face amount, however, accrues at the stated coupon. After all tranches have been retired, the Z bond receives the coupon on its current face amount plus all the prepayments. Trustees ensure that the remaining collateral is large enough at all times so that all tranches get their promised cash flows. Most of the CMOs are rated AAA by the usual rating agencies. To provide the AAA rating, these agencies require that the present value of zero-prepayment cash flows from the collateral at a discount rate equal to the maximum coupon of the bond determines the maximum amount of bonds that will be issued. The difference between the required bond payments and the cash flow received from the collateral is called the residual and is retained by the issuer of CMOs. Figure 9-9 illustrates a sequential CMO deal.

CMO Planned Amortization Class Structure. In a PAC CMO structure, the tranches are created to provide varying levels of protection from prepayment. In this structure, the collateral's principal is divided into two categories. The first category is designated PAC bonds, and the second category is the companion group.

- The amortization schedule for the PAC bonds remains fixed over a range of prepayment rates measured by a range of PSAs. The more stable amortization schedule of the PAC group is at the expense of the companion group.
- The structure, therefore, allows for many PAC bonds with stable average lives. The companion bonds, on the other hand, have much less stable lives than otherwise similar sequential bonds.

FIGURE 9-9   *Cash Flows to a Sequential CMO Structure*

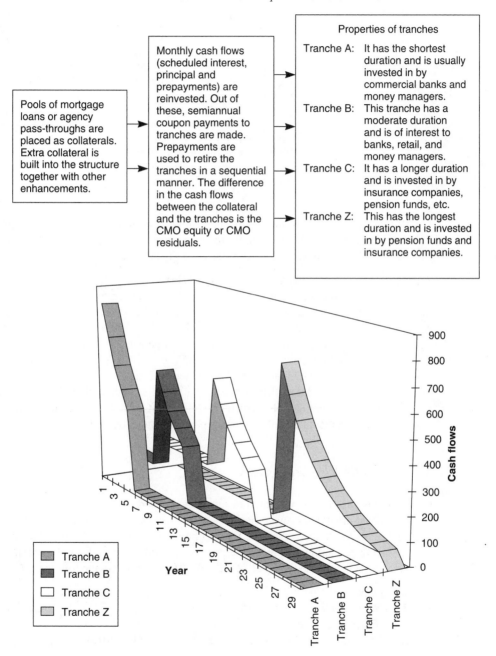

TABLE 9-5
PAC CMO Structure

Tranche	Principal (in $ millions)	Coupon	Average Life (in years)	Yield
PAC-A	60	9.00%	3.50	3 yr T + 70
PAC-B	90	9.00%	8.00	7 yr T + 90
PAC-C	10	9.00%	12.50	10 yr T + 90
PAC-D	30	9.00%	17.00	30 yr T + 100
COMP	100	9.00%	3.00	3 yr T + 250
Z	25	9.00%	18.25	30 yr T + 200

Agency collateral: FNMA
Weighted-average coupon (net): 9.00%
Weighted-average coupon (gross): 9.70%
Pricing speed: 200% PSA

- PAC bonds, because of their more stable amortization schedules, tend to be priced tightly to respective Treasuries. By the same token, bonds in the companion group are priced at much wider spreads relative to Treasuries.

A generic PAC CMO structure is provided in Table 9-5.

As seen in Table 9-5, CMOs can be set up for designing securities that may meet the special needs of different investor groups. A number of CMOs have been issued with tranches that pay coupons at levels tied to the London Interbank Offered Rates (LIBOR). These floating rate CMOs have been popular with commercial banks and foreign institutional investors.

Another type of CMO, known as the targeted amortization class (TAC) CMO, are very similar to PAC CMOs; they also enjoy a specified redemption schedule backed by support tranches in the CMO structure. Unlike PACs, TACs have a longer average maturity when interest rates fall and the prepayments are slower than expected.

VALUATION FRAMEWORK

The basic insight into the valuation of mortgage-backed securities is to recognize that default-free assumable mortgage-backed securities consist of an annuity and a call option that gives the homeowners the right to buy the annuity at a strike price equal to the remaining par amount at any time prior to maturity (from 15 to 30 years). Thus, the factors that determine the value of a fixed-rate mortgage are the following:

- Its coupon
- Time to maturity
- Amortization schedule
- Interest rates on comparable mortgages at the time of valuation

The models for valuing mortgage-backed securities, such as Dunn and McConnell (1981) apply the principles of options pricing. More recent models, notably Buser,

FIGURE 9-10   *Value of Mortgage-Backed Securities, Effect of Interest Rate*

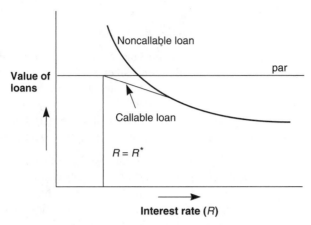

Hendershott, and Sanders (1990), have extended the basic insights, but the principles of valuation have remained the same. Such valuation models assume the following:

1. The expected instantaneous holding-period return on any mortgage is equal to the instantaneous riskless rate plus an instantaneous risk premium. Mathematically, the expected return on the mortgage-backed security $E_t\left[\frac{dV(c, R_t, t)}{V(c, R_t, t)}\right]$ is equal to the risk-less rate R_t plus the risk premium π_t. This leads to

$$E_t\left[\frac{dV(c, R_t, t)}{V(c, R_t, t)}\right] = R_t + \pi_t.$$

    The rate on the mortgage is denoted by c.

2. Mortgage-backed securities are assumed to obey certain boundary conditions. For example, the value of the mortgage-backed security must satisfy two conditions:
    *   As the mortgage-backed security approaches its maturity date T, its value will go to zero

$$V(c, R_T, T) = 0. \tag{9.6}$$

    *   As the interest rates approach ∞, the value of the mortgage-backed security approaches zero

$$\lim_{R_t \to \infty} V(c, R_t, t) = 0. \tag{9.7}$$

    The intuition here is that the mortgage loans are worthless at very high interest rates. Absent the call feature, it is clear that the value of the mortgage-backed security is convex to the origin, as shown in Figure 9-10.

3. The fact that mortgage-backed securities are sold on mortgages that can be prepaid means that we need to impose a condition on the optimal exercise of this prepayment option. We know that the homeowners will tend to prepay the loans

when interest rates decrease to a critical low level R^*. We can capture this condition as

$$\lim_{R_t \downarrow R^*} V(c, R_t, t) = \text{par}. \tag{9.8}$$

The existence of the prepayment feature means that the value of the mortgage-backed securities behave differently at low interest rates. This behavior is sometimes referred to as **compression to par or negative convexity.** When interest rates are close to the coupon of the mortgage-backed security and the volatility of the rates increases, the probability that the call will be exercised increases as well. This may produce a reduction in the price of the mortgage-backed securities.

In the valuation of mortgage-backed securities, we have thus far treated interest rates as the only variable affecting the value of the security and assumed that the mortgage-backed security is default-free. In reality, the fact that some homeowners might default affects the pricing of mortgage-backed securities. If the mortgage-backed security is fully insured and assumable (such as GNMAs), then upon default the guarantor will pay off the mortgage. Thus, the cash flows to mortgage-backed securities are affected by default. For example, defaults that occur during periods of very high interest rates tend to produce a gain for the security holders. When rates are high, the mortgage-backed securities sell below par, but default produces a cash flow equal to par, leading to a windfall gain.

It is also useful to recognize the incentives to voluntary default that the homeowner might have. If the value of the house is relatively high as compared to the value of the mortgage, then the homeowner may not wish to default. If the value of the house is well below the value of the mortgage, the incentive to default is high. This may be thought of as a put option or a walk-away option. The effect of this walk-away option is illustrated in Figure 9-11. Note that when the price of the house drops to a critical value H^*, it is optimal for the homeowner to default on the mortgage.

More recent models of valuing mortgage-backed securities incorporate the house price as a second factor influencing the value. In such models, the value of the mortgage-backed security will be written as a function of both interest rates and house prices, as $V(c, R_t, H_t, t)$.

As $H_t \rightarrow \infty$, the value of the loan approaches that of the default-free loan. It is useful to examine some of the real-life features of mortgages in the context of this formulation. In a recent work, Wang (1995) analyzes mortgage-backed securities in a two-factor setting. The framework used by Wang (1995) for both the one- and two-factor models is presented in Figure 9-12. Note that when the house prices are low, even though the interest rates may be low, there is less of an incentive to prepay the mortgage; the mortgage value may exceed the house value by such a significant amount that the homeowner finds it suboptimal to exercise the option. This suggests that in periods of falling housing prices, the level of prepayments ought to go down. Our argument suggests that housing prices affect the valuation in two distinct ways:

1. At low housing prices, there is a greater incentive to default.
2. At low housing prices, the incentive to refinance also goes down.

FIGURE 9-11   *Value of Mortgage-Backed Securities, House Price, and Default*

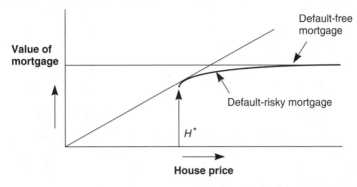

FIGURE 9-12   *Two Models for Valuing Mortgage-Backed Securities*

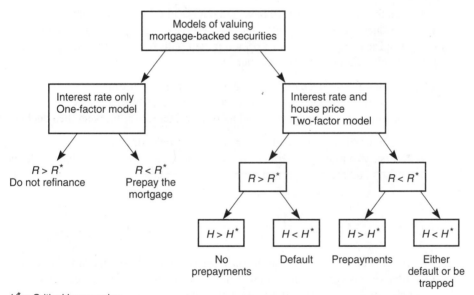

H^* = Critical house price

In addition, housing prices enable us to model situations where depressed house prices, while not inducing immediate default, diminish the incentives to refinance.

Transactions costs in a given pool is yet another feature that we need to incorporate in the valuation framework. Homeowners spend time and resources in their refinancing decisions. Title fees, appraisal fees, and so on, constitute direct costs. There are significant indirect costs as well, which include the time spent in the choice of the mortgage loan and its analysis. It is possible that such transactions costs are dependent on the household and its circumstances. Thus, if the pool has a diverse set of homeowners and their transactions costs are distinct, then the prepayments from such a pool may not be easy to estimate. Note also that transactions costs are incurred by the households but are not received by the investors of mortgage-backed securities. If x_t is the transactions cost faced by the homeowner at date t, then the valuation function should exhibit the following property:

$$V(c, R_t, H_t, t) = \text{par} \qquad \text{if} \qquad V(c, R_{t+}, H_{t+}, t+) \geq \text{par} + x_t$$

$$V(c, R_t, H_t, t) = V(c, R_{t+}, H_{t+}, t+) \qquad \text{if} \qquad V(c, R_{t+}, H_{t+}, t+) < \text{par} + x_t$$

Essentially, these conditions state that the homeowner should refinance if the value (taking into account the transactions costs) associated with that strategy exceeds the value associated with not refinancing. (At each time t, the value of the mortgage is compared with the value associated with prepayments. At an instant after t, which is denoted by $t+$, we examine whether the value of the mortgage is higher than the value associated with prepayments net of transactions costs. We choose the optimal strategy.)

Although the conditions that we have laid out are intuitive, they do not necessarily account for values and prepayments that one observes in real life. For example, the following empirical regularities have been reported with respect to mortgage prepayments but are not accounted for in our framework:

- Prepayment rates for deep discount securities increase over time.
- Prepayment rates for aged premium securities decline over time.
- Prepayment rates on newly originated mortgages increase at first and then decline.

Furthermore, prepayments, as noted earlier, depend on many factors.

It is necessary to modify the framework to obtain a model of valuation that admits these regularities and the richness that prepayments exhibit.

A VALUATION MODEL

The framework we have provided in the previous section may be specialized to calculate quantitative answers for the valuation of various mortgage-backed securities. First, a choice must be made between a single-factor or a two-factor model. Second, an empirical model of prepayments must be chosen. In addition, several specific modeling choices must be made even within this setting; for example, a specific process must be chosen for the interest-rate process.

The procedure used to value most mortgage-backed securities comprises the following steps:

1. An interest-rate process is specified.
2. An empirical model of prepayments is specified and estimated to determine the level of prepayments as a function of three or more factors, including the interest rate as a factor.

3. Monte Carlo simulation procedures are then used to simulate interest-rate paths from the interest-rate process chosen in step (1).
4. Each path is subdivided into 360 monthly intervals for a pool consisting of 30-year mortgages.
5. For each month along each path, three cash flows are identified:
    (a) scheduled interest payments,
    (b) scheduled principal payments, and
    (c) prepayments, which are fed from the empirical model of prepayments.
6. The total cash flows along a given path are discounted back using the appropriate zero-coupon rates that are applicable to that path.
7. This process is repeated for a number of paths (usually thousands of paths), and for each path, the price (sum of discounted cash flows) is determined.
8. The average of all the prices is computed; suitable variance-reduction procedures are then applied. (See Part III for a discussion of variance-reduction procedures.)

We now can compute the cash flows at each node. These cash flows include scheduled interest payments, scheduled principal payments, and prepayments. This allows us to generate monthly cash flows in each simulated path. We then discount the cash flows at the zero-coupon interest rates $z_t(i)$ that is relevant for each month t along path i as shown next.

Given the one-period (monthly) rates, the relevant zero rates are easily computed. The zero rate for n periods in path i is denoted by $z_n(i)$ and is equal to

$$z_n(i) = \sqrt[n]{[1 + r_1(i)][1 + r_2(i)] \cdots [1 + r_n(i)]},$$

where $r_j(i)$ is the one-period rate at month j in path i.

$$P_{\text{model}} = \frac{1}{N} \sum_{i=1}^{N} \left[\frac{C_1(i)}{1 + z_1(i)} + \frac{C_2(i)}{\{1 + z_2(i)\}^2} + \cdots + \frac{C_N(i)}{\{1 + z_N(i)\}^N} \right],$$

where for any month j, $C_j(i)$ is the cash flow in month j associated with path i. We have 360 monthly cash flows for each path i. When a prepayment occurs retiring the pool in month $i = 300$, the cash flows for subsequent months $C_j(i)$, where $j > 300$, will be equal to zero.

We then discount these cash flows at the relevant zero rate $z_j(i)$. We do this for each path i for a total of N paths and average the discounted values.

We vary z until the model value P_{model} is equal to the market value V of the security. We compute the difference

$$\pi_t = P_{\text{model}} - V.$$

If $\pi_t > 0$, the model price is higher than the market value. This indicates that the security is cheap, according to the model. In order to make the model produce a value equal to V, we need to increase the discount factor. So, we select a $z > 0$ such that the model produces a price equal to the market value. This factor z is referred to as the option-adjusted spread (OAS). A positive OAS indicates that the security is cheap. Conversely, if the OAS is negative, then the security is rich.

$$V = P_{\text{model}} = \frac{1}{N} \sum_{i=1}^{N} \left[\frac{C_1(i)}{1 + z_1(i) + z} + \frac{C_2(i)}{\{1 + z_2(i) + z\}^2} + \cdots + \frac{C_N(i)}{\{1 + z_N(i) + z\}^N} \right],$$

The OAS is used extensively in the industry for determining the relative values of mortgage-backed securities.

MORTGAGE DERIVATIVES

A number of mortgage derivatives are currently offered to institutional investors. We will review some of these derivatives.

Strips

Mortgage strips are obtained by dividing the cash flows from an underlying pool of mortgages or mortgage-backed securities through specified allocation of interest and principal to each strip. For example, we can take a 9% GNMA and create a 5% strip and a 12% strip by allocating more of the underlying collateral to the high-coupon strip. An important feature of such strips is that the rate of prepayments is qualitatively influenced by the weighted-average coupon of the underlying pool. For example, a strip with a coupon of 5% will have a much lower prepayment when the underlying pool has a coupon of 9% than when the underlying pool has a coupon of 12%.

The most basic strips in the mortgage market are the interest-only (IO) strip and the principal-only (PO) strip.

Interest-Only (IO) Strip. IO strips receive all of the interest payments from the underlying collateral and none from the principal. The price movements of IOs are highly sensitive to interest-rate changes. As interest rates drop, prepayments increase as an increasing number of the households begin to buy new homes or refinance existing loans. Since prepayments are allocated to principal, IOs tend to lose their value in periods of falling interest rates. This is in sharp contrast to many fixed-income securities, which tend to appreciate in value as interest rates fall. Conversely, when interest rates increase, prepayments decrease, and the IOs increase in value.

Principal-Only (PO) Strip. PO strips receive all of the principal payments from the underlying collateral and none from the interest. The price movements of POs are also highly sensitive to interest-rate changes. As interest rates drop, prepayments increase as an increasing number of the households begin to buy new homes or refinance existing loans. Since prepayments are allocated to principal, POs tend to increase in value in periods of failing interest rates. When interest rates increase, prepayments decrease, and the POs decrease in value.

REMICs

REMICs are real estate mortgage investment conduits, introduced in the Tax Reform Act of 1986. Prior to the Tax Reform Act, CMOs were issued as debt obligations of the issuer; thus, such issues appeared in a balance sheet as a liability. REMICs, on the other hand, are a legal framework within which mortgage-backed securities are treated as asset sales for tax purposes. REMICs can be structured in a senior-subordinated format. This allows for credit enhancements for mortgage-backed securities with multiple tranches.

CMO Residuals or Equity

As noted earlier, CMO residuals or CMO equity refers to the excess cash flows from the underlying mortgage or collaterals. The excess cash flows are computed over the total cash flows that are paid out to the CMO tranches and the operating expenses. We noted earlier how conservative collateral and reinvestment assumptions are made in structuring CMOs. This means that the actual reinvestment rates and prepayment rates are likely to be more favorable, on average. While CMO residuals are volatile and illiquid, they tend to provide rather unique cash flow properties. CMO equity from a fixed-rate CMO tends to increase when interest rates increase and decrease when interest rates fall.

CONCLUSION

The concept of securitization was further developed in this chapter. We then presented a brief description of mortgage contracts. Both fixed-rate and adjustable-rate mortgage contracts were considered. In mortgage contracts, one of the important features is the ability to prepay. Among the most important factors that influence prepayments are the refinancing rates, age of the mortgage, seasonality, and housing prices. We also discussed measures of prepayments, such as PSAs and CPRs. The concept of mortgage-backed securities, such as GNMAs and CMOs, was then introduced. A valuation framework was presented, which we developed into a simple model of valuing mortgage-backed securities. The concept of option-adjusted spreads (OAS) was developed to identify relatively rich and cheap securities. Mortgage derivatives, such as strips, IOs, and POs, were then described.

PROBLEMS

9.1 Define securitization. Then explain the role of the following in securitization:
   (a) Special purpose vehicle
   (b) Credit enhancement
   (c) Bankruptcy remoteness

9.2   Define negative convexity. How does this feature affect the spread between mortgage-backed securities and Treasuries in periods of falling interest rates?

9.3   Define CMO.

9.4   **(a)** What factors influence prepayments in mortgage-backed securities markets? How do they affect the pricing of mortgage-backed securities, such as GNMAs?

(b) Compare the prepayment risk of a GNMA with that of a Z tranche in a CMO. Which investors will prefer the Z tranche? Which investors will prefer the GNMA? Why?

9.5   Explain the link between mortgage credit and the capital markets. How has the process of securitization affected the availability of credit and liquidity in the mortgage market?

9.6   In a recent CMO deal, an investment bank issued a CMO with four tranches of bonds: bond A, bond B, bond C, and the Z bond. This deal was rated AAA by the rating agencies. The issuer also kept the CMO residual (or the extra collateral).

(a) Explain briefly the risk properties of the Z bond and the CMO residual.

(b) If you are an investor who wishes to buy a security whose performance will be superior in a high interest rate setting, which of these securities will you buy? Why?

(c) If you had the choice of investing in a Z bond or in a AAA strip with the same maturity as the Z bond, under what circumstances will you prefer the Z bond? Why?

9.7   In the financial press, you note that the GNMA yields are about 200 basis points higher than Treasuries with comparable maturities.

(a) On this basis, can we conclude that GNMAs are better investments than Treasuries? Explain your conclusion.

(b) As the interest rates drop, will you expect the yields of GNMA to pick up or drop? Why? Explain your conclusions for premium and discount sectors of GNMA.

9.8   **(a)** Explain the major differences between PAC, TAC, and sequential CMO structures.

(b) In this context, explain the role of the following terms: (i) companion class, (ii) support class.

9.9   Explain the considerations that lead to a AAA-rating for CMO structures.

REFERENCES

Buser, S. A., P. H. Hendershott, and A. B. Sanders 1990. "Determinants of the Value of Call Options on Default-free Bonds." *Journal of Business* 63(1):533–550.

Dunn, K., and J. McConnell 1981. "Valuation of GNMA Mortgage-Backed Securities." *Journal of Finance* 36(3):599–616.

Waldman, M., A. Schwalb, and A. K. Feignberg 1993. "Prepayments of Fifteen-Year Mortgages." *Journal of Fixed Income* 2(4):37–44.

Wang, W. 1995. Analysis of Mortgage-backed Securities. Unpublished Ph.D. Dissertation, Columbia University

Chapter 10

Tax-Exempt Debt Markets

Chapter Objectives

This chapter describes the municipal debt market and municipal debt securities. The goal of the chapter is to provide an overview of this important market. In addition, the following questions are addressed in this chapter:

- What have been the historical spreads between municipal securities, Treasuries, and corporate securities?
- What has been the impact of Tax Reform Acts?
- To what degree are municipal securities tax-advantaged?
- What are general obligation bonds?
- What are revenue bonds?
- What are prefunded issues?
- What is yield burning?
- How does insurance affect municipal debt securities?

INTRODUCTION

States, municipalities, and counties raise the capital that they need by issuing debt securities, which are referred to as municipal debt securities. Such securities tend to have a special tax status. The interest income from municipal debt securities are exempt from federal, state, and, where applicable, city taxes; the capital gains or losses may still be subject to the normal taxation rules that are applicable. This chapter is devoted to the study of municipal debt securities. We begin by describing some of the major municipal debt securities. This is followed by a discussion of the investor base in the municipal securities market. The investor base in this market has changed significantly in the last 20 years. The shapes of the municipal yield curve and the Treasury curve are then discussed. We present evidence that the Tax Reform Act of 1986 and, to a lesser extent, the Tax Act of 1990 account for both the shifts in the investor base and for the change in the slope of the municipal yield curve relative to the Treasury yield curve. Then, the primary and the secondary municipal debt markets are presented. We also describe the practice of advanced refunding and municipal bond insurance.

MUNICIPAL DEBT SECURITIES

There are several major categories of municipal securities.

General Obligation Bond (GO)

A general obligation bond is a security that is backed by the full faith, credit, and taxation powers of the issuer. For example, New York State GO bonds are backed by the various taxes that the state levies. These taxes include income taxes, sales taxes, and excise taxes. Counties and cities tend to rely on property taxes for their GO bonds. Depending on the legal limits on the tax rates that the issuing entity is subjected to, the issue may be either an unlimited tax bond or a limited tax bond. Clearly, unlimited tax issues are made by issuers who may levy taxes at an unlimited rate.

The tax base of the issuing entity and its discretion are important factors in determining the pricing of GO bonds. For example, school districts tend to have a limit on the tax rates that they may charge. The tax base of the issuing city, growth rate of the local economy, and property values are important factors. In addition, the existing level of municipal debt is also a very important consideration in the valuation of GO bonds. Per-capita debt is one of the indicators used to judge the financial soundness of GO bonds.

Revenue Bond

Revenue bonds are issued to fund specific projects; or they are bonds that are protected by the pledge of net revenues from specified projects. The bond issuer will use the revenues generated by the project to service the revenue bond issues. Typical projects funded by revenue bonds are bridges, turnpikes, and airports. Revenue sources from such projects will include tolls and user fees.

Revenue bonds are issued for specific sectoral activities, some of which are listed next.

- *Housing revenue bonds.* These bonds are issued to promote the construction of housing for low- and moderate-income families. The proceeds of the bond issue are typically lent to real estate developers.
- *Utility revenue bonds.* These bonds are issued to support the local utilities, such as gas, water, and electric power systems.
- *Health-care revenue bonds.* These bonds are used to raise money for the construction of hospital and health-care facilities.
- *Double-barreled bonds.* These bonds are backed by two distinct sources of revenues. Part of the cash flows of the debt service come from specified projects and the rest from taxation.

In the valuation of revenue bonds, it is important to examine the net revenue of the project. The operating and maintenance expenses are deducted from the revenues before the money is used to service the revenue bonds. The ratio of the net revenue to the debt-service payments, known as the debt-service coverage, is one of the factors often used to judge the financial soundness of revenue bonds. Often, restrictive covenants are specified to ensure effective debt service.

Municipal Notes

Short-term obligations of municipalities are known as municipal notes. They are interest-bearing securities. The following are some categories of municipal notes:

- **Tax anticipation notes (TAN).** TANs are issued in anticipation of future tax receipts from real estate taxes. Typically, the proceeds are used to finance the operations of the municipality.
- **Bond anticipation notes (BAN).** BANs are issued in anticipation of future sale of long-term bonds. The proceeds are used to finance projects.
- **Grant anticipation notes (GAN).** GANs are issued in anticipation of future federal grants.
- **Revenue anticipation notes (RAN).** RANs are issued in anticipation of future revenues.
- **Construction loan notes (CLN).** CLNs are issued for a specific construction project.

In addition to these municipal notes, there are also tax-exempt commercial paper and variable-rate demand notes. Typically, commercial paper has a maturity of 270 days or less. As in the case of corporate commercial paper, CPs are backed by a line of credit from a bank. Municipal markets also have variable-rate notes and zero-coupon bonds. In addition, municipal bonds are also refunded. Typically, refunding occurs to circumvent restrictive bond covenants or to take advantage of low interest rates. For example, revenue bonds (as we noted earlier) that have restrictive covenants may be refunded by issuing new bonds and using the proceeds to buy Treasury securities to create an escrow fund. Many municipal bonds are issued in a serial form. In such serial issues, level payments are achieved with orderly amortization of principal.

TAX REFORM ACT OF 1986

The interest income from municipal securities are exempt from federal and state taxes. For residents of the municipality, there is also exemption at the local level. With the Tax Reform Act of 1986, significant restrictions have been placed on the tax advantages of several municipal securities. The pricing of municipal securities tends to depend a great deal on their current and expected tax status. The Tax Reform Act of 1986 significantly reduced the tax benefits enjoyed by holders of certain municipal securities. Municipal securities issued for traditional governmental purposes, such as highways and utilities, still enjoy the special tax status. Other municipal issues are now called private-activity bonds, and under the Tax Reform Act, these do not qualify for special tax status unless they are defined as qualified private-activity bonds. Private-activity bonds are those in which 10% or more of the proceeds are used by private entities, and 10% or more of the proceeds are secured by the property used in the private entity's activity. For example, a sports facility could fall into this category. A qualified private-activity bond is one which is issued for prespecified purposes, such as airports or student loans.

The Tax Reform Act lead to a reduction in the maximum personal tax rate from 50% to 28%. However, it also subjected municipal bonds to increased taxes. If a municipal bond issue is not qualified, then it will be subject to alternative minimum tax (AMT). These developments reduced the attractiveness of municipal securities. In 1990, the maximum personal tax rate increased to 33%. This increased the value of municipal securities to high-income individuals.

AN OVERVIEW OF MUNICIPAL DEBT MARKET

In Tables 10-1 and 10-2, we summarize the activities in the municipal debt market from 1991 to 1999. Table 10-1 shows the activity in the municipal bond market, and Table 10-2 provides the corresponding information for the municipal notes market. In this 10-year period, the total dollar amount issued increased from $172 million in 1991 to about $226 million in 1999. The total number of issues increased from 10,932 in 1991 to over 13,000 issues in 1999. In general, the dollar amount of issues of revenue bonds exceeds the dollar amount of issues of general obligation bonds. Fixed-rate bonds far exceeds variable-rate bonds. In Table 10-2, note that the issues of municipal notes, which amounted to 44.8 million in 1991, is just 25% of the municipal bond market. Interestingly, however, the revenue issues were less than general obligations issues in the notes market. Almost all the issues of the municipal notes market represented new money in the municipal notes market. On the other hand, in the municipal bond market, nearly 25% of the issues constituted refunding.

Note from Table 10-1 that negotiated underwriting is used much more than competitive bids in selling and distributing municipal bonds. The use of negotiated method is three times more than competitive bids in the bond market. These methods are equally important in the municipal notes distribution. Bond insurance, letters of credit, and other credit enhancements are widely used in both the bonds and notes markets.

Investors in the Tax-Exempt Market

The tax status of the municipal securities attracts a certain clientele. Individuals with very high tax brackets tend to gravitate to municipal securities when alternative tax shelters are scarce. In a similar way, institutions that pay taxes at rates that are close to their maximum levels will find municipal securities attractive. Commercial banks and fire and casualty insurance companies fall into this category. By the same token, some institutions tend to stay away from the municipal securities market. For example, tax-exempt institutions (that do not pay taxes) have little incentive to hold municipal securities. Pension funds whose earnings are tax-exempt will invest in corporate and Treasury debt securities as opposed to municipal securities.

TABLE 10-1   *A Decade of Municipal Bond Finance*

	1991	1992	1993	1994	1995	1996	1997	1998	1999
Total	$172,443,700	$234,667,200	$292,248,800	$165,033,600	$159,982,500	$185,039,900	$220,640,600	$286,182,900	$226,625,000
Number of Issues	10,932	12,959	14,386	11,239	10,725	12,157	12,644	15,402	13,154
Development	6,215,600	7,983,700	8,845,000	6,850,100	7,588,800	5,829,100	7,817,600	8,380,800	8,801,800
Education	27,359,000	39,806,200	47,817,800	29,766,200	32,769,500	38,771,800	46,087,300	61,662,000	52,692,500
Electric Power	8,947,700	15,719,200	27,787,400	6,406,500	4,938,600	5,937,400	6,467,900	15,618,100	5,171,200
Environmental	7,032,000	9,332,500	13,089,900	10,953,000	8,226,100	7,629,700	9,380,700	12,525,000	10,073,000
Facilities									
Health Care	18,265,000	23,543,800	32,031,700	16,462,100	13,607,700	19,985,500	26,095,900	39,295,900	27,731,300
Housing	14,972,000	14,969,400	14,731,600	15,893,400	16,554,100	17,373,600	19,625,000	20,676,600	20,792,600
Public Facilities	9,241,300	9,281,900	16,828,400	8,496,500	6,735,600	10,122,300	11,006,800	12,834,200	10,673,800
Transportation	16,599,000	26,624,500	28,574,800	14,843,000	16,908,700	16,840,900	24,542,100	31,852,800	23,355,300
Utilities	19,414,300	28,311,600	36,641,200	13,929,400	14,309,300	15,912,500	19,930,600	23,585,500	17,813,700
General Purpose	44,397,800	59,094,400	65,901,000	41,433,400	38,344,100	46,637,100	49,687,000	59,752,000	49,519,800
Tax Exempt	154,456,400	213,341,900	269,672,900	139,415,200	130,634,300	154,514,700	182,532,600	245,571,100	188,013,700
Minimum Tax	13,401,800	15,682,600	13,383,400	16,868,000	18,542,400	20,699,600	24,036,700	24,658,200	23,373,000
Taxable	4,585,500	5,642,700	9,192,500	8,750,400	10,805,800	9,825,600	14,071,300	15,953,600	15,238,300
New Money	117,740,800	111,430,100	96,745,100	114,591,100	111,710,600	123,869,900	137,758,100	160,182,400	158,910,100
Refunding	41,443,900	92,445,700	150,152,000	38,600,900	33,849,600	45,944,000	60,153,300	81,956,700	37,800,400
Combined	13,259,000	30,791,400	45,351,700	11,841,600	14,422,300	15,226,000	22,729,200	44,043,800	29,914,500
Negotiated	129,138,500	187,307,500	234,004,200	112,761,100	115,380,900	134,446,500	166,359,300	214,624,200	166,533,200
Competitive	40,222,700	44,365,400	55,627,900	49,468,300	40,810,500	46,966,900	47,828,700	65,410,200	52,796,800
Private Placements	3,082,500	2,994,300	2,616,700	2,804,200	3,791,100	3,626,500	6,452,600	6,148,500	7,295,000
Revenue	115,333,500	154,188,300	200,694,000	109,266,900	99,615,400	120,684,900	148,340,000	192,651,700	156,417,600
General Obligation	57,110,200	80,478,900	91,554,800	55,766,700	60,367,100	64,355,000	72,300,600	93,531,200	70,207,400

(continued)

TABLE 10-1   Continued

	1991	1992	1993	1994	1995	1996	1997	1998	1999
Fixed Rate	150,810,800	209,414,500	262,337,400	140,761,600	133,926,800	158,562,400	182,617,800	249,060,600	186,555,700
Variable Rate (Short Put)	13,453,700	16,029,400	18,532,400	17,228,800	20,904,000	20,287,600	28,495,800	27,121,700	26,775,600
Variable Rate (Long/No Put)	1,202,700	1,470,300	1,572,300	1,154,300	767,500	1,278,700	1,728,100	1,937,700	2,736,500
Zero Coupon	4,226,800	4,096,600	3,480,500	2,181,800	2,241,700	2,122,700	5,026,600	3,970,300	4,711,500
Linked Rate	2,727,600	3,616,100	6,129,000	3,641,200	1,981,900	2,758,900	2,671,100	4,090,300	5,456,100
Convertible	22,100	40,300	197,200	65,900	160,600	29,600	101,200	2,300	389,600
Bank Qualified	12,451,000	14,524,100	18,155,800	13,638,300	12,857,600	15,271,000	17,459,000	24,049,100	17,472,900
Bond Insurance	51,890,900	80,762,100	107,889,500	61,512,000	68,523,700	85,715,600	107,495,700	145,066,800	104,630,300
Letters of Credit	10,243,700	8,202,100	11,034,400	12,238,900	11,371,200	12,117,500	14,723,100	11,863,100	12,112,300
Insured Mortgages	4,950,500	5,645,100	3,900,500	4,739,400	4,040,500	3,380,700	6,425,000	7,659,100	5,675,300
Surety Bonds	97,300	65,400	124,700	82,400	33,500	160,000	0	0	0
Guaranteed Investment Contracts	0	10,100	223,200	0	0	0	0	0	0
Investment Agreements	313,000	99,700	507,700	247,500	0	0	4,000	20,000	562,900
Private Mortgage Insurance	0	18,600	92,100	6,100	0	0	0	0	0
Certificates of Deposit	0	0	0	10,900	0	0	0	0	0
Collateralization	0	0	0	0	0	0	131,800	28,200	32,800
Other Guaranties	0	17,400	78,400	600	0	0	39,500	0	45,700
State Governments	19,266,400	25,157,500	27,996,500	19,861,800	14,677,000	14,346,500	18,688,600	24,944,200	17,672,100
State Authorities	49,848,400	65,718,200	86,414,100	48,425,600	48,297,900	54,282,400	68,237,800	86,406,000	70,521,500
Municipalities	70,190,200	97,365,700	114,743,000	66,187,800	64,214,100	75,512,400	85,496,800	111,297,800	85,835,100
Local Authorities	28,981,800	41,892,700	57,500,400	27,443,600	29,407,200	35,211,100	43,560,500	56,288,500	46,245,000
Public Colleges	3,584,100	3,847,200	4,751,500	2,483,700	2,560,300	4,533,000	3,274,200	4,649,700	4,083,000
Tribal Governments	0	4,900	3,800	0	357,000	101,500	541,700	235,000	119,300
Direct Issuers	572,800	681,000	839,500	631,100	469,000	1,053,000	841,000	2,361,700	2,149,000

Source: Bond Buyer.

TABLE 10-2   *A Decade of Municipal Note Finance*

	1991	1992	1993	1994	1995	1996	1997	1998	1999
Total	$44,800,300	$42,893,900	$47,353,500	$40,293,300	$38,346,300	$41,695,300	$46,271,100	$34,777,800	$37,062,300
Number of Issues	3,725	3,460	3,745	3,710	4,116	4,003	3,932	3,586	3,737
Development	71,000	110,000	144,700	107,700	37,100	372,100	303,600	43,000	125,700
Education	6,932,500	6,315,200	7,554,900	8,442,400	8,897,500	9,236,000	8,695,900	9,263,200	10,304,400
Electric Power	211,100	98,200	412,600	573,300	228,100	307,800	2,028,400	1,554,800	1,928,300
Environmental Facilities	245,200	119,200	348,100	101,400	108,700	77,300	975,300	64,600	109,200
Health Care	99,900	35,300	93,600	97,500	5,300	173,500	275,500	368,600	213,100
Housing	563,200	314,400	698,900	404,000	188,300	555,600	668,000	1,329,600	2,305,700
Public Facilities	284,500	190,500	291,100	192,000	159,400	337,600	278,700	290,800	372,500
Transportation	1,472,300	987,400	1,421,100	1,084,400	1,702,400	1,188,400	1,897,600	1,762,000	1,277,700
Utilities	1,120,900	538,500	1,848,900	1,327,800	2,579,200	1,416,100	2,135,600	1,025,700	905,400
General Purpose	33,799,700	34,185,200	34,539,600	27,962,800	24,440,300	28,030,900	29,012,500	19,075,500	19,520,300
Exempt	43,603,500	41,887,200	43,288,100	37,812,300	37,269,300	40,753,200	44,448,900	32,244,700	34,647,400
Minimum Tax	325,600	504,700	341,700	267,300	97,900	347,800	443,700	907,900	1,488,600
Taxable	871,200	502,000	3,723,700	2,213,700	979,100	594,300	1,378,500	1,625,200	926,300
Money	44,606,000	42,755,700	47,239,800	40,048,400	38,264,300	41,572,300	45,393,700	33,524,600	37,025,400
Refunding	145,400	135,600	113,700	82,400	82,000	122,900	855,900	579,700	36,900
Combined	48,900	2,600	0	162,500	0	100	21,500	673,500	0
Negotiated	27,344,600	26,849,700	26,283,200	17,356,800	18,853,700	21,688,100	22,382,900	19,023,600	17,625,300
Competitive	16,644,600	15,846,700	20,709,300	22,584,300	19,044,800	19,497,000	22,792,200	14,796,000	18,268,400
Private Placements	811,100	197,500	361,000	352,200	447,800	510,200	1,096,000	958,200	1,168,600
Revenue	3,938,700	2,969,000	10,261,500	8,145,700	7,103,500	9,059,800	12,130,200	8,366,800	9,267,600
General Obligation	40,861,600	39,924,900	37,092,000	32,147,600	31,242,800	32,635,500	34,140,900	26,411,000	27,794,700

(continued)

TABLE 10-2   Continued

	1991	1992	1993	1994	1995	1996	1997	1998	1999
Fixed Rate	41,615,300	38,723,500	41,270,900	35,784,900	30,080,600	35,507,700	35,784,200	28,949,300	32,353,500
Variable Rate (Short Put)	3,018,800	4,090,100	6,082,600	3,773,400	8,215,600	6,119,500	10,280,000	5,371,000	4,608,700
Variable Rate (Long/No Put)	166,200	80,300	0	35,000	100	66,600	71,000	457,500	100,100
Zero Coupon	0	0	0	0	0	1,500	0	0	0
Linked Rate	0	0	0	700,000	50,000	0	135,900	0	0
Convertible	0	0	0	0	0	0	0	0	0
Bank Qualified	3,183,400	2,713,400	3,068,700	3,586,500	3,090,000	5,040,300	5,978,800	5,099,600	5,230,000
Bond Insurance	110,100	12,300	11,700	344,400	377,700	444,200	1,874,500	728,200	1,059,100
Letters of Credit	3,240,200	2,854,800	4,896,700	2,501,900	5,601,800	4,543,800	5,804,700	3,862,100	2,305,500
Insured Mortgages	0	200	400	100	5,900	100	100	160,300	332,100
Surety Bonds	0	0	0	0	0	0	0	0	0
Guaranteed Investment Contracts	0	0	61,000	0	0	0	0	0	10,400
Investment Agreements	0	0	0	0	0	0	0	25,200	50,000
Private Mortgage Insurance	0	0	0	0	0	0	0	0	0
Certificates of Deposit	0	0	0	0	0	0	0	0	0
Collateralization	0	0	0	0	0	0	0	0	0
Other Guaranties	0	0	0	0	0	0	0	0	0
State Governments	18,525,100	20,975,300	16,287,500	12,061,300	7,174,600	15,344,600	13,804,900	6,992,000	7,029,900
State Authorities	3,409,800	2,548,400	5,029,600	4,189,200	5,675,500	4,566,600	7,283,300	7,213,400	6,938,700
Municipalities	20,752,300	18,308,800	23,509,700	21,392,000	22,290,000	18,742,200	21,405,600	18,685,200	19,825,700
Local Authorities	1,552,300	675,900	1,780,000	2,106,900	2,350,700	1,828,000	3,050,100	1,242,600	2,666,300
Public Colleges	560,800	251,000	590,400	443,900	855,000	988,600	602,200	442,100	555,500
Tribal Governments	0	0	0	0	0	0	0	0	0
Direct Issuers	0	134,500	156,300	100,000	500	0	125,000	202,500	46,200

Source: Bond Buyer.

The incentives to hold municipal debt securities have changed over time for some institutions. Prior to the Tax Reform Act of 1986, commercial banks were permitted to deduct interest expenses associated with the purchase of municipal securities, and the interest income from municipal securities were tax-exempt as well. This double advantage was removed after the Tax Reform Act of 1986. In 1983, Congress disallowed the commercial banks from deducting 15% of the municipal carrying costs associated with the purchases of municipal securities. In 1985, the lost deduction increased to 20%. The 1986 tax reform created two classes of municipal securities, bank-qualified municipals and nonqualified municipals. For nonqualified municipal securities, banks are not allowed to deduct interest expenses associated with the purchase. For an issue to be bank-qualified, no more than $10 million may be issued per year, and the proceeds must be used for an essential public purpose. In the case of bank-qualified issues, banks can deduct 80% of the interest paid to the depositors from taxes, provided such funds are used to invest in bank-qualified issues.

To get a better idea of the nature of investors in this market and how it has changed over time, review Table 10-3.

Several noteworthy patterns may be seen in Table 10-3. Commercial banks tended to be net sellers of municipal bonds during the 1980 to 1990 period. Their share fell from 37.30% in 1980 to about 7.20% in 1999. Mutual funds and money market funds increased their combined share from about 6.40% in 1980 to about 30% in 1999. The linchpin of the "buy side" in the municipal debt market continues to be households. Their share varied from 26.20% in 1980 to a peak of 48.50% in 1990. Currently, households account for a little more than one-third of the market. This change in the pattern of ownership is attributable in large part to the tax changes in the 1980s, which we described earlier.

Commercial banks, the dominant buyers in the period 1960 to 1979, have become net sellers in the period 1980 to 1990. Also, individual households, specialty mutual funds, and money market funds have become the dominant buyers.

MUNICIPAL YIELD SPREADS

The tax-exempt status of the municipal securities suggests that the yields of municipal securities should be below the yields of comparable corporate securities and Treasury securities. To a taxable investor, the before-tax return on a corporate security should be high enough that its after-tax return is the same as that of a municipal security that is comparable in its risk characteristics.

Often, this is loosely interpreted as the relationship

$$R_{mT} = R_{cT} \times (1 - \tau), \qquad (10.1)$$

where R_{mT} is the municipal yield, R_{cT} is the corporate yield, τ is interpreted as the marginal tax rate of the marginal investor, and T is the time to maturity. Since we can observe R_{mT} and R_{cT}, it is possible for us to treat τ as the implied tax bracket of the marginal investor. One of the assumptions of this simple relationship is that the implied

TABLE 10-3 *Investors in Municipal Debt Markets (1980–1999 in $ Billions)*

Year	Total Amount Outstanding	Households		Mutual Funds		Money Market Fund		Closed End Funds		Trusts		Commercial Banks		Insurance Co.		Others	
		Amt	%	Amt	%	Amt	%	Amt	%	Amt	%	Amt	%	Amt	%	Amt	%
1980	399.4	104.5	26.20	4.4	1.10	2	0.50	—	—	26	6.50	148.8	37.30	80.5	20.20	33.2	8.30
1981	443.7	131.3	29.60	5.1	1.10	4.4	1.00	—	—	29.6	6.70	154	34.70	83.9	18.90	35.4	8.00
1982	508	170	33.50	8	1.60	13.3	2.60	—	—	31.2	6.10	158.3	31.20	87	17.10	40.2	7.90
1983	575.1	211.2	36.70	13.4	2.30	16.9	2.90	—	—	35.7	6.20	162.1	28.20	86.7	15.10	49.1	8.50
1984	650.6	250.7	38.50	19.1	2.90	24	3.70	—	—	39.9	6.10	174.6	26.80	84.7	13.00	57.6	8.80
1985	859.5	346.4	40.30	34.9	4.10	36.4	4.20	1	0.10	48.2	5.60	231.7	27.00	88.2	10.30	72.7	8.50
1986	920.4	352.6	38.30	67	7.30	64.1	7.00	2	0.20	56.9	6.20	203.4	22.10	101.9	11.10	72.5	7.90
1987	1,010.40	452.5	44.80	74.8	7.40	61.8	6.10	3.3	0.30	63.1	6.20	174.3	17.30	124.8	12.40	55.8	5.50
1988	1,082.30	523.7	48.40	82.9	7.70	66.1	6.10	7.5	0.70	65.9	6.10	151.6	14.00	134.1	12.40	50.5	4.70
1989	1,135.20	547.1	48.20	98.6	8.70	70.1	6.20	12.1	1.10	73	6.40	133.8	11.80	134.8	11.90	65.7	5.80
1990	1,184.40	574.4	48.50	112.6	9.50	84	7.10	14.1	1.20	80.8	6.80	117.4	9.90	136.9	11.60	64.2	5.40
1991	1,272.20	614	48.30	139.7	11.00	90.6	7.10	25.4	2.00	89.9	7.10	103.2	8.10	126.8	10.00	82.6	6.50
1992	1,302.80	585.5	44.90	168.4	12.90	96	7.40	39.7	3.00	96	7.40	97.5	7.50	134.3	10.30	85.4	6.60
1993	1,377.50	551.9	40.10	211.3	15.30	105.6	7.70	51.8	3.80	108.9	7.90	99.2	7.30	146.1	10.60	102.7	7.50
1994	1,341.70	501.5	37.40	207	15.40	113.4	8.50	53.4	4.00	114.2	8.50	97.6	7.30	153.8	11.50	100.8	7.50
1995	1,293.50	457.7	35.40	210.2	16.30	127.7	9.90	59.6	4.60	108.3	8.40	93.4	7.20	161	12.40	75.6	5.80
1996	1,296.00	435.6	33.60	213.3	16.50	144.5	11.10	61.7	4.80	104	8.00	94.2	7.30	175.4	13.50	67.3	5.20
1997	1,367.50	463.6	33.90	219.8	16.10	167	12.20	60.8	4.40	90.7	6.60	96.7	7.10	191.6	14.00	77.3	5.70
1998	1,464.30	475.4	32.50	242.6	16.60	193	13.20	61.7	4.20	89.5	6.10	104.8	7.20	210.9	14.40	86.4	5.90
1999	$1,532.50	$527.50	34.40	$241.50	15.80	$210.40	13.70	$62.40	4.10	$88.40	5.80	$110.70	7.20	$208.90	13.60	$82.70	5.40

Source: Federal Reserve System.

tax bracket should be the same regardless of the maturity T of the corporate and municipal securities. Stated differently, it is assumed here that the spread between the corporate and municipal sectors is the same for all maturities. Even though the relation derived in Equation 10.1 ignores these important considerations, it has one important empirical prediction: As the tax rates fall (increase), the spread between corporates and municipals should narrow (widen) further. Indeed, during the early 1980s when the federal income tax was cut by a significant amount, the spreads narrowed, as can be seen from the evidence presented in Figure 10-1.

Table 10-4 identifies the factors that influence the spreads between municipals on one hand, and corporates and Treasuries on the other. Note that the spread is a function of current and expected tax status; contractual provisions, such as calls, serial features, and puts; liquidity; default risk; and so on. These factors tend to have a differential effect on the spread between Treasuries and municipals depending on the maturity of the securities. For example, the call feature is liable to have a greater effect on a municipal with a longer maturity than on a municipal with a shorter maturity. This suggests that the spread between Treasury and municipals should increase with maturity, holding other factors constant.

TABLE 10-4   *Factors Affecting Municipal Spreads*

Factors	Treasuries	Corporates	Municipals
Credit risk	Absent	Very low	Varies
Interest risk	Varies	Varies	Varies
Liquidity risk	Very low	Moderate	High
Timing risk	None	Low	High
Tax risk	Only federal taxes	Fully taxable	Tax-exempt; future tax changes

FIGURE 10-1   *Yields of Treasuries, Corporates and Municipals*

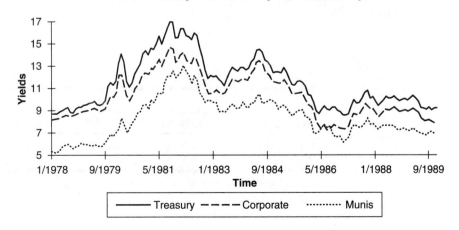

To get a perspective on these issues, examine the empirical evidence on the spreads between municipal and corporate securities for the period January 1978 to March 1991 in Figure 10-1.

Note from Figure 10-1 that the spreads between Treasuries and municipals have varied a great deal, ranging from a low of −33 basis points in 1986 around the tax-reform-act period to a high of 478 basis points in February 1980.

Peek and Wilcox (1986) analyze the behavior of the implied tax brackets for three distinct maturity sectors: one-year, five-year, and ten-year. Their analysis covers 1955 through 1985. For these maturity sectors, they estimate the implied tax rates τ_1, τ_5, and τ_{10}, and they find the regularity that $\tau_1 > \tau_5 > \tau_{10}$. Their evidence points to the facts that the municipal yield curve is steeper than the Treasury yield curve and that the municipal yield curve is upward sloping.

In a more recent study, Farinella and Koch (1994) have suggested that the steep upward-sloping nature of the municipal securities yield curve is no longer descriptive of the market conditions after the Tax Reform Act of 1986. Table 10-5 (taken from their work) indicates that the municipal curve is no longer steeply upward-sloping relative to the Treasury. Note in the table that the spread between the twenty-year and one-year Treasuries was 39 basis points compared to the municipal spread of 136 basis points during the period 1960(I) to 1979(IV). Clearly, the municipal curve was much steeper than the Treasury yield curve during this period. During the 1980(I) to 1986(II) period, the municipal spread was 316 basis points, well in excess of the Treasury spread of 84 basis points. Note, however, that in the post-Tax-Reform-Act-of-1986 period, 1986(III) to 1992(IV), the municipal spread was 211 basis points compared to the Treasury spread of 165 basis points. Clearly, the relative steepness of the municipal curve is much less in this period.

Green (1993) develops a model that is able to explain why the implied tax brackets decrease with maturity. Equation 10.1 can be derived under the assumption that taxable investors are at the margin between taxable and tax exempt debt securities of the same maturity. Green points out, however, that taxable investors are more likely to hold portfolios of taxables that are tax advantaged relative to par bonds with similar pretax cash flows. Using this approach, Green derives implied tax brackets that are consistent with the data.

TABLE 10-5 *Slopes of Yield Curves: Municipal versus Treasury*	*Spread (twenty-year minus one-year)*	*1960(I)– 1979(IV)*	*1980(I)– 1986(II)*	*1986(III)– 1992(IV)*
	Municipal	1.36%	3.16%	2.11%
	Treasury	0.39%	0.84%	1.65%

Source: Farinella and Koch 1994.

ISSUANCE AND PRIMARY MARKET

Most municipal notes (both fixed and variable rate notes) are rated by rating agencies. The rating terminology is shown in Table 10-6. Recall that municipal bonds are also rated, as described in Chapter 7.

Closely linked to the credit reputation of municipal securities is the municipal bonds insurance. There are several large municipal bond insurers: American Municipal Bond Assurance Corporation (AMBAC), Municipal Bond Investors Assurance Corporation (MBIAC), Financial Guarantee Insurance Company (FGIC), and Bond Investors Guaranty Insurance Company (BIG). Rating agencies tend to rate insured municipal bonds at the highest category (Aaa or AAA).

Issuance of municipal securities takes several distinct steps. First, it is important to note that municipal securities do not come under the filing provisions of Securities Act of 1933; thus, they are not registered with the SEC. Second, the issuance of GO bonds typically require the approval of the voters, since taxes collected from the voters are used to service GO bonds. GO bonds are subject to debt ceilings to electoral supervision either via statutes or via referendum.

Issuance of revenue bonds requires feasibility studies by professionals and may carry restrictive covenants. Such covenants may cover many areas. For example, the municipality may have to set the prices and rates at a level sufficient to ensure a surplus over the maintenance expenses in order to provide debt service. The covenants may also specify maintenance standards, insurance requirements, and restrictions on additional issues of debt.

Typically, covenants require the setting up of specific funds into which revenues are placed. This is done to control the priority of distributing revenues. For example, a debt service fund may be set up to ensure that enough money is deposited into it for

TABLE 10-6 *Rating Conventions for Municipal Notes*	Security	Moody's	Standard & Poor's
	Fixed	MIG1	SP-1
	Variable	VMIG1	Strong capacity to
	Description	Best quality	service debt
	Fixed	MIG2	SP-2
	Variable	VMIG2	Satisfactory capacity
	Description	High quality	to service debt
	Fixed	MIG3	SP-3
	Variable	VMIG3	Speculative capacity
	Description	Favorable quality	to service debt
	Fixed	MIG4	
		Adequate quality	
	Variable	VMIG4	

debt service. Similarly, a debt service reserve fund may be set up to ensure that a surplus of a pre-specified amount is set up. Sinking funds may be set up to retire the issue in an orderly fashion and to avoid a large balloon payment at maturity.

Underwriting

New issues of GO and revenue bonds are effected by the issuing municipalities through the primary market, which employs dealers, either through competitive bids or through negotiated sale. Underwriters are dealers who provide a number of functions including pricing of the issue, distribution (reoffer) of the issue, maintenance of a secondary market for the issue, and help in the structuring of the issue to best suit the needs of the issuer.

An important part of underwriting is the official statement, which contains the details about the new issue and about the issuer. One of the roles of the underwriter is to help the issuer prepare this official statement. Underwriters have a major responsibility for verifying the accuracy and truthfulness of the information that is disclosed. The underwriter of an issue makes an implicit recommendation to the investor, and there must be a "reasonable basis" for doing so. The Securities and Exchange Commission has a rule, SEC Rule 15c2-12, that governs the information disclosure. In order to establish a reasonable basis, underwriters will review the official statement, inform customers about any official statements, enter into a binding contract with the issuer to distribute the securities to buy, and reoffer the securities to the public. Underwriters, in addition, use their own research staff, secondary market information, and their past experience with the issuers and other issues of similar characteristics to help form their structuring, pricing, and distribution decisions.

As noted in Tables 10-1 and 10-2, both negotiated underwriting and competitive bids are used for distributing municipal securities.

SECONDARY MARKET

Much like the Treasury market, the municipal secondary markets are OTC or dealer markets. Interdealer brokers deal exclusively with dealers. They do not deal with public customers, carry positions, or underwrite positions. J. J. Kenny and Chapdelaine are two of the biggest interdealer brokers. Such interdealer brokers provide wire services showing the securities that are available for trades. They do this much like the interdealer brokers in the Treasury markets, concealing the identities of the dealers who wish to make those trades. In addition to the interdealer brokers, dealers also have access to the Blue list, which is published daily by Standard and Poor. The **Blue list** contains the interdealer offerings of municipal securities and is a very good indicator of the daily supply in the municipal market. Many dealers subscribe to the Blue list ticker, which enables the dealers to access a specified list of securities. In addition to these sources, Munifacts, a wire service, is provided by *Bond Buyer,* a publication that is active in the municipal market.

Market Conventions

Municipal securities are quoted in terms of yields. The liquidity in this market is poor; hence, the bid-offer spreads can be wide, especially for seasoned issues. The convention in the market is such that a bond selling at a discount is priced relative to its maturity. A bond selling at a premium is priced to its call date, provided it is callable at par. Municipal securities pay semiannual coupons, and accrued interest is computed based on a 360-day year basis.

Advanced Refunding

Many long-term municipal bonds are callable. If a municipality has issued a callable bond and the interest rates go down, the bonds will be called and replaced by cheaper bonds that reflect the lowered interest rates. Often, callable bonds have a **call-protection period.** For example, a 30-year municipal bond may be protected from call for the first 10 years of its life. During this noncall period, the municipality can try to buy back the bonds from the bondholders. This can be done through formal tender offers or open-market purchases. This is a time-consuming operation and may not result in all the bonds to be tendered by the bondholders.

The most common way of retiring a noncallable municipal bond issue is through advanced refunding or by defeasance. In advanced refundings, the municipality issues new bonds that reflect the low market interest rates. The proceeds of this issue are then used to buy a portfolio of U.S. Treasury securities. The income generated by this Treasury portfolio is guaranteed to make timely payments of the existing (noncallable) municipal bonds. All the promised coupon payments and the call price to be paid on the first call date will be met by the cash flows from the Treasury portfolio. This portfolio will be placed in an **irrevocable trust.** Since under advanced refundings the cash flows are backed by Treasury portfolio, such municipal bonds carry a AAA rating even in the absence of bond insurance. Depending on the provisions in the advanced refunding, the bond may or may not be called. The article from *Forbes* (1999) describes some of the risks to the municipal bond investors who invest in advanced-refunded bonds.

The ability to refund this way may present the following **tax arbitrage.** The municipality can issue a tax-exempt 30-year bond at 5% and use the proceeds to buy a Treasury portfolio at a weighted yield of 7% for refunding an old issue. The difference of 200 basis points will constitute risk-free profits. The most favorable conditions for such a tax arbitrage will prevail when long-term municipal bond rates are very low and the short-term to medium-term Treasury yields are much higher. In addition, interest rates have fallen to a point that the present value of the savings associated with advanced refunding is very high. Since 1986, IRS rules have prohibited the municipal bond issuers from engaging in this tax arbitrage. The new rules require that the yield of the Treasury portfolio placed in escrow may not exceed the yield on new municipal issues.

Yield Burning

In order to comply with the IRS, a tax-exempt issuer can pay the difference between the yield of the escrow Treasury portfolio and the yield of new tax-exempt securities. The issuer can also purchase from the Treasury a special issue of State and Local Government Series (SLGS) Treasury securities whose yield will be the same as that of the escrow portfolio. If the provision of IRS is not respected, the IRS can declare the bonds to be not eligible for tax exemption.

Yield burning occurs when a securities dealer artificially inflates the prices of Treasury securities when the dealer sells them to a municipality that is in the process of setting up the escrow portfolio. The inflated price "burns" the yield and helps in circumventing the tax arbitrage provision, thereby depriving the IRS of tax revenue. If the interest savings are sufficiently high, then the municipality is willing to pay a higher price to the security dealer. Yield burning can place the dealer, municipality, and investors in a difficult situation.

Municipal Bond Insurance

As noted in Tables 10-1 and 10-2, a significant amount of municipal debt securities are insured. Often, scheduled interest and principal payments are guaranteed by AAA-rated municipal bond insurers. Such insurances help the investors in two ways. First, even if the issuer gets into financial difficulty, payments are made without any interruption. Second, ratings downgrades of the issuer need not affect the market price of insured municipal debt securities. In most cases, the isurance is provided by monoline insurers who specialize in insuring investment-grade debt issues.

Risky Munis

By Marilyn Cohen

Peace of mind is nice when you buy a bond. Treasurys, of course, have Washington's limitless taxing power to back them up. Among municipal bonds, a number have taken to offering a guarantee called advanced refunding that is just as solid because Treasurys support them. At least these munis look safe on the surface. But they may be riskier than you would expect, so a sharp eye is necessary when buying.

With advanced refunding, the muni issuer sets aside Treasury or other federal securities in an escrow account to ensure timely semiannual interest, as well as principal paybacks. You are not relying on the credit quality of the issuer; you are relying on the sterling collateral provided by Uncle Sam. The county, hospital or city can go bankrupt and you will get your money.

The problem is that some of these munis can be called years early, which is a risk that many bond buyers don't look at. Last year the Gainesville, Fla. municipally owned utility—furnishing everything

Source: M. Cohen, "Risky Munis," Forbes Magazine Online, November 1, 1999. Reprinted by permission of *Forbes Magazine*. © 2001 Forbes 1999.

from electricity to water to sewerage—shocked the muni-bond community by moving to redeem three outstanding advanced-refunded bonds years before their maturity dates. The utility won the City Commission's approval to call the bonds, although it has not done so yet. Other muni issuers are following suit.

Can you imagine buying an 8% or 9% bond at a premium price of 120 or 130 and having it called at par? That is a painful loss. Relatively low interest rates in recent years are the cause. New muni bonds can be floated at a yield around 5%. Obviously, Gainesville would save a bundle if the utility issued new bonds at today's low rates and bought out the current holders. The three Gainesville Regional Utilities issues, which were escrowed in 1983 and are due in 2014, have been paying investors handsomely, between 6.5% and 9.3%.

Like the Gainesville issues, the bonds to worry about probably were advanced refunded before 1985, when rates were higher. Because most investors never see a bond issue's fine print, you may not have a clue of a potential explosion in your portfolio until the bonds are called. Moreover, if you hold bearer bonds, you won't know the bad news until you present your next coupons for payment. Sorry, there won't be one; only a redemption. That means you have gone six months without earning a nickel.

Call-Proof

These municipal bonds won't be called early, their issuers say. They provide added protection from defaults because they are backed by Treasurys or similar securities.

Municipal bond	Coupon	Due date
Los Angeles, Calif. Harbor Department Revenue	7.60%	Oct. 1, 2018
Massachusetts Turnpike Authority	5.00	Jan. 1, 2020
Orange County Florida Water & Sewer	9.50	Oct. 1, 2013
Philadelphia, Pa. Hospital & Higher Education Facilities	6.65	Dec. 1, 2019
Puerto Rico Commonwealth Aqueduct & Sewer	9.00	July 1, 2009

If you are in the market to buy an advanced-refunded issue, you can check out its redemption vulnerability. First, know that these munis come in two flavors: escrowed to maturity and prerefunded. Prerefunded means the bond can be called at a specific point a few years before the maturity date—say, in 2005 for a bond due in 2010. Escrowed to maturity simply means that there's no set call date. Regardless, either kind can be called right now in many cases.

The trick is to identify advanced-refunded bonds whose issuers have said they won't call. A good source for this information is the Bloomberg terminal's municipal bond description page. There, under Refunded Information, it may say "status of call provisions not addressed" or "optional call provisions may be exercised" or "status of call provisions unknown." Do not buy these issues. Or at least have your broker double-check by eyeing the bond indenture to see if the calls have been extinguished without Bloomberg's knowledge. If, on the other hand, the database's description page shows "original call provisions waived," you've got the green light to purchase the securities. See the accompanying table for a sample of advanced-refunded bonds that are safe from calls.

Marilyn Cohen is president of Envision Capital Management, Inc., a Los Angeles Fixed-Income Money Manager.

CONCLUSION

There has been a general erosion in the tax advantages of municipal securities. Still, for investors in the high federal tax bracket, municipal securities still offer attractive returns. Municipal bonds present call risk to investors. This is described in the article from *Forbes* (1999).

PROBLEMS

10.1   Explain the difference between the general obligation bonds and revenue bonds.

10.2   Discuss why the municipal yield curve is steeper than the Treasury yield curve, in general.

10.3   What are the reasons for the relative fall in the steepness of the municipal yield curve relative to the Treasury yield curve after the Tax Reform Act of 1986?

10.4   Discuss why the three major investors in the municipal market are commercial banks, wealthy individuals, and fire and casualty insurers.

10.5   How will changes in future tax policies affect the pricing of municipal bonds?

10.6   Discuss the concept of advanced refunding in the municipal bond markets.

10.7   Why are municipal bonds insured? Who are the major insurers in the municipal bond market?

10.8   The implied tax rate τ is found using the equation

$$R_m = R_T \times (1 - \tau),$$

where R_m is the municipal yield, R_t is the Treasury yield, and τ is the implied tax rate. What are the limitations of this approach? Is it correct to assume that as τ increases, municipal bonds become less attractive investments?

REFERENCES

Farinella, J. A., and T. W. Koch 1994. "Who Took the Slope out of the Municipal Yield Curve?" *Journal of Fixed-Income* 4(2):59–65.

Green, R. C. 1993. "A Simple Model of the Taxable and Tax-Exempt Yield Curves." *The Review of Financial Studies* 6:233–264.

Peek, J., and J. A. Wilcox 1986. "Tax Rates and Interest Rates on Tax-Exempt Securities." *New England Economic Review:* (January/February):29–41.

Chapter 11

Emerging Debt Markets

Chapter Objectives

This chapter provides a brief overview of emerging debt markets. We describe the risks associated with investing in emerging debt markets.

The following issues are addressed as well:

- What is the effect of the Russian default on emerging debt markets?
- What are some recent institutional developments that may potentially improve the process of resolving financial distress?
- What are Brady bonds? What are the features of Brady bonds?
- What is EMBI?

HOW IMPORTANT IS THE EMERGING DEBT MARKET?

The term **emerging markets** is used to describe economies of developing nations. Countries in Latin America, Africa, the Middle East, Asia, and eastern Europe fall into this category. In the last two decades, the emerging markets have become a significant constituency in the global debt markets. Traditionally, emerging markets have relied on bank loans and loans from institutions, such as the International Monetary Fund (IMF) and the World Bank. Over the last two decades, however, the publicly traded bonds issued by emerging economies have started to grow at a much more rapid pace. The private market financing to emerging markets can be broken down across (a) regions, (b) financing type, such as bonds, equities, and loans and (c) borrower type, such as sovereign, public, and private. In Table 11-1 we present the regional breakdown for the period 1994 to 1998.

The flow of capital to Asia started to slow down sharply after the East Asian crisis in 1997. This drop took place in the third quarter of 1997, causing the flow to level off in 1997 and to dip significantly in 1998 when the Russian default occurred. Table 11-2 shows that the bond market has become more important than the loan market in sovereign debt. The issuance of bonds dropped sharply in late 1997 and in 1998 due to the East Asian and Russian crises. Table 11-3 shows the types of borrowers in the emerging debt markets. Private borrowers account for over 50% of borrowing in most years, followed by sovereign and public borrowers.

In Table 11-4, we summarize the composition of the market in greater detail for 1996. Note that the sovereign bonds and loans account for nearly 85% of the market. Of the sovereign markets, the bonds markets account for bulk of the debt securities.

TABLE 11-1

Private Market Financing to Emerging Markets by Regions (in Billions of Dollars and in Percentages)

	1994	1995	1996	1997	1998
Asia	84.6 (62.2%)	86.9 (55%)	118.5 (54.3%)	127.5 (44.6%)	34.1 (22.9%)
Western Hemisphere	26.2 (19.3%)	36.2 (22.9%)	63.1 (28.9%)	90.3 (31.6%)	64.6 (43.5%)
Middle East	10.8 (7.9%)	8.7 (5.5%)	9.9 (4.5%)	16.0 (5.6%)	9.2 (6.2%)
Africa	3.3 (2.4%)	9.3 (5.9%)	5.6 (2.5%)	14.8 (5.2%)	4.4 (3.0%)
Europe	11.2 (8.2%)	16.8 (10.6%)	21.3 (9.7%)	37.5 (13.1%)	36.1 (24.3%)

Source: IMF 1999.

TABLE 11-2

Private Market Financing to Emerging Markets by Financing Type (in Billions of Dollars and in Percentages)

	1994	1995	1996	1997	1998
Bonds	61.3 (45.0%)	63.7 (40.4%)	111.3 (51.0%)	138.2 (48.3%)	78.2 (52.7%)
Equities	18.0 (13.3%)	11.2 (7.1%)	16.4 (7.5%)	24.8 (8.7%)	9.9 (6.7%)
Loans	56.7 (41.7%)	82.9 (52.6%)	90.7 (41.5%)	123.2 (43.0%)	60.4 (40.7%)

Source: IMF 1999.

TABLE 11-3

Private Market Financing to Emerging Markets by Types of Borrowers (in Billions of Dollars and in Percentages)

	1994	1995	1996	1997	1998
Sovereign	18.2 (13.4%)	25.4 (16.1%)	41.8 (19.1%)	48.2 (16.8%)	48.7 (32.8%)
Public	38.2 (28.1%)	48.2 (30.6%)	53.8 (24.6%)	73.2 (25.6%)	31.9 (21.5%)
Private	79.5 (58.5%)	84.2 (53.3%)	122.8 (56.2%)	164.8 (57.6%)	68.0 (45.8%)

Source: IMF 1999.

TABLE 11-4

Composition of Bond Markets as of December 1996

Security	Percentage Outstanding
Sovereign—Bradys	18
Sovereign—Other US$ bonds	20
Sovereign—Local currency	36
Sovereign—Loans	9
Corporate	16

Source: Bernstein and Pericook, Jr., 1998.

The Brady bonds are those bonds that came about through the restructuring of sovereign loans. We discuss this important segment in detail later. The trading volume in the emerging debt markets exceeded $5 trillion in 1996. More than half of the trading volume was accounted for by the Brady bonds. These bonds were created by restructuring sovereign bank loans. We will discuss Brady bonds in detail later in the chapter.

In addition to Brady bonds, sovereign issuers have also issued Eurobonds. Unlike Brady bonds, Eurobonds tend to be less liquid because of their smaller issue sizes. The bid-offer spreads of Eurobonds tend to be higher than those of Brady bonds as well.

WHAT IS DIFFERENT ABOUT SOVEREIGN DEBT?

Sovereign loans and bonds are quite unlike a bank loan to a corporate borrower or a debt security issued by a corporation. Corporate debt and sovereign debt differ in many important dimensions. Corporate debt is a contract between the borrower and the lender that is a legally enforceable claim. Should there be a default (triggered by either a nonpayment or a nontimely payment of contractual obligations), the lender has the legal right to take action against the borrower. Usually, such action is taken within the framework of a bankruptcy code. Through the bankruptcy code, the lender is able to formally access the assets of the borrower. We have seen in the study of corporate debt contracts the key provisions of the bankruptcy code and how they prove to be valuable to corporate lenders. In fact, the success of corporate bond markets depends crucially on the effectiveness of the bankruptcy code.

The sovereign debt contract presents major challenges in ensuring that the lenders will have access to the assets of the borrower. The borrowing country may default on its contractual obligations without the lender having any recourse to the assets of the sovereign borrower. In many instances, the borrowing country has defaulted, and the lenders have little choice other than to renegotiate their loans. Often the lenders had to accept a writedown of their loans. The Russian default in the summer of 1998 is a case in point.

Why do lenders, such as commercial banks and fixed-income asset managers, extend credit to sovereign borrowers? The existing explanations are based on costs of access in the future to global credit markets. This is sometimes referred to as reputational costs. Since sovereign borrowers are likely to be repeat borrowers, they care about future access to credit markets, which can become costly if they were to default in earlier rounds of borrowings. The second explanation is based on the potential for retaliatory actions by the lender by way of sanctions and trade barriers. The crux of the problem in sovereign lending is the inability of the lenders to enforce the contractual terms credibly. With corporate debt, the outside option of bankruptcy or liquidation is credible, and it disciplines the borrower. There is much less credibility in sovereign debt markets due to the absence of a well-defined bankruptcy procedure and the inability to access the collateral in the event of financial distress. This would imply that the sovereign spreads should be higher than other similar corporate securities. This appears to be the case. Empirical work on sovereign spreads suggests that sovereign spreads are much higher than similarly rated domestic (U.S.) corporate debt. We show in Figure 11-1 the sovereign spreads and spreads on high-yield securities. Notice how the sovereign spreads are consistently higher than high-yield spreads.

The following is an excerpt from the IMF (1999) report on the conditions that led to the Russian default.

Russia: The Feeding Frenzy

The actions announced by the Russian government on August 17, 1998, came as a major surprise to the financial markets, even though Russia had been downgraded by one rating agency (Moody's) in March 1998 and then by all three major agencies in May or early June, and despite the fact that yields on Russian securities clearly reflected a substantial default risk. In explaining their large positions in Russian assets, market participants have typically noted that they relied on the proposition that Russia was too important a country for the major industrial countries and the international financial institutions to allow it to collapse. In this sense, moral hazard clearly played a role in the buildup of claims on Russia in a way that cannot realistically be said for any of the other crisis countries. But in addition to (or in combination with) this moral hazard, there is also clear evidence that Russia represents a case where many investors bought securities that they did not fully understand, and where they did so in the face of developments that should have raised concerns.

Between March 1998 and July 1998, there was an enormous buildup in the outstanding stock of sovereign Russian eurobonds. This buildup, which added to the large positions of nonresidents in GKOs and OFZs (ruble-denominated domestic government securities) and other Russian instruments, reflected five separate bond issues: one in March, one in April, two in June, and one in July as part of the GKO exchange. As a result, the stock of eurobonds rose from $4.6 billion to $15.9 billion in just five months. What is notable is that these bond sales and massive growth in nonresidents' holdings of Russian assets occurred in the face of downgrades in Russia's credit rating and in sharp increases in yields that indicated a substantial probability of default (see also Annex V, on the review of ratings during the crises). For example, before the first issue of 1998 in March, the yield spread on the benchmark June 2007 bond stood at about 490 basis points. By late June, when the outstanding stock of eurobonds had risen from $4.6 billion to $9.4 billion, the yield spread had increased to about 750 points, and Russia was rated four notches below investment grade by Moody's and Standard and Poor's. By late July, after the issuance of a further $6.4 billion of bonds in the debt exchange (or $4.8 billion at market value, since the bonds were issued with submarket coupons) the yield spread had risen to around 900 points. By August 14, just before the announcement of the devaluation and debt moratorium, the yield spread had risen to about 1,800 basis points and Russia was rated by the two leading agencies as five or six notches below investment grade.

For many investors, the sharp rise in yields was viewed more as a buying opportunity than as an indicator of possible default. Each of the first four eurobond issues in 1999 was substantially oversubscribed, and in the case of the GKO exchange it has been argued that the reason why a larger proportion of eligible GKOs was not exchanged was that GKO holders expected that they would make large capital gains as GKO yields fell when others tendered their holdings and reduced the outstanding stock. Market participants talk of "feeding frenzies" at the time of new Russian issues, and of demand from a wide range of investors with little knowledge of Russia. Indeed, one eurobond issue—the April issue of

Source: IMF (1999).

Lit 750 million ($420 million) in 5-year bonds—was targeted at Italian retail investors seeking the high yields that had been previously available on Italian debt. And in the case of the London Club debt, the number of holders of the restructured notes (IANs) and loans (PRINS) had grown from about 400 "traditional" creditors (mostly banks) at the time of the original agreement to several thousand, many of which had little understanding of the legal nature of the instruments they held. The widely dispersed holdings of these instruments and the lack of understanding of the inherent risks was reflected in difficulties in contacting and seeking agreement among creditors in the negotiations over the London Club debt in late 1998 and early 1999. Similarly, some investors in MinFins (domestically issued dollar-denominated debt) appear to have lacked a full understanding of their legal status, including the jurisdiction in which they were issued. A range of other Russia-linked securities were also offered in the first half of 1998 by other issuers. These included euro-ruble issues (notes with principal and interest payments payable in dollars, but based on the value of the ruble) from several supranational institutions (the IFC, European Bank for Reconstruction and Development (EBRD), and Inter-American Development Bank (IADB)) that were sold to yield-seeking investors (and which were swapped to provide low cost dollar financing to their issuers). There were also ruble-linked notes such as a May 1998 issue by an Italian investment bank of Lit 750 billion of 10-year bonds that yielded an above-market coupon of 6.4 percent, but with a clause that the coupon would go to zero in the event of a Russian default: the clause was triggered in August 1998, and holders were left with a zero-coupon bond worth about only 60 percent of face value. More generally, there was a whole range of structured notes with payments linked, sometimes with leverage, to the payment flows on GKOs and other Russian securities. The large falls in prices of these securities, the disappearance of a market in many cases, and the legal uncertainty over some instruments contributed to the deterioration in sentiment for other emerging market assets following the Russian default.

FIGURE 11-1 *Yield Spreads on Emerging Market and U.S. High Yield Bonds*[1] *(in Basis Points, Weekly Average)*

Source: IMF. "International Capital Markets: Developments, Prospects and Key Policy Issues," September 1999.
[1]EMBI excludes Russia from the start of 1998.

INSTITUTIONAL BACKDROP

The institutional background associated with sovereign debt differs in many respects from corporate debt markets. For the sovereign loan markets, there are two organizations that deal with the process of restructuring troubled sovereign loans. They are known as the London Club and the Paris Club. The focus of the London Club is to help restructure the loans extended by commercial banks to sovereign borrowers. The members of the London Club are basically the lending commercial banks, and they meet periodically to restructure loans. On the other hand, the Paris Club focuses exclusively on bilateral and multilateral loans from one country to another. The members of the Paris Club are the lending nations, and they meet periodically to restructure troubled bilateral and multilateral loans.

The London and Paris Clubs are focused on loans rather than bonds. More recently, contractual safeguards have been designed for lenders to sovereign borrowers in the bond markets. One of the key provisions currently being debated is the collective action clauses [CACs], which are meant to assist in the resolution of defaults in sovereign bond markets. The CACs have three important provisions:

1. **Modifying the terms of the bond contract:** This provision allows the terms of the bond contract, such as coupon payments, to be modified through a majority approvel of bondholders. If a two-thirds or three-fourths majority by value of voting approve the changes, then it becomes a binding modification for all bondholders.
2. **Collective Representation Provisions:** This provides a formal forum in which the views of the issuer and the representatives of the bondholders can be heard.
3. **Sharing Clauses:** These clauses limit direct action against the borrower. They provide for a sharing of proceeds among the bondholders that acts as a deterrent to direct action.

In addition to these contractual provisions, many sovereign borrowers waive their sovereign immunity and agree to be brought to court in the event of financial distress. In practice, this waiver of sovereign immunity may not be tremendously useful inasmuch as the access to the collateral of the sovereign borrower remains remote. When Russia defaulted in 1998, the losses to the creditors amounted to over $6 billion. A report by the U.S. ratings agency Standard and Poor's indicates that only one government, Ecuador, defaulted in 1999, compared with five in 1998. The value of sovereign debt in default was $102 billion, nearly unchanged from 1998. In the context of this, it is reasonable to expect that the bondholders will protect themselves by designing the sovereign debt contracts to minimize their exposure. We will investigate this issue next.

BRADY BONDS

Brady bonds were created when sovereign loans under default were written down and converted into bonds. Mexico was the first country to participate in the creation of Brady bonds (leading to Mexican Bradys). Through a process of debt reduction in exchange for some economic reforms, several Brady bonds were created. Loans that were exchanged for debt at par were known as par Brady bonds. Loans wherein the principal amount was reduced by 35% to 50% of the face value were exchanged for discount bonds. Besides debt reduction through writedown of the face value, bonds were issued at below-market coupon rates, and in some cases, new money was lent. By converting loans to bonds, Brady bond markets attracted a larger investor base. In order to make the Brady bonds sufficiently attractive to investors, a portion of the scheduled payments have been collateralized using U.S. Treasury strips. To get a sense of how Brady bonds are structured, let us review Table 11-5. This table is taken from Bernstein and Penicook (1998). Latin American countries account for almost 85% of the total Brady bonds market estimated at $121 billion. The biggest issuers are Brazil, Argentina, and Mexico.

Several design features are worthy of note. First, most of the bond issues have a grace period. During the grace period, the principal is not amortized. This feature helps to mitigate defaults that may be induced by liquidity problems. A significant majority of the debt issues appear to be floating rate debt. This has the effect of reducing the duration of the debt issues and lowering the market risk of the bonds. Note also that a vast majority of the bond issues provide for a partial capitalization of interest payments. This is also a design feature to avoid liquidity-induced defaults. The idea behind explicitly specifying these features is that the lenders can price the value of these features into the spreads.

EMERGING MARKET SPREADS

In order to assess the risk associated with emerging market debt, we need to look at their spreads. It is useful to focus on broad indices in this context. To the extent that the bonds are in the same currency, the spread gives an estimate of the risk premium, which is (among other things) a compensation for the incremental credit risk present in the emerging debt markets. Several emerging market bond indices have been developed to track the performance of this asset class. Perhaps the most widely followed index is the one assembled by J.P. Morgan. The indexes are constructed by restricting attention to certain instruments and countries. Specific weighting schemes are used in putting together the indices. The article from Cunningham (1999) shows the different indices prepared by J.P. Morgan and how they are constructed.

The spreads in the emerging markets have fluctuated dramatically over the years. In particular, the spreads are extremely sensitive to the macroeconomic performance of countries. Key factors that appear to influence the spreads include vulnerability of the country's currency. This depends on the ratio of short-term debt to its international reserves. The higher this ratio, the more vulnerable the currency. Spreads also depend on such factors as dollar-denominated export growth rate, stability of the banking system, and political risks. In Figure 11-1, we noted that the spreads in EMBI dramatically widened around the time of the Russian default.

TABLE 11-5   *Bonds Issued under Loan Restructuring*

Restructuring Plan	Issue Exchange Data	Instruments Issued	Maturity (yrs) Grace (yrs)	Rate Type	Principal Collateral	Interest Collateral	Principal Reduction	Interest Reduction	Debt Conv/New Money	Interest Arrears
Mexico Aztec Exchange	May 1988	Aztec 2008 bond	20 bullet	Floating	◆	◆				
Brazil Parallel	Nov. 1988	New money bond	11/4	Floating					◆	
Financing agreement	Aug. 1989	Exit bond	25/11	Fixed				◆	◆	
Mexico Brady	Feb. 1990	New money bond	15/7	Floating					◆	
	March 1990	Par bond	30 bullet	Fixed	◆	◆		◆		
		Discount bond	30 bullet	Floating	◆	◆	◆			
Philippines 1989–1990 Financing agreement	May 1990	New money bond	15/8	Floating					◆	
Costa Rica Brady	May 1990	Principal bond A	20/11	Fixed		◆		◆		
		Principal bond B	25/16	Fixed				◆		
		Interest bond A	15/0	Floating						◆
		Interest bond B	15/0	Floating						◆
Venezuela Brady	Dec. 1990	DCB DL	17/7	Floating					◆	
		DCB IL	18/7	Floating					◆	
		FLIRB	17/7	Mixed				◆		
		Par bond	30 bullet	Fixed	◆	◆		◆		
		Discount bond	30 bullet	Floating	◆	◆	◆			
		New money A	15/7	Floating					◆	
		New money BP	15/7	Floating					◆	
		New money BNP	15/8	Floating					◆	
Uruguay Brady	Dec. 1990	DCB	16/7	Floating					◆	
		New money note	15/7	Floating					◆	
Nigeria Brady	Jan. 1992	Par bond	30 bullet	Fixed	◆	◆		◆		
Philippine Brady	Dec. 1992	Par bond	28 bullet	Step up	◆	◆		◆		
		DCB	17/5	Floating					◆	
		FLIRB	15/7	Mixed				◆		
Argentine Brady	April 1993	Par bond	25 bullet	Step up	◆	◆		◆		
		Par bond	30 bullet	Step up	◆	◆		◆		
		Discount bond	30 bullet	Floating	◆	◆	◆			
		PDI bond	12/3	Floating						
Brazil Brady	Dec. 1991	IDU bond	8/1	Floating		◆				◆
		C bond	20/10	Fixed	◆	◆	◆			◆
	April 1994	Discount bond	30 bullet	Floating	◆	◆	◆			
		Eligible interest bond	12/3	Floating						◆

TABLE 11-5 *Continued*

Restructuring Plan	Issue Exchange Data	Instruments Issued	Maturity (yrs) Grace (yrs)	Rate Type	Principal Collateral	Interest Collateral	Principal Reduction	Interest Reduction	Debt Conv/New Money	Interest Arrears
		DCBs	18/10	Floating		♦			♦	
		FLIRBs	15/9	Mixed	♦♦	♦♦		♦		
		Par bond	30 bullet	Step up	♦	♦		♦		
		New money bond	15/7	Floating					♦	
Jordan Brady	Dec. 1993	Discount bond	30 bullet	Floating	♦	♦	♦			
		PDI bond	12/3	Floating						♦
		Par bond	30 bullet	Step up	♦	♦		♦		
Dominican Republic Brady	Aug. 1994	Discount bond	30 bullet	Floating	♦	♦	♦			
		PDI bond	15/3	Floating		♦				♦
Bulgaria Brady	July 1994	Discount bond	30 bullet	Floating	♦	♦	♦			
		FLIRB	18/8	Mixed		♦		♦		
		IAB	17/7	Floating						♦
Poland Brady	Oct. 1994	Discount bond	30 bullet	Floating	♦	♦	♦			
		Par bond	30 bullet	Step up	♦	♦	♦	♦		
		PDI bond	20/7	Step up						♦
		DCB	25/20	Step up			♦		♦	
		New money bond	15/10	Floating					♦	
Ecuador Brady	Dec. 1994	Par RSTA bond	30 bullet	Step up	♦	♦	♦			
		Interest equalization	10/1	Floating						♦
	Feb. 1994	Par bonds	30 bullet	Step up	♦	♦		♦		
		Discount bonds	30 bullet	Floating	♦	♦	♦			
		PDI bonds	20/10	Floating						♦
Panama Brady	July 1996	FLIRB bonds	18/5	Mixed		♦		♦		
		PDI bonds	20/10	Floating						♦

Source: Bernstein, R. and J.A. Penicook, Jr. (1998). "Emerging Market Debt: Practical Portfolio Considerations," in *Emerging Markets Capital Flows* (Richard Levich, Ed.). Kluwer Academic Publishers, Norwell, MA. Reprinted with permission.

DCB Debt conversion bond

FLIRB Front-loaded interest reduction bond

PDI Past due interest

IDU Interest due and unpaid

IAB Interest accrual bond

RSTA Revolving short-term trade agreements

♦ Interest is partially capitalized over first six years

♦♦ Collateral will phase in over time

Criteria for Country and Asset Inclusion in J.P. Morgan's Emerging Market Bond Indices

This box sets out the criteria for asset and country inclusion in J. P. Morgan's Emerging Market Bond Indices. Table A lists the countries covered along with the market capitalisation and face value of each of the notional portfolios.

The EMBI tracks returns and spreads on Brady bonds and some other restructured sovereign debts. It covers most Brady bonds issued by countries rated BBB-/Baa3 or lower by Standard & Poor's and Moody's—one definition of emerging economies. Bonds covered must have a face value of over US$500 million, at least $2\frac{1}{2}$ years to maturity and be liquid in the sense of having prices that are widely quoted by brokers. At end-August 1999, the EMBI covered assets with a face value of US$111 billion, in other words the bulk of the total stock of Brady bonds.

The EMBI+ tracks returns on a wider range of instruments—sovereign US$-denominated bonds. Again, the measure covers bonds issued by countries rated BBB-/Baa3 or lower by Standard & Poor's and Moody's. And again, the measure excludes bonds which are not large enough (face value must be over US$500 million), mature too soon (minimum of $2\frac{1}{2}$ years to maturity) or are not judged to be sufficiently liquid.

The EMBI(Global) is a newly released index, designed to track returns on a yet-wider range of emerging economy instruments. The definition of emerging economy is broader—covering all countries classified as low or middle income by the World Bank and any others which have restructured sovereign debts over the past ten years. As with the other indices, this measure only covers instruments with a face value of over US$500 million and at least $2\frac{1}{2}$ years to maturity. Bonds must also pass a liquidity test— there must be a daily price available from either J. P. Morgan or another source—though the liquidity criteria are less restrictive than for the EMBI or EMBI+.

The EMBI(Global constrained) was released alongside the EMBI(Global). It is based on the same pool of assets, for the same set of emerging economies. It differs from the EMBI(Global) because it excludes a portion of the instruments issued by the largest countries (those whose eligible instruments exceed US$5 billion in face value). The rationale for restricting exposure to individual countries is to provide a benchmark for those investors who face limitations on the amount of portfolio exposure they can take to individual issuers.

Source: A. Cunningham, Emerging Economy Spread Indices and Financial Stability in Financial Stability Review (November 1999). Bank of England.

TABLE A *Comparison of J. P. Morgan Index Criteria and Coverage*

	EMBI	EMBI+	EMBI(Global)	EMBI(Global Constrained)
Overview (30/8/99)				
Market capitalisation	US$72 billion	US$131 billion	US$170 billion	US$99 billion
Face value	US$111 billion	US$199 billion	US$244 billion	US$136 billion
Instrument coverage				
Class of assets	Brady bonds/other restructured	All sovereign/quasi-sovereign US$-denominated bonds		
Min face value	US$500 million	US$500 million	US$500 million	US$500 million
Min maturity	2½ years	2½ years	2½ years	2½ years
Liquidity	Widely quoted prices		Daily price quotes from at least one broker	
Country coverage				
Criteria	Rated BBB-/Baa3 or lower by both Standard & Poor's and Moody's		Classified as low or middle income by World Bank, and/or having restructured sovereign debts within the past ten years or has restructured debts outstanding	
No. countries	11	16	27	27
Countries covered				
Latin America	Argentina	Argentina	Argentina	Argentina
	Brazil	Brazil	Brazil	Brazil
			Chile	Chile
		Colombia	Colombia	Colombia
	Ecuador	Ecuador	Ecuador	Ecuador
	Mexico	Mexico	Mexico	Mexico
	Panama	Panama	Panama	Panama
	Peru	Peru	Peru	Peru
	Venezuela	Venezuela	Venezuela	Venezuela
Asia			China	China
			Malaysia	Malaysia
		Philippines	Philippines	Philippines
		South Korea	South Korea	South Korea
			Thailand	Thailand
Eastern Europe	Bulgaria	Bulgaria	Bulgaria	Bulgaria
			Croatia	Croatia
			Hungary	Hungary
	Poland	Poland	Poland	Poland
	Russia	Russia	Russia	Russia
Other			Algeria	Algeria
			Greece	Greece
			Ivory Coast	Ivory Coast
			Lebanon	Lebanon
		Morocco	Morocco	Morocco
	Nigeria	Nigeria	Nigeria	Nigeria
			South Africa	South Africa
		Turkey	Turkey	Turkey

The tendency of the sovereign debt markets to "move together" in a period of crisis can also be seen by examining the spreads in U.S. dollar-denominated Eurobonds issued by emerging economies. This is shown in Figure 11-2.

Notice how the Russian default produced a highly correlated increase in the spreads of almost all emerging market debt. This is a general "flight to quality" phenomenon in which investors sell low credit quality debt and invest the proceeds in highly liquid and safe securities, such as Treasury bills and bonds. This leads to a significant liquidity risk in the emerging debt markets. The bid-offer spreads widen, and it becomes difficult if not outright impossible to unwind positions. To get a perspective on the liquidity risk, let us review Figure 11-3.

Notice the dramatic increase in the bid-offer spreads of Brady bonds around the time of the Russian default. Also, during this time, the U.S. Treasury markets were viewed as "safe havens." As a consequence, the Treasury prices went up, and the spreads between on-the-run and off-the-run Treasuries widened, reflecting the desire of investors to invest in liquid assets. This flight to quality or "flight to liquidity" phenomenon is discussed in Dupont and Sack (1999). The following excerpt discusses this liquidity crisis.

In calculating the spreads of Brady bonds, it is especially important to recognize that the benchmark Treasury securities are bullet securities with no optionalities. On the other hand, as noted in Table 11-5, emerging-market bonds have a grace period, step-up coupons, capitalization of interest payments, partial collateralization, etc. These factors must be valued into the price of emerging-market debt. In the market, two conventions are followed. One is to compute the spread ignoring the collateral. The other measure, known as **stripped yield,** computes the price after stripping the collateral from the bonds.

FIGURE 11-2 *Secondary Market Yield Spreads on U.S. Dollar-Denominated Eurobonds by Selected Emerging Markets*[1] *(in Basis Points)*

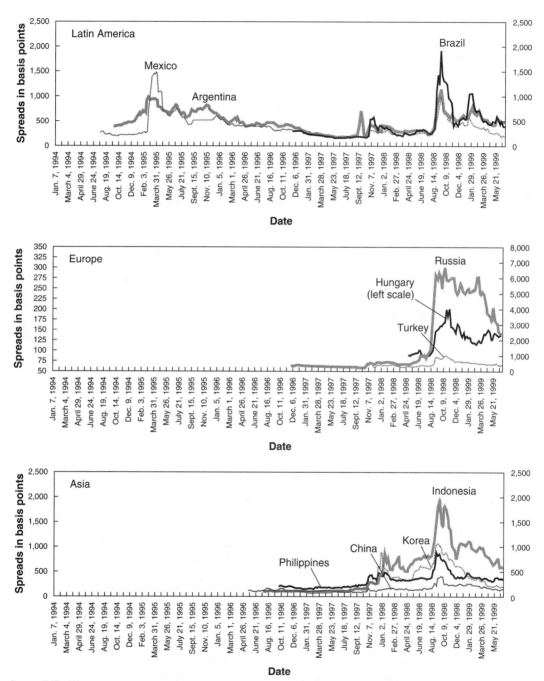

Source: IMF 1999.

[1]Latin America: Republic of Argentina bond due December 3, United Mexican States bond due September 2, and Republic of Brazil bond due November 1. Europe: National Bank of Hungary bond due April 3, Republic of Turkey bond due May 2, and Ministry of Finance of Russia bond due November 1. Asia: People's Republic of China bond due November 3, Republic of Indonesia bond due August 6, Republic of Philippines bond due October 16, and Korea Development Bank bond due November 3.

FIGURE 11-3 *Bid-Ask Spreads in Emerging Bond Markets (As Percent of Bond Prices)*

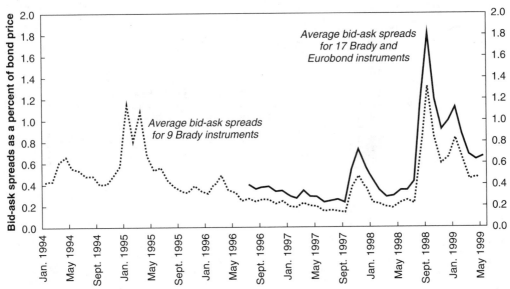

Source: Staff calculations based on data from J.P. Morgan; IMF 1999.

The Flight to Quality and Treasury Yields

Treasury securities generally have lower yields than other fixed-income products because of their safety and liquidity. At times, the market's concern about risk and liquidity has become pronounced, resulting in a "flight to quality" into Treasury securities despite their lower yields.

Such a flight occurred in the fall of 1998. After the devaluation of the Russian ruble in August of that year and subsequent difficulties in other emerging-market economies, investors' aversion toward risk appeared to intensify. That sentiment was reinforced by the prospect of a default by Long-Term Capital Management, a prominent hedge fund that in August and September had sustained sharp losses from its investment positions. By generating sizable losses for the firm's counterparties and forcing the abrupt unwinding of the firm's extensive positions in the Treasury and other markets, a default could have significantly disrupted markets.[1]

Liquidity in many markets declined sharply over this period, with bid-offer spreads widening and large transactions becoming more difficult to complete. Anecdotal reports suggest that bid-offer spreads on Treasury securities widened from their normal levels of 1.6¢ or less per $100 to as high as 16¢ for on-the-run issues and 25¢ for off-the-run issues. Moreover, investors showed a dramatic preference for the greater liquidity offered by on-the-run issues. Yield spreads between the most recently issued and second most recently issued securities (the liquidity premium on on-the-run securities) widened sharply, as investors were willing to hold the more liquid securities at lower yields (chart).

The increased concern about liquidity and the reduced willingness of investors to bear risk also caused a widening of spreads between other fixed-income securities and Treasury securities. The widening affected even highly rated debt. Market strains began to subside following the Federal Reserve inter-meeting policy easing on October 15, 1998. Soon thereafter, bid-offer spreads on Treasury securities, premiums for on-the-run issues, and yield spreads between government-sponsored enterprise and Treasury securities began to decline.

Liquidity premium on on-the-run five-year
Treasury security

Yield spread on AA corporate bond index
over on-the-run five-year Treasury note

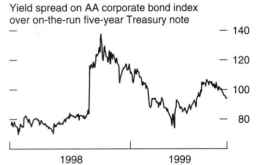

Source: Bloomberg.
Note: Data are daily and extend through October 1999.

Source: Dupont and Sack 1999.

[1]*Hedge Funds, Leverage, and the Lessons of Long-Term Capital Management,* Report of the President's Working Group on Financial Markets (April 1999).

PROBLEMS

11.1 What are some of the factors that influence the spreads between emerging-market bonds and Treasury securities with similar characteristics?

11.2 Briefly explain Brady bonds. What are the important contractual provisions in Brady bonds?

11.3 What are collective action clauses? How do they help sovereign lenders in the bond markets?

11.4 Explain briefly the functions of the London Club and the Paris Club.

11.5 What is your understanding of flight to quality or flight to liquidity?

REFERENCES

Bernstein, R., and J.A. Penicook, Jr. 1998. Emerging Market Debt: Practical Portfolio Considerations, in Emerging Markets Capital Flows. In Emerging Markets Capital Flows. Edited by Richard Levich. Norwell, MA: Kluwer Academic Publishers.

Cunningham, A. 1999. Emerging Economy Spread Indices and Financial Stability. *Financial Stability Review* (November). Bank of England.

Dupont, D., and B. Sack. 1999. "The Treasury Securities Market: Overview and Recent Developments." Federal Reserve Bulletin (December): 785–806.

International Capital Markets: Developments, Prospects and Key Policy Issues. (September 1999). International Monetary Fund.

Levich, R. 1998. *Emerging Markets Capital Flows.* Norwell, MA: Kluwer Academic Publishers.

Chapter 12

Portfolio-Management Techniques

Chapter Objectives

This chapter describes the portfolio-management principles that are relevant to pension funds, insurance companies, and portfolio- and asset-management companies. We discuss how the asset-management practices are intertwined with the liability structure of the company. We address the following questions:

- What is the nature of the liabilities of pension plans, insurance companies, and commercial banks? How do they affect their asset-management practices?
- What are matched-funding techniques?
- What is immunization?
- How are portfolios indexed?
- What is the concept of portfolio insurance?

INTRODUCTION

Fixed-income portfolios account for a significant part of the money management sector, which includes mutual funds, pension funds, insurance companies, and other money management firms, including hedge funds. A number of issues are in overall portfolio-management activity. These issues are best understood in the context of the risks of fixed-income securities, discussed in Chapter 1. The portfolio should be assembled to achieve an appropriate balance between the objectives that have been set out for the portfolio-management firm and the various dimensions of risks that are present in different sectors of the fixed-income markets. For example, if the objective of the portfolio manager is to provide for the safety of capital and liquidity, then the composition of the portfolio should be more heavily weighted toward the Treasury, agency, and high-grade corporate sectors of the fixed-income markets. On the other hand, if the objective of the portfolio manager is to provide high growth, then other sectors, such as strips and mortgage-backed securities, are more relevant.

Portfolio management is guided to a certain extent by the underlying liabilities, the degree depending on the nature of the underlying business. At one extreme, portfolios are managed to maximize the expected return subject to some constraints on the level of risk—in such portfolio management situations, liabilities do not play a very active part. The sponsor of a pension plan may assign part of the pension assets to a

371

professional money manager for a prespecified period with the expectation that the re-turns on the assets will be maximized during that period. In such a case, the liabilities (pension obligations) do not enter directly in the portfolio-management problem faced by the professional money manager. If the value of the assets fall, however, sooner or later the sponsor of the pension plan will exert pressure on the money manager to generate a surplus over the liability. Thus, the liabilities will start to dictate the asset-management problem. At the other extreme, portfolio selection may be entirely dictated by the liabilities. An example of this would be the dedicated portfolio construction, where a minimum-cost portfolio is constructed to meet a defined schedule of liabilities. This is typical of municipalities and local governments that invite bids from dealers for dedicated portfolios to implement bond defeasence and capital expenditures.

NATURE OF THE UNDERLYING BUSINESS AND PORTFOLIO MANAGEMENT

We now investigate how portfolio management is affected by the nature of the busi-ness that needs asset management and the underlying economic function that the port-folio manager has to provide.

Pension Funds

For pension plans, the portfolio manager is one of many managing the pension funds of a firm, and the overriding concern is to make sure that the funds are managed to meet the pension liabilities. The penalty for not meeting the liability should be high, and the incentives for building a surplus should be great. Pension liabilities (obligations) are long-term and are reasonably predictable. Such factors as mortality and employee turnover typically influence pension obligations. Actuaries are quite conservative and may value liabilities by using discount rates that are not necessarily reflected in the market yields on fixed-income securities of a similar duration. The implications for such a discrepancy for portfolio management are discussed fully later in the chapter. The liabilities are typically correlated with future wages, which are in turn correlated with the stock market. Liabilities are also long-dated with a high duration; thus, the lia-bility has both interest rate and equity exposure. First, to get an appreciation of the as-sets that are under the management of pension plans, review Tables 12-1 and 12-2.

Table 12-3 summarizes the key features of the liabilities of pension plans. Re-member that the assets are typically managed by a number of professional money managers.

Insurance Companies

Insurance companies have a product mix consisting of guaranteed investment con-tracts (GICs), insurance policies, annuities, and so on. The proceeds from the sale of such products must then be invested in assets in such a way as to maximize profits. The link between assets and liabilities should be rather tight in the asset-allocation

TABLE 12-1   *Growth of Pension Assets (in Billions of U.S. Dollars)*

Year	1950	1960	1970	1980	1982	1984	1986	1987	1988	1989
Assets of Private Pension Plans	13	57	153	627	787	1,000	1,349	1,464	1,634	1,836
Assets of Public Pension Plans	12	34	88	275	361	487	638	706	814	950

Source: U.S. Federal Reserve Board.

Flow of funds accounts and EBRI tabulations based on American Council of Life Insurance data.

TABLE 12-2 *Defined Benefits (DB) and Defined Contribution (DC) Plans*		DB Plan		DC Plan	
	Year	Assets*	Percent	Assets*	Percent
	1950	45	88.24	6	11.76
	1955	92	85.19	16	14.81
	1960	153	82.26	33	17.74
	1965	270	79.18	71	20.82
	1970	323	76.54	99	23.46
	1975	360	74.23	125	25.77
	1981	574	72.20	221	27.80
	1990**	902	68.02	424	31.98
	2000**	1,453	65.10	779	34.90

Source: EBRI Databook on employee benefits.

*In billions of 1984 U.S. dollars

**Projected estimates

TABLE 12-3   *Pension Plan Liabilities*

Plan	Liability
Defined contribution plans	Pay as you go. Money is placed by investors in assets and portfolios of their choice.
Defined benefits plan	Long-dated liabilities. Highly interest-rate sensitive and correlated with future wages. Asset allocation and funding are regulated. Turnover in the labor market, mortality, etc.

policies used by the insurance companies. If the assets provide a better return than the cost associated with meeting the obligations under GICs, insurance products, and annuities, then the insurance company makes a profit. Sometimes the spread between the return on assets and the cost of meeting the liabilities is boosted by assuming additional credit risk (by investing in junk bonds, for instance) or by assuming illiquidity (by investing in real estate, for example) or by lack of diversification. Table 12-4 summarizes the key features of the liabilities of insurance companies.

TABLE 12-4   *Insurance Company Liabilities*

Nature of Insurance	*Liability*
Life insurance	Annuities, GICs, life-insurance products. Interest-rate sensitive. They also depend on mortality rates and demographic factors. Insurance products have optionlike features, which affect the interest-rate exposure significantly.
Property insurance	The liabilities are related to industry and project-specific risks. Liabilities require very close management and technical knowledge.

The liabilities tend to have a very strong interest-rate exposure. Many of the products sold by insurance companies have several contractual provisions that qualitatively alter the interest-rate exposure. For example, whole-life insurance policies that are offered by insurance companies often extend a line of credit to the insured individual. Such loans also provide a cap on the borrowing costs. The net effect of these provisions is that when the interest rates increase, the policy options increase in value. Another example of an option that an insured individual has is to buy additional insurance at prespecified rates. Other insurance products, such as GICs, may also contain specified options. In these cases, insurance companies have sold policy options whose values are extremely sensitive to interest-rate changes.

Banks and Financial Institutions

Traditionally, banks and financial institutions borrow in the short-term maturity sector. Typically, they issue CDs or floating-rate notes (FRNs) that are indexed to short-term interest rates. The proceeds are then loaned out to projects that have longer maturities. Here, the primary source of risk is the possibility that the shape of the yield curve might shift. In particular, the possibility that the curve might become inverted poses a big threat to the profitability of the bank. Advanced techniques, such as securitization, are used to alleviate this risk, in part. In addition, the nature of the bank's business automatically entails the assumption of credit risk (the experience of U.S. Banks with Latin American loans is an obvious case in point) and illiquidity (such as a real estate portfolio). Table 12-5 summarizes the key features of bank liabilities.

Portfolio Management

We have considered three important segments of portfolio-management industry. Depending on the segment, the liability of the firm will influence the asset-allocation process to a greater or lesser extent. There are also tax-related incentives for some of these segments not to invest in certain areas of fixed-income markets. For example,

TABLE 12-5
Bank Liabilities

Bank Activity	*Liabilities*
Domestic loans and deposits	Credit risk, yield-curve risks. Generally illiquid.
Foreign loans and liabilities	Foreign-exchange risks, interest-rate risks.
Investment portfolio	Varying credit and liquidity.

TABLE 12-6   *Portfolio Management Considerations*

Dimension	*Portfolio Management Implications*
Liability characteristics	If the penalty for not meeting the liability is very high, then portfolio management is pinned down almost entirely by the features of the liabilities. In other extreme cases, assets may be managed as per stated policies, as in certain mutual funds.
Tax status	Special tax incentives may induce certain preferences in portfolio management (e.g., pension funds may prefer corporates and avoid municipals).
Charter and legal restrictions	Diversification across different sectors. Short sale restrictions. Ability to trade in derivatives.
Operating policies	Stated policies may require investment in only certain sectors.

pension funds are tax-exempt and as a consequence do not generally invest in tax-exempt municipal bond markets. Similar incentives exist for insurance companies as well.

In addition, there are legal and regulatory restrictions on asset allocation. For example, plan charters tend to impose restrictions on the percentage of assets that may be placed in any one sector of the fixed-income market.

Broadly, we may characterize the important aspects of portfolio management as in Table 12-6.

We will explore next different portfolio-management techniques used extensively in the industry. First, we will consider matched-funding portfolio-management strategies. In this category are (1) dedicated-portfolio policies, (2) immunization policies, (3) horizon matching, and (4) contingent immunization policies. Then, we will explore other policies, such as indexation and portfolio insurance, which are much more dynamic and have greater flexibility in their implementation. These strategies are used extensively in practice. An article from *Pension World* (Zirky and Mackey 1993) illustrates the relevance of these strategies to institutional investors.

Pension Plan Funding Strategies: Defining Terms

By Emad A. Zirky and Robert M. Mackey

Mitchell Hutchins

New York

Matched funding investment strategies are used to fund pension plan liabilities. There seems to be a degree of confusion, within the Taft-Hartley community, as to the meaning of some of the terms used to describe the process. The following information is offered to give a clearer understanding of each strategy, as well as to explain the appropriate application of each technique.

The amount of future pension fund benefit obligations is typically estimated using actuarial projections of such variables as life expectancies, future salaries, inflation, and time of service. Two factors make the funding status of these liabilities more important today than ever before:

1) The amount of these obligations, which approaches the total net worth of the sponsors for some of the more mature plans; and,

2) The reporting requirements under FASB 87.

The Financial Accounting Standards Boards' (FASB) Statement 87 requires corporations to "mark-to-market" the value of their pension obligations. This means that corporations must use existing market rates of interest to discount the future liabilities and arrive at a present value for these obligations. In addition, FASB 87 requires this present value to be compared with the pension assets to arrive at a funded status (surplus or deficit) of the pension plan. This status must be reported on the balance sheet, and any changes in this status reported on the income statement. Matched-funding strategies are an ideal means of controlling the risk of this funded status.

There are four fixed income investment strategies which are used to help meet the future benefit obligations:

1) Dedication: fixed income portfolio structured so that cash flow (interest + maturities) is available as pre-determined obligations become payable.

2) Horizon-matching: fixed income portfolio constructed to match interest rate sensitivity of the liabilities while at the same time having a dedicated structure for the nearer term obligations.

3) Immunization: fixed income portfolio structured for a fixed period to meet a predetermined target amount. Matches interest rate sensitivity of the assets to the liabilities.

4) Dollar-duration matching: same as immunization, but does not assume that the value of the assets and liabilities are equal.

In deciding which strategy is most suitable, we must look at the nature of the future obligation. For these purposes, it is useful to distinguish between two categories of pension fund liabilities: retired-lives benefits and active-lives benefits.

Future Retiree Payments

As the name implies, retired-lives benefits consist of the future payments to be made to current retirees. Here, the benefits are set—with the exception of any future cost-of-living adjustments which may be made—and the only estimation to be made is with regard to mortality. Since these obligations can be estimated with a high degree of confidence, dedication that matches these obligations with cash flows from the portfolio is an appropriate strategy.

A flexible, less costly solution is a strategy known as horizon-matching. This technique utilizes a portfolio of assets constructed to match the interest rate sensitivity of the liabilities while cash-matching the nearer term, more predictable obligations. In this way, benefit payments can be made directly from the cash flow of the portfolio, while the elimination of the strict cash-matching in the later years provides greater flexibility in incorporating new or revised liabilities should the need arise. In addition, this more flexible structure is less expensive than strict dedication, and it allows greater opportunity in adding value to the portfolio. Matched funding techniques are somewhat less precise, but still useful when applied to active-lives benefits.

The Projected Payments

Active-lives benefits refer to the projected payments to be made to employees who haven't yet retired. Since benefits typically increase with salary and years of service, these obligations are much more difficult to predict. For this reason, dedication is generally inappropriate for the funding of active-lives benefits, but immunization, which matches the interest rate sensitivity of the assets with that of the liabilities, can be a useful strategy. While immunization, from a total return perspective, is advantageous only when rates are "high," from a risk management perspective, it is always a valuable tool. Regardless of the level of interest rates, a portfolio of assets that matches the interest rate sensitivity of the liabilities represents the riskless posture with respect to the funding status of the pension plan.

In addition, from a total return perspective, we must be careful in our determination of the attractiveness of current interest rate levels. While interest rates have certainly retreated from their highs of the early 80s, current rates are still significantly above their all-time historical averages. Horizon-matching, which again combines dedication and immunization, can also be useful if the sponsor wishes to fund near-term payments from the portfolio.

Finally, a strategy which is appropriate when the liabilities are not fully match-funded (fixed-income assets less than the present value of the liabilities) is known as dollar-duration matching. Typically, a sponsor will wish to allocate some portion of the plan assets to equities or other assets in the hopes of earning higher returns than those which might be available in the fixed-income markets. Dollar-duration matching, like immunization, matches the interest rate sensitivity of the assets to that of the liabilities. However, while classical immunization assumes the values of the assets and liabilities are equal, dollar-duration matching considers the relative values of the assets and liabilities and adjusts for any difference.

For example, if a pension fund has assets equal to its liabilities (i.e., it is fully funded), but wishes to allocate one-half of the assets to equities, a dollar-duration matched portfolio would require assets with an interest rate sensitivity equal to twice that of the liabilities.

Offset by Value Change

While the dollar allocation to fixed-income securities would be only one-half of the present value of the liabilities, a change in the present value of the liabilities due to a change in interest rates would be offset by an equal change in the value of the fixed-income (dollar-duration matched) portfolio.

It should be kept in mind that these strategies have applications regardless of the current funded status of the plan. For overfunded plans, matched-funded strategies can be used to hedge the interest rate risk of the liabilities (i.e., fully match-fund the liabilities).

The sponsor can then invest the surplus as aggressively as desired without fear of endangering the funded status of the plan. With underfunded plans, a dollar-duration matched strategy can be used to match the interest rate sensitivity of the liabilities while the sponsor attempts to make up the deficit.

Horizon-matching can also be used in conjunction with a dollar-duration matching strategy regardless of the plan's funded status, if it is desired that benefit payments be made from the cash flow of the portfolio.

MATCHED FUNDING

Dedicated Portfolios

In a number of situations, corporations, local governments, and other institutions are faced with the task of funding a stream of liabilities in the future. In the case of corporations, the liability could be the obligations associated with the pension plans that are in place. The sponsoring firm may have to fund a stream of projected benefits that are payable to retiring employees. The firm may either buy guaranteed investment contracts (GICs) or fund them by buying a suitable portfolio of assets. GICs are typically offered by insurance companies. For a local government, the problem may be one of funding projected capital expenditures to build a highway or a bridge, for example. Matched-funding techniques are used in such situations.

A dedicated portfolio consists of buying a minimum-cost portfolio from a universe of securities subject to restrictions on callability, credit quality, sectors, and so on. The universe of assets may be defined as in Table 12-7. The choice of admissible securities is based on several considerations. First, the universe should not include any security that has significant uncertainty about the timing of future cash flows or about the magnitude of future cash flows. This consideration rules out floating-rate notes, bonds that are callable before the liabilities are due, and mortgage-backed securities that carry significant prepayment risks. Second, the universe should be chosen to ensure a minimum acceptable level of credit risk. Typically, this means that only investment-grade securities are included in the universe of securities. While Treasuries naturally satisfy this requirement, they are also the most expensive choice. Typically, agency securities and corporates of investment credits may be safely included. To the extent possible, the universe should include securities that minimize reinvestment risks. This feature should call for strips whose maturities come closest to the liability dates. Finally, there is no need to include securities that mature after the last payment date in the liability schedule. Transaction costs, bid-offer spreads, and so on may also be incorporated in the solution procedure.

We will illustrate these basic concepts in the context of simple examples.

TABLE 12-7			
Universe of Securities	*Security*	*Contractual Features*	*Credit Risk*
	U.S. Treasury	Noncallable	Negligible
	Strips	Noncallable	Negligible
	Agency	Noncallable	Low
	Investment-grade corporates	May be callable	Moderate
	Junk bonds		Risky

Example 12-1:

Consider the problem of funding a stream of pension liabilities consisting of $100 million per year for the next three years. Consider a liability schedule facing the corporation over the next three years with the cash flows due at the end of every year, as shown in Table 12-8. Typically, such a liability schedule will come from the institutions that need to fund the cash outlays associated with capital expenditures or bond-defeasence activities.

We will assume that the universe of securities consists of three coupon bonds and three strips, as shown in Table 12-9. The matched-funding strategy then consists of finding the minimum-cost portfolio of assets from the universe specified in Table 12-9, subject to the condition that all the liabilities are met.

From Table 12-9, we can determine the strip rates as follows: the price of strip 1 should equal its discounted face value. Hence,

$$94.3396 = \frac{100}{(1 + y_1)},$$

or
$$y_1 = 6\%.$$

Similarly, the price of strip 2 implies that

$$85.7339 = \frac{100}{(1 + y_2)^2},$$

or
$$y_2 = 8\%.$$

Finally, the price of strip 3 implies a three-year strip rate y_3 such that

$$75.1315 = \frac{100}{(1 + y_3)^3},$$

or
$$y_3 = 10\%.$$

TABLE 12-8 *Liability Schedule* *(in Millions of Dollars)*	*Year 1*	*Year 2*	*Year 3*
Liabilities	100	100	100

TABLE 12-9   *Universe of Securities, Example 12-1*

Security	*Price at* *Year 0*	*Cash Flow* *at Year 1*	*Cash Flow* *at Year 2*	*Cash Flow* *at Year 3*
Bond 1	100.6520	10	10	110
Bond 2	95.5480	8	8	108
Bond 3	105.7561	12	12	112
Strip 1	94.3396	100	0	0
Strip 2	85.7339	0	100	0
Strip 3	75.1315	0	0	100

Using the concepts developed in Chapter 5, we can calculate the implied spot rates for years 1, 2, and 3 from the coupon-bond prices in Table 12-9. If r_1, r_2, and r_3 are the implied spot rates, then the coupon-bond prices must satisfy:

$$100.6520 = \frac{10}{1 + r_1} + \frac{10}{(1 + r_2)^2} + \frac{110}{(1 + r_3)^3}, \tag{12.1}$$

$$95.5480 = \frac{8}{1 + r_1} + \frac{8}{(1 + r_2)^2} + \frac{108}{(1 + r_3)^3}, \tag{12.2}$$

and

$$105.7561 = \frac{12}{1 + r_1} + \frac{12}{(1 + r_2)^2} + \frac{112}{(1 + r_3)^3}. \tag{12.3}$$

Solving Equations 12.1, 12.2, and 12.3 we can verify that $r_1 = y_1$, $r_2 = y_2$, and $r_3 = y_3$.

The simplest strategy is to buy the relevant strips to fully fund the liabilities. In this problem, this strategy will be to buy 100 units of each strip. The total cost of this strategy is

$$94.3396 + 85.7339 + 75.1315 = 255.20.$$

Is there a cheaper alternative? In a world where there are no arbitrage opportunities, the present value of the liabilities should be always equal to the present value of assets that we buy to fund. In Table 12-9, the prices are chosen so that there are no arbitrage opportunities. The spot rates indicated by the three coupon bonds for the maturities 1, 2, and 3 years are precisely the same as the strip rates for those maturities, respectively.

The cash flows from the dedicated portfolio will match the liabilities dollar for dollar under the most conservative reinvestment assumptions. Clearly, as we relax the credit quality and permit more aggressive reinvestment assumptions, we will find a lower-cost portfolio. The true cost, however, may be higher. Portfolios may be rededicated from time to time as spreads change. The problem may then be solved as a linear programming problem, for which efficient algorithms are currently available for computation. Consider the matched-funding strategy posed formally as a linear programming problem next.

Example 12-2:

Choose n_i such that

$$\min_{\{n_1, n_2, \dots, n_N\}} \sum_{i=1}^{N} n_i P_{i0}$$

subject to the funding constraints shown next:

$$\sum_{i=1}^{N} n_i x_{i1} \geq 100,$$

$$\sum_{i=1}^{N} n_i x_{i2} \geq 100,$$

and

$$\sum_{i=1}^{N} n_i x_{i3} \geq 100,$$

where P_{i0} is the price of security i at date 0, x_{i1} is the cash flow from security i at date 1, etc. We choose n_i, the number of each security to buy at date 0, to fully fund the liabilities at all future dates. We might also wish to specify additional constraints $n_i \geq 0$. For Example 12-1, the constraints take the form:

$$n_1 10 + n_2 8 + n_3 12 + n_4 100 + n_5 0 + n_6 0 \geq 100$$

$$n_1 10 + n_2 8 + n_3 12 + n_4 0 + n_5 100 + n_6 0 \geq 100$$

$$n_1 110 + n_2 108 + n_3 112 + n_4 0 + n_5 0 + n_6 100 \geq 100.$$

Let

$$x = n_1 100.652 + n_2 95.5479 + n_3 105.7561 + n_4 94.3396$$

$$+ n_5 85.7334 + n_6 75.1315$$

be the total cost. Then, we pick n_i ($i = 1, 2, \ldots, 6$) so that $n_i \geq 0$ and the total cost x is minimized. See Table 12-10 for the optimal allocation.

The solution for this simple linear programming problem follows: The total cost of this strategy is the same as the strategy of buying the three strips.

From Table 12-10 and the bond prices in Table 12-9, we can compute the total cost of the dedicated portfolio as follows:

$$0.2065(100.6520) + 0.2291(95.5480) + 0.1839(105.7561) + 0.9389(94.3396)$$

$$+ 0.9389(85.7339) + 0.3194(75.1315) = 255.20.$$

Thus, the cost of this portfolio is the same as buying the strips.

TABLE 12-10	Security	Allocation
Optimal Allocation, Example 12-2		
	Bond 1	0.2065
	Bond 2	0.2291
	Bond 3	0.1839
	Strip 1	0.9389
	Strip 2	0.9389
	Strip 3	0.3194

In Example 12-2, the spot rates and the strip rates are identical, and as a result, there is no improvement in the cost of the dedicated portfolio. In reality, as we have seen in Chapter 5, spot rates differ from strip rates. Such factors as liquidity and taxes introduce the differences. This means that the inclusion of both bonds and strips should produce an improvement in the cost of the dedicated portfolio.

Example 12-3:

Consider a slightly different universe, but admit the possibility that the spot rates differ from strip rates (Table 12-11).

For Example 12-3, we note that the strip rates are exactly as before, so $y_1 = 6\%$, $y_2 = 8\%$, and $y_3 = 10\%$. This is because the strip prices in Table 12-11 are the same as the ones in Table 12-9. The bond universe and their prices in Table 12-11 have changed. This will produce different implied spot rates. We use the bond prices in Table 12-11 to set up the following conditions:

$$100 = \frac{10}{1 + r_1} + \frac{110}{(1 + r_2)^2} + \frac{0}{(1 + r_3)^3} \tag{12.4}$$

$$95 = \frac{8}{1 + r_1} + \frac{8}{(1 + r_2)^2} + \frac{108}{(1 + r_3)^3} \tag{12.5}$$

$$105 = \frac{12}{1 + r_1} + \frac{12}{(1 + r_2)^2} + \frac{112}{(1 + r_3)^3}. \tag{12.6}$$

Solving Equations 12.4 through 12.6, we get the implied spot rates as $r_1 = 8.11\%$, $r_2 = 10.10\%$, and $r_3 = 10.06\%$.

Since the implied spot rates are higher than the strip rates, we expect the minimum-cost portfolio to consist of more bonds based on our analysis.

The optimal allocation from the linear programming formulation is shown in Table 12-12. Note the reduction in cost that is brought about by the inclusion of bonds in the universe, as compared to the cost of funding using strips alone.

The minimum-cost portfolio is valued at $0.8117(100) + 0.8929(105) + 0.8117(94.3396) = 251.49$, which is less than the cost of buying the strips to fund the liabilities.

Example 12-3 is admittedly simple. The complications that typically arise in the context of real-life dedications include reinvestment rates, transaction costs, and subsequent rededications.

Reinvestment Rates. The formulation so far assumes that the coupon dates and redemption dates coincide with the dates on which cash flows are due to meet the liabilities. It is often the case that the liability payment dates are different from the coupon payment dates. Under these circumstances, we need to forecast the reinvestment rates at which cash flows from bonds will be carried forward until the liabilities become due.

TABLE 12-11   *Universe of Securities, Example 12-3*

Security	Price at Year 0	Cash Flow at Year 1	Cash Flow at Year 2	Cash Flow at Year 3
Bond 1	100.000	10	110	0
Bond 2	95.000	8	8	108
Bond 3	105.0000	12	12	112
Strip 1	94.3396	100	0	0
Strip 2	85.7339	0	100	0
Strip 3	75.1315	0	0	100

TABLE 12-12

Optimal Allocation, Example 12-3

Security	Allocation
Bond 1	0.8117
Bond 2	0.00
Bond 3	0.8929
Strip 1	0.8117
Strip 2	0.00
Strip 3	0.00

Example 12-4:

Let us reformulate Example 12-2 by assuming that the coupon dates and the maturity dates of securities occur at dates 0.5, 1.5, and 2.5, whereas the liabilities are due at dates 1, 2, and 3. The formulation of the linear programming problem is modified as follows:

$$\min_{\{n_1, n_2, \ldots, n_N\}} \sum_{i=1}^{N} n_i P_{i0}$$

subject to the funding constraints:

$$\sum_{i=1}^{N} n_i x_{i1} \times (1 + R)^{0.5} \geq 100,$$

$$\sum_{i=1}^{N} n_i x_{i2} \times (1 + R)^{0.5} \geq 100,$$

and

$$\sum_{i=1}^{N} n_i x_{i3} \times (1 + R)^{0.5} \geq 100,$$

where P_{i0} is the price of security i at date 0, x_{i1} is the cash flow from security i at date 1, etc. We assume that cash flows can be reinvested at a rate R.

TABLE 12-13   *Effect of Reinvestment-Rate Assumption on Minimum-Cost Portfolio*

Security	Reinvestment Rate					
	1%	*2%*	*3%*	*4%*	*5%*	*6%*
Bond 1	0.376	0.642	0.572	0.310	0.308	0.307
Bond 2	0.400	0.161	0.068	0.073	0.071	0.070
Bond 3	0.000	0.066	0.252	0.502	0.500	0.498
Strip 1	0.925	0.905	0.892	0.884	0.879	0.875
Strip 2	0.925	0.905	0.892	0.884	0.879	0.875
Strip 3	0.149	0.036	0.000	0.000	0.000	0.000
Minimum cost	253.36	252.1	250.74	249.83	248.52	247.20

It should be clear that the reinvestment-rate assumption will affect the minimum cost of the portfolio, as well as its composition in general. Note that as the assumed reinvestment rate increases, the minimum cost of the portfolio decreases. Table 12-13 illustrates the effect of the reinvestment rate on the composition and the cost of the minimum-cost portfolio. Note that the minimum-cost portfolio changes as the reinvestment-rate assumptions change. Strips are an integral part of the dedicated portfolio for all reinvestment rates. Bonds become a part of the dedicated portfolio only at certain reinvestment rates.

Transactions Costs. Another problem that is important in dedicated-portfolio problems is the transactions costs and the bid-offer spreads that are encountered when securities are transacted. Using linear programming formulations, most reasonable transactions-costs specifications are easily incorporated.

Rededication. Once the dedicated portfolio is constructed, the initial optimal-funding policy has been found. This does not mean that the original portfolio will continue to be the optimal portfolio as the levels of interest rates and the spreads across markets and maturities change through time. So, as a practical matter, it is useful to reevaluate the optimality of the original portfolio from time to time. In addition, there may be opportunities for rededication when there are qualitative shifts in yields and the shape of the yield curve, and in intermarket spreads.

Immunization

Note that the dedicated-portfolio technique gives the portfolio manager little room for manipulation. Once the universe is defined and the inputs are prepared, the asset allocation becomes fairly straightforward; the policy has, in general, little upside potential. An alternative portfolio-management technique, that is popular in the fixed-income portfolio sector, is the immunization technique.

Running an immunized portfolio assumes the following:

- The present value of the assets must match the present value of the liabilities.
- The duration (or interest-rate sensitivity) of the assets must match the duration of the liabilities.

- The assets must have a dominance pattern over the liabilities for prescribed changes in yields. This dominance pattern requires that certain second-order effects, such as convexity of assets, exceed those of the liabilities. This issue was discussed in Chapter 5 in detail.

Unlike dedicated portfolios, immunization requires dynamic portfolio rebalancing over time. Also, the possibility of unanticipated deficits is greater in the immunization setting, compared to the dedicated-portfolio setting.

We will illustrate the immunization concept, continuing to develop our example.

Example 12-5:

In Table 12-9, we assume that the yield to maturity of strip 1 is 6%, of strip 2 is 8%, and of strip 3 is 10%. Let us consider the immunization strategy using strip 3. The duration of liability when the market yields are at 10% is $D = 1.942$. In Table 12-14, we show the duration of the liability at yield levels varying from 0% to 18%. Note that the duration of strips is always equal to its remaining time to maturity. In order to immunize the liability, the duration of the liability must be equal to the duration of the strip. In order to do this, we impose the following condition:

$$0 = \frac{n_3 P_3}{V_p} D_3 + \frac{P_L}{V_p} D_L, \tag{12.7}$$

where n_3 is the number of strip 3, P_3 is the price of strip 3 (= 75.1315), D_3 is the duration of the strip (= 3), and P_L is the market value of liabilities (= 248.69). The total value of the portfolio is

$$V_p = n_3 P_3 + P_L.$$

Solving for n_3, we get

$$n_3 = -\frac{P_L}{V_p} D_L \times \frac{V_p}{P_3 D_3} \tag{12.8}$$

$$n_3 = -\frac{248.69}{V_p} \times 1.94 \times \frac{V_p}{3 \times 75.1315} = -2.14. \tag{12.9}$$

Note that once we select the number of strips to buy to immunize the liability schedule, the market value of the strip is also automatically determined. This means that while we are able to match the duration of the liability with that of the asset (strip 3), the funding of the liability is still at risk—we have provided a hedge for price risk but not for cash-flow funding. The market values of the liability and the asset are shown in Table 12-14 for different interest rate scenarios. Note that the price risks are hedged reasonably. As time passes, the liabilities will become due. For example, at date 1, a cash outflow of 100 will be required. This should be met by selling the requisite amount of strip 3 and rebalancing the position to immunize the liabilities once again.

TABLE 12-14   *Present Value of Liabilities and Assets as a Function of Discount Rates*

	0%	1%	2%	3%	4%	5%	6%
Value of liability	300.00	294.10	288.39	282.86	277.51	272.32	267.30
Duration of liability	2.00	1.99	1.99	1.98	1.97	1.97	1.96
Value of bond 1	130.00	126.47	123.07	119.80	116.65	113.62	110.69
Duration of bond 1	2.77	2.77	2.76	2.76	2.76	2.75	2.75
Value of bond 2	124.00	120.59	117.30	114.14	111.10	108.17	105.35
Duration of bond 2	2.81	2.80	2.80	2.80	2.79	2.79	2.79
Value of bond 3	136.00	132.35	128.84	125.46	122.20	119.06	116.04
Duration of bond 3	2.74	2.73	2.73	2.72	2.72	2.72	2.71
Value of Strip 1	100.00	99.01	98.04	97.09	96.15	95.24	94.34
Duration of Strip 1	1.00	1.00	1.00	1.00	1.00	1.00	1.00
Value of Strip 2	100.00	98.03	96.12	94.26	92.46	90.70	89.00
Duration of Strip 2	2.00	2.00	2.00	2.00	2.00	2.00	2.00
Value of Strip 3	100.00	97.06	94.23	91.51	88.90	86.38	83.96
Duration of Strip 3	3.00	3.00	3.00	3.00	3.00	3.00	3.00

	7%	8%	9%	10%	11%	12%
Value of liability	262.43	257.71	253.13	**248.69**	244.37	240.18
Duration of liability	1.95	1.95	1.94	**1.94**	1.93	1.92
Value of bond 1	107.87	105.15	102.53	**100.00**	97.56	95.20
Duration of bond 1	2.75	2.74	2.74	**2.74**	2.73	2.73
Value of bond 2	102.62	100.00	97.47	**95.03**	92.67	90.39
Duration of bond 2	2.79	2.78	2.78	**2.78**	2.77	2.77
Value of bond 3	113.12	110.31	107.59	**104.97**	102.44	100.00
Duration of bond 3	2.71	2.71	2.70	**2.70**	2.69	2.69
Value of Strip 1	93.46	92.59	91.74	**90.91**	90.09	89.29
Duration of Strip 1	1.00	1.00	1.00	**1.00**	1.00	1.00
Value of Strip 2	87.34	85.73	84.17	**82.64**	81.16	79.72
Duration of Strip 2	2.00	2.00	2.00	**2.00**	2.00	2.00
Value of Strip 3	81.63	79.38	77.22	**75.13**	73.12	71.18
Duration of Strip 3	3.00	3.00	3.00	**3.00**	3.00	3.00

	13%	14%	15%	16%	17%	18%
Value of liability	236.12	232.16	228.32	224.59	220.96	217.43
Duration of liability	1.92	1.91	1.91	1.90	1.90	1.89
Value of bond 1	92.92	90.71	88.58	86.52	84.53	82.61
Duration of bond 1	2.73	2.72	2.72	2.71	2.71	2.71
Value of bond 2	88.19	86.07	84.02	82.03	80.11	78.26
Duration of bond 2	2.77	2.77	2.76	2.76	2.76	2.75
Value of bond 3	97.64	95.36	93.15	91.02	88.95	86.95
Duration of bond 3	2.69	2.68	2.68	2.67	2.67	2.67
Value of Strip 1	88.50	87.72	86.96	86.21	85.47	84.75
Duration of Strip 1	1.00	1.00	1.00	1.00	1.00	1.00
Value of Strip 2	78.31	76.95	75.61	74.32	73.05	71.82
Duration of Strip 2	2.00	2.00	2.00	2.00	2.00	2.00
Value of Strip 3	69.31	67.50	65.75	64.07	62.44	60.86
Duration of Strip 3	3.00	3.00	3.00	3.00	3.00	3.00

Let us summarize the advantages and disadvantages of immunization strategy as compared to the dedicated-portfolio strategy:

- Immunization strategy has a much greater flexibility. The portfolio manager has the choice of selecting a wide range of assets to immunize the liability schedule. In Example 12-5, then, although we chose strip 3, any other combination of assets could have been chosen.
- The position must be rebalanced to meet cash outflows, as well as to account for the changes in the duration of the liability schedule due to the passage of time.

Example 12-6:

We can combine strip 1 and strip 3 to create an asset portfolio that approximately matches the present value of the liability, as well as the duration of the liability as shown in Table 12-15. The analysis that was presented in Chapter 5 showed that this barbell portfolio has a greater convexity; hence, it will have a dominance pattern over the liability schedule that we have.

TABLE 12-15   *Immunization Using Strips 1 and 3*

	# strip 1 = 1.45		# strip 3 = 1.59			
	0%	*1%*	*2%*	*3%*	*4%*	*5%*	*6%*
Value of liability	300.00	294.10	288.39	282.86	277.51	272.32	267.30
Duration of liability	2.00	1.99	1.99	1.98	1.97	1.97	1.96
Value of strip 1	145.00	143.56	142.16	140.78	139.42	138.10	136.79
Duration of strip 1	1.00	1.00	1.00	1.00	1.00	1.00	1.00
Value of strip 3	159.00	154.32	149.83	145.51	141.35	137.35	133.50
Duration of strip 3	3.00	3.00	3.00	3.00	3.00	3.00	3.00
Total value of strips	304.00	297.89	291.99	286.28	280.77	275.45	270.29

	7%	*8%*	*9%*	*10%*	*11%*	*12%*
Value of liability	262.43	257.71	253.13	248.69	244.37	240.18
Duration of liability	1.95	1.95	1.94	1.94	1.93	1.92
Value of strip 1	135.51	134.26	133.03	131.82	130.63	129.46
Duration of strip 1	1.00	1.00	1.00	1.00	1.00	1.00
Value of strip 3	129.79	126.22	122.78	119.46	116.26	113.17
Duration of strip 3	3.00	3.00	3.00	3.00	3.00	3.00
Total value of strips	265.31	260.48	255.80	251.28	246.89	242.64

	13%	*14%*	*15%*	*16%*	*17%*	*18%*
Value of liability	236.12	232.16	228.32	224.59	220.96	217.43
Duration of liability	1.92	1.91	1.91	1.90	1.90	1.89
Value of strip 1	128.32	127.19	126.09	125.00	123.93	122.88
Duration of strip 1	1.00	1.00	1.00	1.00	1.00	1.00
Value of strip 3	110.19	107.32	104.55	101.86	99.27	96.77
Duration of strip 3	3.00	3.00	3.00	3.00	3.00	3.00
Total value of strips	238.51	234.51	230.63	226.86	223.21	219.65

HORIZON MATCHING

Thus far, we have presented two approaches to portfolio management. The dedicated-portfolio approach left the portfolio manager little room for manipulation. The major advantage of this approach is that the liabilities will always be met. The immunization approach provided the portfolio manager a great deal more flexibility. This flexibility, however, comes at a price: There is a greater risk that the cash outflows may not be met. In addition, the underlying assumptions that are implicit in the approach (such as parallel shifts in the yield curve) may not be valid during any given period, leading to variations in performance. Horizon matching combines the portfolio-dedication approach and the immunization approach.

The essential features of horizon matching may be summarized as follows:

- It is a hybrid of the matched-funding and immunization techniques.
- The relevant horizon (say, 30 years) is split into two parts. Part 1 may consist of a 10-year horizon, and part 2 may consist of the remaining 20 years.
- The first part of the liabilities will be managed via matched funding, and the second part will be managed via immunization.

The underlying reasoning behind horizon matching is the belief that liabilities over the short term can be predicted with greater precision than the liabilities over the long term.

Contingent Immunization

In contingent immunization strategies, the manager of pension assets takes more risks. In a 16%-yield setting, he or she may accept a required return of 14%. This requires a lower market-value of assets.

Example 12-7:

Consider a pension plan that has a $100 million portfolio. In five years, assuming a 16% rate, it will grow to be $210 million. But by accepting a 14% return, the target portfolio value after five years is only $192 million. In a 16% yield environment, this is attained by setting aside only $91.50 million for investment. This leaves a cushion of $8.50 million for active management.

Immunized portfolio strategies are quite popular in the industry. The article that follows, from *Pensions and Investments* (Barr 1994), illustrates this. The top money managers and the assets under their management are also shown.

Strong Market Boosts Immunized Portfolios
By Paul G. Barr

Despite a 25% jump in total assets of dedicated and immunized portfolios for managers in the *Pensions & Investments* 1994 directory of money managers, interest by pension executives continues to be minimal, managers say.

Total assets among the top 25 dedicated and immunized managers rose 25.1% to $67.12 billion, from $53.66 billion in the previous year's survey.

Metropolitan Life Insurance Co., New York; Prudential Fixed Income Advisors, Short Hills, N.J.; and J.P. Morgan Investment Management, New York, held steady as the three largest managers, managing $13.4 billion, $10.4 billion, and $7 billion, respectively.

Pacific Investment Management Co., Newport Beach, Calif., had a huge increase in dedicated and immunized assets under management, climbing $2.6 billion to $3.1 billion. But James Muzzy, managing director, said PIMCO really doesn't seek that type of business.

The gains in 1993 were a single client in a special situation, he said.

Fidelity Investments, Boston, also showed a big jump, rising to $1.7 billion, from $222 million last year, when it did not rank on the Top 25 chart.

Managers among the Top 25 who were interviewed said most of the increase in assets probably resulted from the strong performing fixed-income market in 1993.

Any growth in assets would not have come through new clients, said John Werring, president, Prudential Fixed Income Advisors.

Although Prudential Fixed Income's managers are seeing some interest in strategies that attempt to match the durations of a plan sponsor's assets and liabilities, strictly dedicated and immunized portfolios are receiving very little interest, he said.

Likewise, Thomas Shively, chief investment officer of fixed income for State Street Research & Management Co., Boston, said that, if anything, sponsors are "unwinding" pure dedicated and immunized bond portfolios.

State Street Research ranked 10th this year, with $1.81 billion in dedicated/immunized assets under management.

As interest rates took their recent long trip downward, pension executives saw the asset side of their dedicated and immunized portfolios climb, managers said. Eventually, many sponsors sold off those portfolios to capture those gains.

1993's strong fixed-income market—the Salomon Broad Bond Index rose 9.9%—gave dedicated and immunized portfolios a strong enough boost that they probably rose about 20%, managers estimated.

Because dedicated and immunized portfolios generally have a duration that is longer than the market—to match the duration of a pension plan's liabilities—market movements for immunized portfolios usually are greater. (Duration is a widely used measure of the cash flows from a fixed-income investment.)

But a decision last year by the Securities and Exchange Commission that could result in higher valuations of some plan sponsors' liabilities, could raise plan sponsor interest in matching fund assets to liabilities.

Source: *Pensions & Investments* (May 16, 1994) pp. 16, 96.

(continued)

Pension executives have been undergoing a "steady learning process" regarding a plan's funding level, and relating their assets to liabilities, said Robert Whalen, managing director, CIGNA Investments, Inc., Hartford, Conn. The late 1993 decision by the SEC to enforce a market-based rate for valuing liabilities might have speeded that some, he said.

Mr. Werring of Prudential Fixed Income said that while strict immunized and dedicated portfolios are not getting much interest, a looser version—duration matching—is. In these portfolios, a manager would build a portfolio that is benchmarked against the duration of the liabilities of the plan sponsor, and try to add value trading against that duration.

There are some instances, though, where immunization strategies are being used in an indirect way among pension executives, managers say.

When a plan sponsor purchases an insurance annuity to cover its pension obligations, the insurance company selling the annuity uses immunized portfolios, State Street Research's Mr. Shively said. For instance, a sponsor shedding a major division may want to get that pension liability off of its books and will purchase an annuity to cover its obligation.

CIGNA offers such annuities, but the firm hasn't seen a lot of activity in that area either, Mr. Whalen said.

Top 250 Managers Ranked by Total Assets

Firm	$ millions	Firm	$ millions	Firm	$ millions
1. Fidelity Investments	258,400	22. Massachusetts Mutual	58,770	39. Equitable Real Estate	38,677
2. Bankers Trust	184,452	23. John Hancock		40. Bank of America	36,434
3. Merrill Lynch Asset	159,900	Financial	58,457	41. Capital Guardian Trust	35,454
4. State Street Bank &		24. Federated Investors	57,204	42. Brinson Partners	35,047
Trust	157,854	25. PNC Investment		43. Massachusetts	
5. Wells Fargo Nikko	150,711	Mgmt.	56,000	Financial	34,590
6. Metropolitan Life	128,200	26. Prudential Asset	55,700	44. Mellon Capital	34,570
7. Alliance Capital	115,276	27. INVESCO North		45. Boatman's Trust	34,043
8. J.P. Morgan	109,801	America	53,450	46. Templeton Worldwide	34,032
9. Capital Research	103,363	28. Pacific Investment	53,001	47. First Nat'l Bank/	
10. Scudder, Stevens &		29. TCW	48,553	Chicago	34,000
Clark	96,264	30. Goldman Sachs Asset	47,990	48. UBS Asset New York	33,600
11. Putnam Investments	90,898	31. First Fidelity		49. Morgan Stanley Asset	33,401
12. Wellington Mgmt.	82,248	Bancorporation	47,916	50. Lincoln Nat'l	
13. Vanguard Group	80,300	32. Boston Co. Asset	44,420	Investment	32,857
14. Northern Trust	77,125	33. T. Rowe Price	43,870	51. Aetna Life Guaranteed	32,665
15. NBD Bank	75,733	34. Principal Financial		52. Loomis Sayles	32,325
16. Citibank Global	75,000	Group	42,959	53. U.S. Trust/New York	32,153
17. Dreyfus	74,272	35. Travelers Insurance	41,300	54. Banc One	30,363
18. Kemper Financial	69,310	36. Morgan Grenfell	41,174	55. HSBC	30,234
19. NationsBank	61,200	37. GE Investments	40,436	56. Miller Anderson	
20. New York Life	60,567	38. Mitchell Hutchins		Sherrerd	30,026
21. CIGNA Investments	59,005	Asset	38,899	57. National City	29,754

Top 250 Managers Ranked by Total Assets

Firm	$ millions	Firm	$ millions	Firm	$ millions
58. Neuberger & Berman	29,305	98. Prudential Fixed		137. MacKay-Shields	10,631
59. Hartford Life	28,970	Income	17,183	138. Trusco Capital	10,500
60. Oppenheimer Capital	28,834	99. Bank of New York	16,745	139. Harris Investment	10,365
61. Stein Roe & Farnham	28,736	100. Lord Abbott	16,607	140. Allmerica Financial	10,300
62. Transamerica	28,223	101. Fiduciary Trust	16,526	141. CoreStates	
63. Chancellor Capital	27,827	102. Payden & Rygel	16,000	Investment	10,280
64. Mellon Bond	27,604	103. Bank of Boston	16,000	142. Smith, Barney,	
65. AMP	27,208	104. Barrow, Hanley,		Shearson	9,963
66. Lincoln Capital Mgmt.	26,321	Mewhinney	15,987	143. Dimensional Fund	
67. Wilmington Trust	25,784	105. Rowe Price-Fleming		Advisors	9,863
68. Fleet Investment		Int'l	15,435	144. Columbia Circle	
Advisors	25,518	106. Woodbridge Capital	15,400	Investors	9,846
69. Phoenix Home Life	25,137	107. PanAgora Asset	15,175	145. Midlantic Nat'l Bank	9,800
70. Fayez Sarofim	25,078	108. Nationwide Insurance	15,116	146. STW Fixed Income	9,681
71. Twentieth Century	24,938	109. Continental Asset	15,019	147. Yamaichi Int'l	9,628
72. Delaware Mgmt. Co.	24,500	110. Baillie Gilford		148. First of America	
73. RCM Capital	24,481	Overseas	14,982	Investment	9,446
74. Daiwa Int'l	23,888	111. Ark Asset Mgmt.	14,939	149. Newbold's Asset	9,411
75. Great-West Life	23,557	112. First Quadrant	14,682	150. Strong Asset	9,382
76. Jennison	23,102	113. Nikko Capital	14,527	151. Wilshire Associates	9,339
77. Sanford C. Bernstein	22,998	114. Weiss, Peck & Greer	13,798	152. Mercantile-Safe	
78. First Union Nat'l Bank	22,800	115. Independence		Deposit	9,313
79. State Street Research	22,486	Investment	13,720	153. Invista Capital	9,156
80. Standish, Ayer &		116. SunBank Capital	13,700	154. Copley Real Estate	9,001
Wood	22,253	117. Investment Advisors	13,480	155. Portfolio Group	8,935
81. Aeltus Investment		118. Columbia Mgmt.	13,293	156. Provident Life &	
Mgmt.	21,875	119. Grantham Mayo		Accident	8,783
82. First Bank System		v. Otterloo	13,129	157. UMB Financial	
Trust	21,547	120. Provident Investment	13,079	Advisors	8,693
83. Janus Capital	21,462	121. Smith Breeden	13,055	158. MIMLIC Asset	8,678
84. Norwest Investment	21,443	122. Salomon Brothers	12,936	159. First Interstate/Calif.	8,421
85. Brown Brothers		123. Piper Capital	12,772	160. Barnett Banks Trust	8,255
Harriman	21,330	124. Nicholas-Applegate	12,521	161. Integra Trust	8,188
86. BlackRock Financial	20,860	125. Firstar Investment	12,376	162. Capitoline Investment	8,149
87. G.T. Capital	20,731	126. J&W Seligman	12,208	163. Glenmede Trust	8,044
88. Lazard Freres	20,673	127. McMorgan	12,120	164. Munder Capital	8,000
89. CS First Boston	20,570	128. Dodge & Cox	11,648	165. LaSalle Advisors	7,800
90. BEA	20,540	129. Schroder Capital	11,623	166. JMB Institutional	
91. ANB Investment &		130. ASB Capital	11,586	Realty	7,692
Trust	20,098	131. Barings	11,449	167. Back Bay Advisors	7,624
92. Fischer Francis Trees	19,741	132. Western Asset	11,204	168. Public Financial	7,610
93. Society Asset	19,647	133. Pacific Mutual Life	11,169	169. General American Life	7,608
94. Duff & Phelps	19,608	134. Smith Barney Capital	11,037	170. Denver Investment	
95. IDS Advisory	18,746	135. Continental		Advisors	7,525
96. Seligman Henderson	18,503	Assurance	11,013	171. Continental Bank	7,378
97. Wachovia Investment	17,950	136. Criterion Investment	10,854	172. Warburg, Pincus	7,000

(continued)

Top 250 Managers Ranked by Total Assets

Firm	$ millions	Firm	$ millions	Firm	$ millions
173. Fifth Third Bancorp	6,987	201. Sears Investment	5,661	228. Sit Investment	4,744
174. Dunedin Fund		202. American United Life	5,478	229. NWQ Investment	4,713
Managers	6,939	203. Lowe, Brockenbrough	5,456	230. Certus Financial	4,700
175. Lombard Odier Int'l	6,804	204. Franidin Portfolio	5,422	231. Union Capital	4,652
176. Van Kampen Merritt	6,700	205. Global Advisors	5,416	232. LaSalle Street Capital	4,604
177. Mutual of America	6,700	206. RREEF Funds	5,409	233. Aldrich, Eastman &	
178. Cursitor-Eaton Asset	6,675	207. Oechsle Int'l	5,377	Wallch	4,580
179. Old Kent Financial	6,500	208. Washington Square	5,358	234. William R. Blair	4,559
180. Merus Capital	6,495	209. Nomura Capital	5,304	235. Kemper Asset	4,505
181. Heitmen Advisory	6,421	210. Chicago Title & Trust	5,288	236. Corporate Property	4,500
182. Batterymarch Financial	6,386	211. WorldInvest	5,254	237. Gabelli Asset	4,451
183. Martin Currie	6,314	212. AMR Investment		238. BSS Asset	4,370
184. Bear Stearns	6,310	Services	5,247	239. Sirach Capital	4,368
185. Mississippi Valley	6,300	213. T. Rowe Price Stable	5,205	240. Brundage, Story &	
186. Yarmouth Capital	6,250	214. National Asset	5,202	Rose	4,362
187. Shawmut	6,226	215. Qualivest Capital	5,119	241. Protective Life	
188. Voyageur Asset Mgmt.	6,220	216. Lehman Brothers		Insurance	4,315
189. Shields Asset	6,204	Global	5,113	242. Commerce Bank	4,297
190. Cooke & Bieler	6,200	217. Lynch & Mayer	5,109	243. Wright Investors	
191. IDS Institutional	6,150	218. Harris Associates	5,076	Service	4,214
192. AON Advisors	6,088	219. Clay Finlay	5,009	244. Manning & Napier	4,200
193. OFFITBANK	6,078	220. Prudential Real Estate	4,934	245. Atlantic Portfolio	
194. Eagle Asset	6,050	221. Luther King Capital	4,924	Analytics	4,147
195. Mellon Equity	5,983	222. Capital Growth Mgmt.	4,904	246. Concert Capital	4,135
196. Balcor	5,837	223. David L. Babson	4,831	247. Public Storage	4,000
197. Morley Capital	5,773	224. Avatar Investors	4,821	248. Advanced Investment	3,872
198. Hotchkis & Wiley	5,715	225. Value Line Asset	4,813	249. Commerz Int'l	3,858
199. United of Omaha	5,704	226. Meridian Investment	4,765	250. United Capital	3,801
200. M&I	5,666	227. Nicholas	4,757	**Total**	**5,938,130**

INDEXATION

Another portfolio-management policy that is extensively used in the industry is the indexation policy. Under this policy, fixed-income portfolio managers will attempt to replicate or outperform the return experience of a chosen index over a prespecified period in future.

In some ways, it is natural to link the performance of the manager of a fixed-income portfolio to the performance of an otherwise identical fixed-income portfolio. If, during a given performance period, the Treasury index with a duration of five years produced a return of, say 5%, then it is reasonable to expect a manager of a fixed-income portfolio with a similar duration to do as well, if not better. The performance evaluation becomes simpler in indexation policies. In addition, by defining a benchmark index to serve as a reference point, the money manager is forced to operate within a broad set of acceptable parameters. For example, if the index used is drawn from domestic Treasuries and investment-grade corporates, then the portfolio manager is expected to operate within these two sectors of the fixed-income markets.

Indexation policy requires the following:

* The choice of a specific index to be used as the performance benchmark.
* The performance period over which the portfolio manager will be managing the indexed portfolio.
* The flexibility level that is acceptable to the money manager and to the investors. This may cover the frequency of transactions, derivatives transactions, repo transactions, security lending, etc.

Indexation Method

Let us define R_I as the index return. We will consider a simple fixed-income portfolio consisting of bullet securities only. Assume that the portfolio consists of N securities. Let R_j be the return on security j. Let x_j be the fraction of security j in the fixed-income portfolio. Note that $\sum_{j=1}^{N} x_j = 1$. Then the portfolio return may be stated as

$$R_p = x_1 R_1 + x_2 R_2 + \cdots + \cdots + x_N R_N. \qquad (12.10)$$

Note that all the returns over a future time period are random. Therefore, we have to work with expected returns and the variability of expected returns. Taking expectations from Equation 12.10, we get

$$E[R_p] = x_1 E[R_1] + x_2 E[R_2] + \cdots + \cdots + x_N E[R_N]. \qquad (12.11)$$

In an indexation problem, it is the difference between the expected return of the indexed portfolio and that of the index that matters. Therefore, we define $\mu_I = E[R_I]$ and $\pi = R_p - R_I$ as the excess return of the portfolio over the index. Then, we may compute the difference in the expected return as follows. Let $\mu_p = E[\pi]$ and $\mu_j = E[R_j] - E[R_I]\ \forall\ j$. Then,

$$\mu_p = [\mu_p - \mu_I] = x_1 \mu_1 + x_2 \mu_2 + \cdots + \cdots + x_N \mu_N. \qquad (12.12)$$

In a similar way, we can compute the variance. Let us define

$$\sigma_j^2 = \mathrm{Var}\{R_j - R_I\}$$

and

$$\sigma_{jk} = \mathrm{Cov}\{R_j - R_I, R_k - R_I\}.$$

Then

$$\sigma_p^2 = \mathrm{Var}\{R_p - R_I\} = \mathrm{Var}\left\{\sum_{j=1}^{N} x_j (R_j - R_I)\right\}.$$

It is easy to verify that

$$\sigma_p^2 = \sum_{j=1}^{N} x_j^2 \sigma_j^2 + 2 \sum_{j=1}^{N} \sum_{k=1, k>j}^{N} x_j x_k \sigma_{jk}. \tag{12.13}$$

Formally, the indexation problem may be stated as a quadratic programming problem in which the variance of the tracing error is minimized subject to the constraints that are normally imposed on security holdings. Formally this is

$$\min_{x_1, x_2, \ldots, x_N} \sigma_p^2 = \sum_{j=1}^{N} x_j^2 \sigma_j^2 + 2 \sum_{j=1}^{N} \sum_{k=1, k>j}^{N} x_j x_k \sigma_{jk}$$

subject to the constraints

$$\sum_{j=1}^{N} x_j = 1$$

and

$$x_j \geq 0, \quad \forall\, j = 1, 2, \ldots, N.$$

Index funds are offered as strategies to money that is placed by institutions in defined benefits and defined contribution plans. The article from *Institutional Investor* (Rohrer 1994) that follows shows Wells Fargo alone accounted for over $20 billion in assets in the defined contribution plans. A significant part of that was under indexation.

Wells Fargo's Quantum Leap

The bank's special-purpose trust company aims to make structured products a force in 401(k)s.

By JULIE ROHRER

In the 1970s Wells Fargo Bank's money management subsidiary pioneered practical applications of modern portfolio theory to defined-benefit plans, virtually revolutionizing the pension industry. Now Wells is poised to launch a trust company dedicated to defined-contribution plans that could have considerable impact on the 401(k) business.

Currently awaiting final regulatory approval, Wells Fargo Defined Contribution Trust Co. is a joint venture between the bank's 401k MasterWorks recordkeeping and administrative services operation and its Wells Fargo Nikko Investment Advisors money

Source: J. Rohrer, "Wells Fargo's Quantum Leap," *Institutional Investor,* September 1994, pp. 195–196. This copyrighted material is reprinted with permission from Institutional Investor, Inc., 488 Madison Avenue, New York, NY 10022.

management arm, which offers a broad range of structured investment products. By combining the administrative and money management functions in one unit, the new company should bring even greater focus to Wells's rapidly growing defined-contribution effort. Having added close to $4 billion in 401(k) assets to its $15 billion in defined-contribution assets under management in 1993, Wells ranked fifth among the top 401(k) dollar gainers in this magazine's annual Pension Olympics (*Institutional Investor,* May 1994).

Wells Fargo Nikko is today the largest manager of quant products. Nobody offers more index funds—100-plus varieties (eight in the U.S. equity markets alone)—or tactical-asset-allocation strategies. Wells's latest version of the latter features five diversified Stagecoach LifePath funds that are geared to particular 401(k) participants' planned retirement dates. Index funds and tactical-asset-allocation strategies total some $136 billion of the bank's $165 billion in tax-exempt assets.

What's good for defined-benefit plans, reason Wells officials, should be good for 401(k) participants. Says Donald Luskin, Wells Fargo Nikko managing director: "The defined-contribution market is in some ways like the defined-benefit market of the 1970s. It's searching for its identity and professionalism."

What do 401(k) plan participants need? "Fundamental building blocks of investing, with enough markets represented to provide legitimate asset allocation choices—index funds are quite natural to do that," contends Wells Fargo Nikko chief executive officer Frederick Grauer. Take that a step further to encompass plan participants who don't feel comfortable determining their own investment mix and you have tactical-asset-allocation strategies popping up as a logical solution.

Washington apparently agrees with this assessment. The Federal Retirement Thrift Investment Board, formed by the Federal Employers Retirement System Act of 1987, requires that the equity assets of its savings plan be invested in "a portfolio designed to replicate the performance of a commonly recognized index." Since 1988 $7 billion of the plan's $22 billion in assets have been managed in a Wells equity index fund that tracks the Standard & Poor's 500 and in a commingled U.S. debt index fund that tracks the Lehman Brothers Aggregate Bond index. The remainder is in short-term Treasuries issued to the plan.

In the private sector Koch Industries' 401(k) plan has invested all of its $225 million in assets in Wells Fargo funds. They include an S&P 500 index fund, a money market fund, an S&P 400 index fund, a structured guaranteed-investment-contract bond fund and a tactical-asset-allocation strategy. Koch's manager of foundations and investments, Janice Dollman, says the company wanted conservative options for its 401(k), since the plan is a supplement to a defined-benefit fund.

Wells's crucial commitment to the 401(k) market came in 1988 when it began building its own systems to develop an integrated full-service recordkeeping and administrative capability to complement its investment products. Launched in 1989, 401k MasterWorks today provides 140 companies representing plan assets of more than $4 billion (and 175,000 participants) with recordkeeping and trustee services, employee-benefits consulting, employee communications and education services as well as investment management and investment funds. MasterWorks has yet to lose a client for service reasons, asserts Alan Kizor, the Wells executive vice president who's in charge of the unit.

(continued)

Ironically, Wells hadn't been a major defined-benefit recordkeeper, having abandoned the master-trust business in 1984. That was a blessing in disguise, says Kizor: Instead of straining to adapt master-trust systems to 401(k) reporting, Wells based the MasterWorks system on the bank's IRA accounts; that tracking process proved to be ideally adaptable to the needs of individual 401(k) participants. In the mid-1980s, before daily valuation became a buzzword in the industry, Wells was the largest IRA bank in the country, with thousands of "little trust [IRA] accounts" invested in pooled funds managed by Wells Fargo Nikko. "We had to build proprietary systems to enable individuals to move their IRA money on a daily basis from one fund to another," notes Kizor.

MasterWorks' target market is larger plans of at least 500 participants. Wisely, it has not restricted its business to sponsors that also use Wells Fargo Nikko investment funds; this flexibility has helped to add several clients to its roster. Nevertheless, confides Kizor, "we have yet to take on a single situation where the plan sponsor doesn't use at least one [Wells Fargo Nikko] fund."

From day one MasterWorks permitted plan participants to access their accounts 24 hours a day through an automated voice-response system or to talk to a human being by phone from 6:00 a.m. to 6:00 p.m., Pacific time. About 97 percent of calls to reps get answered within 30 seconds, says Kizor. What's more, participants can conduct business in any one of seven languages: English, Spanish, Taiwanese, Cantonese, Russian, French or Hebrew.

Today daily valuation is almost a given for 401(k) service providers, but, as Koch's Dollman testifies, MasterWorks "actually does daily. We have 18 [distinct] payrolls a month." Wells's system accounts for each payroll the day it is made, so plan deductions or contributions are also recorded on the day they're made. That's a flexibility not all providers could offer, Dollman points out. Says Wells's Kizor, "I'd had no idea there were so many definitions of the word 'pay.' "

MasterWorks guarantees that quarterly statements will be back within ten days of the end of a quarter. Otherwise, says Kizor, "we refund your previous quarter's recordkeeping fees." Loans are expedited practically instantaneously. Dollman observes that a loan requested by a participant in Koch's 401(k) was in the person's hands in four working days.

Many 401(k) plan sponsors, of course, are committed to active management. Fidelity Investments is not exactly quaking in its boots yet. What's more, major players have their own line of quant products to offer 401(k) participants, particularly a wide range of tactical-asset-allocation funds. These are already popular among plan sponsors because they take a key decision-making process out of the unsure hands of plan participants.

But if index funds and other structured products invade the defined-contribution market to the extent that they have the defined-benefit market, Wells should have little to complain about. "This is an important business for Wells Fargo," emphasizes vice chairman Clyde Ostler.

The bank's brand recognition can't hurt its marketing pitch either. A recent publication, "World's Greatest Brands: A Review by Interbrand" (published by John Wiley & Sons), evaluates the world's top-selling brands on a number of criteria. Fidelity Investments and Vanguard Group are nowhere to be found among the top 100 names. Only one bank—Wells Fargo—makes the list.

PORTFOLIO INSURANCE

Portfolio insurance is a dynamic portfolio-management policy in which a floor level is established below which the pension assets will not fall. The strategy provides for some upside potential as well. This strategy is best illustrated in the context of pension funds asset allocation.

The valuation of pension obligations is a nontrivial issue in defined-benefits (DB) plans. The accumulated pension obligation (ABO), a measure used in the industry, provides a lower bound and is the dollar amount that the company will be expected to pay if the plan is terminated immediately. The projected benefits obligation (PBO) takes into account the growth rate of wages for current employees and is, therefore, greater than the ABO. These measures are, in turn, used to determine whether a plan is underfunded or overfunded. Most pension portfolios are managed by professional money managers. The sponsor of the pension plan is interested in managing the portfolio in order to meet the promised pension obligations (ABOs or PBOs) at any time. The requirement that the assets in the pension plan must always be above the ABO or PBO is illustrated in Figure 12-1. Notice that in the figure the pension assets, for the most part, have been above pension liabilities.

If the penalty for not meeting the liabilities is infinite, then the following portfolio allocation policy is optimal:

- At each point, take the surplus of the pension assets over the liability. This surplus can be invested in a mean-variance efficient portfolio without regard for the liabilities of the pension plan.

FIGURE 12-1 *Pension Asset Allocation*

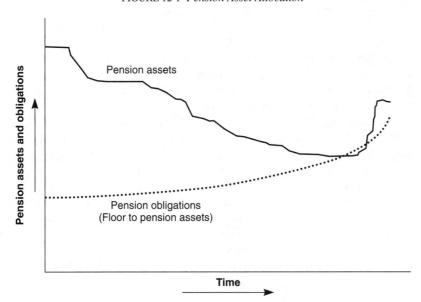

- The remaining assets will be invested to precisely replicate the liabilities of the pension plan. If the pension liabilities are known with certainty (an unlikely situation), then the remaining assets can be placed in a dedicated portfolio. If, on the other hand, the pension liabilities are correlated with future wages (as is likely to be the case in most defined-benefits plans), then these assets will be placed in a portfolio of equity and fixed-income sectors that is maximally correlated with pension liabilities.

In the fixed-income sector, portfolio insurance strategies are more difficult to implement. The reason for this is the lack of a liquid futures contract on a basket of fixed-income securities. This is not a problem in most equity markets; stock-index futures contracts are traded extensively around the world and are fairly liquid. The development of futures contracts in many benchmark maturities in the Treasury sector and the liquidity in options on futures contracts have made the implementation of portfolio insurance strategies in the fixed-income sector (especially in the Treasury market) less difficult. Currently, futures contracts are available on two-year, five-year, ten-year, and thirty-year benchmark maturities. In addition, options are traded on ten-year T-note futures, as well as on T-bond futures contracts. The lack of comparable futures and options in corporate and mortgage-backed securities areas means that only cross-hedging is possible for these sectors.

How can these contracts be used to implement a synthetic portfolio insurance policy on a diversified fixed-income portfolio? The following steps could lead to a reasonable portfolio insurance policy:

1. The portfolio's risk properties should first be summarized. Summary measures that are typically used include the duration, PVBP, and convexity.
2. The horizon over which the portfolio insurance is in effect must be specified along with the level of protection that is needed.
3. A portfolio of futures contracts should be chosen from each benchmark maturities such that
   (a) the price changes in the futures portfolio are highly correlated with the price changes in the underlying fixed-income portfolio, and
   (b) the risk properties of the fixed-income portfolio are closely matched by the risk properties of the futures portfolio.
   The presence of delivery options in futures contracts makes this a particularly difficult task. (This part of the portfolio insurance is much simpler in equity markets, where stock-index futures contracts tend to be settled in cash.)
4. A strike price of the synthetic put option should be chosen that is consistent with the level of protection that is needed.
5. The replicating portfolio of the synthetic put option on the fixed-income portfolio should then be implemented by trading in the portfolio of futures contracts. This will require the use of options-pricing models to compute the delta of the synthetic put at each instant in order to implement the futures trades. Steps 4 and 5 should be implemented using the techniques developed in Chapter 14.

CONCLUSION

In this chapter, we have developed various portfolio-management techniques that are widely used in the fixed-income area. The concepts of dedicated-portfolio construction and immunized portfolios were developed in detail. In addition, such concepts as horizon matching, contingent immunization, and portfolio insurance were also described. Bond indexes are used to gauge and direct the performances of portfolios. Indexation strategies were also presented in this chapter.

PROBLEMS

12.1   What are GICs? Describe the institutions that are likely to be attracted to GICs.

12.2   When would a dedicated-portfolio strategy be preferred to alternatives such as immunization or indexation? Why?

12.3   A new city municipality is funding a capital project which requires an outlay of $4 million per year for the next five years and an estimated $5 million per year thereafter for another five years. The projections for the next five years are firm, but there is some uncertainty about the projections beyond that. Describe the funding strategies that the city can use. Assume that it can raise capital by issuing general obligations bonds.

12.4   Portfolio insurance provides downside protection, as well as upside potential. Explain why, despite these advantages, some investors pursue other strategies, such as indexation or immunization.

REFERENCES

Barr, P. G. 1994. "Strong Market Boosts Immunized Portfolios." *Pensions & Investments* (May 16):16, 96.

Rohrer, J. 1994. "Wells Fargo's Quantum Leap." *Institutional Investor* (September):195–196.

Zirky, E. A., and R. M. Mackey 1993. "Pension Plan Funding Strategies: Defining Terms." *Pension World* (August):40–41.

Part III

Fixed-Income Derivatives and Risk Management

Chapter 13

An Overview of
Derivatives Markets

Chapter Objectives

This chapter provides an overview of listed and dealer derivative markets. In addition, specific situations are presented illustrating how such derivatives can be used in practical applications. The following issues and questions are addressed in this chapter:

- What are the differences between listed and OTC derivatives?
- What is the distribution of credit risk in the derivatives market?
- What are Asian options and how are they used in practice?
- What are options on swaps and how can they be used?
- What are the most recent developments in fixed-income derivatives?

INTRODUCTION

During the last 25 years, derivative markets have developed in a number of areas of capital markets. Today, managers can trade in derivative products that are customized to manage specific exposures in interest rates, currencies, commodities, and equity markets. Derivative markets reflect varying levels of complexity and customization. At one extreme, there are derivative markets, such as the equity stock options listed on the Chicago Board of Options Exchange (CBOE), which are fairly simple and standardized derivative contracts backed by Options Clearing Corporation (OCC) to ensure contract integrity. At the other extreme, dealer derivative contracts, such as interest-rate swaps and OTC options to enter into interest-rate swaps, are also available. Such derivative contracts are highly customized and are backed by the capital allocated by the dealers. Clearly, the credit reputation of the dealer is a critical component in ensuring product integrity.

In this chapter, we will provide an overview of derivatives markets in general and of the fixed-income derivatives markets in particular. The purpose of this overview is to get a perspective on the rich variety of derivative markets that are available to the corporate and investment community and how such markets offer improved risk-management capabilities. Our focus will be largely on the derivative markets applied to the financial sector. We shall, however, explore some commodity-related derivatives, such as commodity swaps and commodity-linked bonds.

There are two categories of derivative markets, listed derivatives markets and dealer derivative markets. This classification helps in understanding the distinct roles played by these markets and how one complements the other.

Listed derivatives are traded in centralized exchanges. Examples of listed derivatives markets include Chicago Mercantile Exchange (CME), Chicago Board of Trade (CBOT), London International Financial Futures Exchange (LIFFE), etc. We will survey listed exchanges briefly in this chapter. In addition to listed exchanges, there are decentralized markets where derivatives are traded. These are known as **dealer derivatives markets** or over-the-counter (OTC) derivatives markets. We compare and contrast the listed markets and OTC markets later in the chapter.

LISTED DERIVATIVES MARKETS

Since the advent of futures trading on financial instruments (such as interest rates, stock indices, and foreign currencies) in the early 1970s on the Chicago Board of Trade (CBOT) and the Chicago Mercantile Exchange (CME), listed derivatives have registered an impressive growth in the volume of trading and the breadth of coverage of underlying markets. To get an appreciation of the range of these markets, we first provide some of the largest international exchanges and the contracts that are widely traded.

In the websites listed at the end of this chapter, readers can find the range of products and services that are offered by listed derivatives exchanges. In the body of this chapter, we will provide an overview of some of the important contracts and highlight their salient features. We start with the Chicago Board of Options Exchange products.

At the Chicago Board of Options Exchange (CBOE), interest rate options are traded. Major interest rate options at the CBOE and their contractual provisions are shown in Table 13-1. Note that options are available for the benchmark government yields at 91-days, 5-year, 10-year, and 30-year maturity sectors.

TABLE 13-1   *Interest Rate Options*

Symbols:

	Standard Options	*Exercise Settlement Value*	*LEAPS December 2001*
13-week Treasury bill	IRX	SSX	ZXB
5-year Treasury note	FVX	FVS	ZXV
10-year Treasury note	TNX	TNS	ZXN
30-year Treasury bond	TYX	TYS	ZXT

Underlying: IRX is based on the discount rate of the most recently auctioned 13-week U.S. Treasury bill. The new T-bill is substituted weekly on the trading day following its auction, usually a Monday. FVX, TNX, and TYX are based on 10 times the yield-to-maturity on the most recently auctioned five-year Treasury note, ten-year Treasury note, and thirty-year Treasury bond, respectively. LEAPS are long-dated options that expire in approximately two to three years from the date of initial listing. Options are European-style exercise and are available in up to three near-term months followed by three additional months from the March quarterly cycle. LEAPS expire in December of the expiration year.

Multiplier: $100

Strike Price Intervals: $2\frac{1}{2}$ points. A 1-point interval represents 10 basis points. (The standard strike price table applies to five-point intervals; codes U-Z are used for fractional strike prices.)

Premium Quotation: Stated in points and fractions. One point equals $100. The minimum tick for series trading below 3 is $\frac{1}{16}$ ($6.25) and for all other series, is ($12.50).

Expiration Date: Saturday immediately following the third Friday of the expiration month.

Expiration Months: IRX—Three near-term months plus two additional months from the March quarterly cycle (March, June, September, and December). FVX, TNX, TYX—Three near-term months plus three additional months from the March quarterly cycle. LEAPS expire in December of the expiration year.

Exercise Style: *European*—Interest rate options may generally be exercised only on the last business day before the expiration date.

Settlement of Option Exercise: The exercise-settlement values of interest rate options (symbols above) are based on the "spot yield" on the last trading day as reported by the Federal Reserve Bank of New York at 2:30 P.M. Central Time. (Spot yield refers to the annualized discount rate on the most recently issued T-bill or yield-to-maturity on the most recently issued T-notes or T-bond.) Exercise will result in delivery of cash on the business day following the expiration date. The exercise-settlement amount is equal to the difference between the exercise-settlement value and the exercise price of the option, multiplied by $100.

Position and Exercise Limits: IRX options and LEAPS—The aggregate position and exercise limits are 5,000 contracts on the same side of the market. FVX, TNX, TYX options, and LEAPS—The aggregate position and exercise limits are 25,000 contracts on the same side of the market. A hedge exemption for public customers may be available for certain diversified portfolios that may expand the limit.

Margin: Purchases of puts or calls with nine months or less until expiration must be paid for in full. Writers of uncovered puts or calls must deposit / maintain 100% of the option proceeds* plus 15% of the aggregate contract value (current index level × $100) minus the amount by which the option is out-of-the-money, if any, subject to a minimum for calls of option proceeds* plus 10% of the aggregate contract value and a minimum for puts of option proceeds* plus 10% of the aggregate exercise price amount. (*For calculating maintenance margin, use option current market value instead of option proceeds.) Additional margin may be required pursuant to Exchange Rule 12.10.

CUSIP Numbers: IRX - 124918, FVX - 124951, TNX - 124952, TYX - 124953.

Last Trading Day: Trading in interest rate options will ordinarily cease on the business day (usually a Friday) preceding the expiration date.

Trading Hours: 7:20 A.M. to 2:00 P.M. Central Time (Chicago time).

Source: http://www.cboe.com/products/prodspec/i-rateop.htm

TABLE 13-2   *CBOT Products*

Treasury bond futures	Treasury bond futures and options
Ten-year futures and options	Five-year futures and options
Two-year futures and options	Municipal bond futures and options
Fed fund futures	Inflation-indexed futures and options
PCS CAT insurance options	Flexible options
Electricity contracts	

Source: CBOT.

These options offer rich interest-rate risk management strategies to fixed-income portfolio managers, issuers, and dealers. For example, a portfolio manager buying a 30-year Treasury bond may wish to sell a call option on the 30-year Treasury bond (shown in Table 13-1). This strategy generates additional income from the proceeds of the option sale. If subsequently the interest rates go down and the bond prices consequently go up, the call option will get exercised, and this will limit the profitability. Hence, depending on the view of the portfolio manager, various options strategies can be customized. We review these possibilities in detail in the next chapter. While CBOE focuses on options, other exchanges tend to offer both futures contracts and options contracts. The definitions of options contracts and futures contracts are presented in Chapters 14 and 15, respectively. In this chapter, we review some of the most actively traded futures and options contracts.

At CBOT, many important interest-rate futures contracts and options are traded. Table 13-2 shows the major products that are actively traded at CBOT. All options at CBOT are traded on underlying futures contracts, unlike the CBOE options described in Table 13-1. Note that CBOT offers futures and options on inflation-indexed interest rates, municipal bonds, Fed funds, and the coupon benchmarks in the Treasury markets.

Table 13-2 illustrates the broad coverage of CBOT products. For the underlying Treasury markets, futures contracts are available for all benchmark maturities (two-year, five-year, ten-year, and thirty-year). In addition, options on futures contracts are also available. (See Chapter 14 for a definition of options on futures contracts and how they can be valued.) In addition, CBOT offers a Fed fund futures contract, which is at the "front-end" of the Treasury yield curve. (Chapter 2 provides a detailed discussion of the Fed funds market.) Table 13-3 summarizes the provisions of Fed fund futures. Fed fund futures are quite useful in summarizing the market's expectations of the central bank's actions. CBOT offers futures and options on Treasury inflation-indexed bonds or TIPS. The municipal bond futures and options at the CBOT are very valuable to players in the tax-exempt fixed-income markets. This contract is based on a broad portfolio of underlying municipal bonds and hence are particularly attractive to municipal bond portfolio managers. Table 13-4 highlights the provisions of muni bond con-

TABLE 13-3   *Thirty-Day Fed Funds Futures*

Trading unit	$5 million
Deliverable grades	
Price quote	
Tick size	Increments of $\frac{1}{2}$ of $\frac{1}{100}$ of 1% of $5 million on a 30-day basis ($20.84)
Daily price limit	150 basis points (variable trading limits of 225 basis points); no limit in the spot month
Contract months	First 25 calendar months (and the next two months in the March, June, September, December cycle thereafter)
Last trading day	Last business day of the delivery month
Last delivery day	
Trading hours	Open outcry: 7:20 A.M. to 2:00 P.M. Chicago time, Monday through Friday. Trading in expiring contracts closes at noon on the last trading day.

Source: http://www.cbot.com/cbot/www/prod_detail/0,1499,14+58+140+30,00.html

TABLE 13-4   *Municipals Index Futures*

Trading unit	$1,000 times the closing value of The Bond Buyer™ municipal bond index. A price of 90-00 reflects a contract size of $90,000.
Deliverable grades	
Price quote	Points ($1,000) and 32nds of a point; for example, 85-16 equals $85\frac{16}{32}$
Tick size	$\frac{1}{32}$ of a point ($31.25/contract)
Daily price limit	Three points ($3,000/contract) above or below the previous day's settlement price (expandable to $4\frac{1}{2}$ points)
Contract months	March, June, September, December
Last trading day	Seventh business day preceding the last business day of the delivery month
Last delivery day	
Trading hours	Open outcry: 7:20 A.M. to 2:00 P.M. Chicago time, Monday through Friday. Trading in expiring contracts closes at noon on the last trading day.
Settlement	Municipal bond index futures settle in cash on the last day of trading. Settlement price equals The Bond Buyer™ municipal bond index value on that day.

Source: http://www.cbot.com/cbot/www/prod_detail/0,1499,14+58+140+31,00.html

tracts at CBOT. The expanding agency markets have led to the development of agency futures contracts highlighted in Table 13-5. The design of this contract is very similar to the Treasury bond futures contract which is highlighted in Table 13-6. Agency futures contracts are helpful in hedging issuances of agency debt securities and in risk management of portfolios of agency debt.

TABLE 13-5   *Ten-Year Agency Futures*

Trading unit	One Fannie Mae® Benchmark Note^SM or Freddie Mac Reference Note^SM having a face value of $100,000 at maturity.
Deliverable grades	
Price quote	
Tick size	One-half or $\frac{1}{32}$ of 1 point ($15.625), rounded up to the nearest full cent.
Daily price limit	Regular limits of 3 points ($3,000) with expandable limits of $4\frac{1}{2}$ points ($4,500). Limits are lifted on the second business day preceding the first day of the delivery month.
Contract months	The first five consecutive contracts in the March, June, September, and December quarterly cycle.
Last trading day	Seventh business day preceding the last business day of the delivery month. The expiring contract ceases trading at 12:00 noon (Chicago time) on the last day of trading.
Last delivery day	
Trading hours	Open outcry: 7:20 A.M. to 2:00 P.M., Monday through Friday, Chicago time.
Settlement	
Delivery standards	Noncallable Fannie Mae benchmark notes or Freddie Mac reference notes maturing at least $6\frac{1}{2}$ years but not more than $10\frac{1}{4}$ years (i.e., original maturity) from the first day of the delivery month, an original issuance of $3 billion or greater, and semiannual fixed-coupon payments are eligible for delivery. The invoice price of a deliverable issue at settlement equals the futures settlement price multiplied by the conversion factor, plus accrued interest. The conversion factor is the price of the delivered note with a $1.00 par value yielding 6.00% to maturity.
Delivery methods	Federal Reserve book-entry, wire-transfer system.

Source: http://www.cbot.com/cbot/www/prod_detail/0,1499,14+58+140+39,00.html

In the Chicago Mercantile Exchange (CME), several important interest rate derivatives are traded. Table 13-7 provides a list of widely traded interest-rate products at the CME. Perhaps the most important contract at CME is the Eurodollar futures contract, which we will discuss in detail in Chapter 15. The CME also trades futures and options on agency debt, as well as on several emerging market debt instruments. The detailed contractual specifications can be obtained from the website of the Chicago Mercantile Exchange that is provided at the end of this chapter.

In Tables 13-8 and 13-9, we describe some of the listed options on U.S. Fixed-Income Securities and International Fixed-Income Securities. The list provided is illustrative but does not cover the whole range of products available in these exchanges. It is useful to note that the underlying maturity ranges from 90 days (T-bill) to 30 years (T-bond). Typically, the contracts in each country cover benchmark maturities in each

TABLE 13-6   *U.S. Bonds Futures*

Trading unit	One U.S. Treasury bond having a face value at maturity of $100,000 or multiple thereof
Deliverable grades	U.S. Treasury bonds that, if callable, are not callable for at least 15 years from the first day of the delivery month or, if not callable, have a maturity of at least 15 years from the first day of the delivery month. The invoice price equals the futures settlement price times a conversion factor plus accrued interest. The conversion factor is the price of the delivered bond ($1 par value) to yield 8%. Beginning with the March 2000 contracts, the conversion factor will be the price of the delivered bond ($1 par value) to yield 6%.
Price quote	Points ($1,000) and 32nds of a point; for example, 80-16 equals $80\frac{16}{32}$
Tick size	One–thirty-second of a point ($31.25/contract); par is on the basis of 100 points
Daily price limit	Three points ($3,000/contract) above or below the previous day's settlement price (expandable to $4\frac{1}{2}$ points). Limits are lifted the second business day preceding the first day of the delivery month.
Contract months	March, June, September, December
Last trading day	Seventh business day preceding the last business day of the delivery month
Last delivery day	Last business day of the delivery month
Trading hours	Open outcry: 7:20 A.M. to 2:00 P.M. Chicago time, Monday through Friday. Trading in expiring contracts closes at noon on the last trading day.

Source: http://www.cbot.com/cbot/www/prod_detail/0,1499,14+58+140+24,00.html

TABLE 13-7

Interest Rate Derivatives at the Chicago Mercantile Exchange (CME)

1. Eurodollar futures
2. Eurodollar futures options
3. Thirteen-week U.S. Treasury bill futures
4. Options on 13-week U.S. Treasury bill futures
5. One-month LIBOR futures
6. One-month LIBOR options
7. Fed funds rate futures
8. Ten-year agency note futures
9. Ten-year agency note options
10. Five-year agency note futures
11. Five-year agency note options
12. Mexican par Brady bonds futures
13. Mexican par Brady bond options
14. Argentine FRB bond futures/options
15. Argentine Brady (par) bond futures/options
16. Brazilian C bonds futures/options
17. Brazilian EZ bonds futures/options

TABLE 13-8   *Listed Options on U.S. Fixed-Income Securities*

Underlying Asset/Exchange	Contract Details	Expiry Date	Position Limits
Thirty-year T-bond $100,000 par, minimum tick $\frac{1}{64}$, tick size 15.625, CBT	First three contracts, M, J, S, D. Two-point strike intervals.	Noon on the last Friday at least five business days prior to the first business day of the delivery month	Three points daily price limit. Exercise by 6:00 P.M. on the last trading day. Automatic exercise for intrinsic of 2 points or more.
Ten-year T-note $100,000 par, minimum tick $\frac{1}{64}$, tick size 15.625, CBT	First three contracts, M, J, S, D. Two-point strike intervals.	Noon on the last Friday at least five business days prior to the first business day of the delivery month	Three points daily price limit. Exercise by 6:00 P.M. on the last trading day. Automatic exercise for intrinsic of 2 points or more.
Five-year T-note $100,000 par, minimum tick $\frac{1}{64}$, tick size 15.625, FINEX	First two contracts, M, J, S, D. One-point strike intervals.	1:00 P.M. on the last Friday at least five business days prior to the first business day of the delivery month	No daily price limit. Exercise by 6:00 P.M. on the last trading day. Automatic exercise for intrinsic of 0.5 points or more.
Muni-bond index $100,000 par, minimum tick $\frac{1}{64}$, tick size 15.625, FINEX	First three contracts, M, J, S, D. One-point strike intervals.	1:00 P.M. on the last Friday at least five business days prior to the first business day of the delivery month	Three points daily price limit. Exercise by 6:00 P.M. on the last trading day. Automatic exercise for in-the-money options.
Ninety-day Eurodollar $1,000.000 par, minimum tick 0.01%, tick size 25.00, CME, LIFFE, SIMEX	First eight contracts, M, J, S, D. Quarter-point strike intervals.	Simultaneously with the close of trading in the underlying futures (usually the third Monday of the contract month)	No daily limits. 500 futures equivalent position. Automatic exercise for in-the-money options.
Ninety-day T-bill $1,000,000 par, minimum tick 0.01%, tick size 25.00, CME	First four contracts, M, J, S, D. Quarter-point strike intervals.	Last business day of the week, preceding by at least six business days the first business day of the contract month	No daily limits. 5,000 futures equivalent position. No automatic exercise for in-the-money options.

country. Usually, the most actively traded futures contracts in global fixed-income markets are on government benchmark debt securities. To a lesser extent, this is the case with options or futures contracts as well. A notable exception is the Eurodollar futures contracts and options, or Eurodollar futures, which are very actively traded. Chapter 16 contains an extensive treatment of this important market. With the advent of the Euro as the common currency, many of the futures and options contracts are now redesigned to settle in Euros.

TABLE 13-9   *Listed Options on International Fixed-Income Securities*

Underlying Asset/Exchange	*Contract Details*	*Expiry Date*	*Position Limits*
France			
MATIF 10-year FF500,000 par, minumum tick 0.01%, tick size FF50	First four contracts, M, J, S, D. One-point strike intervals.	4:00 P.M. on the last Friday of the month prior to the delivery month of the future	No daily limits. Automatic exercise of in-the-money options.
MATIF 90-day FF500,000 par, minimum tick 0.01%, tick size FF125	First three contracts, M, J, S, D. 10-basis-point strike intervals.	3:30 P.M. on the last trading day of the underlying futures	No daily limits. Automatic exercise of in-the-money options.
Germany			
LIFFE 10-year DM250,000 par, minimum tick 0.01%, tick size DM25	First three contracts, M, J, S, D. One-point strike intervals.	4:00 P.M. six business days prior to the first business day of the delivery month	No daily limits. Automatic exercise of in-the-money options.
LIFFE 90-day EuroDM DM1,000,000 par, minimum tick 0.01%, tick size DM25	First two contracts, M, J, S, D. Quarter-point strike intervals.	4:10 P.M. the second business day preceding the third Wednesday of the delivery month	No daily limits. Automatic exercise of in-the-money options.
MATIF 90-day EuroDM DM1,000,000 par, minimum tick 0.01%, tick size DM25	First four contracts, M, J, S, D. Quarter-point strike intervals.	3:50 P.M. the second business day preceding the third Wednesday of the delivery month	No daily limits. Automatic exercise of in-the-money options.
United Kingdom			
LIFFE 20-year Gilt Sterling 500,000 par, minimum tick $\frac{1}{64}$, tick size 7.8125	First four contracts, M, J, S, D. Two point strike intervals.	4:15 P.M. six business days prior to the first business day of the delivery month	No daily limits. Automatic exercise of in-the-money options.
LIFFE 90-day Sterling 500,000 par, minimum tick 0.01%, tick size 12.5	First three contracts, M, J, S, D. Quarter-point strike intervals.	3:30 P.M. on the last trading day of the underlying futures	No daily limits. Automatic exercise of 1 point plus in-the-money options.
Japan			
TSE 10-year bonds Yen 100,000,000 par, minimum tick 0.01%	First two contracts, M, J, S, D. One-point strike intervals.	3:00 P.M. the last business day of the month prior to the delivery month; trading is allowed till 4:30.	No daily limits. No automatic exercise of in-the-money options.

DEALER DERIVATIVES MARKETS

An overview of dealer derivatives markets is provided in Table 13-10. Note that interest rate contracts account for more than 60% of the notional amounts as of the end of 1999. In terms of gross market value, they account for nearly 50% of the global OTC

TABLE 13-10   *The Global Over-the-Counter (OTC) Derivatives Markets*[1]
(Amounts Outstanding in Billions of U.S. Dollars)

	Notional Amounts				Gross Market Values			
	End June 1998	End Dec. 1998	End June 1999	End Dec. 1999	End June 1998	End Dec. 1998	End June 1999	End Dec. 1999
Grand Total	**72,143**	**80,317**	**81,458**	**88,201**	**2,580**	**3,231**	**2,628**	**2,813**
A. Foreign exchange contracts	**18,719**	**18,011**	**14,899**	**14,344**	**799**	**786**	**582**	**662**
Outright forwards and forex swaps	12,149	12,063	9,541	9,593	476	491	329	352
Currency swaps	1,947	2,253	2,350	2,444	208	200	192	250
Options	4,623	3,695	3,009	2,307	115	96	61	60
B. Interest rate contracts[2]	**42,368**	**50,015**	**54,072**	**60,091**	**1,160**	**1,675**	**1,357**	**1,304**
FRAs	5,147	5,756	7,137	6,775	33	15	12	12
Swaps	29,363	36,262	38,372	43,936	1,018	1,509	1,222	1,150
Options	7,858	7,997	8,562	9,380	108	152	123	141
C. Equity-linked contracts	**1,274**	**1,488**	**1,511**	**1,809**	**190**	**236**	**244**	**359**
Forwards and swaps	154	146	198	283	20	44	52	71
Options	1,120	1,342	1,313	1,527	170	192	193	288
D. Commodity contracts[3]	**451**	**415**	**441**	**548**	**38**	**43**	**44**	**59**
Gold	193	182	189	243	10	13	23	23
Other	258	233	252	305	28	30	22	37
Forwards and swaps	153	137	127	163	—	—	—	—
Options	106	97	125	143	—	—	—	—
E. Other[4]	**9,331**	**10,388**	**10,536**	**11,408**	**393**	**492**	**400**	**429**
GROSS CREDIT EXPOSURE[5]					**1,203**	**1,329**	**1,119**	**1,023**
Memorandum item:								
Exchange-traded contracts[6]	*14,792*	*13,932*	*14,440*	*13,522*	—	—	—	—

Source: Bank for International Settlements.

[1]All figures are adjusted for double-counting. Notional amounts outstanding have been adjusted by halving positions vis-à-vis other reporting dealers. Gross market values have been calculated as the sum of the total gross positive market value of contracts and the absolute value of the gross negative market value of contracts with non-reporting counterparties. [2]Single-currency contracts only. [3]Adjustments for double-counting estimated. [4]For end-June 1998: positions reported by non-regular reporting institutions in the context of the triennial Central Bank Survey of Foreign Exchange and Derivatives Market Activity at end-June 1998; for subsequent periods: estimated positions of non-regular reporting institutions. [5]Gross market values after taking into account legally enforceable bilateral netting agreements. [6]Sources: FOW TRADEdata; Futures Industry Association; various futures and options exchanges.

derivatives markets! In comparison to the total OTC derivatives (notional amount) of $88,201 billion, the exchange traded derivatives amounts to $13,522 billion. It is, therefore, evident that the dealer market is more than six times as big as the listed derivatives market. Table 13-11 highlights the key differences between listed and dealer derivatives markets.

Some Dealer Derivatives

Dealer derivatives vary widely with respect to underlying asset, maturity, style, and contingency provisions. To illustrate their versatile nature, Tables 13-12 and 13-13 list examples of some of the varied dealer derivative products (drawn from industry publications).

TABLE 13-11   *Listed Derivatives versus Dealer Derivatives*

Dimension of the Contract	Listed Derivatives	Dealer Derivatives
Liquidity	Typically excellent for nearby contracts. Domestic contracts have greater liquidity.	Typically not as liquid as listed contracts but can be good in certain markets.
Size	Fixed by exchange rules.	Can be customized.
Credit risk	Clearinghouse guarantees.	Dealer capital coupled with credit enhancements.
Contractual provisions (maturities, exercise, etc.)	Standardized	Customized

TABLE 13-12   *Dealer Derivatives, Options*

Contract or Product	Features
Asian options	Arithmetic average of prices or arithmetic average of strike prices. Value of Asian options depend on the path of the underlying asset price until exercise.
Forward-start options	A standard (call) option is granted at a future date with prespecified strike price and maturity (executive stock options).
Chooser options	The buyer decides after a specified time whether the option is a call or a put.
Barrier options	The option's payoffs depend on whether during its life the underlying asset reached a prespecified value (down-and-out options).
Lookback options	The buyer can look back during the life of the option to select the strike price or the best underlying asset price.

TABLE 13-13   *Dealer Derivatives, Hybrids*

Contract or Product	*Features*
Bonds with equity kickers	These bonds are issued to provide an upside potential to investors (convertible bonds, warrants, and unit packages of stocks and bonds).
Warrants	Issuing firm sells warrants that the investor may use to buy from the issuer a prespecified number of shares of common stock at specified prices. Life ranges from two years to ten or more years. Although typically issued with bonds, warrants are detachable. OTC dealers make a secondary market.
Index-linked debt	
S&P index notes	These notes pay a fixed interest rate, but their principal is linked to S&P 500 index.
Liquid-yield option notes (LYONs)	Zero-coupon notes where the principal is tied to NYSE composite index. Subject to a minimum.
Bonds with imbedded options	
Put bonds	The buyer may put the bond back to the issuer at par at designated times.
Callable bonds and MBS	These bonds may be called by the issuer depending on the state of the economy (interest rates, seasonality, etc.).

MOTIVATION FOR DERIVATIVES

In this section, we provide several illustrative examples of the importance of derivatives in the risk-management strategies of corporations.

Swaps

Interest rate swaps are widely used by financial institutions to manage risk. In Chapter 16 we describe in detail interest rate swaps and their applications. We wish to illustrate here a simple application to motivate the use of derivatives in risk management. Consider a bank with the following simplified balance sheet:

Assets	*Liabilities*
$100 million 10-year loan @8%	$100 million 6-month CD @5%

The bank has issued $100 million of six-month CDs yielding 5% and used the proceeds to extend a 10-year loan at a fixed rate of 8%. For simplicity, we assume that the loan is noncallable. The bank has to re-finance the CD every six months and this presents a source of risk. Typically, the bank CD rates are tied to London interbank of-

FIGURE 13-1   *Swap Contract*

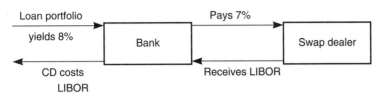

fered rate (LIBOR). Let us assume that the bank has a CD rate equal to LIBOR. Then the bank can use a swap contract to manage its risk. Let us say that a 10-year swap pays 7% fixed in exchange for LIBOR. Then the bank can enter into the swap contract shown in Figure 13-1.

The bank is able to hedge its re-financing costs by receiving LIBOR from the swap dealer. In turn, the bank has to pay 7%. This is not a problem as the loan produces an income of 8%. Now the bank is left with the *credit risk* of the counterparties: the party that has taken the loan and the swap dealer who is the counterparty to the swap transaction.

Asian Options on CP

The first illustration deals with Asian Options on London Interbank offered rates (LIBOR). Consider a AAA-rated corporation that routinely issues commercial paper (CP) every 90 days. Such issues may be made to fund working capital needs and short-term liquidity demands. Given the business operations of the firm, it may be necessary for the firm to schedule periodic issuance over the planning period. As of January 30, 1994, the treasurer of this corporation knows that the firm will be actively in the CP market. To simplify matters, let us assume that, each time, the firm issues a 30-day CP. The current rate for the firm in the CP market is 30 days LIBOR minus 10 basis points. Let us further assume that the firm's credit standing is not going to change in a qualitative way over the next six months, so that the spread relative to 30 days LIBOR may be assumed to be 10 basis points for the planning period. Under these circumstances, it is clear that the risk faced by the firm is the possibility that 30 days LIBOR may go up over the next six months. The exposure to the possibility of increased rates on the respective issuance dates poses the risk of increased cost of capital.

One strategy is to hedge each issue. This can be done by using Eurodollar futures contracts or options on Eurodollar futures contracts. (Think through how you would use these markets.) As pointed out earlier, however, these contracts are standardized and may not suit the issue dates that the treasurer has to deal with. Furthermore, liquidity is currently only significant for contracts whose underlying asset is 90 days LIBOR. If a six-month view is taken by the treasurer, then it may make sense to consider buying a call option on the average of the 30 days LIBOR on the issuance dates. The payoff of such an option may be represented as

$$c = \max\left(0, \{w_1 l_1 + w_2 l_2 + w_3 l_3 + w_4 l_4 + w_5 l_5 + w_6 l_6 - k\}\right), \qquad (13.1)$$

TABLE 13-14 *Commercial Paper Issue Schedule, January 30, 1994*	*Issue Date*	*Amount (in Millions of Dollars)*	*LIBOR on Issue Date*
	2/15/1994	100	l_1
	3/15/1994	200	l_2
	4/15/1994	200	l_3
	5/15/1994	100	l_4
	6/15/1994	200	l_5
	7/15/1994	200	l_6

where w_i represents the weight attached to the LIBOR on issue date i, and l_i is the LIBOR on that issue date. Using the values given in Table 13-14, l_i can be easily calculated. For example,

$$l_1 = \frac{100}{1000} = 0.10.$$

Naturally, $\Sigma_{i=1}^{6} w_i = 1$. Let us think of the strike rate k of the option as the current 30 days LIBOR. Furthermore, let us assume that the option expires on the last issue date and is on a notional principal of the aggregate amount of $1,000 million.

This option gives the issuing corporation several choices.

If the weighted-average rate turns out (expost) to be, say, 3.5% (annualized) and the strike rate is 3% (annualized), the option pays 50 basis points on the notional principal as shown next:

$$\frac{50}{100} \times \frac{1}{100} \times \frac{30}{360} \times 1,000,000,000 = \$416,666.67. \tag{13.2}$$

If the option is American-style, it can be exercised on any issue date with the provision that the payoff at exercise will be the difference between the weighted-average of the LIBOR until the exercise date and the strike rate. If the LIBOR goes up for the period until the first three issue dates and then starts to decline, the issuer may exercise early.

The Asian option is extremely valuable as a strategy. Although this example considered an issuer of short-term paper, the strategy is similar in other markets.

Options on Foreign-Exchange Swaps

The second application deals with the use of a derivative known as options on swaps. Options on a swap are referred to as **swaptions** and represent the right to enter into a swap on or before a specified date at currently determined terms. Such options may be either European- or American-style. If the buyer of the swaption has the right to pay a fixed rate in the swap (upon exercise), it is called a **payer's swaption.** If the buyer of the swaption has the right to receive a fixed rate, it is called a **receiver's swaption.**

Note that such options may be structured with fixed and floating legs in different currencies. Options on foreign-currency swaps are defined in a similar way.

Consider a U.S. firm that has bid for a government project to build a plant or a highway in a foreign country. This creates a capital-budgeting problem. If the bid is successful, the bidder will be awarded the project. Winning the project will result in a future stream of cash flows denominated in the foreign currency. If the bid fails, nothing happens.

In such a situation, the firm faces a contingent foreign-currency exposure. This rules out the strategy of selling the future foreign-currency receipts forward. Buying a swaption, in which the firm has the right to pay the foreign currency and receive the domestic currency, makes a lot of sense. The firm can use the anticipated foreign currency receipts to fund the swap liability and receive the U.S. dollars receipts at currently agreed-upon terms. We expect that this option will only be exercised if the firm wins the bid. Of course, even if the firm loses the bid, the swaption can be exercised as long as it finishes in-the-money.

Quantos—Foreign Equity Investment without Foreign-Exchange Risk

U.S. investors buying (say) German stocks are exposed to two sources of risk, equity risk in the German market and foreign-currency risk due to shifts in the deutsche mark/dollar relationship. Consider a forward contract that allows U.S. investors to buy German stocks. The future payoffs of these contracts will be translated into U.S. dollars at currently determined exchange rates. Such forward contracts are known as guaranteed exchange-rate contracts or **Quantos.**

Let S be the current German stock price in deutsche marks, X be the predetermined exchange rate of dollars and deutsche marks, K be the forward price in deutsche marks at which the investor can buy the stock, and S^* be the stock price when the forward contract matures at date t. Then, the payoff of the Quanto is

$$f = X \times (S^* - K). \tag{13.3}$$

Note that the payoff at date t is uncertain, since the German stock price S^* at date t is unknown. The exchange rate, however, is fixed now at X deutsche marks per dollar. Obviously, $f \geq 0$ or $f \leq 0$, depending on the stock price at date t in relation to the forward price K.

Quantity adjusting options are also available to institutions. These dealer derivatives function as follows: Quanto options give the buyer the right to foreign assets (stocks or bonds) at predetermined strike prices. The payoffs (if any) from such options are converted from foreign currencies at currently agreed-upon exchange rates. For example, in our example, the payoffs of the Quanto option will be

$$c = X \times \max \{(S^* - K), 0\}. \tag{13.4}$$

In Chapter 14 we provide a method for valuing such options.

| | | Cash Flow | Cash Flow |
Position	Investment	When $S^* \geq 70$	When $S^* < 70$
Naked	−7000	S^*	S^*
Protected	$-(7000 + P)$	S^*	70

TABLE 13-15

Portfolio Insurance

P = put premium

Listed or OTC Put Options in Portfolio Insurance

One of the most widely used strategies in the derivatives market is portfolio insurance. Simply stated, the idea is to buy or synthesize a put option on a portfolio to insure it. Chapter 14 contains a detailed description of options.

For example, an investor holding 100 shares of IBM stock wishes to protect himself against the possibility that the stock price may fall over the next month. If the stock is selling at $70 per share, then by buying a one-month put option at a strike price of $70, the investor has assured himself of full protection. To see why this is the case, compare the naked (uninsured) position and the protected (insured) position in Table 13-15. For the protected position, when the stock price after a month, denoted by S^*, is greater than 70, the investor can participate in the upside potential net of the put premium P; when the stock price is below 70, the put can be exercised to ensure that the terminal cash flow is always 70. This strategy provides complete or full insurance. Option at a strike price of $70 may be expensive. If a put option with a strike price of $68 is purchased, then it is less expensive. Such an option is known as an out-of-the-money option. It provides a less-effective insurance but is also less costly.

Likewise, bonds can be protected by buying OTC put options of prespecified maturities. Note that the cost of insurance depends on the level of protection, as well as the volatility of the underlying asset that is being insured: The greater the volatility, the higher the cost of insurance. This idea is presented in Figure 13-2.

In Figure 13-2, σ refers to the volatility (or the riskiness) of the underlying stock, and K refers to the strike price of the option. Chapter 14 explains how such factors affect the value of options.

Commodity Swaps in Risk Management

Commodity swaps are a strategy to reduce risk by exchanging cash flows from realized spot rates for cash flows from a predetermined fixed price. Consider the case of the Energy Products Corporation (EPC), which is engaged in the production of crude oil. The projected monthly production of EPC is 10 million barrels for the next six months. The crude oil is sold to refiners who process the crude oil to produce refined products such as jet fuel. Most of the crude oil production of EPC is sold in the spot market; forward agreements extend only to small maturities and cover a very small part of the production. The quality of the crude produced is similar to that of West Texas Intermediate (WTI) crude oil but is not identical. The crude oil prices at which EPC sells its output fluctuate a great deal. The WTI crude oil futures prices on the

FIGURE 13-2   *Effect of Level of Protection and Volatility in Portfolio Insurance*

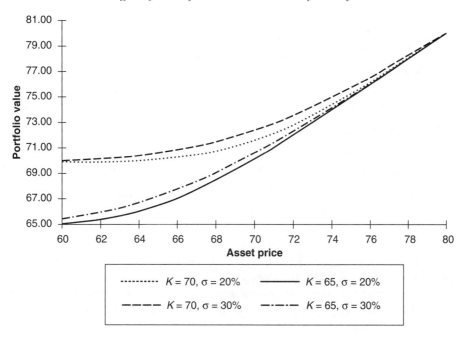

New York Mercantile Exchange (NYMEX) provide a very good proxy for the price risk experienced by EPC. The Treasurer of EPC reviews the production schedule on February 8, 1994, and is concerned by the fact that the crude oil price exposure has led to significant fluctuations in the working capital requirements recently. The investment bankers for EPC have suggested the possible use of dealer derivatives known as commodity swaps. They have also suggested the use of Asian options.

In Figure 13-3, we illustrate a commodity swap by this producer. In this swap transaction, the producer is entering into a swap on a notional principal of 10 million barrels of crude oil. Every month, the producer sells the oil in the spot market. The average price realized in the spot market is paid to the banker through the swap on a notational principal of 10 million barrels per month, and the banker pays the currently agreed-upon fixed price per barrel (in this case $20 per barrel).

Another alternative to the producer is an Asian option. For EPC, the following features should be present in the Asian option:

• The Asian option will be based on a daily average of NYMEX futures prices. On the exercise date, EPC will get the difference between the average NYMEX futures price (until the exercise date) and the strike price. Note that EPC is interested in an Asian put option that gives the right to sell the output valued at an average price at a currently agreed-upon fixed strike price. This structure is ideal if the daily sales are uniform and there are no seasonal patterns within a month.

FIGURE 13-3   *Commodity Swap*

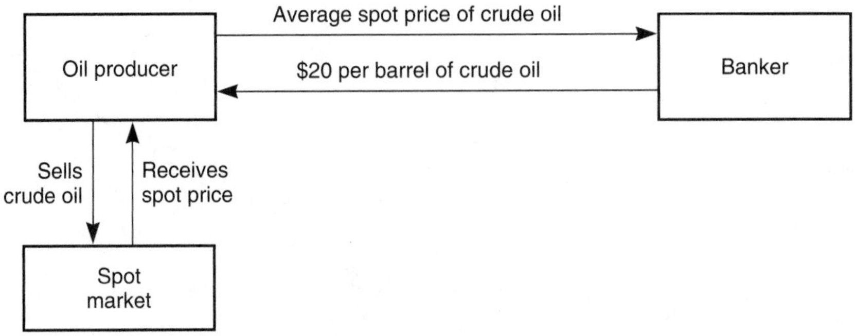

Notes:

1. Every month, the producer sells the oil in the spot market. The average of the spot price in the spot market is paid to the banker through the swap on a notional principal of 10 million barrels every month.

2. The bank pays a fixed price of $20 per barrel.

- The strike price can be chosen to reflect the risk perceptions of the senior management of EPC. An out-of-the money Asian option is less expensive but provides less of a hedge. It is better to present the cost of several strike-price structures and of the implied hedge protection as measured by the delta of the Asian option.

OTHER CLASSIFICATIONS OF DERIVATIVES

From the standpoint of the relationship between the payoffs of the derivatives and the path taken by an underlying state variable, we can classify derivatives into two groups: path-independent dealer derivatives and path-dependent derivatives.

If a standard European call option is priced on the S&P 500 index, then we are only interested in what happened to the S&P 500 index at maturity. It is path-independent. On the other hand, if a lookback call is priced, we need to know the entire path of the S&P 500 index prices. It is path-dependent. Figure 13-4 illustrates the difference. This figure tracks three prices relating to the S&P 500 index:

- the S&P 500 index price,
- the average S&P 500 index price, and
- the maximum S&P 500 index price.

Path-Independent Derivatives

A path-independent security is one whose promised cash flows at any time depend only on the prices and rates at that time. In particular, the promised cash flows do not depend on the history of the prices and rates. Dealer options on bonds, interest-rate swaps, caps, and forward rate agreements fall into this category as do most listed options, forwards, futures, swaps, and dealer derivatives. Path-independent dealer derivatives may be European or American and are easy to price. In Chapter 14 we review the theory behind the pricing of path-independent securities.

FIGURE 13-4   *Stock Price, Average Price, and Maximum Price of the S&P 500 Index*

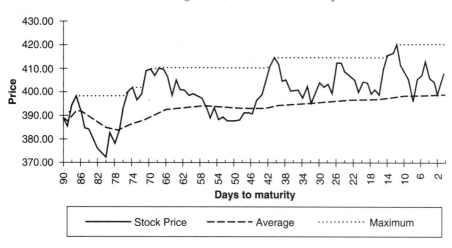

Path-Dependent Derivatives

A path-dependent security is one whose promised cash flows at any time depend not only on the prices and rates at that time but also on the history of prices and rates until that date. Asian options and lookback options are examples in this category. Path-dependent dealer derivatives are usually priced using Monte Carlo simulation techniques.

We list some of the path-dependent derivatives in Table 13-12, and discuss three of them below. The valuation of such exotic options is undertaken in Chapter 14.

Asian Options. This path-dependent option is very popular in the financial community. The payoff of an Asian option depends not only on the underlying asset price on the exercise date but also on the average price of the underlying asset during a pre-specified period during the life of the option. The motivation for buying and selling such an option has already been discussed. An Asian call option will have the payoff distribution

$$c_{\text{Asian}} = \max\left(0, \frac{\sum_{i=1}^{n} S_i}{n} - K\right), \tag{13.5}$$

where S_i, $i = 1, 2, \ldots, n$ are the observed prices of the underlying asset at regular intervals (daily, weekly, monthly, etc.). An Asian put will have the payoff distribution:

$$p_{\text{Asian}} = \max\left(0, K - \frac{\sum_{i=1}^{n} S_i}{n}\right). \tag{13.6}$$

Sometimes, average strike-price options, which are conceptually very similar to Asian options, are traded by the dealer community. The strike price is chosen to be the average of the underlying asset price over a prespecified period during the life of the option. This average strike price is then applied to the terminal asset price at exercise date. The average strike-price call will have the payoff distribution

$$
c_{\text{average}} = \max\left(0, S_n - \frac{\sum_{i=1}^{n} S_i}{n}\right). \tag{13.7}
$$

The average strike-price put will have the payoff distribution

$$
P_{\text{average}} = \max\left(0, \frac{\sum_{i=1}^{n} S_i}{n} - S_n\right). \tag{13.8}
$$

Barrier Options. We noted that the value of an Asian option depends on the history of underlying asset prices because of the fact that the exercise payoff depends on the historical average. In the case of barrier options, the payoffs depend not only on the terminal price of the underlying asset price but also on whether the underlying asset price reached a certain barrier price, specified exogenously in the contract, during the life of the option. Two examples of such barrier options are given next.

Down-and-Out Call Options. These are options that behave exactly like a standard call option except that the option is automatically extinguished prior to its stated expiry date if the underlying asset price drops below the barrier boundary known as the knockout boundary. When the boundary is reached, a rebate is paid to the owner of the option. The payoffs can be formally represented as

$$
c_{\text{down-and-out}} = \max\,(0, S^* - K) \quad \text{if} \quad \forall \quad \tau \leq T \quad S(\tau) > H.
$$

If the knock-out boundary H is hit for the first time prior to the maturity date, then the option is worth $c_{\text{down-and-out}} = R$, where R is the rebate.

Up-and-Out Call Options. These are options that act exactly like standard calls except that when an upper knock-out boundary is reached, the option is automatically extinguished, and a rebate R is paid. The payoffs can be formally represented as

$$
c_{\text{up-and-out}} = \max\,(0, S^* - K) \quad \text{if} \quad \forall \quad \tau \leq T \quad S(\tau) < H.
$$

If the knock-out boundary H is hit for the first time prior to the maturity date, then the option is worth $c_{\text{up-and-out}} = R$, where R is the rebate.

In a similar way down-and-in options and up-and-in options can be defined.

Lookback Options. A lookback call option provides the buyer of the option with the right to the difference between the highest underlying asset price that was reached during the life of the option and the prespecified strike price. Similarly, a lookback put option gives the buyer the right to the difference between the strike price and the lowest underlying asset price that was reached during the life of the option.

The payoffs of lookback options may be represented formally as

$$c_{lookback} = \max \left[0, \max \left(S_0, S_1, \ldots, S_n\right) - K\right]$$

$$p_{lookback} = \max \left[0, K - \min \left(S_0, S_1, \ldots, S_n\right)\right]$$

In the payoff functions shown previously, $S_1, S_2, \ldots, S_n$ represent the realized underlying asset prices during the life of the option.

DERIVATIVES AND RISK MANAGEMENT

Recent losses in the derivatives market are summarized in this section to provide a perspective on the sources of risk in derivatives transactions. A number of highly reputable banks and investment banks have suffered extensive losses in recent times due to improper risk management and control practices.

MBS Market

- J. P. Morgan in 1992 lost close to $200 million U.S. dollars in the mortgage-backed securities market. It was widely understood that their model of prepayments produced incorrect option-adjusted spreads.
- In 1987, Merrill Lynch lost about $350 million in stripped mortgage-backed securities due to incorrect pricing.

In these two instances, the problem seems to have arisen from proprietary trading activities that used an incorrect model to price the securities. There are two sources of risks here: model risk, and data and validation risk.

Bank Debt

- Westpac, an Australian Bank, lost close to $1 billion after writing off bad debts.
- Similar write-offs occurred in many U.S. banks after the Latin American countries defaulted.
- Many U.S. and Japanese banks held large amounts of real estate portfolios, which resulted in substantial write-offs when the commercial real estate market soured.
- Barclays in 1992 made a provision of close to $350 million against a loan that was extended to a British property developer.

There are three sources of risks here: (1) credit risk and lack of contractual control, (2) liquidity and lack-of-diversification risk, and (3) management failure.

Derivatives

- In 1994, Procter and Gamble lost close to $200 million in interest-rate swap transactions arranged by Bankers Trust Company.
- Recently, Kidder Peabody detected that in the government-bond trading area several fictional trades had been sent to the computer system (for phantom forward reconstitutions), resulting in General Electric taking a write-off totaling nearly $250 million.
- Metallgesellschaft, a German trading firm, lost $1 billion in commodities and derivatives trading.

There are three sources of risks here: (1) derivatives-risk management and reporting risk, (2) accounting and verification risk, and (3) risk and speculative limits.

Responses to Improper Risk Management

The global value of derivative trading was estimated at around $88 trillion as shown in Table 13-10. To protect against potential defaults, large loan reserves are held by international banks. Financial institutions are required to maintain risk-adjusted capital. There is an increased emphasis on disclosure of the true financial health of any company, including the off-balance-sheet liabilities. The clients, auditors, rating agencies, and other constituencies are increasingly looking for detailed and transparent accounting systems based on up-to-date prices. **Chapter 19 is devoted to risk measurement and management. There we will examine the different sources of risk and how it can be measured and managed.**

REGULATION OF DERIVATIVES

A number of agencies are involved in the oversight of the derivative markets. The Commodity Futures Trading Commission (CFTC), The Securities and Exchange Commission (SEC), and the Federal Reserve play important roles in regulating these markets. Given the global links of the dealer and listed derivatives markets, foreign governments and their agencies frequently coordinate regulatory issues that affect the functioning of these markets. The interest-rate and currency swaps markets, futures, and options with multiple global listings are obvious examples.

In the United States, as well as in other countries, listed derivatives are subject to regulatory oversight. In fact, the listing requirements are imposed before a derivative may be listed in an exchange. An important ingredient that ensures the financial viability of derivative instruments is the clearinghouse.

Listed futures contracts are marked-to-market daily. The features of markup to market, margins, price limits, and position limits protect the integrity of such derivatives markets. In dealer markets, the credit rating of the dealer, the capital assigned to the derivatives business, and the contractual provisions (such as up-front collaterals, discretionary marking-to-market, contingency provisions, etc.) protect the integrity of such markets.

A detailed treatment of regulation is beyond the scope of this text. We provide several references which provide a detailed treatment of this topic.

CONCLUSION

This chapter provided an overview of listed and dealer derivatives markets. We provided examples of how some exotic derivatives may be used to manage the risks encountered in certain financing and business activities. A perspective of the growth of the dealer derivative markets and the distribution of risks in such markets was also provided.

PROBLEMS

13.1   Explain the major differences between the listed derivative and the dealer derivative markets.

13.2   A corporation is planning to issue $100 million par amount of floating rate notes indexed to 180 days LIBOR, one month from now. Its rate on the floater is LIBOR minus 10 basis points, payable every six months. If the corporation wishes to hedge against the possibility of a rise in short-term interest rates, what are the alternatives that are open to it in (1) the listed derivative markets and (2) the dealer derivative markets? Under what conditions will the corporation choose the dealer markets over listed markets?

13.3   What are the differences between a lookback call and an Asian call option?

13.4   Consider the risk faced by a producer of crude oil.

   (a) Articulate the conditions under which such a producer can use the NYMEX crude oil futures contracts to hedge the price risk.

   (b) Explain the circumstances under which the producer might use commodity swaps.

   (c) When would the producer prefer Asian options?

13.5   Dealers offer caps on interest rates, such as the six-month London Interbank offered rates (LIBOR).

   (a) Give examples of institutional investors who are buyers of this derivative.

   (b) Characterize the economic conditions under which they will buy such derivatives.

13.6   Options on stock indexes are offered by exchanges and by dealers in the OTC market. Assume that two identical stock index options are available, one in the listed market and one in the OTC market. Are investors indifferent to the choice of these two options? Explain your answer.

13.7   Increasingly, corporate treasurers are confronted with the use of derivatives in their day-to-day activities, as well as in policy matters. Some of the activities of a corporate treasurer are listed in the following:

Treasury Activity	*Outlook*
CP issue	Bearish on rates
Pension asset allocation	Some upside with a floor equal to accumulated benefits obligations
Foreign exchange exposure in a foreign subsidiary	Highly volatile earnings and foreign exchange rates

Discuss the use of derivatives in each of these activities.

REFERENCES

Antl, B., ed. 1986. *Swap Finance,* vol. 2. London: Euromoney Publications.

Bank for International Settlements 1988. *International Convergence of Capital Measurement and Capital Standards.* Basle, Switzerland.

Cox, J., and M. Rubinstein 1983. *Options Market.* Englewood Cliffs, NJ: Prentice-Hall.

Darby, M. R. 1994. Over-the-Counter Derivatives and Systemic Risk to the Global Financial System. National Bureau of Economic Research Working Paper Series, No. 4801.

Davis, K., and I. Harper 1991. *Risk Management in Financial Institutions.* Sydney: Allen and Unwin.

Global Derivatives Study Group 1993. *Derivatives; Practices and Principles.* Washington, D.C.: Group of Thirty.

Hull, J. 1989. *Options, Futures and Other Derivative Securities.* Englewood Cliffs, N.J.: Prentice Hall.

"The regulation of OTC derivatives," Testimony of Chairman Alan Greenspan, Before the Committee on Banking and Financial Services, U.S. House of Representatives July 24, 1998.

Sacks, P., and S. Crawford 1991. *New Products, New Risks.* New York: Harper Business.

Walmsley, J. 1988. *The New Financial Instruments.* New York: John Wiley.

SOME USEFUL WEBSITES

1. http://www.bis.org (Bank for International Settlements)

2. http://www.isda.org (International Swap and Derivatives Association)

3. http://www.cboe.com (Chicago Board of Options Exchange)

4. http://www.cbot.com (Chicago Board of Trade)

5. http://www.cme.com (Chicago Mercantile Exchange)

6. http://www.forexdirectory.net

Chapter 14

Options Pricing Theory with Applications to Fixed-Income Markets

Chapter Objectives

This chapter provides an overview of options contracts and options markets in the United States and abroad. Basic no-arbitrage propositions and put-call parity relationships are derived. Chapter 14 will help the reader to understand and answer the following questions:

- What are options on bonds and options on futures contracts?
- What are some commonly used option strategies?
- What are some of the key no-arbitrage relationships for options?
- Which factors determine the value of options?
- What are the put-call parity relationships for options on bonds, options on futures, etc.?
- How are binomial and Black and Scholes formulas obtained and used?
- How can Monte Carlo simulation techniques be used for valuing options?
- How are interest rate options priced?
- What are the ways in which the risks of options are quantified? The concept of delta, gamma, vega, and theta.

In addition, this chapter illustrates the central ideas using worked out examples. The results developed in this chapter are valuable for the valuation of corporate bonds and mortgage-backed securities that have optionlike features. These securities are taken up in later chapters.

INTRODUCTION

In this chapter, a self-contained account of options in equity and fixed-income securities markets will be provided. First, the contracts will be defined and some institutional perspectives will be offered. Then the focus will shift to the no-arbitrage restrictions and the pricing procedures that have been developed for such options. In addition, examples will be provided showing how such options can be used in risk-management applications.

So far, we considered the analysis of Treasury securities that are mostly non-callable. As we saw in Chapter 5, however, even in the Treasury market there are some callable issues. In order to analyze such issues, it is essential to develop some key results in options pricing. This is because a callable Treasury bond provides a call option to the Treasury, and this option will be exercised by the Treasury should the interest rates on similar bonds fall below that coupon. So, the investors would value such callable bonds as a portfolio of an otherwise identical noncallable bond minus the value of a call option that they have provided to the Treasury. As we move to the other sectors of fixed-income markets, such as corporate bond markets and mortgage-backed securities markets later in the book, it will be noted that more optionlike features are present in these markets. For example, many corporate bonds are callable, some provide a put option to the investor, etc. It will turn out that the default risk in corporate bonds can be modeled using option pricing techniques. We will show that the homeowners have the right to prepay their mortgage loan. This is nothing but a call option to "call away" their loan when mortgage rates fall. This option is at the center of pricing mortgage-backed securities.

For these reasons it is logical to develop the valuation of options and the terminology used in options literature at this stage. We proceed to do this next.

CONTRACT: DEFINITION AND TERMINOLOGY

Options are contracts that give the owner (buyer) the right but not the obligation to do something. For this right, the buyer pays a fixed price, which is referred to as the **option premium.** The sellers of options have a corresponding obligation to meet the financial responsibilities in the event the buyer decides to exercise or sell his right. Options that give the right to buy an underlying asset are known as **call options.** Options that give the right to sell an underlying asset are known as **put options.** When options may be exercised only at maturity, they are termed **European.** If they may be exercised at any time prior to (and including) maturity, they are called **American.**

Calls and Puts

A call option is a contract that gives its owner the right but not the obligation to buy a fixed number of a specified security at a fixed price at any time on or before a given date.

The following terminology is used in the context of options:

Exercise: the act of invoking the right.

Underlying security: the specified security on which the option exists.

Strike price: the fixed price at which the buyer has the right to buy.

Expiration date: the date on which the option (right) expires.

Premium: the market price of the option contract.

The buyer of the call can, at any time, exercise the option or retain the option or sell the option at the concurrent market price. On the expiration date, the buyer has to exercise it or sell it (these strategies are equivalent on expiry date) or let it expire.

In Figure 14-1 and Figure 14-2, we illustrate the transactions associated with call options and the alternatives available to the buyer and seller. Figure 14-1 illustrates the initial transaction. The buyer pays the call premium to the seller (writer) and receives the option. Upon exercise (as Figure 14-2 shows) the buyer pays the strike price and surrenders the call option to the seller. In turn, the seller delivers the underlying security. This is an example of an option that settles by physical delivery. In options that are cash settled, instead of delivering the underlying security, the seller will pay the cash value of the underlying security.

The market price of the option on the expiry date depends only on the underlying asset price and the strike price. Let K be the strike price and P^* be the market price of the underlying security on the expiration date. Then c^*, the value of the call (on the underlying security) on its expiration date, depends on whether the option will be exercised or will be allowed to expire. To exercise the option, the buyer of the option pays K, receives the underlying security, and sells the underlying security for P^*. This only makes sense when $P^* > K$. On the other hand, if $P^* \leq K$ it is better to let the option expire.

FIGURE 14-1   *Initial Transaction*

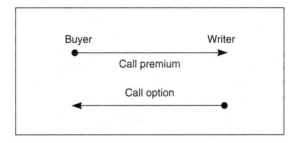

FIGURE 14-2   *Exchange at Option Exercise*

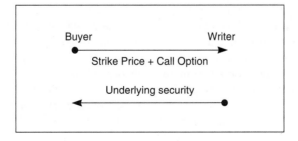

Thus, we can write the option's value on the expiry date succinctly as

$$c* = \begin{cases} P* - K & \text{if } P* > K \\ 0 & \text{if } P* \leq K \end{cases}$$

or more succinctly,

$$c* = \max [0, P* - K]. \tag{14.1}$$

On the expiry date, there is no difference between exercising and selling. If the exercise value is more than the market price, then it is possible to buy the option and exercise it immediately and make arbitrage profits. In a similar way, if the exercise value is less than the market price, then it is possible to sell the option, borrow the strike price, and buy the stock. If the option is exercised, then one delivers the stock and receives the strike price. This leads to riskless profits. If the option is not exercised, the position leaves a cash flow equal to the call premium.

Example 14-1 illustrates a dealer option on a Treasury bond.

Example 14-1:

> **Pricing date:** t = May 6, 1993
> **Underlying security:** $1 million par of 7.25%, 5/15/2016 T-bond
> **Price of underlying security:** $P = 110 \frac{10}{32}$
> **Strike price:** $K = 110$
> **Expiration date:** T = June 6, 1993
> **Call premium:** $c = 2.00$ ($20,000)
> **Style:** European

The dealer here is offering a European call option to customers with a maturity of one month and the option is slightly in-the-money (i.e., $P > K$). Typically, there will be a bid-offer spread at which the dealer will stand ready to buy or sell the option. The quote is 2.00, but the dollar amount is $2 \times 10,000 = 20,000$, since the quotes are in percentages of a million-dollar par amount. (The price of the underlying bond, $110 \frac{10}{32}$, is multiplied by 10,000 to get a dollar price of the bond as $110 \frac{10}{32} \times 10,000 = 1,103,125$.)

A put option is a contract giving its owner the right, but not the obligation, to sell a fixed number of a specified security at a fixed price at any time on or before a given date.

The market price of the option on the expiry date depends only on the underlying asset price and the strike price. Let K be the strike price and $P*$ be the market price of the underlying security on the expiration date. Then, $p*$, the value of the put (on one of the underlying securities) on its expiration date, depends on whether the option will be exercised or will be allowed to expire. To exercise the option, the buyer of the option receives K and delivers the underlying security. It makes sense to exercise when $P* < K$. If $P* \geq K$ it makes sense to let the option expire.

Thus, we can write the option's value on the expiry date succinctly as

$$p^* = \begin{cases} 0 & \text{if } P^* \geq K \\ K - P^* & \text{if } P^* < K \end{cases}$$

or

$$p^* = \max [0, K - P^*]. \tag{14.2}$$

At any time t prior to the maturity date of the option, let P be the value of the underlying asset. When $P \gg K$, call options are said to be **deep-in-the-money.** If $P > K$, then the calls are said to be **in-the-money.** When $P = K$, the calls are said to be **at-the-money.** Usually, when $P \approx K$, the calls are referred to as **near-the-money** options.

In Figure 14-3, we show what happens when the call option is exercised. We assume that the strike price of the option is \$120 per share and that the option is on 100 shares. The buyer of the option pays the strike price (\$120 per share) and surrenders the option. The writer of the option will deliver 100 shares of IBM. Figure 14-4 shows the initial transaction. The buyer pays the put premium to the writer, and the writer delivers the put option to the buyer. Figure 14-5 shows transactions at maturity.

In a similar manner, when $P < K$, calls are referred to as **out-of-the-money** options. When $P \ll K$, calls are referred to as **deep-out-of-the-money options.** Corresponding terminology is used to describe put options.

FIGURE 14-3   *If the Call Option Is Exercised*

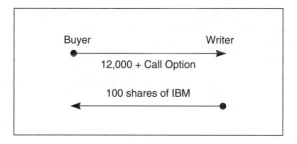

FIGURE 14-4   *Initial Transaction*

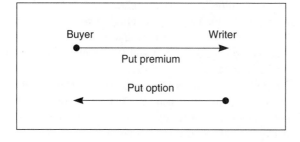

FIGURE 14-5   *Subsequent Exchange at Option Exercise*

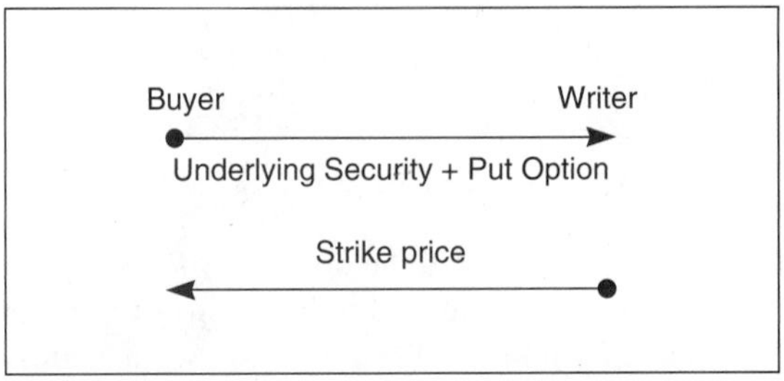

The call and put premiums are also separated into intrinsic values and time values. The **intrinsic value of a call** is max $[0, P - K]$. If the call premium is c, then the **time value of a call** is $c - \max [0, P - K]$. In a similar way, the **intrinsic value of a put** is defined as max $[0, K - P]$. The **time value of a put** is $p - \max [0, K - P]$, where p is the put premium. Usually, the option premium is greater than the intrinsic value. The difference between the two represents the time value of the option.

Example 14-2:

> **Pricing date:** $t =$ May 5, 1995
> **Underlying security:** \$1 million par of 8.00%, 2/15/2023 T-bond
> **Price of underlying security:** $P = 100 \frac{9}{32}$
> **Strike price:** $K = 101$
> **Expiration date:** $T =$ August 15, 1995
> **Put premium:** $p = 2.00$ (\$20,000)
> **Style:** American
>
> This put option is in-the-money (since $K > P$) by $\frac{23}{32}$. Its intrinsic value is $101 - 100 \frac{9}{32} = \frac{23}{32}$. The time value of the option is $2.00 - \frac{23}{32} = 1 \frac{9}{32}$.

Institutional Arrangements

We now turn to the institutional arrangements designed to ensure the integrity of the contracts.

Listed options are supported by clearinghouses. This arrangement delinks the seller of the option from the buyer. The **clearinghouse** interposes itself between the buyers and sellers and acts as sellers to the buyers and vice versa. The contract integrity therefore depends on the solvency and the credit worthiness of the clearinghouse and not on the individual buyers or sellers.

The options markets are organized in centralized exchanges where a number of competing floor traders or brokers and market makers participate. There is a separation of roles. Market makers are permitted to trade only for their own accounts and are not permitted to act on behalf of customers; they bring their own capital and provide liquidity to the exchange. Floor brokers, on the other hand, are only permitted to execute the orders of customers; in effect, they act as the representative of the customer and are not permitted to trade for their own accounts. The floor brokers and market makers are members of the options exchanges. In addition to the floor brokers and market makers, there are order-book officials who are employees of the exchange and who handle the orders of public customers.

Classification of Options

Options may be classified along several dimensions. If options are classified based on who offers them, they are either over-the-counter (OTC) options or listed options. OTC options (also referred to as dealer options) are offered by dealer. It should be noted that OTC options are more customized, less liquid, and are driven by the dealer's capital that is assigned to the options business.

Options that are traded at the Chicago Board of Options Exchange (CBOE), the Chicago Board of Trade (CBT), and other centralized exchanges are known as listed options. Listed options are more standardized, more liquid, and are driven by the clearinghouse guarantees.

Options may also be classified according to the underlying assets: foreign exchange (FX) options, index options, equity options, options on futures contracts, options on bonds, options on interest rates, etc. Options may be explicit or implicit. Sellers of futures contracts have the option to choose which asset to deliver and when to deliver; these seller's options are reflected in the futures price, and such options are **implicit.** Similarly, in deciding to accept or reject a project, the corporate controller has the option of accepting the project now or later. Each project is in competition with itself postponed; by delaying the project, we give up the positive NPV today, but we may get a better draw on interest rates leading potentially to a lower cost of capital. In addition, we get more information about the project's cash flows and costs as the time passes. We could list other examples of options, but the point should be clear: Options are present in everyday choices.

Options are also present in most corporate contracts. Compensation packages typically include stock options, and corporate bonds are issued with call features, conversion options, sinking fund options, and so on. Such options are called imbedded options.

We need to understand the following:

- The presence of such options
- The motivation for such options
- How to value such options

FACTORS DETERMINING AN OPTION'S VALUE

In this section, we will examine the determinants of an option's value. Recall that the intrinsic value of a call is max $[0, P - K]$ and that of a put is max $[0, K - P]$. Clearly, a call's intrinsic value increases in the underlying asset price and decreases in the strike price.

TABLE 14-1

*Factors in American
Options*

Factor	Call	Put
Market price (P)	↑	↓
Strike price (K)	↓	↑
Volatility (σ)	↑	↑
Riskless interest rate (r)	↑	↓
Time to expiration (t)	↑	↑
Dividend yield (d)	↓	↑

TABLE 14-2

*Factors in European
Options*

Factor	Call	Put
Market price (P)	↑	↓
Strike price (K)	↓	↑
Volatility (σ)	↑	↑
Riskless interest rate (r)	↑	↓
Time to expiration (t)	?	?
Dividend yield (d)	↓	↑

The option premium is, in general, greater than the intrinsic value. We enumerate the factors that influence the American and European options markets in Tables 14-1 and 14-2. The effect of increasing each factor while holding all the other factors fixed is also shown as an arrow pointing in the direction of its impact on the option premium. The following is a brief discussion of each factor:

P: The current market price of underlying security is clearly a major determinant of the option premium. As the market price increases, the value of a call option increases and that of the put decreases.

K: The strike price of an option clearly influences its value. The call's value decreases with the strike price, and the put's value increases with the strike price.

σ: The volatility of the underlying security is another major factor. As the volatility increases, the probability of extreme outcomes increases. For a call option, extreme values on the upside places the option in-the-money, and the holder benefits by either selling the option or exercising it; extreme outcomes on the downside are not of concern, since the loss on the downside is bounded by the call premium. Similar arguments show that a put also benefits from increased volatility.

r: The riskless interest rate is also an important factor in the determination of an option's value. The holder of a call option has to pay the strike price to exercise the option and must set the present value of the strike price aside in the bank in order to make this payment at maturity. As the riskless rate increases, the holder of the call needs to set aside less money in the bank in order to pay the strike price at the maturity date of the option. Hence, the call value increases with the riskless rate of interest. Conversely, the put value decreases with the riskless rate.

t: The time to maturity of the option plays two distinct roles. First, as the maturity increases, there is more time for the volatility effect to play out. This affects both calls and puts favorably. Second, as the maturity increases, the effect of the riskless rate takes on a bigger role; this favorably affects the call but adversely affects the put option. So, we can say that as the time to maturity increases, the call value increases. For puts, the direction depends on whether the put is European or American. For an American put, as the time to maturity increases, the value increases. We cannot be unequivocal about the value of European put options as the time to maturity increases. For European call options, when dividends are paid by the underlying asset during the life of the option, we cannot be certain about the effect of time to maturity.

d: Coupon payments or dividends play a role in affecting the value of options. Loosely speaking, the payment of a coupon reduces the full price of the bond. The value of the call (put) depends on the design of the contract. Typically, the options on a bond are specified such that the holder will have to pay (receive) the strike price plus the accrued interest in order to receive (deliver) the underlying bond. This effectively means that the accrued interest or the coupon becomes a wash in computing the payoffs of the option. We will examine this in greater detail later in the chapter.

Note that the expected return on the underlying security is not a factor in determining option premium.

TRADING STRATEGIES

Options enable investors to obtain a variety of payoff distributions in future. Such risk-return patterns are not easy to create without options. In this section, we describe some of the trading strategies extensively used by practitioners in capital markets.

Cox and Rubinstein (1985) define four classes of options-trading strategies:

1. Uncovered (naked) positions
2. Covered or hedged positions
3. Spreads
4. Combinations

Uncovered Positions

First, we take up uncovered positions. There are four such positions: long call, long put, short call, and short put. (See Table 14-3.) The payoffs associated with each position on the maturity date of the option are shown in Figures 14-6 through 14-9. Note that in each figure, we show not only the payoffs at the maturity date of the option but also the payoffs when the options have three months to maturity. This provides a useful contrast and also provides a distinction between the time value and intrinsic value.

TABLE 14-3   *Summary of Uncovered-Positions Strategies*

Classification	*Features*
Long call	Bullish view. Downside-limited call premium. Upside unlimited in principle. Break-even level is the premium paid plus the strike. (See Figure 14-6.)
Long put	Bearish view. Downside-limited put premium. Upside limited to the current underlying asset price at initiation. Break-even price is the strike minus the premium. (See Figure 14-7.)
Short call	Neutral to bearish view. Downside unlimited. Upside limited to the call premium. Break-even level is premium paid plus the strike. (See Figure 14-8.)
Short put	Neutral to bullish view. Downside limited to the underlying asset price (at initiation less the premium). Upside limited to the put premium. Break-even level is the strike minus the premium. (See Figure 14-9.)

FIGURE 14-6   *Long Position in a Call Option*

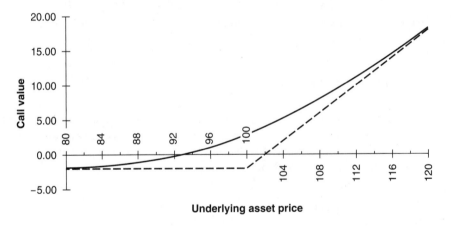

Uncovered positions are essentially speculative positions. Using the replicating-portfolio concepts, it is possible to precisely characterize the nature of the risk associated with these positions as will be shown later.

In Figures 14-6 to 14-9, we assume that the call premium at the time of purchase or sale is 2.00 and that of the put is 1.80. In addition, we assume that the underlying asset price and the strike price of these options are the same at 100. In each of the options positions described, there are break-even points that separate the profitable regions from the other regions. For example, in Figure 14-6, the buyer of the call paid 2.00. At maturity, the underlying asset price has to be at least 102 for the buyer of the option to break even. It is easy to recognize that the option has no time value at maturity; all the value is represented by the intrinsic value. When the option has three months left to maturity, the option has both time value and intrinsic value.

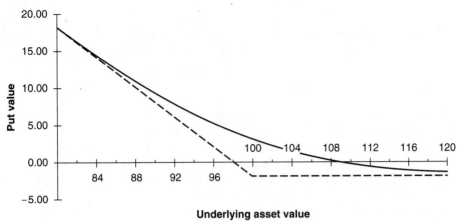

FIGURE 14-7   *Long Position in a Put Option*

Position value at maturity and at three months prior to maturity.

Initial put premium = 1.80; strike = 100

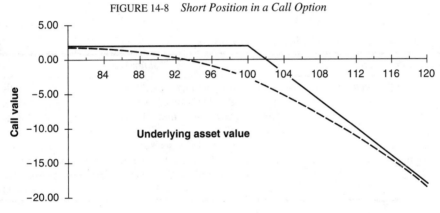

FIGURE 14-8   *Short Position in a Call Option*

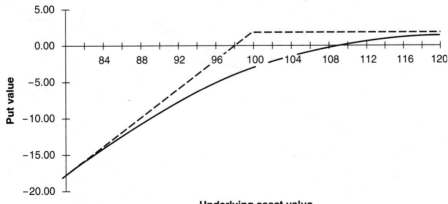

FIGURE 14-9   *Short Position in a Put Option*

Call value at maturity and at three months prior to maturity.

Initial premium = 2.00; strike = 100

The break-even price for a long position in the put option is 98.20. The underlying asset price will have to drop to this level for the put buyer to break even at maturity.

Covered (Hedged) Positions

The hedged positions (see Table 14-4) are frequently employed by professional portfolio managers in mutual funds, pension funds, and hedge funds. The strategy of buying the underlying asset and writing a call option is referred to as the buy-write strategy and is frequently employed in the industry; by writing a call at a strike of 102 and buying the asset at 100, the manager is able to take in the call premium and enjoy the upside potential up to 102. If the underlying asset price goes above 102, the call is in-the-money, and the underlying asset is called away. The buy-write strategy is illustrated in Figure 14-10.

The strategy of buying the underlying asset and buying a put option on the underlying asset is an insurance strategy. This is illustrated in the payoff diagram in Figure 14-11.

TABLE 14-4   *Summary of Covered-Positions Strategies*

Classification	*Features*
Buy-write (buy underlying and write call)	Neutral and low volatility view. Downside is cushioned by call premium. Upside is capped by the strike price. Break-even level is the strike price minus the premium received. (See Figure 14-10.)
Protective put (buy put and buy the underlying asset)	Insured position; underlying asset is insured at the strike less the premium paid. Upside potential is the same as the underlying asset less the put premium. Break-even price is the strike price plus the underlying asset price at initiation. (See Figure 14-11.)

FIGURE 14-10   *Buy-Write Policy*

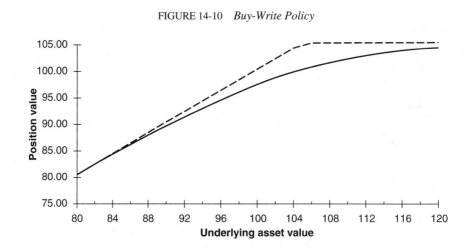

Short positions in call and put options carry considerable risk; there is always the possibility that the buyer will exercise the option prior to the maturity date of the option.

Spreads and Combinations

The last two classes of options-trading strategies, spread positions and combinations, are presented in Tables 14-5 and 14-6.

FIGURE 14-11   *Protective Put*

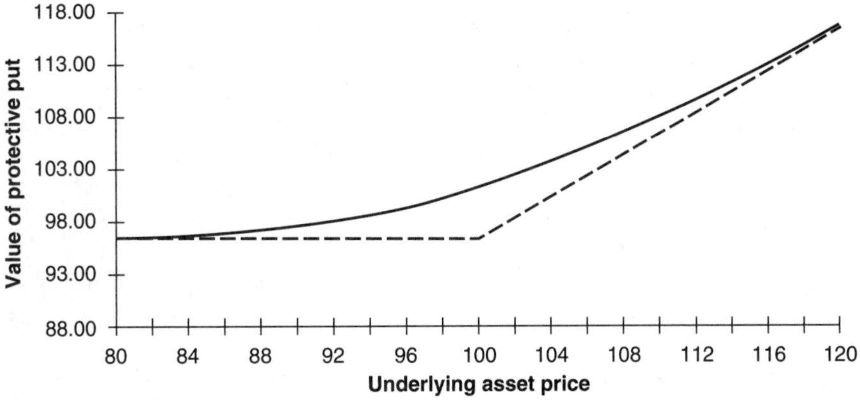

TABLE 14-5   *Summary of Spread Strategies*

Classification	Features
Vertical spreads (VS)	
Bullish VS (buy $c(K_1)$ and write $c(K_2)$)	Position requires positive outlay. Moderately bullish. Break-even price is $K_1 + c(K_1) - c(K_2)$. Downside limited.
Bullish VS (buy $p(K_1)$ and write $p(K_2)$)	Same.
Bearish VS (buy $c(K_2)$ and write $c(K_1)$)	Position generates income. Mildly bearish.
Bearish VS (buy $p(K_2)$ and write $p(K_1)$)	Position generates income. Mildly bearish.
Time spreads (buy call $c(K_1)$ and sell call $c(K_1)$ with different maturities)	Position can be structured so as to generate a cash inflow or an outflow.

TABLE 14-6   *Summary of Combinations*

Classification	Features
Straddle (buy call $c(K_1)$ and buy put $p(K_1)$ with same maturities ($S = K_1$))	Position requires a positive outlay. Makes money for a strong move on either side.
Strangle (buy call $c(K_3)$ and buy put $p(K_1)$ with same maturities ($S = K_2$))	Position requires a positive outlay. Makes money for a strong move on either side.

NO-ARBITRAGE RESTRICTIONS

The absence of riskless arbitrage means that the prices of options should satisfy certain relationships. These appear in Merton (1973), an important paper on options pricing.

Lower Bounds

Lower bounds specify levels below which no options may sell. If these bounds are violated, then there are riskless arbitrage opportunities. The lower bounds can be formulated as follows:

- $c \geq 0$ and $p \geq 0$. If the options premiums are negative, then the buyer of the option will be paid a positive sum. This is inconsistent with no arbitrage.
- $c \geq P - K$ (for American calls) and $p \geq K - P$ (for American puts), where P is the underlying asset price. If these restrictions are not met, then the optimal strategy is to buy the options and immediately exercise them.

Put-Call Parity

An important relation in options-pricing theory is known as the **put-call parity relationship.** In this section, we state and prove the put-call parity results for options on bonds (stocks) and futures contracts.

In Table 14-7, we provide the basic recipe that may be used to verify that the calls on puts on stocks and bonds satisfy the parity relation. Note that transactions 2, 3, and 4 in Table 14-7 together exactly replicate transaction 1, which is a long position in call. To prevent arbitrage, we must have

$$c = p + P - \frac{K}{(1 + R)^{T-t}} \tag{14.3}$$

TABLE 14-7 Put-Call Parity for Options on Stocks or Bonds	Transaction Today	Investment Today	$P^* \geq K$ Date T	$P^* < K$ Date T
	1. Buy the call	$-c$	$P^* - K$	0
	2. Buy the put	$-p$	0	$K - P^*$
	3. Buy the bond	$-P$	P^*	P^*
	4. Borrow the present value of the strike	$\dfrac{K}{(1+R)^{T-t}}$	$-K$	$-K$
	Total of $(2) + (3) + (4)$	$-p - P + \dfrac{K}{(1+R)^{T-t}}$	$P^* - K$	0

Note that the put-call parity stated previously means that an at-the-money call option on stock will be more expensive than an at-the-money put. To see why this is true, set $P = K$ and note that the put-call parity is

$$c = p + P - \frac{P}{(1 + R)^{T-t}} > p,$$

when $R > 0$. This relationship is modified when there are intermediate payments on the underling security, such as coupons or dividends. In interpreting the put-call parity for options on bonds, we must regard K as the strike price inclusive of accrued interest on the expiration date, and P is the full price of the bond inclusive of accrued interest.

We illustrate the put-call parity with Example 14-3.

Example 14-3:

> **Pricing date:** t = February 15, 1995
> **Underlying security:** $1 million par of 8.00%, 2/15/2023 T-bond
> **Price of underlying security:** $P = 100\frac{9}{32}$
> **Strike price:** $K = 100$
> **Expiration date:** T = June 15, 1995
> **Call premium:** $c = 4.20$ ($42,000)
> **Put premium:** $p = 2.00$ ($20,000)
> **Style:** European
> **Financing rate:** $r = 6\%$
> **Accrued interest:** $ai_t = 0$

Let us set up the transactions which will replicate the call option by buying other securities, as shown next in Table 14-8. The maturity of the option is 120 days. The transactions indicate that the call's payoffs are exactly replicated by buying the put, buying the underlying bond, and borrowing the present value of the strike price. The difference between the price of the call, 4.20, and the value of the portfolio of put, bond, and the amount borrowed that replicates the call, 4.18, is negligible.

TABLE 14-8   *Put-Call Parity for Options on a T-Bond (Example 14-3)*

Transaction Today	Investment Today	$P^* \geq K$ Date T	$P^* < K$ Date T
1. Buy the call	−4.20	$P^* - 100$	0
2. Buy the put	−2.00	0	$100 - P^*$
3. Buy the bond	$-100\frac{9}{32}$	P^*	P^*
4. Borrow the present value of the strike	$\dfrac{100}{(1+0.06)^{\frac{120}{365}}} = 98.1025$	−100	−100
Total of (2) + (3) + (4)	$-2 - 100.28125 + 98.1025 = -4.18$	$P^* - 100$	0

TABLE 14-9   *Put-Call Parity for Options on Bonds with Coupons*

Transaction Today	Investment Today	Dividends Date s	$P^* \geq K$ Date T	$P^* < K$ Date T
1. Buy the call	$-c$		$P^* - K$	0
2. Buy the put	$-p$		0	$K - P^*$
3. Buy the bond	$-P$	d	P^*	P^*
4. Borrow the present value of strike	$\dfrac{K}{(1+R)^{T-t}}$		$-K$	$-K$
5. Borrow the present value of dividend	$\dfrac{d}{(1+R)^{s-t}}$	$-d$		
Total of (2) + (3) + (4) + (5)	$-p - P + \dfrac{K}{(1+R)^{T-t}} = \dfrac{d}{(1+R)^{s-t}}$		$P^* - K$	0

Consider now a situation when at date s, where $t \leq s \leq T$, there is a cash flow d from the underlying security. This might arise because the underlying bond pays a coupon during the life of the option. The put-call parity in such a case may be derived as shown in Table 14-9.

The put-call parity relationship is

$$c = p + P - \frac{K}{(1 + R)^{T-t}} - \frac{d}{(1 + R)^{s-t}}. \tag{14.4}$$

For bond options, we regard d as coupon payments. Typically, for bond options, the buyer of the option pays the strike price plus accrued interest when the option is exercised. In turn, the underlying bond is delivered. Since the market convention is to work with the flat price B_t of the bond, we may write the put-call parity for bond options as

$$c = p + (B_t + a_t) - \frac{\hat{K} + a_T}{(1 + R)^{T-t}} - \frac{d}{(1 + R)^{s-t}}, \tag{14.5}$$

where the full price at t is P, which equals the flat price B_t plus the accrued interest a_t. The option has a flat strike price of $\hat{K}$, and the person exercising the option at date T will pay the flat strike price plus the accrued interest at date T, which is a_T.

Example 14-4:

In this example, we determine the price of a call given the price of a put, the underlying bond, and the financing rate, using the put-call parity relation.

> **Pricing date:** t = February 17, 1987
> **Underlying security:** $1 million par of 7.50%, 11/15/2016 T-bond
> **Price of underlying security:** $P = 98.625$
> **Strike price:** $K = 100$

TABLE 14-10 *Put-Call Parity for Options on a T-bond with Coupons (Example 14-4)*

Transaction Today	Investment Today	Coupon Date s	$P^* \geq K$ Date T	$P^* < K$ Date T
1. Buy the call	$-c$		$P^* - K$	0
2. Buy the put	-5		0	$100.64 - P^*$
3. Buy the bond	-100.575	3.75	P^*	P^*
4. Borrow the present value of strike	$\dfrac{100 + 0.64}{(1.06)^{\frac{118}{365}}}$		-100.64	-100.64
5. Borrow the present value of coupons	$\dfrac{3.75}{(1.06)^{\frac{87}{365}}}$	-3.75		
Total of (2) + (3) + (4) + (5)	$-5 - 100.575 + 98.762$ $+ 3.698 = -3.12$		$P^* - 100.64$	0

Expiration date: T = June 15, 1987
Call premium: c = ??
Put premium: p = 5.00 ($50,000)
Style: European
Financing rate: (R =) 6%
Coupon date: s = 5/15/1987
Accrued interest at t: $(a_t) 1.95 \left[\frac{94}{2 \times 181} \times 7.5 = 1.95 \right]$

Accrued interest at T: $(a_T) 0.64 \left[\frac{31}{2 \times 181} \times 7.5 = 0.64 \right]$

Note that the put-call parity shown in Table 14-10 produces the call price 3.12.

If both the call and the put on the bond are at-the-money, so that $B_t = \hat{K}$, then we have

$$c = p + (B_t + a_t) - \frac{B_t + a_T}{(1 + R)^{T-t}} - \frac{d}{(1 + R)^{s-t}}. \tag{14.6}$$

Note that even if the bond does not pay any coupons during the life of the option (so that $d = 0$), the relation between the at-the-money call and put will depend on the shape of the yield curve. To see this, set $d = 0$ and write the put-call parity for at-the-money options as

$$c = p + (B_t + a_t) - \frac{B_t + a_T}{(1 + R)^{T-t}}. \tag{14.7}$$

The accrued interest of the bond reflects the coupons (yields) in the long end of the yield curve, and R is the short-term financing rate. In a positively sloped yield curve, the increase in accrued interest $a_T - a_t$ far exceeds the financing costs:

$$(B_t + a_t) \times [(1 + R)^{T-t} - 1].$$

This may be rewritten as

$$c = p + \frac{(B_t + a_t) \times \{(1 + R)^{T-t} - 1\} - (a_T - a_t)}{(1 + R)^{T-t}}. \tag{14.8}$$

Clearly, **when the carry is positive, the at-the-money put option on a bond is more expensive than the at-the-money call option.**

Options on Futures Contracts

A long position in a call option on a futures contract gives the right to take a long position in an underlying futures contract at a currently determined futures price on or before the maturity date of the option. When the option is exercised, a *long* position in the underlying futures contract is opened in the account of the investor who exercised the option. (Note that the value of futures contract opened is zero.) The difference between the prevailing futures price and the strike price is paid to the investor.

A long position in a put option on a futures contract gives the right to take a short position in an underlying futures contract at a currently determined futures price on or before the maturity date of the option. When the option is exercised, a *short* position in the underlying futures contract is opened in the account of the investor who exercised the option. The value of the futures contract opened is zero. The difference between the strike price and the prevailing futures price is paid to the investor.

For options on futures contracts, the put-call parity relationship may be derived as shown in Table 14-11.

This leads to the put-call parity relation for options on futures,

$$c = p + \frac{H - K}{(1 + R)^{T-t}}. \tag{14.9}$$

Note that an at-the-money call on futures is identical in price to an at-the-money put option. We illustrate the put-call parity relation for options on futures in Example 14-5.

TABLE 14-11 *Put-Call Parity for Options on Futures*	Transaction Today	Investment Today	$H^* \geq K$ Date T	$H^* < K$ Date T
	1. Buy the call	$-c$	$H^* - K$	0
	2. Buy the put	$-p$	0	$K - H^*$
	3. Buy the futures	0	$H^* - H$	$H^* - H$
	4. Lend the present value of $(H - K)$	$-\dfrac{H - K}{(1+R)^{T-t}}$	$H - K$	$H - K$
	Total of (2) + (3) + (4)	$-p - \dfrac{H - K}{(1+R)^{T-t}}$	$H^* - K$	0

Example 14-5

In this example, we determine the price of a put, given the price of a call, the underlying futures, and the financing rate, using the put-call parity relation.

> **Pricing date:** $t =$ February 17, 1987
> **Underlying security:** T-bond futures (March 1987)
> **Futures Price:** $H = 99.35$
> **Strike price:** $K = 100$
> **Expiration date:** $T = 06/15/1987$
> **Call premium:** $c = 5.00$
> **Put premium:** $p =$??
> **Style:** European
> **Financing rate:** $(R =)\ 6\%$

The steps are shown in Table 14-12. The put premium can be calculated from the equation:

$$p + \frac{99.35 - 100}{(1.06)^{\frac{118}{365}}} = 5.$$

Solving, we get $p = 5 + 0.64 = 5.64$.

It is important to note that the put-call parity relations hold only for European options. Further, in deriving the put-call parity relation for options on futures, we have assumed that the futures contracts are not marked to market every day.

Alternatively, we could have assumed that all future one-period interest rates are known. Then, as Cox, Ingersoll, and Ross (1981) and Richard and Sundaresan (1981) have shown, forward and futures prices are the same and the put-call parity relation previously shown goes through even when futures are marked to market. As a practical matter, the empirical effect of marking to market seems to be unimportant for short maturities.

TABLE 14-12   *Put-Call Parity for Options on Futures (Example 14-5)*

Transaction Today	Investment Today	$H^* \geq K$ Date T	$H^* < K$ Date T
1. Buy the call	-5	$H^* - 100$	0
2. Buy the put	$-p$	0	$100 - H^*$
3. Buy the futures	0	$H^* - 99.35$	$H^* - 99.35$
4. Lend the present value of $(99.35 - 100)$	$-\dfrac{99.35 - 100}{(1.06)^{T-t}}$	$99.35 - 100$	$99.35 - 100$
Total of $(2) + (3) + (4)$	$-p - \dfrac{99.35 - 100}{(1.06)^{T-t}}$	$H^* - 100$	0

Upper Bounds

Upper bounds specify levels above which no options may sell. If these bounds are violated, then there are riskless arbitrage opportunities.

- $c \leq P$ and $p \leq K$. The call premium must be less than the underlying asset price, and the put premium must be below the strike price of the option. Note that $0 \leq c \leq P$; hence, if $P = 0$, $c = 0$.
- The lower-boundary condition may be tightened as shown next.

$$c \geq P - \frac{K}{(1 + R)^{T-t}} - \frac{d}{(1 + R)^{s-t}} \tag{14.10}$$

This condition follows from the put-call parity relation and the fact that $p \geq 0$.

- $c(K_2) \leq c(K_1)$ and $c(t_2) \geq c(t_1)$, where $K_2 > K_1$ and $t_2 > t_1$. Note that if $c(K_2) > c(K_1)$, there is a riskless arbitrage; we will write the option $c(K_2)$ and buy the other, netting an income of $c(K_2) - c(K_1) > 0$. If the written call is exercised, we can always exercise the call that we purchased. This action will net an additional income of $K_2 - K_1$. This condition holds for both American-style and European-style options. In a similar way, if $c(t_2) < c(t_1)$, there is an arbitrage opportunity; we will buy $c(t_2)$ and sell $c(t_1)$, netting an income of $c(t_1) - c(t_2) > 0$. If the options are American, then any time the written option is exercised, we can either sell or exercise the option that we purchased to make money or break even.

We summarize in Table 14-13 the key no-arbitrage bounds that were developed originally in Merton (1973).

Optimal Early Exercise

The flexibility of American options, permitting the holder to exercise at any time prior to the expiry date, make them more attractive than their European counterparts. In this section, we consider the optimal early exercise strategies for American calls and puts.

Early Exercise of American Calls. The optimal premature exercise of American call options is based on the trade-off between the present value of dividends achieved by exercising the call and the present value of the interest on the strike price given up by exercising it. Since any exercise strategy that calls for exercise prior to the payment of dividends results in foregone interest, it is by definition suboptimal. Hence, the best time to exercise an option early is just prior to the exdividend date. Whenever the present value of dividends exceeds the present value of the interest on the strike price, you must exercise the option; otherwise, you should sell it.

To verify these claims, we can use the bounds that were developed earlier (see Table 14-13). The logic works as follows:

- The call is worth $c \geq (P - K)$, in general. (If $c < (P - K)$, then we will buy the call and immediately exercise it to make money.)

TABLE 14-13   *Summary of No-Arbitrage Bounds*

Underlying Asset	Bounds	Style (A or E)
Lower bounds	$c \geq 0$	A and E
	$c \geq P - K$	A
	$c \geq P - \dfrac{K}{(1+R)^{T-t}} - \dfrac{d}{(1+R)^{s-t}}$	A and E
	$p \geq 0$	A and E
	$p \geq K - P$	A
	$p \geq \dfrac{K}{(1+R)^{T-t}} + \dfrac{d}{(1+R)^{s-t}} - P$	A and E
Upper bounds	$c \leq P$	A and E
	$p \leq K$	A and E
	$p \leq \dfrac{K}{(1+R)^{T-t}}$	E
Other bounds	$c(K_1) \geq c(K_2)$ if $K_2 > K_1$	A and E
	$p(K_1) \leq p(K_2)$ if $K_2 > K_1$	A and E
	$c(K_1) - c(K_2) \leq K_2 - K_1$	A and E
	$c(K_1) - c(K_2) \leq \dfrac{K_2 - K_1}{(1+R)^{T-t}}$	E
	$p(K_2) - p(K_1) \leq K_2 - K_1$	A and E
	$p(K_1) - p(K_2) \leq \dfrac{K_2 - K_1}{(1+R)^{T-t}}$	E
	$c(K_2) \geq \lambda c(K_1) + (1-\lambda)c(K_3)$	A and E
	$p(K_2) \geq \lambda p(K_1) + (1-\lambda)p(K_3)$	A and E
Early exercise rules	Never exercise the call if $PV(\text{int}) > PV(d)$. Never exercise the put if $PV(\text{int}) < PV(d)$.	

Note: $\lambda = \frac{K_3 - K_2}{K_3 - K_1}$. (We derive the early exercise conditions in a later section of the chapter.) We assume that $K_3 > K_2 > K_1$.

- If $c > P - K$, then it makes sense to sell the call and realize c rather than exercising and realizing just $P - K$.
- So, we need to identify the conditions under which $c = P - K$ so that the exercise value is the option value. To identify such circumstances, let us consider when $c = P - K$ will lead to possible riskless arbitrage.

  Suppose $c = P - K$. Then consider the following self-financing strategy: buy the call, short the underlying asset, and lend the strike price to earn interest. This position makes money, as long as the underlying asset does not make any cash payments.

  If a cash payment is made, then the short seller must make restitution.

- Hence, we may conclude that $c > P - K$ on all days except on the exdividend dates and the expiration date.

A consequence of this logic is that if the underlying asset never pays any dividends during the life of the option, then $c > P - K,$ and it is preferable to sell the option rather than to exercise it. Thus, we conclude that a call option on a stock not paying dividends during the option's life should never be exercised. A necessary condition for an American call to be exercised is that the underlying security must make some cash payments during the option's life. Note that even if dividends are paid, as long as the interest earned on the strike price is sufficient to make restitution of the dividends, it is still optimal to hold the option and not exercise it.

Define the present value of interest on the strike price as

$$PV(\text{int}) \equiv \frac{K \times (1 + R)^{T-t} - K}{(1 + R)^{T-t}}.$$

Let the present value of dividends be defined as

$$PV(d) = \frac{d}{(1 + R)^{s-t}}.$$

From the lower bound conditions in Table 14-13, we know that

$$c \geq P - \frac{K}{(1 + R)^{T-t}} - \frac{d}{(1 + R)^{s-t}}.$$

This may be rewritten as

$$c \geq P - K + PV(\text{int}) - PV(d).$$

Note that if $PV(\text{int}) - PV(d) > 0,$ then $c > P - K,$ and it is not optimal to exercise the call. For sufficiently large dividends, we will encounter cases in which $c = P - K$ and which call for optimal exercise of the call option.

Early Exercise of American Puts. An American put may be optimally exercised even in the absence of dividend payments. To see why this is the case, let us first note from the put-call parity relation that

$$p = c - P + \frac{K}{(1 + R)^{T-t}} + \frac{d}{(1 + R)^{s-t}}.$$

This holds for European options. We can rewrite the previous equation as

$$p = c - P + K - PV(\text{int}) + PV(d).$$

Now consider an American put. For an American put, the following inequality must hold:

$$p \geq c - P + K - PV(\text{int}) + PV(d).$$

When early exercise is optimal, its value should be $p = K - P.$ Using the condition previously stated, if $c + PV(d) - PV(\text{int}) > 0,$ then $p > K - P;$ hence, early exercise is not optimal. Take the extreme case when $PV(d) = 0.$ Then, if $c < PV(\text{int}),$ it may be optimal to exercise the put option. Note that c in this context is a European call. As the strike price K increases, the value of a European call c will fall, but $PV(\text{int})$ will increase. This suggests that when K is sufficiently high, the put will be exercised.

In this section, we considered bounds that are the consequence of no arbitrage. To get a precise relationship between the value of an option and its determinants, we need to place additional structure on the valuation problem.

CONCEPT OF NO ARBITRAGE

The **principle of no arbitrage** says that two perfect substitutes that are freely traded have to sell at the same price in the absence of frictions, such as transactions costs, short-sale constraints, taxes, etc. This simple concept also has been referred to as the **absence of free lunch,** or the **law of one price.** In the context of fixed-income securities markets, this concept has tremendous relevance. In valuing bonds of different maturities and contractual provisions, we must ensure that there are no arbitrage opportunities. In other words, it should not be the case that some combination of bonds may be used to replicate the cash flows of some other bond at a lower cost. At a first glance, it may appear that there are no perfect substitutes that are simultaneously traded; hence, one might conclude that this concept is of limited value. As we will show in this chapter, however, by using specific trading strategies it is possible to create perfect substitutes. We will show that it is possible to replicate the payoffs of options on bonds by trading in the underlying bond and either lending or borrowing money on an overnight basis. We will formalize these ideas next.

Concept of State Prices

Consider a simple setting in which at date $t = 0$, a bond is selling at price P. At date $t = 1$, it can either sell at uP with a probability q or sell at dP with a probability $1 - q$. We denote the bond price uP at date 1 as an "up state" and the bond price dP at date 1 as a "down state."

$$
\begin{array}{ccc}
 & & uP \\
 & \nearrow & \\
P & & \\
 & \searrow & \\
 & & dP \\
t = 0 & \quad & t = 1
\end{array}
$$

We assume that $u > 1 + R > d$, where R is the riskless rate of interest (such as 4% or 0.04). Let us define $r = 1 + R$. The expected return on this bond defined by

$$
E(\overline{R}) = \frac{quP + (1 - q)dP}{P} = qu + (1 - q)d.
$$

In a similar manner, we can compute the variance of the return on the bond

$$\sigma^2(\tilde{R}) = [q\{u - E(\overline{R})\}^2 + (1 - q)\{d - E(\overline{R})\}^2].$$

This expression for the variance of the return on the bond can be simplified as

$$\sigma^2(\tilde{R}) = [q(1 - q)](u - d)^2.$$

The volatility of the return can then be obtained by taking the square root:

$$\sigma(\tilde{R}) = [q(1 - q)]^{\frac{1}{2}}(u - d).$$

Since we have assumed a riskless asset, this asset will produce a payoff distribution:

$$
\begin{array}{ccc}
 & & r \\
 & \nearrow & \\
1 & & \\
 & \searrow & \\
 & & r \\
t = 0 & & t = 1
\end{array}
$$

Consider a security that pays one dollar at date $t = 1$ in the up state and nothing in the down state. We will label this security **primitive security 1.** Let its price at date 0 be denoted by π_u. Consider another security that pays one dollar at date $t = 1$ in the down state and nothing in the up state. Let its price at date 0 be denoted by π_d. We will call this security **primitive security 2.**

The payoffs of the bond can be replicated using the primitive securities by the strategy illustrated in Table 14-14.

We are able to exactly replicate the cash flows of the bond at day $t = 1$ in both the up state and the down state by buying uP of the primitive security 1 and dP of the primitive security 2. This portfolio of primitive security 1 and primitive security 2 creates a perfect substitute for the bond. These substitutes must sell for the same price. Hence, at date 0 we must have

$$P = \pi_u uP + \pi_d dP.$$

Canceling out P and simplifying, we get

$$\pi_u u + \pi_d d = 1. \tag{14.11}$$

TABLE 14-14 *Pricing Bonds*	*Transaction at Date 0*	*Investment at Date 0*	*Cash Flows at Date 1 in Up State*	*Cash Flows at Date 1 in Down State*
	1. Buy the bond	P	uP	dP
	2. Buy uP units of the primitive security 1	$\pi_u uP$	uP	0
	3. Buy dP units of the primitive security 2	$\pi_d dP$	0	dP

Note that by buying one unit of primitive security 1 and one unit of primitive security 2 we get one dollar at date 1, no matter which state occurs. The present value of this dollar at date 0 is $\frac{1}{r}$; hence, we have

$$\pi_u + \pi_d = \frac{1}{r}. \qquad (14.12)$$

Solving (4.11) and (14.12), we get the prices of primitive security 1 and primitive security 2 (also known as state prices):

$$\pi_u = \frac{r - d}{r(u - d)} \qquad (14.13)$$

$$\pi_d = \frac{u - r}{r(u - d)} \qquad (14.14)$$

Example 14-6 gives a concrete illustration.

Example 14-6:

Let $P = 100$, $u = 1.07$, $R = 0.02$, and $d = 0.98$. This leads to the following evolution of bond prices.

$$
\begin{array}{ccc}
 & & 107 \\
 & \nearrow & \\
100 & & \\
 & \searrow & \\
 & & 98 \\
t = 0 & & t = 1
\end{array}
$$

Let us further assume that the probability of an up move is $q = 0.5$, and the probability of a down move is $1 - q = 0.5$.

We can then compute the state prices π_u and π_d as shown in Equations 14.15 and 14.16, respectively.

$$\pi_u = \frac{1.02 - 0.98}{[1.02 \times (1.07 - 0.98)]} = 0.435730 \qquad (14.15)$$

$$\pi_d = \frac{1.07 - 1.02}{[1.02 \times (1.07 - 0.98)]} = 0.544662 \qquad (14.16)$$

Example 14-7:

Table 14-15 illustrates how the primitive securities can be used to exactly replicate the cash flows of bond 1. Together, the total value of the primitive securities that are needed to replicate the bond is

$$0.43573 \times 107 + 0.544662 \times 98 = 100.$$

Note that this is precisely equal to the value of the bond. What do the prices of primitive security 1 and primitive security 2 represent? In effect, they represent

TABLE 14-15   *Pricing Bond 1*

Transaction at Date 0	Investment at Date 0	Cash Flows at Date 1 in Up State	Cash Flows at Date 1 in Down State
1. Buy the bond	P	107	98
2. Buy 107 units of the primitive security 1	0.435730×107	107	0
3. Buy dP units of the primitive security 2	0.544662×98	0	98

the present values of receiving one dollar at date 1 contingent on the occurrence of a certain state. The prices of such securities (state prices) are fundamental in the valuation of other securities.

Example 14-8:

We can use the prices of primitive securities to value any bond available for trading. Consider for example bond 2 with the following payoff distribution.

$$
\begin{array}{ccc}
 & & 103 \\
 & \nearrow & \\
\hat{P} & & \\
 & \searrow & \\
 & & 98.5 \\
t = 0 & t = 1 &
\end{array}
$$

What is the price $\hat{P}$ of this bond? The price of bond 2 is the sum of the following:

- The present value of $103 in the up state

$$\pi_u \times 103 = 0.43573 \times 103 = 44.88017.$$

- The present value of $98.5 in the down state

$$\pi_d \times 98.5 = 0.544662 \times 98.5 = 53.64924.$$

Adding these two present values together gives:

$$44.88017 + 53.64924 = 98.52941.$$

Hence, bond 2 should sell at 98.52941 to be consistent with the pricing of bond 1.

No Arbitrage and Bond-Price Dynamics

If bond 1 and bond 2 are priced to preclude arbitrage possibilities, then the evolution of these bond prices must satisfy certain conditions.

The expected return on bond 1 is

$$\frac{q \times 107 + (1 - q) \times 98}{100} = 1.025000.$$

The expected return on bond 2 is

$$\frac{q \times 103 + (1 - q) \times 98.5}{98.52941} = 1.022537.$$

Note that the expected returns on bond 1 and bond 2 differ. Does this mean that the bonds are not fairly priced? To see that, even though the expected returns on these bonds differ, they are priced fairly, let us compute for each bond the market price of risk

$$\phi_b = \frac{E(R_b) - r}{\sigma_b},$$

where $E(R_b)$ is the expected return on bond b, and σ_b is the volatility of the returns on bond b.

Example 14-9:

Let us compute the market price of risk of bond 1. The expected return on bond 1 is

$$E(R_1) = \frac{[quP + (1 - q)dP]}{P} = qu + (1 - q)d = 1.025. \qquad (14.17)$$

The volatility of the returns of bond 1 is
$$\sigma_1 = [q(1 - q)(u - d)^2]^{\frac{1}{2}} = .045. \qquad (14.18)$$

The market price of risk for bond 1 is

$$\phi_1 = \frac{1.025 - 1.02}{0.045} = .111111. \qquad (14.19)$$

Example 14-10:

Let us compute the market price of risk of bond 2. Note that in the up state the price of the bond is 103. Its price at date 0 is 98.52941. This means that the up move factor $\hat{u} = \frac{103}{98.52941} = 1.045373$. The price of the bond in the down state is 98.5. Therefore, the down move factor $\hat{d} = \frac{98.50}{98.52941} = .999702$. The expected return on bond 2 is

$$E(R_2) = \frac{[q\hat{u}\hat{P} + (1 - q)\hat{d}\hat{P}}{\hat{P}} = q\hat{u} + (1 - q)\hat{d} = 1.022537. \qquad (14.20)$$

The volatility of the returns of bond 2 is
$$\sigma_2 = [q(1 - q)(\hat{u} - \hat{d})^2]^{\frac{1}{2}} = 0.022836. \qquad (14.21)$$

The market price of risk for bond 2 is

$$\phi_2 = \frac{1.022537 - 1.02}{0.022836} = 0.111. \qquad (14.22)$$

We see from Equations 14.19 and 14.20 that the market prices of risk for bond 1 and bond 2 are the same. In other words, bond prices should evolve in such a way as to ensure that

$$\phi_1 = \frac{E(R_1) - r}{\sigma_1} = \phi_2 = \frac{E(R_2) - r}{\sigma_2}.$$

This is a general implication of no arbitrage in capital markets.

Relationship between State Prices and No Arbitrage

Using the state prices, the value of bond 2 is 98.52941. How do we know that there are no-arbitrage opportunities between bond 1 and bond 2? To verify this, let us consider a simple replicating-portfolio strategy in which we replicate the cash flows of bond 2 using bond 1 and the riskless asset that provides a return of 2%.

Example 14-11:

At date 0, we buy $\frac{1}{2}$ units of bond 1 and lend $\$\frac{49.5}{1.02}$ at 2% interest rate. (Precisely how we arrived at these numbers will be explained shortly.) The total investment in this portfolio is

$$\frac{1}{2} \times 100 + \frac{49.5}{1.02} = 98.52941. \tag{14.23}$$

Note that the cost of this portfolio is exactly equal to the price of bond 2, whose cash flows we are trying to replicate.

Let us consider the payoffs from this strategy next. In the up state at date $t = 1$, the value of this portfolio follows:

- $\frac{1}{2}$ units of bond 1 is worth $\frac{1}{2} \times 107 = \$53.5$.
- The money that was lent is worth $\frac{49.5}{1.02} \times 1.02 = \$49.5$.
- So the total amount in the up state is

$$\frac{1}{2} \times 107 + \frac{49.5}{1.02} \times 1.02 = 103.$$

This is precisely the value of bond 2 in the up state. In the down state at date $t = 1$, the value of this portfolio follows:

- $\frac{1}{2}$ units of bond 1 is worth $\frac{1}{2} \times 98 = \$49$.
- The money that was lent is worth $\frac{49.5}{1.02} \times 1.02 = \$49.5$.
- So the total amount in the up state is

$$\frac{1}{2} \times 98 + \frac{49.5}{1.02} \times 1.02 = 98.5.$$

Note that this is precisely the value of bond 2 in the down state.

Thus, this portfolio has exactly replicated the cash flows of bond 2 in date 2 both in the up state and in the down state; hence, we have created a perfect substitute. This must sell for the same price as bond 2. The investment in this portfolio, as shown earlier, is equal to 98.52941. This is, therefore, the price of bond 2.

We have just verified a very important principle: **Whenever we can find state prices and value securities using state prices, then such a pricing procedure is free from arbitrage.**

Precisely how did we compute the number of bonds 1 to buy and the amount of money to loan out at date $t = 0$? At date $t = 0$, let us buy Δ units of bond 1 and place B dollars in a bank account earning an interest rate of $1 + R$. The motivation for these transactions is simple; to replicate bond 2, it seems reasonable to take a long position in bond 1, as we expect the bond 1 price to go up when the bond 2 price goes up, and vice versa. Why do we lend money? Note that bond 2 is less volatile than bond 1. When bond 1's price goes up to 107, bond 2's price goes up only to 103. Similarly, when bond 1's price goes down to 98, bond 2's price goes down only to 98.5. To achieve this lowered fluctuation, we place some money in a safe bank account. The total investment, I, in this strategy is

$$I = \Delta \times 100 + B. \tag{14.24}$$

At date 1 in the up state, this portfolio is worth

$$I_u = \Delta \times 107 + B \times 1.02. \tag{14.25}$$

We would like the value of this portfolio to exactly match the value of bond 2; hence, we set

$$I_u = \Delta \times 107 + B \times 1.02 = 103. \tag{14.26}$$

The value of this portfolio in date 1 in the down state is worth

$$I_d = \Delta \times 98 + B \times 1.02. \tag{14.27}$$

This should exactly replicate the value of bond 2 in the down state. Therefore, we have

$$I_d = \Delta \times 98 + B \times 1.02 = 98.5. \tag{14.28}$$

We solve the two equations 14.27 and 14.28 to get the values of $\Delta = \frac{1}{2}$ and $B = \frac{49.5}{1.02}$. Using these values in Equation 14.25, we get the investment $I = 98.52941$.

Risk-Neutral Pricing

In a world where investors are risk neutral, they are satisfied with an expected return equal to the riskless rate of return. Is there a probability p under which bond 1 and bond 2 will provide just the riskless rate of return? For bond 1, this would mean:

$$\frac{uP \times p + dP \times (1 - p)}{P} = r.$$

Solving, we find that

$$p = \frac{r - d}{u - d}. \tag{14.29}$$

Note that this risk-neutral probability p may be written in terms of the state price π_u as

$$p = \pi_u \times r.$$

In a similar manner, we may write

$$1 - p = \pi_d \times r.$$

For bond 1, we get

$$p = \frac{1.02 - 0.98}{1.07 - 0.98} = .444444 \tag{14.30}$$

and

$$1 - p = 0.555556. \tag{14.31}$$

Note that if we use the risk-neutral probabilities to compute the expected return of bond 2, we get

$$\frac{103 \times p + 98.5 \times (1 - p)}{98.52941} = 1.02.$$

This indicates that all bonds are priced to provide the riskless rate of return under the risk-neutral probability. We can also write the pricing derivation in the following manner:

1. Price of bond 1 is given by

$$P = \pi_u uP + \pi_d dP.$$

2. Using the relationship between π_u and p, and π_d and d we can write this as

$$P = \frac{puP + (1 - p)dP}{r}.$$

3. $puP + (1 - p)dP$, however, is the expected value of the bond price at date $t = 1$, where the expectation is taken with respect to the risk-neutral probability p. Thus, we can write the pricing formula as

$$P = \frac{E_p[\tilde{P}]}{r}, \tag{14.32}$$

where $E_p[\cdot]$ is the expectations operator with respect to the risk-neutral probability measure p.

This gives us a very simple pricing procedure. First, we find the risk-neutral probability p. We then calculate the expected future cash flows under the risk-neutral probability. Finally, this expected value is discounted at the riskless rate to compute the price of the security. This pricing rule is especially convenient for valuing securities by Monte Carlo simulation techniques, as we show later in the text.

Note that in our analysis, the original probability q does not play a direct role in pricing the bonds. It is the risk-neutral probability that matters. We will develop these ideas further in this chapter in the context of the term structure of interest rates. All our analyses thus far have been conducted in a two-date setting. In order to provide a true setting for term-structure analysis, it is necessary to develop an intertemporal framework that extends beyond a two-date setting to a multiperiod setting. The next section analyzes the processes that can be used to describe the behavior of bond prices and interest rates through time.

PRICING BY REPLICATION

Under certain assumptions, options-pricing theory shows that the payoffs distribution of options can be replicated by trading in a certain way in the underlying asset coupled with riskless lending or borrowing.

Are call options on T-bonds riskier than T-bonds? How can an asset that gives all the upside and limited downside be riskier than the underlying asset? We will show that the concept of replication gives us a much better framework in which to think about such questions.

Steps in Constructing Replicating Portfolios

Consider how we go about replicating a call option T-bond. First, we recognize that however we construct the replicating portfolio, it must be the case that as the bond price goes up, the value of the portfolio goes up as well. This is because the call on the bond will appreciate in value as the bond price increases. This indicates that the replicating portfolio will have a long position in the T-bond.

We can refine this further. For a deep out-of-the-money call option, bond-price increases will hardly affect the call premium. Hence, the replicating portfolio of a deep out-of-the-money call should have no bonds. By the same token, the premium of a deep in-the-money call option will increase by a dollar if the underlying bond price increases by a dollar. Hence, the replicating portfolio for a deep in-the-money option should have one bond per option. These observations indicate that the replicating portfolio has to constantly modify its exposure to the bond-price risk depending on whether the option is in-the-money or out-of-the-money. Further, when the option is at-the-money, the replicating portfolio should have one-half bond in it.

The number of underlying assets in the replicating portfolio for an option on a single unit of the underlying asset is known as the *delta* of the option and is denoted by Δ.

Consider the example in Figure 14-6. A three-month at-the-money call option on a bond had a premium of 2.00. To replicate this at-the-money option, we need to buy one-half bond, which will cost 50.00. Given that the replicating portfolio must exactly duplicate all the properties of the option, it is clear that its cost can be only 2.00. This means that 48.00 must be borrowed in addition to the out-of-pocket investment of 2.00 to buy the necessary bonds.

To summarize: To replicate a call option on a bond (stock), we borrow money to buy delta bonds (stocks). As the bond (stock) price increases and the option goes in-the-money, we borrow more money and buy more bonds (stocks), progressively increasing the number of bonds (stocks) to one when the option is deep in-the-money. As the bond (stock) price decreases and the option goes out-of-the-money, we sell bonds (stocks) progressively, decreasing the number of bonds (stocks) to zero when the option is deep out-of-the-money.

Note that if the underlying asset were to pay dividends or coupons it will reduce the cost of replicating the call option. In the case of underlying assets, such as stocks and bonds, we can easily identify the cash flows from assets as dividends or coupons. Later, we will show that underlying assets, such as futures, have an *implicit dividend yield* which is the financing rate. Likewise, underlying assets, such as foreign currency, has an implicit dividend yield equal to the foreign rate of interest.

A Binomial Model for Bond Options

Let the full price (flat plus accrued) of the bond behave according to the following binomial tree:

$$
\begin{array}{ccc}
 & & uP \\
 & \nearrow & \\
P & & \\
 & \searrow & \\
 & & dP \\
t=0 & & t=1
\end{array}
$$

We will assume throughout that the probability of an up move is q and that of a down move is $1 - q$, irrespective of the level of the underlying asset price.

Consider now a call option on this bond at a strike price of K. Let this option expire on date $t = 1$. We can observe P directly, and we will estimate u and d from the volatility of the underlying bond as indicated later in this chapter.

The option value behaves according to the following binomial tree:

$$
\begin{array}{ccc}
 & & c_u = \max (uP - K, 0) \\
 & \nearrow & \\
c & & \\
 & \searrow & \\
 & & c_d = \max (dP - K, 0) \\
t=0 & & t=1
\end{array}
$$

Assume that the option expires at $t = 1$. In the up state, the option is worth $c_u = \max (uP - K, 0)$, and in the down state, the option is worth $c_d = \max (dP - K, 0)$. We wish to determine what the option is worth, c, at date $t = 0$.

Let us borrow B at a rate $r = 1 + R$ and buy Δ of the underlying bond. Then this portfolio will have the following properties:

$$\Delta uP - Br$$
$$\nearrow$$
$$\Delta P - B$$
$$\searrow$$
$$\Delta dP - Br$$
$$t = 0 \qquad t = 1$$

In the up state, the portfolio is worth $\Delta uP - Br$, and in the down state, the portfolio is worth $\Delta dP - Br$. We want our portfolio to replicate the call at date $t = 1$ in both the states. Hence,

$$c_u = \Delta uP - Br$$
$$\nearrow$$
$$\Delta P - B$$
$$\searrow$$
$$c_d = \Delta dP - Br$$
$$t = 0 \qquad t = 1$$

We thus have two conditions:

$$c_u = \Delta uP - Br$$

$$c_d = \Delta dP - Br.$$

Note that we know c_u and c_d and can solve for Δ and B. We get

$$\Delta = \frac{c_u - c_d}{(u - d)P} \tag{14.33}$$

and

$$B = \left[\frac{c_u d - c_d u}{(u - d)} \right] \times \frac{1}{r}. \tag{14.34}$$

To preclude arbitrage, the replicating portfolio must sell for the same price as the call at date $t = 0$; hence,

$$c = \Delta P - B = \frac{pc_u + (1 - p)c_d}{r}, \tag{14.35}$$

where

$$p = \frac{r - d}{u - d}.$$

If interest rate r is continuously compounded, then the probability

$$p = \frac{e^{r\Delta t} - d}{u - d},$$

where Δt is the time in years between two consecutive points in time and r is the annu-alized continuously compounded rate. When the underlying asset pays a continuous dividend yield of δ, the probability

$$p = \frac{e^{(r-\delta)\Delta t} - d}{u - d}.$$

Equation 14.35 is the well-known binomial options-pricing formula. If the option is American, then we must check to see whether early exercise is optimal. We do this by comparing the value of c in Equation 14.35 with the exercise value $P - K$ and choosing the maximum of the two. The formula makes intuitive sense. We take the ex-pected value of the option, using the probability factor p, and discount the resulting payoff at the riskless rate.

Consider now the expected return of the underlying bond under the probability p:

$$\frac{p \times uP + (1 - p) \times dP}{P}.$$

Substituting for p and simplifying, we get the expected return equal to r, the risk-less rate. **The probability parameter p, therefore, is known as the risk-neutral probability.**

Example 14-12:

The full price of the bond at $t = 0$ is 100. On date $t = 1$, the price can either go to $100 \times 1.08 = 108.00$ in the up state or go down to $100 \times \frac{1}{1.08} = 92.593$ in the down state. Assume that the riskless rate is 5%. Assume that a call option on this bond is traded at date $t = 0$, maturing at date $t = 1$. It has a strike price of 100. De-termine the replicating-portfolio, risk-neutral probability p, and the option price c.

The bond price behaves as follows:

$$
\begin{array}{ccc}
 & & 108.00 \\
 & \nearrow & \\
P = 100 & & \\
 & \searrow & \\
 & & 92.593 \\
t = 0 & & t = 1
\end{array}
$$

The call option price distribution is

$$
\begin{array}{ccc}
 & & c_u = 8.000 \\
 & \nearrow & \\
c & & \\
 & \searrow & \\
 & & c_d = 0.000 \\
t = 0 & & t = 1
\end{array}
$$

Using Equation 14.33 gives

$$\Delta = \frac{c_u - c_d}{(u - d)P} = \frac{8.000 - 0.000}{(1.08 - 0.92593)100} = 0.5192.$$

In a similar way, using Equation 14.34 gives

$$B = \left[\frac{c_u d - c_d u}{u - d} \right] \times \frac{1}{r}$$

$$= \left[\frac{8.000 \times 0.92593 - 0.0000 \times 1.08}{1.08 - 0.92593} \right] \times \frac{1}{1.05}$$

$$= 45.789$$

Hence, we borrow $45.7886 to buy 0.5192 shares to replicate the call option. Finally, using Equation 14.35, we get

$$c = \Delta P - B = 0.5192 \times 100 - 45.789 = 6.131.$$

The risk-neutral probability is

$$p = \frac{r - d}{u - d} = \frac{1.05 - 0.92593}{1.08 - 0.92593} = 0.805.$$

If r is continuously compounded and the time interval between $t = 0$ and $t = 1$ is one year, then

$$p = \frac{e^{0.05(1)} - 0.92593}{1.08 - 0.92593}$$

$$= \frac{1.05127 - 0.92593}{1.08 - 0.92593} = \frac{0.12534}{0.15407} = 0.8135.$$

We will work through the example with discrete compounding.

This strategy will also carry over many periods. Consider the options-pricing problem when the option expires at date $t = 2$.

$$
\begin{array}{ccccc}
 & & & & u^2P \\
 & & & \nearrow & \\
 & & uP & & \\
 & \nearrow & & \searrow & \\
P & & & & udP \\
 & \searrow & & \nearrow & \\
 & & dP & & \\
 & & & \searrow & \\
 & & & & d^2P \\
t = 0 & t = 1 & & t = 2 &
\end{array}
$$

The payoffs of the option on bond follow:

$$c_{uu} = \max\ (0,\ u^2P - K)$$

$$c_u$$

$$c$$

$$c_{ud} = \max\ (0,\ udP - K)$$

$$c_d$$

$$c_{dd} = \max\ (0,\ d^2P - K)$$

$$t = 0 \qquad t = 1 \qquad\qquad t = 2$$

First, we determine the value of the option c_u in the up state at date $t = 1$:

$$c_u = \frac{pc_{uu} + (1 - p)c_{ud}}{r}.$$

If early exercise is permitted (if the option is American), then

$$c_u = \max\left[uP - K, \frac{pc_{uu} + (1 - p)c_{ud}}{r}\right]. \tag{14.36}$$

In a similar way,

$$c_d = \frac{pc_{ud} + (1 - p)c_{dd}}{r}.$$

Again, if early exercise is permitted, the value of the option in the down state is

$$c_d = \max\left(dP - K, \frac{pc_{ud} + (1 - p)c_{dd}}{r}\right). \tag{14.37}$$

Once we have figured out the values at date $t = 1$ for the up state and the down state, we can determine the call premium at $t = 0$:

$$c = \max\left[P - K, \frac{pc_u + (1 - p)c_d}{r}\right]. \tag{14.38}$$

Example 14-13:

We illustrate now the problem considered in Example 14-12 for two periods. The bond prices evolve as shown next.

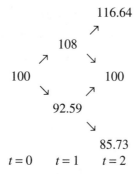

$$t = 0 \qquad t = 1 \qquad t = 2$$

Then the payoffs of the option on the bond are

$$c_{uu} = 16.64$$

$$c_u = 12.76$$

$$c = 9.78 \qquad c_{ud} = 0$$

$$c_d = 0$$

$$0$$

$$t = 0 \qquad\qquad t = 1 \qquad\qquad t = 2$$

The value of the option c_u in the up state at date $t = 1$ is

$$c_u = \frac{pc_{uu} + (1 - p)c_{ud}}{r} = \frac{0.805 \times 16.64 + 0.195 \times 0}{1.05} = 12.76.$$

In a similar way,

$$c_d = \frac{pc_{ud} + (1 - p)c_{dd}}{r} = 0.0.$$

Once we have figured out the values at date $t = 1$ for the up state and the down state, we can determine the call premium at $t = 0$:

$$c = \max\left(P - K, \frac{pc_u + (1 - p)c_d}{r} \right)$$

$$= \frac{0.805 \times 12.76 + 0.195 \times 0}{1.05}$$

$$= 9.78$$

We illustrate how the binomial model can be implemented in a spreadsheet. Figure 14-12 indicates the basic parameters of the model and how u, d, r, and p

FIGURE 14-12   *Implementing Binomial Options Pricing Model*

	A	B	C	D	E	F	G	H	I	J	K	L
1												
2												
3												
4												
5												
6			S	100				Inputs to the model			=EXP(D9*SQRT(D8/I7))	
7			K	100				n	10			
8			T	0.25				u	1.0321281		=1/I8	
9			VOL	20%				d	0.968872			
10			D	0				r	1.002002		=EXP(D11*(D8/I7))	
11			R	8%				p	0.5237441			
12											=(I10-I9)/(I8-I9)	
13												
14												
15												
16												
17												

Example: Underlying asset price = 100;
Strike = 100;
Volatility = 20%;
Financing rate = 8%;
Time to maturity = 0.25 years;
Dividends = 0.

FIGURE 14-13   *Underlying Asset Price Lattice*

	A	B	C	D	E	F	G	H	I	J	K	L	M	N
11														
12		=C14*I8												
13			0	1	2	3	4	5	6	7	8	9	10	
14			100.000	103.213	106.529	109.951	113.484	117.130	120.893	124.777	128.786	132.924	137.194	0
15				96.887	100.000	103.213	106.529	109.951	113.484	117.130	120.893	124.777	128.786	1
16					93.871	96.887	100.000	103.213	106.529	109.951	113.484	117.130	120.893	2
17						90.949	93.871	96.887	100.000	103.213	106.529	109.951	113.484	3
18		=C14*I9					88.118	90.949	93.871	96.887	100.000	103.213	106.529	4
19								85.375	88.118	90.949	93.871	96.887	100.000	5
20									82.718	85.375	88.118	90.949	93.871	6
21										80.143	82.718	85.375	88.118	7
22											77.648	80.143	82.718	8
23												75.231	77.648	9
24													72.889	10

are calculated for a step size n = 10. Figure 14-13 builds the lattice of asset prices for ten steps. The easiest way to complete this worksheet is to copy the formula in cell D14 across E14: M14. Then, the formula in cell D15 across the relevant range of the entire worksheet. Figure 14-14 provides the option lattice. Here, we work backward. We begin in cell M30. The value of put is the strike price (in cell D7 in Figure 14-12) minus the stock price (in cell M14 in Figure 14-13). We copy this formula from M30 to M39. We step back to cell L30. We apply the formula shown in Figure 14-14 and copy it across the relevant range.

The recursive structure of the formula allows us to determine the call premium for options which may have several periods to maturity. For *European options,* these recursive arguments lead to the simple formula:

$$c = P\Phi(a; n, p') - \frac{K}{r^n}\Phi(a; n, p), \qquad (14.39)$$

where $p' = p \times \frac{u}{r}$ and a is the minimum number of up moves that the underlying asset price must make in order for the option to end in the money at maturity—it

FIGURE 14-14 *Option Lattice*

	A	B	C	D	E	F	G	H	I	J	K	L	M	N	O
25															
26															
27								=MAX(D7-L14,(I11*M30+(1-I11)*M31)/I10)							
28															
29							Option Price Lattice							=max(D7-m14,0)	
30			0	1	2	3	4	5	6	7	8	9	10		
31	Value of Put		3.18	1.86	0.92	0.35	0.08	0.00	0.00	0.00	0.00	0.00	0.00	0	
32	By Binomial Method			4.65	2.90	1.55	0.64	0.16	0.00	0.00	0.00	0.00	0.00	1	
33	(AMERICAN PUT)				6.60	4.39	2.55	1.18	0.33	0.00	0.00	0.00	0.00	2	
34						9.05	6.43	4.07	2.12	0.70	0.00	0.00	0.00	3	
35							11.88	9.05	6.23	3.69	1.48	0.00	0.00	4	
36								14.62	11.88	9.05	6.13	3.11	0.00	5	
37									17.28	14.62	11.88	9.05	6.13	6	
38										19.86	17.28	14.62	11.88	7	
39											22.35	19.86	17.28	8	
40												24.77	22.35	9	
41													27.11	10	
42															

is the smallest integer greater than $\left(\ln \frac{K}{Pd^n}\right) / \left(\ln \frac{u}{d}\right)$. The function $\Phi(a; n, p)$ represents the cumulative binomial distribution function, which denotes the cumulative probability of getting at least a up moves in a total of n steps using the probability factor p or p'.

Options on Futures

Most listed options in the fixed-income markets are on futures contracts. It is, therefore, important to understand how these options are on future prices and in what ways they differ from OTC options, which are typically on underlying bonds or interest rates.

Let the futures price evolve according to the following binomial tree:

$$
\begin{array}{ccc}
 & & uH \\
 & \nearrow & \\
H & & \\
 & \searrow & \\
 & & dH \\
t=0 & & t=1
\end{array}
$$

Consider now a call option on this futures contract at a strike price of K. Let this option expire on date $t = 1$. We can observe H and we will estimate u and d from the volatility of the underlying futures contract.

The option value behaves according to the following binomial tree:

$$
\begin{array}{ccc}
 & & c_u = \max(uH - K, 0) \\
 & \nearrow & \\
c & & \\
 & \searrow & \\
 & & c_d = \max(dH - K, 0) \\
t=0 & & t=1
\end{array}
$$

We will assume that the option expires at $t = 1$. In the up state, the option is worth $c_u = \max(uH - K, 0)$, and in the down state, the option is worth $c_d = \max(dH - K, 0)$. We wish to determine what the option is worth (C) at date $t = 0$.

The strategy that we developed in the context of bond options in the construction of a replicating portfolio needs to be modified. Let us consider how we will go about replicating a call option futures contract. First, we recognize that however we construct the replicating portfolio, it must be the case that as the futures price goes up, the value of the portfolio goes up. This is because the call on the futures will appreciate in value as the futures price increases. This indicates that the replicating portfolio will have a long position in the underlying futures contract.

We can refine this further. For a deep out-of-the-money call option, futures price increases will hardly affect the call premium. Hence, the replicating portfolio of a deep-out-of-the-money call should have no futures. By the same token, the premium of a deep-in-the-money call option will increase by a dollar if the underlying futures price increases by a dollar. Hence, the replicating portfolio for a deep-in-the-money option should have one futures per each option.

These observations indicate that the replicating portfolio has to constantly modify its exposure to the futures price risk depending on whether the option is in-the-money or out-of-the-money. Further, when the option is at-the-money, the replicating portfolio should have one-half futures in it. As before, the number of underlying assets in the replicating portfolio for an option on a single unit of the underlying asset is denoted by Δ.

Let us say that a three-month at-the-money call option on futures had a premium of 2.00. To replicate this at-the-money option, we need to buy one-half futures, which will be costless to initiate. Given that the replicating portfolio must exactly duplicate all the properties of the option, it is clear that it must cost only 2.00. This means that 2.00 must be set aside in Treasury bills (or lent) in order to replicate the futures option.

To summarize: to replicate a call option on a futures, we lend money to buy T-bills and also to buy Δ futures contracts. As the futures price increases and the option goes in-the-money, we buy more futures progressively and increase the number of futures to one when the option is deep-in-the-money. Note that the initial futures position will throw off cash flows from mark to market, which will be swept into T-bills—we lend more money as the option gets deeper in-the-money. As the futures price decreases and the option goes out-of-the-money, we sell futures, progressively decreasing the number of futures to zero when the option is deep-out-of-the-money. We sell T-bills to meet the variation margin calls. As time elapses, futures contract approaches its maturity, where it must converge to the underlying spot price. So implicitly the futures price loses its carry at a continuous rate equal to the financing rate.

Let us lend $\$B$ at a rate $r = 1 + R$ and buy Δ of the underlying futures. Then this portfolio will have the following properties:

$$\Delta(uH - H) + Br$$
$$\nearrow$$
$$B$$
$$\searrow$$
$$\Delta(dH - H) + Br$$
$$t = 0 \qquad\qquad t = 1$$

In the up state, the portfolio is worth $\Delta(uH - H) + Br,$ and in the down state, the portfolio is worth $\Delta(dH - H) + Br.$ We want our portfolio to replicate the call at date $t = 1$ in both the states. Hence,

$$c_u = \Delta(uH - H) + Br$$

$$\nearrow$$

$$B$$

$$\searrow$$

$$c_d = \Delta(dH - H) + Br$$

$$t = 0 \qquad\qquad t = 1$$

We thus have two conditions:

$$c_u = \Delta(uH - H) + Br$$

$$c_d = \Delta(dH - H) + Br.$$

Note that we know c_u and $c_d,$ and can solve for Δ and $B.$ We get

$$\Delta = \frac{c_u - c_d}{(u - d)H} \tag{14.40}$$

and

$$B = \frac{c_u(1 - d) + c_d(u - 1)}{(u - d)r}. \tag{14.41}$$

To preclude arbitrage, the replicating portfolio must sell for the same price as the call at date $t = 0$; hence,

$$c = B = \frac{pc_u + (1 - p)c_d}{r}, \tag{14.42}$$

where

$$p = \frac{1 - d}{u - d}. \tag{14.43}$$

Equation 14.42 is the binomial futures options-pricing formula. If the option is American, then we must check to see whether early exercise is optimal. We do this by comparing the value of c in Equation 14.42 with the exercise value $H - K$ and choosing the maximum of the two.

$$c = \max\left[H - K, \frac{pc_u + (1 - p)c_d}{r}\right] \tag{14.44}$$

The formula makes intuitive sense. We take the expected value of the option, using the probability factor $p,$ and discount the resulting payoff at the riskless rate.

We can verify this formula even for an option that has many periods to maturity. **Call options on futures may be optimally exercised prematurely even when it is**

suboptimal to exercise call options on the underlying spot asset. This may be developed as follows.

Let us suppose that the option is in-the-money at date $t = 1$, no matter which state occurs. Then, $c_u = uH - K$ and $c_d = dH - K$. Substituting these values in the pricing formula, Equation 14.44, we get

$$c = \max\left[H - K, \frac{p(uH - K) + (1 - p)(dH - K)}{r} \right].$$

Note that when we substitute for $p = \frac{1-d}{u-d}$ in the previous equation, we get

$$c = \max\left[H - K, \frac{H - K}{r} \right].$$

Clearly, the payoffs associated with early exercise at date $t = 0$ outweigh the value associated with waiting and exercising the option later. It is possible to verify this for put options on futures contracts as well.

We can now extend the analysis to cases in which the options have more than one period to their maturity date. To illustrate the idea, let us consider the options-pricing problem, when the option expires at date $t = 2$.

$$
\begin{array}{ccccc}
 & & & & u^2H \\
 & & & \nearrow & \\
 & & uH & & \\
 & \nearrow & & \searrow & \\
H & & & & udH \\
 & \searrow & & \nearrow & \\
 & & dH & & \\
 & & & \searrow & \\
 & & & & d^2H \\
 & t=0 & t=1 & & t=2
\end{array}
$$

The payoffs of the option on the bond follow:

$$
\begin{array}{cccc}
 & & & c_{uu} = \max(0, u^2H - K) \\
 & & \nearrow & \\
 & c_u & & \\
 & \nearrow & \searrow & \\
c & & & c_{ud} = \max(0, udH - K) \\
 & \searrow & \nearrow & \\
 & c_d & & \\
 & & \searrow & \\
 & & & c_{dd} = \max(0, d^2H - K) \\
t=0 & t=1 & & t=2
\end{array}
$$

First, we determine the value of the option c_u in the up state at date $t = 1$:

$$c_u = \frac{pc_{uu} + (1 - p)c_{ud}}{r}.$$

If early exercise is permitted (if the option is American), then

$$c_u = \max\left[uH - K, \frac{pc_{uu} + (1 - p)c_{ud}}{r} \right]. \qquad (14.45)$$

In a similar way,

$$c_d = \frac{pc_{ud} + (1 - p)c_{dd}}{r}.$$

Again, if early exercise is permitted, the value of the option in the down state is

$$c_d = \max\left[dH - K, \frac{pc_{ud} + (1 - p)c_{dd}}{r} \right]. \qquad (14.46)$$

Once we have figured out the values at date $t = 1$ for the up state and the down state, we can determine the call premium at $t = 0$:

$$c = \max\left[H - K, \frac{pc_u + (1 - p)c_d}{r} \right]. \qquad (14.47)$$

Example 14-14:

Suppose that the futures price on a bond is at 100 now. The up move factor is estimated to be 1.10, and the down move factor is 0.909. A call option on a futures contract is traded now. The strike price of the option is 100, and the option will expire two periods from now. If the volatility of the futures prices is estimated at 12%, what is the value of the option now? (Assume that the one-period riskless rate is 5%).

The evolution of the futures price follows:

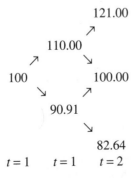

$$
\begin{array}{ccccc}
 & & & & 121.00 \\
 & & & \nearrow & \\
 & & 110.00 & & \\
 & \nearrow & & \searrow & \\
100 & & & & 100.00 \\
 & \searrow & & \nearrow & \\
 & & 90.91 & & \\
 & & & \searrow & \\
 & & & & 82.64 \\
t = 1 & & t = 1 & & t = 2
\end{array}
$$

The value of the call at maturity follows:

$$
\begin{array}{ccccc}
 & & & & 21.00 \\
 & & & \nearrow & \\
 & & c_u & & \\
 & \nearrow & & \searrow & \\
 c & & & & 0.00 \\
 & \searrow & & \nearrow & \\
 & & c_d & & \\
 & & & \searrow & \\
 & & & & 0.00 \\
 t = 1 & & t = 1 & & t = 2
\end{array}
$$

The risk-neutral probability is

$$
p = \frac{1 - 0.909}{1.1 - 0.909} = 0.47644.
$$

The value of the option at $t = 1$ in the up node is

$$
c_u = \frac{0.47644 \times 21 + (1 - 0.47644) \times 0}{1.05} = 9.5288.
$$

Note that if the option is American, its immediate exercise value will be $110 - 100 = 10$. This exceeds the value of waiting and exercising at $t = 2$; hence, $c_u = 10.00$. The value of the option at $t = 1$ in the down node is zero as the option ends worthless even if the futures price were to go up. So, $c_d = 0.00$.

The value of the option at $t = 0$ is

$$
c = \frac{0.47644 \times 10 + (1 - 0.47644) \times 0}{1.05} = 4.537524.
$$

The value of the call over time follows:

$$
\begin{array}{ccccc}
 & & & & 21.00 \\
 & & & \nearrow & \\
 & & c_u = 10.00 & & \\
 & \nearrow & & \searrow & \\
 c = 4.54 & & & & 0.00 \\
 & \searrow & & \nearrow & \\
 & & c_d = 0.00 & & \\
 & & & \searrow & \\
 & & & & 0.00 \\
 t = 0 & & t = 1 & & t = 2
\end{array}
$$

Note that the only thing that changes in the current formulation compared to the formulation of options on bonds is that the risk-neutral probability is given by Equation 14.43 as opposed to $p = \frac{r-d}{u-d}$. The recursive structure of the formula allows us to

TABLE 14-16

Risk-Neutral Probabilities

Underlying Security	*Probability*	*Restrictions*
Common stock (no dividends)	$p = \dfrac{r-d}{u-d}$	$u > r > d$
Common stock (dividend yield δ)	$p = \dfrac{r(1-\delta)-d}{u-d}$	$u > r(1-\delta) > d$
Futures contract	$p = \dfrac{1-d}{u-d}$	$u > 1 > d$
Spot currency (foreign interest rate r^*)	$p = \dfrac{\frac{r}{r^*}-d}{u-d}$	$u > \dfrac{r}{r^*} > d$

TABLE 14-17

Continuous Compounding of Risk-Neutral Probabilities

Underlying Security	*Probability*
Common stock (no dividends)	$p = \dfrac{e^{r\Delta t}-d}{u-d}$
Common stock (dividend yield δ)	$p = \dfrac{e^{(r-\delta)\Delta t}-d}{u-d}$
Futures contract (Implicit dividend yield is r. Set $\delta = r$ in the common stock formula.)	$p = \dfrac{1-d}{u-d}$
Spot currency (Implicit dividend yield is r^*, which is the foreign interest rate. Set $\delta = r^*$ in the common stock formula.)	$p = \dfrac{e^{(r-r^*)\Delta t}-d}{u-d}$

determine the call premium for options that have several periods to maturity. In fact, the binomial formula derived earlier applies to this case as well, once p has been redefined. Table 14–16 provides the appropriate risk-neutral probabilities for various underlying assets. Here we assume discrete compounding.

With continuous compounding, the risk-neutral probabilities will look as shown in Table 14-17.

Risk-Neutral Pricing

Generally speaking, we can show that the no-arbitrage pricing is equivalent to finding the risk-neutral probabilities. Table 14-16 provides the risk-neutral pricing probabilities for some important options.

Note that in the application of the binomial options-pricing procedure, we are obliged to specify the number of time steps into which we have divided the life of the option. For example, we used two time steps and three time steps in our previous illustrations. At a pragmatic level, it could be argued that n, the number of time steps, should be such that we get sufficiently accurate answers. In an important paper, Cox, Ross, and Rubinstein (1979) show how to use the binomial approach to obtain the

Black and Scholes (1973) options-pricing formula as a limiting case. Their arguments are summarized next.

Let $T - t$ be the life of the option in years. Subdivide the life of the option into n time steps. Define $h = \frac{T-t}{n}$. Consider the annualized riskless rate of interest $1 + R$. Its allocation to the subintervals will be governed by the relation:

$$(1 + \hat{R}) = (1 + R)^{\frac{T-t}{n}}.$$

Cox, Ross, and Rubinstein (1979) select

$$u = \frac{1}{d} = e^{\sigma\sqrt{\frac{T-t}{n}}}, \tag{14.48}$$

where σ is the volatility of the underlying asset returns, $T - t$ is the time to maturity of the option in years, n is the number of time steps into which the option is divided, and e is the base of natural logarithm. They let the probability $q = 0.5 + 0.5\frac{\mu}{\sigma}\sqrt{\frac{T-t}{n}}$, where μ is the expected rate of return on the underlying asset. Then as $n \to \infty$, the options-pricing formula converges to the Black and Scholes formula:

$$c = PN(d_1) - Ke^{-r(T-t)}N(d_2),$$

where $N(d_1)$ is the cumulative normal density evaluated at d_1, and $N(d_2)$ is the cumulative normal density evaluated at d_2. Moreover,

$$d_1 = \frac{\ln\left(\frac{P}{K}\right) + \left(r + \frac{\sigma^2}{2}\right)(T - t)}{\sigma\sqrt{T - t}}$$

and

$$d_2 = d_1 - \sigma\sqrt{T - t}.$$

Example 14-15:

Consider a bond with a price $P = 102$. A call option on this bond is available at a strike price of 101 with a maturity of six months. The financing rate is 5%, and the volatility of the bond returns is estimated at 25%. Determine the value of the call option.

Note that $T - t = 0.5$ years. We can compute

$$d_1 = \frac{\ln\left(\frac{102}{101}\right) + \left(0.05 + \frac{0.25^2}{2}\right)0.5}{0.25\sqrt{0.5}} = 0.28554$$

and

$$d_2 = d_1 - \sigma\sqrt{T - t} = 0.28554 - 0.25\sqrt{0.5} = 0.10876.$$

Using the Black and Scholes options-pricing formula, we get

$$c = PN(d_1) - Ke^{-r(T-t)}N(d_2)$$

$$= 102N(0.28554) - 101e^{-0.05\times0.5}N(0.10876).$$

From the normal distribution tables, we note that $N(0.286) = 0.612386$ and $N(0.109) = 0.543306$. Then the call value is

$$c = 102 \times 0.612386 - 101e^{-0.05 \times 0.5} \times 0.543306 = 8.944.$$

Using the table of risk-neutral probabilities (Table 14-16), we can derive the Black and Scholes options-pricing formula for options on futures, foreign currencies, and so on. One of the most useful adjustments to the basic options-pricing formula of Black and Scholes is the Merton (1973) proportional-dividend model. The formula derived by Merton follows:

$$c = P_e^{-\delta(T-t)}N(d_1) - Ke^{-r(T-t)}N(d_2), \tag{14.49}$$

where δ is the proportional rate of dividend payout, $N(d_1)$ is the cumulative normal density evaluated at d_1, and $N(d_2)$ is the cumulative normal density evaluated at d_2. Moreover,

$$d_1 = \frac{\ln\left(\frac{P}{K}\right) + \left(r - \delta + \frac{\sigma^2}{2}\right)(T - t)}{\sigma\sqrt{T - t}}$$

and

$$d_2 = d_1 - \sigma\sqrt{T - t}.$$

We show how the Black and Scholes formula can be implemented in EXCEL in Figure 14-15.

Now let us consider an example in which the underlying asset pays dividends.

FIGURE 14-15   *Black and Scholes Model*

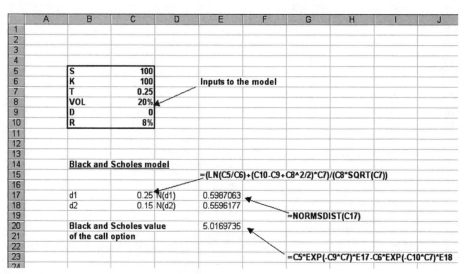

Example 14-16:

Consider a stock with a price $P = 102$. A call option on this stock is available at a strike price of 101 with a maturity of six months. The financing rate is 5%, and the volatility of the bond returns is estimated at 25%. Assume that the dividend yield of the stock is 4%. Determine the value of the call option.

Note that $T - t = 0.5$ years. We can compute

$$d_1 = \frac{\ln\left(\frac{102}{101}\right) + \left[0.05 - 0.04 + \frac{0.25^2}{2}\right](0.5)}{0.25\sqrt{0.5}} = 0.172406$$

and

$$d_2 = d_1 - \sigma\sqrt{T - t} = 0.172406 - 0.25\sqrt{0.5} = -0.00437.$$

From the normal distribution tables, we note that $N(0.172406) = 0.568441$, and $N(-0.00437) = 0.498256$. Then the call value is

$$c = 102e^{-0.04 \times 0.5} \times 0.568441 - 101e^{-0.05 \times 0.5} \times 0.498256 = 7.751475.$$

In Figure 14-16 we show this example in a worksheet.
In a similar way, options on futures can be valued by using the formula

$$c = He^{-r(T-t)}N(d_1) - Ke^{-r(T-t)}N(d_2), \tag{14.50}$$

FIGURE 14-16   *Implementing Example 14-16 in EXCEL*

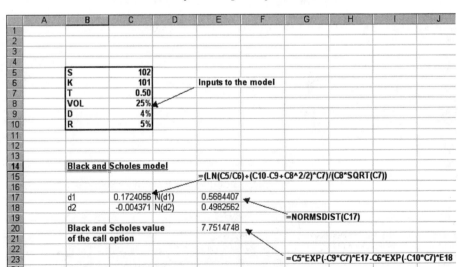

where $N(d_1)$ is the cumulative normal density evaluated at d_1, and $N(d_2)$ is the cumulative normal density evaluated at d_2. Moreover,

$$d_1 = \frac{\ln\left(\frac{H}{K}\right) + \frac{\sigma^2}{2}(T-t)}{\sigma\sqrt{T-t}}$$

and

$$d_2 = d_1 - \sigma\sqrt{T-t}.$$

This is known as Black's formula. It is widely used in the valuation of options on futures and interest-rate caps. Note that the Black's options pricing formula in Equation 14.50 can be obtained from the Black and Scholes formula in Equation 14.49 by the following steps:

1. Replace P in Equation 14.49 by the futures price H everywhere, including in the formula for d_1.
2. Replace the dividend yield δ in Equation 14.49 and in the formula for d_1 by r.

Note that the Black and Scholes model is valid generally only for European options. The binomial model is valid for both European and American options.

We can use the Black and Scholes model to compute implied volatility (Fig. 14-17). This is the volatility at which the Black and Scholes model price is equal to the market price of the option. This is illustrated next.

FIGURE 14-17   *Implied Volatility*

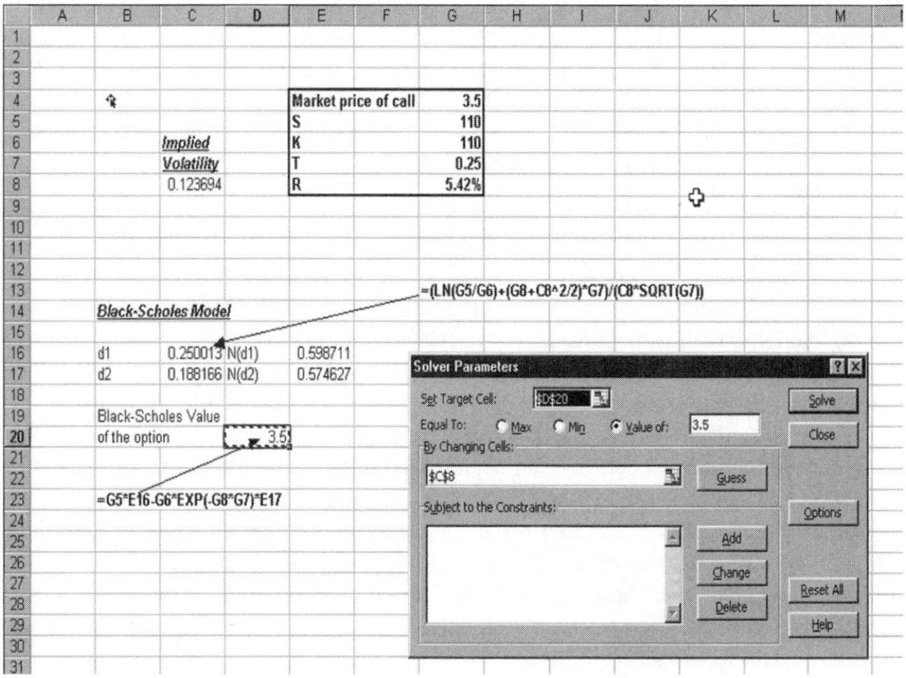

FIGURE 14.18   *Binomial Approximation to the Black and Scholes Value*

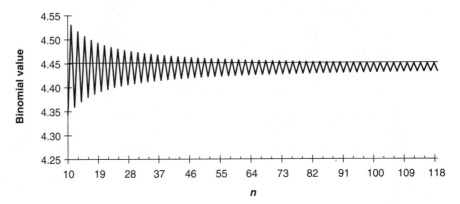

TABLE 14-18   *Binomial Approximation of European Option Values*

Volatility		n = 10 Maturity (days)			n = 50 Maturity (days)			n = 100 Maturity (days)		
		30	60	90	30	60	90	30	60	90
0.20	95	5.90	6.76	7.68	5.88	6.83	7.66	5.88	6.82	7.67
	100	2.43	3.56	4.47	2.48	3.62	4.54	2.48	3.63	4.55
	105	0.75	1.57	2.46	0.72	1.62	2.44	0.73	1.62	2.44
0.25	95	6.24	7.48	8.56	6.27	7.46	8.50	6.26	7.47	8.47
	100	2.99	**4.34**	5.42	3.04	**4.42**	5.52	3.05	**4.43**	5.53
	105	1.15	2.41	3.49	1.20	2.39	3.41	1.19	2.38	3.38
0.30	95	6.65	8.22	9.46	6.69	8.16	9.34	6.69	8.13	9.34
	100	3.54	5.12	6.37	3.61	5.22	6.49	3.62	5.23	6.50
	105	1.66	3.24	4.50	1.67	3.17	4.36	1.68	3.13	4.37

Accuracy of Binomial Model. Let us examine how accurate the binomial options-pricing model is with respect to the parameter n. Note that when $n = 1$ at the option's maturity, there are two possible outcomes for the underlying asset: uP and dP. When $n = 2$, there are three outcomes: u^2P, P, and d^2P. (Remember that $udP = P$.)

The values of the binomial model, theoretically, should converge to the Black and Scholes value as n approaches ∞. In Figure 14-18, we show the binomial values for $n = 10, 11, \ldots, 100$. The Black and Scholes value is also shown for reference.

Note that the binomial model provides a very good approximation of the Black and Scholes value for European options, even with $n = 50$ or less. The pattern of the error also suggests that there may be efficient computational algorithms for implementing the binomial options-pricing model. Tables 14-18 and 14-19 provide illustrations of the Black and Scholes values and the binomial values for a set of options.

TABLE 14-19			Maturity (days)		
Black and Scholes					
Option Values	Volatility	Price	30	60	90
	0.20	95	5.88	6.84	7.68
		100	2.49	3.65	4.58
		105	0.73	1.64	2.45
	0.25	95	6.27	7.47	8.49
		100	3.06	**4.45**	5.56
		105	1.19	2.38	3.40
	0.30	95	6.70	8.15	9.35
		100	3.63	5.25	6.53
		105	1.69	3.15	4.37

MONTE CARLO SIMULATION

The derivation of the binomial and the Black and Scholes options-pricing models illuminates an important feature of options pricing: The original probability distribution is not the relevant one. We can exchange the original probability measure with a risk-neutral probability measure. Then, using the risk-neutral probability measure, we can take the expected value of the option and discount this expected value at the riskless rate of interest. This insight was originally formulated by Cox and Ross (1976), and later formally developed into the broader implication of no arbitrage by Harrison and Kreps (1978).

This allows us to use Monte Carlo simulation techniques to price certain types of options and contingent claims. Consider a European call option maturing on date T with a strike price of K. Let us denote the current time by 0; thus, the time to maturity is T years.

Let us suppose that the bond price P_t has a true expected return (mean) of μ and a volatility of σ^2. Furthermore, let us assume that P_t is drawn from a lognormal distribution. These assumptions are consistent with the ones employed in the binomial and the Black and Scholes models.

The life of the option $[0, T]$ is first divided into N steps as $\{0 \equiv t_0 < t_1 < \cdots < t_N \equiv T\}$. This means that $t_i - t_{i-1} \equiv \Delta t \equiv \frac{T}{N}$. In mathematical terms, the bond price at P_T at date T is given by

$$\ln P_T = \ln P_0 + \sum_{i=1}^{N} \left[\left(\mu - \frac{1}{2}\sigma^2 \right) \Delta t + \sigma\sqrt{\Delta t}\,\tilde{z} \right]. \qquad (14.51)$$

In Equation 14.51 $\tilde{z}$ is a standard normal variable. Under the risk-neutral probability principle, we can change the probability measure and write the relevant pricing distribution as

$$\ln P_T = \ln P_0 + \sum_{i=1}^{N} \left[\left(r - \frac{1}{2}\sigma^2 \right) \Delta t + \sigma\sqrt{\Delta t}\,\tilde{z} \right]. \qquad (14.52)$$

TABLE 14-20

Pricing Options by Simulation

Path Number	Terminal Bond Price	Option Value at Maturity
1	P_T^1	$c^1 = \max(0, P_T^1 - K) \times (1 + r)^{-T}$
2	P_T^2	$c^2 = \max(0, P_T^2 - K) \times (1 + r)^{-T}$
. . .	. . .	. . .
. . .	. . .	. . .
. . .	. . .	. . .
M	P_T^M	$c^M = \max(0, P_T^M - K) \times (1 + r)^{-T}$

Note that Equation 14.51 differs from Equation 14.52 since we have replaced the expected return μ by the riskless rate r. Using a random number generator, we can now generate independent paths as follows. First, we generate N draws to determine P_T for path 1 from Equation 14.52. Note that this is done by generating N draws of $\tilde{z}$ (one for each time interval), which is a standard normal variable. We can write Equation 14.52 as

$$P_T = P_0 \times e^{\sum_{i=1}^{N}[(r - \frac{1}{2}\sigma^2)\Delta t + \sigma\sqrt{\Delta t}\tilde{z}]}.$$

Next, we repeat this procedure to generate M paths. For each path, we determine P_T. Then, we perform the calculations as shown in Table 14-20. The value of the option is

$$c = \frac{c^1 + c^2 + \cdots + c^M}{M}. \tag{14.53}$$

We illustrate this concept in Example 14-17.

Example 14-17:

Consider a bond with a price $P = 102$. A call option on this bond is available at a strike price of 101 with a maturity of one month. The financing rate is 5%, and the volatility of the bond returns is estimated at 25%. Determine the value of the call option.

Any bond price path can be generated as

$$\ln P_T = \ln P_0 + \sum_{i=1}^{N}\left[\left(r - \frac{1}{2}\sigma^2\right)\Delta t + \sigma\sqrt{\Delta t}\tilde{z}\right].$$

Let us take the life of the option ($\frac{1}{12}$ years) and subdivide it into $N = 100$ intervals. Then, the formula for the price path becomes

$$\ln P_T = \ln 102 + \sum_{i=1}^{100}\left[\left(0.05 - \frac{1}{2}0.25^2\right)\Delta t + 0.25\sqrt{\Delta t}\tilde{z}\right].$$

Remember that $t_i - t_{i-1} \equiv \Delta t \equiv \frac{1/12}{100}$. We will generate many such paths. For each of those paths we will identify the payoffs of options. They will then be discounted back and averaged.

In Tables 14-21 and 14-22 we show several sample paths: along path 1 in Table 14-21 all realizations of $\bar{z}$ are shown. The terminal bond price is 96.66 in path 1 as shown in Table 14-22 and, therefore, the option is out-of-the-money. Along path 3, the terminal stock price is 111.53, and the option is in-the-money and has a value of 10.53 at maturity. We take the discounted value of the option for each path and average them to get an option value of 4.06.

In the procedure presented here, we have the value of the underlying asset at maturity for each path. This can be used to determine the value of option at maturity for each path. Using this information, we can construct a histogram or a frequency distribution of option values at maturity as shown in Figure 14-19. Note that in more than 50% of the paths the option ends up out-of-the-money at maturity. In a few paths, however, the option ends up deep-in-the-money at maturity. The average of the option values across all paths leads to a value of 4.06.

Variance-Reduction Procedures

The difficulty with the simulation procedure outlined in the preceding section is that the value we obtain tends to have a large variation from sample to sample. If we are trying to estimate the true value c of the call option through repeated samplings $\{c^1, c^2, \ldots, c^M\}$, then the sample mean of the option value is simply

$$\hat{c} = \frac{c^1 + c^2 + \cdots + c^M}{M}. \tag{14.54}$$

Note that variance of the estimated call price from the simulation procedure is inversely related to M. Increasing M beyond a certain number becomes computationally unattractive. To avoid this, some variance-reduction procedures are used.

Example 14-18:

Using Example 14-17, we create another set or estimates $\{c^{1*}, c^{2*}, \ldots, c^{M*}\}$ by replacing $\bar{z}$ with $-\bar{z}$. This will lead to an option value of 3.54 in Example 14-17. We then take the average of the estimates

$$\bar{c}_i = \frac{c^i + c^{i*}}{2} = \frac{4.06 + 3.54}{2} = 3.80.$$

The sample-mean estimate by this averaging rule is

$$\hat{\hat{c}} = \frac{\bar{c}_1 + \bar{c}_2 + \cdots + \bar{c}_M}{M}.$$

The variance of this estimate of the call option is less than half of that of the first estimate $\hat{c}$. More sophisticated variance-reduction procedures have been developed in the literature which have not been addressed here. See Boyle (1977) and some of the references cited in that paper.

TABLE 14-21 *Simulated Standard Normal Variable* ($\tilde{z}$)

	Path 1	Path 2	Path 3	Path 4	Path 5	Path 6	Path 7	Path 8	Path 9	Path 10
$z1$	1.59	1.50	−0.19	−0.44	0.63	1.14	0.56	2.08	0.39	−0.85
$z2$	0.33	−1.48	0.07	−0.91	0.13	0.59	−2.16	−0.59	1.41	0.27
$z3$	0.15	−0.67	0.16	1.00	0.81	0.78	−1.05	1.63	0.34	0.07
$z4$	0.13	−1.07	0.47	1.17	−0.91	−1.35	1.17	0.31	0.21	−2.23
$z5$	−0.01	−0.74	−0.06	1.21	−0.48	−0.73	0.78	2.91	1.54	−0.54
$z6$	1.06	−0.14	0.52	−0.10	−0.39	−0.19	0.60	−0.03	1.31	1.27
$z7$	−0.10	1.19	0.63	1.27	0.05	−2.14	1.28	−0.65	−0.62	−1.05
$z8$	1.38	0.73	−0.32	−1.94	−0.48	−0.92	−0.17	0.06	−1.32	−0.82
$z9$	−0.40	−0.59	1.19	−1.60	0.03	1.14	−1.36	0.15	−0.43	−0.41
$z10$	0.88	−0.11	1.89	1.15	1.35	0.75	−1.22	−0.52	0.46	0.10
. . .	−1.05	0.86	0.26	0.54	−1.93	−0.49	0.65	1.50	−0.31	−1.10
. . .	0.07	0.64	−0.70	−0.05	0.10	−0.04	−0.21	−0.26	−0.37	0.32
. . .	−0.01	0.19	0.12	1.37	0.68	0.19	−0.82	−0.80	−0.37	−0.51
. . .	0.90	−0.93	−1.71	0.28	1.07	−0.08	0.00	0.07	−0.09	1.23
. . .	0.92	1.55	0.80	−1.05	−0.48	0.53	0.01	0.77	0.54	0.81
. . .	0.42	−0.66	0.27	0.14	−1.56	1.29	0.13	1.23	−1.39	−0.97
. . .	−1.13	−1.13	1.11	−1.55	1.23	0.72	0.65	−0.19	0.71	−0.09
. . .	−0.28	−1.38	−0.27	0.04	0.77	−0.64	−2.09	0.14	0.67	0.07
. . .	−0.21	−1.91	−0.03	−0.15	−0.26	−0.92	−1.29	−0.43	0.80	−1.92
. . .	−0.35	−0.73	0.32	−1.59	0.33	0.54	−0.23	−1.69	0.88	−0.67
. . .	0.54	−1.48	1.04	−0.72	− 0.33	−0.97	−0.11	−0.81	0.38	−1.85
. . .	−0.33	0.48	−0.26	0.67	−0.34	0.26	0.62	2.18	−0.26	1.18
. . .	0.56	−0.68	0.18	0.68	−0.21	−0.42	0.39	0.00	−1.40	−2.06
. . .	0.14	1.47	−0.19	1.24	0.44	−0.94	0.17	1.41	−2.04	−0.10
. . .	−1.21	−0.59	−0.65	1.58	−0.45	−0.25	−0.33	0.71	0.27	0.82
. . .	−1.68	−1.03	−0.12	−0.29	0.12	−0.65	0.69	−0.71	0.81	1.00
. . .	−0.07	1.01	0.56	0.98	0.79	2.45	0.33	−0.99	−1.44	0.90
. . .	−0.97	0.20	−0.78	0.56	−0.29	−0.80	0.58	−0.79	−0.61	−0.99
. . .	0.74	−2.17	0.58	−1.38	0.58	0.33	1.40	−1.47	0.91	0.59
. . .	−0.58	1.50	−1.22	−1.59	0.24	1.45	−0.27	−0.85	1.58	−0.24
. . .	0.17	0.67	0.05	0.37	−0.57	0.85	1.71	0.91	−0.17	1.84
. . .	−0.62	−2.34	−0.20	0.08	1.31	1.93	0.85	1.27	−0.49	−1.14
. . .	0.75	0.11	1.05	0.19	−0.13	−0.95	−1.57	0.13	−0.85	0.25
. . .	0.32	−0.28	−0.83	0.14	−0.63	1.15	−0.68	0.93	0.32	−0.59
. . .	−1.36	−0.82	0.41	1.83	−0.77	1.27	−1.04	−0.81	−1.25	−1.03
. . .	−0.89	−0.62	0.84	−0.41	−0.28	−0.02	−1.16	0.94	−0.77	−0.98
. . .	−3.32	0.67	−0.26	2.04	−0.01	−1.18	−0.27	0.42	0.04	0.40
. . .	−0.09	−0.22	1.70	−0.03	1.37	0.15	−0.36	0.78	−0.01	0.06
. . .	−0.05	−0.24	2.08	−1.77	0.07	0.01	−0.15	1.46	−0.10	0.83
. . .	0.34	−0.68	0.20	0.68	−0.92	−0.51	−0.04	−0.30	0.04	0.64
. . .	−0.68	0.75	−0.40	−1.17	−1.85	2.20	−0.51	0.11	0.05	−0.93
. . .	−1.17	−1.57	−1.18	1.15	0.34	−0.68	−0.46	−1.47	−0.76	−0.96
. . .	0.46	−1.31	0.35	−0.90	1.29	0.18	1.22	−1.59	−0.25	0.56
. . .	0.97	−0.47	0.18	0.27	1.22	−1.45	−0.51	−1.37	−0.54	0.26
. . .	−0.38	0.35	−1.75	0.58	0.14	−0.49	−1.41	0.33	−1.55	−1.06
. . .	2.75	−1.01	−1.30	0.80	−0.36	0.40	−0.21	0.36	0.27	0.99
. . .	−0.82	−0.78	−0.81	−0.19	1.40	−0.29	0.07	0.80	0.02	0.53
. . .	0.36	1.50	−0.53	0.28	0.15	−0.81	0.68	−0.76	−0.40	−0.24
. . .	−0.46	1.06	−0.42	−2.27	−2.32	−0.53	−2.09	−0.59	−0.79	1.05
. . .	0.49	1.65	−1.48	1.92	−2.24	0.14	0.58	−2.02	0.56	−0.31

480

TABLE 14-21   *Continued*

	Path 1	Path 2	Path 3	Path 4	Path 5	Path 6	Path 7	Path 8	Path 9	Path 10
. . .	−0.45	0.07	1.01	−1.17	−0.95	−0.78	−0.07	−1.59	−1.06	−0.82
. . .	0.45	−0.59	−1.15	1.75	0.76	0.02	1.05	−0.06	−0.57	−0.41
. . .	−0.13	−1.43	0.53	−0.31	1.35	−0.18	0.21	−0.26	−0.21	0.08
. . .	−1.23	0.57	−1.21	−0.07	0.29	−0.24	−0.67	1.66	2.14	−0.06
. . .	−1.04	−0.78	−0.35	0.20	−0.30	1.40	−1.58	−1.04	0.23	1.33
. . .	−0.16	1.16	−0.31	1.70	0.77	0.69	0.36	0.11	0.45	0.70
. . .	−0.15	0.52	−0.41	1.90	−0.07	−1.35	0.02	−1.46	0.20	2.15
. . .	0.33	−0.28	−0.43	−0.65	−0.21	2.40	−1.40	2.79	−0.31	−0.54
. . .	0.73	0.13	−0.27	0.51	0.09	0.19	1.60	−0.39	−0.95	−0.31
. . .	−0.17	−0.74	−0.07	0.35	0.28	−0.31	−0.64	0.72	−1.07	0.79
. . .	0.14	−0.01	−0.41	−0.45	0.61	−0.81	1.41	−0.92	−0.80	−0.86
. . .	−0.88	−0.90	2.25	1.02	−1.93	−1.92	−0.10	−0.92	−0.03	−1.31
. . .	−0.33	−0.08	0.01	0.15	−3.52	−1.25	−0.62	0.10	−0.33	0.45
. . .	−0.48	−0.18	−1.83	−0.25	−0.78	−1.70	−1.26	0.68	0.07	1.82
. . .	0.55	−0.68	0.76	−3.40	0.43	1.11	−0.03	−1.98	0.16	1.79
. . .	−0.21	−0.74	0.26	1.46	0.06	0.83	1.68	0.25	0.43	1.04
. . .	−0.28	−0.71	−0.50	−1.28	0.40	1.34	0.66	1.03	1.92	2.77
. . .	2.30	0.79	−1.96	0.37	0.26	−0.51	1.47	−2.81	1.95	1.12
. . .	0.28	−0.36	0.97	−0.85	−0.42	1.48	0.03	1.75	0.60	0.08
. . .	0.76	−0.91	−1.24	2.41	0.24	0.73	0.12	−1.50	−1.06	1.21
. . .	0.23	−1.55	0.27	0.52	−2.25	−0.05	0.87	−0.62	−0.96	−0.56
. . .	0.65	−0.09	1.15	−0.36	1.38	−0.82	2.41	0.09	−1.35	0.60
. . .	1.18	−0.05	1.73	−0.30	2.57	0.45	−1.39	−2.20	0.77	−0.81
. . .	0.44	1.07	1.76	1.67	0.40	−0.74	0.82	0.57	−0.96	0.00
. . .	−0.71	0.53	0.01	0.90	−0.40	−1.94	0.59	−0.63	0.52	1.13
. . .	−0.31	−1.34	0.25	0.78	0.30	1.49	−0.97	0.04	−1.74	−1.60
. . .	−0.87	−1.03	1.68	1.38	−0.79	−0.25	−0.91	0.03	1.27	2.27
. . .	0.19	1.06	−0.62	0.75	1.96	1.33	1.42	0.35	−1.16	0.19
. . .	−0.89	−1.18	0.11	0.30	0.89	−1.24	0.60	−0.19	1.77	−1.49
. . .	−0.45	−0.27	1.46	−2.38	0.17	−0.23	−1.51	1.12	0.53	−0.61
. . .	−0.32	−0.24	−1.17	0.46	−2.15	−1.38	0.93	0.53	−0.02	−0.93
. . .	−0.98	−0.88	1.35	−1.35	0.84	0.23	1.83	0.02	0.37	−0.75
. . .	−1.99	−1.39	0.91	0.25	0.20	−0.67	−1.10	−1.47	−1.02	0.97
. . .	0.80	0.91	−0.19	0.31	−0.92	1.56	−0.91	1.38	0.71	−0.42
. . .	0.13	−0.25	−0.30	0.49	2.61	1.81	−0.98	−0.29	−0.46	−1.93
. . .	−0.16	1.25	0.44	0.98	−0.05	0.71	1.26	−0.84	0.70	−0.23
. . .	−0.89	0.84	−1.26	−0.79	1.67	0.22	−0.03	1.20	−0.30	−0.34
. . .	0.99	−1.01	0.30	−0.48	0.06	1.00	2.37	2.92	1.07	−0.36
. . .	−0.65	−1.60	−0.26	0.63	−0.14	−0.83	0.37	0.09	0.32	−0.39
$z90$	0.97	0.45	−0.37	1.14	0.24	−0.81	0.63	−0.20	−2.96	0.13
$z91$	−1.29	0.12	2.15	−0.01	−0.03	−0.12	0.38	0.08	0.83	0.67
$z92$	0.18	−0.94	−1.15	0.06	−0.07	−1.73	−1.30	−1.31	0.54	−0.70
$z93$	0.20	0.41	0.54	3.02	−0.06	−0.03	−1.29	1.39	−0.68	−1.05
$z94$	−0.32	0.02	1.44	0.27	−1.40	0.44	0.50	−0.42	0.10	−0.93
$z95$	−0.58	−0.56	1.94	0.45	−1.09	−1.70	1.66	−0.53	0.58	0.16
$z96$	−0.82	−0.74	0.77	−1.86	0.83	0.62	−0.41	−0.10	−0.79	−0.56
$z97$	−0.64	0.01	0.96	0.46	−1.03	0.43	1.22	0.62	0.70	−0.71
$z98$	0.74	−0.55	0.28	0.31	−0.40	−0.15	−0.60	−0.88	−0.50	0.07
$z99$	−0.04	−0.52	0.37	0.92	−0.37	−2.04	−0.46	0.52	0.67	0.05
$z100$	−0.74	1.28	0.66	0.31	−0.45	1.96	1.54	−0.75	0.29	0.96

TABLE 14-22 *Simulated Bond Prices and Option Values*

	1	2	3	4	5	6	7	8	9	10
P0	102	102	102	102	102	102	102	102	102	102
P1	103.17	103.10	101.86	101.68	102.46	102.84	102.41	103.53	102.28	101.38
P2	103.41	102.02	101.91	101.02	102.56	103.27	100.84	103.10	103.32	101.58
P3	103.53	101.53	102.03	101.75	103.16	103.85	100.09	104.31	103.57	101.63
P4	103.63	100.76	102.37	102.61	102.49	102.86	100.94	104.55	103.73	100.02
P5	103.63	100.23	102.32	103.50	102.14	102.32	101.50	106.75	104.88	99.63
P6	104.42	100.13	102.71	103.43	101.85	102.18	101.94	106.73	105.87	100.55
P7	104.35	100.98	103.17	104.37	101.89	100.63	102.88	106.23	105.40	99.79
P8	105.39	101.51	102.93	102.93	101.54	99.97	102.75	106.28	104.41	99.21
P9	105.09	101.08	103.82	101.76	101.57	100.79	101.75	106.40	104.09	98.92
P10	105.75	101.00	105.23	102.61	102.55	101.34	100.87	106.01	104.43	99.00
. . .	104.96	101.63	105.43	103.00	101.14	100.99	101.34	107.15	104.20	98.22
. . .	105.02	102.10	104.90	102.97	101.22	100.96	101.19	106.95	103.92	98.45
. . .	105.01	102.24	104.99	103.98	101.71	101.10	100.60	106.34	103.65	98.10
. . .	105.69	101.56	103.71	104.19	102.49	101.04	100.61	106.40	103.59	98.97
. . .	106.39	102.70	104.31	103.41	102.14	101.43	100.70	106.99	103.99	99.55
. . .	106.72	102.22	104.51	103.52	101.01	102.37	100.70	107.94	102.96	98.86
. . .	105.86	101.39	105.35	102.38	101.90	102.90	101.18	107.79	103.48	98.80
. . .	105.64	100.39	105.15	102.41	102.47	102.43	99.67	107.90	103.98	98.85
. . .	105.48	99.03	105.13	102.29	102.28	101.76	98.76	107.57	104.58	97.50
. . .	105.22	98.51	105.37	101.14	102.53	102.16	98.60	106.28	105.24	97.03
. . .	105.63	97.47	106.16	100.62	102.29	101.46	98.52	105.67	105.53	95.76
. . .	105.38	97.81	105.96	101.10	102.04	101.65	98.96	107.33	105.34	96.57
. . .	105.80	97.34	106.10	101.60	101.89	101.35	99.24	107.33	104.29	95.16
. . .	105.91	98.37	105.96	102.50	102.22	100.67	99.36	108.42	102.77	95.09
. . .	104.99	97.96	105.47	103.67	101.89	100.49	99.12	108.98	102.97	95.66
. . .	103.74	97.24	105.38	103.46	101.98	100.03	99.62	108.43	103.57	96.35
. . .	103.69	97.95	105.80	104.19	102.56	101.80	99.85	107.66	102.51	96.98
. . .	102.98	98.09	105.21	104.61	102.35	101.22	100.27	107.06	102.07	96.29
. . .	103.53	96.58	105.65	103.59	102.78	101.46	101.28	105.93	102.74	96.70
. . .	103.10	97.63	104.73	102.41	102.96	102.52	101.08	105.29	103.91	96.53
. . .	103.22	98.10	104.77	102.69	102.54	103.15	102.33	105.98	103.78	97.82
. . .	102.77	96.46	104.62	102.74	103.51	104.59	102.95	106.95	103.42	97.02
. . .	103.32	96.54	105.41	102.89	103.41	103.88	101.80	107.05	102.80	97.20
. . .	103.56	96.35	104.79	102.99	102.95	104.73	101.30	107.76	103.03	96.79
. . .	102.56	95.78	105.10	104.35	102.39	105.70	100.56	107.14	102.11	96.08
. . .	101.90	95.36	105.74	104.05	102.19	105.68	99.73	107.87	101.55	95.41
. . .	99.51	95.82	105.55	105.58	102.18	104.80	99.53	108.20	101.58	95.69
. . .	99.45	95.67	106.84	105.56	103.19	104.91	99.28	108.81	101.58	95.73
. . .	99.42	95.51	108.45	104.24	103.25	104.92	99.17	109.95	101.50	96.30
. . .	99.66	95.05	108.61	104.74	102.57	104.54	99.14	109.72	101.53	96.75
. . .	99.18	95.57	108.30	103.87	101.22	106.20	98.79	109.80	101.57	96.11
. . .	98.35	94.50	107.39	104.73	101.47	105.69	98.46	108.65	101.02	95.45
. . .	98.68	93.62	107.66	104.06	102.41	105.83	99.33	107.42	100.84	95.83
. . .	99.37	93.30	107.80	104.26	103.31	104.74	98.97	106.37	100.45	96.01
. . .	99.10	93.54	106.46	104.69	103.42	104.37	97.97	106.63	99.34	95.29
. . .	101.08	92.86	105.48	105.30	103.15	104.68	97.82	106.90	99.54	95.96
. . .	100.49	92.35	104.87	105.15	104.19	104.46	97.87	107.52	99.55	96.33
. .	100.75	93.35	104.47	105.37	104.31	103.86	98.35	106.94	99.27	96.17
. . .	100.42	94.06	104.16	103.67	102.59	103.47	96.89	106.49	98.71	96.89
. . .	100.77	95.18	103.06	105.11	100.96	103.58	97.30	104.96	99.11	96.67

TABLE 14-22 *Continued*

	1	2	3	4	5	6	7	8	9	10
.. . .	100.45	95.23	103.81	104.23	100.28	103.00	97.25	103.77	98.36	96.11
. . .	100.78	94.83	102.96	105.55	100.82	103.01	97.99	103.72	97.96	95.83
. . .	100.68	93.87	103.35	105.32	101.81	102.88	98.14	103.54	97.82	95.88
. . .	99.80	94.25	102.46	105.27	102.02	102.71	97.67	104.78	99.33	95.84
. . .	99.06	93.73	102.21	105.42	101.80	103.74	96.57	104.00	99.49	96.77
. . .	98.95	94.52	101.98	106.72	102.37	104.26	96.83	104.08	99.81	97.25
. . .	98.84	94.87	101.69	108.18	102.32	103.26	96.84	103.00	99.96	98.76
. . .	99.08	94.68	101.38	107.68	102.17	105.06	95.87	105.09	99.74	98.39
. . .	99.60	94.77	101.19	108.08	102.24	105.20	96.98	104.79	99.06	98.17
. . .	99.48	94.27	101.14	108.35	102.45	104.97	96.53	105.34	98.31	98.73
. . .	99.58	94.26	100.85	108.00	102.90	104.36	97.52	104.65	97.75	98.12
. . .	98.96	93.66	102.49	108.79	101.49	102.94	97.45	103.97	97.73	97.21
. . .	98.73	93.61	102.50	108.91	98.96	102.02	97.02	104.04	97.50	97.52
. . .	98.39	93.49	101.16	108.72	98.41	100.79	96.15	104.55	97.55	98.81
. . .	98.78	93.04	101.71	106.10	98.72	101.59	96.13	103.08	97.66	100.08
. . .	98.63	92.54	101.90	107.22	98.76	102.20	97.29	103.27	97.96	100.83
. . .	98.43	92.08	101.53	106.24	99.05	103.19	97.76	104.04	99.32	102.86
. . .	100.07	92.60	100.12	106.53	99.23	102.81	98.79	101.97	100.72	103.69
. . .	100.27	92.36	100.82	105.88	98.93	103.91	98.82	103.26	101.16	103.75
. . .	100.82	91.76	99.93	107.72	99.10	104.46	98.90	102.15	100.39	104.66
. . .	100.99	90.75	100.12	108.13	97.52	104.42	99.52	101.70	99.71	104.25
. . .	101.47	90.69	100.96	107.85	98.49	103.81	101.25	101.77	98.75	104.70
. . .	102.33	90.66	102.22	107.62	100.32	104.15	100.25	100.18	99.29	104.10
. . .	102.66	91.36	103.52	108.92	100.61	103.60	100.85	100.59	98.62	104.10
. . .	102.14	91.71	103.53	109.62	100.33	102.17	101.28	100.13	98.99	104.95
. . .	101.91	90.83	103.72	110.24	100.54	103.27	100.57	100.16	97.76	103.75
. . .	101.28	90.17	104.98	111.33	99.97	103.09	99.92	100.19	98.66	105.45
. . .	101.42	90.86	104.52	111.93	101.39	104.08	100.94	100.44	97.84	105.59
. . .	100.77	90.10	104.61	112.18	102.03	103.16	101.38	100.31	99.09	104.47
. . .	100.45	89.92	105.71	110.28	102.16	102.99	100.29	101.12	99.47	104.02
. . .	100.23	89.77	104.83	110.65	100.60	101.98	100.96	101.50	99.45	103.34
. . .	99.53	89.20	105.85	109.59	101.21	102.15	102.29	101.52	99.72	102.78
. . .	98.11	88.32	106.54	109.79	101.36	101.67	101.50	100.45	98.99	103.50
. . .	98.68	88.89	106.40	110.04	100.69	102.82	100.84	101.45	99.50	103.19
. . .	98.77	88.74	106.17	110.43	102.59	104.16	100.13	101.25	99.17	101.77
. . .	98.66	89.54	106.51	111.20	102.56	104.70	101.04	100.64	99.67	101.60
. . .	98.03	90.08	105.56	110.58	103.79	104.86	101.02	101.50	99.46	101.36
. . .	98.74	89.43	105.78	110.21	103.84	105.62	102.75	103.65	100.23	101.10
. . .	98.28	88.41	105.59	110.70	103.74	104.99	103.03	103.72	100.46	100.82
P90	98.97	88.70	105.32	111.62	103.92	104.39	103.49	103.57	98.36	100.92
P91	98.06	88.78	106.96	111.61	103.90	104.30	103.77	103.64	98.95	101.41
P92	98.19	88.19	106.08	111.66	103.85	103.02	102.81	102.67	99.34	100.90
P93	98.33	88.45	106.50	114.10	103.81	102.99	101.87	103.70	98.85	100.15
P94	98.11	88.46	107.61	114.32	102.77	103.32	102.23	103.39	98.93	99.49
P95	97.70	88.11	109.12	114.70	101.98	102.07	103.46	103.00	99.34	99.61
P96	97.13	87.65	109.73	113.18	102.59	102.52	103.16	102.93	98.78	99.21
P97	96.69	87.65	110.49	113.56	101.84	102.84	104.06	103.38	99.28	98.71
P98	97.21	87.31	110.71	113.81	101.54	102.72	103.62	102.73	98.92	98.75
P99	97.18	86.99	111.01	114.57	101.28	101.24	103.28	103.11	99.40	98.79
P100	96.66	87.79	111.53	114.82	100.95	102.67	104.43	102.56	99.61	99.47

(continued)

TABLE 14-22   *Continued*

	1	2	3	4	5	6	7	8	9	10
Min Price	96.66	86.99	99.93	100.62	97.52	99.97	95.87	100.13	97.50	95.09
C = Call Value	0.00	0.00	10.53	13.82	0.00	1.67	3.43	1.56	0.00	0.00
Discounted C	0.00	0.00	10.49	13.77	0.00	1.66	3.41	1.56	0.00	0.00
Average	4.06									
L = Lookback	0.00	0.80	11.60	14.21	3.44	2.70	8.56	2.43	2.10	4.38
Discounted L	0.00	0.80	11.55	14.15	3.42	2.69	8.52	2.42	2.09	4.36
Average	5.71									

FIGURE 14-19   *Histogram of Option Values in 100 Trials*

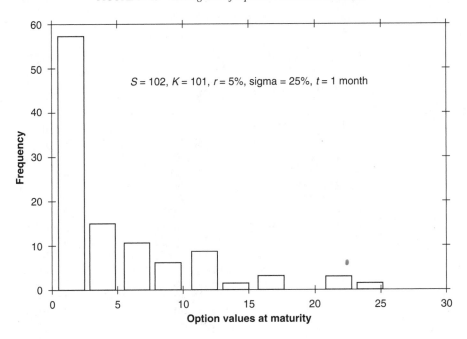

In Example 14-18, recall that the option value with variance reduction is 3.80. Had we used the Black and Scholes model, we would have obtained an option price of 3.68. We are off by 12 pennies. By using more paths, we can reduce the error even further. This is shown next. To illustrate how the simulation results behave as we increase the number of paths, we present Table 14-23. Throughout, we have subdivided the life of the option into 100 intervals.

As we can see, the accuracy improves significantly at first and then tapers off quickly.

Table 14-21 also provides the value of the normal random variable in *each path* along *all* subintervals besides the maturity date. If our objective is just to value ordi-

TABLE 14-23
Ordinary Call Option on Bond

Number of Paths	Option Value
100	3.800
200	3.782
500	3.687
1,000	3.708
10,000	3.664

TABLE 14-24
Lookback Call Option on Bond

Number of Paths	Option Value
100	5.278
200	5.727
500	5.462
1,000	5.347
10,000	5.517

nary calls and puts, we do not need all this information. In fact, there is no need to generate such information for valuing ordinary options. It is more efficient just to work with simulated prices just at maturity for each path.

Suppose, however, we are interested in valuing exotic options, such as lookback options or Asean options. These are described in Chapter 13 in detail. A lookback option provides at maturity

$$\max \, [P_T - \min_i \{P_i\}, \, 0],$$

where $\min_i \{P_i\}$ is the minimum of the underlying asset price during the life of the option. In Table 14-21, note that for each path we can explicitly compute $\min_i \{P_i\}$. For example, in path 1 $\min_i \{P_i\} = 96.66$. Hence, the payoff of the lookback option in path 1 is $P_T - \min_i \{P_i\} = 96.66 - 96.66 = 0$. For path 3, $P_T - \min_i \{P_i\} = 111.53 - 99.93 = 11.60$. Averaging across all paths and discounting, we get the value of the lookback to be 5.71. We provide the results for lookback options for various simulation runs in Table 14-24 (after variance reduction).

Monte Carlo procedures are quite powerful in many applications. A number of problems in corporate bonds and mortgage-backed securities can be solved using Monte Carlo simulation techniques.

We now examine the risk measures used in the options literature.

Option-Price Sensitivity

Delta Risk. As the underlying factors (such as the bond price, exchange rate, futures price, or spot-exchange rate) change, the value of the derivative asset changes as well. This exposure is called the **delta risk** and is denoted by Δ_i. Using the options-pricing models, we can calculate these option-price sensitivities.

The first variable in the risk management of options is the option delta. It is formally defined as:

$$\Delta_C = \frac{\partial C}{\partial S}$$

$$\Delta_P = \frac{\partial P}{\partial S}.$$

The delta of an option (in a model of options pricing) measures the price change in an option for a small change in the value of the underlying asset (such as the spot rate). Intuitively, we expect the delta of a call to be positive and the delta of a put to be negative. Moreover, we expect the delta to change as the value of the underlying asset changes.

Note that the same derivative asset may have more than one delta. For example, a convertible bond may have a delta with respect to the underlying stock price and another with respect to the overall interest rates. In concrete terms, if the delta of a derivative asset is 0.5, then for a full-point change in the underlying factor, the derivative asset's value will change by one-half point. The behavior of delta as a function of the underlying asset's value is shown in Figure 14-20.

The delta risk is always measured in the context of a specific model. Hence, the risk-management system is only as good as the models used to produce such risk measures.

The real-risk management problem in the derivatives area has less to do with the measurement of delta risk than with the fact that the deltas of derivative assets are, as a rule, constantly changing. This calls for a very dynamic and active risk or position management. Often, this is the biggest qualitative difference between other risk-management systems and derivative risk-management systems. In particular, the system requirements of a such a dynamic risk-management program follow:

- Real-time data and analytics from more than one market (underlying asset markets and derivative assets market)

FIGURE 14-20   *Delta of a Call Option on a Futures Contract*

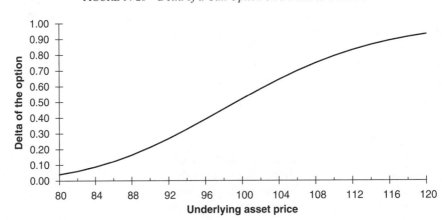

- The ability to aggregate risks across different derivatives and report positions
- The ability to mark-to-market the book using several pricing models on real-time data

The delta risk of the overall book in a certain derivative asset class (say, options on the OEX index) can be easily aggregated and reported. This turns out to be important in both risk measurement and management. For example, if Δ_i is the delta of option i (put or call, different strike prices, and different maturities) and the book has x_i such options, then the delta risk of the entire book (denoted by Δ_p) may be written

$$\Delta_p = \sum_{i=1}^{n} x_i \times \Delta_i. \tag{14.55}$$

Once the book's delta is measured by the previously shown aggregation scheme, we find a suitable hedging instrument, such as MMI futures or S&P 500 futures and take an offsetting position so that the delta of the book is exactly offset by the delta of the hedging instrument. Such a policy is known as a **delta-neutral hedge policy.**

Note that some of the Δ_i will be positive and some will be negative; thus, the book is likely to contain some natural hedges. This raises a very important risk-management question about how frequently each trade should be hedged. At one extreme, we can propose that each trade should be neutrally hedged as soon as the trade is executed. At the other extreme, we can propose that the trades should be unhedged until the end of the day, and then the portfolio of trades should be hedged once neutrally. The optimal hedge policy actually lies between these two extremes and is dependent on the rate of change of the delta risk. This leads us to the gamma risk measure.

Gamma Risk. The delta risk of derivative securities change as the market conditions in the underlying factors change. The rate of change of delta is known as the **gamma risk** of the derivative product. This is denoted by the symbol Γ.

Formally,

$$\Gamma_C = \frac{\partial \Delta_C}{\partial S}$$

$$\Gamma_P = \frac{\partial \Delta_P}{\partial S}.$$

The gamma of an option is the change in the delta of the option for a small change in the value of the underlying asset.

The Δs of derivative assets change constantly. The larger the Γ, the more dramatic will be the movements in the Δ of the derivative asset for a given change in the market conditions of the underlying factor. In mathematical terms, Δ is the first derivative of the derivative asset's price function with respect to the underlying factor, and Γ is the second derivative. Stated differently, Γ is the Δ of the delta function.

As with the delta risk, some derivative positions will have a positive gamma risk, and others will have a negative gamma risk. Intuitively, if an upward movement in the

FIGURE 14-21   *Gamma of Calls and Puts*

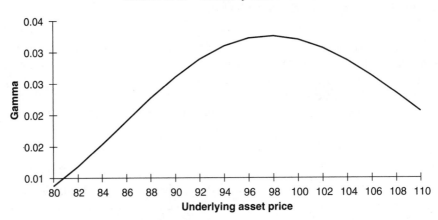

underlying factor causes the delta (with respect to that factor) of the derivative asset to increase and a downward movement causes the delta of the derivative asset to decrease, then such a position has a positive gamma. On the other hand, if an upward movement in the underlying factor causes the delta (with respect to that factor) of the derivative asset to decrease and a downward movement causes the delta of the derivative asset to increase, then such a position has a negative gamma. The behavior of gamma is shown in Figure 14-21.

In a way similar to the aggregation of delta risk, we can aggregate and measure the overall gamma risk of a book within the same derivative asset class. For example, if Γ_i is the gamma of option i (put or call, different strike prices, and different maturities) and the book has x_i such options, then the gamma risk of the entire book (denoted by Γ_p) may be written

$$\Gamma_p = \sum_{i=1}^{n} x_i \times \Gamma_i. \tag{14.56}$$

It is worth pointing out that when the book has a positive gamma, the down-side risk is bounded or limited. The profile of profits typically assumes a U shape, which approaches a V shape as the derivative positions approach maturity. On the other hand, if the position has a negative gamma, the risk profile is such that the losses are not bounded. Clearly, summarizing and measuring risk this way enables managers to understand and thus to respond to risks better.

Once the book's delta and its gamma are measured by the aggregation schemes shown previously, we find two suitable hedging instruments, such as MMI futures or S&P 500 futures, and listed options and take an offsetting position so that the delta of the book is exactly offset by the combined delta of the two hedging instruments and the gamma of the book is exactly offset by the combined gamma of the two hedging instruments. Such a policy is known as a **delta-and-gamma-neutral hedge policy.**

FIGURE 14-22   *Theta of a Call Option*

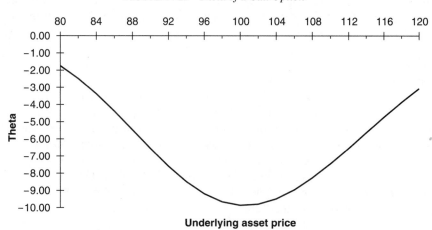

Underlying asset price

The trade-offs associated with the frequency of hedging trades apply here as well. Intuitively, however, it should be clear that a delta-and-gamma-neutral position is less vulnerable to infrequent hedging than a delta-neutral position.

Typically, all derivative positions have a limited term to maturity. For listed options and futures, it is typically of the order of a few days to a few weeks. For warrants and convertibles, the maturity period typically extends to several years. The book of derivatives typically tends to either appreciate in value or depreciate in value as the time passes, even when the underlying factors do not change. This leads us to the next measure of risk.

Theta Risk. The rate of change in the value of a derivative asset as the time passes is known as the **theta risk** of the asset and is denoted by θ. Formally,

$$\theta_C = \frac{\partial C}{\partial t}$$

$$\theta_P = \frac{\partial P}{\partial t}.$$

The theta of an option measures the change in the option value due to the passage of time. A positive theta position indicates that the book will lose value with time. The behavior of theta is graphed in Figure 14-22.

Once again, we can aggregate the overall theta of the book in a manner similar to delta and gamma risk. Define $\theta_i = \frac{\partial c_i}{\partial t}$. Then, we can aggregate the theta risk as

$$\theta_p = \sum_{i=1}^{n} x_i \times \theta_i. \tag{14.57}$$

Rho Risk. The sensitivity of the derivatives book to changes in the financing rates is called the **rho risk** and is denoted by ρ. This is an important policy measure in risk management.

Volatility Risk. By far the most important source of risk is the market volatility risk. There are two levels at which this risk is present.

First, the measures of volatility may be crude—sample unconditional standard deviations are often used in the industry. This measure, while simple, ignores time-series properties, such as volatility clustering, autoregression, and possible heteroscedasticity, that are present in various markets. More sophisticated estimation procedures, such as ARCH (autoregressive and conditional heteroscedastic) and GARCH models, are needed to minimize this source of risk, which I will call as the **estimation risk.** Using the listed options markets, it is possible to construct implied volatilities and aggregate those according to the "smile effect" or "the volatility skew." Usually, the weighting of such implied volatilities is obtained using measures, such as the elasticity or vega of the options, which is the sensitivity of the option premiums with respect to the changes in the underlying volatilities.

The second source of risk arises when a constant volatility estimate is used in the pricing model, when the market volatility is random. This is the **model misspecification risk.** This risk results from mispricing the options and using the incorrect hedge recipes that flow from such misspecifications.

The volatility factor is denoted by σ, and the vega risk is denoted by $\Omega_i = \frac{\partial c_i}{\partial \sigma}$. We can aggregate the volatility risk as before. Using an options pricing model allows these sensitivities to be calculated.

A full treatment of the risk management problem is presented in Chapter 18.

CONCLUSION

This chapter provided an overview of listed and OTC options markets. In addition to a survey of key contracts, we also developed basic propositions, such as put-call parity relations, no-arbitrage restrictions, and basic pricing approaches. In addition, early exercise conditions were developed for American options. We also developed basic options strategies and their associated payoff diagrams. Valuation approaches, such as binomial, Black and Scholes, and Monte Carlo simulation procedures, were also developed. The price sensitivity of options, such as Δ, Γ, Θ, and vega measures for individual options, as well as portfolios of options, were obtained and interpreted.

PROBLEMS

14.1. Evaluate the following statements. Explain each of your conclusions as precisely as possible. Provide, wherever possible, an analytical argument to support your answer.

(a) American options on futures should never be prematurely exercised.

(b) A call option on a portfolio of bonds is more valuable than a portfolio of call options on each of the bonds in the portfolio.

(c) An at-the-money six-month call option on a long bond that does not pay coupons during the life of the options should be at least as valuable as an at-the-money six-month put option on the same bond.

(d) In the absence of dividend payments during the life of the option, an American put should never be prematurely exercised.

14.2. Solve this problem without using options-pricing software. A 30-day call option (European-style) was offered by a dealer on 100 shares of IBM stock. The following terms apply:

- Stock price = 60.00
- Strike price = 58.00
- Financing rate = 5% per annum
- Volatility of IBM = 20% annualized

IBM was not expected to pay dividends over the next 30 days.

(a) Determine the value of this option.

(b) What is the probability that the option will end in-the-money when it expires?

(c) Determine the composition of the hedge portfolio. Show all the key steps.

14.3. Spreadsheet Problem. The following data are available on Digital stock.

- Stock price = 40.00
- Volatility of Digital stock = 25% annualized

Digital never pays dividends. You are required to price a 30-day at-the-money American put option on Digital stock. Assume that you are going to implement a binomial options-pricing model in which you intend to divide the life of the option into 30 steps. The annualized interest rate is 3%.

(a) Write a spreadsheet file (name the file put.wk1 or put.xls) to value the binomial options-pricing model.

(b) Determine the value of the put option and its delta.

(c) Turn in the spreadsheet file with complete documentation.

14.4. The following table contains the book of options trades of a bank's equity-index trading desk. Determine the net exposure of this desk in terms of the underlying S & P 500 index and construct a delta-neutral hedge position. Assume that the market price of the options are fair so that the implied volatility of each option is the relevant volatility at which the option is priced. Assume a dividend yield of 3% and a financing rate of 3%.

Underlying Asset and Price (S&P 500 Index)	Option Type (Premium)	Long or Short Number	Strike Price	Maturity
462.35	Call (7.00)	Long 100	460	30 days
462.35	Call (10.50)	Long 200	460	60 days
462.35	Put $\left(9\frac{5}{8}\right)$	Long 300	460	90 days

REFERENCES

Black, F., and M. Scholes 1973. "The Pricing of Options and Corporate Liabilities." *Journal of Political Economy* 81:637–659.

Boyle, P. P. 1977. "Options: A Monte Carlo Approach." *Journal of Financial Economics* 4:323–338.

Cox, J. C., and S. A. Ross 1976. "The Valuation of Options for Alternative Stochastic Processes." *Journal of Financial Economics* 3:145–166.

Cox, J. C., and M. Rubinstein 1985. *Options Markets*. Englewood Cliffs, NJ: Prentice-Hall.

Cox, J. C., J. E. Ingersoll, and S. A. Ross 1981. "The Relation between Forward Prices and Futures Prices." *Journal of Financial Economics* 9:321–346.

Cox, J. C., S. A. Ross, and M. Rubinstein 1979. "Options Pricing: A Simplified Approach." *Journal of Financial Economics* 7:229–263.

Harrison, J. M., and D. M. Kreps 1978. "Martingales and Arbitrage in Multiperiod Security Markets." *Journal of Economic Theory* 20:381–408.

Merton, R. C. 1973. "Theory of Rational Options Pricing." *Bell Journal of Economics and Management Science* 4:141–183.

Richard, S., and M. Sundaresan 1981. "A Continuous-Time Model of Forward and Futures Prices in a Multigood Economy." *Journal of Financial Economics* 9:347–372.

Chapter 15

Treasury Futures Contracts

Chapter Objectives

This chapter introduces the reader to the forward and futures markets. After a concise treatment of these markets, this chapter provides a detailed discussion of the Treasury bond futures contract. The theoretical underpinnings of pricing are presented; conversion factor, basis, carry, and delivery options are treated in detail. The following questions are addressed:

- What are forward and futures contracts? What are the differences between these contracts?
- What is open interest?
- What is marking-to-market and why is it important?
- What is meant by positive carry or negative carry?
- How can one identify the cheapest deliverable bond to the T-bond futures contract?
- What are delivery options and how are they valued?
- How can T-bond futures contracts be used to hedge interest-rate risk?
- How can the duration of a fixed-income portfolio be increased decreased using T-bond futures contracts?

INTRODUCTION

The forwards market and the futures market provide a mechanism for dealing with the uncertainty in commodity and asset prices that we encounter in our daily lives. Recall that assets can be bought and sold in the spot market (e.g., the stock market, where we could buy or sell shares of stock almost instantaneously) or in forwards and futures markets in which investors, producers, and buyers transact for *deferred* delivery.

A farmer expecting a crop of oats in a few months faces the possibility of a reduction in the price of oats in the market. If possible, he wants to sell his crop at a price that has been agreed upon at the time of production or at a stage when the size of his crop can be predicted with some accuracy. The farmer typifies a hedger who sells futures or is **short** in the deferred delivery market. Such a participant is sometimes referred to as a **short hedger.**

On the other hand, a corporation, such as Quaker Oats, that has to buy oats in futures to meet its production needs, wants to protect itself against the possibility of an increase in the price of oats. Thus, Quaker Oats wants to buy, at a currently established price, the quantity of oats dictated by its production needs. The corporation typifies an investor who buys futures or is **long** in the deferred delivery markets. Such an investor is known as the **long hedger.**

It is easy to see why the producers of oats and the buyers of oats want to reduce, if not eliminate, price uncertainty from their business decisions by engaging in contracts that set prices now but deliver goods later. Forward trading serves precisely this purpose. By selling forward oats at a currently determined price, the farmer eliminates price uncertainty from his or her business decisions. By buying forward at an agreed-upon price now, Quaker Oats eliminates price uncertainty from its production-planning decisions. Thus, forward trading facilitates the coordination of the production plans of the various buyers and sellers in various commodity and asset markets. This example is typical of producers of most commodities.

In a similar way, in financial markets, managers and traders face price uncertainty. The manager of a pension-fund portfolio that is fully invested in an equity portfolio is rightfully concerned about the possibility of a drop in equity prices. He or she may, therefore, protect the value of the portfolio by selling forward stock index contracts at a price now. Market makers who expect equity prices to go up are willing to buy the equity at a currently determined price. Forward trading enables investors with different expectations about price changes to execute transactions now for settlement later, as specified in the contract.

Although we motivated forward trading from the vantage point of producers of commodities, buyers of commodities, portfolio managers, and traders, there are others who benefit from forward trading. Individuals who have an opinion about the future price movements in an asset market may speculate in forward trading. By providing an avenue for such speculators to express their market view through forward trading, the forward market prices reflect a consensus view of the future price of the asset. This role is sometimes referred to as the **price-discovery role** of forward market. Note that the speculators may not (and typically do not) have any position in the underlying asset. In addition to short hedgers, long hedgers, and speculators, there are **arbitrageurs** who take advantage of any anomalies between spot prices and the prices that are set in the forward market. A market maker in government bonds may also sell or buy forward if he or she believes that the spot and futures prices enable him or her to lock in riskless profits.

HISTORY OF FORWARD AND FUTURES TRADING

The concept of deferred delivery agreements is not a recent one. In the latter half of the nineteenth century, the Chicago Board of Trade began trading in futures contracts. Interest in academic literature concerning futures markets dates from the early 1920s. Discussions of forward trading and the desirability of forward markets to improve the efficiency of resource allocation can be found in Keynes (1930) and subsequently in the classic *Value and Capital* (Hicks 1939). The development of this market has been steady since its appearance in the 1860s, but the growth has been phenomenal since the introduction of financial futures contracts. The Chicago Mercantile Exchange introduced foreign currency futures contracts, which may be properly viewed as the first financial futures contracts to be traded. This proved to be the catalyst for the subsequent explosive growth in futures contracts with financial instruments as the underlying assets. A detailed treatment of the development of futures markets is not attempted in this book. The interested reader may consult Carlton (1984) and Silber (1981), as well as the references cited in these papers.

Table 15-1 summarizes the significant developments in the history of the futures markets. The passage, in 1922, of the Grain Futures Act brought futures trading directly under the regulation of the federal government. (See Anderson [1984] for a detailed treatment of regulation of futures contract innovation in the United States.) It also officially authorized the trading of futures in grains, livestock, and oilseeds. Subsequently, several futures contracts covering a variety of underlying goods, such as eggs, cocoa, rubber, and pork, were traded with varying degrees of success. This was followed by some amendments to the Grains Futures Act in 1936. The year 1965 saw the introduction of live cattle futures contracts. In 1972, IMM of the Chicago Mercantile Exchange introduced the first financial futures, a foreign currency futures contract, in which the underlying asset was the spot exchange rate itself. This was followed by several successful innovations in financial futures contracts. In 1978, the Chicago Board of Trade introduced the Treasury bond futures contracts. In 1982, stock index futures contracts were introduced.

From a regulatory perspective, 1974 was an important year. The Commodity Futures Trading Commission (CFTC) was set up in this year to provide guidelines for contract designation. Although the CFTC was originally intended to be the body responsible for regulating all futures trading, several other agencies have also tended to

	Year	Event
TABLE 15-1	1922	Enactment of Grain Futures Act by Congress
Major Developments in the Futures Markets	1923	Authorized trading in corn, wheat, cotton, coffee, and sugar
	1936	Commodity Exchange Act
	1965	Live cattle futures contracts
	1972	Introduction of foreign currency futures. The first financial futures contracts.
	1974	Creation of Commodity Futures Trading Commission (CFTC)
	1978	Trading of U.S. Treasury bond futures contracts
	1982	Trading in stock index futures contracts and Eurodollar time deposits
	1982	Futures Trading Act
	1984	Options on futures contracts

exercise their power in the regulation of futures trading. The Treasury department, the Securities and Exchange Commission (SEC), and the Federal Reserve have all from time to time influenced the conduct of futures trading in various markets. Anderson (1984) and Kane (1984) provide a discussion of the regulatory structure and the impact of such competition between different agencies.

The Futures Trading Act of 1982 attempted to define the jurisdiction of the SEC and the CFTC in the matter of futures regulation. At the risk of oversimplification, it can be said that the CFTC was given the jurisdiction over futures contracts on goods and those contracts on securities for which a cash-settlement procedure is used, while the SEC was given the jurisdiction over futures contracts on securities for which a physical delivery system is used. These agencies play a role in many policy issues, such as setting margins and protection against manipulation. In 1984, options were introduced on futures contracts as underlying assets. As of 1987, options were traded actively on stock index futures, foreign currency futures, Treasury futures, and commodity futures contracts.

The impressive growth of futures contracts is evidenced by the diversity of the assets on which futures contracts are currently traded. In addition, exchanges all over the world offer futures contracts on different underlying assets. We have provided in Chapter 13 a summary of the range of the futures contracts that are currently actively traded.

FORWARD CONTRACTS

An investor who buys (sells) a forward contract agrees to buy (sell) one unit of the underlying asset at a specified future time, called the maturity date. The price at which the purchase will be made is called the forward price. The forward price is determined when the contract is written; it is specified in the contract and does not change over the life of the contract. An investor who has agreed to buy is said to be long in the forward market, and the investor who has agreed to sell is said to be short in the forward market. The forward price is chosen so that the purchaser of the forward contract, the long position, pays and receives nothing when the contract is written. At the time of maturity, the long position receives one unit of the asset or its cash value, which is delivered by the seller of the forward contract, the short position. On the maturity date, the short position receives the forward price specified in the contract.

Cash Flows from Forward Contracts

Let us consider an investor who has established a long position in one forward contract on an asset at time t. Assume that the contract matures at time $s > t$. Let $G_t(s)$ be the forward price at time t, V_j be the cash value of the spot asset at time j, and R_j be one plus the riskless rate of interest between time j and time $j + 1$. Table 15-2 presents a summary of the cash flows arising out of the long position in a forward contract.

TABLE 15-2	Date	Forward Price	Cash Price	Interest Rates	Cash Flows from Forward
Cash Flows from a Forward Contract	t	$G_t(s)$	V_t	R_t	0
	$t+1$	$G_{t+1}(s)$	V_{t+1}	R_{t+1}	0
	$t+2$	$G_{t+2}(s)$	V_{t+2}	R_{t+2}	0
	$t+3$	$G_{t+3}(s)$	V_{t+3}	R_{t+3}	0
	$\ldots$	$\ldots$	$\ldots$	$\ldots$	$\ldots$
	$\ldots$	$\ldots$	$\ldots$	$\ldots$	$\ldots$
	s	$G_s(s)$	V_s	R_s	$G_s(s) - G_t(s)$
	Total				

Example 15-1:

A forward contract on crude oil was entered into at date t to buy crude at a price of $20 per barrel for settlement at date s, which is three days from date t. The forward price and cash price of crude oil are shown in the following table. Also shown are the cash flows from the forward contract.

Date	Forward Price	Cash Price	Cash Flows from Forward
t	20	18	0
$t+1$	21	$19\frac{1}{2}$	0
$t+2$	22	$21\frac{1}{2}$	0
$s=t+3$	$21\frac{1}{2}$	$21\frac{1}{2}$	$21\frac{1}{2} - 20 = 1\frac{1}{2}$

Note that there are no cash flows during t through $t + 2$. As the cash price of oil increases, clearly the forward contract to buy at $20 becomes much more valuable. Its full value is only realized on settlement date. Conversely, if the cash price had fallen below $20, the forward contract to buy at $20 would have become a financial obligation. Once again, all the losses will only be settled on the settlement date.

The value of a forward contract fluctuates between the time it is written and the time it matures. When the contract is written, it has no value, but on the maturity date, the long realizes a profit or loss equal to the difference between the cash price and the contracted forward price. Between the writing and the maturity, the value of a forward contract will fluctuate because the value of the right to buy at the forward price written in the contract changes as the cash price changes.

Note that on the maturity date s, the forward price $G_s(s)$ must necessarily be equal to the spot price V_s. Were this not the case, it would be possible to make arbitrage profits: if $G_s(s) > V_s$, then we could sell forward, buy spot, and close out by making delivery. These transactions would produce a profit of $G_s(s) - V_s$. In a similar way, if $G_s(s) < V_s$, then we could buy forward, sell spot, and close out by taking delivery. These transactions would produce a profit of $V_s - G_s(s)$.

Example 15-2 illustrates the issues that are involved.

Example 15-2:

On March 12, XYZ Corporation agrees to buy 1,000 barrels of crude oil from West Texas Intermediate (WTI) at a price of $19 per barrel with the understanding that the crude oil will be delivered to Cushing, Oklahoma, on May 12, a period of 60 calendar days from March 12. Assume that the financing costs amount to 8.0% annualized. If 30 days later, the crude oil forward price is quoted at $17 per barrel, what is the value of the forward contract to XYZ Corporation? It should be clear that XYZ Corporation has a forward contract (at a forward price of $19) with a negative value. XYZ can dispose of it only by paying compensation to a third party. This can be accomplished by selling forward at a forward price of $17 on April 12. At maturity date, the physical delivery of oil from the original forward contract is used to cover the short position in the second forward contract that was established on April 12. The loss on May 12 is

$$(\$17 - \$19) \times 1000 \equiv \$2000.$$

The present value of the contract as of April 12 is

$$\frac{2000}{\left(1 + \frac{.08 \times 30}{360}\right)} \equiv 1986.75.$$

The fluctuation in the value of a forward contract is due to the fact that forward contracts are not marked to market. The futures contracts, which we describe next, are marked to market, and their value after they are marked to market is always zero.

FUTURES CONTRACTS

An investor who takes a long (short) position in a futures contract agrees to buy (sell) specified units of the underlying asset (or its cash value) on a specified maturity date at a currently specified futures price. The futures price is determined when the contract is written and is specified in the contract. The futures price is set so that no payment is made when the contract is written; that is, at initiation, the futures contract has a zero market value. As the contract matures, however, the investor must make or receive daily installment payments toward the eventual purchase of the underlying asset. The total of the daily installments and the payment at maturity will equal the futures price set when the contract was initiated. (This definition is based on Richard and Sundaresan [1981].)

The daily installments are determined by the daily change in the futures price. If the futures price goes up, then the investor who is long in the futures contract receives a payment from the investor who is short that equals the change in the daily futures price. This process is called **marking-to-market** on futures exchanges.

The effect of marking-to-market is to rewrite the futures contract each day at the new futures price. Hence, the value of the futures contract after the daily settlement will always be zero since the value of a newly written futures contract is zero. When the contract matures, the long will have already paid or received the difference between the initial futures price and the futures price at the maturity time. With these payments to his or her credit, he or she will have a balance due equal to the futures price at the maturity time. However, the value of a futures contract written at the maturity time for immediate delivery must be zero. Therefore, at maturity, the futures price must equal the current spot price: The balance due is simply the current spot price at the maturity time.

Cash Flows from Futures

It is useful to consider the cash flows from a futures more formally at this stage. Consider an investor who has established a long position in one futures contract on an asset at time t. Assume that the contract matures at time $s > t$. Let $H_t(s)$ be the futures price at time t, V_j be the cash value of the spot asset at time j, and R_j be the one plus the riskless rate of interest between time j and time $j + 1$. In Table 15-3, we have presented the cash flows from the long position in a futures contract.

Recall that at maturity date s of a futures contract, the futures price must be exactly equal to the cash price. In other words, $H_s(s) = V_s$. (Note that the sum of the cash flows in the last column of Table 15-3 is $H_s(s) - H_t(s)$, which is the same as $V_s - H_t(s)$.) This means that if the futures price is higher than the cash price at maturity and the investor sells futures and buys cash and effects delivery, the investor can make riskless profits. Similarly, if the futures price is less than the cash price and the investor buys futures and sells cash, the investor can make riskless profits.

TABLE 15-3 Cash Flows from a Futures Contract	Date	Future Price	Cash Price	Interest Rate	Cash Flows from Futures
	t	$H_t(s)$	V_t	R_t	0
	$t + 1$	$H_{t+1}(s)$	V_{t+1}	R_{t+1}	$H_{t+1}(s) - H_t(s)$
	$t + 2$	$H_{t+2}(s)$	V_{t+2}	R_{t+2}	$H_{t+2}(s) - H_{t+1}(s)$
	$t + 3$	$H_{t+3}(s)$	V_{t+3}	R_{t+3}	$H_{t+3}(s) - H_{t+2}(s)$
	. . .	. . .	. . .	. . .	. . .
	. . .	. . .	. . .	. . .	. . .
	s	$H_s(s)$	V_s	R_s	$H_s(s) - H_{s-1}(s)$
	Total				$H_s(s) - H_t(s)$

Exceptions to the rule that the futures price must equal the cash price occur whenever the futures contracts provide either the short or the long with some delivery options. These exceptions are fully treated in the context of specific futures markets later.

The holder of a futures position receives or pays cash on a daily basis. An investor with a long (short) position receives (pays) cash flows when the futures prices increase, and pays (receives) cash flows when the futures prices fall. If the future interest rates are random, this introduces a reinvestment risk. If cash is fully invested in interest-bearing securities, then a margin call resulting from unfavorable changes in futures prices will force the investor to liquidate some of the assets to post the additional margin. The opportunity cost of this is unknown at the time the futures position is initiated. Similarly, any receipts of cash due to favorable changes in futures prices will have to be reinvested at rates unknown at time t. As a result, we may expect the futures prices at time t to not only embody the expectations about the future cash price V_s at time s but also the path of one-period interest rates between time t and time s.

Example 15-3:

Consider a futures contract to buy crude oil entered into at date t for settlement at date s, which is three days from date t. Let us assume for simplicity that the futures settle by cash on date s to the crude oil price at date s. The futures and cash prices, as well as the cash flows from futures contracts, are shown in the following table.

Date	Futures Price	Cash Price	Cash Flows from Futures
t	20	18	0
$t+1$	21	$19\frac{1}{2}$	1
$t+2$	22	$21\frac{1}{2}$	1
$s = t+3$	$21\frac{1}{2}$	$21\frac{1}{2}$	$-\frac{1}{2}$

Note that as the cash price increases, the futures price increases as well. This coupled with the marking-to-market feature leads to cash inflows at dates $t + 1$ and $t + 2$. From $t + 2$ to $t + 3$ future price fell by $\frac{1}{2}$. This resulted in a loss of $\frac{1}{2}$. The sum of the cash flows from futures (in the last column) is the same as in the forward contract in Example 15-1. Only, in the case of futures, it is paid out in installments.

Design Features

The definition of the futures contract and the discussion of the contract presented in Table 15-3 captures the essential features of futures contract. There are, however, several real-life features of such contracts.

Delivery Specifications. The exchanges must decide whether the futures contract calls for physical delivery or cash settlement. In addition, the exchanges must decide on the set of assets that can be used by the investors to satisfy the delivery requirements. The delivery parameters, such as location, timing, and quality, have to be specified in detail; these issues are resolved on a case-by-case basis. There are also some common considerations that underlie the choice of delivery specifications.

First, the delivery specifications must be such that the deliverable assets are in competitive supply so that no single economic agent acting alone or a group of dominant agents acting in collusion will be able to corner the supply of deliverable assets. The principal implication of this is the design requirement that, in the case of commodity futures contracts, the deliverable set includes several grades of commodities. For futures contracts on financial assets, such as Treasury bonds or Treasury notes, many bonds and notes issued by the Treasury qualify for delivery. While such a design feature mitigates the problem of corners, it introduces a different problem. With so many deliverable assets, the maturity futures price will tend to track the price of cheapest deliverable asset. At the time of contracting, however, investors do not know which asset will be the cheapest when the contract expires. This introduces another element of uncertainty. Exchanges have attempted to deal with this problem by standardizing the assets that may be delivered against a futures contract. For example, in the case of T-bond futures contracts, the Chicago Board of Trade (CBOT) has stipulated that the standard grade is the 8%, 20-year bond issued by the Treasury. The deliverable set, however, includes all the bonds issued by the Treasury that have 15 years or more to first call date or maturity. CBOT then standardizes these bonds through a system of conversion factors that attempt to equalize the bond prices and the futures price that has been adjusted by the conversion factor of the bonds. Futures prices track the cheapest deliverable asset's price; as a consequence, the delivery of more expensive bonds is suboptimal. These issues are taken up for detailed analysis later in the book.

The choice between physical delivery and cash settlement is also a nontrivial one. Both types of contracts are popular in the market place. The S&P 500 futures contract are closed out by cash settlement, whereas the T-bond futures contract are closed out by physical delivery. Both are extremely successful contracts. Cash settlement, when coupled with an underlying asset, such as the S&P 500 index, which is not easily subject to manipulations, ensures complete convergence of the futures price to a competitively determined cash price at maturity. This turns out to be a desirable feature in futures contracts when they are used for hedging. Cash settlement is characteristic of equity futures contracts, and physical settlement is characteristic of debt futures contracts.

It is worth noting that only a tiny percentage of futures contracts are closed by physical delivery, and most of them are offset prior to the maturity date. This should come as no surprise, as the diversity of deliverable grades makes taking physical delivery less attractive. A further reduction in incentive to take delivery is attributable to the fact that the short may effect delivery on any business day of the delivery month, typically with short notice. This flexibility is called the timing option implicit in futures contracts.

Many futures contracts permit the short some flexibility in the choice of the location of physical delivery as well. This is referred to as the location option imbedded in futures contracts.

Price Limits. The exchanges may impose price limits. These limits stipulate the range of futures prices within which trading will be sustained in the futures markets. When the futures prices reach the limit, the investor is locked into his or her position and cannot offset. Typically, the limits are removed during the delivery months of the futures contract.

Margins. Exchanges set margins to ensure that the investor has sufficient equity to meet any adverse price moves. This, in conjunction with marking-to-market and price limits, minimizes the risk of nonperformance by investors who take futures positions. In much of the analysis in the book, we assume that the initial margin requirements to open a futures position can be met by posting interest-bearing securities. This turns out to be a realistic assumption, although in many instances a small percentage of the margin will have to be posted in cash. Once the initial margin level falls to a prespecified level, called the maintenance margin, margin calls will result. This usually happens when the futures prices move in an adverse manner relative to the established futures position for several consecutive days. When this happens, the investor must restore the margin level to the initial margin level by posting cash.

Here, we have merely sketched some of the important design features of futures contracts. A detailed analysis of the design features is taken up on a case-by-case basis later. Tables 15-4 and 15-5 show examples of the *Wall Street Journal* listings of the future price quotations for actively traded futures contracts. On April 8, 1987, the open

TABLE 15-4

Futures Quotations S&P 500 Index Futures Prices

Prices	September 2000	December 2000	March 2001
Open	150,360	152,500	154,750
High	150,820	152,750	155,790
Low	149,500	151,800	154,040
Settlement	150,080	152,320	154,650
Open interest	370,809	14,779	1,389

TABLE 15-5

Futures Quotations T-Bond Futures

Prices	March 2001	June 2001
Open	$104\frac{23}{32}$	$104\frac{30}{32}$
High	$105\frac{10}{32}$	$105\frac{6}{32}$
Low	$104\frac{17}{32}$	$104\frac{16}{32}$
Settlement	$104\frac{20}{32}$	$104\frac{18}{32}$
Open interest	405,867	2,289

price for the June contract was 303.20; this is the price at which the first transaction was executed. The highest price on April 8 for the June contract was 306.10, and the lowest price on that day was 295.50. In general, the settlement price is a representative price within the range of the market at the end of the day; in the case of S&P 500 futures, it is simply the closing price. The change in the settlement price from the previous day is also reported for each contract. This is useful information, as marking-to-market is based on the settlement prices. In addition, the lifetime-high and lifetime-low prices are reported. Open interest is the number of outstanding contracts on the previous day. For the June contract, the open interest stood at 99,315. Note that the open interest falls rapidly as one moves into more distant maturity futures contracts. This is typical of most futures contracts. Total volume is the number of contracts traded on any day. For the S&P 500 index futures on April 8, this was 91,721 contracts. The total open interest across all contracts, as well as the change in this quantity over the previous day, are also reported.

Typically, a number of maturity dates are available for trading. In the case of S&P 500 index futures, only three maturities were available. The maturities for the Eurodollar time-deposit futures contracts extend up to two years, with one contract maturing every quarter. The size of the S&P 500 futures, also indicated in the *Wall Street Journal* report, is 500 times the index. By posting an initial margin of $10,000, it is possible to establish a long (short) position in one S&P futures contract. (By 1995, however, this had increased to $20,000. Margins can be changed at the discretion of the exchange depending on market conditions.) In effect, this is equivalent to taking a long position in 500 shares of the index, as far as the exposure to S&P 500 index price changes are concerned. Indeed, we will show later that buying futures is equivalent to borrowing and buying the underlying asset.

FORWARD CONTRACTS VERSUS FUTURES CONTRACTS

Forward contracts differ from futures contracts in a number of ways:

- Forwards are not marked-to-market, as are futures contracts. This alone is sufficient to cause a difference in the forward prices and futures prices in the presence of interest rate uncertainty.
- Forwards are typically entered into by institutions either on a bilateral basis, as in the case of the oil industry, or through extensive OTC markets, as in the case of foreign currency markets. Futures contracts, on the other hand, are traded in centralized open outcry exchanges in which bid-offer prices are established.
- The difference in the market organization, in turn, requires different institutional arrangements for ensuring performance. In the futures markets, anyone with a reasonable amount of capital can participate. Exchanges have clearinghouses that monitor the performance of participants through the system of marking-to-market, margins, and margin calls that force the participants to respond quickly to adverse price movements. If any investor is unable to respond, that investor's open position is correspondingly reduced and ultimately extinguished. The clearinghouses

have capital that they can rely on to meet any residual shortfall. This mechanism is necessary in order for the open outcry markets to function; there is no time in such a market to conduct extensive credit checks on investors. In forward markets, the situation is quite different. In the bilateral contracts prevalent in the oil industry, for example, the corporations receive sufficient information about the credit risk that they face in forward contracting. This enables them to design the necessary contractual terms to protect themselves from any nonperformance contingencies. In OTC forward markets, high capital requirements and collateral requirements are enforced to screen investors with high credit risks.

- Forward contracts, especially the ones in bilateral settings, specify precise terms concerning the deliverable grades, location, and delivery dates. The goal in such a contracting process is delivery. This aspect differs sharply from the delivery specifications of futures contracts, which provide the short with the many imbedded options we have discussed previously.

Under what circumstances will one prefer forward contracting over futures contracting? When might one expect both markets to coexist, and when might one dominate the other? The answers to these questions depend in good part on the contractual features that we have described previously. Economic agents who wish to take delivery of the underlying good at a future date for further processing at some location will prefer the delivery terms associated with forward contracts. The familiarity of such economic agents with one another's credit risks, delivery capabilities, and so on, makes forward contracting viable and, indeed, preferable to futures contracting. The continued existence of forward contracts in the oil industry is a case in point. The existence of OTC forward markets in foreign currencies is an indication that such markets have a role that cannot be duplicated by futures contracts. As a rule, it is difficult to offset forward contracts in the foreign currency market. Here it is difficult to compare forwards to foreign currency futures markets. In foreign currency markets, forward rates are quoted according to conventions that differ from the futures quotations. The spot quotes are written out to the appropriate number of decimal places. The forward quotes are then expressed in points, by which they sell at a discount or premium. This convention is in contrast with the practice in the futures markets where the futures prices are also written out to the appropriate decimals. It is also worth remembering that forward quotes are given for standard fixed maturities; 30, 60, and 90 days are the most common. Fixed maturities of six months and a year or more are less common. This practice makes the comparison of forwards and futures a bit more difficult, due to the fact that futures contracts have a fixed delivery month and their days to maturity change every day.

TREASURY FUTURES CONTRACTS

A considerable increase in the volatility in interest rates occurred after the shift in the Fed's policy in October 1979. This was seen earlier in the text. The interest rates have tended to fluctuate a great deal since that shift. This increased volatility has posed significant risks for issuers, financial intermediaries, and investors.

TABLE 15-6

Margin Requirements for Treasury Futures

Contract	Initial Margin	Maintenance Margin
Five-year T-note	$1,000	$750
Ten-year T-note	$1,500	$1,000
T-bond	$3,000	$2,500
T-bill	$1,500	$1,200

To successfully manage such risks, it is necessary to have hedging vehicles in the marketplace. The introduction of Treasury bill futures contracts in the International Monetary Market in January 1976, Treasury bond futures contracts in the CBT in August 1977, Treasury note (ten-year) futures contracts in the CBT in 1982, and the recent introduction of Treasury note (five-year) futures contracts in CBT and NYCE are, in part, a response to these factors. In this section, the specifications of Treasury futures contracts will be described. T-bond futures contracts and their specifications will be analyzed in detail. Since the Treasury note futures are similar to Treasury bond futures, the analysis for the Treasury bond futures applies to the note contracts as well.

The Treasury bill futures contract listed at the IMM was one of the liquid contracts until the introduction of the Eurodollar futures contract. The Treasury bond (T-bond) futures contract of the Chicago Board of Trade (CBT) continues to be one of the most liquid futures contracts ever traded. CBT also lists a Treasury note futures contract whose specifications are almost identical to the T-bond futures contract, except that the underlying nominal asset is a 10-year note. The margin requirements needed to open positions in these contracts are shown in Table 15-6. The margins indicated are exchange-specified minimum amounts; the actual transactions may entail higher margins.

Treasury Bill Futures Contracts

The salient features of the T-bill futures contract are provided in Table 15-7. The deliverable asset to the T-bill futures is a $1,000,000 face value Treasury bill that has 90 days to maturity. The invoice price is computed using the following formula:

$$P = 1,000,000 \times \left[1 - d \times \left(\frac{\tau}{360} \right) \right], \tag{15.1}$$

where d is the discount rate (expressed in decimals) at the maturity date of the futures, τ is the time to maturity of the T-bill, and P is the invoice price. This convention is based on the fact that U.S. T-bills are sold on a discount basis. The discount rate d is calculated as

$$d = \frac{(100 - P)}{100} \times \frac{360}{\tau}, \tag{15.2}$$

where 100 is the face value of the T-bill, P is the market value, and τ is the time to maturity. The settlement prices of futures are quoted as 100 minus the discount rate in

TABLE 15-7 *IMM Treasury Bill Futures Contract*

Trading unit	$1,000,000 face value of U.S. Treasury bills deliverable during the months traded
Months traded	March, June, September, December
Deliverable grade	U.S. Treasury bills with 90 days to maturity
Delivery method	Federal Reserve book-entry wire-transfer system
Price quote	On a discount basis
Minimum price change	0.01 = $25
Daily price limit	60 basis points or $1,500
Hours of trade	8:00 A.M. to 2:00 P.M. Chicago time
Last trading day	The day before the first delivery day
Delivery date	First day of spot month on which the 13-week Treasury bill is issued, and the one-year Treasury bill has 13 weeks to maturity
Ticker symbol	TB

percent, which applies to bills delivered on the settlement date. Thus, a futures price of 93.50 indicates a discount rate of 6.50%. An investor who is short as of the delivery date in a Treasury bill futures contract may deliver either a 90-day T-bill, a 91-day T-bill, or a 92-day T-bill. The short will receive upon delivery of a 90-day T-bill an amount that will be computed using Equation 15.1 as

$$1,000,000 \times \left[1 - 0.065 \times \frac{90}{360} \right] = 983,750.$$

Thus, the discount convention in the cash market is also followed in the futures market. However, the Eurodollar futures are quoted with an add-on market convention. To make the appropriate comparisons, it is necessary to convert discount yields to add-on yields as shown in Equation 15.3.

$$d = \frac{(100 - P)}{P} \times \frac{360}{\tau}, \tag{15.3}$$

where y is the add-on yield equivalent. The discount convention allows the convergence of futures prices on T-bills to converge to the price of the deliverable T-bill at the maturity date of futures contract. Hence, the comparison of futures and forward prices is conceptually valid, but the add-on convention used in the Eurodollar futures market makes this comparison much more difficult.

Forward and Futures Rates. The existence of a liquid spot market in bills means that investors can synthetically create forward rates. If the synthetically created forward rates differ from the futures rates, after accounting for transactions costs and risks, then arbitrage profits are possible. To this end, we first illustrate how the Treasury spot markets can be used to borrow and lend at forward rates. Table 15-8 illustrates a strategy to borrow at a future date T_1 at a currently known forward rate, $f_t^b(T_1, T_2)$.

TABLE 15-8   *Borrowing at Forward Rate*

Transaction on Current Date	Investment on Current Date t	Maturity Date, First Bill T_1	Maturity Date, Second Bill
Buy the bill that matures on T_1	$-b(t, T_1)$	1	0
Sell the bill that matures on T_2	$b(t, T_2)$		-1
Borrow the difference until T_2	$b(t, T_1) - b(t, T_2)$		$-\dfrac{b(t,T_1)-b(t,T_2)}{b(t,T_2)}$
Total investment	0		
Total cash flow		1	$-\dfrac{b(t,T_1)}{b(t,T_2)}$

The forward rate is given by the following expression:

$$f_t^b(T_1, T_2) = \frac{b(t, T_1)}{b(t, T_2)}.$$

In the computation of forward rates, bid prices are to be used for the bill maturing on T_2 and ask prices for the bills maturing on T_1. The borrowing is also assumed to take place at the offer rate. Using the concept of spot rates of interest, let R_1 be the spot rate of interest between t and T_1, and let R_2 be the spot rate of interest between t and T_2. Then,

$$b(t, T_1) = \frac{1}{(1 + R_1)^{T_1 - t}}$$

and

$$b(t, T_2) = \frac{1}{(1 + R_2)^{T_2 - t}}.$$

Hence, the rate that we have locked in is

$$f_t^b(T_1, T_2) = \frac{b(t, T_1)}{b(t, T_2)} = \frac{\frac{1}{(1+R_1)^{T_1-t}}}{\frac{1}{(1+R_2)^{T_2-t}}}.$$

Simplifying, we get

$$f_t^b(T_1, T_2) = \frac{(1 + R_2)^{T_2 - t}}{(1 + R_1)^{T_1 - t}}.$$

Example 15-4:

The prices of two T-bills and their maturities are shown in the following tables. What is the forward rate that can be locked in for the purposes of borrowing between July 25, 1996, and April 3, 1997?

The bill prices in the table are obtained using the formula in Equation 15.1. The borrowing rate between July 25, 1996, and April 3, 1997, is 4.022%.

Settlement May 2, 1996	Security	Maturity	Bid (Discount)	Offer (Discount)
	T-bill	July 25, 1996	4.96%	4.94%
	T-bill	April 3, 1997	5.33%	5.31%

Transaction on May 2, 1996	Investment on May 2, 1996	July 25, 1996 Cash Flows	April 3, 1997 Cash Flows
Buy the bill maturing on July 25, 1996 @ 4.94%	−0.98847	1	0
Sell the bill maturing on April 3, 1997 @ 5.33%	0.95025		−1
Borrow the difference until April 3, 1997	0.03822		−0.04022
Total	0	1	−1.04022

TABLE 15-9   *Lending at Forward Rate*

Transaction on Current Date	Investment on Current Date T_1	Maturity Date, First Bill T_2	Maturity Date, Second Bill
Sell the bill that matures on T_1	$b(t, T_1)$	−1	0
Buy the bill that matures on T_2	$-b(t, T_1)$		1
Lend the difference until T_2	$-[b(t, T_1) - b(t, T_2)]$		$\dfrac{b(t,T_1) - b(t,T_2)}{b(t,T_2)}$
Total investment	0		
Total cash flow		−1	$\dfrac{b(t,T_1)}{b(t,T_2)}$

In a similar manner, Table 15-9 illustrates a strategy for lending at a future date T_1 at a forward rate, $f_t^l(T_1, T_2)$.

Example 15-5:

For the T-bills provided in the previous example, what is the forward rate that can be locked in between July 25, 1996, and April 3, 1997, for lending purposes?

The idea is essentially similar to the previous example, except that we will sell the T-bill maturing on July 25, 1996, at 4.96% and buy the T-bill maturing on April 3, 1997, at 5.31% and lend the difference as shown in the following table.

Transaction on May 2, 1997	Investment on May 2, 1997	July 25, 1996 Cash Flows	April 3, 1997 Cash Flows
Sell the bill maturing on July 25, 1996 @ 4.96%	0.98843	−1	0
Buy the bill maturing on April 3, 1997 @ 5.31%	−0.95044		1
Lend the difference until April 3, 1997	−0.03799		0.03997
Total	0	−1	1.03997

The appropriate lending rate that can be locked in between July 25, 1996, and April 3, 1997, is 3.997%.

In the computation of forward rates, ask prices are used for the bill maturing on T_2 and bid prices for the bills maturing on T_1. The lending is also assumed to take place at the bid rate. In the absence of bid-offer spreads and transactions costs, the two forward rates will coincide. Note that for someone who already has long positions in the bills some of these transactions are easy to enter into.

The existence of the T-bill futures market allows one to perform these transactions with relative ease. Note that these transactions are not necessary if the objective is to simply lock in a forward rate; by selling futures contracts on T-bills, an investor could lock in his or her borrowing cost. In a similar way, by buying the T-bill futures, an investor could lock in his or her lending costs. If the futures rates differ significantly from the forward rates, then arbitrage profits are possible.

Applications of T-bill Futures. T-bill futures may be used in a variety of risk-management situations. Dealers who make a market in T-bills, CDs, and commercial paper may find it desirable to hedge their inventory positions by selling T-bill futures. Alternatively, they may buy T-bill futures to lock in their acquisition cost of future purchases of T-bills. In addition, T-bill futures allows dealers to effectively arbitrage between forward rates and futures rates. In this context, underwriters of short-term money market securities may find T-bill futures an attractive vehicle for protecting their price risk until the securities are distributed. For commercial banks and savings and loan associations, T-bill futures provide a tool for asset-liability management. For individual investors and institutional investors, such as pension funds and mutual funds, T-bill futures provide a way to better manage their risk positions.

Treasury Bond and Treasury Note Futures Contracts

The salient features of the T-bond futures contract are provided next. In Table 15-10, contractual provisions for Treasury bond futures are indicated. The T-bond futures contract and its design has been extensively copied and adopted by a number of exchanges. The gilt futures contract at LIFFE, the French government bond contract at

MATIF, the Bund futures contract on the German government bond, and the Japanese government bond contract have used the design specifications of CBT's U.S. T-bond futures contract extensively. The contractual specifications for T-bond futures, long gilt futures, German Bund futures, and the Japanese Government Bond futures are shown in Tables 15-10 to 15-13, respectively.

The contract in Table 15-10 has a par value of $100,000. The contract also permits the delivery of many eligible underlying securities. The reason why several securities are eligible for delivery is easy to explain—if only one security were permitted for delivery, it would be easy for one or two institutions to corner the supply of that security and create a scarcity that then would lead to the manipulation of the market. There is, however, a drawback to permitting many securities to be delivered. Each se-

TABLE 15-10   *U.S. Treasury Bond Futures*

Trading unit	One U.S. Treasury bond having a face value at maturity of $100,000 or multiple thereof
Deliverable grades	U.S. Treasury bonds that, if callable, are not callable for at least 15 years from the first day of the delivery month or, if not callable, have a maturity of at least 15 years from the first day of the delivery month. The invoice price equals the futures settlement price times a conversion factor plus accrued interest. The conversion factor is the price of the delivered bond ($1 par value) to yield 8%.
	Beginning with the March 2000 contracts, the conversion factor will be the price of the delivered bond ($1 par value) to yield 6%.
Price quote	Points ($1,000) and 32nds of a point; for example, 80-16 equals $80\frac{16}{32}$.
Tick size	One-thirty-second of a point ($31.25/contract); par is on the basis of 100 points.
Daily price limit	Three points ($3,000/contract) above or below the previous day's settlement price (expandable to $4\frac{1}{2}$ points). Limits are lifted the second business day preceding the first day of the delivery month.
Contract months	March, June, September, December
Delivery method	Federal Reserve book-entry wire-transfer system
Last trading day	Seventh business day preceding the last business day of the delivery month
Last delivery day	Last business day of the delivery month
Trading hours	Open Outcry: 7:20 A.M.–2:00 P.M. Chicago time, Monday through Friday.
	Project A®: Afternoon session 2:15 to 4:30 P.M. Chicago time, Monday through Thursday.
	Overnight session 6:00 P.M. to 5:00 A.M. Chicago time, Sunday through Thursday.
	Day session 5:30 A.M. to 2:00 P.M. Chicago time, Monday through Friday.
	Trading in expiring contracts closes at noon on the last trading day.
Ticker symbol	Open Outcry: US
	Project A®: ZB

Source: Chicago Board of Trade.

TABLE 15-11   *Long Gilt Contracts*

Long Gilt Future	
Unit of trading	£100,000 nominal value notional gilt with 7% coupon
Delivery months	March, June, September, December, such that the nearest three delivery months are available for trading
First notice day	Two business days prior to the first day of the delivery month
Last notice day	First business day after the last trading day
Delivery day	Any business day in delivery month (at seller's choice)
Last trading day	11.00 Two business days prior to the last business day in the delivery month
Quotation	Per £100 nominal
Minimum price movement	0.01
(Tick size and value)	(£10)
LIFFE CONNECT™ trading hours	08.00–8.00
Trading platforms	LIFFE CONNECT™ central order book applies price/time priority trading algorithm, basis trade facility, block trade facility
Minimum block trade threshold	See block trade facility—contract minimum size thresholds.

Contract Standard: Delivery may be made of any gilts on the list of deliverable gilts in respect of a delivery month, as published by the exchange on or before the tenth business day prior to the first notice day of such delivery month. Holders of long positions on any day within the notice period may be delivered against during the delivery month. All gilt issues included in the list will have the following characteristics:

- Having terms as to redemption such as provide for redemption of the entire gilt issue in a single installment on the maturity date falling not earlier than 8.75 years from, and not later than 13 years from, the first day of the relevant delivery month;
- Having no terms permitting or requiring early redemption;
- Bearing interest at a single fixed rate throughout the term of the issue payable in arrears semiannually (except in the case of the first interest payment period which may be more or less than six months);
- Being denominated and payable as to the principal and interest only in pounds and pence;
- Being fully paid or, in the event that the gilt issue is in its first period and is partly paid, being anticipated by the board to be fully paid on or before the last notice day of the relevant delivery month;
- Not being convertible;
- Not being in bearer form;
- Having being admitted to the official list of the London Stock Exchange;
- Being anticipated by the board to have on one or more days in the delivery month an aggregate principal amount outstanding of not less than £1.5 billion which, by its terms and conditions, if issued in more than one tranche or tap or issue, is fungible.

Exchange Delivery Settlement Price (EDSP): The LIFFE market price at 11.00 on the second business day prior to settlement day. The invoicing amount in respect of each deliverable gilt is to be calculated by the price factor system. Adjustment will be made for full coupon interest accruing as at settlement day.

Recent Changes:

- For the March 1998 delivery month (and previous delivery months), the notional coupon was 9%.
- Up to and including the June 1998 delivery month, the unit of trading was £50,000 nominal.
- The tick size for the June 1998 delivery month switched to $\frac{1}{100}$th of a point from the close of business on May 8, 1998, from $\frac{1}{32}$.
- The tick value for the June 1998 delivery month, from the close of business on May 8, 1998 until expiry, was £5. Up to May 8, the tick value was £7.8125.
- Prior to December 1998, contract maturity bracket 10 to 15 years.

(continued)

TABLE 15-11   *Continued*

Long Gilt Option	
Unit of trading	One long gilt futures contract
Expiry months	March, June, September, December (nearest two available for trading) plus two additional serial months, such that four expiry months are available for trading, which include the nearest three consecutive calendar months.
Delivery day / Exercise day / Expiry day	Delivery on the first business day after the exercise day. Exercise by 17.00 on any business day, brought forward to 10.45 on the last trading day. Expiry at 10.45 on the last trading day.
Last trading day	10.00 Six business days prior to the first day of the expiry month
Quotation	Multiples of 0.01
Minimum price movement	0.01
(Tick size and value)	(£10)
Trading hours	08.02–16.18
Trading platforms	LIFFE CONNECT™ central order book applies a pro rata trading algorithm but with priority given to the first order at the best price subject to a minimum order volume and limited to a maximum volume cap.
Minimum block trade threshold	See block trade facility—contract minimum size thresholds.

Contract Standard: Assignment of one long gilt futures contract for the expiry month at the exercise price. The futures delivery month associated with each option expiry month shall be

- March in respect of January, February, and March expiry months;
- June in respect of April, May, and June expiry months;
- September in respect of July, August, and September expiry months;
- December in respect of October, November, and December expiry months.

Exercise Price Intervals: £0.50 eg £102.00, £102.50, etc.

Introduction of New Exercise Prices: Thirteen exercise prices will be listed for each new series. Additional exercise prices will be listed when the long gilt futures contract settlement price is within £0.50 of the sixth highest or lowest existing exercise price, or as deemed necessary by the exchange.

Option Price: The contract price is not paid at the time of purchase. Option positions, as with futures positions, are marked-to-market daily, giving rise to positive or negative variation margin flows. If an option is exercised by the buyer, the buyer is required to pay the original contract price to the clearinghouse, and the clearinghouse will pay the original option price to the seller on the following business day. Such payments will be netted against the variation margin balances of buyer and seller by the clearinghouse.

Recent Changes:

- The tick size for June 1998 delivery month switched to $\frac{1}{100}$th of a point from the close of business on May 8, 1998 from $\frac{1}{64}$ previously.
- The tick value for the June 1998 delivery month from the close of business on May 8, 1998, and until expiry was £5. Up to the close of business on May 8, the tick value was £7.8125.
- Up to and including the June 1998 long gilt delivery months onward, the exercise price interval was £1.00 eg £102.00, £103.00, etc.

For further information, please contact bonds@liffe.com.

Source: LIFFE.

TABLE 15-12   *German Government Bond (Bund) Contracts (Denominated in Euro)*

German Government Bond (Bund) Future

Unit of trading	€100,000 nominal value notional German government bond with 6% coupon[1]
Delivery months	March, June, September, December, such that the nearest three delivery months are available for trading
Delivery day	Tenth calendar day of delivery month. If such a day is not a business day in Frankfurt then the Delivery Day will be the following Frankfurt business day.
Last trading day	12.30 Frankfurt time Two Frankfurt business days prior to the delivery day
Quotation	Per €100 nominal value
Minimum price movement	0.01
(Tick size and value)	(€10)
LIFFE CONNECT™ trading hours[1]	07.00–18.00
Trading platforms	LIFFE CONNECT™ central order book applies price/time priority trading algorithm, basis trade facility, block trade facility
Minimum block trade threshold	See block trade facility—contract minimum size thresholds.

[1]For the March 2000 delivery months onward (for delivery months June, September, and December, the notional coupon was 4%).

Contract Standard: LIFFE CONNECT™ central order book applies price/time priority trading algorithm, basis trading facility, block trade facility.

Contract Standard: Delivery may be made of any Bundesanleihen with $8\frac{1}{2}$ to $10\frac{1}{2}$ years remaining maturity as at the tenth calendar day of the delivery month, providing that any such Bund has a minimum amount in issue of €2,000,000,000 as listed by LIFFE. Delivery may be made via accounts at (i) Deutsche Börse Clearing AG[2]; (ii) Euroclear; or (iii) Cedel S.A.

Exchange Delivery Settlement Price (EDSP): The LIFFE market price at 12.30 Frankfurt time on the last trading day. The invoicing amount in respect of each deliverable Bund[3] is to be calculated by the price factor system. A final list of deliverable bunds and their price factors will be announced by the exchange 10 market days prior to the last trading day of the delivery month. Adjustments will be made for full coupon interest accruing as at the delivery day.

[2]Previously named Deutscher Kassenverein AG.

[3]For the purpose of the contract, Bund means *Anleihe der Bundesrepublik Deutschland.*

(continued)

TABLE 15-12 *Continued*

German Government Bond (Bund) Option

Unit of trading	One Bund futures contract
Expiry months	March, June, September, December (nearest two available for trading) plus two additional serial months, such that four expiry months are available for trading, which include the nearest three consecutive calendar months.
Delivery day / Exercise day / Expiry day	Delivery on the first business day after the exercise day.
	Exercise by 17.00 on any business day, brought forward to 10.45 on the last trading day
	Expiry at 10.45 on the last trading day
Last trading day	10.00
	Six business days prior to the first day of the expiry month
Quotation	Multiples of €0.01
Minimum price movement	0.01
(Tick size and value)	(€10)
Trading hours[1]	07.02–16.15
Minimum block trade threshold	See block trade facility—contract minimum size thresholds.

[1]Unless otherwise indicated, all times are London times.

Trading Platforms: LIFFE CONNECT™ central order book applies a pro rata trading algorithm but with priority given to the first order at the best price subject to a minimum order volume and limited to a maximum volume cap.

Contract Standard: Assignment of one Bund futures contract for the expiry month at the exercise price. The futures delivery month associated with each option expiry month shall be

> March in respect of January, February, and March expiry months;
> June in respect of April, May, and June expiry months;
> September in respect of July, August, and September expiry months;
> December in respect of October, November and December expiry months.

Exercise price intervals €0.50 eg €90.00, €90.50, etc.

Introduction of New Exercise Prices: Nine exercise prices will be listed for each new series. Additional exercise prices will be listed when the Bund futures contract settlement price is within €0.25 of the fourth highest or lowest existing exercise price, or as deemed necessary by the exchange.

Option Price: The contract price is not paid at the time of purchase. Option positions, as with futures positions, are marked-to-market daily giving rise to positive or negative variation margin flows. If an option is exercised by the buyer, the buyer is required to pay the original contract price to the clearinghouse, and the clearinghouse will pay the original option price to the seller on the following business day. Such payments will be netted against the variation margin balances of buyer and seller by the clearinghouse.

For further information, please contact bonds@liffe.com.

Source: LIFFE.

TABLE 15-13   *Japanese Government Bond (JGB) Contract*

Japanese Government Bond Future

Unit of trading	¥100,000,000 face value notional long-term Japanese government bond with 6% coupon
Delivery months	March, June, September, December, such that two delivery months are available for trading.
Delivery day	Next business day*
Last trading day	16.00
	One business day prior to Tokyo Stock Exchange last trading day
Quotation	Per ¥100 face value
Minimum price movement	0.01
(Tick size and value)	(¥10,000)
LIFFE CONNECT™ trading hours	07.00[1]–16.00
Trading platforms	LIFFE CONNECT™ central order book applies price/time priority trading algorithm.

[1]Unless otherwise indicated, all times are London times. The JGB Contract opens at 8.00 on Tokyo Stock Exchange holidays.

Contract standard: *All open positions on LIFFE at the close of a business day will be closed out automatically at the first subsequent opening price on the Tokyo Stock Exchange (TSE) for the same delivery month and cash settlement made accordingly through variation margin. Unless deferred as a result of there being no TSE opening price (e.g., in the event of a TSE holiday), settlement will be on the next business day.

Price Limit:
1. ¥2.00 from Tokyo Stock Exchange closing price. If limit is hit, price limits are removed one hour later for the remainder of the day.
2. No limit during the last hour of trading on each day.

For further information, please contact bonds@liffe.com.

curity will have a different coupon and maturity, and the compensation upon the delivery of a security depends on the conversion factor of that security—the price (per dollar par) at which the security will provide a yield to maturity or call of 6%. This is a rough way to equalize the relative desirability of delivering any one eligible security. As we will show later, this procedure leads to certain biases in the delivery strategies.

Table 15-14 contains the open interest and prices of the Treasury bond and the 10-year Treasury note contracts. Note that the open interest declines rapidly as the maturity date of futures increases. The depth of the market is typically concentrated in the first two maturity months. The September 2000 T-bond contract had an open interest of about $41 billion, indicating an extraordinary amount of liquidity.

TABLE 15-14   *Interest Rate*

Treasury Bonds (CBT)-$100,000; pts. 32nds of 100%)

	Open	High	Low	Settle	Change	Lifetime High	Lifetime Low	Open Interest
Sept	99-25	100-11	99-23	100-03 +	10	100-12	88-19	414,340
Dec	99-27	100-11	99-24	100-04 +	11	100-11	88-31	30,899
Mr01	100-04	100-12	100-03	100-06 +	12	100-12	88-06	1,498

Est vol 150,000; vol Thu 133,157; open int 447,374, +8,683.

Treasury Notes (CBT)-$100,000; pts. 32nds of 100%

	Open	High	Low	Settle	Change	Lifetime High	Lifetime Low	Open Interest
Sept	99-165	99-27	99-135	99-235 +	7.5	100-07	94-22	531,112
Dec	99-145	99-24	99-135	99-21 +	7.0	100-04	96-075	80,213

Est vol 110,000; vol Thu 126,531; open int 611,350, +7,572.

Source: wsj: Aug. 21, 2000.

New Developments

Recently, CBOT changed the deliverable grade to a 6% standard. Until recently (prior to March 2000 contract), the delivery standard used to be 8%. The rationale for this change is explained in the following excerpted CBOT article.

6% Coupon: The Chicago Board of Trade Is Changing

Beginning with the March 2000 contract, the notional coupons of the CBOT® Treasury bond, 10-year, 5-year, and 2-year Treasury note futures contracts will change from 8% to 6%. In addition, the deliverable basket of securities for the 5-year Treasury note will be expanded to include one additional security. The 6% March 2000 Municipal Bond contract listing will be announced at a later date.

These changes will affect many aspects of the fixed-income contracts, including the level of futures prices, cheapest-to-deliver status, embedded delivery option values, calendar spreads (especially the Dec 99–Mar 00 spreads), basis point values, and implied volatility levels.

The Chicago Board of Trade's response to global market participants whose consensus supported these changes included extensive research and industry trade calls. Among the findings:

- Reducing the notional coupon to 6% would better reflect the current yield environment.
- The 6% coupon would increase duration, making it a more effective instrument for those hedging the long end of the yield curve.
- Increasing the optionality in the futures contract would be more attractive to the basis and relative value traders.

Delivery Options in Treasury Bond Futures. It is important to fully understand the T-bond futures contract specification in order to determine the relationship between the futures prices and Treasury bond prices. A seller of a T-bond futures contract has a great deal of flexibility or many delivery options during the delivery month.

The short may deliver any bundle of prespecified Treasury bonds sometime during the delivery month, so long as the investor has not offset his or her short position.

The Treasury bond futures contract closes for the day at 2:00 P.M. Chicago time. The Treasury bond market, however, is a dealers' market. Indeed, as long as bond dealers are willing to execute orders, the bond market may be considered open. The clearinghouse of the CBOT accepts delivery during the delivery month until 8:00 P.M. Chicago time. These observations mean that an investor who has an open short position in T-bond futures as of 2:00 P.M. Chicago time during the delivery month has the option to deliver any combination of the deliverable issues until 8:00 P.M. Chicago time. If the deliverable issues were to experience a significant price decline during the 2:00 P.M. to 8:00 P.M. period, this option will be of considerable value to the investor who is short. This option is known as the "wild-card" delivery option in T-bond futures contracts. The key is that the invoice price is fixed at 2:00 P.M. and does not change until the next day of trading. The investor may elect to delay delivery by waiting. This strategy permits the investor to participate in any potential price declines in the 2:00 P.M. to 8:00 P.M. period next day. In essence, the investor who is short on the first day of the delivery month has a sequence of six-hour put options during each day of the delivery month until the last day of futures trading. Each put provides the right to sell a bundle of deliverable issues until 8:00 P.M. at an invoice price set at 2:00 P.M. Upon expiration, the investor gets another put at a different invoice (strike) price the next day at 2:00 P.M. The T-bond futures ceases trading seven business days prior to the last business day of the contract month. Thus, the wild-card option provides the short with a sequence of approximately 15 daily put options.

It is easy to see the directional impact of the wild-card option on T-bond futures price. Since the short has the flexibility associated with the wild-card feature, the long will enter into the futures transaction only if the futures price is discounted by the value of the sequence of put options represented by the wild-card feature. Thus, the effect of wild-card option, in a rational setting, is to reduce the futures price by the fair value of the option.

The T-bond futures contract ceases trading seven business days prior to the last business day of the contract month. The clearinghouse, however, accepts delivery until the last business day of the month. Between the last day of futures trading and the last delivery date, bond prices fluctuate in the marketplace, but the futures price stays fixed at its closing level as of the last trading day. This feature of the Treasury bond futures contract is called the end-of-the-month option. The holder of a short position in Treasury bond futures has considerable flexibility during this period. He or she has a timing option that permits him or her to select any day during this period to effect delivery. Furthermore, holders have a quality option that permits them to select any bundle of deliverable bonds from among approximately 30 deliverable issues.

Note that the design of T-bond futures contract provides several implicit options to the short. This is typical of many futures contracts, as we have seen. These delivery options have important effects on the relationship between futures prices and cash prices.

FIGURE 15-1   *Deliveries to T-Bond Futures Contract (December 1977–March 1991)*

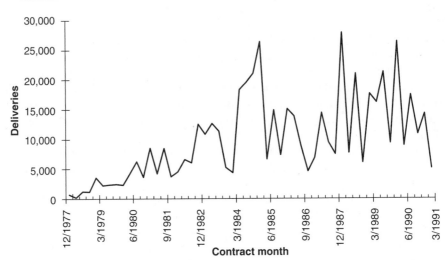

Empirical Evidence on Deliveries. In this section, we present some evidence on actual deliveries made to the T-bond and T-note futures contracts during the period 1977 through 1987, based on the data provided by Commodity Futures Trading Commission (CFTC). This section draws heavily from Broadie and Sundaresan (1992).

Although more than 90% of the open interest is settled by offset in both Treasury bond and Treasury note futures markets, the actual deliveries made in these markets are, nevertheless, economically significant. Figure 15-1 depicts the actual deliveries made in each contract month traded since the inception of the Treasury bond futures contract. In Figure 15-2, the actual deliveries for the Treasury note contract are placed. In Table 15-15, we provide some summary statistics for these figures.

In Figure 15-3, the distribution of deliveries in the Treasury bond futures market has been aggregated across all contracts during the normal yield-curve parts of the sample period, December 1977 to June 1987. The striking fact apparent in the distribution is that deliveries are almost always delayed until the last few days of the delivery month; in this sample period, about 90% of the deliveries were made during the last five days of the delivery month. A significant volume of deliveries also occurred around the last day of futures trading. This is due to **positive carry.**

Figure 15-4 provides the distribution of deliveries when the yield curve is inverted or downward-sloping. Note that more percentage is delivered in the earlier part of the delivery month. **The carry is negative, and this favors early delivery.** On the other hand, the availability of the quality option, wild-card option, and end-of-the-month option favors later delivery. The trade-offs determine the optimal delivery strategy.

The pattern of deliveries for the Treasury note futures contract is similar to that of the Treasury bond futures contract. If anything, the tendency to postpone deliveries until the last delivery date is even stronger for Treasury note futures contracts.

FIGURE 15-2   *Deliveries to T-Note Futures Contract (September 1982–March 1991)*

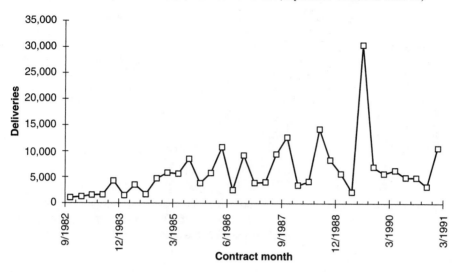

TABLE 15-15   *Deliveries of Bonds and Notes*

Statistic	Treasury Bonds	Treasury Notes
Sample period	Dec. 1977 to June 1987	June 1982 to June 1987
Number of contract months	39	20
Average face delivered	$7.62 billion	$4.84 billion
Maximum face delivered	$26.38 billion	$10.77 billion
Minimum face delivered	$0.20 billion	$1.06 billion

FIGURE 15-3   *Timing of Deliveries of T-Bonds, Normal Yield Curve*

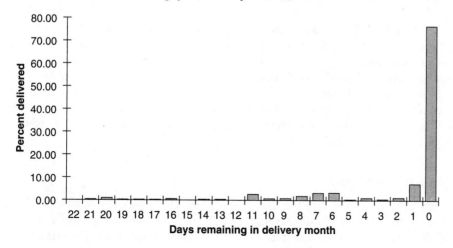

FIGURE 15-4   *Timing of Deliveries of T-Bonds, Inverted Yield Curve*

ANALYSIS OF A SPECIFIC CONTRACT: SEPTEMBER 2000 T-BOND CONTRACT

To better understand the pricing and delivery strategies, we analyze here a specific T-bond futures contract that expired on September 2000.

Seller's Option in the September 2000 Contract

For the September 2000 futures contract, the first delivery date was September 1, 2000, and the last delivery date was September 29, 2000. The contract expired in September 2000.

Any T-bond that has a minimum of 15 years to its maturity date or (if callable) to its first call date is eligible for delivery. There are many T-bonds that satisfy this broad requirement, and the seller of the T-bond futures has the option of deciding which combination of eligible T-bonds should be delivered. This is the **quality option.**

The delivery of a specific deliverable bond into the futures market results in the payment of an invoice price. The option of selecting a specific bundle of deliverable bonds is with the short. The aggregate face value of the T-bonds must be equal to $100,000 for each futures contract.

Invoicing Deliveries

A key delivery parameter is the conversion factor. The underlying premise is that the futures price must be adjusted upward if the T-bond delivered has a coupon in excess of 6% and adjusted downward if the delivered T-bond has a coupon of less than 6%.

The exact formula for the computation of the conversion factor follows:

$$CF = \frac{1}{\left(1 + \frac{y}{2}\right)^{\frac{x}{6}}}\left[\frac{c}{2} + \left(\frac{c}{0.06}\left[1 - \frac{1}{\left(1 + \frac{0.06}{2}\right)^{2N}}\right] + \frac{1}{\left(1 + \frac{0.06}{2}\right)^{2N}}\right)\right] - \frac{c}{2}\frac{6 - x}{6},$$

where CF is the conversion factor, c is the coupon expressed in decimals, N is the full number of years to maturity or first call date, and x is the number of months by which maturity exceeds N rounded down to the nearest quarter. Clearly, $x = 0, 3, 6,$ or 9. The formula provides CF directly when $x = 0, 3,$ or 6. When $x = 9$ the formula becomes

$$CF = \frac{1}{\left(1 + \frac{y}{2}\right)^{\frac{1}{2}}}\left[\frac{c}{2} + \left[\frac{c}{0.06}\left[1 - \frac{1}{\left(1 + \frac{0.06}{2}\right)^{2N+1}}\right] + \frac{1}{\left(1 + \frac{0.06}{2}\right)^{2N+1}}\right]\right] - \frac{c}{4}.$$

We illustrate the computation of the conversion factor in two specific examples.

Example 15-6:

1. As of the first delivery date (September 1, 2000), compute the time to the maturity date of the bond, and round it down to the nearest quarter.
2. For the $9\frac{7}{8}\%$ T-bond, the relevant maturity is 15 years.
3. Compute the value of a $9\frac{7}{8}\%$ T-bond with 15 years to maturity such that it will yield 6.0% to maturity. This is 1.3798 for the $9\frac{7}{8}\%$ T-bond.

Example 15-7:

1. As of the first delivery date (September 1, 2000), compute the time to the maturity date of the bond, and round it down to the nearest quarter.
2. For the $5\frac{1}{4}\%$ T-bond, the relevant maturity is 28 years and 3 months.
3. Compute the value of a 5.25% T-bond with 28 years and 3 months such that it will yield 6% to maturity. This is 0.8984 for the 5.25% T-bond.

We illustrate the calculations next using the conversion factor formulae.

1. Computing the conversion factor of 5.25%, 2/15/2029 Treasury bond to September 2000 futures contract.

Coupon	5.25%
Yield	6%
N	28
x	3
CF	0.8984

$$CF = \frac{1}{\left(1 + \frac{0.06}{2}\right)^{\frac{3}{6}}}\left[\frac{0.0525}{2} + \left(\frac{0.0525}{0.06}\right)\left\{1 - \frac{1}{\left(1 + \frac{0.06}{2}\right)^{2\times 28}}\right\} + \frac{1}{\left(1 + \frac{0.06}{2}\right)^{2\times 28}}\right]$$

$$- \frac{0.0525}{2}\frac{6 - 3}{6} = 0.8984$$

2. Computing the conversion factor of 9.875%, 11/15/2015 Treasury bond to September 2000 futures contract.

Coupon	9.875%
Yield	6%
N	15
x	0
CF	1.3798

$$CF = \frac{1}{\left(1 + \frac{0.06}{2}\right)^{\frac{0}{6}}} \left[\frac{0.09875}{2} + \left(\frac{0.09875}{0.06}\right)\left\{1 - \frac{1}{\left(1 + \frac{0.06}{2}\right)^{2\times15}}\right\} + \frac{1}{\left(1 + \frac{0.06}{2}\right)^{2\times15}} \right]$$

$$-\frac{0.09875}{2}\frac{6-0}{6} = 1.3798$$

The conversion factor is used to determine the invoice price, which is the compensation paid for delivering a contract-grade bond. First, the futures price is multiplied by the conversion factor of the bond. Then the accrued interest is added to determine the invoice price.

To calculate the invoice price that will be paid in the futures market, let us assume that the delivery occurs on September 29, 2000. The futures price is $100\frac{3}{32}$.

Example 15-8:

Table 15-16 illustrates the factors involved in the calculation of the invoice price for the 14% T-bond. The invoice price is

$$100.09375 \times 1.3798 + 3.6763 = 141.7857.$$

Example 15-9:

In a similar way, Table 15-17 illustrates the factors for calculating the invoice price for the 5.25% T-bond.

$$100.09375 \times 0.8984 + 0.6420 = 90.5662$$

The conversion factors of all the deliverable bonds are shown in Table 15-18.

Basis in T-Bond Futures

A concept that is widely used in the analysis of the T-bond contract is the basis. Let P_t be the flat price of the deliverable T-bond, CF be its conversion factor, and $H_t(s)$ be the futures price at date t for maturity at date s. Recognizing that futures contracts permit delivery on any business day of the delivery month, we will interpret s as the last business day of the delivery month in a positive-carry market and interpret s as the first business day of the month in a negative-carry market. The **basis** B_t is defined as

$$B_t = P_t - CF \times H_t(s).$$

TABLE 15-16		
September 2000 Futures $9\frac{7}{8}\%$ T-Bond Invoice Price Calculations	Futures price	$100\frac{3}{32}$
	Coupon	$9\frac{7}{8}\%$
	Maturity	11/15/2015
	Conversion factor	1.3798
	Accrued interest as of September 29, 2000	3.6763
	Invoice price	141.7857

TABLE 15-17		
September 2000 Futures $5\frac{1}{4}\%$ T-Bond Invoice Price Calculations	Futures price	$100\frac{3}{32}$
	Coupon	5.25%
	Maturity	2/15/2029
	Conversion factor	0.8984
	Accrued interest	0.6420
	Invoice price	90.5662

If t happens to be in the delivery month, then by the no-arbitrage principal, we must have $B_t > 0$. If this were not the case, by simultaneously selling the futures and immediately delivering, one could lock in riskless profits.

Determination of Delivery

We now analyze the optimal delivery strategies for the September 2000 futures contract. Let us say that on August 21, 2000, we wish to determine the optimal delivery strategy for the September 2000 futures contract. From the contractual specifications laid out in our discussion thus far, we have the following conclusions:

- Eligible Treasury bonds can be delivered on any day from September 1, 2000, to September 29, 2000.
- The last day of futures trading will be March 20, 1987, leaving seven business days (23, 24, 25, 26, 27, 30, and 31) for the completion of the delivery process.
- As noted in Table 15-18, T-bonds that are eligible for delivery to the March futures must have 15 years or more to maturity as of Sep 1, 2000, if they are non-callable. If callable, they must have at least 15 years to the first call date.

Table 15-18 lists all deliverable T-bonds to the September 2000 futures contract as of August 2000.

To better understand the pricing of Treasury futures contract, we now develop the concept of cash-and-carry arbitrage.

Cash-and-Carry Arbitrage Principle. The cash-and-carry principle is a pricing principle that is widely used in the industry. The logic behind this principle works as follows: If the price at which an investor can sell a bond in the forward market (at the

TABLE 15-18 *Treasury Bonds Eligible for Delivery into the CBOT Treasury Bond Futures Contract along with Their Conversion Factors, June 29, 2000*

Bond Number	Coupon	Issue Date	Maturity Date	Cusip Number	Issue ($ B)	6% Conversion Factors			
						June 2000	September 2000	December 2000	March 2001
1	$5\frac{1}{4}$	11/16/98	11/15/28	912810FF0	10.0	0.8984	0.8989	0.8991	0.8996
2	$5\frac{1}{4}$	02/16/99	02/15/29	912810FG8	10.0	0.8982	0.8984	0.8989	0.8991
3	$5\frac{1}{2}$	08/17/98	08/15/28	912810FE3	10.0	0.9326	0.9327	0.9331	0.9332
4	6	02/15/96	02/15/26	912810EW4	12.0	1.0000	0.9999	1.0000	0.9999
5	$6\frac{1}{8}$	11/17/97	11/15/27	912810FB9	10.0	1.0166	1.0166	1.0164	0.0165
6	$6\frac{1}{8}$	02/17/98	11/15/27	912810FB9	10.0	1.0166	1.0166	1.0164	1.0165
7	$6\frac{1}{8}$	08/16/99	08/15/29	912810FJ2	10.0	1.0171	1.0169	1.0170	1.0168
8	$6\frac{1}{4}$	08/16/93	08/15/23	912810EQ7	10.8	1.0310	1.0307	1.0306	1.0304
9	$6\frac{1}{4}$	02/15/94	08/15/23	912810EQ7	11.1	1.0310	1.0307	1.0306	1.0304
10@	$6\frac{1}{4}$	02/15/00	05/15/30	912810FM5	10.0	1.0344	1.0344	1.0342	1.0342
11	$6\frac{3}{8}$	08/15/97	08/15/27	912810FA1	10.0	1.0498	1.0495	1.0495	1.0491
12	$6\frac{1}{2}$	11/15/96	11/15/26	912810EY0	10.0	1.0656	1.0654	1.0650	1.0649
13	$6\frac{5}{8}$	02/18/97	02/15/27	912810EZ7	10.5	1.0824	1.0820	1.0818	1.0813
14	$6\frac{3}{4}$	08/15/96	08/15/26	912810EX2	10.0	1.0981	1.0976	1.0973	1.0968
15	$6\frac{7}{8}$	08/15/95	08/15/25	912810EV6	11.2	1.1126	1.1119	1.1116	1.1109
16	$7\frac{1}{8}$	02/16/93	02/15/23	912810EP9	9.0	1.1379	1.1370	1.1364	1.1355
17	$7\frac{1}{8}$	05/17/93	02/15/23	912810EP9	8.3	1.1379	1.1370	1.1364	1.1355
18	$7\frac{1}{4}$	05/15/86	05/15/16	912810DW5	18.8	1.1261	1.1250	1.1236	1.1225
19	$7\frac{1}{4}$	08/17/92	08/15/22	912810EM6	10.0	1.1516	1.1506	1.1499	1.1489
20	$7\frac{1}{2}$	11/15/86	11/15/16	912810DX3	18.9	1.1542	1.1529	1.1513	1.1500
21	$7\frac{1}{2}$	08/15/94	11/15/24	912810ES3	10.6	1.1902	1.1895	1.1885	1.1877
22	$7\frac{5}{8}$	11/15/92	11/15/22	912810EN4	9.7	1.1980	1.1971	1.1958	1.1949
23	$7\frac{5}{8}$	02/15/95	02/15/25	912810ET1	10.8	1.2072	1.2061	1.2053	1.2042
24	$7\frac{7}{8}$	02/15/91	02/15/21	912810EH7	10.7	1.2195	1.2180	1.2167	1.2151
25	8	11/15/91	11/15/21	912810EL8	32.2	1.2383	1.2370	1.2354	1.2341
26	$8\frac{1}{8}$	08/15/89	08/15/19	912810ED6	19.9	1.2390	1.2371	1.2355	1.2336
27	$8\frac{1}{8}$	05/15/91	05/15/21	912810EJ3	11.3	1.2502	1.2488	1.2470	1.2456
28	$8\frac{1}{8}$	08/15/91	08/15/21	912810EK0	11.3	1.2518	1.2502	1.2488	1.2470
29	$8\frac{1}{2}$	02/15/90	02/15/20	912810EE4	9.9	1.2851	1.2830	1.2812	1.2790
30	$8\frac{3}{4}$	05/15/87	05/15/17	912810DY1	17.5	1.2879	1.2855	1.2828	1.2803
31	$8\frac{3}{4}$	05/15/90	05/15/20	912810EF1	9.3	1.3156	1.3136	1.3113	1.3093
32	$8\frac{3}{4}$	08/15/90	08/15/20	912810EG9	20.0	1.3178	1.3156	1.3136	1.3113
33	$8\frac{7}{8}$	08/15/87	08/15/17	912810DZ8	13.4	1.3038	1.3010	1.2985	1.2957
34	$8\frac{7}{8}$	02/15/89	02/15/19	912810EC8	18.7	1.3187	1.3161	1.3138	1.3112
35	9	11/15/88	11/15/18	912810EB0	8.1	1.3298	1.3275	1.3247	1.3223
36	$9\frac{1}{8}$	05/15/88	05/15/18	912810EA2	8.3	1.3383	1.3357	1.3328	1.3302
37	$9\frac{1}{4}$	02/15/86	02/15/16	912810DV7	6.9	1.3250	1.3216	1.3185	—
38	$9\frac{7}{8}$	11/15/85	11/15/15	912810DT2	6.2	1.3835	1.3798	—	—
39	$10\frac{5}{8}$	08/15/85	08/15/15	912810DS4	5.7	1.4533	—	—	—
				Number of eligible issues:	39	39	38	37	36
				Dollar amount eligible for delivery:	458.0	458.0	452.2	446.1	439.2

Source: CBOT.

FIGURE 15-5   *Financing Bonds (Transaction as of August 21, 2000)*

Trader finances a deliverable T-bond *and* sells futures now.

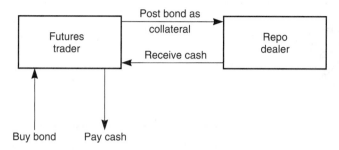

maturity date of the forward contract) is higher than the cost of financing the bond, then the investor should sell forward and finance the bond. Otherwise, the investor should buy forward and sell the bond in a repurchase transaction. Let us consider a strategy in which the trader finances a deliverable T-bond and sells futures as of August 21, 2000, shown in Figure 15-5.

In order to effect such a trade, a bond trader first gathers information about the following aspects of the trade:

- The price of the bond, its accrued interest, and its coupon dates. These factors are crucial to the profitability of the trade. The accrued interest is what the trader gets if the trader is long in the bond.
- The status of the bond in the market for repurchase agreements. If the bond trades special in the repo market, the financing cost of that bond may be substantial. Once again, this is central to the profitability of the trade.
- The futures price is obviously the major determinant of the compensation that the trader may expect to receive should the trader decide to deliver or offset.

If we make several key assumptions, we can regard the futures contract as a forward contract.

- Markets are frictionless and there are no taxes.
- Each bond is priced to reflect the present value of its future cash flows.
- Only one T-bond is eligible for delivery and is available in plentiful supply.
- The financing rate is a constant; overnight repos and term repos may be entered into at the same rate.

Let the forward price at date t for settlement at date T be $G_t(T)$. The analysis is summarized in Table 15-19. Note that the total cash flows at T will be zero because the forward price converges to the cash price: $G_T(T) = P_T$. Equivalently, the basis at maturity is zero. Then, to preclude arbitrage, it must follow that the investment at t must be zero as well. The investment at t, however, is equal to

$$-(P_t + ai_t) + PV_t(G_t(T)) + PV_t(ai_T) + PV_t\left(\frac{c}{2}\right) = 0.$$

TABLE 15-19   *Cash-and-Carry Arbitrage*

Transaction at t	Cash Flow at t	Coupon Date s	Maturity Date T
1. Sell Forward	0		$(G_t(T) - G_T(T))$
2. Buy the Bond –	$(P_t + ai_t)$		
Receive coupon		$\frac{c}{2}$	
Receive market value of bond at T			$P_T + ai_T$
3. Borrow $PV_t(\frac{c}{2})$	$PV_t(\frac{c}{2})$	$-\frac{c}{2}$	
4. Borrow $PV_t(ai_T)$	$PV_t(ai_T)$		$-ai_T$
5. Borrow	$PV_t(G_t(T))$		$-G_t(T)$
Total cash flow at s and T		0	0

If the financing rate is assumed to be constant at a level r, then the expression may be written as

$$G_t(T) = (P_t + ai_t) \times \left(1 + r \times \frac{T - t}{360}\right) - ai_T - \frac{c}{2} \times \left(1 + r \times \frac{T - s}{360}\right).$$

Quite often, the quantity on the right-hand side of the expression is referred to as the forward price, reflecting the fact that the cash-and-carry arbitrage ignores the marking-to-market feature and the fact that the seller's delivery options are ignored.

Let

$$\text{Forward Price} = G_t(T) \equiv (P_t + ai_t) \times \left(1 + r \times \frac{T - t}{360}\right) - ai_T - \frac{c}{2} \times \left(1 + r \times \frac{T - s}{360}\right).$$

The forward price is computed under the assumption that there is only one deliverable bond and that the bond has to be delivered on the last day of futures trading. As we know from the discussion of T-bond futures specifications, these assumptions are restrictive; many bonds are deliverable, and there are significant flexibilities in the timing of deliveries. As a result of ignoring these options that the short has in the futures market, the computed forward price tends to be higher than the futures price. In other words, because of the options that the short has in the futures market, he or she is willing to sell bonds for deferred delivery at a lower (futures) price than he or she would in the forward market, which assumes that the short has no flexibility.

Note that the transactions in Table 15-19 demonstrate how a short position in a forward contract can be hedged by borrowing and buying the underlying deliverable bond. In fact, the hedging strategy is a fully financed position in the underlying bond. This implies that a long position in a T-bond forward contract is equivalent to borrowing and buying the underlying T-bond. Likewise, a short position in the T-bond forward contract is equivalent to shorting the T-bond and placing the proceeds in a riskless asset. Note that such transactions will be executed in the repo markets discussed earlier in the text.

For T-bond futures contracts, similar arguments can be made. We must use the cheapest deliverable bond to execute the equivalent transactions. A short position in

FIGURE 15-6   *Unwinding the Trade*

Trader delivers the bond by closing out repo; thus, he or she closes short position in futures.

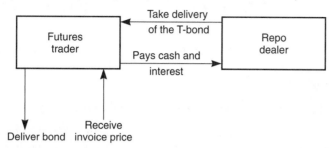

T-bond futures can be hedged by borrowing and buying the cheapest deliverable bond (say, bond X). All the delivery options belong to the seller and, as such, the short position carries little risk. If some other T-bond (say, bond Y) becomes cheap to deliver, the existing T-bond X can be sold, and bond Y can be purchased. Since Y is cheaper than X, the short position will make money.

On the other hand, a long position in T-bond futures has many risks. Since all delivery options are with the seller, the long will not know which bond might be delivered and when.

In addition, the delivery in the futures market on the maturity date or the delivery date will produce a revenue equal to the invoice price (excluding accrued interest), which is

$$CF \times H_t(T).$$

The forward price represents the price at which the bond can be sold forward to break even. The invoice price represents the actual revenue by willing the bond in the futures market. Therefore, the difference between the forward price of the bond and the invoice price measures the profit or loss associated with the strategy of selling futures and borrowing and buying the bond. This difference is what is known as the **basis after carry** (BAC). The transactions on the delivery date to unwind the positions in futures and bond markets are shown in Figure 15-6. This concept is widely used by bond traders who study the spread between futures and forward prices. The basis after carry measures the net cost of carrying the bond in a repurchase transaction and delivering it into the futures market and receiving the invoice price. If the basis and basis after carry are negative, then profits are realized by this arbitrage strategy. Typically, the basis and basis after carry are positive, as Table 15-20 illustrates. The basis after carry is also positive for all deliverable bonds.

Note that the basis after carry can be split into two components: the basis and the carry.

$$BAC_i = (P_t + ai_t) \times \left(1 + r \times \frac{T - t}{360}\right) - ai_T - \frac{c}{2} \times \left(1 + r \times \frac{T - s}{360}\right) - CF_i \times H_t(T).$$

Intuitively, we can write BAC as

$$BAC_i = [P_t - CF_i \times H_t(T)] - \left[ai_T - ai_t + \frac{c}{2} \times \left(1 + r \times \frac{T-s}{360} \right) \right]$$

$$+ (P_t + ai_t) \times r \times \frac{T-t}{360},$$

which says that

$$BAC = Basis - Reinvested\ Cash\ Inflows + Financing\ Costs.$$

When the carry is positive, BAC is less than the basis; otherwise, it is greater than the basis. Traders can minimize their losses by delaying delivery in a positive carry market if there are no adverse price movements.

It is worth remembering that when BAC < 0 there will be arbitrage opportunities. This requires selling futures, and borrowing and buying the cheapest bond for delivery. The bond transaction will be positioned through a repo desk. On the other hand, if BAC > 0, there is no riskless arbitrage opportunity; if we try to buy futures and short the cheapest bond, there is always the risk that on the delivery month some other bond might become cheaper to deliver. If this were to happen, that bond will be delivered, and the short position will have to be covered, perhaps at a considerable cost.

Usually, the traders use the basis after carry of a deliverable bond to determine which bond is cheapest to deliverable issue (CDI) or the cheapest to deliver (CTD). On a daily basis, the basis after carry is calculated for each deliverable issue, and the issue that has the lowest basis after carry is identified as the CDI. In the computations of basis after carry, a financing rate of 6.05% is assumed for all T-bonds.

A related concept is the implied repo rate. This concept computes the internal rate of return associated with the strategy of selling T-bond futures, and borrowing and buying an eligible T-bond and delivering it to the futures market at maturity. In the expression that we derived for the basis after carry, we set BAC = 0 and solve for $r = r^*$ as the implied repo rate. The resulting expression for the implied repo rate is

$$r^* = \frac{\left[CF_i \times H_t(T) - P_{it} + ai_T + \frac{c}{2} - ai_t \right]}{\left[(P_{it} + ai_t) \times \frac{T-t}{360} - \frac{c}{2} \times \frac{T-s}{360} \right]}. \tag{15.4}$$

Equation 15.4 is valid when there is a coupon payment at date s prior to the maturity date T of the futures contract. If there is no coupon payment, then the equation can be simplified by setting $c = 0$ to get the implied repo rate as:

$$r^* = \frac{[CF_i \times H_t(T) + ai_T - (P_{it} + ai_t)]}{[P_{it} + ai_t]} \times \frac{360}{T-t}.$$

After we identify the cheapest bond to the September 2000 T-bond futures, we work out an example or implied repo rate.

In Table 15-20, we present the basis after carry calculations for each deliverable bond to the September 2000 futures contract. Note that bond 17, which is the $7\frac{1}{2}\%$,

TABLE 15-20 *Cheapest Deliverable Treasury Bond Analysis (Wall Street Journal Prices dated 8/21/2000)*

Settlement Date 08/21/00		September 2000 Futures 100.09375			Final Delivery Date 09/29/00		First Day of Delivery 9/1/00				

Bond Number	Coupon	Maturity	Price (Flat) in Decimals— (Accrued Not Included)	Accrued Interest	YTM	PVBP $ per Million Par	Modified Duration in Years	Conver. Factor	Basis in Ticks (32nds)	Repo Rate	Forward Price	Basis after Carry (32nds)
1	5.250%	11/15/28	91.81250	1.3981	5.845%	1288	13.82	0.8989	58.82	6.42%	91.90	61.76
2	5.250%	2/15/29	91.93750	0.0856	5.834%	1295	14.08	0.8984	64.42	6.42%	92.02	67.10
3	5.500%	8/15/28	94.96875	0.0897	5.868%	1313	13.81	0.9327	51.56	6.42%	95.05	54.07
4	6.000%	2/15/26	101.09375	0.0978	5.916%	1317	13.02	0.9999	32.32	6.42%	101.16	34.49
5	6.125%	11/15/27	103.09375	1.6311	5.895%	1378	13.16	1.0166	42.83	6.42%	103.17	45.37
6	6.125%	8/15/29	104.25000	0.0999	5.820%	1436	13.76	1.0169	78.87	6.42%	104.33	81.32
7	6.250%	8/15/23	103.78125	0.1019	5.946%	1277	12.29	1.0307	19.67	6.42%	103.84	21.59
8	6.250%	5/15/30	108.00000	1.6644	5.688%	1512	13.79	1.0344	142.82	6.42%	108.10	146.03
9	6.375%	8/15/27	106.34375	0.1039	5.902%	1404	13.19	1.0495	41.45	6.42%	106.41	43.52
10	6.500%	11/15/26	107.78125	1.7310	5.912%	1400	12.79	1.0654	36.52	6.42%	107.85	38.85
11	6.625%	2/15/27	109.50000	0.1080	5.911%	1423	12.98	1.0820	38.35	6.42%	109.56	40.28
12	6.750%	8/15/26	111.00000	0.1101	5.916%	1425	12.83	1.0976	36.39	6.42%	111.06	38.22
13	6.875%	8/15/25	112.25000	0.1121	5.929%	1410	12.55	1.1119	30.58	6.42%	112.30	32.28
14	7.125%	2/15/23	114.37500	0.1162	5.956%	1356	11.84	1.1370	18.19	6.42%	114.42	19.51
15	7.250%	5/15/16	112.81250	1.9307	5.981%	1096	9.55	1.1250	6.63	6.42%	112.84	7.58
16	7.250%	8/15/22	115.71875	0.1182	5.958%	1352	11.67	1.1506	17.63	6.42%	115.76	18.82
17	7.500%	11/15/16	115.56250	1.9973	5.987%	1136	9.66	1.1529	5.26	6.42%	115.59	5.99
18	7.500%	11/15/24	119.90625	1.9973	5.939%	1461	11.98	1.1895	27.03	6.42%	119.96	28.73
19	7.625%	11/15/22	120.37500	2.0306	5.958%	1401	11.44	1.1971	17.69	6.42%	120.42	19.07
20	7.625%	2/15/25	121.68750	0.1243	5.934%	1485	12.19	1.2061	30.86	6.42%	121.73	32.11
21	7.785%	2/15/21	122.28125	0.1269	5.897%	1363	11.14	1.2180	11.75	6.42%	122.31	12.59
22	8.000%	11/15/21	124.28125	2.1304	5.967%	1400	11.07	1.2370	14.89	6.42%	124.31	15.89
23	8.125%	8/15/19	124.28125	0.1325	5.970%	1315	10.57	1.2371	14.57	6.42%	124.29	14.70
24	8.125%	5/15/21	125.31250	2.1637	5.978%	1389	10.90	1.2488	10.09	6.42%	125.34	10.91
24	8.125%	8/15/21	125.56250	0.1325	5.972%	1401	11.14	1.2502	13.61	6.42%	125.58	14.03
25	8.500%	2/15/20	128.71875	0.1386	5.984%	1368	10.62	1.2830	9.55	6.42%	128.71	9.40
26	8.750%	5/15/17	128.90625	2.3302	5.989%	1251	9.53	1.2855	7.54	6.42%	128.89	7.08
27	8.750%	5/15/20	131.78125	2.3302	5.983%	1403	10.46	1.3136	9.54	6.42%	131.79	9.71
28	8.750%	8/15/20	131.96875	0.1427	5.986%	1414	10.70	1.3156	9.13	6.42%	131.96	8.86
29	8.875%	8/15/17	130.46875	0.1447	5.991%	1273	9.75	1.3010	7.90	6.42%	130.44	6.87
30	8.875%	2/15/19	131.96875	0.1447	5.991%	1351	10.23	1.3161	7.53	6.42%	131.95	6.84
31	9.000%	11/15/18	133.12500	2.3967	5.988%	1350	9.96	1.3275	8.02	6.42%	133.11	7.66
32	9.125%	5/15/18	133.93750	2.4300	5.991%	1333	9.78	1.3357	7.75	6.42%	133.92	7.16
33	9.250%	2/15/16	132.59375	0.1508	5.990%	1215	9.16	1.3216	9.92	6.42%	132.54	8.09
34	9.875%	11/15/15	138.37500	2.6298	5.996%	1241	8.80	1.3798	8.50	6.42%	138.31	6.39

11/15/2016 bond, is the cheapest to deliver with a basis after carry of 5.99 ticks. The next cheapest is bond 34, which is the $9\frac{7}{8}\%$, 11/15/2015 bond with a basis after carry of 6.39 ticks. Note that the bonds that are cheap to deliver tend to have relatively high coupons and low maturity.

In this section, it was assumed that the financing rates are known and that there are no timing options to the short. The ability of the short to deliver any one or a combination of T-bonds was accounted for only indirectly by the basis after carry, which considers T-bonds, one at a time, for delivery consideration. These assumptions are relaxed by using interest rate models, such as the Black, Derman, and Toy model discussed in Chapter 17.

Coupon Bias in Deliveries. We have shown that for the March 1987 T-bond contract, high-coupon bonds were cheaper to deliver. Is there a general coupon bias? To address this question, we examine the circumstances under which low-coupon bonds or high-coupon bonds may be cheaper to deliver. To do this, we vary the yield from 1% to 15% in Figure 15-7.

We compute the ratio of price to the conversion factor for the high-coupon and the low-coupon bonds. Consider the ratio

$$\frac{P_i}{\mathrm{CF}_i} \; \forall \; i.$$

At yield levels below r^* we find that the high-coupon bond has a lower ratio. This suggests that at higher yields, low-coupon long-maturity bonds are cheaper to deliver. Conversely, at low yields, high-coupon, short-maturity bonds are cheaper to deliver. The economic reasoning behind this is the following. As rates fall, all bonds appreciate in price, but low-coupon, long-maturity bonds tend to become relatively more expensive; hence, it is cheaper to deliver high-coupon, short-maturity bonds. In a similar manner, as the rates go up all bonds become cheap, but the low-coupon, long-maturity bonds tend to become cheaper than the high-coupon, short-maturity bonds. As a con-

FIGURE 15-7   *Effect of Yields on CTD*

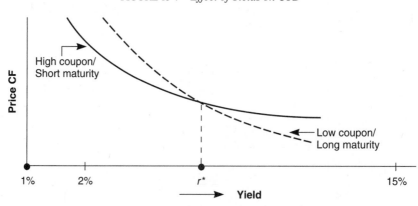

sequence, low-coupon, long-maturity bonds are delivered during periods of high interest rates.

Broadie and Sundaresan (1992) examine whether futures prices are bid down by
the value of the options present in futures contracts. Using a single-factor model, they
conclude that delivery options are important and that they affect the futures price. If
the delivery options implicit in the futures market have economic value, then a rational
agent will assume a long position in the futures contract only if the investor sells at a
discount relative to the forward price where there are no such options. From an empirical standpoint, the difference between the cash price and the adjusted futures price (invoice price) as of the first delivery date gives us the market value of the wild-card and
end-of-the-month options.

They find that the discounts are of the order of 9 to 16 ticks for Treasury bonds
and 13 ticks for Treasury notes on the first delivery date. For the expiry date of futures, the discounts for Treasury bonds average about 6 to 9 ticks and for Treasury
notes about 6 ticks.

Example 15-10:

September 2000 T-bond futures is quoted at 100.09375. The deliverable bond
7.50%, 11/15/2016 is selling at a flat price of 115.56250 for settlement on
8/21/2000. The conversion factor of this bond is 1.1529. Determine its implied
repo rate. If the actual repo rate is 6.42%, is there an arbitrage?

The accrued interest on 8/21/2000 = ai_t = 1.9973.
The accrued interest on 9/29/2000 = ai_T = 2.7921.
The futures price $H_t(T)$ = 100.09375.
The conversion factor = CF_i = 1.1529.
The cash price of the bond = P_{it} = 115.5625.

Since there is no coupon between 8/21/2000 and 9/29/2000 (which is the delivery
date), we can set $c = 0$ in Equation 15.6 to solve for the implied repo

$$r^* = \left(\frac{[1.1529 \times 100.09375 + 2.7921 - (115.5625 + 1.9973)]}{115.5625 + 1.9973} \right) \times \frac{360}{39}$$

$$= 4.95\%.$$

We show how to implement this in Figure 15-8.

Using T-Bond Futures to Hedge Bonds

Portfolio managers use T-bond futures to hedge interest rate risk. To illustrate how
this is done let us consider the following example:

Example 15-11:

Refer to Table 15-20. You have a long position in $100 million par value of bond
34. How many T-bond futures must you sell in order to remain neutrally hedged?

FIGURE 15-8   *Implied Repo Rate (Wall Street Journal Prices dated 8/21/2000).*

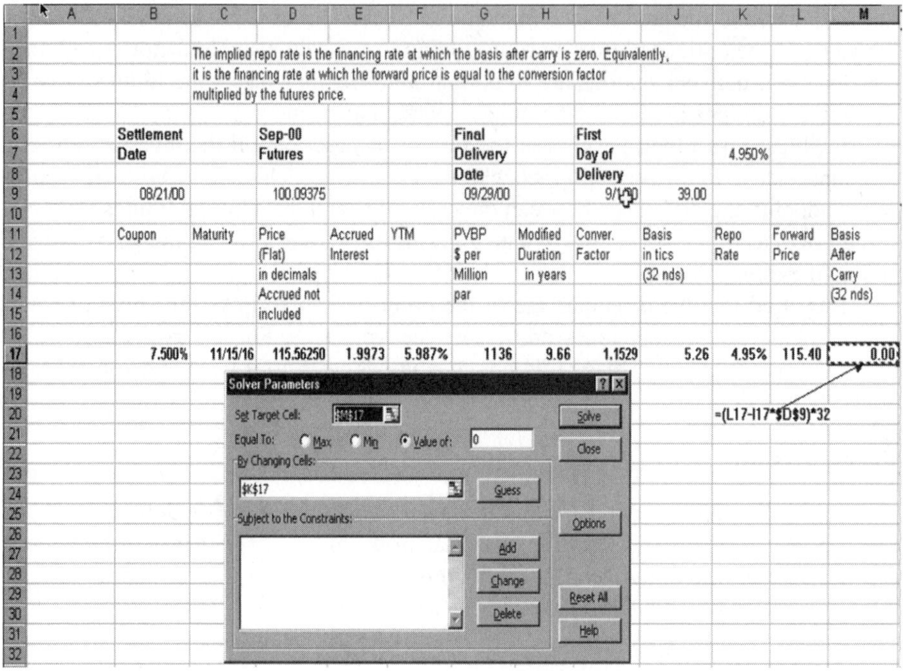

To answer this question, let us note that for the cheapest bond, the basis after carry is 5.99 ticks, which can be thought of as the market value of delivery options.

$$\text{Basis After Carry} = \text{Forward Price} - \text{CF} \times \text{Futures Price}$$

Let us assume that the basis after carry *for the cheapest bond* is zero. Then,

$$\text{Forward Price} = \text{CF} \times \text{Futures Price}. \tag{15.5}$$

This implies that

$$\text{PVBP (Forward Price)} = \text{CF} \times \text{PVBP (Futures Price)}.$$

But

$$\text{Forward Price} = (P_t + a_t)\left[1 + r\,\frac{T-t}{360}\right] - a_T - \frac{c}{2}\left[1 + r\,\frac{T-s}{360}\right].$$

By changing the yield by one basis point on each side, we get

$$\text{PVBP (Forward Price)} = \text{PVBP}\left(\begin{array}{c}\text{Cash Price of}\\ \text{Cheapest Bond}\end{array}\right) \times \left[1 + r\,\frac{T-t}{360}\right]. \tag{15.6}$$

Combining Equations 15.5 and 15.6, we get

$$\text{PVBP (Futures Price)} = \frac{1}{CF}\,\text{PVBP [Cash Price of Cheapest Bond]} \times \left[1 + r\,\frac{T-t}{360}\right].$$

Using the information from Table 15-20, we get

$$\text{PVBP (Futures Price)} = \frac{1}{1.1529} \times 1136 \times \left[1 + 0.0642 \times \frac{39}{360}\right]$$

$$= 992.1944/\text{million par}.$$

We must, however, remember that the par value of T-bond futures is \$100,000; hence, to get a million par, we must scale up the number futures by a factor of 10.

To hedge neutrally bond 34 in Table 15-20 we must set

$$\text{PVBP (bond 34)} = \text{Number of Futures} \times \text{PVBP (Futures)}.$$

This implies from Table 15-20 that

$$100 \times 1,241 = \text{Number of Futures} \times 992.1944 \text{ (Subject to a scale factor of 10)}$$

$$\text{Number of Futures} = \frac{100 \times 1,241}{992.1944}$$

$$= 125.01763.$$

Scaling it up by 10, we conclude that 1,250 futures contracts must be sold to effect the desired hedge.

CONCLUSION

In this chapter, we have defined futures and forward contracts and identified some important differences between these two deferred delivery agreements. This chapter also provided some conditions under which both markets may play useful functions. A historical perspective of the markets was provided, leading to their current configuration. We then examined in detail the Treasury futures contracts and the delivery options that are contained in them.

PROBLEMS

15.1   Define the following terms: (i) open interest, (ii) volume of trading, (iii) clearinghouse, (iv) price limits.

15.2   What are the differences between cash settlement and physical deliveries in the futures markets? Why do we observe physical deliveries in the Treasury futures and cash settlement in the equity index futures?

15.3   Define (i) basis and (ii) basis after carry. What do these concepts attempt to capture?

15.4   Describe the seller's options in a Treasury futures contract. How do these options affect the basis after carry? What would be the basis after carry in the absence of the seller's options? Why?

15.5 (a)   Generally, we find that the Treasury futures prices decline with maturity in an upward-sloping yield curve. Why?

(b)   Under the same circumstances, equity index futures tend to increase with maturity. Why?

15.6   The market price of a 30-year T-bond (6.25% coupon, August 15, 2023, maturity) is quoted at $103\frac{14}{32}$ for settlement on September 24, 1993.

(a)   Calculate (i) the yield to maturity (compounded semiannually) and (ii) the value of an 0.01 per $1 million par amount.

(b)   Determine the conversion factor for this bond to the December 1993 T-bond futures contract.

15.7   For the T-bond in Problem 13.6, the financing costs (term repo to the end of December) are relatively stable at 3.0% (annualized) in the repo market.

(a)   A bond trader wishes to carry a 25 million face amount of this bond until December 31, 1993. What is the minimum price at which he will be able to sell this security on December 31, 1993, to break even? Why?

(b)   On September 24, 1993, the December T-bond futures was quoted at $120\frac{2}{32}$. Compute (i) the basis and (ii) the basis after carry. Is there an opportunity for arbitrage? If there is an arbitrage possibility, set up the trade that will enable you to reap arbitrage gains.

15.8   Present the term structure of futures prices (futures prices versus delivery month) for (i) the crude oil futures markets and (ii) the T-bond futures markets. Explain the pattern that you observe.

REFERENCES

Anderson, R. 1984. "The Regulation of Futures Contracts Innovations in the United States." *Journal of Futures Markets* 4:297–332.

Black, F. 1976. "The Pricing of Commodity Contracts." *Journal of Financial Economics* 3:167–179.

Broadie, M., and S. Sundaresan 1992. "The Pricing of Timing and Quality Options: An Application to Treasury Bond and Treasury Note Futures Market." Columbia University Working Paper.

Carlton, D. 1984. "Futures Markets: Their Purpose, Their History, Their Growth, Their Successes and Failures." *Journal of Futures Markets* 4:237–271.

Cox, J., J. Ingersoll, and S. Ross 1981. "The Relation between Forward Prices and Futures Prices." *Journal of Financial Economics* 9(4):321–346.

Garbade, K. D., and W. L. Silber 1983. "Futures Contracts on Commodities with Multiple Varieties: An Analysis of Premiums and Discounts." *Journal of Business* 56:249–271.

Gay, G. D., and S. Manaster 1984. "The Quality Option Implicit in Futures Contracts." *Journal of Financial Economics* 13:353–370.

Gay, G. D., and S. Manaster 1986. "Implicit Delivery Options and Optimal Delivery Strategies for Financial Futures Contracts." *Journal of Financial Economics* 16:41–72.

Hicks, J. 1939. *Value and Capital: An Enquiry into Some Fundamental Principles of Economic Theory.* 2d ed. Oxford: Oxford University Press.

Jarrow, R., and G. Oldfield 1981. "Forward Contracts and Futures Contracts." *Journal of Financial Economics* 9(4):373–382.

Kane, E. 1984. "Regulatory Structure in Futures Markets: Jurisdictional Competition between the SEC, the CFTC and Other Agencies." *Journal of Futures Markets* 4:367–384.

Keynes, J. 1930. *A Treatise on Money.* New York: Harcourt Brace and Company.

Kilcollin, T. E. 1982. "Difference Systems in Financial Futures Markets." *Journal of Finance* 37:1183–1197.

Livingston, M. 1984. "The Cheapest Deliverable Bond for the CBT Treasury Bond Futures Contract." *Journal of Futures Markets* 4:161–172.

Richard, S., and M. Sundaresan 1981. "A Continuous Tune Model of Forward Prices and Futures Prices in a Multigood Economy." *Journal of Financial Economics* 9(4):347–371.

Silber, W. 1981. "Innovation, Competition and New Contract Design in Futures Markets." *Journal of Futures Markets* 1(2):123–155.

Chapter 16

Eurodollar Futures and Swaps

Chapter Objectives

This chapter describes the Eurodollar futures markets and the interest-rate swap markets. These two markets are shown to be tightly aligned. The Eurodollar contract, its specifications, and its applications are illustrated with specific examples. In addition, the following questions are addressed:

- What are Eurodollar futures contracts, and where are they traded?
- How can Eurodollar futures contracts be used to swap from floating-rate liabilities into fixed-rate liabilities?
- What are TED spreads?
- What is an interest-rate swap? How is it priced?
- What are swap spreads? What factors influence them?
- Why have swap spreads widened from 1998 to 2000?
- What is the impact of the swap dealer's credit reputation on the swap bid-offer spreads?
- How can swaps be used to manage risk?

INTRODUCTION

In this chapter, we provide a description of the Eurodollar time deposits and the Eurodollar futures contracts. The cash settlement feature of Eurodollar futures is described, and its implications for swapping from floating to fixed-rate liabilities are investigated. This is followed by a discussion of the spread between Eurodollar futures contracts and Treasury bill futures contracts. This spread, known as the TED spread, is used by investors in their trading strategies. Options on Eurodollar futures contracts are discussed next. The use of such options to create caps, floors, and collars on London Interbank Offered Rates (LIBOR) is illustrated through examples. We then define interest rate swaps and describe the evolution of the swap market and swap-related derivatives. Risk characteristics of interest-rate swaps are then examined. Two approaches for the valuation of swaps are presented: The first approach uses forward rates and the second approach uses the par bond curve concept. Risk management of swaps and the credit risk of swaps are investigated next. Finally, the chapter analyzes the swap spreads and presents some empirical evidence on spreads.

EURODOLLAR FUTURES CONTRACTS

Eurodollar deposits are dollar deposits maintained outside the United States. Generally, they are exempt from the Federal Reserve regulations that apply to the domestic deposits markets. The rates that apply to Eurodollar deposits in interbank transactions are known as the London Interbank Offered Rates (LIBOR). The LIBOR spot market is active in maturities ranging from a few days to 10 years. The depth of the market is especially great in the three-month and six-month maturity sectors.

The market for Eurodollar deposits is among the largest financial markets with many participating institutions. In fact, many other financial markets, such as the swap markets and the commercial paper markets, to name just two, regard LIBOR as benchmarks in setting their relevant rates.

The Eurodollar futures contract introduced by the Chicago Mercantile Exchange is currently one of the most actively traded futures contracts in the United States and in the world. This contract settles to 90-day LIBOR, which is the yield derived from the underlying asset that is the 90-day Eurodollar time deposit. This method of computing the futures price is unique and is a departure from the futures-pricing formulations in the literature. Since the price-to-yield transformation is not linear, the pricing of futures contracts on yields does not follow directly from the pricing of the corresponding futures. More importantly, it also renders the standard implied forward rates calculations from the LIBOR term structure different from the futures price; such forward rates apply only to situations where the forward and futures contracts are on asset prices and not to situations where the contracts are on yields.

Currently, Eurodollar futures contracts with virtually identical specifications are traded at the International Monetary Market (IMM) in Chicago, the Singapore International Monetary Exchange (SIMEX), and the London International Financial Futures Exchange (LIFFE). Proposals are currently well under way to list Eurodollar futures contracts in Tokyo as well. IMM and SIMEX also have common clearing systems, whereby Eurodollar futures positions that are established in one exchange can be offset in the other.

Table 16-1 gives a sample of Eurodollar futures contracts.

Calculating Yields in the Cash Market

In the Eurodollar time deposit market, deposits are traded between participating banks for maturities ranging from a few days to several years. On the trade date, the banks negotiate on principal, interest, and maturity. The settlement date is typically two London business days after the trade date. On the settlement date, the principal amount is sent by the lender to the borrower. On the maturity date, principal plus the interest is sent by the borrower to the lender. Interest on Eurodollar time deposits is calculated on actual/360 basis as Example 16-1 illustrates.

TABLE 16-1   *Eurodollar Futures Contracts, August 21, 2000*

EURODOLLAR (CME) - $1 million; pts of 100%

	Open	High	Low	Settle	Chg	Yield Settle	Chg	Open Interest
Sept	93.28	93.29	93.28	93.28	....	6.72	....	581,308
Oct	93.15	93.16	93.15	93.15	+ .01	6.85	− .01	11,334
Nov	93.14	93.14	93.14	93.14	+ .02	6.86	− .02	3,039
Dec	93.11	93.13	93.10	93.12	+ .01	6.88	− .01	546,312
Ja01	93.20	93.21	93.20	93.21	....	6.79	....	136
Mar	93.15	93.21	93.14	93.19	+ .04	6.81	− .04	492,154
June	93.12	93.19	93.11	93.18	+ .05	6.82	− .05	288,398
Sept	93.12	93.18	93.10	93.16	+ .04	6.84	− .04	228,932
Dec	93.05	93.11	93.03	93.09	+ .04	6.91	− .04	172,199
Mr02	93.10	93.17	93.09	93.15	+ .04	6.85	− .04	138,429
June	93.10	93.16	93.09	93.14	+ .03	6.86	− .03	104,259
Sept	93.10	93.15	93.09	93.14	+ .03	6.86	− .03	97,231
Dec	93.05	93.09	93.03	93.08	+ .03	6.92	− .03	75,557
Mr03	93.08	93.15	93.08	93.13	+ .03	6.87	− .03	72,088
June	93.08	93.13	93.06	93.11	+ .03	6.89	− .03	49,690
Sept	93.07	93.11	93.05	93.10	+ .02	6.90	− .02	48,757
Dec	93.00	93.05	92.99	93.03	+ .02	6.97	− .02	38,281
Mr04	93.04	93.09	93.03	93.07	+ .02	6.93	− .02	37,435
June	93.01	93.06	93.00	93.04	+ .02	6.96	− .02	39,243
Sept	92.98	93.03	92.97	93.01	+ .02	6.99	− .02	32,268
Dec	92.90	92.94	92.89	92.93	+ .02	7.07	− .02	29,510
Mr05	92.94	92.98	92.93	92.97	+ .02	7.03	− .02	23,507
June	92.91	92.95	92.90	92.94	+ .01	7.06	− .01	16,488
Sept	92.88	92.93	92.88	92.91	+ .01	7.09	− .01	11,882
Dec	92.80	92.85	92.80	92.84	+ .01	7.16	− .01	8,776
Mr06	92.84	92.89	92.84	92.87	+ .01	7.13	− .01	8,210
June	92.81	92.86	92.81	92.84	+ .01	7.16	− .01	6,856
Sept	92.78	92.83	92.78	92.81	+ .01	7.19	− .01	6,472
Dec	92.70	92.75	92.70	92.74	+ .01	7.26	− .01	6,676
Mr07	92.74	92.79	92.74	92.77	+ .01	7.23	− .01	5,247
June	92.71	92.76	92.71	92.74	+ .01	7.26	− .01	4,172
Sept	92.68	92.73	92.68	92.71	+ .01	7.29	− .01	3,369
Dec	92.60	92.65	92.60	92.64	+ .01	7.36	− .01	4,786
Mr08	92.64	92.69	92.64	92.67	+ .01	7.33	− .01	3,930
June	92.61	92.66	92.61	92.64	+ .01	7.36	− .01	4,223
Sept	92.58	92.63	92.58	92.61	+ .01	7.39	− .01	3,895
Dec	92.50	92.55	92.50	92.54	+ .01	7.46	− .01	2,998
Mr09	....	....	....	92.57	+ .01	7.43	− .01	2,337
June	....	....	....	92.54	+ .01	7.46	− .01	2,250
Sept	....	....	....	92.51	+ .01	7.49	− .01	1,948
Dec	....	....	....	92.43	+ .01	7.57	− .01	1,540
Mr10	....	....	....	92.47	+ .01	7.53	− .01	1,395
June	....	....	....	92.43	+ .01	7.57	− .01	1,165

Est vol 259,053; vol Thu 189,483; open int 3,218,682, −12,240.

Source: *Wall Street Journal,* August 21, 2000.

Note: The total open interest is 3,218,682 contracts. Each contract has an underlying par value of $1 million of a 90-day time deposit. This represents an extremely liquid market.

Example 16-1:

One million dollars is borrowed for 45 days in the Eurodollar time deposit market at a quoted rate of 5.25% (annualized). What is the interest due after 45 days?

$$\text{Interest} = \$1,000,000 \times 0.0525 \times \frac{45}{360}$$

$$= \$6,562.50$$

We can generalize from this example so that τ is the time to maturity in days between the settlement date t and the maturity date s. Let $l_t(\tau)$ be the LIBOR quoted on a principal amount $b(t, s)$ at date t. We will choose $b(t, s)$ so that it grows to $1 at date s. Then, the dollar interest earned (using Example 16-1) is

$$I = b(t, s) \times l_t(\tau) \times \frac{\tau}{360}. \tag{16.1}$$

Rearranging

$$l_r(\tau) = \frac{360}{\tau} \left[\frac{I}{b(t, s)} \right]. \tag{16.2}$$

Remember that the principal $b(t, s)$ borrowed is chosen at t such that

$$1 = b(t, s) + I. \tag{16.3}$$

Using Equation 16.3 to eliminate I in Equation 16.2, we get

$$l_r(\tau) = \frac{360}{\tau} \left[\frac{I}{b(t, s)} - 1 \right]. \tag{16.4}$$

To compare the return on Eurodollar time deposits with the return on other securities, it is useful to construct the continuously compounded return as well.

Example 16-2:

What is the continuously compounded return on the Eurodollar time deposit in Example 16-1?

The continuously compounded yield, denoted by y, is

$$y = \frac{365}{\tau} \ln \left[\frac{P + I}{P} \right],$$

where P is the principal borrowed, I is the dollar interest earned, and τ is the time to maturity in days.

$$y = \frac{365}{45} \ln \left[\frac{1,000,000 + 6,562.50}{1,000,000} \right]$$

$$= 5.306\%$$

Note that cash market yield is higher than the quoted LIBOR.

Having examined the yield calculations in the Eurodollar cash (deposit) market, we turn to the Eurodollar futures settlement next.

Eurodollar Futures Settlement to Yields

A key feature of Eurodollar futures contract is how they are settled at maturity. The futures contract settles by cash on its maturity date with no delivery or timing flexibilities to either the investor who is short or to the investor who is long. On the expiration date, which is the second London business day before the third Wednesday of the maturity month, the contract settles by cash to LIBOR using the following procedure.

On the expiration date, the clearinghouse determines the LIBOR for three-month Eurodollar deposits on two different times, the time of termination of trading and at a randomly selected time within 90 minutes of the termination of trading. The determination of the LIBOR is done via a sampling procedure. The clearinghouse selects, at random, 12 reference banks from a list of no less than 20 participating banks. Each bank provides a quotation to the clearinghouse on the LIBOR applied to three-month Eurodollar time deposits. The clearinghouse eliminates the highest two quotes and the lowest two quotes and computes an arithmetic average of the remaining eight quotes of the LIBOR. This is regarded by the clearinghouse as the LIBOR for that time. The final settlement price of the Eurodollar futures contract is obtained by performing this LIBOR computation at the two times indicated previously and then subtracting the arithmetic mean of the computed LIBOR (rounded to the nearest basis point) from 100.

Thus, at maturity, futures price (by design) converges to $100 \times (1 - \text{LIBOR})$ where the LIBOR is expressed in decimals with a resolution of a basis point. For example, an 8.01% (annualized) LIBOR will be expressed as 0.0801. Equivalently, 100 minus the Eurodollar futures price will converge to the three-month LIBOR. Figure 16-1 illustrates the convergence process for the December 1988 futures contract. A summary of Eurodollar futures features is in Table 16-2.

Several factors about the Eurodollar futures contracts in Table 16-1 deserve special attention. First, Eurodollar futures extend until 2002, more than seven years from November 1994. The contract is heavily used for hedging and synthesizing interest-rate swaps, FRAs, and other swap-related derivatives. We will explore such uses later. Second, note that the open interest in the December 1994 maturity is 366,000 contracts, each with a par amount of $1 million. This represents a tremendous amount of liquidity for institutional investors. In fact, liquidity until 1999 is fairly good. The total volume of trading in this futures market was nearly 750,000, representing a par amount of $750 billion. We have also computed the quantity called the **implied interest rate** in Table 16-1; this is 100 minus the futures price. For example, corresponding to the December 1994 futures price of 93.80, the implied interest rate is $100 - 93.80 = 6.20$.

We now relate the Eurodollar futures settlement price to the 90-day LIBOR on the settlement (maturity) date of the futures contract. As in the cash market calculations, we will standardize the principal amount $b(t, s)$ at date t so that at maturity we get a total (principal + interest) of $1. Note that for the Eurodollar futures contract maturing on date s, the relevant principal is $b(s, s + 90)$ since the contract settles to 90-day LIBOR at date s.

FIGURE 16-1   *Eurodollar Futures Rates and the Three-Month LIBOR*

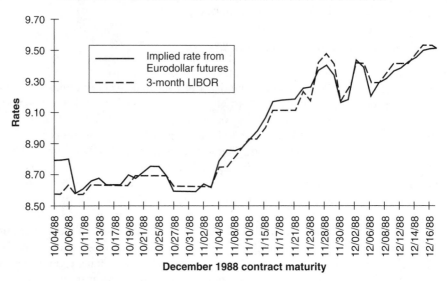

TABLE 16-2	Underlying instrument	Three-month Eurodollar time deposits
Eurodollar Futures	Contract size	$1,000,000 U.S. face value
Contracts	Contract months	March, June, September, December
	Minimum price change	0.01 = $25
	Trading hours	8:20 A.M. to 3:00 P.M. (EST)
	Delivery terms	Cash settlement on last trading day; settlement based on LIBOR
	Last day of trading	Two London business days before third Wednesday of delivery month

Let $l_s(90)$ denote the three-month LIBOR (annualized) at date s. LIBOR on a Eurodollar time deposit with a maturity of τ days is defined using a money-market convention according to the formula:

$$l_s(\tau) = \frac{360}{\tau}\left(\frac{I}{b(s, s+\tau)} - 1\right). \tag{16.5}$$

The Eurodollar futures price $H_s(s)$ at maturity date s is

$$H_s(s) \equiv 100 \times [1 - l_s(90)]. \tag{16.6}$$

This follows from the add on settlement feature of the Eurodollar futures contract described earlier. The resulting Eurodollar futures price is in percentages of a one million face amount of a 90-day time deposit. The market resolution is a basis point worth $1,000,000 \times \frac{1}{100} \times \frac{1}{100} \times \frac{90}{360} = \$25$.

We will illustrate the use of Eurodollar futures in synthesizing LIBOR-based swaps through a simple example. Remember that the Eurodollar futures price settles to 90-day LIBOR, $l_s(90)$, at maturity date s, as in Equation 16.6.

Example 16-3:

Consider the case of a December 1987 Eurodollar futures contract. This contract matured on December 14, 1987, at a settlement price of 91.62. The 90-day LIBOR on that day stood at 8.38%. The maturity price was $100 - 8.38 = 91.62$.

This settlement feature of Eurodollar futures is unique and is known as the **add on settlement** feature. Contrast this with the discount settlement feature used in the Treasury bill futures market (see Chapter 13).

Example 16-4:

The Eurodollar futures prices are in percentages of a one million face amount of a 90-day time deposit. The market resolution is a basis point that is worth $1,000,000 \times \frac{1}{100} \times \frac{1}{100} \times \frac{90}{360} = \$25$. Thus, if the Eurodollar futures price moves from 92.58 to 92.62 in one day, the dollar value of that move of 4 basis points is $4 \times 25 = \$100$ per contract.

Example 16-5:

Consider a firm that has floating-rate liabilities indexed off a 90-day LIBOR on a face amount of $100 million. The firm would like to swap these into a stream of fixed-rate liabilities. Assume that the liability schedule facing the firm as of January 2, 1987, is as shown in Table 16-3. Liabilities are assumed to fall due each quarter on the maturity dates of Eurodollar futures contracts.

The schedule of the Eurodollar futures prices as of January 2, 1987, is shown in Table 16-4. The ex-post settlement prices of these futures contracts on their respective maturity dates is shown in Table 16-5. The implied rate of interest $r_t(s_i) = 100 - H_t(s_i)$ is also indicated for each futures contract. Note that the implied rate of interest for each contract is known as of date t, January 2, 1987.

By selling a portfolio of futures contracts (called a **strip of futures**) on date t, it is possible for the firm to convert its floating liabilities into a stream of currently known liabilities as given by the implied rates of interest. To see this clearly, review Table 16-6, where the firm has sold a strip of 100 futures contracts.

The firm at date t sells a strip of Eurodollar futures contracts maturing on dates $s_i (i = 1, \ldots, 4)$. The payoffs from futures contracts (ignoring marking-to-market)

TABLE 16-3 Schedule of Floating Liabilities	t	s_1	s_2	s_3	s_4
	1/2/1987	3/16/1987	6/15/1987	9/14/1987	12/14/1987

TABLE 16-4	$H_t(s_1)$	$H_t(s_2)$	$H_t(s_3)$	$H_t(s_4)$
Schedule of Eurodollar Futures Prices, January 2, 1987	93.95	93.95	93.86	93.68
	6.05%	6.05%	6.14%	6.32%

TABLE 16-5	$H_{s_1}(s_1)$	$H_{s_2}(s_2)$	$H_{s_3}(s_3)$	$H_{s_4}(s_4)$
Eurodollar Futures Prices at Maturity	93.50	93.77	92.50	91.62
	6.50%	6.23%	7.50%	8.38%

TABLE 16-6 *Swap Execution*

Transaction	t 1/2/1987	s_1 3/16/1987	s_2 6/15/1987	s_3 9/14/1987	s_4 12/14/1987
	Sell 100 of each futures				
Cash flow from futures		6.50 − 6.05 × 250,000 = 112,500	6.23 − 6.05 × 250,000 = 45,000	7.50 − 6.14 × 250,000 = 340,000	8.38 − 6.32 × 250,000 = 515,000
Liabilities		−6.50 × 250,000 = −1,625,000	−6.23 × 250,000 = −1,557,500	−7.50 × 250,000 = −1,875,000	−8.38 × 250,000 = −2,095,000
Total		−6.05 × 250,000 = −1,512,500	−6.05 × 250,000 = −1,512,500	−6.14 × 250,000 = −1,535,000	−6.32 × 250,000 = −1,580,000

will be the date t futures price minus the settlement futures price. For example, the payoff from the March 1987 contract on date s_1 will be $[H_t(s_1) - H_{s_1}(s_1)] \times 2,500 \times 100$. On March 16, 1987, the Eurodollar futures price settled at 93.50. Therefore, the payoff is $(93.95 - 93.50) \times 2,500 \times 100 = \$112,500$. From Table 16-5, it is clear that the LIBOR increased during this period, and as a result, the futures prices fell. The profits from futures prices enabled the firm to lock in the rates that were determined at date t. The Eurodollar futures market permitted the firm to lock in, at date t, the known rates as shown in the bottom cell of Table 16-6.

Swap Rate Calculations

The effective rate that is locked in by the firm is the swap rate and is computed as follows. Intuitively, the swap rate is the fixed rate that is paid on the same dates as the floating payments with a present value equal to that of the floating payments. From Tables 16-4 and 16-6, we see that the rates locked in as of date t were 6.05 for s_1, 6.05 for s_2, 6.14 for s_3, and 6.32 for s_4. These rates were known at date t, as seen from Table 16-4. Intuitively, we will expect that the effective fixed rate (swap rate) locked in at date t will be a weighted average of these rates implied by Eurodollar futures contracts. We proceed to compute this next.

Let $b(t, j)$, $(j = 1, \ldots, 4)$ be the discount functions quoted at date t for various future dates j. Then the swap rate x payable at each date s_i must satisfy the equality

$$x[b(t, s_1) + b(t, s_2) + b(t, s_3) + b(t, s_4)]$$
$$= r_t(s_1)b(t, s_1) + r_t(s_2)b(t, s_2) + r_t(s_3)b(t, s_3) + r_t(s_4)b(t, s_4). \tag{16.7}$$

The left-hand side of the previous equation calculates the present value of paying $x\%$ at dates s_1, s_2, s_3, and s_4. The right-hand side calculates the present value of paying the implied interest rates from Eurodollar futures contracts set at t but paid at the reset dates s_1, s_2, s_3, and s_4. The implied interest rates at date t are known from Table 16-4 as $r_t(s_1) = 6.05\%$, $r_t(s_2) = 6.05\%$, $r_t(s_3) = 6.14\%$, and $r_t(s_4) = 6.32\%$. Once we calculate the discount factors $b(t, s_1)$, $b(t, s_2)$, $b(t, s_3)$, and $b(t, s_4)$, we can solve for the effective swap rate x from the previous equation. We write out explicitly the effective swap rate x in Equation 16.8. Note that Equation 16.8 may be regarded as a swap valuation model. Once we plug in the implied interest rates and discount rates, the swap rate is readily obtained. The actual calculation of the discount rates is computationally more involved, but we illustrate a simple procedure next.

The swap rate x is

$$x = \frac{r_t(s_1)b(t, s_1) + r_t(s_2)b(t, s_2) + r_t(s_3)b(t, s_3) + r_t(s_4)b(t, s_4)}{[b(t, s_1) + b(t, s_2) + b(t, s_3) + b(t, s_4)]}. \tag{16.8}$$

Equation 16.8 simply requires that in a swap, the fixed rate x must have the same present value (shown on the left-hand side) as the floating payments (which, by virtue of Eurodollar futures settlement feature, is given by the right-hand side).

Example 16-6:

In the context of Example 16-5, the swap rate is easily calculated. On January 2, 1987, the LIBOR of different maturities were as shown in Table 16-7. The discount factors are calculated using the formula

$$b(t, j) = \frac{1}{1 + \text{LIBOR} \times \frac{y}{360}}, \tag{16.9}$$

where y is the maturity in days of LIBOR.

TABLE 16-7   *Schedule of LIBOR and Discount Functions, January 2, 1987*

	Three-Month s_1	*Six-Month* s_2	*Nine-Month* s_3	*Twelve-Month* s_4
LIBOR	6.3125%	6.25%	6.25%	6.25%
Days	73	164	255	346
Discount	0.9874	0.9723	0.9576	0.9433

At date t we obtain LIBOR quotes for settlement at the reset dates s_1, s_2, s_3, and s_4. Using this information, which is reported in Table 16-7, we can calculate the discount factors for each reset date. We illustrate the discount rate calculations for date s_1.

$$y = \text{\# days between } t \text{ and } s_1$$

$$= \text{Difference between March 16, 1987 and January 2, 1987}$$

$$= 73 \text{ days}$$

LIBOR at date t for settlement at date s_1 is 6.3125%.

Using Equation 16.9, we get the discount factor as

$$b(t, s_1) = \frac{1}{1 + 0.063125 \times \frac{73}{360}} = 0.9874.$$

This information as well as the discount factors for reset dates s_2, s_3, and s_4 are provided in Table 16-8. The LIBOR data upon which our calculations are based is also given.

Alternatively, the discount rates can be calculated using Eurodollar futures prices. This approach is shown in Table 16-8.

The zero price for the maturity 3/16/1987 is calculated exactly as shown earlier. To calculate the zero price for maturity 6/15/1987, we need to calculate the implied futures rate between 3/16/1987 and 6/15/1987. This is 6.05%. This rate applies to loans starting at 3/16/1987 and maturing at 6/15/1987 for a loan maturity of 91 days. The relevant zero price for maturity at 6/15/1987 is obtained as follows:

$$\frac{1}{1 + 0.063125 \cdot \frac{73}{360}} \times \frac{1}{1 + 0.06050 \cdot \frac{91}{360}} = 0.972489.$$

In a similar manner, the relevant zero price for maturity 9/14/1987 is

$$\frac{1}{1 + 0.063125 \cdot \frac{73}{360}} \times \frac{1}{1 + 0.06050 \cdot \frac{91}{360}} \times \frac{1}{1 + 0.06050 \cdot \frac{91}{360}} = 0.957841.$$

TABLE 16-8   *Schedule of Eurodollar Futures Prices and Discount Rates on January 2, 1987*

Eurodollar Futures or Spot LIBOR	Implied Futures Rate or Spot LIBOR	Maturity Date of Futures or LIBOR	Number of Days from the Settlement	Zero Price	Days between Futures Settlement
	6.3125%	3/16/87	73	0.9874	
93.95	6.0500%	3/16/87	73	0.9725	91
93.95	6.0500%	6/15/87	164	0.9578	91
93.86	6.1400%	9/14/87	255	0.9432	91
93.68	6.3200%	12/14/87	346		

Proceeding in this manner, we can compute the relevant discount factors. Using these discount functions, the swap rate x is

$$= \frac{6.05\% \times 0.9874 + 6.05\% \times 0.9723 + 6.14\% \times 0.9578 + 6.32\% \times 0.9433}{0.9874 + 0.9723 + 0.9578 + 0.9433}$$

$$= \frac{23.69749}{3.8606} = 6.1383\%.$$

The swap rate x is 6.1383%, based on the discount functions and the implied rates of interest at date t.

Eurodollar Futures versus Swap Markets

While Eurodollar futures contracts may be used to execute swaps and they contain information about swap rates, institutions find it much easier to execute swaps by contacting swap intermediaries. There are good reasons as to why this is the case. With Eurodollar futures, the convergence to LIBOR is on the maturity date. This is ideal if the reset date and payment date coincide with the maturity date. For other swap structures, Eurodollar futures can not be used in so direct a manner. On the other hand, the swap market is well organized, and the transactions are easily arranged. The credit risks are more easily factored into the contract. It is also easy to customize the swap contract to suit the needs of contracting parties: arbitrary indices, reset frequencies, and payment dates may be easily fitted into the swap contract.

However, the existence of Eurodollar futures markets and the swap rates implicit in Eurodollar futures force a tight link between swap rates and Eurodollar rates. The arbitrage possibilities between the two markets ensures a greater efficiency in the swap market. Since most swap intermediaries hedge their risks in the Eurodollar market, the rates in these markets are linked closely. It should also be noted that Eurodollar futures on 30-day LIBOR is traded at IMM, though this contract is less active compared to the 90-day LIBOR contract.

Intermarket Spreads

In this section, we will explore intermarket spread strategies using Eurodollar futures and T-bill futures contracts. These strategies are referred to as **TED spreads.** Consider the data presented in Table 16-9.

The TED spread and the prices of Eurodollar and T-bill futures are shown for December 1987 maturity in Figures 16-2 and 16-3, respectively. These contracts move parallel to each other, for the most part. The T-bill contract tracks the prices of deliverable T-bills. Such bills are free from default risk. The Eurodollar futures contracts track the LIBOR, and when the banking industry undergoes a downturn, LIBOR rates will increase significantly. Generally, any shock to the economy that significantly affects the banking sector will affect the LIBOR and, hence, the Eurodollar futures prices. These arguments are best illustrated by reviewing the TED spread around the stock market crash of 1987, as shown in Figure 16-4.

TABLE 16-9   *T-Bill and Eurodollar Futures*

Date	T-Bill Futures	Euro-dollar Futures	TED Spread	Date	T-Bill Futures	Euro-dollar Futures	TED Spread	Date	T-Bill Futures	Euro-dollar Futures	TED Spread
06/01/87	91.90	93.10	120.00	08/05/87	92.32	93.66	134.00	10/09/87	90.85	92.33	148.00
06/02/87	91.55	92.82	127.00	08/06/87	92.30	93.64	134.00	10/12/87	90.84	92.34	150.00
06/03/87	91.74	92.97	123.00	08/07/87	92.31	93.64	133.00	10/13/87	90.94	92.41	147.00
06/04/87	91.78	93.01	123.00	08/10/87	92.33	93.66	133.00	10/14/87	90.65	92.11	146.00
06/05/87	91.88	93.17	129.00	08/11/87	92.39	93.71	132.00	10/15/87	90.54	92.05	151.00
06/08/87	91.87	93.20	133.00	08/12/87	92.44	93.75	131.00	10/16/87	90.44	92.05	161.00
06/09/87	91.81	93.19	138.00	08/13/87	92.58	93.82	124.00	10/19/87	90.64	92.50	186.00
06/10/87	91.86	93.24	138.00	08/14/87	92.59	93.85	126.00	10/20/87	91.80	93.80	200.00
06/11/87	91.94	93.26	132.00	08/17/87	92.55	93.84	129.00	10/21/87	92.06	93.93	187.00
06/12/87	92.23	93.50	127.00	08/18/87	92.41	93.73	132.00	10/22/87	92.40	94.19	179.00
06/15/87	92.24	93.59	135.00	08/19/87	92.35	93.67	132.00	10/23/87	92.23	93.97	174.00
06/16/87	92.23	93.59	136.00	08/20/87	92.39	93.66	127.00	10/26/87	92.54	94.28	174.00
06/17/87	92.33	93.67	134.00	08/21/87	92.33	93.59	126.00	10/27/87	92.36	94.08	172.00
06/18/87	92.28	93.63	135.00	08/24/87	92.31	93.51	120.00	10/28/87	92.34	94.15	181.00
06/19/87	92.28	93.66	138.00	08/25/87	92.36	93.53	117.00	10/29/87	92.47	94.23	176.00
06/22/87	92.41	93.75	134.00	08/26/87	92.32	93.47	115.00	10/30/87	92.42	94.12	170.00
06/23/87	92.39	93.68	129.00	08/27/87	92.16	93.32	116.00	11/02/87	92.29	93.98	169.00
06/24/87	92.26	93.59	133.00	08/28/87	92.07	93.25	118.00	11/03/87	92.42	94.13	171.00
06/25/87	92.35	93.68	133.00	08/31/87	92.07	93.31	124.00	11/04/87	92.50	94.18	168.00
06/26/87	92.22	93.62	140.00	09/01/87	92.01	93.26	125.00	11/05/87	92.69	94.24	155.00
06/29/87	92.28	93.69	141.00	09/02/87	91.84	93.13	129.00	11/06/87	92.63	94.13	150.00
06/30/87	92.31	93.69	138.00	09/03/87	91.84	93.14	130.00	11/09/87	92.56	94.01	145.00
07/01/87	92.40	93.78	138.00	09/04/87	91.65	92.97	132.00	11/10/87	92.54	94.02	148.00
07/02/87	92.51	93.88	137.00	09/08/87	91.47	92.83	136.00	11/11/87	92.48	94.00	152.00
07/06/87	92.51	93.89	138.00	09/09/87	91.53	92.89	136.00	11/12/87	92.50	93.96	146.00
07/07/87	92.56	93.90	134.00	09/10/87	91.62	92.98	136.00	11/13/87	92.42	93.77	135.00
07/08/87	92.56	93.90	134.00	09/11/87	91.71	93.03	132.00	11/16/87	92.37	93.80	143.00
07/09/87	92.46	93.86	140.00	09/14/87	91.69	92.94	125.00	11/17/87	92.43	93.93	150.00
07/10/87	92.60	93.95	135.00	09/15/87	91.59	92.91	132.00	11/18/87	92.45	94.04	159.00
07/13/87	92.55	93.93	138.00	09/16/87	91.61	92.91	130.00	11/19/87	92.53	94.17	164.00
07/14/87	92.66	94.00	134.00	09/17/87	91.62	92.94	132.00	11/20/87	92.49	94.12	163.00
07/15/87	92.51	93.87	136.00	09/18/87	91.73	93.03	130.00	11/23/87	92.45	94.06	161.00
07/16/87	92.54	93.93	139.00	09/21/87	91.69	93.02	133.00	11/24/87	92.41	93.99	158.00
07/17/87	92.60	93.97	137.00	09/22/87	91.79	93.09	130.00	11/25/87	92.37	94.00	163.00
07/20/87	92.58	93.96	138.00	09/23/87	91.78	93.08	130.00	11/27/87	92.19	93.99	180.00
07/21/87	92.49	93.82	133.00	09/24/87	91.64	92.92	128.00	11/30/87	92.32	94.17	185.00
07/22/87	92.43	93.76	133.00	09/25/87	91.59	92.84	125.00	12/01/87	92.27	94.12	185.00
07/23/87	92.36	93.70	134.00	09/28/87	91.58	92.81	123.00	12/02/87	92.24	94.24	200.00
07/24/87	92.30	93.64	134.00	09/29/87	91.42	92.70	128.00	12/03/87	92.25	94.32	207.00
07/27/87	92.29	93.63	134.00	09/30/87	91.40	92.69	129.00	12/04/87	92.25	94.36	211.00
07/28/87	92.28	93.55	127.00	10/01/87	91.39	92.72	133.00	12/07/87	92.12	94.07	195.00
07/29/87	92.29	93.56	127.00	10/02/87	91.45	92.77	132.00	12/08/87	92.07	94.03	196.00
07/30/87	92.34	93.62	128.00	10/05/87	91.35	92.64	129.00	12/09/87	92.05	94.07	202.00
07/31/87	92.31	93.59	128.00	10/06/87	91.26	92.60	134.00	12/10/87	91.91	94.03	212.00
08/03/87	92.17	93.51	134.00	10/07/87	91.16	92.58	142.00	12/11/87	91.79	94.05	226.00
08/04/87	92.17	93.54	137.00	10/08/87	90.95	92.38	143.00	12/14/87	91.62	94.04	242.00

FIGURE 16-2   *TED Spread during 1986 to 1987*

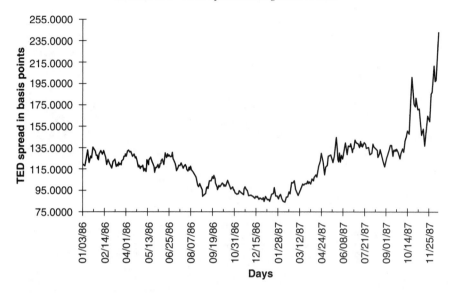

FIGURE 16-3   *Eurodollar and T-Bill Futures Prices*

Note that the TED spread widened significantly around the time of stock market crash. In fact, market participants tend to use the TED spread as a mechanism to incorporate some of their market views. As the enclosed article from Barrons by Andrew Bary suggests, market participants bet on the yield gaps between bank deposits and risk-free Treasuries using TED spreads. This spread tends to widen in times of financial crisis and tighten in periods of stability.

FIGURE 16-4   *TED Spread around Crash of 1987*

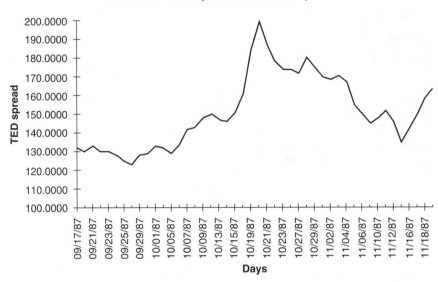

Has Greenspan Given the Green Light to Buying Bonds with Borrowed Money?

BY ANDREW BARY

The leveraged bond trade may be returning with a vengeance. From 1991 through 1993, buying bonds with gobs of borrowed money became one of the most lucrative games in financial history as the Federal Reserve kept short-term rates at the lowest levels in a generation. During that long period of easy money, formerly unknown Wall Street bond traders and hedge-fund operators became grotesquely wealthy by purchasing massive amounts of 4% and 5% Treasury securities and financing them with money borrowed at 3%.

That game came to an abrupt halt a year ago when the Fed began raising short-term rates. But with Fed Chairman Alan Greenspan signaling Wednesday that the central bank may be done tightening, the leveraged bond trade started to look a lot more appealing.

The two-year Treasury note, long the security of choice with the speculative set, surged on Wednesday after Greenspan's comments, as its yield fell nearly 20 basis points to 6.85%. And at the market peak Thursday, the two-year yielded just 6.73%, 30 basis points below its closing level on the prior Friday and off nearly a full percentage point since the start of the year. The two-year note ended the week at 6.84%

Speculation ran through the market Wednesday and Thursday that hedge funds and other speculators were putting back their old leveraged positions. "I think the trade is coming back," says Jim Bianco, director of research at Arbor Trading Group in Barrington, Ill.

He detects signs of increased two-year note speculation in the sharply narrowing yield gap between the two-year and the three-month T-bill. Bianco notes that since the end of December, the two-year note yield has fallen dramatically while the rate on the three-month T-bill has actually increased, to 5.72%. "This is one of the largest divergences in history," Bianco says, noting that the two securities usually move in the same direction. Bianco ventures that the two-year note has moved so much because speculators can finance it profitably with 6% short-term money, while the T-bill can't be leveraged profitably at today's rates.

Some wags said Greenspan's comments amounted to a hedge-fund bailout. "The macro guys got killed in the carry trade last year. They need some help," said one hedge-fund manager.

Positive Carry

It's not hard to see why the two-year note appeals to a leveraged speculator right now. It yields nearly a point above the 6% Fed funds rate, providing the holder with a spread known as positive carry. Until recently, there was plenty of positive carry in this trade, but also a lot of risk because the Fed was ratcheting up short rates. But if the Fed is just one tightening step away from being finished, the danger in the two-year is greatly reduced.

It's difficult for small investors to emulate the big boys because bond dealers normally won't sell Treasuries to individuals with just 5% down. But risk-taking investors can traffic in the highly liquid Eurodollar futures market in Chicago. Eurodollars offer the same play as the two-year note. Bullish investors can buy Eurodollar futures, particularly the December 1995 and March 1996 contracts, while bears can sell them.

The TED Spread

Betting on the yield gap between bank deposits and risk-free Treasuries has been popular with speculators for over a decade. The spread tends to widen in times of financial crisis, and tighten in periods of calm. The usual way to play this relationship is through the "TED," a reference to the spread between Treasury bill futures and Eurodollar futures.

Since the start of the year, there has been a dramatic narrowing in the TED of about $\frac{1}{4}$-percentage-point, as the Orange County bond liquidations ended and as the credit markets rallied. In the past week alone, two-year swap spreads, a proxy for the TED, tightened nearly 10 basis points to 22 basis points, a big move in a usually stable spread.

At mid-week, when the TED spread hit its narrowest point, some Wall Street dealers and others supposedly put on massive arbitrage trades, betting the spread would eventually reverse. These traders bought two-year Treasury notes and sold "strips" of Eurodollar futures extending out two years, or they bought two-year notes and sold the fixed side of interest-rate swaps. One sign of huge arbitrage activity was a big jump of nearly 100,000 contracts in Eurodollar open interest on Wednesday and Thursday. That rise in open interest is equivalent to $100 billion of Eurodollar futures.

"This is a great risk-reward trade," one bond dealer said Friday. He figures the trade works under several scenarios: If Mexico's financial troubles deepen, if the U.S. economy slows, or if the U.S. bond market moves sharply lower. It probably loses, however, if the Fed can engineer a soft landing for the economy.

(continued)

With the bond rally of 1995 has come a marked improvement in the derivative mortgage securities market. Institutional investors who wouldn't go near volatile stuff like inverse floaters and principal-only strips have been nibbling lately because these instruments offer a leveraged bet on lower rates.

For bullish individuals with a stomach for risk, there are three closed-end bond funds that provide a nearly pure play on mortgage derivatives. The TWC/Dean Witter Term Trust 2000, TWC/Dean Witter Term Trust 2002 and TWC/Dean Witter Term Trust 2003 all had a lousy 1994. And their share prices got walloped after dividend cuts last month.

These derivative-laden funds, sold by Dean Witter and managed by Trust Co. of the West, have come under so much pressure because angry brokers have been getting their clients out.

The selling, however, may present an opportunity because the funds trade at discounts of about 15% to their net asset values, versus premiums of 10% a year ago. "The TCW funds are among the few closed-end bond funds I've been buying lately," says Thomas Herzfeld, head of Thomas Herzfeld Advisors, a closed-end fund specialist. The TWC/Dean Witter Term Trusts 2000 and 2003 finished Friday at $6\frac{5}{8}$, while the TWC/Dean Witter Term Trust 2002 ended at 7.

Given their current discounts and portfolio composition, these funds could reward patient investors with double-digit returns in a benign market. But, as the original investors, who paid $10 a share, learned, the trio do carry more risk than the typical mortgage mutual fund.

As the article from *Barron's* illustrates, buying the two-year note and selling Eurodollar futures is a trade in which the investor is betting that the spread between LIBOR and two-year Treasury yield will widen. To see this, let us first note that if LIBOR increases (after the execution of the trade), the Eurodollar futures price will go down. This will benefit the investor who is short in Eurodollar futures contracts. Likewise, if the Treasury yields were to go down, the investor will benefit from his or her long position in the two-year note. This is an example of a trade that will make money when there is a flight to quality in which investors liquidate their investments in banks and fly to "safe" assets, such as Treasury securities. During the Japanese bank failures in the late 1990s and the Russian default in 1998, investors exhibited their preference for Treasury securities.

Options on Eurodollar Futures Contracts

Calls and puts are traded on Eurodollar futures contracts. These contracts are listed at the IMM in the Chicago Mercantile Exchange. The settlement feature of the Eurodollar futures implies that a call option on Eurodollar futures is equivalent to a put option on LIBOR. Likewise, a put option on Eurodollar futures is equivalent to a call option on LIBOR.

To see this clearly, let us consider the data in Table 16-10. On May 9, 1996, the Eurodollar futures price is 94.48. Several calls and puts are available on the June

TABLE 16-10

Options on
Eurodollar Futures
Trade Date: 5/9/96
Eurodollar Futures
(June 1996) 94.48

Strike	Call	Put
93.75	0.73	r
94.00	0.48	r
94.25	**0.24**	0.01
94.50	0.04	0.06
94.75	0.01	**0.27**
95.00	r	0.52

Eurodollar futures contract. It is important to note that these options settle by cash at maturity, and they expire on the same day as the underlying futures contract. Let us examine the call with a strike price of 94.25. At maturity, this call will pay an amount equal to

$$\max [0, H - 94.25],$$

where H is the Eurodollar futures price at maturity. We know that $H = 100 - \text{LIBOR}$ from Equation 16.6. Using this, we get the payoff of the call option on Eurodollar futures to be

$$\max [0, 5.75 - \text{LIBOR}].$$

This is also the payoff of a put option on LIBOR with a strike rate of 5.75%. From Table 16-10, we find that this call costs 24 basis points. Each basis point costs $25 so that the value of this option is $24 \times 25 = \$600$.

In a similar way, the put with a strike price of 94.75 will pay at maturity an amount equal to

$$\max [0, 94.75 - H],$$

where H is the Eurodollar futures price at maturity. Since at maturity, the Eurodollar futures price settles to LIBOR by the condition $H = 100 - \text{LIBOR}$, we can rewrite the payoff of the put at maturity as

$$\max [0, \text{LIBOR} - 5.25].$$

This is the payoff of a call option on LIBOR with a strike rate of 5.25%. From Table 16-10, we find that this put option costs 27 basis points. Its cost is $27 \times 25 = \$675$.

Caps, Floors, and Collars on LIBOR

Eurodollar futures and options on Eurodollar futures can be used to customize different return-risk profiles for investors who have assets or liabilities denominated in LIBOR. Consider Table 16-11 in which we examine scenarios at the maturity of Eurodollar futures contract where LIBOR can vary from a low of 3% to a high of 8%. Note that the Eurodollar futures price, as a consequence of its settlement to LIBOR, varies from a high of 97.00 to a low of 92.00. In Table 16-11, we have described the net payoffs of a long position in call initiated at a cost of 0.24; a long position in put

TABLE 16-11　*Payoffs of Options on Maturity Date Under Different Scenarios*

LIBOR	3.0%	3.5%	4.0%	4.5%	5.0%	5.5%	6.0%	6.5%	7.0%	7.5%	8.0%
Futures Price	97.00	96.50	96.00	95.50	95.00	94.50	94.00	93.50	93.00	92.50	92.00
Call											
(Strike=94.25)	2.51	2.01	1.51	1.01	0.51	0.01	−0.24	−0.24	−0.24	−0.24	−0.24
Put											
(Strike=94.75)	−0.27	−0.27	−0.27	−0.27	−0.27	−0.02	0.48	0.98	1.48	1.98	2.48
Long Futures											
@ 94.48	2.52	2.02	1.52	1.02	0.52	0.02	−0.48	−0.98	−1.48	−1.98	−2.48
Short Futures											
@ 94.48	−2.52	−2.02	−1.52	−1.02	−0.52	−0.02	0.48	0.98	1.48	1.98	2.48

initiated at a cost of 0.27; a long position in futures initiated at a futures price of 94.48; and a short position in futures initiated at a futures price of 94.48. For example, when the futures price is 97.00, the put ends up out-of-the-money, leading to a loss of 0.27, whereas a long position in futures yields $(97.00 − 94.48) = 2.52$.

Example 16-7:

How can investors use these contracts to synthesize different return-risk profiles? Consider an issuer who has liabilities denominated in LIBOR. The cost per million dollars par amount of the liability is directly proportional to LIBOR for this issuer. For example, when LIBOR is 6%, the cost will be

$$1,000,000 \times 0.06 \times \frac{90}{360} = 15,000.$$

Suppose the issuer believes that LIBOR has a good chance of going above 5.25%. Then the issuer can buy a put option on Eurodollar futures at a strike price of 94.75. The total costs with and without the put are shown in Table 16-12. Note that for LIBOR levels above 5.25%, the cost is capped out at

$$= 1,000,000 \times 0.0525 \times \frac{90}{360} + 27 \times 25$$

$$= \$13,800.$$

This establishes a **cap** on the total cost.

If LIBOR goes below 5.25%, the issuer is able to take advantage of the falling LIBOR, although the cost of the put option diminishes the advantage of falling rates. The payoffs of the positions are shown in Figure 16-5.

Example 16-8:

What if the issuer believes that the LIBOR is likely to go up by a moderate amount but is willing to bet that it is unlikely to go down below 5.75%? The strategy of

TABLE 16-12   *Constructing Caps, Floors, and Collars on LIBOR*

LIBOR	−3.0%	−3.5%	−4.0%	−4.5%	−5.0%	−5.5%
Total cost						
(per million)	−7,500.00	−8,750.00	−10,000.00	−11,250.00	−12,500.00	−13,750.00
Buy a put						
(Strike=94.75)	−675.00	−675.00	−675.00	−675.00	−675.00	−50.00
Total cost						
(with the put)	−8,175.00	−9,425.00	−10,675.00	−11,925.00	−13,175.00	−13,800.00
Write a call	−6,275.00	−5,025.00	−3,775.00	−2,525.00	−1,275.00	−25.00
Total cost	−13,775.00	−13,775.00	−13,775.00	−13,775.00	−13,775.00	−13,775.00
Buy a put and						
write a call	−6,950.00	−5,700.00	−4,450.00	−3,200.00	−1,950.00	−75.00
Total cost	−14,450.00	−14,450.00	−14,450.00	−14,450.00	−14,450.00	−13,825.00

LIBOR	−6.0%	−6.5%	−7.0%	−7.5%	−8.0%
Total cost					
(per million)	−15,000.00	−16,250.00	−17,500.00	−18,750.00	−20,000.00
Buy a put					
(Strike=94.75)	1,200.00	2,450.00	3,700.00	4,950.00	6,200.00
Total cost					
(with the put)	−13,800.00	−13,800.00	−13,800.00	−13,800.00	−13,800.00
Write a call	600.00	600.00	600.00	600.00	600.00
Total cost	−14,400.00	−15,650.00	−16,900.00	−18,150.00	−19,400.00
Buy a put and					
write a call	1,800.00	3,050.00	4,300.00	5,550.00	6,800.00
Total cost	−13,200.00	−13,200.00	−13,200.00	−13,200.00	−13,200.00

FIGURE 16-5   *Constructing a Cap on LIBOR*

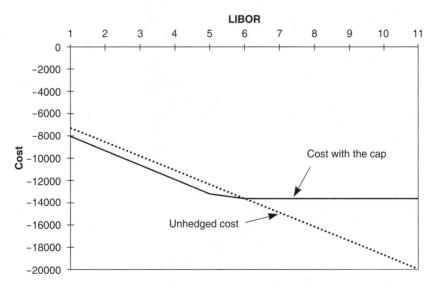

FIGURE 16-6   *Constructing a Floor on LIBOR*

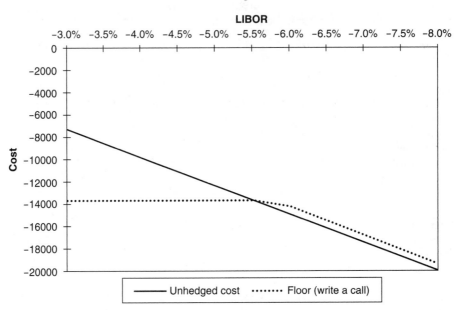

writing a call at a strike of 94.25 will produce an income of 24 × 25 = $600 per million par. If LIBOR goes up, the issuer ends up keeping the call premium as the call finishes out-of-the-money. This cushions the cost of the liability. If LIBOR goes down, the call ends up in-the-money. For example, if LIBOR = 5%, we can see from Table 16-12 that the cost is $1,000,000 \times .05 \times \frac{90}{360} = \$12,500$, but the call is worth $[5.75 - 5.00] = 0.75$ or 75 basis points. This is equal to 75 × 25 = $1275; hence, the total cost becomes 12,500 + 1,275 = 13,775. In fact, for all levels of LIBOR below 5%, the cost is 13,775. The payoffs are shown in Figure 16-6. This establishes a **floor** on the cost.

Let us say that the issuer would like to cap LIBOR by buying a put option on Eurodollar futures but would like to finance a part of this purchase by selling a call option on Eurodollar futures. In this case, the issuer would like to get a cap if LIBOR were to go up but is willing to give up some of the gains if LIBOR were to go down. This is known as a **collar** on LIBOR. Note from Table 16-11 that this strategy locks in a total cost of 13,200 when LIBOR goes above 5.75% and a total cost of 14,450 when LIBOR goes below 5.25%. This is illustrated in Figure 16-7.

We can thus use Eurodollar futures and options on Eurodollar futures to create swaps, caps, floors, and collars on LIBOR. Since futures and options on Eurodollars are listed in exchanges, they tend to be standardized with a limited set of maturities, strike prices, and so on. Also, they are mostly indexed to 90-day LIBOR. In order to get better customization, it is necessary to go to the dealer markets.

FIGURE 16-7   *Constructing a Collar on LIBOR*

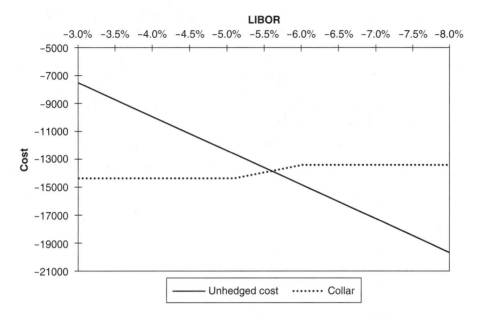

TABLE 16-13

USD Cap and Floors Mid-Volatilities (September 8, 2000. Closing Prices as of 3:00 P.M. EST)

Cap and Floors Spot Mid-Volatilities	
1 year	10.250
2 year	13.300
3 year	14.800
4 year	15.600
5 year	15.900
7 year	16.150
10 year	15.800
15 year	14.350
20 year	13.100

Source: Tullett & Tokyo Liberty Inc.

Valuation of Caps

Black's model of options on futures is widely used in the cap markets. In fact, in the cap market, market makers quote bid-offer spreads in terms of implied volatility. Black's model is the basis for computing implied volatility in the cap market. Some illustrative volatility quotes are shown in Table 16.13 for caps and floors ranging from 1 to 20 years in maturity.

Example 16-9:

Consider a cap on three-month LIBOR. Let R denote the three-month LIBOR, and let the cap rate be set at 5%. Let the notional principal be N. The cap is reset every three months. The payoff of the cap on a reset date is

$$N \frac{1}{4} \max [0, R - 5\%].$$

Suppose that the cap rate is K and that the interest payments are made at times as shown in the following timeline:

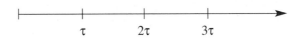

The payment at the next reset is based on LIBOR at the previous reset. That is, R_k is the rate set at $k\tau$, and the amount paid at $(k + 1)\tau$ is given by

$$\frac{1}{4} N \max [0, R_k - K],$$

where N is the notional principal.

Let the forward rate between $k\tau$ and $(k + 1)\tau$ be denoted by F_k. Then the payoff of the cap can be written as of $k\tau$ as

$$N \frac{\tau}{1 + F_k \tau} \max [0, R_k - K].$$

Recognizing that at $k\tau$, $R_k = F_k$ and applying Black's model, we can price the caplet as

$$\frac{N\tau}{1 + \tau F_k} e^{-rk\tau} [F_k N(d_1) - K N(d_2)],$$

where

$$d_1 = \frac{\ln \left[\dfrac{F_k}{K} \right] + \dfrac{1}{2} k\tau \sigma_F^2}{\sigma_F \sqrt{k\tau}};$$

$$d_2 = d_1 - \sigma_F \sqrt{k\tau}.$$

Figure 16-8 shows how to implement the Black's model on a spreadsheet. Figure 16-9 illustrates the calculation of implied volatility.

We can compute the implied volatility by equating the market price to the model price. In Figure 16-9, the implied is 15.18%.

FIGURE 16-8   *Cap Valuation*

						Caplet 1	Caplet 2	Caplet 3	Caplet 4
Settlement Date:				8/10/98					
Model used:				Black's Model					
Derivative:				CAPS					
INPUTS TO THE MODEL						Caplet 1	Caplet 2	Caplet 3	Caplet 4
Forward curve:					$d1=$	-0.4966	0.3632	0.8556	1.2058
					$d2=$	-0.5416	0.2996	0.7777	1.1158
Maturity	0.25	0.5	0.75	1	$N(d1)=$	0.309721	0.641781	0.803891	0.886053
Forward					$N(d2)=$	0.294033	0.617753	0.781615	0.867746
Rates	5.50%	5.75%	6.00%	6.25%					
						116.9041	509.0195	999.4206	1520.011
Terms:					CAP				
1 Notional	1000000				VALUE	**3145.36**	0.315%		
2 Index	3								
Maturity					✧				
3 Volatility	9.00%				Market				
4 Strike	5.63%				Value	4000			
5 Riskless rate	5.50%								

FIGURE 16-9   *Implied Volatility from Caps*

						Caplet 1	Caplet 2	Caplet 3	Caplet 4
Settlement Date:		8/10/98							
Model used:		Black's Model							
Derivative:		CAPS							
INPUTS TO THE MODEL						Caplet 1	Caplet 2	Caplet 3	Caplet 4
Forward curve:					$d1=$	-0.2698	0.2501	0.5499	0.7641
					$d2=$	-0.3457	0.1428	0.4184	0.6123
Maturity	0.25	0.5	0.75	1	$N(d1)=$	0.393646	0.598764	0.7088	0.777596
Forward					$N(d2)=$	0.364773	0.556778	0.662178	0.729828
Rates	5.50%	5.75%	6.00%	6.25%					
						270.9359	739.0497	1240.229	1749.785
Terms:					CAP				
1 Notional	1000000				VALUE	**4000.00**			
2 Index	3								
Maturity									
3 Volatility	15.18%				Market				
4 Strike	5.63%				Value	4000			
5 Riskless rate	5.50%								
					Implied Volatility	15.18%			

INTEREST-RATE SWAPS

Transactions in which two parties agree to make periodic payments to one another computed on the basis of specific interest rates on a notional principal amount are known as interest-rate swaps. In most interest-rate swaps, there are two legs or payments; the payment made by one counterparty is based on a floating rate of interest,

FIGURE 16-10   *A Five-Year Intermediate Interest-Rate Swap*

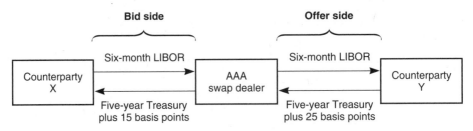

such as the LIBOR, while the payment made by the other counterparty is based on a fixed rate of interest or a different floating interest rate. Participants in the swap market use interest-rate swaps to transform one type of interest liability into another. The swap transaction is used as a tool to manage their interest-rate exposure or to lock in a predetermined profit level.

In Figure 16-10, the basic structure of interest-rate swap is depicted. The counterparty Y borrows in the floating-rate market by issuing a five-year floater (say, at the LIBOR plus 1%), which is reset every six months; and counterparty X borrows in the fixed-rate market by issuing a five-year note (say, at 12%). They then enter into a swap transaction with a AAA swap dealer. The swap allows Y to receive a six-month LIBOR every six months. In turn, Y will pay a fixed rate of the five-year Treasury plus 25 basis points. Let us assume that the five-year Treasury is yielding 11%. Then the cost to Y will be 11.25% + 1% = 12.25%.

Counterparty X pays floating-rate swap payments of the six-month LIBOR and receives from the swap dealer the five-year Treasury plus 15 basis points. The total cost for X is 12% − 11.15% + LIBOR or LIBOR + 75 basis points.

The swap will turn out to be beneficial if Y's borrowing cost in the fixed-rate market exceeds 12.25% and X's borrowing cost in the floating-rate market exceeds the LIBOR plus 75 basis points. Usually, the floating-rate borrower (X) will be a corporation and the fixed-rate borrower (Y) will be a bank. If the bank is in a better position to monitor and manage the risks of X, then a bilateral contract, such as swap, may benefit both parties. For example, Y may have an informational advantage relative to the typical floating-rate lender. Moreover, Y is in the business of evaluating the risks of borrowers and, as a result, may have acquired greater monitoring and risk-management skills over time. In addition, Y also has an equilibrium supply of borrowers with differing borrowing requirements. As a result, Y's search costs are lower in terms of identifying and matching two counterparties with complementary borrowing needs. For this service, Y typically gets a fee. The advantages of better information and lower transactions costs (of monitoring, for instance) are reflected in the swap transaction.

The foregoing observations suggest that it is necessary to admit differential information and the costs of monitoring and searching to rationalize a swap transaction.

Swaps can also be arranged to manage the risk of specific asset or liability exposures. An **asset swap,** for example, combines an existing asset, such as a bond or

FIGURE 16-11   *Asset Swap*

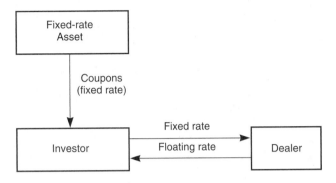

a note, with a swap to create a different risk-return profile. Consider an investor who owns a fixed-rate asset. He can engage in an interest rate swap as shown in Figure 16-11.

The investor swaps the coupons with the swap dealer for floating rate revenues. If the fixed-rate asset held by the investor is highly illiquid, then the swap may allow the investor to "trade" the cash flows of this illiquid asset at a competitive floating rate.

The underlying asset used in an asset swap can be a zero-coupon bond, CMO, or a premium or a discount bond. This implies that the swap payments and netting of cash flows between the counterparties can vary to suit the needs of the counterparties. If the asset is a mortgage-backed security, then it will be paying monthly cash flows that go toward interest and amortizing principal payments. Such assets can be combined with **index amortizing swaps,** where the notional principal is amortized to precisely mirror the assets's remaining principal amount. Index amortizing swaps use the following terms:

- *Notional principal amount* is the original amount at the beginning of the swap.
- *Lock-Out Period* is the period during which there is no amortization of the notional amount. This is specified on the trade date of the swap.
- *Stated final maturity* is the expiry date of the swap. The swap may amortize to zero before this date.
- *Amortization Schedule* applies to the notional principal after the lock-out period and is specified in the index amortization swap. It typically depends on the levels of some chosen interest rate index.

The amortization rate is computed at the beginning of each reset period (after the lock-out period) based on the level of the interest-rate index. The interest-rate index used can be chosen from LIBOR (three months or six months) or any benchmark Treasury rates (2, 3, 5, 10, or 30). Table 16-14 is an illustration of the amortization schedule in an index amortizing swap.

Some swaps have a **clean up call,** whereby the swap can be called away if the remaining notional amount drops to about 5% of the original amount.

TABLE 16-14		
Amortization Schedule	Notional amount:	$500,000,000
	Lock-out period:	3 years
	Final maturity:	6 years
	Reset:	Quarterly
	Index:	3-month LIBOR

Three-Month LIBOR	Amortization/Period
4.50%	100%
5.50%	15%
6.50%	5%
7.50%	0%

FIGURE 16-12   *Index Amortizing Swaps*

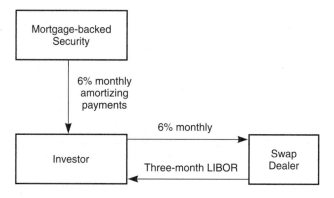

As the swap structure in Figure 16-12 shows, the investor has hedged the position in the asset through the swap. As rates drop, the asset prepays, but the swap also increases the amortization rate.

Diversity of Swap Contracts

In addition to the size of the swap markets, the diversity of contracts that are structured in the market bears some attention. Swaps are structured on different underlying instruments with different maturity dates. To gain a perspective on the diversity of this market, examine Table 16-15. There are five basic types of swaps. Fixed-to-floating in the same currency, floating-to-floating in the same currency, their counterparts across two currencies, and currency swaps that are fixed-to-fixed. In addition, there are markets that are closely related to swap markets.

• Interest-rate caps. This agreement caps the interest obligations at a predetermined rate for a prespecified period of time. For example, firm A agrees to sell a cap on a three-month LIBOR at 6.5% for every quarter for the next two years. In return, firm B pays firm A an agreed-upon compensation.

TABLE 16-15   *Diversity of Swaps Market*

Type of Swap	*Term of Swap*	*Remarks*
Interest-rate swaps	2 to 10 years	Same currency, one party pays fixed and the other pays floating.
Basis swaps	2 to 7 years	Same currency, parties pay floating cash flows keyed to different indices.
Currency swaps, fixed-to-fixed	2 to 10 years	Different currencies, both pay fixed-interest payments.
Currency swaps, fixed-to-floating	2 to 10 years	Different currencies, one pays fixed and the other floating.
Currency swaps, floating-to-floating	2 to 10 years	Different currencies, both pay floating interest payments.

- Swaptions. Bank A may sell an option to bank B, whereby bank B will have the option to enter into a swap any time before a predetermined date at predetermined terms of exchange.
- Floor. An investor holding a portfolio of floating-rate notes whose coupons are indexed to LIBOR might wish to buy a floor on LIBOR. If the floor rate is 6% and LIBOR falls below 6%, then the difference is paid to the investor on the agreed-upon notional principal.

The swap-related products, such as caps, floor, and swaptions, are dealer market products. Since they are highly customized, they differ from the caps and floors discussed earlier in the context of options on Eurodollar futures contracts. These Eurodollar futures options are standardized (90-day LIBOR, fixed strike prices and maturities) and are not liquid beyond six months.

Risk Characteristics of Swaps

In general, swaps are subject to three distinct sources of risk: interest-rate risk, default risk, and foreign currency risk. These components of risk interplay in subtle ways that must be understood to manage the total risk of swaps. To put these risk characteristics of swaps into proper perspective, consider some broad risk questions for the matched swap transaction in Figure 16-10. In a matched swap transaction, the intermediary has brokered the swap. In this case, the intermediary faces no interest-rate risk in the absence of default by either of the two parties. The floating-rate borrower ends up with a fixed-rate obligation, which means that his or her risk is the same as a fixed-rate note with a coupon of 12.25% with the same term and liquidity features (so long as there is no default). In a similar way, the fixed-rate borrowers ends up with floating obligations at a cost of the LIBOR plus 75 basis points. His or her risk is the same as that of a floating-rate borrower with the reset dates and payment dates as specified in the swap contract (so long as there is no default).

There is a positive probability of default in swaps, but the impact of default is drastically different for the three players in Figure 16-10. For the intermediary, default by one counterparty moves the transaction from a matched book to a forward contract.

To see this, let us assume that the floating-rate borrower defaults. Then the intermediary will have to pay 11.15% and accept a payment of the LIBOR from the solvent counterparty. This is obviously a forward purchase of the LIBOR, which may either have a positive or negative value at the time of default. For the counterparty that defaulted, the effect of default is to move the transaction from a forward contract to a straight floating-rate debt contract. Of course, the precise outcome will depend on the contingency provisions that were written into the swap contract. For the solvent counterparty, the effect should have no consequences, as the financial intermediary performs the role of a clearinghouse.

The default risk in a swap can be quite important and can arise due to a number of factors. A swap defect by Hammersmith and Fulham in the late 1980s occurred when the swap agreement was declared unlawful. As the enclosed article by Cohen (1989) shows, the default risk can be quite significant.

When Fingers Get Burned

NORMA COHEN reports on the implications of local councils' interest rate swaps

When the London borough of Hammersmith was finally barred last February by the Department of the Environment from making payments due under its interest rate swap and options contracts, it opened up a legal Pandora's box that it has since been unable to close.

The immediate issue is over the right of local authorities to conduct capital markets operations—whether the purpose is for reducing interest rate risk or for raising revenues.

Initially, the consideration appeared to be a political one. The Conservative Government objected to authorities using fee income from the capital markets to escape from Whitehall's restrictions on local council spending.

However, in the process of making a political point, the DoE has unleashed the spectre of a series of lawsuits between banks, local government, central government and money brokers that could swamp the courts for years to come. It has also called into question the legality of swaps with all non-corporate entities, such as UK building societies, which have only recently begun to use the swap markets to reduce their own exposure to volatile interest rates.

Larger building societies are specifically permitted under current UK law to conduct capital markets operations aimed at reducing risk. But when they agree to a swap, bankers have no way of knowing what its actual purpose is. Therefore, any transaction with a building society could be at risk.

The Corporations Act of 1988 affirms that swap agreements entered into in good faith with corporate borrowers are sound. But there is no such safe harbour for noncorporate entities. This category includes any mutually-owned organisation such as a friendly society or charitable trust or any quasi-governmental body which uses capital market instruments.

"This is the most significant legal question for the swaps market since it began in the early 1980s," said Mr. Michael Canby, a partner at Linklaters and Paines and a specialist in capital markets transactions. The total market in interest rate swaps was the equivalent of $1,010 billion at the end of 1988, according to the International Swap Dealers Association. Of that, $52.27bn were interest rate swaps in sterling.

At the height of its activities in interest rate swaps, Hammersmith alone accounted for nearly 10 per cent of the sterling market. While swaps with local authorities account for only a small portion of overall swaps business, the market has been badly shaken by the realisation that contracts are not inviolate after

Source: *Financial Times* (September 6, 1989). Reprinted by permission.

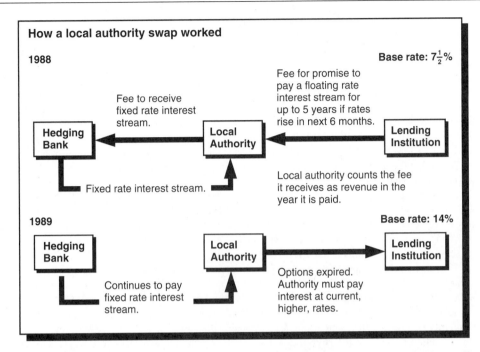

How a local authority swap worked

1988   **Base rate: 7½%**

Fee to receive fixed rate interest stream.

Fee for promise to pay a floating rate interest stream for up to 5 years if rates rise in next 6 months.

Hedging Bank   **Local Authority**   **Lending Institution**

Fixed rate interest stream.

Local authority counts the fee it receives as revenue in the year it is paid.

1989   **Base rate: 14%**

Hedging Bank   **Local Authority**   **Lending Institution**

Continues to pay fixed rate interest stream.

Options expired. Authority must pay interest at current, higher, rates.

all. This has caused bankers in the UK and abroad to reassess all their swap counterparties in an effort to plug the legal loopholes.

On October 4, the High Court will consider a request by the District Auditor to rule all of Hammersmith's interest rate swap and options contracts *ultra vires*—outside its legal jurisdiction. The auditor will argue that the council never had the legal authority to enter into contracts that at one time had a notional principal value of about £5bn, and will ask the court to rule all of them void. Such a ruling would mean that payments to bank counterparties, estimated at about £186m over the next five years if interest rates remain stable, will not need to be paid. Hammersmith, a Labour-controlled council, has already said it does not intend to contest the auditor's case.

However, the banks to whom the fees are owed have mounted a vigorous legal challenge to the auditor's charges, enlisting the services of the most expensive legal advice in the City of London to defend the right of Labour-controlled Hammersmith to engage in capital markets activities.

But whatever the High Court decides, the matter will not be laid to rest.

If the swaps are ruled legal, it will force local authorities to pay huge sums to bankers. This could spell financial ruin for several local authorities, raising the question of whether local governments can go bankrupt and whether the central government has any obligation to stand behind them if they do.

If the swaps are all ruled illegal, as the Audit Commission insists, bankers stand to lose hundreds of millions of pounds, not just from Hammersmith but from every authority which has arranged similar transactions. It will hobble local authorities—and potentially all non-corporate entities—in their efforts to use the capital markets to raise funds and reduce risk.

If the court rules that some of the transactions are legal—a view that many bankers privately believe is the most likely—it will leave the judge to decide which of the banks must be paid and which need not. This will leave the banks, which have presented a united front on the matter up until now, to fight it out among themselves over which transactions are the legal ones. The court proceedings are likely to make

(continued)

public some unwelcome details about how each bank does business, possibly exposing some sloppy lending practices.

Bankers and their legal advisers agree that it is unlikely that the DoE, when it provoked the crisis last February by refusing to sanction payments by Hammersmith to its bankers, understood the far-reaching consequences of its actions.

While some cynical bankers argue that the DoE intended to punish the banking community for its tacit assistance in local authorities' fund-raising efforts, it is more likely that the Department simply did not have the technical expertise to allow it to foresee all the problems which would unfold.

In February, Mr Nicholas Ridley, the Environment Secretary at the time, declined a request by Hammersmith to be allowed to make payments without its councillors becoming subject to fines or disqualification. The action provoked a crisis, forcing Hammersmith and four other local councils to hold up millions of pounds in payments to banks.

The action did not come out of the blue. In July 1988, the District Auditor for Hammersmith—Deloitte Haskins and Sells—told Hammersmith that it believed its activities in the swaps and options markets were probably illegal and that it should begin winding down its position and seek further legal advice. While Hammersmith did seek legal advice in July 1988 and wind down its portfolio, it continued to make payments under existing contracts.

In 1988, the Audit Commission circulated legal opinions it had sought with respect to interest rate swap and option agreements. While the Commission's leading counsel felt that those swaps entered into for purposes of managing debt were probably legal, he took the view that those entered into for the purpose of raising fee income were probably not. The Commission's junior counsel took the view that all local authority swap and options agreements were probably illegal.

In presenting the case to the High Court, the Audit Commission and Deloitte Haskins & Sells are taking the view of the Commission's junior counsel and asking that all of Hammersmith's transactions be ruled *ultra vires*. This position is likely to be the starting point for a series of legal battles:

- If the High Court rules in favour of the District Auditor, the lenders will continue to appeal until all avenues are exhausted.
- Bankers have already begun to comb through their local authority swap and options portfolios for those transactions in which the local authority was the net beneficiary—in other words, the bank made a net payment instead of receiving one in return. The banks will then sue the local authorities for return of these proceeds, arguing that those contracts were *ultra vires* as well.
- Banks are also considering whether to proceed against the money brokers which arranged the transactions on their behalf.

The role of the money brokers is somewhat complex since they only acted as middlemen. Banks habitually demanded to know the name of the local authority they were matched with, with many refusing transactions linked to rate-capped boroughs. But bankers still argue that they dealt with the brokers in good faith, believing brokers would not match them to illegal transactions.

What the banks knew and when they knew it remains a central issue in the whole case. The banks' affidavit before the High Court argues that the Audit Commission never specifically told them that the transactions were illegal and they had no reason to believe they were. Therefore, even if swaps and options are deemed to be off limits for councils in the future, it is unfair to punish banks retrospectively.

Furthermore, the bankers say, the Local Government Act of 1972 does not require them to ask local councils in advance whether the transaction is legal. But several banks did wonder whether the transactions were legal. Several banks and securities houses had sought counsel's advice in 1987 and 1988 about the advisability of entering into swap and options transactions with local authorities. Linklaters and Paines, for instance, had come to the conclusion several years ago that the authorities might be exceeding their competence by entering into those transactions and advised clients accordingly.

The integrity of the clearing process is a function of the capital adequacy of the intermediary and its credit-worthiness. It is in this context that the rules pertaining to the capital adequacy of swap market makers proposed by Federal Reserve and the Bank for International Settlements (BIS) have some important implications. We examine them later in this chapter.

In a foreign currency swap, there is a foreign currency risk exposure as well. In the absence of default, the intermediary has a matched position; when there is default, the transaction moves into an open forward contract on foreign currency, in addition to the intermediary assuming the interest-rate risk. For the solvent counterparty, there is no change in the transaction when there is default. For example, a U.S. company pays £1 million sterling and receives $2 million U.S. at an exchange rate of two dollars per pound sterling. This transaction will be reversed at a later date that is specified in the contract now.

The risk characteristics associated with reset dates, payment dates, index maturity, and cash flows are less easy to characterize without formal arguments. If the floating leg of the swap resets frequently and does not have many optionlike features, then the risk of the swap may be shown to be essentially that of the fixed side plus the face amount outstanding under some simplifying assumptions. We show that this is the case later in the chapter.

Valuation of Swaps

In this section, a framework is developed for the valuation of swaps. Although the discussion will primarily focus on interest-rate swaps, the insights are applicable to other swap contracts.

The valuation of floating-rate payments in swaps has received some attention recently in the academic literature. Cox, Ingersoll, and Ross (1980) and Ramaswamy and Sundaresan (1986) have developed arbitrage-free models of pricing floating-rate payments. Ramaswamy and Sundaresan (1986) develop a continuous-time model of pricing floaters that are subject to default risk. The model accommodates collars, drop lock, and conversion features, but requires continuous resets and payments. Interest-rate swaps have also begun to attract formal analyses. See Bicksler and Chen (1986); Smith, Smithson, and Wakeman (1986, 1988); Turnbull (1987); and Sundaresan (1991). Cooper and Mello (1991) study the default risk of swaps. They study, in a partial equilibrium setting, the default risk of swaps, the spreads due to default, and the possible wealth transfers due to swaps.

The valuation of swaps requires precise specification of the timing of resets and payments. In addition, we need to specify the index maturity to which floating payments are linked. As before, let s_i be the ith reset date. Let τ be the index (LIBOR) maturity. Furthermore, let $t_p(s_i)$ be the payment date associated with the reset date s_i. Most interest rate swaps are known as generic interest rate swaps. In such swaps, typically the floating index is six-month LIBOR so that $\tau = 6$ months. Also in these swaps, the reset date (s_i) precedes the payment date $t_p(s_i)$ by exactly the index maturity τ (six months). Generic interest rate swaps are particularly easy to value. The settlement date in such swaps are typically the first reset dates. We illustrate the general principles of valuing generic interest rate swaps with a simple example next.

Example 16-10:

Table 16-16 shows the prices of zero-coupon bonds (strips) and their yields as of August 25, 1995. What is the swap rate on a two-year generic interest rate swap? Assume that the floating rates reset every six months. The first reset occurs on August 25, 1995. The credit risk of the counterparties can be ignored.

In the first approach, we will calculate the six-month forward rates for every reset date. Then, we will calculate the present value of all these forward rates. The fixed-rate which has the same present value is the swap rate. We will illustrate these calculations now.

As of August 25, 1995, the six-month spot rate is 5.50%. This is the rate to which the floating leg is reset. At date $t = 6$, the floating leg will pay 5.50%. This should be discounted back to $t = 0$ by using the six-month zero price at $t = 0$, which is 0.9732. The discounted value is $0.0550 \times 0.9732 = 0.0535$. This is shown in Table 16-17.

At date $t = 0$, we can calculate the six-month forward rate that will prevail from $t = 6$ to $t = 12$. This rate, $f_o(6, 12)$ is given by

$$\left[1 + \frac{0.0550}{2}\right]\left[1 + \frac{f_o(6,\ 12)}{2}\right] = \left[1 + \frac{0.0570}{2}\right]^2.$$

TABLE 16-16

Valuation of Swaps

	Zero yields on 8-25-1995 Settlement Date 8/25/95		
Maturity (in months)	*Percentage Yield*	*Zero Prices*	*Percentage Forward Rates*
6	5.50	0.9732	5.5000
12	5.70	0.9453	5.9002
18	5.90	0.9165	6.3006
24	6.20	0.8850	7.1026
30	6.50	0.8522	7.7044

TABLE 16-17   *Pricing a Two-Year Swap*
Method 1: Set PV of Floating Equal to PV of Fixed

	0	6	12	18	24	Time
		$t = 6$	$t = 12$	$t = 18$	$t = 24$	*Sum*
Floating payments		5.50%	5.90%	6.30%	7.10%	
Zero prices		0.9732	0.9453	0.9165	0.8850	3.7201
PV (float)		0.0535	0.0558	0.0577	0.0629	0.2299
Total:		0.2299				
Swap rate: (0.22991)/3.7201 = 6.1802%						

Thus, $f_o(6, 12) = 5.90\%$. The floating leg will reset to this rate at $t = 6$ but will actually pay this amount at $t = 12$. So, the present value at $t = 0$ of receiving 5.90% at $t = 12$ is

$$0.059 \times 0.9453 = 0.0558.$$

This is shown in Table 16-17.

We can also calculate the relevant forward rates to which the floating leg will reset at $t = 12$ and $t = 18$ for payments at $t = 18$ and $t = 24$, respectively. The present value of all floating payments is 0.2299 as shown in Table 16-17. Suppose that the fixed-leg of the swap pays x (in decimals) at dates $t = 6, 12, 18,$ and 24. Then the present value of these fixed payments is

$$x[0.9732 + 0.9453 + 0.9165 + 0.8850] = 3.7201x.$$

Setting the present value of floating leg equal to the present value of fixed leg, we get

$$3.7201x = 0.2299$$

or $$x = 0.061802.$$

Hence, the effective swap rate is $x = 6.1802\%$.

Another approach to pricing interest-rate swaps is to replicate the cash flows of the swap. Consider the two-year generic interest-rate swap in the example. Every six months, the floating leg of this swap pays the six-month rate that prevailed on the last reset date. The floating leg can be replicated as follows: take $1 at date $t = 0$ and invest it into the prevailing six-month rate. At date $t = 6$, we get $1 plus the six-month rate. The six-month rate that we receive at $t = 6$ exactly replicates what we would have received in the floating leg of the swap at $t = 6$. Next, with the $1 remaining at $t = 6$, we can invest in the six-month rate at $t = 6$. At $t = 12$, this strategy will produce a cash flow of $1 plus the six-month interest rate that prevailed at $t = 6$. We can keep this interest at $t = 12$ (which exactly replicates the cash flow of the floating leg at $t = 12$) and roll $1 at $t = 12$ into the then prevailing six-month rate. Proceeding this way, we will get the cash flows described in Table 16-18. Let i_6, i_{12}, and i_{18} be the six-month interest rates at dates $t = 6, 12,$ and 18, respectively.

Note that our strategy cost us $1 at $t = 0$ and produced cash flows of i_0 at $t = 6$, i_6 at $t = 12$, i_{12} at $t = 18$, and $1 + i_{18}$ at $t = 24$. This is exactly what the floating leg of the swap would have paid except that at $t = 24$, the floating leg will not pay the balloon of $1. In order to account for this, we issue a zero-coupon bond at $t = 0$ maturing at $t = 24$. This produces a cash inflow equal to the price of the zero-coupon bond at $t = 0$ but produces an outflow of $1 at $t = 24$ (to pay the balloon). We summarize these transactions in Table 16-19. If the fixed-leg pays x at each date, then its present value is

$$x[b(0, 6) + b(0, 12) + b(0, 18) + b(0, 24)].$$

TABLE 16-18

$t = 0$	$t = 6$	$t = 12$	$t = 18$	$t = 24$
1. Invest \$1 in six-month rate	Receive \$(1 + 0.055)			
2.	Keep 0.055 as interest and roll \$1 into six-month rate at $t = 6$	Receive \$(1 + i_6)		
3.		Keep i_6 as interest and roll \$1 into six-month rate at $t = 12$	Receive \$(1 + i_{12})	
4.			Keep i_{12} as interest and roll \$1 into six-month rate at $t = 18$	Receive \$(1 + i_{18})
Cash flows received	$i_0 = 5.5\%$	i_6	i_{12}	$1 + i_{18}$

TABLE 16-19　*Arbitrage Recipe*

$t = 0$	$t = 6$	$t = 12$	$t = 18$	$t = 24$
Cost: \$1 (from Table 16-18)				
Cash flows (from Table 16-18)	i_0	i_6	i_{12}	$1 + i_{18}$
Issue a zero-coupon bond maturing at $t = 24$				
Proceeds: $b(0, 24)$				-1
Net cash flows $1 - b(0, 24)$	i_0	i_6	i_{12}	i_{18}

Since the present value of floating cash flows must equal the present value of fixed cash flows, we get

$$1 - b(0, 24) = x[b(0, 6) + b(0, 12) + b(0, 18) + b(0, 24)]$$

or

$$1 = x[b(0, 6) + b(0, 12) + b(0, 18) + b(0, 24)] + b(0, 24). \qquad (16.10)$$

Note in Equation 16.10 that the right-hand side is the present value of all the fixed (coupon) payments plus the present value of the balloon payments. Equation 16.10 says that the present value is equal to 1. In other words, the swap rate, x, is the two-year par bond yield. This provides us with another approach to valuing swaps. We il-

TABLE 16-20   *Pricing a Two-Year Swap*
Method 2: Valuing by the Par Bond Yield

			Settlement Date 8/25/95			
			Coupon Bond Prices			
			c = 5%		*c = 6.1802%*	
Maturity (in months)	*Percent Yield*	*Zero Prices*	*Cash Flows*	*PV*	*Cash Flows*	*PV*
6	5.50	0.9732	2.5	2.43309	3.0901	3.007397
12	5.70	0.9453	2.5	2.3633684	3.0901	2.921218
18	5.90	0.9165	2.5	2.2911892	3.0901	2.832002
24	6.20	0.8850	102.5	90.71711	103.0901	91.23937
			Sum	97.80		100.00

lustrate this approach for the following swap example. In Table 16-20, we have tried a coupon of 5% (annualized). The present value of this bond is

$$2.5 \times 0.9732 + 2.5 \times 0.9453 + 2.5 \times 0.9165 + 102.5 \times 0.8850,$$

which is equal to 97.80. The bond sells at a discount. When the coupon is set at 6.1802%, it sells at par. Clearly, this is the swap rate. Both approaches led us to the same conclusion. In addition, as shown earlier, we can value swaps using Eurodollar futures. We illustrate in Example 16-11 how to value a forward swap using Eurodollar futures.

Example 16-11:

The settlement date is February 25, and the Eurodollar futures prices are shown in Table 16-21. Based on this information, how will you determine the one-year swap rate on a *forward swap* that starts on March 19, 2000 and ends on March 19,

TABLE 16-21
Eurodollar Futures Prices

SD	*2/25/00*
Maturity	*Settlement*
03/19/00	93.798
06/19/00	93.480
09/19/00	93.255
12/19/00	93.025
03/19/01	92.920
06/18/01	92.820
09/17/01	92.765
12/17/01	92.700
03/18/02	92.735
06/17/02	92.725
09/16/02	92.720
12/16/02	92.655

FIGURE 16-13   *Eurodollar Futures Strips and Their Use in Swap Pricing*

	C	D	E	F	G	H	I	J	K	L	M
1											
2											
3											
4		Today's date		2/24/00							
5											
6		Settlement date		2/25/00							
7											
8					Spot LIBOR from 2/25 to 3/19						
9											
10							100/(1+F14*(D14-F6)/360)				
11											
12		Maturity	Futures	Forward	Forward	Zero	Zero	Day Count			
13			Price	Rate	Price	Price	Yield	30/360			
14	1	03/19/00		6.040%	99.616	99.616	5.861%	24	=DAYS360(F6,D16)		
15	2	06/19/00	93.798	6.203%	98.440	98.061	6.279%	114			
16	3	09/19/00	93.480	6.520%	98.361	96.454	6.474%	204			
17	4	12/19/00	93.255	6.745%	98.324	94.837	6.597%	294			
18	5	03/19/01	93.025	6.975%	98.286	93.212	6.700%	384			
19	6	06/18/01	92.920	7.080%	98.242	91.573	6.814%	473			
20	7	09/17/01	92.820	7.180%	98.217	89.941	6.908%	562	=((100/H16)^(180/J16)-1)*2		
21	8	12/17/01	92.765	7.235%	98.204	88.325	6.973%	652			
22	9	03/18/02	92.700	7.300%	98.188	86.725	7.021%	743			
23	10	06/17/02	92.735	7.265%	98.197	85.161	7.072%	832			
24	11	09/16/02	92.725	7.275%	98.194	83.623	7.114%	921			
25	12	12/16/02	92.720	7.280%	98.193	82.112	7.142%	1,011			
26	13	03/17/03	92.655								
27											

2001? The swap's reset date precedes the payment date by one quarter. Assume that the start date is the first reset date. Assume that the spot LIBOR between February 25, 2000, March 19, 2000, is 6.040%.

Eurodollar futures prices are rounded to three decimals. In calculations, we have used the actual prices.

Since the payment date *follows* the reset date by one quarter, we need to use the Eurodollar futures price for maturity March 19, 2000 (start date) to determine the forward rate on June 19, 2000 (the first payment date). In Figure 16-13, the forward rate at June 19, 2000, is 100 − 93.798 = 6.203 (rounded up). The actual spot LIBOR is used for computing the forward price between the settlement date and March 19, 2000. In Figure 16-14 we show some sample calculations that are based on the data from Figure 16-13. Based on such calculations we construct Figure 16-15, which shows how to compute the forward swap rate.

RISK MANAGEMENT OF SWAPS

Commercial banks and investment banks act as intermediaries in many swap transactions. The swap books of intermediaries present unique risk-management problems. Until a suitable counterparty is found, an intermediary "warehouses" the swap without having arranged an offsetting swap and thereby assumes the position of a

FIGURE 16-14   *Sample Calculations*

	A	B	C	D	E	F	G	H	I	J
2										
3										
4										
5										
6							=100/(1+0.0604*(23/360))			
7										
8										
9	0	Zero price for 2/25 to 3/19				99.615594				
10		100/[1+0.06040*(24/360)]								
11							=(100-E17)/100			
12	1	Forward rate between 9/19 and 12/19								
13		(100-93.255)/100				0.06745				
14										
15	2	Forward price between 9/19 and 12/19								
16										
17		100/[1+0.0.06745*(91/360)]				98.323596				
18										
19	3	Zero price for maturity on 12/19					=100/(1+S13*(91/360))			
20		This is the same as the								
21		zero price for 9/19 times the forward price								
22		between 9/19 and 12/19:								
23										
24		[96.454] times [98.324]/100				94.837142				
25										
26							=H16*G17/100			
27										
28										

FIGURE 16-15   *Forward Swap Rate (Details)*

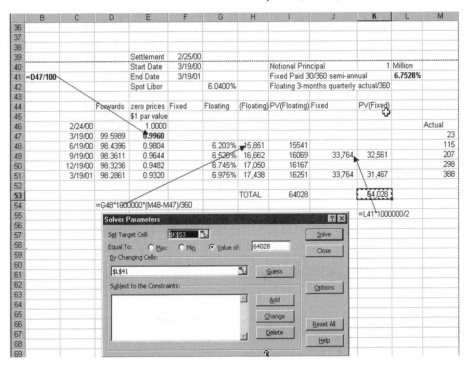

	B	C	D	E	F	G	H	I	J	K	L	M
36												
37												
38												
39				Settlement	2/25/00							
40				Start Date	3/19/00			Notional Principal		1	Million	
41	=D47/100			End Date	3/19/01			Fixed Paid 30/360 semi-annual			6.7528%	
42				Spot Libor		6.0400%		Floating 3-months quarterly actual/360				
43												
44			Forwards	zero prices	Fixed	Floating	(Floating)	PV(Floating)	Fixed		PV(Fixed)	
45				$1 par value								
46		2/24/00		1.0000								Actual
47		3/19/00	99.5989	0.9960								23
48		6/19/00	98.4396	0.9804		6.203%	15,851	15541				115
49		9/19/00	98.3611	0.9644		6.528%	16,662	16069	33,764	32,561		207
50		12/19/00	98.3236	0.9482		6.745%	17,050	16167				298
51		3/19/01	98.2861	0.9320		6.975%	17,438	16251	33,764	31,467		388
52												
53							TOTAL	64028		64,028		
54				=G48*1000000*(M48-M47)/360								
55										=L41*1000000/2		

Solver Parameters

Set Target Cell: K53

Equal To: ○ Max   ○ Min   ● Value of: 64028

By Changing Cells:

L41

Subject to the Constraints:

[Solve]   [Close]   [Guess]   [Options]   [Add]   [Change]   [Delete]   [Reset All]   [Help]

counterparty. In addition to acting as an intermediary to match two counterparties, intermediaries usually assume the credit risks of both counterparties. The credit risks of the counterparties make the swaps somewhat idiosyncratic and make it difficult to organize a liquid secondary market.

The size of the swap book in many cases runs into hundreds of millions or even billions of dollars. The diversity of indices used and such contractual features as options to extend or cancel, caps, and floors make risk measurement and management a difficult task. The Federal Reserve and BIS guidelines issued recently impart a sense of urgency to the tasks of risk measurement and risk management. We provide some highlights of the guidelines next to provide a perspective on the issue of risk management of swaps.

Federal Reserve-BIS Guidelines for Swaps

The Federal Reserve and the Bank for International Settlements have proposed sweeping guidelines for the risk measurement of swaps. These guidelines require the calculation of the marked-to-market value of all interest-rate swaps. In order to perform this task, it is necessary to have a theoretically sound model of swap valuation.

A key concept in the proposed guidelines is the replacement cost of swaps. This is computed by adding only the positive marked-to-market values. To this replacement cost is added a measure of the future potential increases in credit exposure. This future potential exposure measure is calculated by multiplying the total notional value of the contracts by one of the credit conversion factors in Table 16-22.

No potential exposure is calculated for single-currency interest-rate swaps in which payments are made based on two floating-rate indices, that is, floating-to-floating or basis swaps. The credit exposure on these contracts is evaluated solely on the basis of their marked-to-market value. Exchange-rate contracts with an original maturity of 14 days or less are excluded. Instruments traded on exchanges that require daily payment of variation margin are also excluded. The only form of netting recognized is netting by novation. **Netting by novation** is a contract between two counterparties under which any obligation to each other to deliver a given currency on a given date is automatically amalgamated with all the other obligations for the same currency and value date, legally substituting one single-net amount for the previous gross obligations.

TABLE 16-22 *Credit Conversion Factors*	*Remaining Maturity*	*Interest-Rate Swaps*	*Foreign Currency Swaps*
	One year or less	0.0%	1.0%
	Over one year	0.5%	5.0%

In a market that is liquid, bid-offer spreads are small, and the task of marking-to-market is simple. However, swap contracts that are illiquid do not always have a liquid secondary market, and the determination of their value requires two important considerations. First, an appropriately tested swap-valuation model is necessary to perform the task of valuation. Second, the valuation should be done by an agent who has no vested interest in either overstating or understating the value of the swap positions. For example, if the swap desk finds that marking-to-market results in a substantial charge to its profits, it may not report it, fearing adverse senior management action.

Management of the Credit Risk of Swaps

The credit risk associated with swaps is an important component of the overall risk of swaps. The management of credit risk proceeds along two distinct lines:

1. Contractual provisions, contingencies, documentation, and collaterals.
2. Diversification of the swap book across industry segments and market segments.

Much of credit-risk management rests with the structuring of the swap agreements, contingency provisions, termination provisions, and collateral requirements. Usually collateral in the form of readily marketable securities are demanded from the participant with weaker credit to guard against potential credit risk.

In setting aside the capital needed to support swap activities, it is first necessary to mark the swaps to market, so as to correctly determine the replacement cost of swaps. This requires a properly calibrated model for valuing swaps in general.

Once this is done and the interest-rate exposure is properly hedged, as indicated in the previous section, the credit risk of the book has to be aggregated. For this it is useful to subdivide the swaps into two groups: one in which the intermediary is paying fixed and the other in which the intermediary is paying floating. Within each of these groups, swaps must be further classified across different credit-risk categories, and then marked-to-market and aggregated within those credit-risk classifications. This will enable the management of the swap book to identify which of the swap agreements have significant replacement costs due to deteriorating credit risk and to what extent the swap book is reasonably matched. Marking-to-market will effectively indicate the health of the swap book upon the termination of each swap agreement (voluntary or involuntary) in the book. If there is a net loss, then the capital set aside should be sufficient to meet those losses.

Just how important is the credit risk? ISDA conducted a study over the 10-year period 1981 to 1991 in which they found that the losses amounted to about $358 million. As a fraction of the notional principal, this is 0.0115%, a small amount. This is not a proper way to estimate the credit loss. The notional principal of a swap often significantly overestimates the true value of the swap. On a mark-to-market basis, the loss percentage was 0.46%. We enclose an article by Liebowitz (1990) to illustrate some issues concerning default risk in swaps.

Will the ISDA Default Study Impress the Regulators?

Losses are low, but conclusion may miss the point

By MICHAEL LIEBOWITZ

The International Swap Dealers Association's valiant attempt last week to depict the swaps business as a relatively danger-free zone provoked more questions than it actually answered.

The results of a quick-and-dirty survey, commissioned last spring by ISDA, executed by the group's chief accountants, Arthur Andersen & Co., and unveiled at a conference at the Plaza Hotel in New York, elicited a certain smug feeling among the conferees that swaps are indeed safe and represent a better risk than, say, bank loans.

While the accuracy and fairness of the study are not in dispute, some observers noted that it did not go far enough. In particular, it did not address the concerns of regulators who want to know what would happen during a collapse of large portfolios where counterparties took major hits.

Based on a survey of swap dealers representing over 70% of the $4.34 trillion swap market, the study found that cumulative losses over a ten-year period ending last year amounted to only $358.36 million, or 0.0115% of the total notional amount. At the urging of several ISDA members, the true number against which to reflect these loss figures is the gross mark-to-market value of the swaps. This number came to $77.49 billion, so the loss percentage came to 0.46%.

"The losses were relatively small," said Malcolm Basing, chairman of ISDA and a managing director at Swiss Bank Corp., in an interview. "It fits in with our day-to-day observations [that] the swaps business is well managed and credit exposure is well controlled."

The study concluded that gross claims on a mark-to-market value amounted to $539.29 million, of which $126.49 million was recovered from sales, transfers, settlements and liquidation of collateral.

Hammersmith & Fulham

The largest percentage of the loss predictably resulted from swaps involving UK local authorities, which backed out of certain swap agreements last year, claiming they were void after the House of Lords ruled that such financial transactions were illegal. Total losses emanating from UK councils ran up to $177.74 million, or nearly 50% of the total losses.

To many who remember the first days of the Hammersmith & Fulham dispute, the numbers presented in the survey seemed a trifle low. Early estimates of the losses sustained by counterparties to the UK authorities reached as high as £600 million. But Basing was quick to defend the survey's figure, stating that those estimates were only the replacement value of the portfolios, "not necessarily the losses."

"There have been a lot of out-of-court settlements, and so clearly the numbers would be reduced by that," he said. "Secondly, it is difficult to say whether the press estimates were accurate. The survey does underline that [the UK authorities loss] was a problem, but the message is the same. Even if the total writeoffs [from the UK] were 50% bigger, it would still be negligible."

Failures Managed Easily

The remaining large losses were broken down as follows: corporations, $94.53 million (or 26.38%); non-dealer financial institutions, $60.14 million (or 16.78%); and savings and loans, $20.28 million (or 5.66%).

The moral behind the default study was that whatever large-scale failures have occured, they were easily managed and barely caused a ripple in the huge market. The swap community enjoys discussing the ease with which the portfolios of Drexel Burnham Lambert, Development Finance Corp. of New Zealand, Bank of New England and British and Commonwealth Merchant Bank were dismantled.

In each case, none of the defaults was caused by problems in their swaps books, but rather wholly external events unrelated to swaps. For the most part, these institutions had relatively well managed and balanced books, and did not really test the market's ability to sustain a collapse of a large portfolio. As Basing put it: "We are not surprised by the number. If you think about it, defaults like DFC at the end of the day were handled fairly. The losses were modest in size."

Undoubtedly, the study was intended to impress the regulators, including Federal Reserve Board officials, who were present at last week's conference. It is not clear in the end whether the study will appease the regulators at all, since it doesn't address the sort of "what-if" questions they are posing.

The Fed, the Securities and Exchange Commission and the Government Accounting Office are all preparing studies of the derivatives markets in one form or another. The SEC last month passed a new rule that requires hitherto unregulated affiliates and holding companies of brokerage companies to file quarterly financial reports with the agency on positions in futures, real estate and derivatives.

When reached for comment, SEC commissioner Mary Schapiro said she had not yet read the study, but reiterated her earlier claims that derivative instruments still represent a "big worry."

However, she added, "I think I have always tried to say that the concern is we don't really know how big the risk is.

"It could be the biggest risk [in the financial system] or not such a big one. The regulators need to get a handle on it."

The credit risk and interest-rate risk interact in subtle ways. In order to examine this further, it is useful to examine the marked-to-market value of the swap book for different term structure scenarios and credit-risk assumptions. Monte Carlo simulation techniques and a two-state variables (credit risk and interest-rate risk) approach grounded in a contingent claims pricing framework can be used to accomplish this task.

SWAP SPREADS

The difference between the fixed rate on a swap and the yield of the underlying Treasury benchmark with the same maturity is known as the swap spread. Swap spreads as of July 10, 2000, are presented in Table 16-23. For the 10-year maturity, the Treasury benchmark yielded 6.037%. The swap spread on the bid side was 117 basis points. Therefore, the bid swap rates was 6.037 + 1.170 = 7.207%. The swap spread on the offer side was 118 basis points; hence, the swap offer rate was 6.037 + 1.180 = 7.217%. Note that the swap rates are quoted against three-month LIBOR. The 30-year swap rates were 7.196% (bid) and 7.206% (offer) with a swap spread of 131 (bid) and 132 (offer) basis points, respectively.

To get a perspective on swap spreads, we look at the historical data in Table 16-23 from 1988 to 1991 and later at 1997 to 2000. Note that the 10-year swap spread during 1988 to 1991 varied from 60 to 100 basis points.

TABLE 16-23   *Swap Spreads*

USD Medium-Term Swap Spreads
July 10, 2000 Closing Prices as of 3 P.M.EST

			Mid Yield	Spread		Rate(30/360E)SA Fixed (vs 3 month LIBOR)			
				Bid	Offer	Bid	Offer		
2 year	6.375 June 02		6.300	79.50	80.50	7.095	7.105	*LIBOR Setting*	
3 year		*	6.242	86.50	87.50	7.107	7.117		*(A/360)*
4 year		*	6.184	93.50	94.50	7.119	7.129	1 month	6.63000
5 year	6.75 May 05		6.126	101.00	102.00	7.136	7.146	3 month	6.74500
6 year		*	6.108	104.25	105.25	7.151	7.161	6 month	6.95375
7 year		*	6.090	107.75	108.75	7.168	7.178		
8 year		*	6.073	110.75	111.75	7.180	7.190		
9 year		*	6.055	113.75	114.75	7.192	7.202	*Spreads vs. 10 year*	
10 year	6.50 Feb. 10		6.037	117.00	118.00	7.207	7.217	*Bid*	*Offer*
11 year		*	6.029	119.00	120.00	7.219	7.229	118.25	119.25
12 year		*	6.022	120.50	121.50	7.227	7.237	118.99	119.99
13 year		*	6.014	121.75	122.75	7.232	7.242	119.49	120.49
14 year		*	6.007	122.75	123.75	7.234	7.244	119.73	120.73
15 year		*	5.999	123.75	124.75	7.237	7.247	119.98	120.98
20 year		*	5.962	126.75	127.75	7.229	7.239	119.20	120.20
25 year		*	5.924	129.00	130.00	7.214	7.224	117.68	118.68
30 year	6.25 May 30		5.886	131.00	132.00	7.196	7.206	115.90	116.90
40 year	6.25 May 30		5.886	127.50	129.50	7.161	7.181	112.40	114.40

Source: Tullett & Tokyo Liberty.

*Interpolate

Factors That Influence Swap Spreads

The following factors influence swap spreads:

1. The prevailing and the expected spread between the financing rate and the London interbank offered rates or the LIBOR-GC spread (GC stands for general collateral repo rate) is an important factor affecting the swap spreads.

   Dealers hedge open positions in swaps using either the Eurodollar futures contracts or Treasury securities. For swaps with a maturity of five years or more, it is reasonable to think that Treasury securities are used as hedging instruments given unavailability or the poor liquidity of Eurodollar futures for such a maturity range.

   A dealer who receives fixed in the swap will hedge by shorting the underlying Treasury. This way the swap spread is locked in, and the dealer's incremental cost is the difference between LIBOR (which he or she pays) and the reverse repo rate (that he or she earns on the cash collateral). As this spread widens, the cost associated with the hedge increases, and the dealer will want a higher swap spread to compensate for this cost. This is illustrated in Figure 16-16. The swap dealer hedges his or her swap by shorting the benchmark Treasury. Let us say that the Treasury benchmark is yielding 6.0%, resulting in a swap spread of 50 basis points. The dealer's income and expenses are summarized in Table 16-24.

   A dealer who pays fixed in the swap will hedge by going long in the underlying Treasury. Once again, the swap spread is locked in and the dealer's incremental income is the difference between LIBOR (which he receives) and the repo rate (that he pays on the cash borrowed). As this spread widens the income associated

FIGURE 16-16   *Swap Hedging Costs*

TABLE 16-24		
Swap Hedging Costs	Swap fixed leg	+ 6.50%
	Swap floating leg	− LIBOR
	Short Treasury	− 6.00%
	Long cash proceeds	+ Repo
	Total income:	0.50% − (LIBOR-repo)

Note: The total income to the dealer decreases as the LIBOR-repo spread increases. The dealer will then demand a swap spread of more than 50 basis points to recoup his or her losses.

FIGURE 16-17   *Swap Hedging Costs*

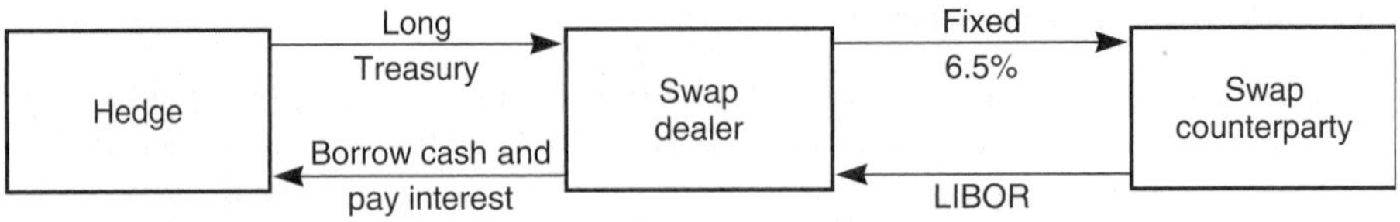

TABLE 16-25

Swap Hedging Costs

Swap floating leg	+ LIBOR
Short Treasury	+ 6.00%
Long cash proceeds	− Repo
Swap fixed leg	− 6.50%
Total income:	**− 0.5% + (LIBOR-repo)**

Note: The total income to the dealer increases as the LIBOR-repo spread increases. The dealer will then be willing to pay a swap spread of more than 50 basis points.

with the hedge increases and the dealer will be willing to pay a higher swap spread. Any event that causes the Treasury security to go special should have a widening effect on swap spreads. Likewise, an expected increase in LIBOR should also contribute to a widening of swap spreads. This can be seen from Figure 16-17. The swap dealer hedges his or her swap by going long in the benchmark Treasury. Let us say that the Treasury benchmark is yielding 6.0%, resulting in a swap spread of 50 basis points. The dealer's income and expenses is summarized in Table 16-25.

We, therefore, conclude that the swap spread should be increasing in the prevailing and expected LIBOR-GC spread.

2. **Liquidity factor or the systemic risk factor:** The second important variable that can influence the swap spread is the liquidity factor. In hedging swaps, dealers might short Treasury securities when they receive fixed in the swap. During the time the hedge is in place, dealers are vulnerable to a "flight to quality" or "flight to liquidity" of the sort that took place during the Russian default in the fall of 1998. Such liquidity factors can have effects on both the financing rates and the market prices of Treasury securities. On-the-run Treasury securities will become relatively more expensive when compared with otherwise similar off-the-run Treasury securities. This market price effect can be conveniently captured by the yield spread between on-the-run and off-the-run Treasury securities. In addition, the repo rates of the more liquid security will trade special, further affecting the spread between LIBOR and the financing rates.

We may, therefore, conclude that the swap spread should increase when the yield spread between on-the-run and off-the-run Treasury securities increase. This is to compensate the dealers for the increased cost of hedging their swap positions in which they receive fixed. In case of dealers who pay fixed in the swap, their hedge will require them to go long in the benchmark Treasury. If there is a flight to liquidity during this period, the dealers hedging costs will decline. This is because they can sell the Treasury at a higher price when they unwind the hedge, or the dealers can enjoy a lower borrowing cost, as their collateral will trade special in the repo market. As a consequence, they will be willing to pay a higher fixed rate in the swap. Hence, no matter how we look at it, the swap spread should increase with the yield spread between on-the-run and off-the-run Treasury securities. We will refer to the yield spread between on-the-run and off-the-run Treasury as the liquidity factor.

We conclude that the swap spread should be increasing in the liquidity factor as reflected by the prevailing and expected spread between the yield of off-the-run and on-the-run Treasury benchmark securities.

3. **Credit risk in the bank sector:** Banks influence swap spreads in two important ways. First, banks actively use the swap market for their asset-liability management purposes. Banks use swaps to convert their floating-rate assets into fixed. This makes them a receiver of fixed in the swap market. The level of their participation, therefore, influences swap spreads. In addition, the London interbank offered rate is determined by the British Bankers Association (BBA). (The details of LIBOR fixing are readily found in *http://www.bba.org.uk.*) Since LIBOR is typically the index used in the floating leg of swaps, the overall or systemic risk of the banks influence swap spreads as well. The panel contributes rates to BBA, and the rates are ranked. Only the rates in the middle quartiles are used in a simple arithmetic averaging process to fix LIBOR. Therefore, LIBOR reflects the *average* credit quality of this contributing panel of banks and how BBA makes adjustments to this panel as the credit reputation of these banks changes. From the perspective of understanding the swap spreads, the following aspects of LIBOR are critical. First, LIBOR reflects the *average* credit risk of the panel banks. As the average credit quality falls, we may expect LIBOR to go up as investors demand a higher compensation for assuming increased credit risk. Second, while LIBOR reflects the average credit quality of the panel of banks, the swap contract is typically "credit enhanced." Daily losses in swaps are met by posting collateral on a daily basis. On each payment date, the losses and gains are netted, and the position is marked to market. To a first approximation, then, it seems reasonable to assume that the swap has little or no credit risk. It then follows that the swap rate must increase when the average credit quality of the panel banks decreases! This conclusion has important implications for valuing swaps and understanding swap spreads. This line of reasoning suggests that the

modeling of credit risk is important in the valuation of swaps not because we believe that the swap has credit risk, but only because the panel of banks in LIBOR fixing has default risk.

An important caveat to the arguments presented should be recognized. If the bank sector as a whole were to experience a serious systemic risk exposure of the sort that occurred following the hedge funds failures in the fall of 1998, then investors will become more risk averse. As a result, swap spreads will inherit a default risk premium.

4. **Demand supply factors:** Swaps are used by many institutions, including corporate issuers, banks, investors in asset swaps, and the federal agencies. The issuance activities and the asset-liability management needs of these institutions will have an important effect on swap spreads. In addition, the current efforts of the Treasury to reduce the supply of Treasury securities may also have an impact on swap spreads. I will briefly explore these factors. Our ability to test these factors will be somewhat limited, since such an effort will require the collection of data on new issue volumes in corporate market, agency market, banks, treasury buybacks, etc. Swap spreads are sensitive to the ratio of the level of government debt outstanding to the level of nonfinancial corporate debt outstanding. Such a relationship, if reliable, may point to a structural shift in swap spreads (and perhaps a tighter link to corporate spreads) given the projected budget surplus in the United States.

    a. **Corporate issuance activity:** When corporate debt spreads tighten, new issues of corporate debt increase, and there will be a greater demand to receive fixed in the swap. This should drive *down* the swap spreads. Corporations tend to issue more debt securities to buyback equity (this has been a major activity in the last few years) or when they anticipate a rate hike or when they see productive opportunities.

        Swap spreads and the new issue volumes of corporate debt should be *negatively* related.

        It is also correct to say that the corporate spreads and swap spreads should be positively correlated. This statement, however, may be *self-referential* to the extent that corporate spreads are priced off the swap curve. The recent problems of using Treasury as the benchmark may accentuate the correlation between swap spreads and corporate spreads purely from benchmarking considerations.

    b. **Agency activities:** As the Treasury markets shrink, agencies are rushing in to fill the breech. Their benchmark programs and the ballooning agency issues should have an impact on swap spreads. Agencies actively use the swap markets to convert fixed-to-floating or vice versa. The volume of agency issues and their mortgage-backed securities portfolio should be a big factor in swap spreads, but no unambiguous sign could be attached to swap spreads as a result of the activities of the agencies in the swap market. This is because potentially the agencies could be on either side of swap transactions. They may in fact attempt to arbitrage any opportunities in the swap market.

Structural Changes

The two (related) structural issues that may influence the swap spreads are (1) the benchmark problem and (2) the liquidity factor.

1. **The benchmark problem:** Traditionally, Treasuries were the benchmark for the pricing of swaps and corporate securities. With the budget surplus and the active buybacks of the Treasury securities, the market is facing some uncertainty about the status of Treasury as a benchmark. This problem is particularly severe in the long end of the yield curve. The scarcity of the Treasury has led to the benchmark programs by the agencies. Many players in the market look to the swap curve as a benchmark.

2. **The liquidity factor:** Examining the proxies of liquidity, it appears as if the liquidity in the market has undergone a structural change. This is related to the active policies pursued by the Treasury in reducing debt, cancellation of some benchmarks, and the reduction in the frequency of issues of some benchmarks, etc. The spread between on-the-run and off-the-run Treasury securities has increased. Generally, Treasuries have become more scarce, leading to illiquidity. This has influenced swap spreads.

Figure 16-18 shows how the swap spreads have widened since August 1998.

FIGURE 16-18 *Swap Spreads*

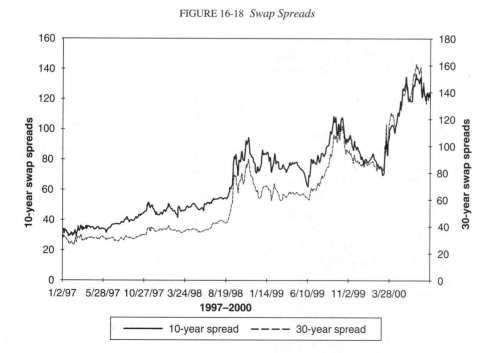

FIGURE 16-19   *Swap Spreads versus Shape of the Yield Curve*

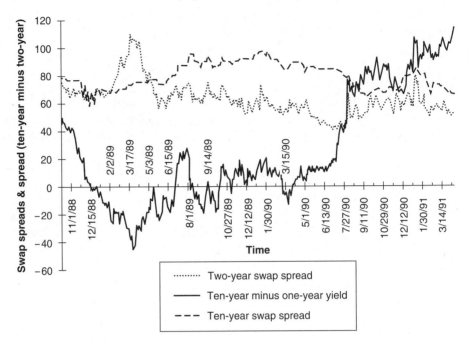

The swap spreads of a AAA dealer are plotted in Figure 16-19 for the period 1988 to 1991, for two-year and ten-year swaps. Also plotted is the spread between the ten-year and two-year Treasury on-the-run securities for the same period. Note that during November 1988 through May 1989, this spread was negative, and the Treasury yield curve was inverted. The swap spreads corresponding to the ten-year swaps were below the swap spreads for the two-year swaps during this period of inverted yield curve. Generally, the Treasury yield curve was upward-sloping for the rest of the period, and the ten-year swap spreads were well in excess of the two-year swap spreads.

The difference in the swap spreads significantly narrowed again during the August 1990 through April 1991 period, even though the Treasury yield curve was strongly upward-sloping. This suggests that there are other factors that may be at work. Papers by Grinblatt (1994) and Duffie and Singleton (1995) have examined the swap spreads. Grinblatt has argued that a big factor in the swap spread is liquidity. Duffie and Singleton (1995) provide a framework for valuing swaps with default risk. They report evidence that both default and liquidity are important factors in the determination of swap spreads.

Danger Signs

The swaps market is behaving very oddly. Why?

An unusual thing happened this week in America. The prices of corporate bonds rose. Of late they have proved a dreadful investment—worse by far than government bonds. How much farther their prices will rise depends largely on what happens in the market in which they are priced: the swaps market. That market is in turmoil.

Swaps are the glue that binds together the world's financial system. First developed in the early 1980s, they now dwarf other financial instruments. At the end of last year there were some $46 trillion of swaps outstanding, compared with $5.4 trillion in, for example, international bond markets.

Broadly, swaps come in two forms: interest-rate swaps and currency swaps. Simply put, both allow two parties to exchange cashflows. In a currency swap, the two exchange currencies and re-exchange them at maturity at the same rate. In the meantime they exchange interest payments. In a typical interest-rate swap, one side exchanges a floating-rate obligation (generally based on Libor, the rate at which the best banks lend to each other) for a fixed one.

This simplicity has made swaps, and interest-rate swaps in particular, a very useful tool. They allow banks, for example, to match their assets and liabilities much more closely. If they have lots of short-term floating-rate liabilities (such as savings accounts) but long-term fixed-rate assets (such as loans) they can "swap" long-term assets into short-term ones. Likewise, companies can use swaps to convert fixed-rate debt (which investors might prefer) into floating-rate debt, or vice versa.

The level of the fixed rate in the swap reflects, among other things, the willingness of the market to accept corporate debt rather than government debt, which means that the swap rate is calculated at a spread over government bonds. Euro swap-spreads have risen in recent weeks, but dollar swap-spreads have widened dramatically. Ten-year spreads peaked at the end of May at 140 basis points (hundredths of a percentage point)—a higher spread than ever before (see chart). They have since narrowed, but are still wider than at the height of the financial crisis that followed Russia's default. At times in recent weeks, the swaps market has shut down completely; nobody was willing to receive a fixed rate.

What on earth is going on? There are, broadly, two sets of explanations, one relatively benign, the other emphatically not. The benign view is that the rise in swap spreads is explicable by rising interest rates, greater default risk, and the relative sizes of government- and corporate-bond markets.

Governments are issuing fewer bonds. On optimistic assumptions, America's government could buy back all its debt by 2010. American companies, in contrast, are borrowing hugely. That makes government bonds more valuable, compared with corporate debt. It reflects what Stephen Compton, head of bonds at Schroder Salomon Smith Barney in Europe, calls "the privatisation of the bond markets".

Rising interest rates, too, are partly to blame for widening swap spreads. When the market thinks that interest rates will rise, there is more of an incentive to pay, rather than receive, a fixed rate. That incentive is greater at times when, as now, long-term rates are lower than short-term ones (an "inverted yield curve"). This means that anybody receiving a fixed (long-term) rate and paying a floating one loses money.

Then there is the increase in corporate debt. Credit Suisse First Boston (CSFB) expects American companies to issue as many bonds this year as they did last, when they sold record amounts. Importantly for swap spreads, one reason that firms are borrowing so much is to buy back their shares. So American companies are becoming ever more highly geared, and hence less credit-worthy. Share buy-backs are running at double last year's level and, reckons David Goldman, a strategist at CSFB, will remain in vogue as long as debt is relatively cheap, and firms' managers think that more leverage is good for shareholder value.

Source: The Economist, June 10th 2000.   *(continued)*

Big and ugly

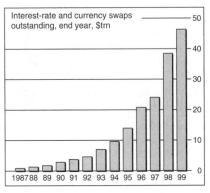

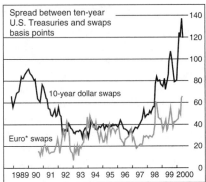

Sources: ISDA; BIS; Credit Suisse First Boston   *D-mark swaps before 1/1/99

If this were not enough, swap-market folk also point accusing fingers at Gary Gensler, under-secretary at the American Treasury. In March, he said that federally sponsored agencies, such as Fannie Mae and Freddie Mac, which everybody assumed were guaranteed by the government, were not. The yield on their debt rose sharply. Since they are the biggest actors in the swaps market, so did swap spreads.

Swap Knot

Taken together, these factors might seem enough to explain what has happened. But James Bianco, who runs an eponymous research firm, thinks they are not. Swap spreads, he points out, have been widening for the past three-and-a-half years—before any of these other factors cropped up. And they do not explain why swap spreads have risen so fast this year.

Mr. Bianco argues that two things dominate the pricing of interest-rate swaps: interest rates and credit concerns. For most of the 1990s swap rates went up and down with interest rates. That relationship has now largely broken down, suggests Mr. Bianco, because markets have become more concerned over risks to the financial system, as a result of the crises of recent years. If Mr. Bianco is right, this has important ramifications: it suggests there are growing worries about the riskiness of the swaps market, based on fears about the health of financial firms—by far the biggest participants.

Pshaw, say critics: there is no credit risk in the swaps market. Forget about those telephone-number figures: no principal amount is exchanged in a swap, so what matters is not the "notional" amount at risk but the cost of replacing the swaps—a far lower number. Moreover, big banks post collateral if they are on the losing side of a swap, thus eliminating even any residual risk.

Really? "Swaps are perceived as riskless. That must be wrong," says a treasurer at a big bank. Unlike futures exchanges, the swaps market looks only at current exposures, not potential ones (futures exchanges demand a dollop of cash up front to cover the second). And the market has grown so much that these potential risks are becoming huge.

So it is at least plausible that people are starting to fret about the banking system. But why might this be a problem in America, of all places? Because it is taking ever more risk to generate the returns demanded by shareholders. Bank lending is growing by 10% at an annual rate, and property lending by 13.5%, its highest rate since 1989. If anything, these rates are accelerating because, after nine years of growth and few defaults, banks' backward-looking risk models tell them that lending is a fine business.

And not just in America. In Europe, too, banks are taking more risk to generate higher returns. At best, the swap market is merely reflecting this increase in risk. At worst, it might be signalling that the world's financial system is in danger of becoming unglued.

SWAP BID-OFFER SPREADS

Sun, Sundaresan, and Wang (1993) examine the effect of the dealer's credit reputation on the bid-offer spreads of swap quotations. Much of this section is drawn from this study.

Tables 16-26 and 16-27 document the swap spreads and the term structure of the swap spreads. These are based on the spreads between swap-offer rates quoted by an AAA-rated swap dealer and the Treasury yields for 605 daily observations in the

TABLE 16-26   *Swap Spreads, October 11, 1988–April 15, 1991*

	Maturity					
Statistic	*Two-year*	*Three-year*	*Four-year*	*Five-year*	*Seven-year*	*Ten-year*
Full sample period (N = 605)						
Mean	64.33	70.84	72.78	76.54	77.49	81.60
SD	12.35	7.65	6.84	8.32	8.20	9.10
t-value	128.05**	227.74**	261.58**	226.16**	232.38**	220.27**
Inverted-yield-curve sample period, (N = 200), December 14, 1988–October 11, 1989						
Mean	74.89	75.56	74.15	76.59	77.34	79.87
SD	13.25	7.78	7.51	9.23	8.78	8.91
t-value	79.71**	137.00**	139.22**	117.10**	124.30**	126.53**

Source: Sun, Sundaresan, and Wang 1993.

**Rejections at the 1% significance level.

The yield curve is defined as inverted when the ten-year Treasury yield is less than the two-year Treasury yield.

TABLE 16-27   *Term Premium of Swap Spread, October 11, 1988–April 15, 1991*

	Maturity				
Statistic	*Three-year*	*Four-year*	*Five-year*	*Seven-year*	*Ten-year*
Full sample period (N = 605)					
Mean	6.52	8.45	12.21	13.16	17.27
SD	7.74	11.76	14.18	14.29	16.44
t-value	23.75**	17.66**	21.16**	22.63**	25.81**
$T^2 (F_{5,600})$	1,605.25 (318.92**)				
Inverted-yield-curve sample period, (N = 200), December 14, 1988–October 11, 1989					
Mean	0.67	−0.74	1.70	2.45	4.98
SD	7.29	14.56	16.77	16.87	17.85
t-value	1.30	−0.72	1.43	2.05**	3.94**
$T^2 (F_{5,195})$	318.19 (62.36**)				

Source: Sun, Sundaresan, and Wang 1993.

**Rejections at the 1% significance level.

The yield curve is defined as inverted when the ten-year Treasury yield is less than the two-year Treasury yield.

TABLE 16-28   *Summary Statistics for Swap-Offer Rates and Bid-Offer Spreads,
October 11, 1988–April 15, 1991*

		Maturity					
	Statistic	*Two-year*	*Three-year*	*Four-year*	*Five-year*	*Seven-year*	*Ten-year*
AAA							
Swap-offer rates	Mean	8.881%	9.004%	9.082%	9.140%	9.251%	9.316%
	SD	0.790%	0.670%	0.580%	0.517%	0.450%	0.416%
Bid-offer spreads (in basis points)	Mean	10	10	10	10	10	10
A							
Swap-offer rates	Mean	8.837%	8.955%	9.052%	9.114%	9.227%	9.290%
	SD	0.778%	0.659%	0.585%	0.518%	0.455%	0.421%
Bid-offer spreads	Mean	4.73	4.74	4.65	4.67	4.79	4.77
(in basis points)	SD	1.19	1.12	1.06	0.90	1.05	0.93

Source: Sun, Sundaresan, and Wang 1993.

Bid-offer spreads are always 10 basis points for a AAA swap dealer.

$N = 605$.

period October 11, 1988, to April 15, 1991. The spreads and term premiums are measured in basis points. The term premiums of the spread are defined as the spread relative to a two-year spread. Note that the spreads are generally increasing with maturity irrespective of the shape of the yield curve. Table 16-28 documents the AAA and A swap-offer rates and bid-offer spreads for the same period. The bid-offer spreads for the AAA swap dealer are always 10 basis points, while the bid-offer spreads for the A swap dealer vary around 4.75 basis points.

Assume that the credit quality of the counterparties is the same for different swap dealers and that the swap contracts do not differ in other dimensions, such as the up-front fee and collaterals. Then, intuitively, the swap-offer rates of AAA-rated dealers should be higher than those of A-rated dealers, while the swap-bid rates of AAA-rated dealers should be lower than those of A-rated dealers. (See Table 16-29.)

Table 16-30 presents the differences between AAA and A swap rates as frequencies.

Reputation of the Investor

Most swap dealers offer swap quotations that are the same irrespective of the credit standing of clients. Usually, an up-front fee is assessed, depending upon the maturity and the notional amount of the swap contract. This fee might vary with the credit standing of clients. Marking-to-market and the posting of marketable collateral may be required of clients whose credit quality decline with time. Clearly, these provisions are integral parts of swap contracts.

In this context, it is useful to note that swap dealers tend to work with an approved list of clients who have been cleared by the credit committee of the swap dealer. For example, the AAA dealer may require that the average credit rating of any counterparties be AA or better; the minimum acceptable credit rating is A. In this case,

TABLE 16-29 *Differences in Swap Rates, October 11, 1988–April 15, 1991 (in Basis Points)*

	Maturity					
Statistic	Two-year	Three-year	Four-year	Five-year	Seven-year	Ten-year
AAA offer rates minus A offer rates						
Mean	4.33	4.96	3.03	2.59	2.68	2.62
SD	5.84	3.63	6.34	4.21	4.09	4.74
t-value	18.22**	33.57**	11.77**	15.13**	16.10**	13.58**
T^2 $(F_{6,599})$			1,497.66 (247.54**)			
A bid rates minus AAA bid rates						
Mean	0.94	0.31	2.31	2.75	2.54	2.62
SD	6.03	3.91	6.34	4.21	4.12	4.77
t-value	3.83**	1.94*	8.96**	16.06**	15.17**	13.50**
T^2 $(F_{6,599})$			482.56 (79.76**)			
AAA mid-market rates minus A mid-market rates						
Mean	1.69	2.32	0.36	−0.08	0.07	0.00
SD	5.91	3.73	6.32	4.18	4.07	4.73
t-value	7.05**	15.33**	1.41	−0.47	0.42	0.00
T^2 $(F_{6,599})$			240.53 (39.76**)			

Source: Sun, Sundaresan, and Wang 1993.

$N = 605$.

*Rejection at 5% significance level.

**Rejection at 1% significance level.

TABLE 16-30 *Frequencies of the Spreads between AAA and A Swap Rates, October 11, 1988–April 15, 1991*

AAA offer rates over A offer rates (percentage)

	Maturity					
Basis Points	Two-year	Three-year	Four-year	Five-year	Seven-year	Ten-year
Above 10	7.11	5.45	1.65	1.16	0.99	0.99
5 to 10	34.21	45.29	21.49	11.90	12.89	6.94
0 to 5	52.89	45.29	67.77	77.85	75.21	82.81
−5 to 0	4.79	3.47	8.10	8.10	9.59	9.09
−10 to −5	0.33	0.17	0.50	0.33	0.83	0.17
Below −10	0.66	0.33	0.50	0.66	0.50	0.00

A bid rates over AAA bid rates (percentage)

	Maturity					
Basis Points	Two-year	Three-year	Four-year	Five-year	Seven-year	Ten-year
Above 10	1.16	0.66	0.99	0.99	1.16	0.00
5 to 10	6.45	3.97	9.42	10.91	10.08	10.41
0 to 5	58.86	54.05	72.07	78.02	76.36	82.31
−5 to 0	26.61	33.22	15.37	8.76	.74	6.12
−10 to −5	7.93	6.78	1.49	0.83	1.49	0.83
Below −10	0.99	1.32	0.66	0.50	0.17	0.33

Source: Sun, Sundaresan, and Wang 1993.

$N = 605$.

it seems reasonable to assume that the credit quality of the counterparties is relatively better for the AAA dealer, which will counteract the AAA dealer's advantage in charging higher bid-offered spreads. Hence, the empirical finding that the AAA swap rates bracket the A swap rates lends stronger support to our hypothesis about the impact of credit ratings on bid-offered spreads.

Options on Swaps or Swaptions

Options that give the right to enter into a swap at a future date at terms that are agreed upon now are known as **swaptions. Payer swaptions** give the right but not the obligation to pay the fixed rate and receive the floating payments on a swap of prespecified tenor. **Receiver swaptions** give the right but not the obligation to receive the fixed rate and pay the floating payments on a swap of prespecified tenor. These particularly valuable instruments hedge a stream of contingent future cash flows.

Example 16-12:

Let us say that a company has bid for a project. If the company wins the bid then the project will produce a stream of 5 million FX per year over the next 10 years. Let us say that the results of the bid will be known in three months.

It can enter into a payer swaption with a three-month maturity, which gives the right to pay 5 million FX per year and receive LIBOR. If the company wins the bid, the swaption will be exercised at maturity, and the FX exposure would be swapped to LIBOR. If the company loses the bid, the swaption can be sold or allowed to expire.

Example 16-13:

Consider a fixed-income portfolio manager who has a callable bond at a coupon of 10%. Yields are falling, and there is a possibility that the bond may be called. Let us say that the call price is 100. The bond's first call date is six months from now, and the bond has 10 years more to maturity from the first call date. How can the portfolio manager hedge the call risk?

The portfolio manager can buy a receiver swaption with six months maturity on an interest rate swap with a maturity of 10 years. The interest rate swap gives will pay a fixed rate equal to the coupon of the callable bond. In exchange, the portfolio manager will have to pay LIBOR. Suppose that the interest rates drop, and the bond gets called at the end of six months. Then the portfolio manager will exercise the swaption and receive the coupon as if he or she still owned the bond. He or she, however, has to pay LIBOR now. This can be done by investing the call price (that he or she would have received when the bond was called) in LIBOR. This way the call can be stripped from callable bonds.

FIGURE 16-20   *Valuing Swaptions*

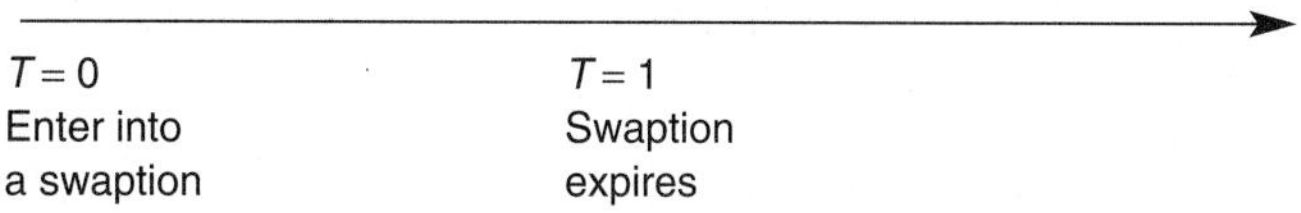

$T = 0$	$T = 1$
Enter into	Swaption
a swaption	expires

The valuation of swaption is illustrated by Figure 16-20. Let us say that a swaption is traded at $T = 0$. The maturity date of the swaption is $T = 1$, and the underlying interest-rate swap has a maturity of five years. Assume for simplicity that the swap pays fixed coupons every year in return for LIBOR. Assume that the strike rate of the swaption is a fixed rate x.

At $T = 1$, we can engage in a swap. This swap rate, y, is the par bond yield at $T = 1$. If instead we can buy a swaption at $T = 0$ at a rate x, then its value at $T = 1$ is the value of a bond that has a coupon rate of x. Consider a swaption on a five-year swap which is generic so that the reset date precedes the payment date by exactly the index maturity. Let us denote the discount factors by d.

Value of a swap on $T = 1$ that pays y:

$$y[d_1 + d_2 + d_3 + d_4 + d_5] - [1 - d_5] = 0.$$

This is because y is the par bond yield.

Value of a swap on $T = 1$ that pays x:

$$x[d_1 + d_2 + d_3 + d_4 + d_5] - [1 - d_5] \neq 0$$

Obviously, the holder of a payer swaption will exercise if

$$x[d_1 + d_2 + d_3 + d_4 + d_5] - [1 - d_5] < 0.$$

Or

$$x[d_1 + d_2 + d_3 + d_4 + d_5] + 1d_5 < 1.$$

His or her payoffs may also be given by the equation

$$\max [0, 1 - \{x[d_1 + d_2 + d_3 + d_4 + d_5] + 1d_5\}].$$

This is an option to sell a five-year bond paying a coupon of x at par.

We can value swaptions as options to sell or buy bonds at a strike price of par. Any bond options pricing model is then a good way to value swaptions. Investors also use Black's model on options on futures to value swaptions. They use the forward swap rate as an input into the Black's model.

Let C = payer swaption, P = receiver swaption, s = tenor of the swap, F = forward rate on the swap, K = strike rate on the swaption, r = financing rate, $T - t$ = time to maturity, m = number of compoundings per year in swap rate, and σ is the volatility of the forward swap rate.

Then the value of the swaption can be found by using the following modified Black's model:

$$C = e^{-r(T-t)}[FN(d_1) - KN(d_2)] \times \frac{1 - \dfrac{1}{\left(1 + \dfrac{F}{m}\right)^{s \times m}}}{F}$$

$$P = e^{-r(T-t)}[KN(-d_2) - FN(-d_1)] \times \frac{1 - \dfrac{1}{\left(1 + \dfrac{F}{m}\right)^{s \times m}}}{F}$$

Example 16-14:

Let us value a two-year payer swaption on a four-year swap with semiannual compounding. Assume a notional principal of $10 million. The forward swap rate on a four-year swap is 7% when it starts two years from now. The strike rate is 7.5%, and the financing rate is 6%. The volatility of the forward swap rate is 20%. See Table 16-31.

Parity Relation

There is a parity relation between the values of (a) payer swaption, (b) receiver swaption and (c) forward swap rate. To see the parity condition, let us examine the payoffs associated with the transactions shown in Table 16-32.

Since a receiver swaption is a put on a bond with a strike of par and a payer swaption is a call on the same bond with a strike of par, we can apply the put-call parity to get the same implication. Table 16-33 shows the put-call parity. It shows that a long position in a put on a bond coupled with a short position in a call replicates a forward swap. Table 16-34 illustrates swaptions quotes.

TABLE 16-31   *Example of Swaption Valuation*

F	7%	d_1	−0.10251		
K	7.50%	$N(d_1)$	0.459178	$N(-d_1)$	0.540822
s	4	d_2	−0.38535		
$T-t$	2	$N(d_2)$	0.34999	$N(-d_2)$	0.65001
Vol.	20%				
r	6%				
Payer swaption value			1.79644% of the notional principal = $179,644.05		
Receiver swaption value			3.32060% of the notional principal = $322,060.34		

TABLE 16-32   *Parity Relation*

$t = 0$	$x > swap\ rate$				$x \leqq swap\ rate$			
	$t = 1$	$t = 2$	$t = 3$	$t = 4$	$t = 1$	$t = 2$	$t = 3$	$t = 4$
1. Enter into a forward swap at a forward rate x.	x-LIBOR	x-LIBOR	x-LIBOR	x-LIBOR	x-LIBOR	x-LIBOR	x-LIBOR	x-LIBOR
2. Buy a receiver swaption.	x-LIBOR	x-LIBOR	x-LIBOR	x-LIBOR	0	0	0	0
3. Sell a payer swaption.	0	0	0	0	x-LIBOR	x-LIBOR	x-LIBOR	x-LIBOR
Hence, it follows that	**Forward Swap = Receiver swaption – Payer Swaption.**							

TABLE 16-33   *Parity Relation*

$t = 0$	$x > swap\ rate$	$x \leqq swap\ rate$
1. Buy a put on a bond paying a coupon rate x.	0	$1 - x[d_1 + d_2 + d_3 + d_4 + 1]$
2. Sell a call on a bond paying a coupon rate x.	$1 - x[d_1 + d_2 + d_3 + d_4 + 1]$	0
Total	Payoff associated with a forward swap at a forward swap rate of x	

TABLE 16-34   *Swaption Volatilities (Mid-Market at-the-Money) July 10, 2000, Closing Prices as of 3:00 P.M. EST.*

Expiry	1 Year	2 Year	3 Year	4 Year	5 Year	7 Year	10 Year	12 Year	15 Year	20 Year	25 Year	30 Year
1 month	11.20	12.70	12.80	12.90	13.00	13.00	13.00	12.50	12.10			
3 month	**11.40**	**13.20**	**13.20**	**13.20**	**13.30**	**13.30**	**13.20**	**12.70**	**12.40**			
6 month	12.50	13.50	13.50	13.40	13.40	13.30	13.20	12.70	12.40			
1 year	**13.65**	**13.90**	**13.70**	**13.60**	**13.50**	**13.35**	**13.20**	**12.50**	**12.20**	**11.50**	**11.20**	**10.90**
2 year	14.90	14.45	14.25	13.90	13.75	13.50	13.20	12.40	12.00	11.20	10.90	10.60
3 year	**14.80**	**14.35**	**14.10**	**13.80**	**13.65**	**13.40**	**13.05**	**12.10**	**11.50**	**10.80**	**10.50**	**10.30**
4 year	14.70	14.20	13.95	13.65	13.45	13.05	12.55	11.80	11.20	10.40	10.10	9.80
5 year	**14.60**	**13.95**	**13.75**	**13.55**	**13.15**	**12.70**	**12.15**	**11.50**	**10.80**	**10.00**	**9.70**	**9.30**
7 year	13.30	12.65	12.45	12.25	11.75	11.35	10.80	10.00	9.30	8.40	8.10	7.80
10 year	**12.20**	**11.40**	**11.10**	**10.60**	**10.30**	**9.80**	**9.40**	**8.80**	**8.20**	**7.50**	**7.00**	**6.50**

Source: Tullett & Tokyo, Inc.

CONCLUSION

We showed several ways interest-rate swaps are priced. Eurodollar futures provide one avenue. Another avenue is to extract the zero prices from the market and work with them. We showed that the spreads between swap rates and Treasury yields, overall, increase significantly with maturities, while the increase is much smaller when the Treasury yield curve is inverted. The bid-offer spreads of market makers are sensitive to their credit reputations. It is interesting to note that Merrill Lynch and several other firms have formed new subsidiaries to engage in the swap business with large clients; these separately capitalized, credit-enhanced subsidiaries have been structured to get a AAA rating. Several other investment banks, including Lehman Brothers and Salomon Brothers, have launched such credit-enhanced subsidiaries. In the equity derivatives market, a self-funded AAA vehicle has been formed by Goldman Sachs.

PROBLEMS

16.1 The Treasurer of XYZ Corporation examines the liability structure of the company on November 1, 1988. He notices that the rollover of commercial paper has been very expensive to the company, as the rates have increased from a low of about 7% in January 1988 to a high of about 8.25% in October 31, 1988. See Figure 16-21. At the same time, the spread between AAA rates (long term) and P1 + six-month CP rates has declined from a high of 310 basis points in January 1, 1988, to 110 basis points in October 31, 1988. See Figure 16-22.

About $200 million worth of floating-rate notes are outstanding in XYZ Corporation's balance sheet. These floaters are plain-vanilla floaters maturing on November 1, 2015, and paying a coupon of six months LIBOR plus a fixed spread of 25 basis points. In fact, November 1, 1988, was a reset date for these floaters. Historically, CP rates and LIBOR are highly correlated; in fact, most CP rates are indexed to the LIBOR.

Concerned by the increase in short-term interest rates, the treasurer of P&G Corporation explores with the company's investment banker, BG, some derivatives-based strategies. BG proposes a five-year interest-rate swap as detailed in Figure 16-23. Essentially, BG proposes that XYZ pay a fixed (swap) rate of a five-year Treasury (T) plus 100 basis points. In turn, every six months, BG will pay XYZ a six-month LIBOR. XYZ is keen to first examine the implications of this swap on the funding costs associated with the floating-rate notes. BG suggests that the notional principal of the swap should be $200 million.

(a) Summarize the advantages and disadvantages of the interest-rate swap from XYZ Corporation's standpoint.

(b) Based on the data, extract the zero rates from LIBOR bond yields. Using these zero rates, price the interest-rate swap. Are BG's quotes reasonable?

(c) XYZ Corporation did the swap on November 1, 1988. Six months later, on May 1, 1989, it decided to reevaluate the swap. As seen in Figure 16-19, the yield curve has become inverted, and XYZ had the option of doing a four-and-a-half-year swap with BG to offset the original swap. On May 1, 1989, after the reset and the payment, determine the marked-to-market value of the swap to XYZ Corporation. Explain your answer.

FIGURE 16-21   *CP Rate Changes*

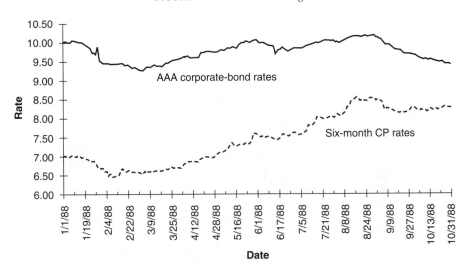

FIGURE 16-22   *Spreads—AAA Bond Rates Minus Six-Month CP Rates*

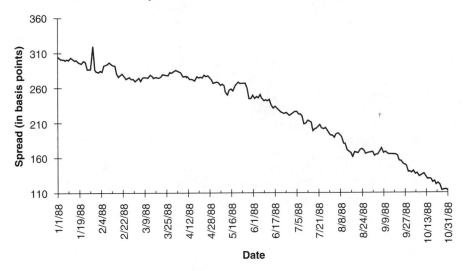

FIGURE 16-23   *Swap Example*

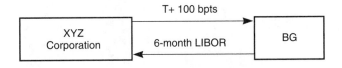

REFERENCES

Alworth, J. 1993. "The Valuation of U.S. Dollar Interest Rate Swaps." *BIS Economic Papers* 35: January. Basle, Switzerland.

Bicksler, J., and A. H. Chen 1986. "An Economic Analysis of Interest Rate Swaps." *Journal of Finance* 41:645–655.

Burghardt, G., T. Belton, M. Lane, G. Luce, and R. McVey 1991. *Eurodollar Futures and Options: Controlling Money Market Risk.* Chicago, IL: Probus Publishing Co.

Cooper, I., and A. S. Mello 1991. "The Default Risk of Swaps." *Journal of Finance* 48:597–620.

Cox, J. C., J. E. Ingersoll, Jr., and S. A. Ross 1980. "An Analysis of Variable Rate Loan Contracts." *Journal of Finance* 35:389–403.

1988. "Capital Adequacy: The BIS Framework and Its Portfolio Implications." *The Journal of International Securities Markets:* 191–218.

Duffie, D., and K. Singleton 1995. "An Econometric Model of the Term Structure of Interest Rate Swap Yields." Graduate School of Business, Stanford University.

Federal Reserve System 1987. "Capital Maintenance: Revision to Capital Adequacy Guidelines." Regulation Y: Docket No. R-0567.

Grinblatt, M. 1994. "An Analytic Solution for Interest Rate Swap Spreads." Working paper, UCLA, Andersen School of Management.

Ramaswamy, K., and S. M. Sundaresan 1986. "The Valuation of Floating-Rate Instruments: Theory and Evidence." *Journal of Financial Economics* 17:251–272.

Smith, C. W., C. W. Smithson, and L. M. Wakeman 1986. "The Evolving Market for Swaps." *Midland Corporate Finance Journal* 3:20–32.

Smith, C. W., C. W. Smithson, and L. M. Wakeman 1988. "The Market for Interest Rate Swaps." *Financial Management* 17:34–44.

Sun, T., S. Sundaresan, and C. Wang 1993. "Interest Rate Swaps: An Empirical Investigation." *Journal of Financial Economics* 36:77–99.

Sundaresan, S. M. 1991. "Valuation of Swaps." In Sarkis J. Khoury, ed., *Recent Developments in International Banking and Finance,* vol. 5. S. J. Khoury, ed. New York: Elsevier Science Publishers.

Turnbull, S. M. 1987. "Swaps: Zero sum game?" *Financial Management* 16:15–21.

Whittaker, J. G. 1987. "Interest Rate Swaps: Risk and Regulation." *Economic Review of the Federal Reserve Bank of Kansas City:* 3–13.

Chapter 17

Models of Yield Curve and Yield Curve Derivatives

Chapter Objectives

This chapter summarizes the important developments in arbitrage-free pricing of securities. We complement the developments in Chapter 14 but focus exclusively on models of term structure and how they can be used to value fixed-income securities and their derivatives. We address the following models:

- Random walk model of interest rates
- Mean-reverting interest rates
- Cox, Ingersoll, and Ross model
- Ho and Lee model
- Hull and White model
- Black, Derman, and Toy model

We show how to calibrate models to market data. Finally, we illustrate the pricing of interest rate derivatives.

INTRODUCTION

We begin with a model of bond prices that is very similar to the developments described in Chapter 14. We assume that the bond price denoted by P follows a simple, multiplicative random walk. Such a process is illustrated below for three points in time: $t = 0, 1,$ and 2.

$$
\begin{array}{ccccc}
 & & & & u^2P \\
 & & & \nearrow & \\
 & & uP & & \\
 & \nearrow & & \searrow & \\
P & & & & udP \\
 & \searrow & & \nearrow & \\
 & & dP & & \\
 & & & \searrow & \\
 & & & & d^2P \\
t=0 & & t=1 & & t=2
\end{array}
$$

Note that the set of possible bond prices increases linearly with time—at date 0, there is one price; at date 1, there are two possible prices (uP and dP); and at date 2, there are 3 possible prices (u^2P, udP, and d^2P). This process is known as the **binomial process** and this has been studied extensively by Cox, Ross, and Rubinstein (1979).

Consider a bond at date t. Assume that we consider a horizon date $T > t$. We can subdivide the life of the bond into n time intervals. Define the length of each subinterval as $h = \frac{(T-t)}{n}$. Consider the annualized riskless rate of interest $1 + R$; its allocation to the subintervals will be governed by the relation:

$$(1 + \hat{R}) = (1 + R)^{\frac{T-t}{n}}.$$

Cox, Ross, and Rubinstein (1979) select

$$u = \frac{1}{d} = e^{\sigma\sqrt{\frac{T-t}{n}}}, \tag{17.1}$$

where σ is the volatility of the underlying asset returns, $T - t$ is the time to the horizon date in years, n is the number of time intervals into which the time to maturity is divided, and e is the base of natural logarithm. They let the probability $q = 0.5 + 0.5\frac{\mu}{\sigma}\sqrt{\frac{T-t}{n}}$, where μ is the expected rate of return on the underlying asset. Then as $n \rightarrow \infty$, it can be shown that the underlying bond price P follows a process that can be described as

$$\frac{dP}{P} = \mu dt + \sigma dz, \tag{17.2}$$

where dz is normally distributed with a mean equal to zero and a variance of dt. The bond price P_T at the horizon date is a random variable. Its properties are summarized by the mean and variance as

$$E\left[\ln\left(\frac{P_T}{P_t}\right)\right] = \mu(T - t)$$

and

$$\sigma^2\left[\ln\left(\frac{P_T}{P_t}\right)\right] = \sigma^2(T - t).$$

In other words, future bond prices are lognormally distributed. This is not a desirable feature; as bonds approach their maturity date, their price should converge to par. This simple requirement is not met by this process.

In practice, this process is used in the industry only in specific applications where convergence to par is not a serious problem. This would be the case if the bond has many years to maturity. There are processes in which convergence to par is satisfied. The process specified in Equation 17.2 is a continuous time limit of the discrete-time binomial process that we considered earlier. Similar processes have been specified for interest rates as well, and we will review some of them.

The derivation of bond prices illuminates an important feature of pricing securities: The original probability distribution is not the relevant one. We can change the original probability measure with a risk-neutral probability measure. Then, using the risk-neutral probability measure, we can take the expected value of the option and discount this expected value at the riskless rate of interest. This insight was originally outlined by Cox and Ross (1976) and later formally developed as a broader implication of no arbitrage by Harrison and Kreps (1978) in an influential paper. This insight also allows us to use Monte Carlo simulation techniques to price certain types of options and contingent claims. (This is taken up in the next chapter to value options.)

VALUATION OF THE YIELD CURVE

The binomial process that we used for describing bond prices can be applied to interest rates as well. Rendelman and Bartter (1980) applied this idea to modeling interest rates behavior.

Binomial Process

We will illustrate the approach in the context of a single-factor model in which the nominal rates follow a binomial process. Consider a simple binomial process for the spot rate of interest.

$$
\begin{array}{ccccc}
 & & & & u^2 r(t) \\
 & & & \nearrow & \\
 & & ur(t) & & \\
 & \nearrow & & \searrow & \\
r(t) & & & & udr(t) \\
 & \searrow & & \nearrow & \\
 & & dr(t) & & \\
 & & & \searrow & \\
 & & & & d^2 r(t) \\
t=0 & & t=1 & & t=2
\end{array}
$$

This process is shown in the discrete-time model of Rendelman and Bartter (1980). We will assume throughout that the probability of an up move is q and that of a down move is $1 - q$, irrespective of the level of the spot rate of interest. More satisfactory processes will be taken up later. Consider a pure discount bond paying a dollar at date 2.

$$
\begin{array}{ccccc}
 & & & & 1 \\
 & & & \nearrow & \\
 & & b^u r(1,2) & & \\
 & \nearrow & & \searrow & \\
b(0,2) & & & & 1 \\
 & \searrow & & \nearrow & \\
 & & b^d(1,2) & & \\
 & & & \searrow & \\
 & & & & 1 \\
t=0 & & t=1 & & t=2
\end{array}
$$

Recall that LEH says that the expected return over one period on any bond should be the same as the one-period rate prevailing at that time. Therefore, by LEH, at date $t = 1$, the following two conditions hold:

$$\frac{1}{b^u(1,2)} = 1 + ur(t)$$

and

$$\frac{1}{b^d(1,2)} = 1 + dr(t).$$

These conditions say that the return at date 1 from holding a one-period bond should be equal to the one-period rate at that node. As a consequence, we can rearrange these two equations to get the bond-price distributions

$$b^u(1,2) = \frac{1}{1 + ur(t)}$$

and

$$b^d(1,2) = \frac{1}{1 + dr(t)}.$$

Working with known cash flows at date $t = 2$, we determined the bond prices at date $t = 1$.

We now proceed in a recursive fashion to date $t = 0$. By LEH, we have

$$\frac{q \times b^u(1,2) + (1 - q) \times b^d(1,2)}{b(0,2)} = 1 + r(t).$$

Rearranging the previous equation and solving for the bond price at date $t = 0$, we get

$$b(0,2) = \frac{q \times b^u(1,2) + (1 - q) \times b^d(1,2)}{1 + r(t)}.$$

Note that we could expand the procedure to any arbitrary future date and compute the pure discount bond prices at date 0 as the sequence $b(0, 1)$, $b(0, 2)$, $b(0, 3)$, $b(0, 4)$, ... $b(0, n)$. In addition, at each future date s in the spot rate tree, we can obtain the entire distribution of yield curve. The ability to get the entire distribution of zero-coupon bond prices is important in the valuation of interest-rate derivatives. We illustrate these ideas in Example 17-1.

Example 17-1:

Given the current one-period rate is 10%, the up move factor $u = 1.25$, the down move factor $d = 0.80$, the probability of an up move is $q = 0.5$, and the evolution of the one-period rates given next.

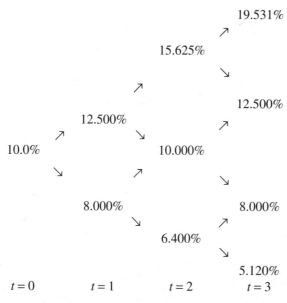

Determine the term structure of interest rates at date $t = 0$ for maturities $T = 1, 2,$ 3, and 4.

We begin by solving for the price of a single-period bond. This bond pays one dollar at date $t = 1$ no matter which state occurs. Therefore, its price at date $t = 0$ is $b(0, 1) = \frac{1}{(1 + 0.10)} = 0.9091$. This is shown as

$$
\begin{array}{c}
\nearrow \quad 1 \\
0.9091 \\
\searrow \quad 1 \\
t = 0 \qquad t = 1
\end{array}
$$

The yield of a one-period bond at date $t = 0$ is 10%.

We now determine the value of a two-period bond. At date $t = 1$, in the up node, the value of the bond is $\frac{1}{1 + 0.125} = 0.8889$. At date $t = 1$, in the down node, the value of the bond is $\frac{1}{1 + 0.08} = 0.9259$. Now that we have the prices of the bond at date $t = 1$, we can move back to date $t = 0$. At date $t = 0$, the expected value of the bond is $(0.8889 \times 0.5 + 0.9259 \times 0.5)$.

The discounted value of this expected price is

$$
b(0, 2) = \frac{[0.8889 \times 0.5 + 0.9259 \times 0.5]}{1.10} = 0.8249.
$$

The yield to maturity of the two-period bond is computed as

$$
0.8249 = \frac{1}{(1 + y_2)^2} \Rightarrow y_2 = 10.10\%.
$$

The evolution of the two-period bond is given next.

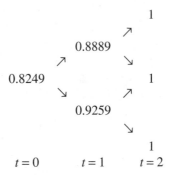

$$
\begin{array}{ccccc}
 & & & & 1 \\
 & & & \nearrow & \\
 & & 0.8889 & & \\
 & \nearrow & & \searrow & \\
0.8249 & & & & 1 \\
 & \searrow & & \nearrow & \\
 & & 0.9259 & & \\
 & & & \searrow & \\
 & & & & 1 \\
t = 0 & & t = 1 & & t = 2
\end{array}
$$

We now proceed to value the three-period bond. At date $t = 2$, at the top node, the value of the bond is $b^{uu}(2, 3) = \frac{1}{1 + 0.15625} = 0.8649$. At date $t = 2$, at the intermediate node, the value of the bond is $b^{ud}(2, 3) = \frac{1}{1 + 0.1000} = 0.9091$. At date $t = 2$, at the lowest node, the value of the bond is $b^{dd}(2, 3) = \frac{1}{1 + 0.0640} = 0.9398$.

Having determined the bond prices at date $t = 2$, we step back to date $t = 1$. At the top node in date 1, the value of the bond is the expected value of the bond in date 2, discounted by the one-period rate at the top node in date 1. This is given by

$$
b^{u}(1, 3) = \frac{[0.5 \times 0.8649 + 0.5 \times 0.9091]}{1 + 0.1250} = 0.7884.
$$

In a similar way, we can determine the price of the bond at date 1, at the lower node as

$$
b^{d}(1, 3) = \frac{[0.5 \times 0.9091 + 0.5 \times 0.9398]}{1 + 0.0800} = 0.8560.
$$

We now step back to date $t = 0$ and determine the value of the three-period bond as

$$
b(0, 3) = \frac{[0.5 \times 0.7884 + 0.5 \times 0.8560]}{1 + 0.1000} = 0.7475.
$$

The yield to maturity of the three-period bond is computed as

$$
0.7475 = \frac{1}{(1 + y_3)^3} \Rightarrow y_3 = 10.19\%.
$$

The evolution is shown by

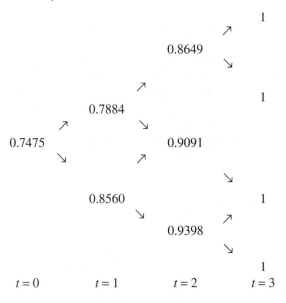

In a similar manner, we can determine the pricing of the four-period bond. The evolution of the four-period bond prices is

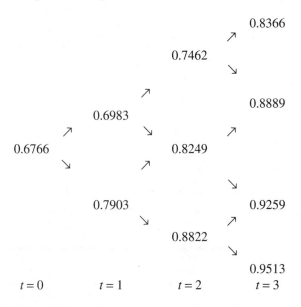

The yield to maturity of the four-period bond is computed as

$$0.6766 = \frac{1}{(1 + y_4)^4} \Rightarrow y_4 = 10.26\%.$$

The term structure of interest rates that we have calculated is recorded in Table 17-1.

In addition to determining the term structure, we also have information on the future yield distributions. For example, we can answer the question: What is the distribution of two-period yields on date 1 (one-period from now)? To address this question, we need to determine $b^u(1, 3)$ and $b^d(1, 3)$. Note that we already have this information from our analysis of the three-period bond pricing. We have determined that $b^u(1, 3) = 0.7884$ and $b^d(1, 3) = 0.8560$. The two-period yields at date 1 can be determined as follows:

$$0.7884 = \frac{1}{(1 + y_2^u)^2} \Rightarrow y_2^u = 12.623\%.$$

In a similar way,

$$0.8560 = \frac{1}{(1 + y_2^d)^2} \Rightarrow y_2^d = 8.084\%.$$

In a way similar to our analysis of bond-price dynamics, we can determine the continuous-time limit of this binomial process for interest rates. It turns out to be the log-normal process

$$dr = r[\mu\, dt + \sigma\, dz].$$

The terminal distribution of the interest rate for any time T is lognormal. Its mean and variance are

$$E\left[\ln\left(\frac{r_T}{r_t}\right)\right] = \mu(T - t)$$

and

$$Var\left[\ln\left(\frac{r_T}{r_t}\right)\right] = \sigma^2(T - t).$$

While our model ensures that the bond prices converge to par at maturity, this process is still unsatisfactory, as it assumes a lognormal distribution at any future date T.

TABLE 17-1 Term Structure	Bond Maturity (Number of Periods)	Bond Price	Yield to Maturity
	1	0.9091	10.00%
	2	0.8249	10.10%
	3	0.7475	10.19%
	4	0.6766	10.26%

This distribution means that some extremely high interest rates can occur in the future. Note that the probability of an up move or a down move is independent of the level of the interest rates. Empirically, interest rates appear to revert to a mean level (possibly a varying mean) of interest rates. This underscores the need to examine alternative processes for interest rates.

We illustrate a mean-reverting interest rate process next. In this process, the interest rate is pulled toward a central value but propagates randomly around the central value.

Mean-Reverting Interest-Rate Process

We present a simple discrete-time process in which the probability of an up move and a down move depend on the level of the interest rates.

Let us assume that the short rate follows a stochastic process specified below:

Upper limit, $r = 2\mu$

Lower limit, $r = 0$

The probabilities associated with each node are dependent on the interest rate at these nodes. These are specified as

$$q[r_t] = 1 - \frac{r_t}{2\mu},$$

and

$$1 - q[r_t] = \frac{r_t}{2\mu}.$$

When the interest rate reaches the upper limit, the probability of a down move is 1. Similarly, when the interest rates reach the lower limit, the probability of an up move is 1. The process has lower and upper limits at 0 and 2μ, respectively. The rates must evolve within these barriers. In the process specified previously, δ represents the amount by which the short rate can go up or go down in the interval $(t, t+1)$. This time interval could be a day, a week, or several weeks. Depending on how the time intervals are divided, the choice of the parameter δ will vary. The process specified affords some flexibility. By choosing the parameter μ suitably, both increasing and decreasing interest-rate scenarios can be modeled in an expectations context. When $r_t = \mu$, the probability of an up move is exactly equal to the probability of a down move. On the other hand, when $r_t < \mu$, the probability of an up move is greater than the probability of a down move, indicating that rates are expected to go up. In a similar manner, when $r_t > \mu$, the probability of an up move is less than the probability of a down move, indicating that rates are expected to go down. Viewed in this context, we may regard the parameter μ to be the long-run mean rate of interest. The location of the current value of the short rate relative to the long-run mean is, therefore, of interest in the bond-pricing problem. Another feature of interest is the speed with which the short rates are expected to approach the long-run mean value. The parameter δ can be interpreted as the speed of adjustment. When δ is large, the short rate r_t approaches the long-run mean interest rate rapidly. On the other hand, if δ is small, the short rate approaches the long-run mean rate sluggishly. The choice of δ, μ, and the current rate r_t provides flexibility in modeling different term-structure scenarios. The interest-rate process we have chosen has a steady state distribution. It can be shown that the mean and the variance of the process (as the number n of movements in the rates approaches infinity) are given by μ and $\frac{\delta\mu}{2}$, respectively. Therefore, by estimating the mean and variance of the interest-rate process using real-life data on interest rates, it is possible to identify the parameters μ and δ, which in turn may be used to generate the interest-rate tree. We provide a simple example to illustrate this model in Example 17-2.

Example 17-2:

Given the current interest rate (one-period) is 10%, the parameter $\delta = 1\%$, and $\mu = 12\%$. Determine the term structure of interest rates at date $t = 0$. The evolution of the one-period interest rates is

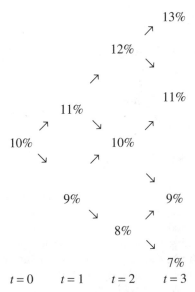

Unlike in the binomial process, the probabilities change at each node of the lattice; hence, we need to keep track of the probabilities. The next lattice shows **the evolution of up move probabilities through time.**

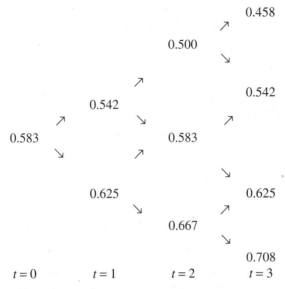

| $t = 0$ | $t = 1$ | $t = 2$ | $t = 3$ |

Note that the probability is exactly 0.5 when the interest rate is equal to 12%, which is the long-run mean. If the rates are below 12%, the probability of an up move increases beyond 0.5; otherwise, it decreases below 0.5.

As we did in the case of the binomial process, we begin by solving for the price of a single-period bond. This bond pays one dollar at date $t = 1$ no matter which state occurs. Therefore, its price at date $t = 0$ is $b(0, 1) = \frac{1}{(1 + 0.10)} = 0.9091$ as shown in the following

$$
\begin{array}{ccc}
 & & 1 \\
 & \nearrow & \\
0.9091 & & \\
 & \searrow & \\
 & & 1 \\
t = 0 & & t = 1
\end{array}
$$

The yield of one-period bond at date $t = 0$ is 10%.

We now proceed to value a two-period bond. At date $t = 1$, at the up node, the value of the bond is $\frac{1}{1 + 0.11} = 0.9009$. At date $t = 1$, at the down node, the value of the bond is $\frac{1}{1 + 0.09} = 0.9174$. Now that we have the prices of the bond at date $t = 1$, we can move back to date $t = 0$ and solve for the price of the two-period bond at date $t = 0$. At date $t = 0$, the expected value of the bond is $(0.9009 \times 0.5830 + 0.9174 \times 0.4170)$.

The discounted value of this expected price is

$$
b(0, 2) = \frac{[0.9009 \times 0.5830 + 0.9174 \times 0.4170]}{1.10} = 0.8253.
$$

The yield to maturity of the two-period bond is computed as

$$0.8253 = \frac{1}{(1 + y_2)^2} \Rightarrow y_2 = 10.076\%.$$

The evolution of the two-period bond is given next.

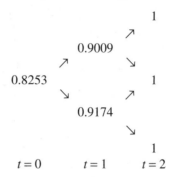

$$t = 0 \qquad t = 1 \qquad t = 2$$

The rest of the analysis is identical to that presented for the binomial process and, therefore, is not repeated here.

We now move to a discussion of models that have been quite influential in the pricing of debt securities and their derivatives. We present two models of interest rates that display mean reversion. The first one is by Vasicek and the second one by Cox, Ingersoll, and Ross. In the Vasicek model, while the interest rates display mean reversion, they can become negative. The volatility of the changes in the interest rates in the Vasicek model is a *constant* over a small interval of time. In contrast, in the Cox, Ingersoll, and Ross model, interest rates never become negative. Furthermore, the volatility of the changes in interest rates is *proportional* to the level of interest rates over a small interval of time.

Vasicek Model

The interest rate process used by Vasicek is

$$dr = r(\mu - r)\,dt + \sigma\,dz.$$

In this process, there are three parameters: μ, the long-run mean of the short-term interest rate; σ^2, the variance parameter; and κ, the speed of adjustment of the short-term interest rate to the long-run mean. The prices of zero-coupon bonds in the Vasicek model can be determined using the following simple formula:

$$b(t, T) = A(T - t)e^{-B(t, T)r_t}$$

Let $\tau \equiv T - t$, the time to maturity of the bond. Then,

$$A(\tau) = \exp\left[\frac{\{B(\tau) - \tau\}\left\{\kappa^2\mu - \dfrac{\sigma^2}{2}\right\}}{\kappa^2} - \frac{\sigma^2 B^2(\tau)}{4\kappa}\right]$$

and

$$B(\tau) = \frac{1 - e^{-\kappa\tau}}{\kappa}.$$

We illustrate the Vasicek model with two examples shown in Figures 17-1 and 17-2. In Figure 17-1, the long-run mean is 12%, and the current short-term interest rate is 10%. As a result, the interest rates are pulled higher, leading to an upward-sloping term structure. The greater the value of the speed of adjustment ($\kappa = 0.1$), the steeper will be the term structure.

In Figure 17-2, the long-run mean interest rate (8%) is *below* the current short-term interest rate. Hence, the interest rates are pulled down, leading to a downward-sloping term structure.

FIGURE 17-1   *Implementing Vasicek Model*

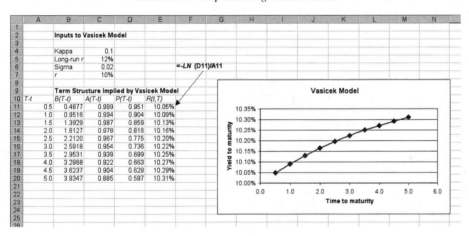

FIGURE 17-2   *Effect of Long-Run Mean Rate*

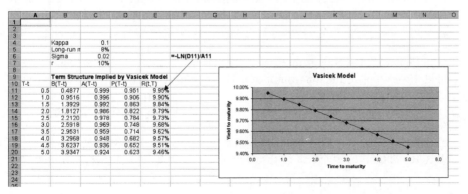

Cox, Ingersoll, and Ross Model

In a model proposed by Cox, Ingersoll, and Ross (1985) (CIR), interest rates follow a mean-reverting process much like the model we presented in the previous section. However, the variance of the changes in interest rates is proportional to the level of the rates.

The interest rate process that they use is represented in the following equation:

$$dr = \kappa(\mu - r)\, dt + \sigma\sqrt{r}\; dz.$$

In this process, there are three parameters: μ, the long-run mean of the short-term interest rate; σ^2, the variance parameter; and κ, the speed of adjustment of the short-term interest rate to the long-run mean. In addition, the parameter λ, which is related to the risk-averse behavior of investors, also affects the bond prices. These parameters must be estimated in order to implement the CIR model.

Prices of discount bonds are determined in the Cox, Ingersoll, and Ross (1985) model using a simple formula. Let the current time be denoted by t; then a bond paying \$1 at time T should be priced as

$$b(t, T) = A(T - t)e^{-B(T - t)r_t} \tag{17.3}$$

Given the parameter τ, representing the time to maturity $T - t$ of a bond, then

$$A(\tau) = \left(\frac{2\gamma e^{(\kappa+\gamma+\lambda)\tau/2}}{2\gamma + (\kappa + \gamma + \lambda)(e^{\gamma\tau} - 1)} \right)^{2\kappa\mu/\sigma^2}$$

$$B(\tau) = \frac{2(e^{\gamma\tau} - 1)}{2\gamma + (\kappa + \gamma + \lambda)(e^{\gamma\tau} - 1)}$$

$$\gamma = \sqrt{(\kappa + \lambda)^2 + 2\sigma^2}.$$

This model can be used to generate different shapes of the yield curve. It is necessary that $2\kappa\mu \geq \sigma^2$ to ensure that the interest rate is positive. In the CIR model, when $r < \frac{2\kappa\mu}{\gamma+\kappa+\lambda}$, the term structure is upward-sloping, and when $r > \frac{\kappa\mu}{\kappa+\lambda}$ the term structure is downward-sloping. For intermediate values of r, the term structure is humped.

We show examples in Figures 17-3 and 17-4. In Figure 17-3, the term structure is downward-sloping. This is because the long-run mean rate (μ) is 5%, and the current interest rate is 10%. Hence, the current rate is pulled *down* toward the long-run mean. The higher the speed of adjustment kappa (κ), the greater will be the inversion of the term structure.

In Figure 17-4, the long-run mean is 25%; hence, the current interest rate (10%) is pulled *higher* toward the long-run mean. This produces a steep upward-sloping yield curve.

Several authors have tested the Cox, Ingersoll, and Ross model. Brown and Dybvig (1986), Gibbons and Ramaswamy (1994), and Pearson and Sun (1994) have examined the model. The fact that the model is driven by only one factor (short rate) means that its ability to capture the richness in the yield curve is somewhat limited. Gibbons and

FIGURE 17-3   *Implementing the CIR Model*

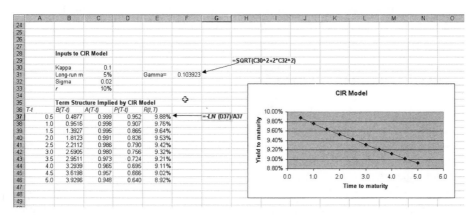

FIGURE 17-4   *Effect of the Long-Run Mean Rate*

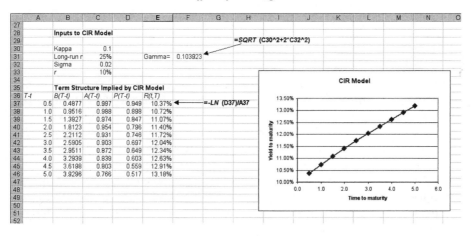

Ramaswamy (1994) estimated the parameters of the model as $\mu = 1.54\%$, $\kappa = 12.43$, $\lambda = -6.08$, and $\sigma = 0.49$. They found that the CIR model that describes the behavior of real returns does a satisfactory job of explaining short-term T-bill returns. In much of the literature, there is a general agreement that single-factor models need to be generalized, perhaps to include three factors: short-term interest rates, the spread between short-term and long-term interest rates (which is a proxy for the slope of the yield curve), and the volatility of interest rates. In the industry, single-factor models are used with an important modification: Some free parameters are added to make the model fit the market data. In the CIR model, we can describe the long-run mean rate $\mu(t)$ as a function of time. Wang (1994) shows that by making $\mu(t)$ a step function, the CIR model can be made to fit the market data. We turn to this class of models next.

CALIBRATION OF MODELS

The models of interest rates that we have presented so far are not calibrated to market data. In other words, the parameters of the models are estimated, and using the estimated parameters, we compute zero prices. These zero prices may or may not correspond to the actual market prices of zeroes. If we believe there are liquid securities which are traded actively with narrow bid-offer spreads, then we would like a model that prices them close to their market values. There is a class of term-structure models that find the parameters from the market data much the same way implied volatilities are computed in equity options, using a process known as calibration. We present three such models of term structure next.

Black, Derman, and Toy Model

We will begin our treatment of the first of these, the Black, Derman, and Toy model, with an illustrative example.

Example 17-3:

Consider a problem in which we want the term-structure model to be calibrated to the market data on one-period and two-period yields and to the volatilities presented in Table 17-2.

In calibrated models, the pricing procedure is turned on its head; normally, term-structure models begin with the spot-rate evolution tree (based on the parameter estimates) and then solve for the term structure as an outcome of applying LEH to the spot-rate tree. This is what we did in the previous section. The outcome of such an exercise will be an output such as Table 17-2. **In the Black, Derman, and Toy model, however, the market data on yields is the input and the spot-rate tree is the output.**

	TABLE 17-2	
Market Data on Yields		

Term to Maturity	Yield to Maturity (Percent)	Volatility (Percent)
1	10.00	
2	11.00	19.00
3	12.00	18.00

To construct the spot-rate tree, we work from the root of the lattice and proceed forward.

$$
\begin{array}{ccccc}
 & & & & r_{uu} \\
 & & & \nearrow & \\
 & & r_u & & \\
 & \nearrow & & \searrow & \\
r & & & & r_{ud} \\
 & \searrow & & \nearrow & \\
 & & r_d & & \\
 & & & \searrow & \\
 & & & & r_{dd} \\
t = 0 & & t = 1 & & t = 2
\end{array}
$$

Given the data provided in Table 17-2, we can determine the prices of zeroes at date $t = 0$. Let $b(0, n)$ be the price of a zero with n years to maturity at date $t = 0$. At node 0, the following conditions exist for a zero that will mature at $t = 2$:

$$
\frac{1}{2} \times \ln\left(\frac{r_u}{r_d}\right) = 0.19. \tag{17.4}
$$

Equation 17.4 sets the volatility of the two-year rates (one period hence) equal to 19%.

$$
\frac{\frac{1}{2} \times \left(\frac{1}{1 + r_u} + \frac{1}{1 + r_d}\right)}{1 + 0.10} = b(0, 2) \tag{17.5}
$$

$$
b(0, 2) = 0.8116
$$

Equation 17.5 sets the price of a two-year zero equal to the one obtained by the LEH. We have assumed that $q = \frac{1}{2}$. Solving Equations 17.4 and 17.5 simultaneously, we get $r_u = 14.319\%$ and $r_d = 9.792\%$.

$$
\begin{array}{ccccc}
 & & & & r_{uu} \\
 & & & \nearrow & \\
 & & 14.318\% & & \\
 & \nearrow & & \searrow & \\
10\% & & & & r_{ud} \\
 & \searrow & & \nearrow & \\
 & & 9.792\% & & \\
 & & & \searrow & \\
 & & & & r_{dd} \\
t = 0 & & t = 1 & & t = 2
\end{array}
$$

We can now construct the tree further forward. We solve for r_{uu}, r_{ud}, and r_{dd} in such a way that when LEH is applied to the tree we get the market prices reflected in Table 17-2. Let $y_u(1, 3)$ be the two-year yield at date $t = 1$ in the "up state." Likewise, let $y_d(1, 3)$ be the two-year yield at date $t = 1$ in the "down state." Using these notations, we write the volatility condition:

$$\frac{1}{2} \times \ln\left[\frac{y_u(1,3)}{y_d(1,3)}\right] = 0.18. \tag{17.6}$$

Equation 17.6 sets the volatility of the three-year rates (one period hence) equal to 18%. In the "up state" at $t = 1$, the rate is $y_u(1, 3)$; and in the "down state" at date $t = 1$, the rate is $y_d(1, 3)$. Also, by no arbitrage, we must have

$$\frac{\frac{1}{2} \times \left\{\frac{1}{[1 + y_u(1, 3)]^2} + \frac{1}{[1 + y_d(1, 3)]^2}\right\}}{1 + 0.10} = b(0, 3), \tag{17.7}$$

where $b(0, 3)$ is the three-period zero price given by

$$b(0,3) = \frac{1}{(1 + 0.12)^3}.$$

We solve the two previous equations to get $y_u(1, 3) = 15.4159\%$ and $y_d(1, 3) = 10.7553\%$.

Note that at $t = 1$ the price of a zero maturing at $t = 3$ can be determined for both the up state and the down state as

$$b_u(1, 3) = \frac{1}{[1 + y_u(1, 3)]^2} = 0.750704$$

and

$$b_d(1, 3) = \frac{1}{[1 + y_d(1, 3)]^2} = 0.81521.$$

In addition, by the LEH, we must also have

$$b_u(1, 3) = \frac{\frac{1}{2} \times \left(\frac{1}{1 + r_{uu}} + \frac{1}{1 + r_{ud}}\right)}{1 + r_u} \tag{17.8}$$

and

$$b_d(1, 3) = \frac{\frac{1}{2} \times \left(\frac{1}{1 + r_{ud}} + \frac{1}{1 + r_{dd}}\right)}{1 + r_d}. \tag{17.9}$$

Also, assuming lognormality, we have

$$r_{ud} = \sqrt{r_{uu} \times r_{dd}}. \tag{17.10}$$

Solving the three previous equations, we get $r_{uu} = 19.4187\%$, $r_{ud} = 13.7669\%$, and $r_{dd} = 9.076\%$. We can construct the yield curve at each node using the zero prices.

$$
\begin{array}{ccccc}
 & & & & 19.4187\% \\
 & & & \nearrow & (j=0) \\
 & & 14.318\% & & \\
 & \nearrow & (j=0) & \searrow & \\
10\% & & & & 13.7669\% \\
 & \searrow & & \nearrow & (j=1) \\
 & & 9.792\% & & \\
 & & (j=1) & \searrow & \\
 & & & & 9.76\% \\
 & & & & (j=2) \\
t=0 & & t=1 & & t=2
\end{array}
$$

We proceed this way to get the entire tree. Once the tree is generated from selected market data, we can use the tree to value any derivative asset that is interest-rate related. A detailed treatment of the discrete-time version of this model in the context of pricing corporate bonds is found in Maloney (1992). We provide a brief description of the general implementation of the Black, Derman, and Toy model next.

Let $t = 0, 1, 2 \ldots, N$ be the time periods, and let $j = 0, 1, 2 \ldots, t$ be the nodes at any time node t. Let $b(t, j, T)$ be the price of a discount bond at date t at node j maturing at date T. Assume that the life of the bond is divided into n periods. Then the Black, Derman, and Toy model may be summarized formally as

$$b(t, j, T) = e^{-r(t, j, T)(T-t)}. \tag{17.11}$$

This equation simply says that the value of a zero is the discounted value of \$1 to be received at date T. This is the price-yield relationship for the zero-coupon bond at date t and state (node) j. The next relationship is the condition that the bonds are priced to eliminate arbitrage opportunities.

$$b(t, j, T) = \{0.5b(t+1, j, T) + 0.5b(t+1, j+1, T)\}b(t, j, t+1) \tag{17.12}$$

This condition is common to all models that are used in the industry to calibrate the model to the market data. In particular, the same condition is used in the Ho and Lee (1986) model and in the Heath, Jarrow, and Morton (1992) model. The Black, Derman, and Toy (1990) model also specifies conditions on the volatility structure,

$$b(t+1, j+1, T) = b(t+1, j, T)^{v(t, T)}, \tag{17.13}$$

where $v(t, T)$ is the volatility factor for a bond with a maturity date T in period $t+1$ as of date t. The volatility factor is given by

$$v(t, T) = e^{[2\sigma(t, T)]}, \tag{17.14}$$

where $\sigma(t, T)$ is the annualized volatility of the yield of a zero-coupon bond maturing at date T as evaluated at date t. As shown earlier, the model takes as market data

$y(0, j, T)$ and $\sigma(0, T)$, where $T = 1, 2, \ldots, N$. Note that at date $t = 0$ there is only one state, so $j = 0$.

When $t = 0$ in Equations 17.12 and 17.13, we first know the relation between $b(1, 0, T)$ and $b(1, 1, T)$ from the volatility structure. Using this in the no-arbitrage condition yields a single nonlinear equation in $b(1, 0, T)$ that can be solved by a univariate Newton-Ralphson iterative search procedure.

To see this clearly, let us rewrite Equations 17.12 and 17.14 for the case when $t = 0$. We get corresponding to Equation 17.12

$$b(0, 0, T) = [0.5b(1, 0, T) + 0.5b(1, 1, T)]b(0, 0, 1).$$

Note that in this equation, $b(0, 0, T)$ is known for all T; hence, the unknowns are $b(1, 0, T)$ and $b(1, 1, T)$. Corresponding to Equation 17.14, we get

$$b(1, 1, T) = b(1, 0, T))^{v(0, T)}.$$

In this equation, $v(0, T)$ is known for all T. Substituting this equation into the previous equation we get

$$b(0, 0, T) = [0.5b(1, 0, T) + 0.5b(1, 0, T)^{v(0, T)}]b(0, 0, 1).$$

This nonlinear equation can be iteratively solved for $T = 1, \ldots, N$ for $b(1, 0, T)$. Once we determine $b(1, 0, T)$, we can utilize that information to determine $b(1, 1, T)$.

When $t \geq 1$, we have a system of two nonlinear equations that again can be solved by a bivariate Newton-Ralphson search procedure. This search is a bit more complicated because for each T we have two nonlinear equations to solve for $b(t, j, T)$. For each t we solve Equations 17.12 and 17.13 simultaneously. We illustrate the idea using the case when $t = 1$. Note that in this case, we get the following two conditions:

$$b(1, j, T) = [0.5b(2, j, T) + 0.5b(2, j + 1, T)]b(1, j, 2)$$

and

$$b(2, j + 1, T) = b(2, j, T)^{v(1, T)}.$$

For $j = 0$ and $j = 1$, the previous system can be solved for $b(2, 0, T)$, $b(2, 1, T)$, and $b(2, 2, T)$. This allows us to get the term structure at $t = 2$ and so on.

Ho and Lee Model

The Ho and Lee (1986) model is developed in a discrete-state, discrete-time framework. The initial (current) term structure is exogenously specified based on market conditions. It is then assumed to be randomly perturbed. This perturbation is effected by allowing the entire term structure to evolve through time as a binomial process. Constraints on the perturbation function are then imposed to preclude pairwise arbitrage between any two bonds. It turns out that this condition alone is insufficient to rule out negative forward rates. As a result, the model still admits arbitrage.

The Ho and Lee model is a novel approach to dynamically modeling the term structure of interest rates. By construction, the model generates bond prices that are calibrated to market data. It also provides a unified preference-independent framework in which to price a wide variety of contingent claims, including futures contracts and options on both the cash instrument and futures contracts.

The price of a bond in state i at time t that pays \$1 at time T is represented by $b(t, i, T)$. The initial term structure $b(0, 0, T)$ is exogenously specified and is assumed to be randomly perturbed. This perturbation is reflected by allowing the entire term structure to evolve through time as a binomial process,

$$
\begin{array}{ccccc}
& & & & b(2, 2, T) \\
& & & \nearrow & \\
& & b(1, 1, T) & & \\
& \nearrow & & \searrow & \\
b(0, 0, T) & & & & b(2, 1, T) \\
& \searrow & & \nearrow & \\
& & b(1, 0, T) & & \\
& & & \searrow & \\
& & & & b(2, 0, T) \\
t = 0 & & t = 1 & & t = 2
\end{array}
$$

where the perturbation functions $h(\tau)$ and $h^*(\tau)$ are defined as follows (where τ is the time to maturity remaining):

$$
b(t + 1, i + 1, T) = \frac{b(t, i, T)}{b(t, i, t + 1)} h(T - (t + 1)) \tag{17.15}
$$

$$
b(t + 1, i, T) = \frac{b(t, i, T)}{b(t, i, t + 1)} h^*(T - (t + 1)) \tag{17.16}
$$

$$
h(0) = h^*(0) = 1.
$$

By dividing Equation 17.15 by Equation 17.16, we get

$$
\frac{b(t + 1, i + 1, T)}{b(t + 1, i, T)} = \frac{h(T - (t + 1))}{h^*(T - (t + 1))}. \tag{17.17}
$$

Assume that the probability that the perturbation will be effected by $h(T)$ is q. Consequently, the probability that the perturbation will be effected by $h^*(T)$ is $1 - q$. The no-arbitrage condition that was used in the Black, Derman, and Toy model is also used here:

$$
b(t, i, T) = \{(1 - q)b(t + 1, i, T) + qb(t + 1, i + 1, T)\}b(t, i, t + 1).
$$

Combining the previous conditions, we get the constraint on the perturbation functions to preclude arbitrage between any two pairs of bonds as

$$
qh(\tau) + (1 - q)h^*(\tau) = 1 \text{ for } \tau, i > 0.
$$

In addition, the following additional conditions are imposed by the Ho and Lee model:

$$h(\tau) = \frac{1}{q + (1 - q)^{\delta\tau}}$$

and

$$h^*(\tau) = \frac{\delta^\tau}{q + (1 - q)^{\delta\tau}}$$

for the constants $0 \geq q \geq 1$ and $0 \geq \delta \geq 1$. We illustrate the Ho and Lee model in Example 17-4.

Example 17-4:

Let us consider the market data presented in Table 17-3. The evolution of the bond prices will be calibrated to this data. We will assume that $q = 0.5$ and that $\delta = 0.99$. Note that we can solve for $h(\tau)$ and $h^*(\tau)$, for $\tau = 1, 2,$ and 3. These values are shown in the following table:

τ	$h(\tau)$	$h^*(\tau)$
1	1.005	.995
2	1.010	.990
3	1.015	.985

The pricing procedure works as follows. The no-arbitrage condition

$$b(0, 0, 2) = [0.5b(1, 0, 2) + 0.5b(1, 1, 2)]b(0, 0, 1)$$

is combined with the perturbation requirement

$$\frac{b(1, 1, 2)}{b(1, 0, 2)} = \frac{h(1)}{h^*(1)}.$$

Solving these two equations, we get $b(1, 0, 2) = 0.92127$ and $b(1, 1, 2) = 0.93508$.

TABLE 17-3			
Market Data on Yields	*Term to Maturity*	*Yield to Maturity (Percent)*	*Bond Price*
	1	8.00	0.92593
	2	8.00	0.85734
	3	8.00	0.79383

We can apply the same principles to solve for $b(1, 0, 3)$ and $b(1, 1, 3)$. The no-arbitrage condition

$$b(0, 0, 3) = \{0.5b(1, 0, 3) + 0.5b(1, 1, 3)\}b(0, 0, 1)$$

is combined with the perturbation requirement

$$\frac{b(1, 1, 3)}{b(1, 0, 3)} = \frac{h(2)}{h*(2)}.$$

Solving these two equations, we get $b(1, 0, 3) = 0.848723$ and $b(1, 1, 3) = 0.865955$.

Having solved for the prices of discount bonds at date $t = 1$, we can move forward to value the prices of bonds at date $t = 2$ for different nodes. The no-arbitrage condition at date $t = 1$ is

$$b(1, 0, 3) = \{0.5b(2, 0, 3) + 0.5b(2, 1, 3)\}b(1, 0, 2).$$

This is combined with the perturbation requirement

$$\frac{b(2, 1, 3)}{b(2, 0, 3)} = \frac{h(1)}{h*(1)}.$$

Solving these two equations, we get $b(2, 0, 3) = 0.91662$ and $b(2, 1, 3) = 0.92588$. In this manner, the entire future distribution of bond prices can be obtained using the Ho and Lee approach.

Ho-Lee Discount Factors		0	1	2	3
	1-Year Zero	0.925926	1		
			1		
	2-Year Zero	0.857339	0.930579	1	
			0.921273	1	
				1	
	3-Year Zero	0.793832	0.865955	0.935231	1
			0.848723	0.925879	1
				0.916620	1
					1

Heath, Jarrow, and Morton Model

The Heath, Jarrow, and Morton (HJM) (1992) model, unlike other models, is based on the evolution of forward rates of interest. Conceptually, the insights of this paper are very similar to the Ho and Lee (1986) model. Unlike the Ho and Lee model, however, the HJM model ensures that the interest rates are always positive. As in the Ho and

FIGURE 17-5   *Heath, Jarrow, and Morton Model, Nonrecombining Tree of Forward Rates*

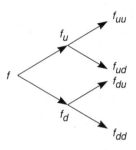

Lee and the Black, Derman, and Toy models, this model enforces the no-arbitrage condition that

$$b(0, 0, j) = [0.5b(1, 0, j) + 0.5b(1, 1, j)]b(0, 0, 1).$$

The no-arbitrage condition means that the evolution of the forward rates are dictated by their volatility structure alone. Unlike the previous models, the HJM model is path dependent. With a path-dependent tree, even with a few steps, many outcomes are possible. If we examine Figure 17-5, we note that after one period from the root of the tree, there are two possible forward rates. After two periods from the root of the tree, there are four possible forward rates: two consecutive up moves lead to f_{uu}, one up move followed by one down move leads to f_{ud}, one down move followed by one up move leads to f_{du}, and two consecutive down moves lead to f_{dd}. In fact, in the HJM model, the number of nodes increases exponentially with time intervals. Thus, with four time intervals in the HJM model, we get $2^4 = 16$ nodes. With seven intervals, we get $2^7 = 128$ nodes. Computationally, the HJM model presents more of a challenge than the other models that we discussed in this chapter. Only a brief presentation of the Heath, Jarrow, and Morton model is given here. See Heath, Jarrow, and Morton (1992) for a detailed presentation. Hull and White (1990) offer another model to value the term structure.

Interest-Rate Derivatives

Interest-rate derivatives range from a simple call option on yields to a complicated structure involving yield-curve swaps in which yields with different maturities are swapped between counterparties. Other interest-rate derivatives include index-amortization swaps, caps, floors, and delivery options in Treasury bond futures contracts. We will illustrate the interest-rate derivatives pricing with an example of a call option on yields.

Consider the task of pricing a call option at date $t = 0$ on a two-period interest rate at a strike rate of $k\%$. Assume that the option is going to expire at date $t = 1$. Assume that the interest rate follows a multiplicative random walk as shown in the following lattice. The probability of an up move is q, and the probability of a down move is $1 - q$.

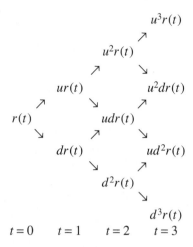

$$t = 0 \qquad t = 1 \qquad t = 2 \qquad t = 3$$

At each node, we can compute the prices of a discount bond, which matures at date $t = 3$. The price distribution is shown in the following price tree:

$$t = 0 \qquad t = 1 \qquad t = 2 \qquad t = 3$$

The price distribution (and hence the yield distribution) is obtained by applying the condition that the expected return on the bond at each node must be equal to the interest rate prevailing at that node. Applying this condition recursively by beginning at $t = 3$, which is the maturity date of the bond, and working backward we can value securities. The pricing equations are

$$\frac{1}{b^{u^2}(2,3)} = 1 + u^2 r(t),$$

$$\frac{1}{b^{ud}(2,3)} = 1 + udr(t),$$

and

$$\frac{1}{b^{d^2}(2,3)} = 1 + d^2 r(t).$$

As a consequence, we can rearrange these three equations to get the bond-price distributions:

$$b^{u^2}(2,3) = \frac{1}{1 + u^2 r(t)},$$

$$b^{ud}(2,3) = \frac{1}{1 + udr(t)},$$

and

$$b^{dd}(2,3) = \frac{1}{1 + d^2 r(t)}.$$

Having obtained the price distributions at date $t = 2$ for the one-period bonds, we step back to date $t = 1$ and obtain the following pricing relationship by using the LEH:

$$\frac{q \times b^{u^2}(2,3) + (1-q) \times b^{ud}(2,3)}{b^u(1,3)} = 1 + ur(t)$$

$$\frac{q \times b^{ud}(2,3) + (1-q) \times b^{d^2}(2,3)}{b^d(1,3)} = 1 + dr(t).$$

Solving the two previous equations, we get the price distributions $b^u(1, 3)$ and $b^d(1, 3)$.

Having obtained the price distributions at date $t = 1$ for the two-period bonds, we step back to date $t = 0$ and obtain the following pricing relationship by using the same condition on expected return as before:

$$\frac{q \times b^u(1,3) + (1-q) \times b^d(1,3)}{b(0,3)} = 1 + r(t).$$

This enables us to solve for $b(0, 3)$.

Corresponding to the price distribution of two-period bond prices $b^u(1, 3)$ and $b^d(1, 3)$ at date $t = 1$, there is a two-period yield distribution. Let $y^u(1, 3)$ be the two-period yield at $t = 1$ in the up state and $y^d(1, 3)$ be the two-period yield at $t = 1$ in the down state. Note that

$$y^u(1,3) = \left[\frac{1}{b^u(1,3)}\right]^{\frac{1}{2}} - 1$$

and

$$y^d(1,3) = \left[\frac{1}{b^d(1,3)}\right]^{\frac{1}{2}} - 1.$$

In a similar way, we can start with a discount bond that matures at date $t = 2$ and solve for its price $b(0, 2)$ at date $t = 0$ and its price distribution at $t = 1$. At date $t = 0$, the two-period yield $y(0, 2)$ is given by

$$y(0,2) = \left[\frac{1}{b(0,2)}\right]^{\frac{1}{2}} - 1.$$

Having obtained the two-period yields, we can set up the two-period yield distribution as shown in the following tree:

$$
\begin{array}{ccc}
& & y^u(1,3) \\
& \nearrow & \\
y(0,2) & & \\
& \searrow & \\
& & y^d(1,3) \\
t=0 & & t=1
\end{array}
$$

The payoffs of the call option at date $t = 1$ follow:

$$
\begin{array}{ccc}
& & C^u = \max\,[0,\, y^u(1,3) - k] \\
& \nearrow & \\
C & & \\
& \searrow & \\
& & C^d = \max\,[0,\, y^d(1,3) - k] \\
t=0 & & t=1
\end{array}
$$

By the LEH, the value of call is

$$C = \max\left[y(0,2) - k, \frac{qC^u + 1(1-q)C^d}{1 + y(0,1)}\right].$$

Example 17-5:

Consider an interest-rate process in which the initial interest rate is 5%, $u = 1.06$, $d = \frac{1}{1.06}$, and $q = 0.5$. Assume that the strike rate on this yield option is 5%. The option is on two-period yields. The option expires at $t = 1$.

$$
\begin{array}{ccccccc}
& & & & & & 5.955\% \\
& & & & & \nearrow & \\
& & & & 5.618\% & & \\
& & & \nearrow & & \searrow & \\
& & 5.30\% & & & & 5.300\% \\
& \nearrow & & \searrow & & \nearrow & \\
5\% & & & & 5.000\% & & \\
& \searrow & & \nearrow & & \searrow & \\
& & 4.717\% & & & & 4.717\% \\
& & & \searrow & & \nearrow & \\
& & & & 4.450\% & & \\
& & & & & \searrow & \\
& & & & & & 4.4198\% \\
t=0 & & t=1 & & t=2 & & t=3
\end{array}
$$

Corresponding to this one-period interest rate process, we can compute the price of a four-period discount bond at date $t = 0$ maturing on date $t = 4$. Its evolution as it approaches maturity is shown next.

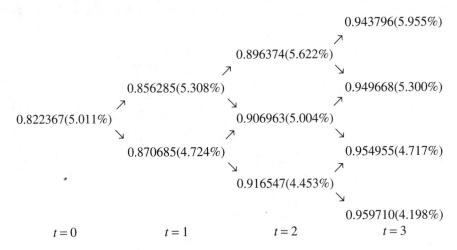

$$
\begin{array}{ccccccc}
 & & & & & & 0.943796(5.955\%) \\
 & & & & 0.896374(5.622\%) & \nearrow & \\
 & & 0.856285(5.308\%) & \nearrow & & \searrow & 0.949668(5.300\%) \\
0.822367(5.011\%) & \nearrow & & \searrow & 0.906963(5.004\%) & \nearrow & \\
 & \searrow & 0.870685(4.724\%) & \nearrow & & \searrow & 0.954955(4.717\%) \\
 & & & \searrow & 0.916547(4.453\%) & \nearrow & \\
 & & & & & \searrow & 0.959710(4.198\%) \\
t = 0 & & t = 1 & & t = 2 & & t = 3
\end{array}
$$

Note that each discount bond price can be converted to a yield, shown in parentheses. For example, we now know that at date $t = 1$, the three-period yield can either be 5.302% or 4.719% with equal probabilities.

In this way, we can construct the lattice for a three-period bond at date $t = 0$. This leads to the following distribution:

$$
\begin{array}{ccccc}
 & & & & b^{u^2}(2, 3) = \\
 & & & & 0.946808(5.618\%) \\
 & & b^u(1, 3) = & \nearrow & \\
 & & 0.901799(\mathbf{5.304\%}) & & \\
b(0, 3) = & \nearrow & & \searrow & b^{ud}(2, 3) = \\
0.863655(5.007\%) & & & & 0.911876(5.000\%) \\
 & \searrow & b^d(1, 3) = & \nearrow & \\
 & & 0.952381(\mathbf{4{,}721\%}) & & \\
 & & & \searrow & b^{d^2}(2, 3) = \\
 & & & & 0.957396(4.450\%) \\
t = 0 & & t = 1 & & t = 2
\end{array}
$$

For the two-period discount bond, at date $t = 0$, the distribution is

$$b^u(1, 2) = 0.949668(5.300\%)$$

↗

$$b(0, 2) = 0.906963(5.00\%)$$

↘

$$b^d(1, 2) = 0.954955(4.717\%)$$

$t = 0$ $\qquad\qquad\qquad\qquad$ $t = 1$

The payoffs of the option can now be determined as

$$c^u = 5.304\% - 5\% = 0.304\%$$

↗

c

↘

$$c^d = 0.000\% = \max\,[4.717\% - 5\%, 0]$$

$t = 0$ $\qquad\qquad\qquad\qquad$ $t = 1$

Thus, the value of the option is

$$\frac{0.304 \times 0.5 + 0.000 \times 0.5}{1.05} = 0.1447.$$

The option is worth 14.47 basis points.

CONCLUSION AND FURTHER READINGS

In this chapter, we have examined the determinants of interest rates. Some evidence was presented on the presence of the Fisher effect in interest rates. Fama (1976, 1990) contains evidence concerning the ability of the term structure to predict future spot rates. He also presents the forecasting power of the term structure concerning inflation. Mishkin (1990a, 1991) has investigated these issues in international and domestic contexts. We also reviewed hypotheses on interest rates. A number of papers have addressed issues relating to hypotheses concerning term structure. Campbell (1986) contains a defense of the traditional models of the term structure. Other papers have been mentioned in our discussion. The conclusions of these papers differ depending on the sample periods chosen by the authors. Some models of term structure were also presented.

PROBLEMS

17.1 Spreadsheet Problem. Use the market data on the yields and volatilities of yields provided in the following table for zeroes with maturities of one to five years.

   (a) Construct the lattice for this market data, and derive the yield curve at each node of the
lattice. In other words, determine r_u, r_d, r_{uu}, r_{ud}, r_{dd}, r_{uuu}, r_{uud}, r_{udd} and r_{ddd}.

Market Data

Maturity	Yield (Percent)	Volatility (Percent)
1	9	20
2	9	19
3	9	18
4	9	17
5	9	16

   (b) Determine the yields of all securities with a maturity of five years or less as applicable
in each node. Treat each period as one year. Assume that the probability $q = \frac{1}{2}$. Use the
Black, Derman, and Toy model for this problem.

   (c) Determine the par bond yield curve out to five years.

17.2 Spreadsheet Problem. Consider the lattice provided in the following example:

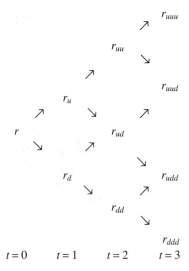

$$t=0 \qquad t=1 \qquad t=2 \qquad t=3$$

Assume that at the root of the tree $r = 10\%$. Assume that the interest rates follow a binomial
process, with $u = 1.1$ and $d = \frac{1}{u}$.

   (a) Determine all the short-term interest rates in the lattice. (Recall that $r_u = ur$, $r_d = dr$, etc.)

   (b) Determine the yields of all securities with a maturity of five years or less as applicable
in each node. Treat each period as one year. Assume that the probability $q = \frac{1}{2}$.

   (c) Compute the state prices. How would you use the state prices to value a two-year bond
paying an annual coupon of 5% and a balloon payment of 100 at the end of two years?

REFERENCES

Black, F., E. Derman, and W. Toy 1990. "A One-Factor Model of Interest Rates and Its Application to Treasury Bond Options." *Financial Analysts Journal* 46(1):33–39.

Brown, S. J., and P. H. Dybvig 1986. "The Empirical Implications of Cox-Ingersoll-Ross Theory of the Term Structure of Interest Rates." *Journal of Finance* 41:617–630.

Campbell, J. Y. 1986. "A Defense of Traditional Hypotheses about the Term Structure of Interest Rates." *Journal of Finance* 41:183–193.

Cox, J. C., and S. A. Ross 1976. "The Valuation of Options for Alternative Stochastic Processes." *Journal of Financial Economics* 3:145–166.

Cox, J. C., J. Ingersoll, and S. Ross 1985. "A Theory of the Term Structure of Interest Rates." *Econometrica* 53:385–407.

Cox, J. C., S. A. Ross, and M. Rubinstein 1979. "Option Pricing: A Simplified Approach." *Journal of Financial Economics* 7:229–263.

Fama, E. F. 1976. "Forward Rates as Predictors of Future Spot-Rates." *Journal of Financial Economics* 3:361–377.

Fama, E. F. 1990. "Term Structure Forecasts of Interest Rates, Inflation and Real Returns." *Journal of Monetary Economics* 25:59–76.

Fama, E. F., and K. French 1993. "Common Risk Factors in the Returns on Stocks and Bonds." *Journal of Financial Economics* 33:3–56.

Fama, E., and M. Gibbons 1982. "Inflation, Real Returns and Capital Investment." *Journal of Monetary Economics* 9(3):297–323.

Gibbons, M. R., and K. Ramaswamy 1993. "The Term Structure of Interest Rates: Empirical Evidence." *Review of Financial Studies* 6:619–658.

Harrison, J. M., and D. M. Kreps 1978. "Martingales and Arbitrage in Multiperiod Security Markets." *Journal of Economic Theory* 20:381–408.

Heath, D., R. Jarrow, and A. Morton 1992. "Bond Pricing and the Term Structure of Interest Rates: A New Methodology for Contingent Claims Valuation." *Econometrics* 60(1):77–105.

Ho, T. S. Y., and S. Lee 1986. "Term Structure Movements and Pricing Interest Rate Contingent Claims." *The Journal of Finance* XLI(5):1011–1029.

Hull, J., and A. White 1990. "Pricing Interest-Rate Derivative Securities." *Review of Financial Studies* 3(4):573–592.

Maloney, K. J. 1992. A Contingent Claims Model of Corporate Security Valuation Using a Realistic Model of Financial Distress. Working paper, Dartmouth University.

Mishkin, F. 1990a. "Can Futures Market Data Be Used to Understand the Behavior of Real Interest Rates?" *Journal of Finance* XLV:245–257.

Pearson, N. D., and T-S. Sun 1994. "Exploiting the Conditional Density in Estimating the Term Structure: An Application to the Cox, Ingersoll and Ross Model." *Journal of Finance* 49(4):1279–1304.

Rendleman, R. J., Jr., and B. J. Bartter 1980. "The Pricing of Options on Debt Securities." *Journal of Financial and Quantitative Analysis* XV(1):11–24.

Wang, C. 1994. "Interest Rate Swaps." Unpublished doctoral dissertation, Columbia Business School, New York, NY.

Chapter 18

Credit Risk

Chapter Objectives

This chapter discusses credit risk, its measurement and modeling. The following issues are addressed in this chapter.

- What constitutes default?
- What is the evidence on default?
- What are some of the important securities that are subject to default risk?
- What are the institutions that help manage default risk?
- How do models of default risk work?

INTRODUCTION

Credit risk is the possibility of *default* by one of the counterparties in a financial transaction. The probability of default affects the future cash flows of the financial transaction; hence, the current market price (or value) of the transaction, which is the **risk-adjusted present value** of future cash flows. Rating agencies define **default** as any missed or delayed disbursement of contractual obligations (interest, sinking funds, or principal), bankruptcy, receivership, or distressed exchanges. As is shown in Table 18-1, during 1996 through 1999, nearly 150 companies defaulted on a total of $44,595.5 million of debt. Each one of these events is an example of a **credit event.** These credit events have occurred in varying proportions in the United States, as can be seen in Figure 18-1.

Each of these credit events is costly: they lead to costly renegotiations, debt service reductions, and potential liquidations. Often, they lead to reorganizations. In such situations, the lender may get less than what was contractually specified. We provide examples of each of these credit events on pages 629 and 630. More often firms miss their contractual obligations or settle with their creditors out of court. Formal bankruptcy procedures are sought typically when negotiations fail to resolve matters.

Default may be the result of a macroeconomic factor, such as recession. It may also be due to company- or industry-specific factors. In general, both these factors are important. They may result in lack of liquidity or insolvency, and both these factors may cause default. Many securities in the capital market are subject to this type of credit risk. We illustrate in Table 18-2 examples of credit-risky securities.

Credit-risky securities come in various forms. Bank loans and bonds are perhaps the most well-known examples of credit-risky securities. As shown in Table 18-2, however, CBOs, CLOs, interest rate swaps, etc. also have credit risk.

TABLE 18-1   *Default Experience, 1996–1999*

Year-to-Date through December 31,	1999	1998	1997	1996
Defaulted debt ($US millions):	$44,595.5	$21,216.6	$9,315.3	$5,927.7
Number of defaulting companies:	147	134	71	31
Moody's Trailing 12-month,				
issuer-based default rate (spec. grade)	5.51%	3.47%	2.04%	1.66%
Moody's trailing 12-month,				
dollar-based default rate (spec. grade)	7.78%	3.32%	2.95%	1.61%

Source: Moody's Special Comment, 2000.

FIGURE 18-1   *Default Type as Percentage of Total, 1982–1997*

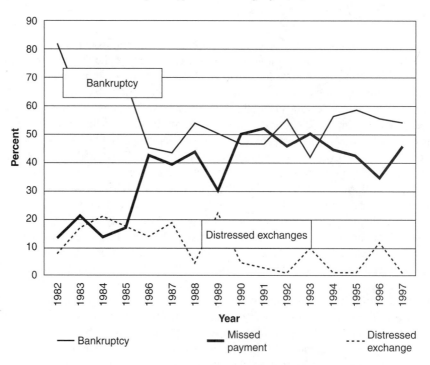

Credit Event: Distressed Exchange Offer

General Media, Inc., Publishing and Entertainment Company
$80.0 million 10.625% Senior Secured Notes, Ser. B due 12/31/2000

General Media, Inc., headquartered in New York, publishes magazines, principally Penthouse and affiliated publications, and produces a number of adult-oriented services via telephone lines and the Internet. The company's operating results have been trending down since the issue of its notes in 1993 due to circulation declines and significant operating costs increases in its publishing sector. Given General Media's financial vulnerability, on May 21, 1999 bondholders agreed to receive $950 in cash for each $1,000 par amount of $28 million of the $80 million outstanding senior secured notes maturing in 2000. The Company was able to complete the redemption of its notes thanks to the sale of its automotive magazines in March, 1999.

Source: Moody's 2000.

04/27/1999 Distressed exchange offer

05/21/1999 Distressed exchange completed: bondholders agreed to receive $950 in cash for each $1,000 par amount of $28 million of the $80 million outstanding senior secured notes maturing in 2000

Credit Event: Missed Installment Payments, Missed Interest Payment, and Chapter 11

Coho Energy, Inc., Oil and Gas Company
$150.0 million 8.875% Guaranteed Senior Subordinated Notes due 10/15/2007

Coho Energy, Inc. (Coho), headquartered in Dallas, Texas, is an independent oil and gas company, which operates primarily in Mississippi and Louisiana. The combination of extremely high leverage, current weak prices, high interest expense, necessary capital expenditures, and moderately declining production following the debt funded acquisition of oil reserves from Amoco in December of 1997, resulted in significant losses in 1998 and first quarter of 1999 and essentially eliminated cash flow. Lack of liquidity led to the company's failure in March 1999 to meet the first of five equal installments toward $89.6 million it owes to the banks (through its subsidiary Coho Resources, Inc.) and the inability to make interest payment due on April 15, 1999 on its senior subordinated notes maturing 2007.

Source: Moody's 2000.

03/02/1999 Missed first installment payment on its borrowing base loan prepayments maturing in 2003 (issued through its subsidiary Coho Resources, Inc.)

04/15/1999 Missed interest payment

08/23/1999 Chapter 11

Credit Event: Chapter 11

Amnex, Inc., Telecommunications Services Company
$15.0 million 8.5% Convertible Subordinated Notes due 9/25/2002

AMNEX, Inc., headquartered in New Rochelle, New York, is an integrated payphone and operator services telecommunications company. Significant losses at its operator services business due to higher network and collection costs prompted the company's decision to shift to the carrier services and payphone business. Restructuring and acquisitions costs led to recurring losses and various covenant violations under its bank facility. AMNEX was unable to obtain additional financing and on May 5, 1999 together with its subsidiary (American Network Exchange. Inc.) it filed for Chapter 11 with the White Plains Bankruptcy Court. At the time of the filing, the parent company reported assets and liabilities of $77 million and $82 million, respectively.

Source: Moody's 2000.
05/05/1999 Chapter 11

Credit Events: Missed Interest Payment, Distressed Exchange Offer, and Bankruptcy Protection

Alpha Shipping Plc, Shipping Company
$175.0 million 9.5% Guaranteed Senior Notes due 2/15/2008

Alpha Shipping Plc (Alpha), incorporated in the Isle of Man with management based in Athens, Greece, is an international shipping company which owns and operates a diversified fleet of drybulk carriers, crude oil, product and chemical tankers, and reefer vessels. Recent depressed freight rate environment in most of the sectors in which the company operates combined with continued high debt burden, not to mention an aging fleet with little realization value, have been detrimental to Alpha's liquidity condition. In spite of a relatively diversified fleet, the company could not generate sufficient cash flows. For the six months ended April 30, 1998, it reported a net loss of $4.5 million compared to a net income of $12 million during the same period a year earlier. Severe liquidity constraint due to unfavorable freight rate volatility led Alpha on February 15, 1999 to abort a 9.5% interest payment on its $175 million senior notes maturing in 2008.

Source: Moody's 2000.
02/15/1999 Missed interest payment
04/30/1999 Distressed exchange offer
06/16/1999 Sought relief under Section 304 of the United States Bankruptcy Code
07/28/1999 Distressed exchange completed: holders of which CSFB, agreed to receive 37 cents on the dollar of the $175 million notes; Alpha's bonds are exchanged for shares in a new company, Eumenides, established to acquire Alpha's vessel-owning subsidiaries

TABLE 18-2   *Credit-Risky Securities*

Type of Credit-Risky Security	Typical Characteristics
Bank loans	Typically senior and secured.
Privately placed debt securities and section 144a issues.	Often junior and unsecured.
Publicly traded debt securities. Issued by corporations and banks, for example.	Can be secured or unsecured. Investment-grade and junk bonds.
Collateralized bond obligations (CBOs). Collateralized loan obligations (CLOs).	Risk depends on the structure, collateral, and credit enhancements.
Interest rate swaps and OTC derivatives.	Mark-to-market, dealer capital, and other credit enhancements.
Credit derivatives.	Depends on the structure.
Sovereign loans and bonds.	Renegotiations, threats of sanctions, availability of seizable collateral, and the presence or absence of IMF as a creditor.

FIGURE 18-2   *Defaulted Debt Recovery Estimates by Seniority and Security of Claim, 1977–1997*

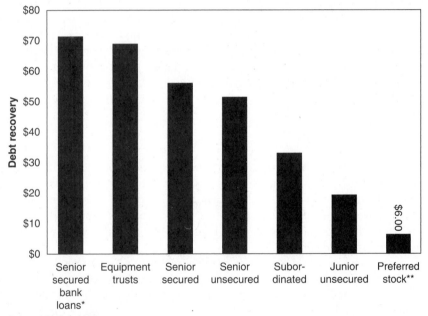

Source: Moody's 2000.
*Estimate based on data from 1989 to 1996.
**Estimate based on data from 1980 to 1997.

Debt securities that are subject to default risk can differ significantly in terms of their seniority in the capital structure, the level of protection they may have by way of security, etc. Depending on their status, the expected recovery rate conditional on default can change. In Figure 18-2, we show the historical recovery rates on various categories of debt instruments. Notice that the bank loans and senior secured debt securities tend to recover about 70% of the par value in the event of default. By contrast, junior unsecured debt instruments have a recovery estimate of just about 20% of their par value.

WHO PRODUCES INFORMATION?

Information about the borrower's financial health come from two sources: **rating agencies and market prices.** We take up each source in turn.

Rating Agencies

Moody's, Standard and Poor, Fitch, etc. produce information about the credit standing of borrowers. Often, borrowers will pay money to have their debt rated. The information produced by the rating agencies change discretely as and when the agencies update their evaluations. Much of the evidence on recovery ratios, defaults, etc. that we have reported came from Moody's. Rating agencies also try to relate defaults to macroeconomic factors. For example, Figure 18-3 illustrates the number of defaults in different subperiods.

Note in Figure 18-3 that the defaults significantly increased during the depression years (1930s). The late 1980s and early 1990s saw again an increase in the number of defaults in the economy. Market-wide factors do play a role in triggering defaults.

Rating agencies also produce information about the probability that a given firm may move from one category of rating into another category. These are known as migration probabilities. We illustrate in Table 18-3 the migration probabilities compiled by Standard and Poor. For example, Table 18-3 suggests that a firm that is rated AAA this year has a 5.62% probability of ending up with a AA rating in one-year's time. This kind of information is extremely useful to investors in credit-risky securities.

Market Prices

Stock prices and bond prices contain valuable information about credit risk. An increase in credit risk translates into lower equity and bond prices, *cetaris paribus.* Market prices change continuously. To the extent that markets are efficient in processing information, we may expect equity prices and yield spreads to provide a better "discovery" of credit risk than other sources. Figure 18-4 shows how yield spreads have reacted to market developments.

A credit event may lead to a lower recovery rate on the loan or bond obligations. So, the investors are interested in determining the *probability of default* (leading to a credit event), as well as the *potential recovery rates* in the event that default occurs. *Together, the probability of default and the recovery rates determine the value of a credit-risky security.*

What factors affect the recovery rates? An important consideration is the relative bargaining positions of lenders and borrowers. This is, in turn, greatly influenced by the underlying bankruptcy code and its enforceability. For example, nonsovereign loans and bonds come under the rubric of a bankruptcy code. On the other hand, sovereign debt does not necessarily fall under a bankruptcy code. This affects the ability of lenders to have access to borrower's collateral in the event of default. Availability of secured collateral and its value under financial distress is yet another factor that influences the recovery rates. The presence of multiple creditors and the existence of

FIGURE 18-3 *Default Frequency*

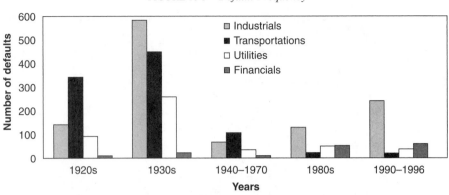

TABLE 18-3 *Standard and Poor's One-Year Transition Rates*

Initial Rating	Rating at Year-End (percent)								
	AAA	AA	A	BBB	BB	B	CCC	D	N.R.
AAA	90.34	5.62	0.39	0.08	0.03	0.00	0.00	0.00	3.54
AA	0.64	88.78	6.72	0.47	0.06	0.09	0.02	0.01	3.21
A	0.07	2.16	87.94	4.97	0.47	0.19	0.01	0.04	4.16
BBB	0.03	0.24	4.56	84.26	4.19	0.76	0.15	0.22	5.59
BB	0.03	0.06	0.40	5.09	76.09	5.82	0.96	0.98	8.58
B	0.00	0.09	0.29	0.41	5.11	74.62	3.43	5.30	10.76
CCC	0.13	0.00	0.26	0.77	1.66	8.93	53.19	21.94	13.14

N.R.—Rating withdrawn.

Source: "Average One-Year Transition Rates," in Standard & Poor's Ratings Performance 2000, p. 12, Table 7 (January 2001). Reprinted with permission of Standard & Poor's Rating Services.

bank debt affect the recovery rates as well. Bank debt is senior and is typically secured. Banks closely monitor their loans. This monitoring is beneficial to other creditors. On the other hand, the fact that the bank debt is secured implies that less collateral is available to other creditors in the event of default.

We are often interested in how the "market" values credit risk. In other words, we want to estimate the compensation that the market wants for assuming credit risk. Often, the yield spread between the credit-risky instrument and an otherwise identical Treasury security (which is presumed to have no credit risk) is used as an estimate. Yield spreads, however, are affected by a number of factors other than just default risk. These factors are

- **Liquidity.** Government securities are more liquid,
- **Taxes.** Government securities are exempt from state and city taxes, and
- **Contractual Provisions.** Government securities are typically noncallable.

Monthly yield spreads during the period 1926 through 1986 are presented in Table 18-4 for AAA bonds and BAA bonds. Note the volatility and the significant

FIGURE 18-4   *BAA Spreads and Risk-Free Yields*

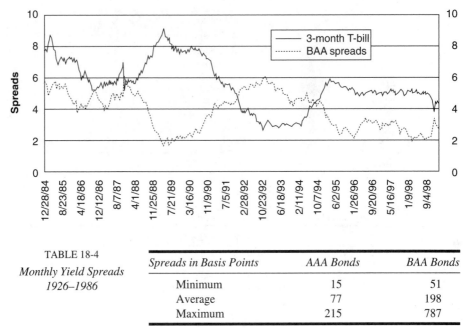

TABLE 18-4
*Monthly Yield Spreads
1926–1986*

Spreads in Basis Points	AAA Bonds	BAA Bonds
Minimum	15	51
Average	77	198
Maximum	215	787

Source: Federal Reserve Bulletin.

levels in the default premium. Spreads are sizable, ranging from 50 to more than 800 basis points. The spreads are highly variable. Default premium and default-free interest rates are negatively correlated.

INSTITUTIONAL ASPECTS

We have already discussed in Part I many of the institutional features of corporate debt market. Bank loans are typically *senior claims and are secured.* Banks monitor the financial health of borrowers and actively manage their loan portfolios. Even syndicated loans have only a few banks; hence, *coordination is easier* in the event of default and renegotiations. On the other hand, publicly traded debt can vary extensively in terms of their seniority, security, and contractual provisions. They are widely held by many bondholders, and as a result, coordination can be difficult in the event of default.

Credit-risky contracts come under the rubric of a bankruptcy code. This code defines the rights and responsibilities of creditors and borrowers in the event of default. Bankruptcy code is a mechanism that anchors the process of coordination, renegotiation, and restructuring a financially troubled borrower and formalizes the access to collateral. The important provisions of the code were discussed in Part I. It is useful to keep the institutional aspects in perspective when evaluating the models of corporate debt, which we describe next.

MODELS OF CREDIT RISK

There are three approaches to modeling credit risk:

1. *Structural Approach:* In this approach, we model the value of the assets of the borrower and the liabilities of the borrower. We determine the trigger level at which the firm's assets will fall below the liability triggering default.
2. *Structural Approach with Strategic Default:* In this approach, we model the value of the assets of the borrower, the liabilities of the borrower, and the bankruptcy code. We determine the incentives that lead to *voluntary default.*

In these two approaches, the focus is on the balance sheet of the borrower and how close the assets are to the trigger level. The focus is on the economic events that lead to the default trigger. *Default in these models is never a surprise.* We know how close the borrower is relative to the default trigger. These models deliver estimates of default probabilities based on the balance sheet information. Market factors can be included in these models.

3. *Reduced Form Models:* In this class of models, we directly model the probability of default and the recovery rates. The focus of these models is the *time to default.* For example, we can assume that the time to default is governed by a Poisson process, where the intensity of the process can depend on some exogenously specified state variables.

By their very nature, default is a *surprise event* in the reduced form models. These models can be calibrated to credit-rating information, such as migration probabilities, and are particularly valuable in the pricing of credit derivatives.

Structural Models of Default

Merton (1974) and Black and Scholes (1973) argued that the equity holders have a valuable put option when they borrow money from bondholders. In case of financial distress, they can hand over the assets to debtholders and "walk away" from their obligations. If the borrower has to access the capital markets repeatedly, then the value of this put is likely to be much lower. This is because the borrower would like to establish and maintain "good reputation" in credit markets. Merton (1974) noted that the corporate borrowers will "walk away" from their debt obligations by putting the firm's assets to the lenders if the value of the implicit put option is high. Using options pricing theory, we can quantify this walk-away option. So, if the assets of the firm are below the present value of the loan obligations, then the stockholders can put the assets to the debtholders at a strike price equal to the present value of their loan obligations. This approach implies the following important relationship:

$$\text{Risky Loan} = \text{Riskfree Loan} - \text{Put Value to Default}$$

or

$$\text{Riskfree Loan} - \text{Risky Loan} = \text{Put Option.}$$

The spread is the value of the put option on the assets of the borrower with a strike price equal to the promised value of debt obligations. Based on our understanding of options pricing, we can assert the following: The spread should increase with volatility. The spread should increase with leverage. The spread typically should increase with time to maturity.

The pricing models developed in Chapter 14 can now be applied to value corporate debt securities. In the pricing of corporate debt securities, options-pricing insights have been used extensively. The design of corporate debt contracts, as well as their valuation, must account for the fact that the managers have the option of walking away from the debtholders. This walk-away option is potent by virtue of the limited liability that owners (stockholders) enjoy. Consider a simplified situation in which firm XYZ has a simple capital structure with n shares of common stock and zero-coupon bonds with a face value of F. Assume that the bonds are due to mature on date T. The current date is t. Let us assume that the markets are frictionless, with no taxes at corporate or personal level. If we were to assume that financial distress and bankruptcy are costless, then we have the value conservation requirement:

$$V = S + D,$$

where V is the total value of the firm, S is the value of equity, and D is the market value of corporate debt. The payoff to the debtholders at time T can be written as follows:

$$\min [F, V_T] = F - \max [0, F - V_T].$$

This is illustrated in Table 18-5.

In writing the payoffs this way, we are assuming that the borrowers will pay the promised amount whenever the promised face value is less than the value of the assets of the firm. If the promised amount is greater than the value of the assets of the firm, we are assuming that the borrowers can hand over the assets of the firm to the lenders and walk away from their obligations. In other words, we are assuming that there are no costs associated with financial distress or bankruptcy.

In this situation, equity can be thought of as a call option on the assets of the firm, with a strike price of F and a maturity of $T - t$. Note that the payoff of the equity may be written as

$$\max (0, V_T - F),$$

where V_T is the value of the assets of the firm at date T, and F is the face value of debt. If σ_v is the volatility of the assets of the firm, then the value of equity can be written (using Black and Scholes pricing model developed earlier in the book) as

$$S = V_t N(d_1) - Fe^{-r(T-t)}N(d_2),$$

TABLE 18-5 *Corporate Debt Pricing*	*Transaction at Date t*	*Cash Flow at Date t*	$V_T \leq F$	$V_T > F$
Buy Equity of the Firm	$-S$	0	$V_T - F$
Buy Bonds of the Firm	$-B$	V_T	F

where $N(d_1)$ is the cumulative normal density evaluated at d_1. Furthermore,

$$d = \frac{\ln\left[\frac{V}{F}\right] + \left(r + \frac{\sigma_V^2}{2}\right)(T - t)}{\sigma_V \sqrt{T - t}}$$

and

$$d_2 = d_1 - \sigma_V \sqrt{T - t}.$$

The value of debt *can be* determined by recognizing that at maturity the bondholders get

$$\min [F, V_T] = F - \max [0, F - V_T].$$

We can think about the value of corporate debt in the following way. Note that the payoff of the risky corporate bond consists of two parts. The first part is F, which is exactly what the buyer of a default-free discount bond will get. The second part is the value of a put option on the assets of the firm with a strike price equal to the face value of corporate debt. Who owns this put option? The equity holders do, which gives them the right to sell the assets of the firm with a strike price equal to the face value of debt. This put option arises by virtue of the limited liability privilege that equity holders enjoy. Substituting for S from the options pricing formula and simplifying, we get the value of corporate debt to be

$$D(V_t, t) = Fe^{-r(T-t)}N(-d_2) - V_t N(-d_1).$$

Here we recognize that the value of debt, D, is a function of the underlying asset value.

Merton (1974) carries this analysis further and computes the default spread between corporate and Treasury discount securities. Let us define the yield to maturity, R, of the corporate discount bond at date t as

$$D(V, t) = Fe^{-R(T-t)}.$$

If r is the default-free, risk-free rate, then the default spread may be defined as $R - r$. Substituting for $D(V, t)$ and simplifying, we get the default spread. The default premium depends on important company-specific factors, such as the leverage, volatility of the underlying assets of the borrower, etc. In addition, the default spread also depends on the default-free interest rate r, which is determined in the market.

$$\text{Default} - \text{Risky Yield} = R = -\frac{\ln D(V, t)}{T - t}$$

$$\text{Default Spread} = -\frac{\ln D(V, t)}{T - t} - r$$

or

$$\text{Spread} = R - r = -\frac{1}{T - t}\ln\{Fe^{-r(T-t)}N(-d_2) - V_t N(-d_1)\} - r$$

To characterize the spread, Merton (1974) used a leverage ratio measure d.

Define the debt ratio as

$$d = \frac{Fe^{-r(T-t)}}{V}.$$

Define the time to maturity as

$$\tau = T - t.$$

Using this measure of leverage, it can be shown that the default premium is increasing in the leverage and in the volatility of the underlying assets of the firm. These implications are shown in Figures 18-5 and 18-6. The behavior of the default premium with respect to the term to maturity depends on whether the leverage is too high or low.

To illustrate these ideas, let us review Figures 18-5 and 18-6. Note that when the leverage ratio is small, the term premium is increasing, as one would expect. When the leverage ratio is very high, however, the short-term debt commands a higher risk premium.

FIGURE 18-5   *Term Premium and Leverage*

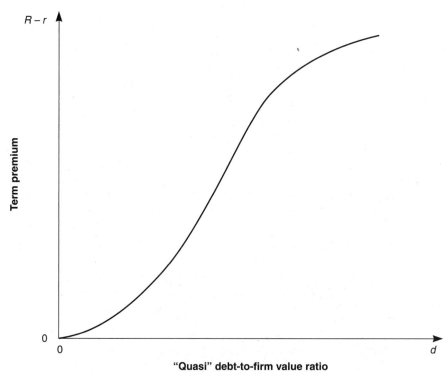

"Quasi" debt-to-firm value ratio

Merton's model requires very high volatility inputs to explain the observed credit spreads. (See Tables 18-3 and 18-4 on credit spreads of BAA bonds.)

In fact, such default premiums are easily calculated in spreadsheets by using binomial methods. The figures presented illustrate that the default spread is increasing in the leverage d and in the volatility of the underlying asset. The effect with respect to time to maturity depends crucially on the degree of the firm's leverage. For firms with a low degree of leverage, default will occur only if the firm value declines substantially, a prospect that is more likely for long maturities than for short maturities. For highly leveraged firms, default will be avoided only if the firm value improves significantly, a prospect that is more likely for higher maturities. Sarig and Warga (1989a) use zero coupons issued by the government and corporations of different credit ratings to study the risk structure of interest rates. They conclude that the shape of the default-risk premiums is strikingly similar to the theoretical predictions of Merton (1974). Their figure as reproduced in Figure 18-7 suggests that the model of Merton (1974) is consistent with the shape of the default-premium structure. Table 18-6 provides the default evidence for various rating categories.

In Merton (1974), two key contractual provisions are specified exogenously. First, the **lower reorganization boundary** is specified. This is the threshold value of the

FIGURE 18-6   *Term Premium and Volatility of Assets*

FIGURE 18-7   *The Term Structure of Risk Premia*

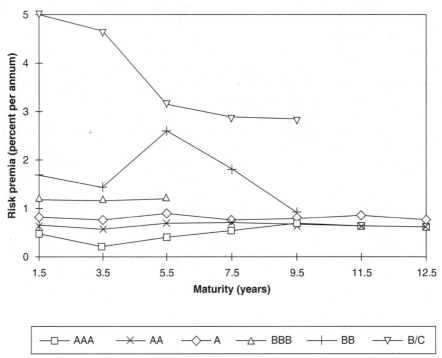

Yield spreads for corporate zero-coupon bonds. February 1985 through September 1987. Maturity numbers (horizontal axis) correspond to the average maturity of each cell in Table 18-6. Average yield spreads are calculated as follows: In each month, the yield to an individual corporate bond has subtracted from it the yield to a zero-coupon government strip with identical maturity. If no government strip with identical maturity existed, the yields on the two strips with maturities most closely bounding the corporate bond were interpolated to obtain the appropriate risk-free zero-coupon yield. These yield differences were then averaged across bonds in a given month and then across time to produce the results.

firm at which the control of the firm transfers from the stockholders to the bondholders. In the context of Table 18-5, bondholders have the right to take over the firm when the value of the firm at maturity date T reaches a level that is less than or equal to F, the promised face amount. Second, the compensation to be received by creditors upon reaching the lower reorganization boundary is specified. The bondholders will receive V_T at date T, once they take over.

Implementing Structural Models in Practice

To implement structural models, we need to estimate the value of the assets of the company, which is very difficult. In addition, we need to figure out the volatility of the assets of the company. There is a way we can extract these two pieces of information

TABLE 18-6   *Yield Spreads for Corporate Zero-Coupon Bonds*

Average yield spreads are calculated over the period February 1985 through September 1987 as follows: In each month, the yield to an individual corporate bond has subtracted from it the yield to a zero-coupon government strip with identical maturity. If no government strip with identical maturity existed, the yield on the two strips with maturities most closely bounding the corporate bond were interpolated to obtain the appropriate risk-free zero-coupon yield. These yield differences were then averaged across bonds in a given month and then across time to produce the results reported for each cell. The unrated column contains bonds from a mixture of ratings and should not be taken to be the lowest rating group. The figures are in percent per annum, and the number of observations is reported below the yield.

Maturity	AAA	AA	A	BBB	BB	B/C	Unrated
0.5–2.5 years	0.410	0.621	0.775	1.326	1.670	4.996	3.081
	21	74	123	48	64	41	38
2.5–4.5 years	0.232	0.562	0.736	1.275	1.495	4.650	3.232
	11	99	251	152	79	117	96
4.5–6.5 years	NA	0.620	0.778	1.405	2.730	3.365	3.197
		114	221	59	58	125	119
6.5–8.5 years	NA	0.620	0.660	NA	1.878	2.959	3.443
		96	138		51	80	119
8.5–10.5 years	0.626	0.575	0.816	NA	0.989	2.912	3.099
	24	69	97		10	10	88
10.5–12.5 years	NA	0.566	0.854	NA	NA	NA	2.478
		64	110				64
12.5 plus years	0.544	0.544	0.740	NA	NA	NA	2.516
	64	501	510				278

Source: Sarig, O., and Warga, A., *Journal of Finance.*

from the market. We observe the equity price in the market. We know that in Merton's model equity is a call option on the assets of the firm with a strike price equal to face value of debt. This leads to the following equation:

$$E = VN(d_1) - Fe^{-r(T-t)}N(d_2).$$

We can also estimate or obtain the implied volatility of equity. Under some simplifying assumptions, we can show that the equity volatility and asset volatility are related through the leverage and the degree to which the option value to default is in-the-money. This relation is shown in the following equation:

$$\sigma_E = N(d_1)\sigma_V \frac{V}{E}.$$

We can solve these two equations simultaneously for the values of V and the volatility of the assets of the firm. Once we have these two variables, we can estimate the probability of default from the model.

Example 18-1:

Let us consider a simple example: the value of equity of a company is $3 million, and it has a single zero-coupon bond outstanding with a face value of $15 million due in 2 years. The implied volatility of the equity of the company is 60%. Based on this information, let us address the following questions:

1.   What is the implied value of the assets of the firm?
2.   What is the implied volatility of the firm's assets?
3.   What is the probability of default by the company at maturity of the debt?

To address these questions, we solve the two equations described earlier in EXCEL. This is shown in Figure 18-8. The solver function allows us to determine the value of the assets of the firm (11.89), as well as the volatility of the assets (16.87%). The (risk-neutral) probability of default is simply $N(-d2)$. In this example, the risk-neutral probability of default is 15.22%. We can compute in standardized units just how far the firm is from defaulting. This is the distance between the value of the assets of the firm (11.89) and the face value of debt (15) standardized in terms of the volatility of the asset value (16.87%). This is sometimes referred to as the distance to default in the industry. In our example it is 1.493.

FIGURE 18-8   *Applying the Model of Merton to Get Probability of Default and Implied Value of the Firm's Assets and Volatility of the Assets*

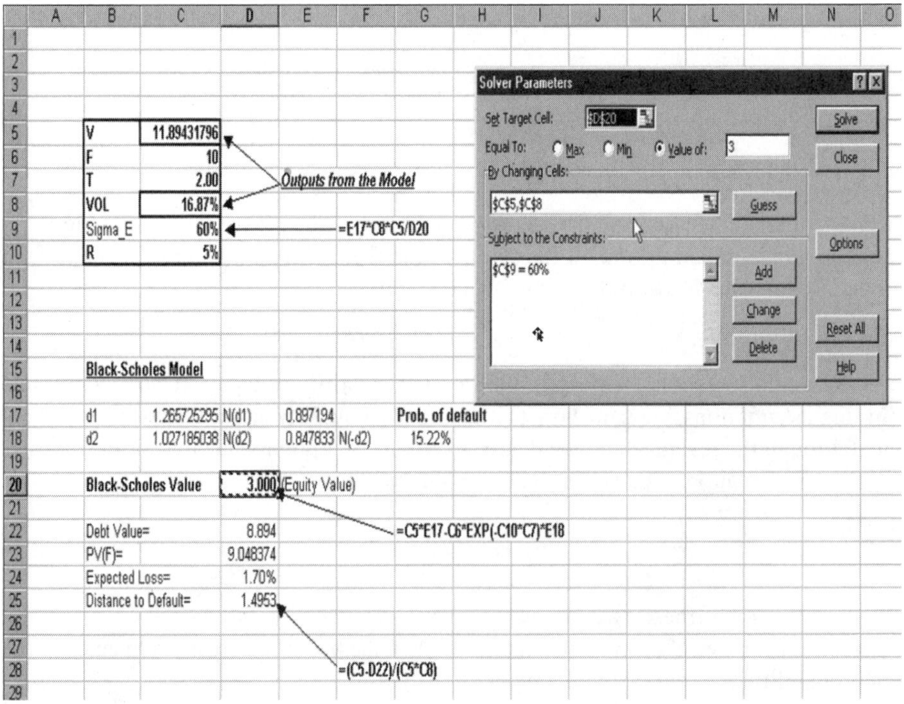

KMV Approach

A company known as KMV Corporation uses the structural approach to calculate the expected default frequency (EDF) for different horizons.

Equity prices are used in conjunction with the balance sheet information to estimate probability of default and distance to default. The probability of default is estimated as shown in Example 18-1. The distance to default is computed from a model similar to Merton. Distance to default is simply

$$\frac{V - D(V, t)}{V \sigma_V}.$$

Empirical evidence suggests that such measures provide good predictive information about future credit rating changes and defaults. Credit risk monitor (which is the name of KMV's product) is built based on this structural model's intuition. They compute the expected default frequency (EDF) which is the probability of default for a horizon ranging from 1 to 5 years.

KMV computed EDF in three steps (shown in Figure 18-9):

1. Calculate the implied asset value and asset volatility using *both* the market data and the company's financial statements.

FIGURE 18-9   *Distance to Default*

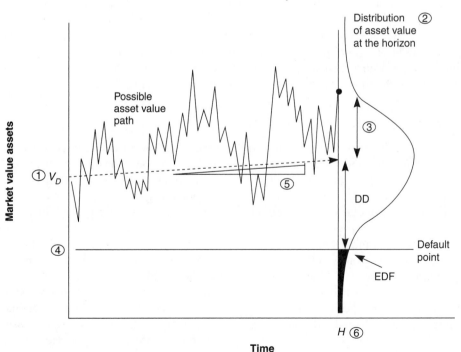

2. Estimate the distance to default as described earlier.
3. KMV uses the historical data on defaults and bankruptcies to determine the EDF given the distance to default.

Subordinated Corporate Debt

In an insightful paper, Black and Cox (1976) have examined the problems associated with the pricing of subordinated debt claims. We will review the basics here. Consider the XYZ company in Table 18-7, and assume that it has two zero-coupon issues due to mature at date T. Assume that one issue is senior with a promised face amount F_1 and another is a junior issue with a promised face amount F_2. We will continue to assume that the process of financial distress and bankruptcy is costless. If we were to denote the value at date t of the equity by S, the senior bonds by B_1, and the junior bonds by B_2, then the value conservation requires that

$$V_t = S + B_1 + B_2.$$

We will also assume that the bondholders have no recourse until date T when their face amount becomes due. (This unrealistic assumption will be removed later, and the pricing implications will become clearer.)

Table 18-7 illustrates the ideas in the pricing of subordinated debt. Note that the payoffs to the senior bondholders may be thought of as a covered call (see Chapter 14 if this is not clear); the senior bondholders own the firm, but they have sold a call on the firm with a strike price equal to the face value F_1 of their debt security. The equity is simply a call on the assets of the firm with a strike price equal to the combined value of the face amount $F_1 + F_2$. By value conservation, we can write the junior debt's value as a portfolio of calls; the subordinated debt is equivalent to a long position in a call with a strike price of F_1 and a short position in a call with a strike price of $F_1 + F_2$. Both calls are on the assets of the firm with a maturity date T.

Safety Covenants

Typically, bond covenanting may specify some net-worth constraints or safety covenants. For example, if at any time l, where $t \leq l \leq T$, the value of the firm V_l were to drop to a level X, then the bondholders have the right to take over the firm and obtain a pre-specified compensation—the actual amount may be written down by a certain amount from the originally promised payments to reflect the costliness of financial distress.

Consider Table 18-8, where there is a single issue of a zero-coupon debt. Let us modify the covenants so that the lower reorganization boundary is X. If this boundary is reached by the firm's value before T, then the bondholders get an amount Y. In this case, the stockholders have a down-and-out option. A down-and-out call option is very similar to a regular call option (discussed in Chapter 14). Unlike a regular call option, however, a down-and-out option automatically expires when the underlying asset reaches a prespecified low value. In the context of the corporate bond pricing problem,

TABLE 18-7   *Subordinated Corporate Debt*

Transaction at Date t	Cash Flow at Date t	$V^* \leq F_1$	$F_1 < V^* \leq (F_1 + F_2)$	$V^* > (F_1 + F_2)$
1. Buy the equity of the firm.	$-S$	0	0	$V^* - (F_1 + F_2)$
2. Buy the senior bonds of the firm.	$-B_1$	V^*	F_1	F_1
3. Buy the junior bonds of the firm.	$-B_2$	0	$V^* - F_1$	F_2

TABLE 18-8   *Safety Covenants*

Transaction at Date t	Cash Flow at Date t	First Date l (when $V_l \leq X$)	Maturity Date ($V_i > X$ for all i)	Maturity Date ($V_i > X$ for all i)
1. Buy the equity of the firm.	$-S$	$\max[X - Y, 0]$	0	$V^* - F$
2. Buy the bonds of the firm.	$-B$	Y	V^*	F

stockholders have a call option but with a safety covenant, the call becomes a down-and-out option: when the value of the firm reaches a low level X, the firm is taken over. Bondholders get Y, and equity holders get $X - Y$ or 0, whichever is higher. Consequently, the bondholders may be thought of as owning the firm, but as having sold a down-and-out option to the stockholders. It is clear from Table 18-8 that the safety covenant allows the bondholders to take over the firm sooner.

So far, financial distress has not been explicitly modeled in the pricing of corporate debt. It is useful to review the empirical evidence on financial distress before we examine corporate debt pricing models that incorporate financial distress.

FINANCIAL DISTRESS AND LIMITATIONS OF MERTON'S MODEL

In Merton's model, financial distress is too simply resolved: debtholders wait until maturity and then if the firm's value is below the face value, they take over the firm without any costs. In reality, debtholders can be much more proactive. They may monitor the firm's financial health frequently before the maturity date. (Safety covenants and sinking funds are ways to do this.) In practice, this is achieved by requiring semi-annual coupons. Every six months, debtholders get a chance to see if there is enough money in the firm to pay coupons.

Usually, there are renegotiations and workouts. In sovereign bond markets, lenders often agree to reschedule the interest and principal payments. There are "debt holidays" that are granted to enable the borrower to recover its financial health. In addition, the process of financial distress can be time-consuming and costly. Chapter 11 is one of the ways financial distress is resolved.

Chapter 7 is invoked for liquidation. There are significant direct and indirect costs of bankruptcy and financial distress. Structural models with strategic default explore how these factors modify the predictions of Merton's model, which is a very important benchmark in much the same way Modigliani-Miller results are in corporate finance. The effect of direct and indirect costs of bankruptcy implies that the borrowers and lenders will seek to avoid these wasteful costs by renegotiating loan contracts.

Over the 1926–1986 period, the yield spreads on high-grade corporates (AAA-rated) ranged from 15 to 215 basis points and averaged 77 basis points; and the yield spreads on BAAs (also investment-grade) ranged from 51 to 787 basis points and averaged 198 basis points. Such spreads can only be accounted for within the Merton model by resorting to implausibly large values of d and σ_V.

Most corporate securities promise coupon payments; indeed, zero-coupon corporate securities are relatively rare, and for good reason. After all, when an investor buys a long-term bond from a corporation, he or she would like to have a periodic credible signal that the corporation is doing well and generating sufficient cash flows to honor its promised coupon obligations; coupons represent such a credible signal. Sinking-fund provisions further enhance the value of the signal by requiring that the balloon payments be periodically reduced.

With a zero-coupon bond, the burden of bankruptcy is placed on the principal payment at maturity and not on the coupon obligations along the way. We can think of situations where the firm is illiquid and unable to meet a promised coupon. To keep the bondholders from taking over the firm, it may sell additional equity or resort to selling assets.

The values of Treasury and corporate bonds are influenced significantly by interest-rate risk. For investment-grade corporate bonds, the bulk of the risk is interest-rate related and not due to credit-related factors. Jones, Mason, and Rosenfeld (1984) conclude that the introduction of stochastic interest rates might improve the performance of such models as Merton (1974). Kim, Ramaswamy, and Sundaresan (1993) confirm that the modeling of stochastic interest rates and cash-flow-triggered financial distress can explain the spreads between corporate and Treasury yields better.

Bankruptcies and financial distress are costly. Such costs have broad ramifications that have been ignored thus far. We will review the empirical evidence later and attempt to incorporate some of these facts into the corporate-pricing model.

STRUCTURAL MODELS WITH STRATEGIC DEBT SERVICE

Central to the understanding of corporate debt is the process by which financial distress is managed. This is especially important for poorly rated debt, which are subjected to a higher probability of incurring financial distress. John (1993) surveys and synthesizes the factors pertaining to financial distress. He proposes that financial distress happens when the liquid assets of the firm are not sufficient to meet the obligations of the firm's debt contracts. Thus, financial distress can be thought of as a mismatch between the firm's current assets and its current obligations. It can be handled in a number of ways:

1. The existing assets can be partially liquidated. This will improve the liquidity of the firm and stave off financial distress. The disadvantage of this approach is that there are also liquidation costs (both direct and indirect).

2. The firm can enter into a process of negotiation with debtholders and reconfigure the debt obligations. This may entail a reduction in the liabilities of the firm or a deferment of the payments. Such debt restructuring will involve the following:
   • Reducing the coupons and/or the principal obligations
   • Increasing the maturity of the debt
   • Accepting the equity of the company in lieu of some of the outstanding obligations.

3. The firm can issue additional claims to achieve the liquidity necessary to avoid financial distress.

Note that the process of managing financial distress involves financial reorganization either on the asset side or on the liability side or both. It can be accomplished either out of court or within the formal bankruptcy codes applicable. The traditional approach to managing financial distress is for either the debtor or the creditor of the distressed firm to file for bankruptcy protection under Chapter 11. The debtor will then have the right to propose a reorganization within 120 days from the filing date. The process of financial reorganization may involve the creditors, and the 120-day period may be extended by the court if it is deemed necessary. The plan is then evaluated by the debtholders who may either accept or reject it. Chapter 7 of the bankruptcy code is used to liquidate the firm if the reorganization plan is not accepted. The liquidation costs associated with court-supervised procedures can be quite high both in terms of the resources and in terms of the time it takes to complete the process.

The key empirical regularities associated with financial reorganizations in the 1980s are well-documented. This section and the next one are drawn heavily from Anderson and Sundaresan (1996). Franks and Torous (1989; 1993) find the following:

• Bankruptcies are costly both because of direct costs and because of disruptions of the firm's activities.
• Bankruptcy procedures give considerable scope for opportunistic behavior by the various parties involved.
• Deviations from the absolute priority of claims are common.

All of this suggests that the lower reorganization boundary of the firm used in Merton (1974) and in Black and Cox (1976) oversimplify real-life reorganizations in many important respects. In an important study, Franks and Torous (1993) point out that the costliness of the formal bankruptcy process creates an incentive for renegotiation of the distressed firm's claims. They report that renegotiations result in substantial deviations from absolute priority that are not favorable to equity. In the renegotiations, some or all holders of the firm's securities agree to restructure their claims. However, despite the incentives to do so, in practice, it often proves impossible to renegotiate claims, resulting in formal bankruptcy and liquidation (Asquith, Gertner, and Scharfstein 1994).

We will illustrate structural models with strategic debt service with a simple example. Consider a firm with an asset value of 100. In one year, the assets can have a value of 110 or 90, as shown in the following distribution. The probability of an up move is q and a downmove is $1 - q$.

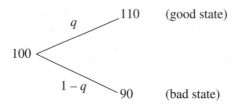

The firm has a zero-coupon bond maturing next year with a par value of 100. Let us assume that if the bondholders invoke Chapter 11 or similar proceedings, it will cost them $15. If this is also known to equity holders, they will realize that the bondholders will *net of* all expenses the following distribution:

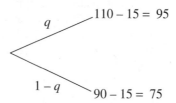

Therefore, there is an incentive for equity holders to pay no more than 95 in the good state and no more than 75 in the bad state. This is called **strategic debt service.** The precise amount that equity holders will pay depends on their bargaining power, their need to access the credit markets again, and so forth. The central idea, however, is that the bondholders may get less than what was promised when there are costs to financial distress. Rational bondholders will anticipate this and will discount the price of corporate debt to reflect potential strategic debt service by equity holders. This was first modeled in Anderson and Sundaresan (1996).

REDUCED-FORM MODELS

In reduced-form models, default is a surprise. Rather than modeling the value of the assets of the firm, in this approach, we directly model the probability of default and the recovery rate conditional on default

For example, let us say that default is a surprise event with a hazard rate $h(t)$. This means the following: If the firm survives at time t, the probability that it will default between t to $t + \Delta t$ is approximately $h(t)\,\Delta t$. Duffie and Singleton (1998) have proposed a model in which $h(t)$ is the hazard rate and L_t is the expected fractional loss in market value if default were to occur at item t. They show that we can construct a default-adjusted short rate, R_t, as follows:

$$R_t = r_t + h_t L_t,$$

where the process R_t is the sum of the default-free short rate r_t and the default-adjusted term $h_t L_t$, which captures the credit risk. Once we have the process for R_t we can price securities similar to the BDT model presented in Chapter 17. The main advantage of this approach is that we can price default-risky discount bonds as if they are default-free *provided* we use the process for R_t to perform discounting.

CREDIT DERIVATIVES

The term **credit derivatives** is used to describe swaps and options designed to either assume or lay off credit risk on some underlying asset or portfolio in return for either interest payments or premium.

Broadly, the participants have been large banks, investment firms, and some insurance companies. The products fall into three categories: (a) credit default options, (b) credit-linked notes, and (c) total returns swaps. Other structures that are not as widely used include credit spread products.

Credit Default Options

As shown in Figure 18-10, bank A is selling the default protection. The term of the option may be equal to the maturity of the bond held by bank B. If a credit event were to occur before the term, then bank A will pay bank B "the credit event payment," which is typically the face value minus the recovery of the par.

In a credit default option structure, bank B is depending on bank A to make the credit event payment. In effect, bank B has taken on some counterparty credit risk to bank A. This risk can be mitigated by a structure known as credit-linked note. This structure is shown in Figure 18-11.

FIGURE 18-10   *Bank B May Hold a Position in Default-Risky Bond*

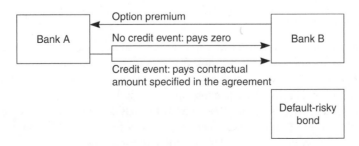

FIGURE 18-11   *Bank B May Hold a Position in Default-Risky Bond*

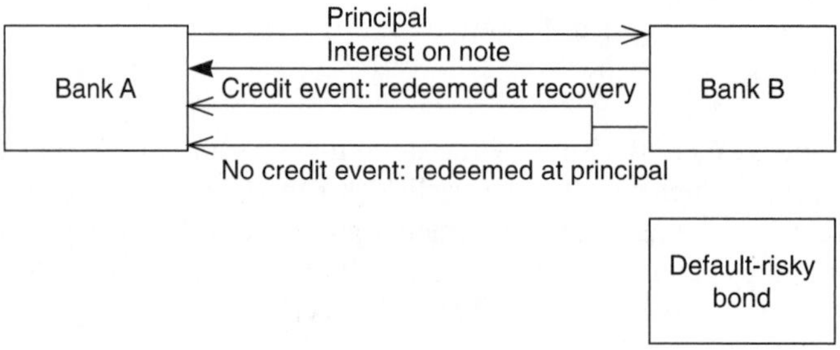

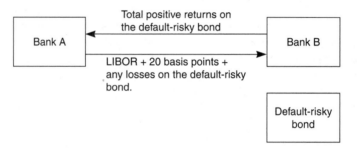

FIGURE 18-12   *Bank B May Hold a Position in Default-Risky Bond*

Credit-Linked Notes

Credit-linked note structure shown in Figure 18-11 can be of the following variety: Bank B issues a 10-year note (linked to the default-risky bond that it may hold). Bank A buys the note at par. If no credit event occurs, the note pays the coupon and expires at par. If there is a credit event on the bond, then the note is redeemed at the recovery value of the bond.

In this structure, bank A has effectively given a collateral by purchasing the credit-linked note for the principal value. Bank B does not have a counterparty exposure to bank A.

Total Returns Swaps

Bank A and B enter into a total return swap on a notional amount equal to the par value of the bond held by bank B. Bank B makes quarterly payments to bank A of all the cash flows from the bond plus any positive mark-to-market value. Bank A pays LIBOR plus a spread plus all the negative mark-to-market value.

An institution invests in an FRN indexed to LIBOR. Simultaneously, the institution executes a total return swap, whereby it agrees to pay LIBOR and receives the total return on a credit-risky asset. This is shown in Figure 18-12.

CONCLUSION

Credit risk has recently attracted more of the attention of regulators and investors. This is due to the failure of some banks and brokerage firms in Japan. In addition, the Russian default and the hedge fund failures in the United States have accentuated the importance of credit risk. In this chapter we have given a brief overview of some of the key issues that underlie credit risk.

PROBLEMS

18.1   Visit the following website: http.//www.moodys.com/cust/default.asp
Review some of the recent ratings actions taken by Moody's.
18.2   Visit the following website: http://www.kmv.com
Evaluate the proposition that stock prices (and hence the EDF) are leading indicators of default.
18.3   What is the difference between Chapter 7 and Chapter 11 of the bankruptcy code?

REFERENCES

Anderson, R. W., and S. M. Sundaresan 1996. "Design and Valuation of Debt Contracts." *Review of Financial Studies* 9(1):37–68.

Asquith, P., R. Gertner, and D. Scharfstein 1994. "Anatomy of Financial Distress: An Examination of Junk-bond Issues." *Quarterly Journal of Economics* 109(3):625–658.

Black, F., and J. C. Cox 1976. "Valuing Corporate Securities: Some Effects of Bond Indenture Provisions." *Journal of Finance* 31:351–368.

Black, F., and M. Scholes 1973. "The Pricing of Options and Corporate Liabilities." *Journal of Political Economy* 81:637–654.

Franks, J., and W. Torous 1989. "An Empirical Investigation of Firms in Reorganization." *Journal of Finance* 44:747–779.

Franks, J., and W. Torous 1993. A Comparison of Financial Recontracting in Workouts and Chapter 11 Reorganizations. ESF Finance Network Working Paper 26.

John, K. 1993. "Managing Financial Distress and Valuing Distressed Securities: A Survey and a Research Agenda." *Financial Management* (Special issue on financial distress) 22(3):60–78.

Jones, E. P., S. P. Mason, and E. Rosenfeld 1984. "Contingent Claims Analysis of Corporate Capital Structures: An Empirical Analysis." *Journal of Finance* 39:611–625.

Kim, I. J., K. Ramaswamy, and S. M. Sundaresan 1993. "Valuation of Corporate Fixed-Income Securities." *Financial Management* (Special issue on financial distress) 22(3):60–78.

Merton, R. C. 1974. "On the Pricing of Corporate Debt: The Risk Structure of Interest Rates." *Journal of Finance* 29:449–470.

Sarig, O., and A. Warga 1989a. "Some Empirical Estimates of the Risk Structure of Interest Rates." *Journal of Finance* 44(5):1351–1360.

Chapter 19

Risk Management

Chapter Objectives

This chapter integrates the concepts of risk developed in the text to provide a framework for measuring and managing risk. The focus of this chapter is to define risk, measure risk, and manage risk in a portfolio context. Such portfolios may be trading portfolios which are typically held for a short period of time (such as a few days or weeks) or investment portfolios which may be held for months. The following issues are addressed in this chapter:

- What is risk?
- What are different sources of risk?
- How can the risk of a portfolio be measured?
- What is the effect of correlation of returns of securities on the risk of a portfolio?
- How does holding period affect risk?
- What is the concept of benchmark equivalents, and how are they used to aggregate risk?
- What is the concept of value-at-risk (VAR)?

INTRODUCTION

The concept of risk is central to players in capital markets. In this text, we have addressed the issue of risk in each chapter as it applies to the market segment discussed in that chapter. For example, in Parts I and II of the text, we looked at the risk of specific segments of fixed-income markets, such as Treasury, options, and corporate and mortgage-backed securities. In Part III of the text, we explored the risk of derivative securities, such as futures and swaps. Chapter 4 addressed the question of measuring the risk of Treasury securities using such concepts as $DV01$, duration, and convexity. Chapter 14 provided measures of risk that are commonly used for options. We noted there that to measure the risk of options, we need options pricing models that allow us to calculate the exposure or the risk of the option for a given change in the price of the underlying security. These measures include the concepts of delta, gamma, and vega. In the context of Chapter 13, we discussed the use of derivatives in risk management situations. Also, in Chapter 16, we explored the risk management issues in the context of interest rate swaps. Treating risk at the level of specific markets as we did in the earlier chapters is extremely useful to managers and traders who take big positions in those markets. They need to understand the risk they are exposed to in order to manage it properly.

655

For senior managers, it is the overall risk of the firm that matters the most. The risks that are taken by managers at various levels (such as divisions or trading desks) must be aggregated in such a way that senior managers are able to assess the following questions:

- Where are concentrations of risk? This needs to be split further into specific categories of concentrations, such as market risk and credit risk.
- Are returns of divisions commensurate with the risk taken by the divisions?
- What is the capital requirement of each division, given its risk exposure?
- Are compensation levels commensurate with the risk-adjusted performance?

This chapter will provide an integrated framework for defining risk, measuring risk, and managing risk. The task of risk management has now become a paramount consideration with the advent of derivative markets and globalization of product and financial markets. To get a perspective on risk management, we examine the fixed-income part of the capital markets.

Note that the fixed-income division is divided into several profit centers. Each profit center has its own risk-return profile. For the senior management, the fixed-income division is just one (perhaps the most important) unit. In addition to fixed-income, there may be other units, such as FX, Equity, Commodities, Syndication, Investment Banking, and so on. The key issue facing the senior management is the ability to understand and react to the overall riskiness of the firm without being swamped by too much information from various reporting divisions. We explore the issues, using the fixed-income unit as an example. The logic of our analysis carries over to other units as well.

Each subdivision of the fixed-income unit is reporting in Figure 19-1 some key information pertaining to risk and return. For example, the Treasury and agency desk is reporting its marked-to-market position value, profit and loss, its overall position in some benchmark equivalents (its position in terms of a benchmark security, such as on-the-run five-year T-note), and the capital needed to cover its credit exposure. Similar reports are submitted by the other reporting units. In a nutshell, such summary reports present senior management with the financial health of its key divisions.

The extent of detail will vary depending on the level at which the risk management problem is looked at. For example, the summary report discussed previously does not indicate the exposure faced by the Treasury and agency desk for a change in the shape of the yield curve. Summary information on the curve risk is presented at a lower level in Figure 19-1, wherein the net position across the yield curve for specific maturity sectors is provided. This information is perhaps more critical to the manager of the Treasury and agency division. At the next lower level, the risk is disaggregated, and a more detailed picture emerges, providing greater detail to the operating manager.

We develop these ideas further in this chapter. First, the concept of risk is defined and some examples provided. Then, the association between risk and return is discussed. Some empirical evidence is presented, which indicates that risk and return go hand in hand. This implies that some exposure to risk is essential in order to obtain higher return. Then we provide categories of risks. Under each category, we discuss issues pertaining to their measurement and management. Important among these categories are the market risk and credit risk. These are treated in considerable detail.

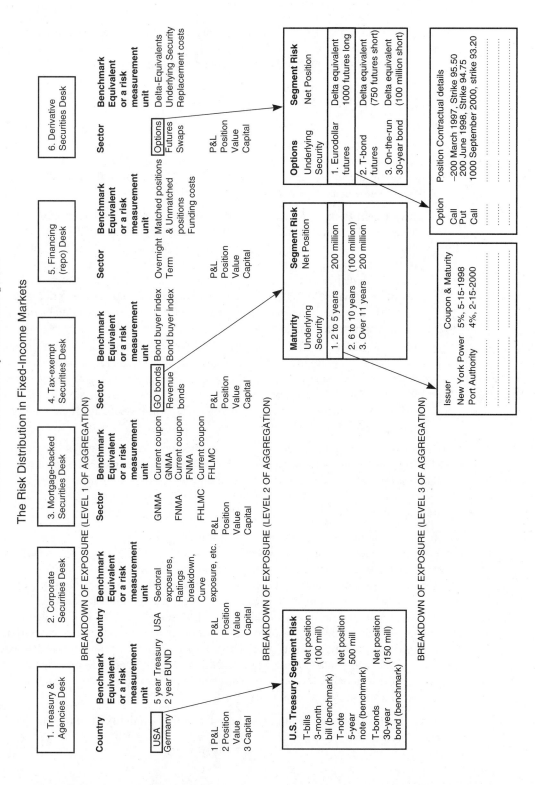

FIGURE 19-1 A Framework for Risk Management

The Risk Distribution in Fixed-Income Markets

The concept of value-at-risk (VAR) is discussed in this context. The VAR calculations are illustrated for cash and derivatives portfolios. We conclude by examining some market responses to the risk management problems.

WHAT IS RISK?

In any economic undertaking there is uncertainty about future outcomes. Risk associated with an economic undertaking is the possibility of suffering a significant economic loss in the future. This definition of risk can be seen in the context of investment and financing as shown next.

Investment Risk　An investment in a project results in future cash flows that are uncertain. The uncertainties in cash flows arise from one's inability to forecast future events (sales growth, defaults, product price, product liabilities, etc.) perfectly. This implies that the return on the project should provide a compensation for the risk that is being taken. This, in turn, leads to the concept of risk-adjusted return on capital (RAROC). Frameworks, such as the capital asset pricing model (CAPM) and arbitrage pricing theory (APT), are used to calculate the risk-adjusted return on capital.

Financing Risk　Financing an activity by issuing a fixed-rate loan may produce an uncertain opportunity cost if future interest rates on such loans were to drop. In this sense, not issuing a fixed-rate loan now (an inaction) may be thought of as a view that future interest rates are going to fall. It is, thus, possible to encounter risk through inaction as well: action or inaction represents a certain view of the future in the relevant markets.

Since risky actions produce uncertain future outcomes, one of the major consequences of risk is the potential for economic loss of profits and/or capital. The main theme is that risk translates to variability in future cash flows and value, which may lead to potential economic losses. The following factors influence the risk of a portfolio or a trading position:

1. The volatility of each security in the portfolio.
2. The position in each security. Here we have to look at the weight of a security as a fraction of the overall portfolio, as well as whether the position is long or short.
3. The correlation structure of securities in the portfolio. The correlation structure interacts with the position (long or short) to significantly influence the risk.
4. The implied or the explicit holding period. In some cases, the holding period may be explicit where the portfolio is held in order to meet a liability (possibly random) at a future point in time. There may be other situations where the assets (such as real estate or emerging market debt) are sufficiently illiquid that the time needed to unwind the position places an implicit holding period that may vary from a few days to several weeks.

Let us address the relationship between risk and the variability of returns in the context of two examples.

Example 19-1:

An investor purchases a zero-coupon bond with a maturity of 30 years. The bond pays no coupons but promises to pay $1,000 at the end of 30 years. At the time of purchase, the yield to maturity of the zero coupon was 8%. The price of the bond is

$$\frac{1,000}{1.08^{30}} = 99.38.$$

This investment action is risky. If the yield to maturity were to fluctuate between 6% and 10%, the value of this bond will fluctuate from a high of 174.11 to a low of 57.31, as shown in Table 19-1.

The return of the asset varies from a high of 75.20% to a low of −42.33%.

As Example 19-1 illustrates, risk often translates to variability of return. In this sense, a higher variability of returns may be thought of as a greater exposure to risk.

Example 19-2:

Let us consider an alternative investment action in which the investor purchases a zero-coupon bond with a maturity of one year. This bond also pays no coupons but promises to pay $1,000 at the end of one year. At the time of purchase, the yield to maturity of the one-year zero coupon was 8%. The price of the bond is

$$\frac{1,000}{1.08^{1}} = 925.93.$$

This investment action is also risky. If the yield to maturity were to fluctuate between 6% and 10%, the value of this bond will fluctuate from a high of 943.40 to a low of 909.09 as shown in Table 19-2. The return of the asset varies from a high of 4.85% to a low of −1.82%.

TABLE 19-1

Investment Risk of a 30-Year Bond

	Yield				
	6%	7%	8%	9%	10%
Price	174.11	131.37	99.38	75.37	57.31
Return	75.20%	32.19%	0.00%	−24.16%	−42.33%

TABLE 19-2

Investment Risk of a One-Year Bond

	Yield				
	3%	4%	5%	6%	8%	10%
Price	970.87	961.54	952.38	943.40	934.58	909.09
Return	4.85%	3.85%	2.86%	1.89%	0%	−1.82%

Inspection of the price fluctuations in Tables 19-1 and 19-2 immediately suggest that the 30-year bond is riskier than the one-year bond. The returns vary from +75.20% to −42.33%. By contrast, the one-year bond returns are fairly stable.

Of course, in the analysis, we have assumed that the yields of the short-term bond and the long-term bonds move in parallel. In reality, as we have seen in Chapter 6, this will not be the case. These examples are used to motivate the idea that the variability of returns and risk go hand in hand.

It is also clear that large changes in yields (of the order of +2% to −2%) tend to occur over a period of several months, in general. Therefore, generally, the longer the holding period, the greater the risk for many transactions.

Normal Distribution

Since risk is about the possibility of suffering a significant economic loss in the future, it is essential to estimate the probability of encountering extreme outcomes in the future. In addition, it is useful to be able to assign some probability that a significant loss can result in any given holding period.

Based on historical returns, it is possible to estimate the volatility and the average return. Using these sample estimates, and assuming that the returns are normally distributed, we can assign probabilities regarding future returns. Normal distribution is a symmetric distribution of returns which can be constructed once the average and the volatility of the returns are specified.

The distribution of returns under the assumption of normality is shown in Figure 19-2. In Figure 19-2, we have assumed that the long-term bond has a mean return of 7% and a volatility of 15%. The short-term bond is assumed to have a mean return of 5% and a volatility of 10%. The relative variability of return for the two bonds is shown in Figure 19-2. Note that the long-term bond has a much greater variation compared to the short-term bond and hence is riskier.

How reasonable is the normality assumption? The evidence appears to suggest that it is at best an approximation of the future behavior of portfolio returns in the equity market. The returns behavior in other markets may deviate from normality. As noted, normal distribution requires us to specify the mean returns of the portfolio and the volatility of the returns of the portfolio. In Figure 19-2, note that when the volatility is higher, more extreme outcomes are realized. This indicates greater risk; hence, for the long-term bond, the curve is flatter. For the short-term bond, the volatility is lower; hence, the curve is narrower, resulting in a more pronounced peak.

Mathematically, the probability density function $\phi(x)$ of a normal distribution describes the probability that the returns will fall within a very narrow band around x and is given below:

$$\phi(x) = \frac{1}{\sqrt{2\pi}\sigma} e^{-\frac{1}{2}\frac{(x-\mu)^2}{\sigma^2}}. \tag{19.1}$$

Given the mean μ and the volatility σ of the return variable x, we can define the standard normal variable $z = \frac{x-\mu}{\sigma}$. The standard normal variable has a mean of zero

FIGURE 19-2   *Risk of Long-Term and Short-Term Bonds*

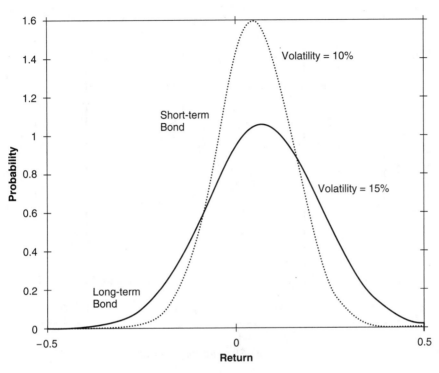

and a volatility of one. The area under the standard normal density function is one. The standard normal density denoted by $n(z)$ is given by

$$n(z) = \frac{1}{\sqrt{2\pi}} e^{\frac{-z^2}{2}}. \tag{19.2}$$

The probability density function can then be integrated to determine the probability that the returns will lie in a certain range. Usually, the range of returns are measured in units of volatility. For example, the probability that the returns will fall within −2.33 units of volatility and +2.33 units of volatility around the mean is 99% in the case of normal distribution. This is shown in Figure 19-3.

The probabilities can be calculated as follows:

$$\text{Probability } (\mu - 2.33\sigma < x < \mu + 2.33\sigma) = \int_{\mu-2.33}^{\mu+2.33\sigma} \frac{1}{\sqrt{2\pi}\sigma} e^{-\frac{1}{2}\frac{(x-\mu)^2}{\sigma^2}} dx \tag{19.3}$$

$$= 0.99.$$

As seen in Equation 19.3, confidence intervals represent the range within which the future returns (or dollar values) are expected to lie with a prespecified probability.

FIGURE 19-3   *Standard Normal Distribution*

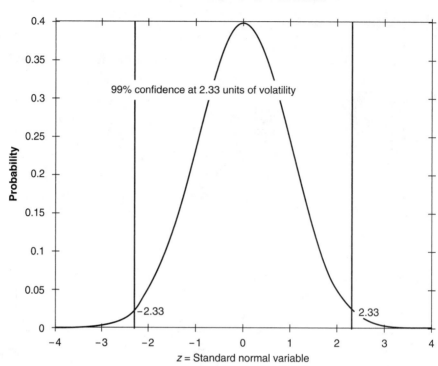

For example, x is expected to lie 99% of the time between $\mu - 2\sigma$ and $\mu + 2\sigma$. Given an estimate of μ and σ, we are able to construct these confidence intervals under the assumption of normality.

Example 19-3:

For the long-term bond, the mean return is 7%, and the volatility is 15%. What is the 99% confidence interval? Assume that these are annualized estimates and that the bond will be held for a period of one year.

Since $\mu = 7\%$ and $\sigma = 15\%$, the confidence intervals are $\mu - 2.33\sigma = 7\% - 2.33 \times 15\% = -27.95\%$ and $\mu + 2.33\sigma = 7\% + 2.33 \times 15\% = 41.95\%$. So, we conclude that the returns will lie 99% of the time between -27.95% and 41.95% in one year's time into the future. Stated slightly differently, we can say that there is only a $\frac{1}{2}\%$ chance that the returns will be below -27.95%.

Can this confidence interval be translated to dollar terms? We explore this in Example 19-4.

Example 19-4:

An investor has $1 million invested in the long-term bond. What is the 99% confidence interval for this investor for a one year horizon?

The confidence intervals for dollar values are obtained by simply multiplying the confidence intervals for returns by the market value of the security.

The lower limit is $-27.95\% \times 1$ million $= 279,500$. The upper limit is $41.95\% \times 1$ million $= 419,500$. One important implication is that the losses can exceed 279,500 only $\frac{1}{2}\%$ of the time. This measure of risk is called the value-at-risk (VAR) in the industry. VAR can be calculated for any specified holding periods.

Holding Period. Normal distribution allows us to estimate the potential losses on a portfolio in a given holding period with some degree of confidence. It turns out that for a holding period of τ years, we can compute the volatility of returns using the formula

$$\sigma(\tau) = \sigma \times \sqrt{\tau}.$$

This allows us to calculate the confidence intervals for any holding period. Implicit in all these calculations is the assumption that our estimated volatility is correct and is representative of the volatility into the future holding periods.

Example 19-5:

An investor has $1 million invested in the long-term bond. What is the 99% confidence interval for this investor for a horizon of 30 days?

Assuming that a year has 252 trading days, we can calculate the relevant volatility for a one-month holding period as

$$\sigma(\tau) = 15\% \times \sqrt{\frac{30}{252}} = 5.175\%.$$

The expected return for this holding period is

$$\mu(\tau) = 7\% \times \frac{30}{252} = 0.833\%.$$

The confidence intervals corresponding to 99% level are $\mu - 2.33\sigma = 0.833\% - 2.33 \times 5.175\% = -11.224\%$ and $\mu + 2.33\sigma = 0.833\% + 2.33 \times 5.175\% = 12.90$. Given that the market value of the investment is $1 million, the intervals corresponding to the value are computed next. The lower limit is $-11.224\% \times 1$ million $= 112,400$. The upper limit is $12.90\% \times 1$ million $= 129,000$.

We have presented some basic concepts in risk measurement. Before we continue these ideas further, it is important to have a perspective on the relationship between risk and return in different segments of the capital markets.

RISK AND RETURN

It is possible to minimize risk by selecting prudent investments, such as Treasury bills in the fixed-income markets. Such a strategy, however, also sharply reduces the return that one might expect to receive. Thus, risk and return are two sides of any portfolio or trading strategy, as we have seen in Chapter 4. For example, we defined concepts, such as bond equivalent yields, current yields, yield to maturity, and rates of return (daily, monthly, annual, and continuous compounding). In addition, as we showed in Chapter 4 and in the earlier sections of this chapter, volatility of security returns may be thought of as a quantitative measure of risk. Based on historical data, we can then construct measures of risk (volatility) and return. To get the perspective that risk and return go hand in hand, let us review some empirical evidence.

This relationship was documented by Ibbotson and Sinqfield (1994). Note in Table 19-3 how the long-term of return of different asset classes bears a direct relation to their riskiness as measured by the volatility. This relationship is based on long-term holding periods and simple buy and hold policies with reinvestment of dividends and coupons. For short-term holding periods with more dynamic trading, the results will obviously differ. The notion, however, that higher expected return requires higher risk-taking is a very general one. The task of risk measurement becomes considerably more complicated when trading is more dynamic.

The time series properties of the returns and risks associated with different asset classes also brings home the point that, on balance, asset classes that provide better return are also subjected to greater variations. This is shown in Figure 19-4.

Note that the equity sector has on average provided better returns than the Treasury bill sector. This, however, has come at the expense of significant fluctuations over time. The Treasury bill sector has provided low returns but has been subjected to much lower variations. With the exception of the period 1979 to 1983, T-bills have been remarkably stable. As noted in Chapters 2 and 3, 1979 through 1983 was a particularly volatile period in the interest rate markets.

TABLE 19-3	Sector	Mean (Percent)	Volatility (Percent)
Risk Return (40-Year Average)			
	1. Common stocks	12.00	21.10
	2. Small company stocks	17.70	35.90
	3. Long-term corporate bonds	5.20	8.50
	4. Long-term government bonds	4.60	8.50
	5. Intermediate-term government bonds	4.90	5.50
	6. T-bills	3.50	3.40
	Inflation	3.20	4.80

FIGURE 19-4   *Equity versus T-bill Returns*

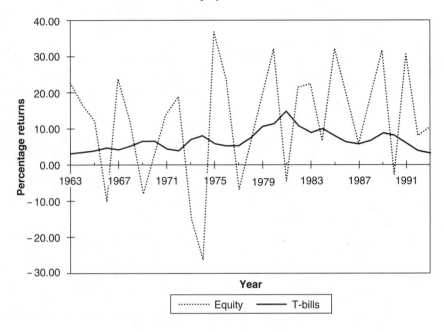

SOURCES OF RISK

Risk arises from a number of sources. These are interdependent, and ultimately the risks manifest themselves in the price or the value of the portfolio (or the transaction) at which the portfolio (or the transaction) can be liquidated. We address the following important categories of risk:

- Market risk
- Credit risk
- Operational risk
- Liquidity risk
- Systemic risk

This way of isolating the sources of risk is useful from a conceptual standpoint. Each source of risk requires careful attention, monitoring, and management.

Market Risk

Perhaps the most central source of risk is the market risk. The market risk of a security or a transaction is the component that is attributable to fluctuations in the price of the security or the value of transaction due to underlying market exposure. Such an exposure can stem from equity markets, interest rates, commodity prices, and foreign exchange markets. For derivatives, risk can arise from more than one of these sources.

For example, a listed option on the S&P 100 index carries with it a significant market risk associated with the U.S. equity market. On the other hand, a hybrid instrument, such as a convertible bond, has both equity and interest-rate risks.

Market risk can also be dependent on the asset-liability structure. A financial institution whose assets have a longer duration than its liabilities may have a significant interest-rate exposure. This is sometimes referred to as the gap risk. In order to clarify issues, we will begin by examining the cash market risks before examining the risk of derivatives.

Cash Market. The concept is probably illustrated best with simple examples in equity and fixed-income markets. Consider simple stock, fixed-income, and derivatives portfolios set up in Tables 19-4, 19-5, and 19-6, respectively. We will first focus on the cash market and later take up the derivatives portfolio for further analysis.

Note that the position risk can be summarized in many ways.

Position Value. One simple way is to simply report the notional amount of the equity and fixed-income positions of the dealer. Thus, we can say that the equity desk has a position value of $10 million, and the fixed-income desk has a position value

TABLE 19-4

Equity Portfolio

Security	Number of Shares	Share Price	Position Value
Stock A	100,000	50	5,000,000
Stock B	200,000	25	5,000,000

TABLE 19-5

Treasury Portfolio

Security	Maturity in Years	Par Amount in Millions	Position Value in Millions
Bond 1	5	100	120
Bond 2	10	50	60

TABLE 19-6   *Derivatives Portfolio*

Security	Maturity in Years	Contract Details	Position Value
Call on Stock A	0.5	Delta = 0.5	2000 options Each option is on 100 shares
Swap (generic)	2	Fixed = 6% Leg Floating = LIBOR Notional Principal = 100 million	2,598,100

of $180 million. This measure has obvious drawbacks: (1) it does not take into account the relative market exposures of different securities in the portfolio, and (2) it is silent on the reinvestment and funding risks that may be present in the portfolio. For example, it is not clear whether the positions have been financed in repo markets. It does capture the obvious fact that the fixed-income market is the dominant part of the book for this dealer measured in terms of the position size. Even for this measure to make sense, it is necessary to ensure that the prices used to compute the position value are not stale. In markets where prices change rapidly, it may even be necessary to mark the position value using real-time prices. Clearly, the systems requirements to do this for dealers who routinely transact in many markets around the world requires careful attention. This is especially a problem in the derivatives book since the position values may depend on assumptions made about the volatility of the underlying securities and on the zero prices that have been extracted to value swaps.

Value-at-Risk (VAR)

Earlier we indicated how the VAR of a security can be measured. Suppose we decide to incorporate some additional features of the securities to refine the measure of risk so that it can be applied to a portfolio. For the equity and fixed-income portfolio, let us incorporate information about variance and covariance of security returns. The variance and covariance information is annualized and presented in Tables 19-7 and 19-8.

VAR of Equity Sector. The total risk of the equity position might be summarized in terms of the variance of the returns of the equity portfolio. This variance, σ_p^2 may be explicitly computed in the following steps. First, the value of the portfolio (position value) is computed as V_p

$$V_p = n_A V_A + n_B V_B, \tag{19.4}$$

where n_A is the number of shares of security A, V_A is the market price of security A, and so on. Then the change in the value of the portfolio ΔV_p may be calculated as

$$\Delta V_p = n_A \Delta V_A + n_B \Delta V_B. \tag{19.5}$$

TABLE 19-7

Variance-Covariance Matrix of Returns, Equity Sector

Security	Stock A	Stock B
Stock A	0.06250	0.00375
Stock B	0.00375	0.02250

TABLE 19-8

Variance-Covariance Matrix of Returns, Fixed-Income Sector

Security	Bond 1	Bond 2
Bond 1	0.02560	0.01536
Bond 2	0.01536	0.01440

The return of the portfolio R_p is $\frac{\Delta V_p}{V_p}$; this is given by

$$R_p = \frac{\Delta V_p}{V_p} = x_A R_A + x_B R_B, \tag{19.6}$$

where R_A is the return on security A, and R_B is the return on security B. In addition, x_A is the fraction of the market value of the portfolio represented by security A and x_B is the fraction of the market value of the portfolio represented by security B.

As we showed earlier, the risk of this portfolio depends on its volatility. So, we first proceed to calculate the volatility of returns. Now the variance of the portfolio return may be computed as

$$\sigma_p^2 = x_A^2 \sigma_A^2 + x_B^2 \sigma_B^2 + 2 x_A x_B \mathrm{cov}(R_A, R_B). \tag{19.7}$$

For the data given in Table 19-4, we can compute $x_A = x_B = 0.5$.

Note in Table 19-7 that the variance of stock A, $\sigma_A^2 = 0.06250$. This implies that the volatility of stock A $\sigma_A = \sqrt{0.0625} = 0.25$. Also note from Table 19-7 that the variance of stock B, $\sigma_B^2 = 0.02250$. This implies that the volatility of stock B $\sigma_B = \sqrt{0.0225} = 0.15$. Finally, note that the covariance of returns from stock A and stock B, $\sigma_{AB} = 0.00375$, but the covariance is related to the correlation coefficient ρ by the formula

$$\sigma_{AB} = \rho \sigma_A \sigma_B.$$

Using this, we can solve for the correlation coefficient ρ as

$$\rho = \frac{\sigma_{AB}}{\sigma_A \sigma_B} = \frac{0.00375}{0.25 \times 0.15} = 0.10.$$

Using these data, we can compute the portfolio variability as

$$\sigma_p^2 = 0.5^2 \times 0.25^2 + 0.5^2 \times 0.15^2 + 2 \times 0.5 \times 0.5 \times 0.10 \times 0.15 \times 0.25$$
$$= 0.023125. \tag{19.8}$$

The volatility of the portfolio return is $\sigma_p = \sqrt{0.023125} = 0.1521$.

The dollar value at risk is expressed in units of standard deviations as

$$\sigma_V = V_p \sigma_p = 10{,}000{,}000 \times 0.1521 \times \sqrt{\frac{1}{252}} = \$95{,}795. \tag{19.9}$$

For a 99% confidence interval, we multiply this by 2.33 to get

$$2.33 \times 95{,}795 = 223{,}201.$$

The dollar value that is at risk is 223,201 in the sense that there is only a half a percent chance that the losses will exceed 223,201 in one day in the equity portfolio. What is the effect of correlation on the overall risk of the equity portfolio? As the correlation increases, the portfolio gets riskier. The reason is simple: with a positive correlation, both securities tend to do well at the same time, and they tend to have poor returns at the same time. This increases the overall riskiness of the portfolio, if the portfolio is

TABLE 19-9

VAR Calculations

Correlation	Variance	Volatility of Equity Portfolio	Dollar Value of Equity at Risk Confidence Levels	
			68%	99%
−0.70	0.008	9.01%	56,782	132,302
−0.60	0.010	10.00%	62,994	146,776
−0.50	0.012	10.90%	68,646	159,946
−0.40	0.014	11.73%	73,867	172,110
−0.30	0.016	12.50%	78,743	183,470
−0.20	0.018	13.23%	83,333	194,167
−0.10	0.019	13.92%	87,684	204,304
0.00	0.021	14.58%	91,829	213,961
0.10	0.023	15.21%	95,795	223,201
0.20	0.025	15.81%	99,602	232,074
0.30	0.027	16.39%	103,270	240,619
0.40	0.029	16.96%	106,812	248,871
0.50	0.031	17.50%	110,240	256,858
0.60	0.033	18.03%	113,564	264,605
0.70	0.034	18.54%	116,794	272,130
	VAR of stock A		78,743	183,470
	VAR of stock B		47,246	110,082

long in both the securities. Table 19-9 illustrates the effect of correlation between securities A and B on the overall riskiness of the portfolio. Note how the diversification effect reduces the risk of the portfolio. The confidence levels are shown for 68% (one unit of volatility) and 99% (2.33 units of volatility).

Do VARs Add? Is it possible for us to simply compute the VAR of security A and the VAR of security B and add them together to get the VAR of the portfolio? If not, what is the bias that we would have introduced by adding the VARs of individual securities to estimate the portfolio VAR?

Let us address these questions by first determining the VAR of individual securities. VAR of stock A is

$$VAR_A = 2.33 \times 0.25 \times 5,000,000 \times \sqrt{\frac{1}{252}} = 183,470.$$

VAR of stock B is

$$VAR_B = 2.33 \times 0.15 \times 5,000,000 \times \sqrt{\frac{1}{252}} = 110,082.$$

Note that the sum of the VARs for 99% confidence over a one day holding period is
$$VAR_A + VAR_B = 293,552.$$

The portfolio VAR is only 223,201. So, we conclude that the VARs are not additive in general. The reason is that the securities are less than perfectly correlated. Note for Table 19-9 that as the correlation increases, the portfolio VAR is approaching the sum of the VARs of the individual securities. This clearly illustrates the benefits of diversification.

By adding the individual VARs, however, we are overstating the VAR of the overall portfolio. This observation applies to Figure 19-1 as well. We can compute the VAR for each division in the fixed-income sector. The VAR for each division should be subject to some risk limits. By adding the VARs of all divisions, we will be significantly overstating the overall riskiness of the fixed-income unit. This arises because the correlation benefits across different divisions of the fixed-income unit are ignored. In a sense, such a calculation will show that the overall risk limit is binding when the overall VAR may be a lot less.

Value-at-Risk of Fixed-Income Sector. In a similar way, we can compute the risk of fixed-income portfolio as well. However, we will approach this problem in two stages. First, we will ignore the information in Table 19-8, which contains the correlation information between the two bonds. Instead, we will just use the information concerning the dollar value of an 0.01 of each fixed-income security.

As shown in Table 19-10, the five-year bond has a $DV01$ of $500 per million, and the ten-year bond has a $DV01$ of $700 per million. The dollar value that is at risk in the fixed-income portfolio is calculated as follows:

$$DV01_p = n_1 DV01_1 + n_2 DV02. \qquad (19.10)$$

Then, the $DV01_p$ is computed as follows:

$$DV01_p = 100 \times 500 + 50 \times 700 = \$85,000. \qquad (19.11)$$

Note that the $DV01$ may be used to construct benchmark or risk equivalents. For example, it is possible to express the risk of the fixed-income portfolio in five-year equivalents as follows: In the example, the $50 million par value of the ten-year bond may be restated in five-year equivalents as $50 \times \frac{700}{500} = 70$ million. Thus, the five-year equivalents for this fixed-income portfolio is $100 + 70 = 170$ million par amount. Often, risk limits are set for fixed-income positions in such equivalents. Such risk limits may give the portfolio manager or the trader some latitude in the choice of securities. This measure, however, assumes that when the five-year rates move by 1 basis point, the ten-year rates also move by 1 basis point. In other words, we assume that the yields move in parallel.

Thus, the dollar value of an 0.01 of the portfolio does not take into account the information about the variances and covariances of the securities which is provided in

TABLE 19-10	Security	DV01
DV01 of Securities	Bond 1	500
	Bond 2	700

Table 19-8. We proceed to do this next. In addition, it must be remembered that the *DV*01 is valid only for a basis point (or a very small) change in yield and does not easily generalize to arbitrary holding periods over which changes can be significant.

As we noted earlier, long-term interest rates tend to be less volatile than short-term interest rates. They are generally positively correlated. In Table 19-8, note that the returns have a strong positive correlation.

For the data given in Table 19-5, we can compute $x_1 = \frac{120}{180} = \frac{2}{3}$ and $x_2 = \frac{60}{180} = \frac{1}{3}$.

Note in Table 19-8 that the variance of bond 1, $\sigma_1^2 = 0.02560$. This implies that the volatility of bond 1, $\sigma_1 = \sqrt{0.0256} = 0.16$. Also note from Table 19-8 that the variance of bond 2, $\sigma_2^2 = 0.01440$. This implies that the volatility of bond 2, $\sigma_2 = \sqrt{0.0144} = 0.12$. Finally, note that the covariance of returns from bond 1 and bond 2, $\sigma_{12} = 0.01536$, but the covariance is given by the formula

$$\sigma_{12} = \rho\sigma_1\sigma_2.$$

Using this, we can solve for the correlation coefficient ρ as

$$\rho = \frac{\sigma_{12}}{\sigma_1\sigma_2} = \frac{0.01536}{0.16 \times 0.12} = 0.80.$$

Now we are in a position to consider the fixed-income portfolio's risk as measured by the variance of the portfolio return. It may be computed as

$$\sigma_p^2 = x_1^2\sigma_1^2 + x_2^2\sigma_2^2 + 2x_1x_2\text{cov}(R_1, R_2). \tag{19.12}$$

We can compute the portfolio variability as

$$\sigma_p^2 = \left[\frac{2}{3}\right]^2 \times 0.16^2 + \left[\frac{1}{3}\right]^2 \times 0.12^2 + 2 \times \frac{2}{3} \times \frac{1}{3} \times 0.80 \times 0.16 \times 0.12 \tag{19.13}$$

$$= 0.01980.$$

This implies a portfolio volatility of $\sigma_p = 0.1407$. We now explicitly recognize that the securities may have changes in yields that are less than perfect. We now compute the VAR of the fixed-income portfolio for a one day holding period (for a 99% confidence level) as follows:

$$VAR(\Delta V_p) = V_p \times \sigma_p = 180,000,000 \times 0.1407 \times 2.33 \times \sqrt{\frac{1}{252}} \tag{19.14}$$

$$= 3,718,001.$$

This is precisely the measure of risk that we have used for the equity portfolio.

VAR for Derivatives

The approach that we have presented for the measurement of risk for the cash market (equity and fixed-income markets) may be easily extended to derivatives as well. Derivative securities (such as options which have a nonlinear payoff in their underlying security's prices), however, present some problems. To illustrate the ideas, turn to the information presented in Table 19-6.

In Table 19-6, we list a book consisting of the option on stock A and a generic interest-rate swap with five years to maturity. What is the appropriate way to measure the risk of such a book? The first thing to note is that the measurement of risk of this book requires an appropriate model of pricing options. In addition, there must be a satisfactory estimation procedure by which the volatility of the underlying asset is estimated. Using inappropriate models or estimation procedures can lead to significant errors in the measurement of risk. For swaps, as seen in Chapter 16, it is essential to estimate the zero prices to be able to determine their replacement costs and their VAR. This implies that we must rely on models for estimating zero prices, such as the ones discussed in Chapter 6. Let us begin with the VAR calculations of options next.

VAR of Options. First, we focus on measuring the risk of the call option whose price we denote by C. For the option we can compute the return as

$$R = \frac{dC}{C}.$$

The return can be slightly rearranged as

$$R = \frac{dC}{dP_A} \frac{dP_A}{P_A} \times \frac{P_A}{C}.$$

By writing the option's return in this manner, it is expressed in terms of the return (R_A) of the underlying security and the delta (δ) of the option. Note that we can now write the option's return as

$$R = \delta \times R_A \times \frac{P_A}{C}.$$

The volatility of the returns is then,

$$\sigma_R = \delta \times \sigma_A \times \frac{P_A}{C}.$$

Just as we did for cash market securities, we need to find the VAR in terms of dollar amounts rather than returns. To do this, we simply multiply σ_R by the market value of the option C and then apply the relevant confidence interval factor L. The VAR for specified confidence level L and a holding period τ years is

$$VAR = L\delta\sigma_A\sqrt{\tau}P_A.$$

Obviously, $L = 2.33$ if the confidence level required is 99%. The VAR of the option (per contract) assuming that each option is on 100 shares (from Table 19-6) is

$$VAR = 2.33 \times 0.5 \times 0.25 \times \sqrt{\frac{1}{252}} \times 100 \times 50 = 91.735.$$

Since the book has 2,000 options, its VAR is $2,000 \times 91.735 = 183,470$. Note that the VAR of the option is simply the VAR of the underlying asset multiplied by the delta of the option. Of course, the delta of the option will depend on the options pricing model used. The VAR analysis for the option assumes that the delta of the option stays at 0.5, which is reasonable for a small holding period. For longer holding periods, such as 30 days, this assumption is unrealistic. The VAR measure for a 30-day holding period is

$$VAR = 2.33 \times 0.5 \times 0.25 \times \sqrt{\frac{30}{252}} \times 100 \times 50 \times 2,000 = 1,004,908.$$

A more reasonable approach is to simulate the underlying asset value for the holding period by determining the value of the option at the end of each scenario and estimating the average across all possible paths. Such an approach will correctly capture the changes in the delta of the derivative instrument. We illustrate this approach for options next.

Monte Carlo Simulation. In the simulation approach, we generate several paths for stock A. For each path, we calculate the value of the option at the end of the holding period (30 days). This way we correctly account for the passage of time, as well as for the fact that in some paths, option will be out-of-the-money and in others, the option will be in-the-money. Clearly, this procedure reflects the changes in delta into the calculations. In order to simulate the prices of stock A, we use the procedure developed in Chapter 14. The risk-neutral price process for A is generated such that the price at a future date T is given by Equation 19.15.

$$\ln P_T = \ln P_0 + \left\{ \left(r - \frac{1}{2}\sigma^2 \right) \Delta t + \sigma \sqrt{\Delta t} \tilde{z} \right\} \qquad (19.15)$$

In Equation 19-15, P_0 is the price of stock A now ($50), r is the riskless rate (assumed to be 5%) and σ is the volatility of the returns of stock A (assumed to be 25% from Table 19-7). The variable $\tilde{z}$ is a standard normal variable with a mean of one and variance of one.

We can write this equation as

$$P_T = P_0 \times e^{\{(r-\frac{1}{2}\sigma^2)\Delta t + \sigma\sqrt{\Delta t}\tilde{z}\}}.$$

Next, we repeat this procedure to generate 300 paths by drawing 300 values of $\tilde{z}$. For each path, we determine P_T. For each path at the end of 30 days, we use the Black-Scholes options pricing model to value the call option. In pricing the option, we assume $r = 5\%$ and $\sigma = 25\%$. The call values are determined for each path. The resulting frequency distribution of call prices is shown in Figure 19-5.

In Table 19-11 we indicate the outcome along each path. The change in the value of the option has been sorted from the lowest realization to the highest realization.

Based on the frequency distribution, we can construct the 99% confidence level. In fact, the simulation results show that the probability that the option will lose value by more than 734,417 is only 1%. The results are shown in Figure 19-6.

Note that the VAR determined using the current delta of the option was 1,004,908, which is significantly higher than the VAR obtained by simulation. This suggests that the VAR procedure used for the cash market (in which payoffs are typically linear) is

FIGURE 19-5   *Distribution of Call on Stock A*

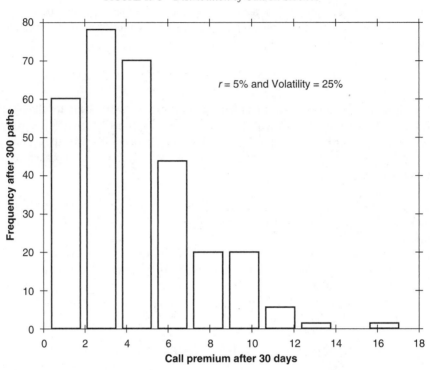

generally inappropriate for securities, such as options (where the payoffs are nonlinear). We now turn to the measurement of VAR for the swap contract in the derivatives book shown in Table 19-6.

VAR of Swaps. The VAR of a swap contract depends on the zero-coupon bond prices needed to calculate the value of the swap. A full-blown treatment of calculating the VAR of a swap is not presented here. We show how the swap can be valued and how the volatility of the swap value depends on the variance-covariance structure of the zero prices.

The generic interest rate swap shown in Table 19-6 has two years to maturity. As discussed in Chapter 16, the valuation of swaps requires the estimation of the zero-coupon bond prices. Let us consider the cash flows of the swap to lay out clearly the steps needed to compute the VAR of swap. The two-year swap given in Table 19-6 has four cash flows as shown in Table 19-12. The next payment date of the swap is three months from now. Thereafter, there are three additional payment dates, each occurring at six month intervals.

Note that the value of the swap, as shown in Chapter 16, is found by calculating the present value of each leg and taking the difference between the two values. The

TABLE 19-11 *VAR by Simulation*

Cumulative Probability	Change in Call Value	Cumulative Probability	Change in Call Value	Cumulative Probability	Change in Call Value
0.003	−788,648	0.170	−472,256	0.337	−287,190
0.007	−755,242	0.173	−470,432	0.340	−285,631
0.010	−734,417	0.177	−463,423	0.343	−279,724
0.013	−718,293	0.180	−459,714	0.347	−271,396
0.017	−707,706	0.183	−456,591	0.350	−270,575
0.020	−704,838	0.187	−451,662	0.353	−269,789
0.023	−696,716	0.190	−450,943	0.357	−269,163
0.027	−695,567	0.193	−448,283	0.360	−267,848
0.030	−681,464	0.197	−442,876	0.363	−263,229
0.033	−677,586	0.200	−437,221	0.367	−260,084
0.037	−676,145	0.203	−429,595	0.370	−258,502
0.040	−676,131	0.207	−421,681	0.373	−254,887
0.043	−672,192	0.210	−419,528	0.377	−248,799
0.047	−671,523	0.213	−418,615	0.380	−248,317
0.050	−667,335	0.217	−414,310	0.383	−240,393
0.053	−665,901	0.220	−402,878	0.387	−240,061
0.057	−638,185	0.223	−402,736	0.390	−239,076
0.060	−632,861	0.227	−400,557	0.393	−237,998
0.063	−629,562	0.230	−398,450	0.397	−234,687
0.067	−617,120	0.233	−397,446	0.400	−232,542
0.070	−614,818	0.237	−392,164	0.403	−215,235
0.073	−613,787	0.240	−392,138	0.407	−195,883
0.077	−608,065	0.243	−387,325	0.410	−192,920
0.080	−593,360	0.247	−383,467	0.413	−191,661
0.083	−589,536	0.250	−379,010	0.417	−188,367
0.087	−576,826	0.253	−377,742	0.420	−187,240
0.090	−576,470	0.257	−377,709	0.423	−182,533
0.093	−570,473	0.260	−375,504	0.427	−181,276
0.097	−570,408	0.263	−373,163	0.430	−176,065
0.100	−569,241	0.267	−371,823	0.433	−175,337
0.103	−565,283	0.270	−371,106	0.437	−172,245
0.107	−558,877	0.273	−367,141	0.440	−163,386
0.110	−553,233	0.277	−358,861	0.443	−152,260
0.113	−548,144	0.280	−355,294	0.447	−149,969
0.117	−542,865	0.283	−344,398	0.450	−148,684
0.120	−522,893	0.287	−344,224	0.453	−143,958
0.123	−521,254	0.290	−342,861	0.457	−142,130
0.127	−514,941	0.293	−340,306	0.460	−136,763
0.130	−506,929	0.297	−331,354	0.463	−135,990
0.133	−506,422	0.300	−326,630	0.467	−133,455
0.137	−504,399	0.303	−324,120	0.470	−131,398
0.140	−499,511	0.307	−316,196	0.473	−125,222
0.143	−498,052	0.310	−312,816	0.477	−121,844
0.147	−487,136	0.313	−310,981	0.480	−109,724
0.150	−487,081	0.317	−309,430	0.483	−106,841
0.153	−485,679	0.320	−309,404	0.487	−105,348
0.157	−482,118	0.323	−307,760	0.490	−100,229
0.160	−477,031	0.327	−298,602	0.493	−96,273
0.163	−474,980	0.330	−293,081	0.497	−95,466

(continued)

TABLE 19-11   *Continued*

Cumulative Probability	Change in Call Value	Cumulative Probability	Change in Call Value	Cumulative Probability	Change in Call Value
0.167	−474,791	0.333	−291,257	0.500	−90,005
0.503	−88,495	0.670	88,308	0.837	388,540
0.507	−86,038	0.673	88,534	0.840	401,414
0.510	−85,636	0.677	97,192	0.843	420,278
0.513	−83,307	0.680	112,778	0.847	445,363
0.517	−81,006	0.683	115,545	0.850	454,745
0.520	−78,257	0.687	118,241	0.853	473,939
0.523	−74,215	0.690	131,621	0.857	497,352
0.527	−72,969	0.693	132,139	0.860	513,377
0.530	−68,669	0.697	132,618	0.863	520,474
0.533	−64,707	0.700	134,498	0.867	567,697
0.537	−64,130	0.703	137,434	0.870	586,906
0.540	−61,210	0.707	137,666	0.873	592,116
0.543	−61,071	0.710	138,124	0.877	610,500
0.547	−57,722	0.713	161,501	0.880	623,734
0.550	−50,640	0.717	161,905	0.883	651,709
0.553	−45,588	0.720	170,871	0.887	698,338
0.557	−37,624	0.723	174,994	0.890	717,967
0.560	−36,122	0.727	177,421	0.893	736,815
0.563	−28,820	0.730	178,381	0.897	755,654
0.567	−26,476	0.733	180,039	0.900	766,961
0.570	−25,884	0.737	186,817	0.903	767,109
0.573	−25,505	0.740	215,565	0.907	773,485
0.577	−24,787	0.743	223,894	0.910	775,022
0.580	−22,383	0.747	226,225	0.913	781,158
0.583	−16,052	0.750	228,115	0.917	783,367
0.587	−15,517	0.753	228,971	0.920	783,428
0.590	−14,408	0.757	233,118	0.923	785,876
0.593	−14,337	0.760	233,775	0.927	804,115
0.597	−10,002	0.763	234,542	0.930	820,710
0.600	−4,938	0.767	236,508	0.933	824,494
0.603	−2,071	0.770	236,681	0.937	826,131
0.607	17,314	0.773	236,912	0.940	847,632
0.610	17,476	0.777	238,144	0.943	905,558
0.613	18,113	0.780	240,621	0.947	917,425
0.617	23,997	0.783	241,328	0.950	983,559
0.620	26,012	0.787	242,575	0.953	1,005,118
0.623	30,844	0.790	259,471	0.957	1,011,531
0.627	36,691	0.793	293,573	0.960	1,037,453
0.630	40,691	0.797	300,552	0.963	1,051,357
0.633	47,650	0.800	303,290	0.967	1,077,121
0.637	55,099	0.803	318,553	0.970	1,083,652
0.640	62,657	0.807	319,207	0.973	1,087,876
0.643	67,111	0.810	321,648	0.977	1,103,643
0.647	68,904	0.813	323,060	0.980	1,218,367
0.650	70,149	0.817	323,469	0.983	1,307,475
0.653	72,077	0.820	333,545	0.987	1,542,662
0.657	73,994	0.823	336,940	0.990	1,597,125
0.660	79,163	0.827	357,724	0.993	1,899,263
0.663	82,819	0.830	361,002	0.997	2,078,484
0.667	88,155	0.833	376,546	1.000	2,280,702

FIGURE 19-6   *VAR of Call Option by Simulation*

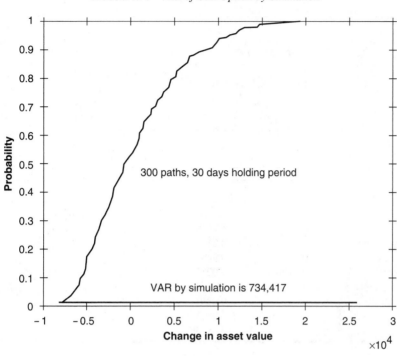

TABLE 19-12

Cash Flows of Swaps

Time	Fixed-Leg	Floating-Leg
$t+3$	$\frac{6\%}{2}$	4%
$t+9$	$\frac{6\%}{2}$	LIBOR
$t+15$	$\frac{6\%}{2}$	LIBOR
$t+21$	$\frac{6\%}{2}$	LIBOR

fixed-leg pays an amount equal to $3\% \times 100{,}000{,}000 = 3{,}000{,}000$ every six months. The present value of the fixed-leg is

$$\text{PV(Fixed)} = 3{,}000{,}000 \times [b(t, t + 3) + b(t, t + 9) + b(t, t + 15) + b(t, t + 21)],$$

where the zero-coupon bond prices at date t for maturities at dates $t + 3$, $t + 9$, $t + 15$, and $t + 21$ are respectively given by $b(t, t + 3)$, $b(t, t + 9)$, $b(t, t + 15)$, and $b(t, t + 21)$. As shown in Table 19-12, the present value of the fixed-leg is

$$\text{PV(Fixed)} = 3{,}000{,}000 \times [0.9901 + 0.9690 + 0.9459 + 0.9211] = 11{,}478{,}300.$$

(The zero prices are reported only up to four decimals. In actual calculations, the zero prices are not approximated to four decimals.)

TABLE 19-13

Valuation of Swaps

	Zero Yields		
Maturity (in Months)	Yield	Zero Prices	Forward Rates (Percent)
3	4.00%	0.9901	4.0000
9	4.25%	0.9690	4.3751
15	4.50%	0.9459	4.8756
21	4.75%	0.9211	5.3763

Pricing a Two-Year Swap

				Time
	3	9	15	21
	$t = 3$	$t = 9$	$t = 15$	$t = 21$
Fixed payments	6.00%	6.00%	6.00%	6.00%
Floating payments	4.00%	4.38%	4.88%	5.38%
Zero prices	0.9901	0.9690	0.9459	0.9211
PV (float)	0.0198	0.0212	0.0231	0.0248
Total PV (float)		**8,880,200**		
PV (fixed)	0.0297	0.0291	0.0284	0.0276
Total PV (fixed)		**11,478,366**		
Value of swap		**2,596,395**		

The value of the floating-leg is easy to determine. Note that at date t, the next floating coupon is already known. This is because we are dealing with a generic interest-rate swap, where the next coupon is reset six months ahead of the payment date. Let us say that the coupon to be paid at $t + 3$ was reset six months earlier (at $t − 3$) at the then prevailing LIBOR of 4.00% (annualized). As discussed in Chapter 16, the value of the present value of the floating-leg can be determined as shown in Table 19-13.

Intuitively, the present value of the floating-leg can be obtained as follows: First, we recognize that the next payment at date $t + 3$ is already set at 4% (annualized). Its present value is

$$2,000,000b(t, t + 3) = 2,000,000 \times 0.9901 = 1,980,200.$$

The subsequent payments in the floating-leg can be replicated by rolling over 100 million at date $t + 3$ in a sequence of six-month LIBOR until maturity. The 100 million that is required at $t + 3$ has a present value at t of

$$100,000,000b(t, t + 3) = 100,000,000 \times 0.9901 = 99,010,000.$$

Since the floating-leg does not pay the balloon payment, we subtract from the par amount the present value of the par amount. The present value of this at t of

$$100,000,000b(t, t + 21) = 100,000,000 \times 0.9211 = 92,110,000.$$

Therefore, the present value of the floating-leg is

$$PV(\text{Floating}) = 2,000,000 b(t, t+3) + 100,000,000[b(t, t+3) - b(t, t+21)],$$

or,

$$PV(\text{Floating}) = 8,880,200.$$

The swap value is the difference between the fixed- and floating-leg, which is $11,478,366 - 8,881,971 = 2,596,395$.

The swap value can be written as a function of the zero-coupon bond prices.

$$S = 3,000,000 \times [b(t, t+3) + b(t, t+9) + b(t, t+15) + b(t, t+21)]$$

$$-[2,000,000 b(t, t+3) + 100,000,000\{b(t, t+3) - b(t, t+21)\}]]$$

The volatility of the swap value σ_s clearly depends on the variance-covarince matrix of the zero prices. As a consequence, the VAR of the swap, in turn, will depend on the variance-covariance matrix of the zero prices. Once σ_s is calculated, the procedure for computing the VAR proceeds exactly as we have done earlier for the cash portfolio.

Modeling Correlation

The stock portfolio can also be analyzed using the simulation technique. One advantage of simulation is that we can model different scenarios that we anticipate. A key consideration is the fact that stock A and stock B are correlated. This correlation must be modeled in the simulation. Consider the equity portfolio in Table 19-4. For this portfolio, let us introduce some basic notations. Let the (2×2) variance-covariance matrix of returns be denoted as Ω. It is given by

$$\begin{bmatrix} \sigma_A^2 & \sigma_{AB} \\ \sigma_{AB} & \sigma_B^2 \end{bmatrix}.$$

Let the weights of the stocks in the portfolio be denoted by the (2×1) vector x

$$\begin{bmatrix} x_A \\ x_B \end{bmatrix}.$$

Then the variance of the stock portfolio can be compactly denoted by

$$\sigma_p^2 = x'\Omega x.$$

The idea behind denoting the portfolio this way is simple. Although we are illustrating the basic ideas with just two securities, the logic goes over even if the portfolio were to contain many securities. We will simply define Ω and x to reflect the characteristics and the number of securities in the portfolio.

The presence of correlation poses a problem in performing simulation. How do we simulate the paths of stock B if we know that its returns are correlated with the returns of stock A? It turns out that this problem can be solved by using a technique known as Cholesky factorization. Simply stated, the Cholesky factorization allows us to simulate each stock's path using standard normal variables after a modification is made to the variance terms. The Cholesky factorization finds a matrix X such that

$$\Omega = X'X.$$

The matrix X turns out to have a nice structure for simulation purposes. In the context of our example X' is

$$\begin{bmatrix} \sigma_A & 0 \\ \rho\sigma_B & \sigma_B\sqrt{1-\rho^2} \end{bmatrix}.$$

Given this factorization, we can implement the simulation as follows:

1. First, we generate a set of standard normal variables $\tilde{z}_A$ and $\tilde{z}_B$ for each stock. We will simulate 300 paths by generating 300 draws of $\tilde{z}_A$ and $\tilde{z}_B$, respectively. Note that $\tilde{z}_A$ and $\tilde{z}_B$ are standard normal variates with a mean of zero and a volatility of one. Also, note that $\tilde{z}_A$ and $\tilde{z}_B$ are not correlated with each other.

2. Using these, we generate the price paths for stocks A and B. The price of stock A at any date T in the future is

$$P_A(T) = P_A(0)e^{\left\{(\mu_A - \frac{1}{2}\sigma_A^2)\Delta t + \sigma_A\sqrt{\Delta t}\tilde{z}_A\right\}}.$$

The expected return of stock A is denoted by μ_A. The price of stock B at any date T in the future will capture the correlation properties as shown next.

$$P_B(T) = P_B(0)e^{\left\{(\mu_B - \frac{1}{2}\sigma_B^2)\Delta t + (\rho\tilde{z}_A + \sqrt{1-\rho^2}\tilde{z}_B)\sigma_B\sqrt{\Delta t}\right\}}$$

The expected return of stock B is denoted by μ_B. Note that we have modified the variance of the security B according to the Cholesky factorization. The price processes of A and B can now be simulated as before except that they now capture the correlation structure as well.

3. It is useful to note that the returns R_A and R_B of the stocks are respectively given by

$$R_A = \ln\left(\frac{P_A(T)}{P_A(0)}\right)$$

and

$$R_B = \ln\left(\frac{P_B(T)}{P_B(0)}\right).$$

Using this definition of returns in the price expressions, we get

$$R_A = \left(\mu_A - \frac{1}{2}\sigma_A^2\right)\Delta t + \sigma_A\sqrt{\Delta t}\tilde{z}_A$$

and

$$R_B = \left(\mu_B - \frac{1}{2}\sigma_B^2\right)\Delta t + \left(\rho\tilde{z}_A + \sqrt{1-\rho^2}\tilde{z}_B\right)\sigma_B\sqrt{\Delta t}.$$

We can easily verify that the variance of R_A is $\sigma_A^2 \Delta t$ and that the variance of R_B is $\sigma_B^2 \Delta t$. In addition, we can verify that the covariance between A and B is $\rho \sigma_A \sigma_B \Delta t$. This shows how the Cholesky factorization can help in setting up the simulation for correlated variables. Programs like Mathematica and Matlab have built-in Cholesky factorization codes. Some technical conditions which are necessary for the factorization to work are not discussed here.

4. We have simulated the behavior of the equity portfolio using 300 paths. At the end of 30 days, we computed the value of the portfolio and determined the change in the value of the portfolio (relative to the beginning value of 10 million) for each path. Then the change in the values was sorted, and a frequency distribution was created. Based on the frequency distribution, the VAR of the portfolio was calculated for a 99% confidence level. The frequency distribution and the VAR are illustrated in Figures 19-7 and 19-8, respectively.

In Figure 19-7, note that the portfolio value changes from a low of about –1.35 million to a high of about 1.75 million in 30 days time. In these simulations, the correlation coefficient was assumed to be 0.10. The implication of this manifests itself into the scatter plot in Figure 19-9, where the prices of stock A are plotted against the returns of stock B.

FIGURE 19-7   *Frequency Distribution of Equity Portfolio*

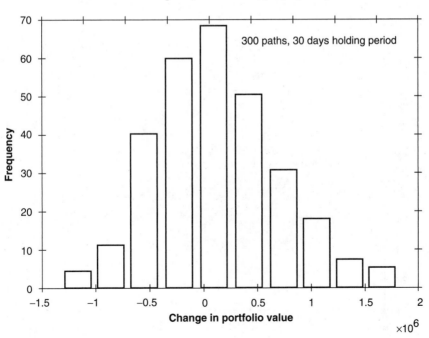

FIGURE 19-8   *VAR of Equity Portfolio by Simulation*

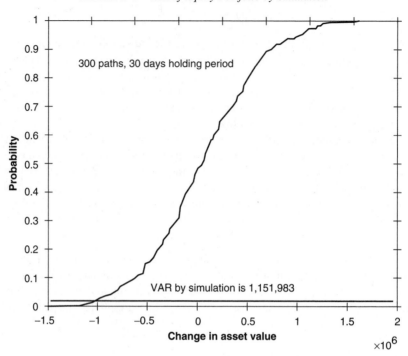

300 paths, 30 days holding period

VAR by simulation is 1,151,983

FIGURE 19-9   *Stock A versus Stock B*

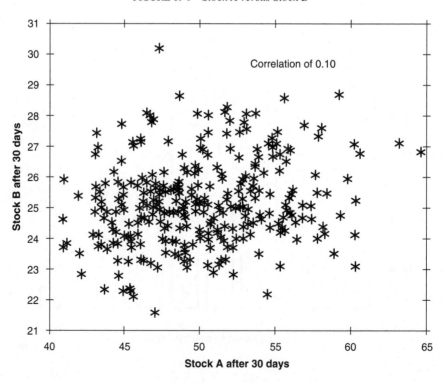

Correlation of 0.10

FIGURE 19-10   *VAR of Equity Portfolio by Simulation*

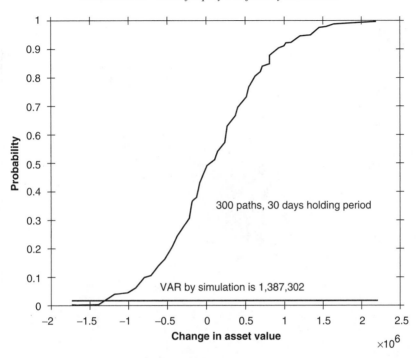

What happens to the VAR when the correlation between stock A and stock B increases to 0.8? Intuition suggests that the VAR should increase. The simulation results are shown in Figures 19-10 and 19-11 under this correlation assumption.

The VAR of the portfolio has increased to a level of 1,387,302, higher than the VAR level of 1,151,963 reached when the correlation was 0.10. Note that with a correlation of 0.8 the future prices (and returns) of stocks A and B are much more closely aligned as shown in Figure 19-11.

Credit Risk

Credit risk arises in practice whenever a counterparty is unable or unwilling to perform in accordance with the prespecified contractual provisions of a transaction, leading to economic losses to the other party. As a simple example, corporation XYZ has taken a three-month loan of $100 million from bank A. The loan calls for the payment of interest and principal after one month totaling $102.5 million. At the end of one month, corporation XYZ fails to pay the full amount. This necessitates certain actions by bank A to recover the amount. These actions are costly, and the outcome is uncertain.

Table 19-14 illustrates a hypothetical interest-rate swap book of a company. As shown in the table, some of the swaps have a positive marked-to-market value, and others have a negative marked-to-market value. Note that the company has engaged in

FIGURE 19-11   *Prices: Stock A versus Stock B*

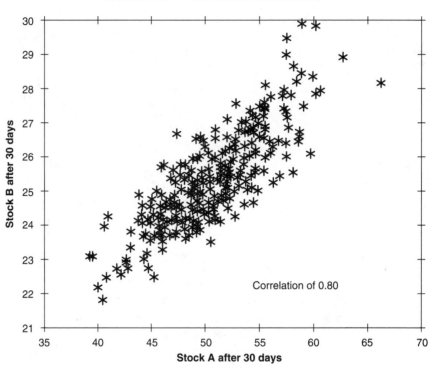

TABLE 19-14

Credit Risk of a Swap Book

Number of Swaps	Swap Maturity	Marked-to-Market Value	Counterparty
1	5	100,000	A
2	4	–200,000	A
3	3	–500,000	X
4	7	1,000,000	Y
5	6	670,000	X

more than one swap with the same counterparty. The notional value of swaps total $500 million. The company has three swaps that have a positive marked-to-market value and two swaps that have a negative marked-to-market value. The total value of positive marked-to-market value swaps is $1,770,000. The total value of the negative marked-to-market value is –$700,000. One way to measure the value of the swap book is 1,770,000 – 700,000 = $1,070,000.

This assumes that there are no defaults by any of the counterparties. In reality, one has to worry about this possibility. Default by a counterparty has an asymmetric effect. If, for example, counterparty Y defaults in swap number four, then the firm potentially stands to lose $1 million. Of course, depending on the swap termination provisions, collaterals, and margins, the loss may be less than that. The idea here is that the firm

TABLE 19-15
Net Credit Risk
of Swaps

Counterparty	Marked-to-Market Value
A	−100,000
X	170,000
Y	1,000,000

will have to find other counterparties to replace the swaps on which the counterparties have defaulted. This is costly when the swap has a positive marked-to-market value to the firm. This suggests that the credit exposure of the firm is the sum of all positive marked-to-market values, which is $1,770,000.

One innovation that is fast becoming an industry practice in many transactions is the concept of netting. Under netting, instead of counterparty X paying 100 million to counterparty Y and counterparty X receiving 90 million from counterparty Y, the difference of 10 million will be paid by X to Y. Netting allows banks in bilateral transactions to set aside much less capital to support credit risk. The concept of netting has been endorsed by regulatory bodies. In addition, several private sector organizations have attempted to standardize the netting procedures. The Exchange Clearing House Organization (ECHO) initiated by several European banks has introduced multilateral netting of spot and forward transactions. The International Swap Dealers Association (ISDA) has instituted the netting arrangement in swap transactions. Netting may actually enable the firm to reduce the credit exposure. We group the net exposure for each counterparty in Table 19-15.

Note that by netting the swap exposures with each counterparty, we find that the firm is able to reduce its exposure further. For the firm, the net exposure with counterparty A is −100,000. The corresponding exposure with counterparty X is 170,000. Thus, the aggregate exposure from credit risk for the firm is $1,170,000.

Typically, firms carry reserves to manage credit exposures. These reserves are a function of the credit quality of the counterparties. Typically, firms may impose a constraint on the average credit quality of the pool of counterparties. For example, some firms require that the average credit rating should be AA or better.

The credit risk, however, depends not only on the credit quality of the counterparties, but also on the diversification (or lack thereof) of counterparties across different industry segments. If a swap dealer has a number of open contracts in one or two industry sectors, then a recession in those sectors can expose the dealer to a greater degree of credit exposure than would otherwise be the case.

The approach behind the measurement of credit risk in our swap example is fairly general. We must price the transactions with each counterparty, utilize netting wherever possible, and focus on the transactions that have a positive marked-to-market value. Typically, many transactions may be marked to a model. This situation also represents model risks. For most derivative contracts (such as options), there are many dimensions of risk, as noted earlier. Generally, a two-step procedure is used for assessing the credit exposure in derivatives transactions. First, we simulate the underlying variables (such as interest rates or futures prices) to determine the payoffs of the derivative asset. Then, we ascribe certain probabilities of default by counterparties. We combine these two sets of information and arrive at a measure of credit exposure. Often, Monte Carlo simulation procedures are used for assessing the credit exposure. In implementing this procedure, it is necessary to obtain and process information about factors that determine the probability of default and the recovery rates in the event of a default. That is,

- The distribution of future interest rates or the market values of the derivative asset. This is accomplished by specifying a stochastic process for the underlying state variables, which may be stock price, interest rates, or volatilities. In a single-state variable model, only one factor will be specified. In two-state variable models, two factors will be specified, and so on.
- The probability of default by the counterparty in the preceding step. This is a function of many factors, such as the overall state of the economy, state of the industry, and company specific factors. Typically, the credit reputation of the counterparty and potential changes in credit reputation convey useful information about the probability of defaults. Moody's and Standard and Poor provide statistics on default rates. One-year default rates are computed by dividing the number of rated issuers defaulting over the calendar year by the number of nondefaulted rated issuers in each rating group. This is shown in Table 19-16. Clearly, Table 19-16 shows the association between credit rating and default rates. In modeling credit risk, it is the future default rates that are of interest.
- The recovery rates associated with defaults. These recovery rates depend on a number of things, such as margins, collaterals, termination provisions, covenants, and seniority. Again, recovery rates have to be forecasted to model the credit risk associated with any transactions.

In the context of interest-rate swaps, the credit exposure over time depends on two factors. The first factor is the passage of time. This implies that over time the number of remaining cash flows in the swap reduces, and as a result the exposure also reduces. The second factor is that at the time of initiation the swap was priced to be zero valued. As time passes, the value of the swap tends to deviate from zero due to changing market conditions. This, in turn, will cause the swap's credit exposure to increase. The tradeoffs typically imply that the credit exposure of the swap increases for a few years before the first effect starts to dominate. After peaking, the credit exposure reduces over the rest of the life of the swap. Note that this is because in interest-rate swaps, there is no balloon payment. In contracts with balloon payments, we would not expect to see this pattern of credit exposure over time.

TABLE 19-16

One-Year Default Rates, 1989–1993

Credit Reputation	1989	1990	1991	1992	1993
Aaa	0.0	0.0	0.0	0.0	0.0
Aa	0.3	0.0	0.0	0.0	0.02
A	0.0	0.0	0.0	0.0	0.01
Baa	0.5	0.0	0.20	0.0	0.16
Ba	2.7	3.3	5.1	0.2	0.5
B	8.6	12.9	13.1	6.4	5.2

Source: Moody's Investor Service.

Operational Risk

This risk arises from improper accounting systems and incorrect settlement of transactions and payments. The operating systems include back-offices dealing with clearance, settlement, order processing, computer, and accounting systems. Typically, an audit department is responsible for overseeing these activities. Operational risk in listed options sometimes occurs in the clearinghouse activities. In traditional banking activities where transactions occur in different time zones, there is an operational risk: one leg of the transaction might be done before the other leg can be completed. A bank may end up delivering the securities before the cash gets paid. This poses a big risk if the transactions run into millions of dollars. Such operational risks are present in large money transfers, which are ever-present in financial transactions. In addition, operational risk also results from the absence of adequate position and risk limits. Even where proper risk limits are present, it is important that they are enforced: traders and managers who do not live by such risk limits should be taken to task.

Perhaps a telling case in point where the operational risks ultimately resulted in the eventual failure of a firm is the Baring Brothers case. The trading activities of one trader in Singapore were not subject to appropriate risk limits. Eventually, the trader was able to build up sufficient losses by piling up his trading positions to the point where the bank collapsed. The accumulated losses in futures markets amounted to about $1.4 billion. A review of the following article indicates that one key problem in the risk management system was the fact that trading and clearing of trades were under the same manager's authority. Segregation of trading and back-office operations (clearing) would have mitigated the problem significantly. It was perhaps equally important that huge positions were permitted without periodic and ad hoc reviews by the senior managers. Such reviews should present information about the VAR of the trade and the potential for significant capital commitments.

Risk Management Gets New Respect
BY PAUL G. BARR

Investment professionals say risk management controls can be improved across the board at financial institutions, although the situation at Barings PLC, London, probably was an extreme case of lax controls.

Barings' unprecedented $1.4 billion loss in futures contracts has financial executives of all stripes questioning the quality of risk management controls in and outside of their firms.

And consultants say investment losses aren't always the first sign of trouble; investment gains sometimes can be just as big a concern. One consultant says pension funds are among the most vulnerable to problems from hidden, excessive risk.

"It kind of wakes you up and makes you realize this can happen to anybody," said Jeremy Dyer, fund manager for Scottish Amicable Investment Managers Ltd., Glasgow, in reference to Baring's speedy collapse.

Source: *Pensions & Investments* (March 20, 1995). Reprinted with permission.

(continued)

Likewise, Francis Petrash, senior manager of risk management technology, Coopers & Lybrand, L.L.P., New York, said Barings' losses are "raising the consciousness" of senior managers on risk management controls.

While the bankruptcy of Orange County, Calif., and the collapse of Askin Capital Management raised questions about risk management, those institutions were not viewed to be as sophisticated as Barings, industry participants say.

"Barings was a well-run firm," but apparently didn't have the controls, said William Michaelcheck, who runs Mariner Partners, an investment partnership in New York. "I don't think there's a firm on earth that's not questioning their systems today," he said shortly after Barings' problems came to light.

Based on press reports, consultants say Barings committed some fundamental risk control errors, particularly if both trading and clearance were under the authority of one person.

Segregation of trading and back-office operations is "something an auditor learns in the first week of class," said David Orszulak, a manager for Price Waterhouse L.L.P., in its investment management and securities operations consulting group, Hartford, Conn. Separating the two is done not only to avoid financial disasters—as happened at Barings—but to avoid the temptation to bend the rules, he said.

And one of the first signs of a possible lapse might not be a catastrophe on the scale of what happened at Barings.

"I'm as much concerned with someone taking a big win as much as taking a big loss," said Scott Lummer, managing director, Ibbotson Associates, Chicago. It's "actually a more severe problem given human nature," he said. When a strategy or trader makes a lot of money, the tendency is to think more money should have been devoted to the strategy or trader, Mr. Lummer said.

Mr. Orszulak said it should be an "equally egregious offense" to make money stretching investment guidelines as it is to lose money doing so. "A wrong is a wrong," he said.

And to find the next Barings, one could perhaps look to the investors who profited trading against Barings' futures positions.

All the money Barings lost was won by others, and those winnings create the potential to confuse fortunate market movement with investment skill, Mr. Lummer said. On the other side of that billion dollars or so profit, "somewhere there's a 'damn we're good;' That's the next Barings," Mr. Lummer said.

Once a manager or trader starts making more money, guidelines are stretched or ignored the next time around. In these cases, supervisors start thinking the trader is skillful, not just lucky, he said.

And without downplaying what happened to Barings, Mr. Lummer said bigger dangers still lie with non-financial, investing institutions, such as pension funds and corporations.

Financial companies "are going to be, by their very nature, having to take risk," he said. "Trading companies, they make money, they lose money, that's going to happen."

But "most pension plans are probably underestimating the risk they are taking," he said. "We have a lot of concerns."

The number of losses at institutions in 1994 from derivatives is greater than what is known, including at pension funds, Mr. Lummer said.

Nonetheless, all companies can do a better job of managing their risk, given that firms selling derivatives or derivatives strategies are going to downplay possible bad outcomes. "Companies are taking exposures that are being soft-peddled" by the managers of the assets, Mr. Lummer said.

Some see equity-linked derivatives and derivative strategies as being the next source of unexpected losses. Mr. Michaelcheck of Mariner Partners said the next big test could come with equity-linked derivative products in the United States, where volatility has been very low in recent years. "I think there are a lot of equity derivatives that haven't been tested yet," he said.

To help prevent unexpected positions being taken, consultants said firms have to set various levels of trading limits beginning with each trader all the way up to firmwide limits.

While most firms have set trading limits, too often they are broken when a trader, manager or strategy becomes successful.

Those guidelines should not be broken, Mr. Lummer said. Perhaps guidelines can be changed for experienced traders, but once they are set, "that's the law, no ifs, ands or buts," he said. The key is defining risk, setting guidelines, and not overstepping them.

Moreover, Mr. Petrash of Coopers & Lybrand said traders and their supervisors should meet regularly to discuss the trader's positions and the potential profits and losses, and the risks being taken.

While computer systems can sometimes be cracked, and accounting numbers played with, using personal interaction and tracking cash flows are two simple ways to keep a stronger handle on a firm's market risk.

On a daily basis, a trader's position sheets should be cross-referenced with the day's trading records, consultants say. Both the supervisor and the trader need to sign off on those positions, and discuss the strategies and possible outcomes related to the positions, Mr. Petrash said.

Moreover, there should be a daily trading exceptions report, which would not necessarily limit a trader's ability to trade, but would flag trades of an unusual size or nature, he said. There also should be regular discussions between a trader and supervisor of how particular trades can be unwound if they prove unprofitable, and what will be the costs of unwinding them, Mr. Petrash said.

Tom Ho, president of Global Advanced Technology Corp., a New York-based fixed-income and risk management consultant, said firms now generally rely too much on risk control systems that look backward, and act as more of a report card. Instead the industry should move to surveillance types of systems that are proactive in seeking out potential deviations from a firm's desired risk, he said.

Mr. Petrash noted a risk management system doesn't act only as a control, but also as a means to profit. They can lead to enhanced opportunities in the marketplace.

While industry professionals were close to undivided on their call for strong controls, the cost of implementing controls is less clear.

The cost of an adequate risk control trading system can run as high as the tens of millions to hundreds of millions of dollars, Mr. Petrash said. It depends on what it is worth for an investment firm's employees to sleep well at night, he said.

Robert D. Arnott, chief investment officer for money manager First Quadrant Corp., Pasadena, Calif., said trading systems are widely available, and not expensive. At the most basic level, "Custodial banks can track aggregate positions," he said.

Greg Pond, president of ADS Associates, Calabasas, Calif., a trading systems firm, said costs vary widely depending on the needs of the institution. His firm has installed its systems and trading software at prices from roughly $350,000 to $3 million.

Another case in point is the ability of some trading units to perform trades where the connection between putative profits from certain trades and actual cash (if any) resulting from such transactions is not properly accounted for in a timely fashion. This happened in the case of the Kidder Peabody situation. In this case, the accounting system for handling certain trades in the strips markets and the government bond markets appeared to have a flaw which was exploited to make paper profits on which the compensation appeared to have been determined. As the following *Business Week* article shows, this practice was allowed over a period of two years, reflecting serious lack of operational and management controls.

Why Didn't Kidder Catch On?

Wall Street is skeptical of the "We wuz robbed" explanation

BY LEAH NATHANS SPIRO,
WITH PHILIP L. ZWEIG IN NEW YORK AND TIM SMART IN NEW HAVEN

Was it simply an isolated incident, a scheme that even the best controls couldn't have detected? Or did it reflect a broad, systemic breakdown?

That is a key issue facing Kidder, Peabody & Co.'s senior managers as they investigate who was behind a two-year, $350 million, phony government bond trading scheme that was disclosed on Apr. 17. Kidder Chief Executive Michael A. Carpenter says he and his top lieutenant, fixed-income head Edward A. Cerullo, were victims of a very sophisticated rogue trader named Joseph Jett, who ran the firm's government bond desk. Jett has been fired, and six other employees were suspended from their jobs. Jett could not be reached for comment.

Carpenter insists that Kidder's controls and risk-management systems are just as good as the rest of the Street's, even though no systems are foolproof: "The altimeter said we were flying at the right altitude, and the compass said we were flying in the right direction, and we banged into the mountain."

Raised Eyebrows

Yet many on Wall Street are skeptical of Carpenter's "We wuz robbed" explanation of what is one of the largest Wall Street losses ever. How could the scheme have gone on undetected since 1991? Why didn't 15-year Kidder veteran Cerullo, who was Jett's boss, have a better handle on how Jett was generating "profits" of $20 million to $40 million a month? And most important, are Carpenter and Cerullo to blame for building a culture at Kidder that kowtowed to superstar traders?

John F. Welch Jr., the tough-guy chief executive of General Electric, which owns Kidder, supports Carpenter. "I think, based on everything I know, Carpenter learned of the situation, attacked it vigorously, and has never tried in any way not to get it out," says Welch. "Do I wish he had a nose that had smelled it earlier? Sure. But that's hindsight." GE took a $210 million charge for the Kidder losses on $1.07 billion in first-quarter earnings.

Yet Welch implies that the mess could have been avoided. "Clearly this man [Jett] couldn't do it alone. People either knowingly made errors or didn't see red flags," says Welch. "No question, when Gary Lynch is through with this investigation, there will be findings" that could lead to further action against employees or their supervisors. Welch is referring to the Kidder-commissioned inquiry being conducted by attorney Lynch.

Lynch is likely to have plenty of questions for Cerullo. A fanatical antismoker who is well-liked and respected at Kidder, Cerullo has had other scrapes with problem traders. In 1991, he was fined $5,000 and censured by the National Association of Securities Dealers for failing to supervise a trader who engineered unauthorized bond transactions. Carpenter backs Cerullo. "He's kicking himself. But I am 100% behind him," says Carpenter. Cerullo declined comment.

Massive Positions

Jett's scheme involved arbitrage trades between the value of pieces of Treasury bonds, called strips, and the recombined bonds. Trouble was, says Kidder, Jett was not generating profit from the slightly greater value of the reconstituted bond, as is usually the practice. Instead, using forward contracts in the strips, he could create much larger bogus profits by exploiting flaws in Kidder's accounting system.

That Jett was allowed to carry out this ploy for such a long time, say Wall Street traders and risk managers, reflects major controls lapses. They claim that if Cerullo truly understood the massive positions Jett must have been taking, he would have questioned Jett about how he was generating such profits. Trading Treasury strips is generally a very low margin area of the fixed-income business, say traders.

Carpenter responds that the profits were not out of line with the real trades on the books and that Cerullo and he were unaware of the phony trades because they accumulated gradually over a period of time. Cerullo "did understand his trading strategy," says Carpenter. But "there didn't seem to be anything terribly out of line. We felt we were running a low-risk, high-margin business."

Kidder may have ignored the lesson learned by Salomon Brothers Inc. in the wake of the 1991 Treasury bond bid rigging scandal: Don't give too much power to traders. When asked whether Cerullo knows how Michael W. Vranos, Kidder's star mortgage-backed trader, generates profits, a senior Kidder official says: "Ed doesn't sit him down and say, 'How did you do it this month?'" But you can be sure such conversations with Kidder traders will occur in the future.

Liquidity Risk

This risk is especially important when the asset portfolio that needs to be funded is highly illiquid. Such illiquid assets might be emerging market debt or real estate or long-dated OTC options. The risk is the inability to fund these asset portfolios. For example, commercial banks hold reserves based on certain assumptions about the proportion of depositors who are likely to withdraw cash. This provides the basis for extension of credit. If their assumptions prove to be incorrect and more depositors decide to withdraw money, the bank will face a liquidity crisis. An extreme example is the case of a bank run. In a run, a significant percent of depositors decide to withdraw their deposits and the bank runs the risk of a failure precipitated by illiquidity.

Often, firms find that they engage in transactions that are not liquid: in other words, there are no active secondary markets in which such contracts may be freely traded. For example, an oil company may sell its output to its institutional customers using long-term forward contracts.

Consider the situation of a firm that has sold long-dated forwards, as shown in Table 19-17. As the price of oil fluctuates in the spot market, the value of these long-dated forward contracts will fluctuate. For example, if the spot price of oil falls to $17.00 per barrel, these forward contracts will be extremely valuable to the firm. Since these are bilateral forward contracts, however, they are not liquid. As a consequence, even though the value of these contracts has increased, the firm is unable to liquidate the contracts and realize their value. Conversely, if the spot price of oil were to increase to $25.00 per barrel, then the value of these forward contracts will decline sharply, even though there are no cash flow implications to the firm until the contracts mature. An opportunity cost of selling the oil at a higher price is clearly present.

The firm may wish to hedge its forward positions using the crude oil futures at NYMEX. In choosing this alternative, it must be aware of the liquidity problems that such large hedges might produce. NYMEX futures do extend to several months, but the liquidity beyond a few months is not that great. As a consequence, the firm must hedge its long-term forward commitments with short-term NYMEX futures. The term structure of the futures prices changes its shape from time to time; the market may be in normal backwardation when distant futures prices are higher than short-dated futures prices; or the term structure may be in contango, wherein longer maturity futures prices are lower than shorter maturity futures prices. Besides, futures prices are marked-to-market. This means that there may be large variation margin calls, leading to significant liquidity problems. Suppose that the firm ends up buying 800,000 barrels worth of futures and the futures prices moved from $20.00 a barrel to $19.50 in one

TABLE 19-17 Long-Term Forwards in Oil	Counterparty	Forward Maturity	Forward Price per Barrel	Amount Sold in Barrels
	A	5 years	20.00	100,000
	X	8 years	21.05	200,000
	Y	2 years	22.15	500,000

day. Then, the variation margin call will be $800,000 \times 0.50 = \$400,000$. Of course, the situation can be more problematic if the term structure of the futures prices moves from contango to normal backwardation when the hedge is in place. This will lead to a rise in distant futures prices, which the firm cannot take advantage of, as it has already locked in prices in long-term forwards, but it will end up paying huge variation margin calls on short-term futures contracts for which the prices have fallen.

The situation described previously is an important one with potentially dire consequences for the financial health of the firm. The case of Metallgesellschaft (MG) is illustrative of this problem. As the following article indicates, MG was using short-term crude oil futures contracts at the NYMEX to hedge its long-term forward commitments to deliver fuel. The resulting funding risk was further accentuated by the need to "roll over" periodically from one short-term future (as it neared expiration) to the next. According to the auditors, the estimated losses as of December 1993 was a little over $1 billion.

Metallgesellschaft

Germany's Corporate Whodunnit

A report on the Metallgesellschaft affair raises more questions than it answers about who was responsible for one of Germany's biggest business fiascos

BERLIN

Just over a year since the near-collapse of Metallgesellschaft (MG), one of Germany's biggest industrial conglomerates, the leading figures in the affair are still trading blows. On January 20th Heinz Schimmelbusch, the firm's former boss, filed a lawsuit in New York alleging that Deutsche Bank and one of its executives, Ronaldo Schmitz, who is the chairman of MG's supervisory board, were in part responsible for the financial troubles that laid the company low. A week later an auditors' report commissioned by MG's shareholders, which include Deutsche, put the blame squarely on Mr. Schimmelbusch and other former MG executives.

Reputations are not the only thing at stake. As they assess the cases, the courts will also, by implication, be judging the fitness of Deutsche and other banks as owners and supervisors of German companies. Doubts about their ability as overseers grew again this week when it emerged that Klöckner-Humboldt-Deutz, an engine maker in which Deutsche has a 36% stake, needs a DM719m ($472m) rescue package. And the Metallgesellschaft affair has become part of the lore about the supposed danger of financial derivatives.

The dispute is about the fuel-trading business of MG Refining & Marketing (MGRM), an American subsidiary of MG, and its huge positions in derivatives (most of which were futures contracts). After it was revealed in December 1993 that the trading arm had run into trouble, Mr. Schimmelbusch and other senior MG managers were removed by the supervisory board. Deutsche Bank and MG's new boss, Kajo

(continued)

Neukirchen, claim that MGRM had been recklessly punting on oil futures. They say that closing out these contracts was the only way to avoid further losses.

MG's former managers take a different view. They argue that the intervention of the supervisory board simply made matters worse, an argument that is supported by two American academics, Merton Miller, a Nobel prize-winning economist, and Christopher Culp, one of his colleagues at the University of Chicago. The two Americans have said that Deutsche and MG's new management doomed what would eventually have turned out to be a profitable trading operation by closing out some of MGRM's contracts when oil prices were plummeting.

Both camps can agree on some aspects of the affair. Nobody, for instance, disputes that MGRM's use of short-term energy futures contracts to hedge long-term commitments to deliver fuel meant that it would have to stump up more collateral on its loss-making futures positions if oil prices fell. They also agree that the scheme required MGRM continuously to sell short-term futures contracts, and to buy new ones. This "rollover" meant that the company might one day have to pay more for new contracts than it made from old ones.

Just this nightmare occurred through much of 1993. By December of that year MGRM had long positions in energy derivatives equivalent to 185m barrels of oil. Rolling over the contracts cost the firm a total of $88m in October and November alone. Here, however, explanations of what happened diverge. MG claims that instead of prolonging its subsidiary's losses, it had to close out its positions. The auditors reckon that MGRM's total loss by the end of December 1993 was just over $1 billion.

It was a self-inflicted wound, contend Messrs Miller and Culp. MRGM's futures were hedging long-term contracts to supply products such as petrol and heating oil for up to a decade at fixed prices which were then higher than those in the spot market. As oil prices fell, dragging down the value of MGRM's futures contracts, the value of the long-term contracts surged, in theory offsetting the losses. Had MGRM persevered, it would have made a profit.

The auditors' report attacks this thesis in two ways. First, it suggests that as early as June 1993 Mr. Schimmelbusch tried in vain to reduce MGRM's positions. The report quotes a memo from Mr. Schimmelbusch dated that month in which MG's former boss asks his chief financial officer, Meinhard Forster, to cut the credit employed by the trading businesses "in a draconian manner if necessary".

Yet MGRM's position jumped from 100m barrels in June to 185m barrels by December. The auditors claim that MGRM was trying to offset losses from its futures positions—a view which Mr. Schimmelbusch apparently shared. According to the auditors, in a meeting in December with members of MG's supervisory board, including Mr. Schmitz, Mr. Schimmelbusch described MGRM's rush to add business as a "double or quits" gamble. He denies that he said this.

Had MG's banks put up more cash, they might have forestalled a forced liquidation. In Mr Miller's view that would have been better than taking a $1 billion loss on a potentially profitable position. The auditors dispute this, too. Their report claims that some 59m barrels-worth of the underlying long-term contracts had a negative value of about $12m. MG counts itself lucky to have escaped these contracts at no cost.

If this claim stands up to scrutiny, then the contracts in question did not gain in value as oil prices fell. That means the futures contracts backing them were hedging nothing. The implication is that they were a pure gamble on energy prices. This is likely to be hotly disputed by those who took the positions. MG's argument will almost certainly not be the last one in this affair. Mr. Schimmelbusch and MGRM's former managers are all pressing ahead with lawsuits. Until these are played out, the Metallgesellschaft affair will continue to haunt Germany's mightiest bank.

LTCM Crisis in 1998

A more recent example of a financial crisis is the collapse of a hedge fund known as the Long-Term Capital Management (LTCM). LTCM, which was formed in 1994, was a hedge fund that leveraged significantly to invest in "relative value" strategies in which the fund attempted to profit from "temporary price discrepancies" between two markets. An example would be a strategy in which the fund might short on-the-run Treasury and go long in off-the-run Treasury when the spread is "well above" historical levels. The motivation is that the spread will narrow and that the trade can be unwound at a profit. Since the profitability without leveraging is relatively small, these trades will be effected with considerable leverage. In August 1998, Russia declared a "debt moratorium" and the credit spreads started to widen dramatically.

LTCM's position on a "marked-to-market" basis became precarious. The firm had to raise capital or sell assets to meet the losses from marking-to-market. Eventually, LTCM was taken over by the creditors under a plan orchestrated by the Federal Reserve Bank of New York.

The following box contains excerpts from the statement of William McDonough, President of the Federal Reserve Bank of New York before the U.S. House of Representatives.

Excerpts from the Statement by William J. McDonough, President, Federal Reserve Bank of New York, before the Committee on Banking and Financial Services, U.S. House of Representatives, October 1, 1998

". . . Perhaps their success went to their heads. Long-Term Capital took on larger and larger positions. They also leveraged their investments at higher levels, returning capital to their investors but not, apparently, reducing risks. We now also know that they took on significant positions in equity markets, through both swap and options contracts. The reputations of the Long-Term Capital partners, as traders and economists, and their initial success, appear to have contributed to so many counterparties' willingness to deal with them.

"While hubris may have set them up for a fall, it was the extraordinary events of August in global markets that appears to have tripped them."

". . . Because of this, during the first two weeks of September, concern about Long-Term Capital was a widespread topic of conversation in financial markets. It is a traditional and essential role for the President and senior officers of the New York Fed to be talking to, and receiving calls from, market participants regarding significant developments and potential dislocations. In fact, the partners at Long-Term Capital called me early in September to notify me of their difficulties and their discussion with investment houses about plans to raise new capital."

(continued)

". . . By Friday, September 18, with the efforts to raise new capital still unsuccessful—and with an increasing number of people now aware of Long-Term's plight because of the efforts to bring in new investors—events seemed to come to a head. With market conditions particularly unsettled that day, I made a series of calls to senior Wall Street officials to discuss overall market conditions. Let me take a moment to put those calls in context. One important objective of the Federal Reserve is to assure financial stability. Particularly in times of stress, it is essential that the Federal Reserve continue to take the pulse of the market. One way to do that is through candid and open communication with key market participants. Everyone I spoke to that day volunteered concern about the serious effect the deteriorating situation of Long-Term could have on world markets."

". . . Also on the 18th, one of the firms that had been working with Long-Term to raise new capital asked the Long-Term Capital partners if the firm could share the information it had with us. The partners at Long-Term Capital responded that they would prefer to present the information themselves and called me to arrange such a presentation."

". . . After conferring with Chairman Greenspan and Secretary Rubin, we agreed that a visit to Long-Term Capital's offices was needed. A team from the New York Fed, led by Peter Fisher, the head of our Markets Group, and joined by Treasury Assistant Secretary Gary Gensler, met with the Long-Term Capital partners at their offices on Sunday, September 20. During this meeting, we learned the broad outlines of Long-Term Capital's major positions in credit and equity markets, the difficulties they were having in trying to reduce these positions in thin market conditions, their deteriorating funding positions and an estimate of their largest counterparty exposures. The team also came to understand the impact which Long-Term Capital's positions were already having on markets around the world and that the size of these positions was much greater than market participants imagined."

The New York Fed's Judgments

". . . Mr. Chairman, I would like now to turn to my second point, and focus explicitly on the question of our judgment that the abrupt and disorderly close-out of Long-Term Capital's positions would pose unacceptable risks to the American economy."

". . . There are several ways that the problems of Long-Term Capital could have been transmitted to cause more widespread financial troubles. Had Long-Term Capital been suddenly put into default, its counterparties would have immediatly "closed-out" their positions. If counterparties would have been able to close-out their positions at existing market prices, losses, if any, would have been minimal. However, if many firms had rushed to close-out hundreds of billions of dollars in transactions simultaneously, they would have been unable to liquidate collateral or establish offsetting positions at the previously-existing prices. Markets would have moved sharply and losses would have been exaggerated. Several billion dollars of losses might have been experienced by some of Long-Term Capital's more than 75 counterparties.

These direct effects on Long-Term Capital's counterparties were not our principal concern. While these losses would have been considerable, and would certainly have adversely affected the firms experiencing them, this was not, in itself, a sufficient reason for us to become involved."

". . . Two factors influenced our involvement. First, in the rush of Long-Term Capital's counterparties to close-out their positions, other market participants—investors who had no dealings with Long-Term Capital—would have been affected as well. Second, as losses spread to other market participants and Long-Term Capital's counterparties, this would lead to tremendous uncertainty about how far prices would move. Under these circumstances, there was a likelihood that a number of credit and interest rate markets would experience extreme price moves and possibly cease to function for a period of one or more days and maybe longer. This would have caused a vicious cycle: a loss of investor confidence, leading to a rush out of private credits, leading to a further widening of credit spreads, leading to further liquidations of positions, and so on. Most importantly, this would have led to further increases in the cost of capital to American businesses."

What Did the New York Fed Do?

". . . At the end of that discussion, 14 banks and securities firms agreed to participate in the recapitalization, with three firms contributing smaller amounts than the other eleven. Two firms declined to participate.

I want to emphasize a few points. First, this was a private sector solution to a private-sector problem, involving an investment of new equity by Long-Term Capital's creditors and counterparties. Second, although some have characterized this as a "bailout", control of the Long-Term Portfolio passed over to this 14 firm creditor group and the original equity holders have taken a severe hit. Finally, no Federal Reserve official pressured anyone, and no promises were made. Not one penny of public money was spent or committed."

Systemic Risk

Interbank and interdealer transactions have grown significantly in many markets. In such situations, one bank or one dealer may be a counterparty to a number of transactions with very many banks and dealers. If, due to a crisis (induced by liquidity, credit or market exposures), that dealer or bank fails in its obligation as a counterparty in various transactions, then a domino effect could result in which several other banks and dealers also end up in a crisis. The ramifications of a systemic failure are extensive. Typically, central banks and regulatory authorities play an active role in trying to prevent such calamities. The capital adequacy requirements, government guarantees, and audits are examples of some policy actions that lower the probability of a systemic failure. In addition, during such episodes, central banks often play an active role in stemming the damage. For example, during the stock market crash of 1987, the Federal Reserve provided liquidity.

Central banks often take actions to avoid systemic risks. Many financial institutions carry implicit or explicit guarantees. The presence of FDIC guarantee helps to prevent a "run" on the banks. Federal Reserve steps up liquidity by timely cuts in its target rate to help the flow of liquidity in a time of crisis. In all these situations, however, regulators will have to weigh the possibility that investors may take excessive risks hoping that the regulators will step in later to bail them out if there is a future crisis due to excessive risk taking.

SYSTEMS AND DATA REQUIREMENTS

Over the last 10 years, risk management has assumed a more important role in money-center banks, investment banks, and security-dealing firms. This is one area where some of the most recent developments in valuation theory and computer hardware and software interact to produce integrated multimarket risk measurement and management systems. Let us review the ingredients of a risk management system.

Data: It is necessary to deliver data (preferably real-time) to firms from many markets in order for firms to measure the positions of securities held. In many situations, transactions are so customized that they cannot be valued using the market data alone; models may be needed to value such transactions. Recall the example of a swap transaction which can only be priced by deriving the zero-coupon bond prices from a specific segment of the fixed-income market. This indicates that the data have to be processed through some preliminary models and statistical methods to generate inputs to the valuation framework. The firm needs to have reliable and timely access to historical data to estimate volatilities and cross correlations.

Valuation models: The measurement of risk is only as good as the models that have been used to generate the measures. This is not a serious problem where the markets are active and the positions and risk measures do not require models for valuation. In most cases, however, models are needed to value positions and assess their risks. Take the example of pricing and measuring the risk of an option on zero-coupon bond yields. Several models may be used for this purpose, including Black and Scholes (1973); Ho and Lee (1986); Black, Derman, and Toy (1990); Cox, Ingersoll, and Ross (1985); and Heath, Jarrow, and Morton (1990).

Even in situations where there is a general agreement on what is the single correct model (and usually there is no agreement on this matter), there is the issue of estimating the parameters that go into the model. Firms using the same model may use different procedures for estimation.

Computer technology: With the advent of global 24-hour trading by many institutions, the technology used to support the trading systems has become the focus. Real-time analytics; better integration of front-office (sales and trading) and back-office (order processing, settlement, clearance, and accounting) systems; use of workstations; and so on have become more and more common in the last decade. A number of data vendors, such as Reuters, Telerate, Bloomberg, and Quotron, have started to offer live data at widely distributed locations. In fact, typically, such data are also supplied with relatively good valuation models, historical information, and analytics. Portfolio management software with the ability to perform marked-to-market valuation and performance measurement are also offered in the market.

Settlement Risk

Settlement risk refers to the possibility that a counterparty is either unable to or unwilling to perform on a contract on the settlement date. This is especially a problem when off-setting payments are involved, as in currency and interest-rate swaps. If A makes the payment but finds out that B has not made the off-setting payment, then A is faced with settlement risk. Differences in the currency of transactions and the time-zones can make the settlement risk quite significant. If Bank A accepts payments from its counterparties and is subsequently closed down by regulators unexpectedly, then the counterparties to this bank will face significant settlement risk if their dues have not been cleared by the bank.

CONCLUSION

Over the years, capital markets have created innovations to more effectively manage risk. Some of these innovations have come at the instigation of regulators; others have come due to technological advances.

In addition, structured transactions and fully funded subsidiaries have been developed to deal with the issue of credit risk. Asset-backed commercial paper programs have enabled issuers with poor credit reputation to take advantage of some of the better quality assets in their balance sheets to issue highly rated paper at a lower cost. This innovation uses a special purpose vehicle (SPV) as discussed in Chapters 1 and 9 with credit and liquidity enhancements. In a similar way, dealers have created fully funded AAA subsidiaries to engage in swap transactions.

The regulators have responded by focusing on auditing financial institutions to ensure that their internal controls, risk measurement systems, and models that are needed to value securities are adequate. The idea that all firms must have satisfactory capital requirements to participate in markets has gained wide acceptance in the regulatory discussions. As noted in Chapter 16, there have been developments in which swap transactions have to be performed with collaterals and discretionary marking to market.

The area of risk management will continue to attract considerable attention from regulators and constituents of financial institutions and dealers. While significant strides have been made in the measurement and management of risk, there are still several open issues. One important issue is the interactions between different sources of risk. When there is a big move in the market, many counterparties become more vulnerable to credit risk. This is also precisely the situation when market liquidity becomes a problem. As a result, we see that the market risk, credit risk, and liquidity risk tend to interact. No satisfactory approaches are available currently to deal with this problem.

PROBLEMS

19.1   The following table lists the swap transactions of a dealer.
(a) Determine the credit exposure of this dealer.
(b) Due to a recession, the credit reputation of all counterparties deteriorated. Examine how the firm should go about making loss reserves. Identify the counterparties against whom the firm has maximum exposure.

Question 1

Number	Swap Maturity	Marked-to-Market Value	Counterparty
1	5	200,000	A
2	4	−40,000	A
3	3	−900,000	X
4	7	1,000,000	Y
5	6	670,000	Y
6	4	800,000	Y
7	2	70,000	X
8	2	170,000	X
9	3	200,000	X
10	4	170,000	A

19.2   What are the ramifications of the Group of 30 recommendations for security dealers? Focus on the data, systems, and modeling issues that need to be addressed.
19.3   You have invested $1 million in a security which has a volatility of 15% (annualized). What is the VAR of this security for a holding period of 30 days at 99% confidence level?
19.4   The variance-covariance matrix of two securities is shown next.

Question 4
VAR of a Portfolio

Security	A	B
A	0.0225	0.0120
B		0.0100

The share price of A is 100 and that of B is 80. Determine the VAR of a value-weighted portfolio of these securities at 99% confidence level for a holding period of one day.
19.5   In Problem 19.3, determine the VAR of an equally weighted portfolio at 99% confidence level for a holding period of one day.

REFERENCES

Barr, P. G. 1995. "Risk Management Gets New Respect." *Pensions and Investments* (March 20):26.

Black, F., and M. Scholes 1973. "The Pricing of Options and Corporate Liabilities." *Journal of Political Economy* 81:637–659.

Black, F., E. Derman, and W. Toy 1990. "A One-Factor Model of Interest Rates and Its Applications to Treasury Bond Options." *Financial Analysts Journal* 46(1):33–39.

1993. *Corporate Finance, Derivatives Supplement.* Euromoney Publications.

Cox, J. C., J. Ingersoll, and S. A. Ross 1985. "A Theory of the Term Structure of Interest Rates." *Econometrica* 53:385–407.

Heath, D., R. Jarrow, and A. Morton 1990. "Bond Pricing and the Term Structure of Interest Rates: A Discrete Time Approximation." *Journal of Financial and Quantitative Analysis* 25(4):419–440.

Ho, T. S. Y., and S. Lee 1986. "Term Structure Movements and Pricing of Interest Rate Contingent Claims." *The Journal of Finance* XLI(5):1011–1029.

Ibbotson and Singfield 1994. "Stocks, Bonds, Bills, and Inflation." *Yearbook,* Ibbotson Associates, Chicago.

1995. "Metallgesellschaft." *Economist* (February 4):71.

Spiro, L. N. 1994. "Why Didn't Kidder Catch On." *Business Week* (May 2):121.

Index